A Programmer's Guide to Java™ Certification

Second Edition

http://www.qaforums.com

A Programmer's Guide to Java™ Certification

Second Edition

A Comprehensive Primer

Khalid A. Mughal
and
Rolf W. Rasmussen

ISBN 81-297-0267-3

First Indian Reprint, 2004
Second Indian Reprint, 2004

This edition is manufactured in India and is authorized for sale only in India, Bangladesh, Pakistan, Nepal, Sri Lanka and the Maldives.

Published by Pearson Education (Singapore) Pte. Ltd., Indian Branch, 482 F.I.E. Patparganj, Delhi 110 092, India.

Printed in India by Pashupati Printers Pvt. Ltd.

To the loving memory of my mother, Zubaida Begum,
and my father, Mohammed Azim.
—K.A.M.

For Olivia E. Rasmussen and
Louise J. Dahlmo.
—R.W.R.

Contents Overview

Contents

List of Figures

List of Tables

List of Examples

Foreword

●●●

Consider the following observations:

- Software continues to become ever more pervasive, ever more ubiquitous in our lives.
- Incompetence seems to be the only thing we can count on in today's world and, especially, in the domain of software.
- The Java programming language has become a lingua franca for programmers all over the world.

One can draw varied conclusions from these comments. One of them is that it is of great importance that programmers working with the Java programming language should be as competent as possible.

The Java certification program is an important effort aimed at precisely this goal. Practitioners looking to obtain such certification need good quality training materials, which brings us to this book.

Programming is still more of an art than a science, and will continue to be so for the foreseeable future. Mastering the intricacies of a large and complex programming language is a challenging task that requires time and effort, and above all experience.

Real programming requires more than just mastery of a programming language. It requires mastery of a computing platform, with a rich set of libraries. These libraries are designed to simplify the task of building realistic applications, and they do. Again, the practitioner is faced with a daunting task.

To address the clear need for professional training material, a plethora of books have been written purporting to tutor programmers in the programming language and platform skills they require.

The choice is as mind boggling as the material within the books themselves. Should one try *Java for Frontally Lobotomized Simians* or *Postmodern Java Dialectics*? The readership for these books is largely self selecting. I trust that if you, the reader, have gotten this far, you are looking for something that is intelligent, yet practical. This book is one of the finest efforts in this crowded arena. It brings a necessary level of academic rigor to an area much in need of it, while retaining an essentially pragmatic flavor.

The material in this book is probably all you need to pass the Java certification exam. It certainly isn't all you need to be a good software engineer. You must continue learning about new technologies. The hardest part of this is dealing with things that are completely different from what you are familiar with. Yet this is what distinguishes the top flight engineer from the mediocre one. Keep an open mind; it pays.

Gilad Bracha
Computational Theologist
Sun Java Software
http://java.sun.com/people/gbracha/

Preface

●●

Writing the Second Edition

The exam for the Sun Certified Programmer for Java 2 (SCPJ2) Platform has changed considerably since the first edition of this book was published. The most noticeable change in the current version of the exam (SCPJ2 1.4) is the removal of GUI and I/O, and the shifting of emphasis toward the core features of the language. In our opinion, the new exam demands an even greater understanding and actual experience of the language, rather than mere recitation of facts. Proficiency in the language is the key to success.

The I/O and GUI topics of the first edition have been eliminated, as they have no relevance for the SCPJ2 exam. These topics are more relevant for the Sun Certified Developer for Java 2 (SCDJ2) Platform exam and, therefore, relegated to a possible future volume on the Developer exam topics.

Since the emphasis of the SCPJ2 exam is on the core features of Java, the second edition provides an even greater in-depth coverage of the relevant topics. The book covers not just the exam objectives, but also supplementary topics that aid in mastering the exam topics.

The second edition is still a one-source guide for the SCPJ2 exam: it provides a mixture of theory and practice for the exam. Use the book to learn Java, pass the SCPJ2 exam, and afterwards, use it as a handy language guide. The book also has an appendix devoted to the SCPJ2 Upgrade exam. To facilitate preparation for the exams, the second edition comes with a CD containing additional resources, including several mock exams developed by Whizlabs Software.

We have taken into consideration the feedback we have received from readers. The many hours spent in handling the deluge of e-mail have not been in vain. Every single e-mail is appreciated and is hereby acknowledged.

Preparing the second edition dispelled all our illusions about second editions being, to put it colloquially, a piece of cake. Every sentence from the first edition has been weighed carefully, and not many paragraphs have escaped rewriting.

UML (Unified Modeling Language) is also extensively employed in this edition. Numerous new review questions have been added. In covering the new topics and expanding the existing ones, new examples, figures, and tables were also specifically created for the second edition.

About This Book

This book provides an extensive coverage of the Java programming language and its core Application Programming Interfaces (APIs), with particular emphasis on its syntax and usage. The book is primarily intended for professionals who want to prepare for the Sun Certified Programmer for Java 2 Platform 1.4 exam (referred to as the SCPJ2 exam), but it is readily accessible to any programmer who wants to master the language. For both purposes, it provides an in-depth coverage of essential features of the language and its core APIs.

There is a great and increasing demand for certified Java programmers. Sun Microsystems has defined the SCPJ2 exam as one that professionals can take to validate their skills. The certification provides the IT industry with the standard to use for hiring such professionals, and allows the professionals to turn their Java skills into credentials that are important for career advancement.

The book helps the reader master all core features of the Java language, and this mastering of the language can culminate in accomplishing the exam. It provides an extensive coverage of all the objectives defined for the exam by Sun. Since the exam objectives are selective, they do not cover many of the essential features of Java. This book provides extensive coverage of additional topics that every Java programmer should master in order to be proficient in this field. In this regard, the book is a comprehensive primer for learning the Java programming language.

This book is *not* a *complete reference* for Java, as it does not attempt to list every member of every class from the Java System Development Kit (SDK) API documentation. Its purpose is not to document the Java SDK APIs. It is also *not* a book on *teaching programming techniques*. Its emphasis is on the Java programming language features, their syntax and correct usage.

The book assumes a background in programming. We believe the exam is accessible to any programmer who works through the book. A Java programmer can easily skip over material that is well understood and concentrate on parts that need reinforcing, whereas a programmer new to Java will find the concepts explained from basic principles.

Each topic is explained and discussed thoroughly with examples, and backed by review questions and exercises to reinforce the concepts. The book is not biased toward any particular platform, but provides platform-specific details where necessary.

Using the Book

The reader can choose a linear or a non-linear route through the book, depending on her programming background. Non-Java programmers wishing to migrate to Java can read Chapter 1, which provides a short introduction to object-oriented programming concepts, and the procedure for compiling and running Java applications. For those preparing for the SCPJ2 exam, the book has a separate appendix providing all the pertinent information on taking the exam.

The table of contents, listings of tables, examples, and figures, and a comprehensive index facilitate locating topics discussed in the book.

In particular, we draw attention to the following features of the book:

Exam and Supplementary Objectives

- Exam objectives are stated clearly at the start of every chapter, together with any supplementary objectives.
- The objectives are defined by Sun and are organized into major sections, detailing the curriculum for the exam.
- The book is organized into chapters that logically follow the order of these major sections.
- The objectives are reproduced in a separate appendix where, for each section of the syllabus, study notes are included to point the reader to topics essential for the exam.
- We believe that the supplementary objectives are important to the ultimate goal of mastering the language.

 ### Review Questions

Review questions are provided after every major topic, in order to test and reinforce the material. These review questions reflect the kind of questions that can be asked on the actual exam. Annotated answers to the review questions are provided in a separate appendix.

Example 0.1 *Example Source Code*

We encourage experimenting with the code examples in order to reinforce the material from the book. These can be downloaded from the book Web site (see p. xxxv).

Java code is written in a mono-spaced font. Lines of code in the examples or in code snippets are referenced in the text by a number, which is specified by using a single-line comment in the code. For example, in the following code snippet, the call to the method.doSomethingInteresting() hopefully does something interesting at (1).

```
// ...
doSomethingInteresting();                                    // (1)
// ...
```

Names of classes and interfaces start with an uppercase letter. Names of packages, variables, and methods start with a lowercase letter. Constants are all in uppercase letters.

Chapter Summary

Each chapter concludes with a summary of the topics, pointing out the major concepts discussed in the chapter.

Programming Exercises

Programming exercises at the end of each chapter provide the opportunity to put concepts into practice. Solutions to the programming exercises are provided in a separate appendix.

Mock Exam

A complete mock exam is provided in a separate appendix, which the reader can try when she is ready. In addition, the accompanying CD contains several mock exams for the SCPJ2 1.4 exam.

Java 2 SDK and API Documentation

A vertical gray bar is used to highlight methods and fields found in the classes of the core Java APIs.

Any explanation following the API information is also similarly highlighted.

In order to obtain optimal benefit from using this book in preparing for the SCPJ2 exam, we strongly recommend installing the latest version (at least 1.4) of the SDK and its accompanying API documentation. The book focuses solely on Java 2, and does not acknowledge previous versions.

Java 2 Platform Upgrade Exam

For those who have taken the Sun Certified Programmer for Java 2 Platform 1.2 Exam, and would like to prepare for the Sun Certified Programmer for Java 2 Platform Upgrade Exam, we have provided an appendix with details of the upgrade exam. The appendix contains the upgrade exam objectives, and for each section of the syllabus, study notes are included to point the reader to topics essential for the upgrade exam. The accompanying CD contains mock exams for the upgrade exam.

Accompanying CD

The accompanying CD contains a wealth of information to help prepare for the exam, and provides numerous mock exams for the candidate to test her skills. The software included simulates near exam-like conditions in order to acquaint the candidate with the exam environment. Appendix H provides details about the contents of the CD.

Book Web Sites

This book is backed by Web sites providing auxiliary material:

> http://www.ii.uib.no/~khalid/pgjc2e/
>
> http://www.awprofessional.com/ (search for ISBN 0201728281)

The contents of the Web sites include the following:

- source code for all the examples and programming exercises in the book
- mock exam engine
- errata
- links to miscellaneous Java resources (certification, discussion groups, tools, etc.)

Information about the Java 2 SDK Standard Edition and its documentation can be found at the following Web site:

> http://java.sun.com/j2se/

The current authoritative technical reference for the Java programming language, *The Java Language Specification, Second Edition* (also published by Addison-Wesley), can be found at this Web site:

> http://java.sun.com/docs/books/jls/

Request for Feedback

Considerable effort has been made to ensure the accuracy of the contents of this book. Several Java professionals have proofread the manuscript. All code examples (including code fragments) have been compiled and tested on various platforms. In the final analysis, any errors remaining are the sole responsibility of the authors.

Any questions, comments, suggestions, and corrections are welcome. Whether the book was helpful or detrimental for your purpose, we would like your assessment. Any feedback is valuable. The authors can be reached by the following e-mail alias:

pgjc2e@ii.uib.no

About the Authors

Khalid A. Mughal

Khalid A. Mughal is an Associate Professor at the Department of Informatics at the University of Bergen, Norway. Professor Mughal is responsible for designing and implementing various courses, which use Java, at the Department of Informatics. Over the years, he has taught Programming Languages (Java, C/C++, Pascal), Software Engineering (Object-oriented System Development), Databases (Data Modeling and Database Management Systems), and Compiler Techniques. He has also given numerous courses and seminars at various levels in object-oriented programming and system development, using Java and Java-related technology, both at the University and for the IT industry. He is the principal author of the book, responsible for writing the material covering the Java topics.

He is also the principal author of an introductory Norwegian textbook on programming in Java (*Java som første programmeringsspråk/Java as First Programming Language*, Cappelen Akademisk Forlag, ISBN 82-02-21782-2, 2002), which he co-authored with Torill Hamre and Rolf W. Rasmussen.

His primary research is in theory, design, and implementation of programming languages and tools (Programming Environments). His current work involves applying Object Technology in the development of learning content management systems. For the past three years he has been responsible for developing and running a web-based programming course in Java, which is offered to off-campus students.

He is a member of the ACM.

Rolf W. Rasmussen

Rolf W. Rasmussen is a Software Engineer, who over the years has worked both academically and professionally with numerous programming languages, including Java. He is employed as System Creator at vizrt, a company that develops solutions for the TV broadcast industry, including real-time 3D graphic renderers, and content and control systems.

He mainly works on control and automation systems, video processing, typography, and real-time visualization. He has in the past worked on clean room implementations of the Java class libraries, and is a contributor to the Free Software Foundation.

He is primarily responsible for developing the review questions and answers, the programming exercises and their solutions, the mock exam, and all the practical aspects related to taking the SCPJ2 exam, presented in this book.

As mentioned above, he is also a co-author of an introductory textbook on programming in Java.

Acknowledgments (First Edition)

A small application for drawing simple shapes is used in the book to illustrate various aspects of GUI building. The idea for this application, as far as we know, first appeared in Appendix D of *Data Structures and Problem Solving Using Java* (M.A. Weiss, Addison-Wesley, 1998).

At Addison-Wesley-Longman (AWL), we would like to thank Emma Mitchell for the support and the guidance she provided us right from the start of this project, Martin Klopstock at AWL for accommodating the non-standard procedure involved in getting the book to the printing press, Clive Birks at CRB Associates for providing the professional look to the contents of this book, and finally, Sally Mortimore at AWL for seeing us over the finishing line. The efforts of other professionals behind the scenes at AWL are also acknowledged.

Many reviewers have been involved during the course of writing this book. First of all, we would like to thank the five anonymous reviewers commissioned by AWL to review the initial draft. Their input was useful in the subsequent writing of this book.

Several people have provided us with feedback on different parts of the material at various stages: Jon Christian Lønningdal, Tord Kålsrud, Kjetil Iversen, Roy Oma, and Arne Løkketangen. Their help is hereby sincerely acknowledged.

We are also very grateful to Laurence Vanhelsuwé, Kris Laporte, Anita Jacob, and Torill Hamre for taking on the daunting task of reviewing the final draft, and providing us with extensive feedback at such short notice. We would like to thank Marit Mughal for reading the manuscript with the trained eye of a veteran English schoolteacher.

We now understand why family members are invariably mentioned in a preface. Without our families' love, support, and understanding this book would have remained a virtual commodity. Khalid would like to thank Marit, Nina, and Laila for their love, and for being his pillars of support, during the writing of this book. Thanks also to the folks in Birmingham for cheering us on. Rolf would like to thank Liv, Rolf V., Knut, and Elisabeth for enduring the strange working hours producing this book has entailed. A special thanks to Marit for providing us with scrumptious dinners for consumption at the midnight hour.

Acknowledgments (Second Edition)

Feedback from many readers helped us to improve the first edition. We would like to thank the following readers for their input in this effort:

Michael F. Adolf, Tony Alicea, Kåre Auglænd, Jorge L. Barroso, Andre Beland, Darren Bruning, Paul Campbell, Roger Chang, Joanna Chappel, Laurian M Chirica, Arkadi Choufrine, Barry Colston, John Cotter, Frédéric Demers, Arthur De Souza, djc, William Ekiel, Darryl Failla, John Finlay, Christopher R. Gardner, Marco Garcia, Peter Gieser, George, Paul Graf, Shyamsundar Gururaj, Ray Ho, Leonardo Holanda, Zhu Hongjun, Kara Van Horn, Peter Horst, Nain Hwu, Kent Johnson, Samir Kanparia, Oleksiy Karpenko, Jeffrey Kenyon, Young Jin Kim, Kenneth Kisser, Billy Kutulas, Yi-Ming Lai, Robert M. Languedoc, Steve Lasley, Winser Lo, Naga Madipalli, Craig Main, Avinash Mandsaurwale, Thomas Mathai, S. Mehra, Yuan Meng, Simon Miller, William Moore, Anders Morch, George A. Murakami, Sandy Nemecek, Chun Pan, Abigail García Patiño, Anil Philip, Alfred Raouf, Peter Rorden, Christian Seifert, Gurpreet Singh, Christopher Stanwood, Swaminathan Subramanian, Siva Sundaram, Manju Swamy, John Sweeney, Harmon Taylor, Andrew Tolopko, Ravi Verma, Per J. Walstrøm, Chun Wang, James Ward, Winky, Chun Wang, Jimmy Yang, Jennie Yip, Yanqu Zhou, and Yingting Zhou.

At the UK office of Addison-Wesley/Pearson Education, we would like to thank our former editor Simon Plumtree for his unceasing support and patience while we slogged on with the second edition. We would also like to acknowledge the help and support of the following professionals, past and present, at the London office: Alison Birtwell, Sally Carter, Karen Sellwood and Katherin Ekstrom. A special thanks to Karen Mosman (who has since moved on to another job) for her encouragement and advice.

During the last lap of getting the book to the printing press, we were in the capable hands of Ann Sellers at the US office of Addison-Wesley/Pearson Education. We would like to acknowledge her efforts and that of other professionals—in particular, Greg Doench, Jacquelyn Doucette, Amy Fleischer, Michael Mullen, and Dianne Russell—who helped to get this book through the door and on to the bookshelf. Thanks also to Mike Hendrickson for always lending an ear when we met at the OOPSLA conferences, and pointing us in the right direction with our book plans.

We would like to thank the folks at Whizlabs Software for their collaboration in producing the contents for the CD accompanying this book. Those guys certainly know the business of developing exam simulators for certification in Java technology.

We were fortunate in having two Java gurus—Laurence Vanhelsuwé and Marcus Green—to do the technical review of the second edition. As he did for the first edition, Laurence came through and provided us with invaluable feedback, from the minutiae of writing technical books to many technical issues relating to the Java programming language. Marcus put the manuscript through his severe certification scrutiny regarding the specifics of the SCPJ2 exam. We are sorry to have upset their plans for Easter holidays, and hasten to thank them most profusely for taking on the task.

We cannot thank enough our own in-house, private copy-editor: Marit Seljeflot Mughal. She diligently and relentlessly read numerous drafts of the manuscript, usually at a very short notice. Marit claims that if she understood what we had written, then a computer-literate person should have no problem whatsoever. This claim remains to be substantiated. If any commas are not used correctly, then it is entirely our fault, in spite of being repeatedly shown how to use them.

We are also indebted to many Java-enabled individuals for providing us valuable feedback on parts of the manuscript for the second edition. This includes Pradeep Chopra, Seema R., and Gaurav Kohli at Whizlabs Software. Unfortunately for us, they only had time to read part of the manuscript. Thanks also to Torill Hamre at the Nansen Environmental and Remote Sensing Center, Bergen, for her useful comments and suggestions. We also thank the following Master students at the Department of Informatics, University of Bergen, for providing useful feedback: Mikal Carlsen, Yngve Espelid, Yngve A. Aas, Sigmund Nysæter, Torkel Holm, and Eskil Saatvedt.

Family support saw us through this writing project as well. Our families have put up with our odd and long working hours, endured our preoccupation and our absence at the dining table. Khalid would like to acknowledge the love and support of his wife, Marit, and daughters, Nina and Laila, while working on this book. Rolf would like to thank Liv, Rolf V., Knut, and Elisabeth for their love, patience and support.

—Khalid A. Mughal,
Rolf W. Rasmussen
March 2003
Bergen, Norway

Basics of Java Programming

1

Supplementary Objectives

- Introduce the basic terminology and concepts in object-oriented programming: classes, objects, references, fields, methods, members, inheritance, aggregation.
- Identify the essential elements of a Java application.
- Learn how to compile and run a Java application.

1.1 Introduction

Before embarking on the road to Java programmer certification, it is important to understand the basic terminology and concepts in object-oriented programming (OOP). In this chapter, the emphasis is on providing an introduction rather than an exhaustive coverage. In-depth coverage of the concepts follows in due course in subsequent chapters of the book.

Java supports the writing of many different kinds of executables: applications, applets, and servlets. The basic elements of a Java application are introduced in this chapter. The old adage that practice makes perfect is certainly true when learning a programming language. To encourage programming on the computer, the mechanics of compiling and running a Java application are outlined.

1.2 Classes

One of the fundamental ways in which we handle complexity is *abstractions*. An abstraction denotes the essential properties and behaviors of an object that differentiate it from other objects. The essence of OOP is modelling abstractions, using classes and objects. The hard part in this endeavour is finding the right abstractions.

A *class* denotes a category of objects, and acts as a blueprint for creating such objects. A class models an abstraction by defining the properties and behaviors for the objects representing the abstraction. An object exhibits the properties and behaviors defined by its class. The properties of an object of a class are also called *attributes*, and are defined by *fields* in Java. A *field* in a class definition is a variable which can store a value that represents a particular property. The behaviors of an object of a class are also known as *operations*, and are defined using *methods* in Java. Fields and methods in a class definition are collectively called *members*.

An important distinction is made between the *contract* and the *implementation* that a class provides for its objects. The contract defines *what* services, and the implementation defines *how* these services are provided by the class. Clients (i.e., other objects) only need to know the contract of an object, and not its implementation, in order to avail themselves of the object's services.

As an example, we will implement different versions of a class that models the abstraction of a stack that can push and pop characters. The stack will use an array of characters to store the characters, and a field to indicate the top element in the stack. Using Unified Modeling Language (UML) notation, a class called CharStack is graphically depicted in Figure 1.1, which models the abstraction. Both fields and method names are shown in Figure 1.1a.

Figure 1.1 *UML Notation for Classes*

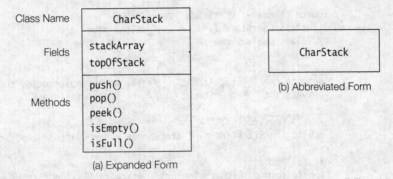

(a) Expanded Form

(b) Abbreviated Form

Declaring Members: Fields and Methods

Example 1.1 shows the definition of the class CharStack depicted in Figure 1.1. Its intention is to illustrate the salient features of a class definition in Java, and not effective implementation of stacks.

A class definition consists of a series of member declarations. In the case of the class CharStack, it has two fields:

- stackArray, which is an array to hold the elements of the stack (in this case characters)

- topOfStack, which denotes the top element of the stack (i.e., index of the last character stored in the array)

The class CharStack has five methods that implement the essential operations on a stack:

- push() pushes a character on to the stack
- pop() removes and returns the top element of the stack
- peek() returns the top element of the stack for inspection
- isEmpty() determines whether the stack is empty
- isFull() determines whether the stack is full

The class definition also has a method-like declaration with the same name as the class, (2). Such declarations are called *constructors*. As we shall see, a constructor is executed when an object is created from the class. However, the implementation details in the example are not important for the present discussion.

Example 1.1   *Basic Elements of a Class Definition*

```java
// Source Filename: CharStack.java
public class CharStack {              // Class name
    // Class Declarations:

    // (1) Fields:
    private char[] stackArray;    // The array implementing the stack.
    private int    topOfStack;    // The top of the stack.

    // (2) Constructor:
    public CharStack(int n) { stackArray = new char[n]; topOfStack = -1; }

    // (3) Methods:
    public void push(char element) { stackArray[++topOfStack] = element; }
    public char pop()              { return stackArray[topOfStack--]; }
    public char peek()             { return stackArray[topOfStack]; }
    public boolean isEmpty()       { return topOfStack < 0; }
    public boolean isFull()        { return topOfStack == stackArray.length - 1; }
}
```

1.3 Objects

Class Instantiation

The process of creating objects from a class is called *instantiation*. An *object* is an instance of a class. The object is constructed using the class as a blueprint and is a concrete instance of the abstraction that the class represents. An object must be created before it can be used in a program. In Java, objects are manipulated through *object references* (also called *reference values* or simply *references*). The process of creating objects usually involves the following steps:

1. Declaration of a variable to store the object reference.
   This involves declaring a *reference variable* of the appropriate class to store the reference to the object.

   ```java
   // Declaration of two reference variables that will denote
   // two distinct objects, namely two stacks of characters, respectively.
   CharStack stack1, stack2;
   ```

2. Creating an object.
   This involves using the new operator in conjunction with a call to a constructor, to create an instance of the class.

   ```java
   // Create two distinct stacks of chars.
   stack1 = new CharStack(10); // Stack length: 10 chars
   stack2 = new CharStack(5);  // Stack length: 5 chars
   ```

   The new operator returns a reference to a new instance of the CharStack class. This reference can be assigned to a reference variable of the appropriate class.

Each object has a unique identity and has its own copy of the fields declared in the class definition. The two stacks, denoted by stack1 and stack2, will have their own stackArray and topOfStack fields.

The purpose of the constructor call on the right side of the new operator is to initialize the newly created object. In this particular case, for each new CharStack instance created using the new operator, the constructor creates an array of characters. The length of this array is given by the value of the argument to the constructor. The constructor also initializes the topOfStack field.

The declaration and the instantiation can also be combined:

```
CharStack stack1 = new CharStack(10),
          stack2 = new CharStack(5);
```

Figure 1.2 shows the UML notation for objects. The graphical representation of an object is very similar to that of a class. Figure 1.2 shows the canonical notation, where the name of the reference variable denoting the object is prefixed to the class name with a colon ':'. If the name of the reference variable is omitted, as in Figure 1.2b, this denotes an anonymous object. Since objects in Java do not have names, but are denoted by references, a more elaborate notation is shown in Figure 1.2c, where objects representing references of CharStack class explicitly refer to CharStack objects. In most cases, the more compact notation will suffice.

Figure 1.2 *UML Notation for Objects*

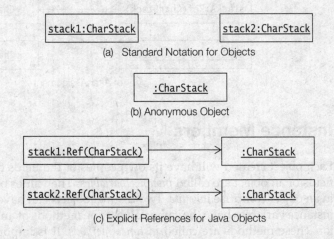

(a) Standard Notation for Objects

(b) Anonymous Object

(c) Explicit References for Java Objects

Object References

A reference provides a handle to an object that is created and stored in memory. In Java, objects can only be manipulated via references, which can be stored in variables. An object can have several references, often called its *aliases*. The object can be manipulated via any one of its aliases.

```
// Create two distinct stacks of chars.
CharStack stackA = new CharStack(12); // Stack length: 12 chars
CharStack stackB = new CharStack(6);  // Stack length: 6 chars

stackB = stackA;                       // (1) aliases after assignment
//(Stack previously referenced by stackB can now be garbage collected.)
```

Two stacks are created in the code above. Before the assignment at (1), the situation is as depicted in Figure 1.3a. After the assignment at (1), reference variables stackA and stackB will denote the same stack, as depicted in Figure 1.3b. Reference variables stackA and stackB are aliases after the assignment, as they refer to the same object. What happens to the stack object that was denoted by the reference variable stackB before the assignment? When objects are no longer in use, their memory is, if necessary, reclaimed and reallocated for other objects. This is called *automatic garbage collection.* (Garbage collection in Java is taken care of by the runtime system.)

Figure 1.3   *Aliases*

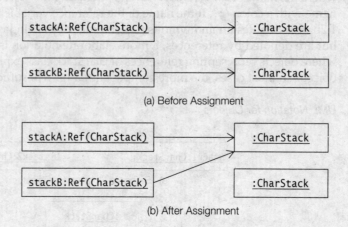

(a) Before Assignment

(b) After Assignment

1.4   Instance Members

Each object created will have its own copies of the fields defined in its class. The fields of an object are called *instance variables.* The values of the instance variables in an object comprise its *state*. Two distinct objects can have the same state, if their instance variables have the same values. The methods of an object define its behavior. These methods are called *instance methods*. It is important to note that these methods pertain to each object of the class. This should not be confused with the implementation of the methods, which is shared by all instances of the class. Instance variables and instance methods, which belong to objects, are collectively called *instance members*, to distinguish them from *static members*, which only belong to the class. Static members are discussed in Section 1.5.

Invoking Methods

Objects communicate by message passing. This means that an object can be made to exhibit a particular behavior by invoking the appropriate operation on the object. In Java, this is done by *calling* a method on the object using the binary infix dot '.' operator. A *method call* spells out the complete message: the object that is the receiver of the message, the method to be invoked, and the arguments to the method, if any. The method invoked on the receiver can also send information back to the sender, via a return value. The method called must be one that is defined for the object.

```
CharStack stack = new CharStack(5);      // Create a stack
stack.push('J');                // (1) Character 'J' pushed
char c = stack.pop();           // (2) One character popped and returned: 'J'
stack.printStackElements(); // (3) Compile time error: No such method in CharStack
```

The sample code above invokes methods on the object denoted by the reference variable stack. The method call at (1) pushes one character on the stack, and the method call at (2) pops one character off the stack. Both push() and pop() methods are defined in the class CharStack. The push() method does not return any value, but the pop() method returns the character popped. Trying to invoke a method printStackElements() on the stack results in a compile-time error, as no such method is defined in the class CharStack.

The dot '.' notation also can be used with a reference to access fields of an object. The use of the dot notation is governed by the *accessibility* of the member. The fields in class CharStack have private accessibility, indicating that they are not accessible from outside the class:

```
stack.topOfStack++;      // Compile time error: topOfStack is a private field.
```

1.5 Static Members

In some cases, certain members should only belong to the class, and not be part of any object created from the class. An example of such a situation is when a class wants to keep track of how many objects of the class have been created. Defining a counter as an instance variable in the class definition for tracking the number of objects created, does not solve the problem. Each object created will have its own counter field. Which counter should then be updated? The solution is to declare the counter field as being static. Such a field is called a *static variable*. It belongs to the class, and not to any object of the class. A static variable is initialized when the class is loaded at runtime. Similarly, a class can have *static methods* that belong only to the class, and not to any objects of the class. Static variables and static methods are collectively known as *static members*, and are distinguished from instance members in a class definition by the keyword static in their declaration.

Figure 1.4 shows the class diagram for the class CharStack. It has been augmented by two static members that are shown underlined. The augmented definition of the CharStack class is given in Example 1.2. The field counter is a static variable declared at (1). It will be allocated and initialized to the default value 0 when the class is loaded. Each time an object of the CharStack class is created, the constructor at (2) is executed. The constructor explicitly increments the counter in the class. The method getInstanceCount() at (3) is a static method belonging to the class. It returns the counter value when called.

Figure 1.4 *Class Diagram Showing Static Members of a Class*

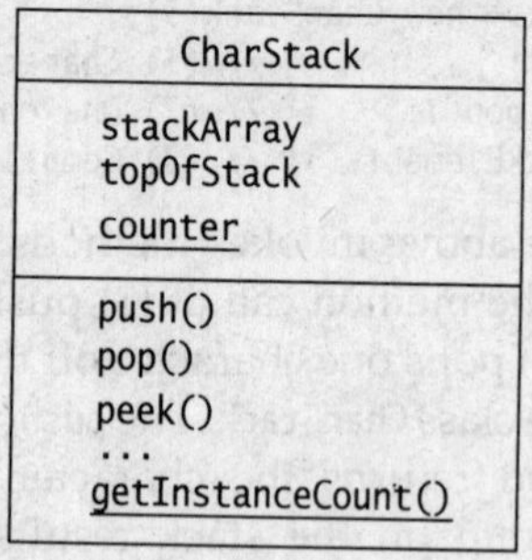

CharStack
stackArray
topOfStack
counter
push()
pop()
peek()
...
getInstanceCount()

Figure 1.5 shows the classification of the members in class CharStack using the terminology we have introduced so far. Table 1.1 at the end of this section, provides a summary of the terminology used in defining members of a class.

Example 1.2 *Static Members in Class Definition*

```java
// Source Filename CharStack.java
public class CharStack {
    // Instance variables
    private char[] stackArray;  // The array implementing the stack.
    private int    topOfStack;  // The top of the stack.

    // Static variable
    private static int counter;                                    // (1)

    // Constructor now increments the counter for each object created.
    public CharStack(int capacity) {                               // (2)
        stackArray = new char[capacity];
        topOfStack = -1;
        counter++;
    }

    // Instance methods
    public void push(char element) { stackArray[++topOfStack] = element; }
    public char pop()              { return stackArray[topOfStack--]; }
    public char peek()             { return stackArray[topOfStack]; }
```

```
                    public boolean isEmpty()        { return topOfStack < 0; }
                    public boolean isFull()         { return topOfStack == stackArray.length - 1; }

                    // Static method                                              (3)
                    public static int getInstanceCount() { return counter; }
                }
```

Clients can access static members in the class by using the class name. The following code invokes the getInstanceCount() method in the class CharStack:

```
    int count = CharStack.getInstanceCount(); // Class name to invoke static method
```

Figure 1.5   *Members of a Class*

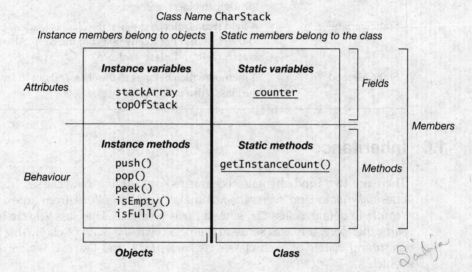

Static members can also be accessed via object references:

```
    CharStack stack1 = new CharStack(10);
    int count1 = stack1.getInstanceCount();   // Reference invokes static method
```

Static members in a class can be accessed both by the class name and via object references, but instance members can only be accessed by object references.

Table 1.1   *Terminology for Class Members*

Instance Members	These are instance variables and instance methods of an object. They can only be accessed or invoked through an object reference.
Instance Variable	A field that is allocated when the class is instantiated, that is, when an object) of the class is created. Also called *non-static field*.
Instance Method	A method that belongs to an instance of the class. Objects of the same class share its implementation.
Static Members	These are static variables and static methods of a class. They can be accessed or invoked either by using the class name or through an object reference.
Static Variable	A field that is allocated when the class is loaded. It belongs to the class and not to any object of the class. Also called *static field* and *class variable*.
Static Method	A method which belongs to the class and not to any object of the class. Also called *class method*.

1.6   Inheritance

There are two fundamental mechanisms for building new classes from existing ones: *inheritance* and *aggregation*. It makes sense to *inherit* from an existing class Vehicle to define a class Car, since a car is a vehicle. The class Vehicle has several *parts*; therefore, it makes sense to define a *composite object* of class Vehicle that has *constituent objects* of such classes as Motor, Axle, and GearBox, which make up a vehicle.

Inheritance is illustrated by an example that implements a stack of characters that can print its elements on the terminal. This new stack has all the properties and behaviors of the CharStack class, but it also has the additional capability of printing its elements. Given that this printable stack is a stack of characters, it can be derived from the CharStack class. This relationship is shown in Figure 1.6. The class PrintableCharStack is called the *subclass*, and the class CharStack is called the *super-class*. The CharStack class is a *generalization* for all stacks of characters, whereas the class PrintableCharStack is a *specialization* of stacks of characters that can also print their elements.

Figure 1.6 *Class Diagram Depicting Inheritance Relation*

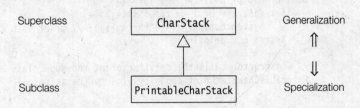

In Java, deriving a new class from an existing class requires the use of the extends clause in the subclass definition. A subclass can *extend* only one superclass. The subclass inherits members of the superclass. The following code fragment implements the PrintableCharStack class:

```
class PrintableCharStack extends CharStack {                           // (1)
    // Instance method
    public void printStackElements() {                                // (2)
        // ... implementation of the method...
    }

    // The constructor calls the constructor of the superclass explicitly.
    public PrintableCharStack(int capacity) { super(capacity); }      // (3)
}
```

The PrintableCharStack class extends the CharStack class at (1). Implementing the printStackElements() method in the PrintableCharStack class requires access to the field stackArray from the superclass CharStack. However, this field is *private* and therefore not accessible in the subclass. The subclass can access these fields if the accessibility of the fields is changed to *protected* in the CharStack class. Example 1.3 uses a version of the class CharStack, which has been modified accordingly. Implementation of the printStackElements() method is shown at (2). The constructor of the PrintableCharStack class at (3) calls the constructor of the superclass CharStack in order to initialize the stack properly.

- -

Example 1.3 *Defining a Subclass*

```
    // Source Filename: CharStack.java
    public class CharStack {
        // Instance variables
        protected char[] stackArray;  // The array that implements the stack.
        protected int    topOfStack;  // The top of the stack.

        // The rest of the definition is the same as in Example 1.2.
    }

    // Source Filename: PrintableCharStack.java
    public class PrintableCharStack extends CharStack {                // (1)
```

```
    // Instance method
    public void printStackElements() {                                // (2)
        for (int i = 0; i <= topOfStack; i++)
            System.out.print(stackArray[i]); // print each char on terminal
        System.out.println();
    }
    // Constructor calls the constructor of the superclass explicitly.
    PrintableCharStack(int capacity) { super(capacity); }             // (3)
}
```

Objects of the PrintableCharStack class will respond just like the objects of the Char-Stack class, but they will also have the additional functionality defined in the subclass:

```
PrintableCharStack aPrintableCharStack = new PrintableCharStack(3);
aPrintableCharStack.push('H');
aPrintableCharStack.push('i');
aPrintableCharStack.push('!');
aPrintableCharStack.printStackElements();     // Prints "Hi!" on the terminal
```

1.7 Aggregation

When building new classes from existing classes using *aggregation*, a composite object is built from other constituent objects that are its parts.

Java supports aggregation of objects by reference, since objects cannot contain other objects explicitly. The fields can only contain values of primitive data types or references to other objects. Each object of the CharStack class has a field to store the reference to an array object that holds the characters. Each stack object also has a field of primitive data type int to store the index value that denotes the top of stack. This is reflected in the definition of the CharStack class, which contains an instance variable for each of these parts. In contrast to the constituent objects whose references are stored in fields, the values of primitive data types are stored in the fields of the composite object. The *aggregation* relationship is depicted by the UML diagram in Figure 1.7, showing that each object of the CharStack class will have one array object of char associated with it.

Figure 1.7 *Class Diagram Depicting Aggregation*

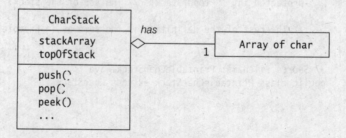

1.8 Tenets of Java

- Code in Java must be encapsulated in classes.
- There are two kinds of values in Java: object references and atomic values of primitive types.
- References denote objects that are created from classes.
- Objects can only be manipulated via references.
- Objects in Java cannot contain other objects; they can only have references to other objects.
- Deletion of objects is managed by the runtime system.

 Review Questions

1.1 Which statement is true about a method?

Select the one correct answer.

(a) A method is an implementation of an abstraction.
(b) A method is an attribute defining the property of a particular abstraction.
(c) A method is a category of objects.
(d) A method is an operation defining the behavior for a particular abstraction.
(e) A method is a blueprint for making operations.

1.2 Which statement is true about an object?

Select the one correct answer.

(a) An object is what classes are instantiated from.
(b) An object is an instance of a class.
(c) An object is a blueprint for creating concrete realization of abstractions.
(d) An object is a reference to an attribute.
(e) An object is a variable.

1.3 Which line contains a constructor in this class definition?

```
public class Counter {                                           // (1)
    int current, step;

    public Counter(int startValue, int stepValue) {              // (2)
        set(startValue);
        setStepValue(stepValue);
    }

    public int get() { return current; }                         // (3)

    public void set(int value) { current = value; }              // (4)

    public void setStepValue(int stepValue) { step = stepValue; } // (5)
}
```

Select the one correct answer.

(a) Code marked with (1) is a constructor.
(b) Code marked with (2) is a constructor.
(c) Code marked with (3) is a constructor.
(d) Code marked with (4) is a constructor.
(e) Code marked with (5) is a constructor.

1.4 Given that Thing is a class, how many objects and how many reference variables are created by the following code?

```
Thing item, stuff;
item = new Thing();
Thing entity = new Thing();
```

Select the two correct answers.

(a) One object is created.
(b) Two objects are created.
(c) Three objects are created.
(d) One reference variable is created.
(e) Two reference variables are created.
(f) Three reference variables are created.

1.5 Which statement is true about an instance method?

Select the one correct answer.

(a) An instance member is also called a static member.
(b) An instance member is always a field.
(c) An instance member is never a method.
(d) An instance member belongs to an instance, not to the class as a whole.
(e) An instance member always represents an operation.

1.6 How do objects pass messages in Java?

Select the one correct answer.

(a) They pass messages by modifying each other's fields.
(b) They pass messages by modifying the static variables of each other's classes.
(c) They pass messages by calling each other's instance methods.
(d) They pass messages by calling static methods of each other's classes.

1.7 Given the following code, which statements are true?

```
class A {
    int value1;
}

class B extends A {
    int value2;
}
```

Select the two correct answers.

(a) Class A extends class B.
(b) Class B is the superclass of class A.
(c) Class A inherits from class B.
(d) Class B is a subclass of class A.
(e) Objects of class A have a field named value2.
(f) Objects of class B have a field named value1.

1.9 Java Programs

A Java program is a collection of one or more classes, with one of them containing the program's execution starting point. A Java *source file* can contain more than one class definition. The Java 2 SDK enforces the rule that at the most one class in the source file has public accessibility. The name of the source file is comprised of the name of this public class with .java as extension. Each class definition in a source file is compiled into a separate *class file*, containing *Java byte code*. The name of this file is comprised of the name of the class with .class as an extension. All programs must be compiled before they can be run. The Java 2 SDK provides tools for this purpose, as explained in 1.10 Sample Java Application.

1.10 Sample Java Application

An *application* is what is normally called a program: source code that is compiled and directly executed. In order to create an application in Java, the program must have a class that defines a method called main. The main() method in the class is the starting point for the execution of any application.

Essential Elements of a Java Application

Example 1.4 is an example of an application in which a client uses the CharStack class to reverse a string of characters.

Example 1.4   *An Application*

```java
// Source Filename: Client.java
public class Client {

    public static void main(String[] args) {

        // Create a stack
        CharStack stack = new CharStack(40);

        // Create a string to push on the stack
        String str = "!no tis ot nuf era skcatS";
```

```java
        int length = str.length();
        System.out.println("Original string: " + str);

        // Push the string char by char onto the stack
        for (int i = 0; i<length; i++) {
            stack.push(str.charAt(i));
        }

        System.out.print("Reversed string: ");
        // Pop and print each char from the stack
        while (!stack.isEmpty()) {
            System.out.print(stack.pop());
        }
        System.out.println();
    }
}

// Source Filename: CharStack.java
public class CharStack {
    // Same as in Example 1.2.
}
```

Output from the program:

```
Original string: !no tis ot nuf era skcatS
Reversed string: Stacks are fun to sit on!
```

- -

The public class Client defines a method with the name main. To start the application, the main() method in this public class is invoked by the Java interpreter, also called the Java Virtual Machine (JVM). The main() method should be declared as follows:

```java
public static void main(String[] args) {
    // ...
}
```

The main() method has public accessibility, that is, it is accessible from any class. The keyword static means the method belongs to the class. The keyword void means the method does not return any value. The parameter list, String[] args, is an array of strings used to pass information to the main() method when the application is started.

Compiling and Running an Application

Java source files can be compiled using the Java compiler tool javac, which is part of the Java 2 SDK.

The source file Client.java contains the definition of the Client class. The source file can be compiled by giving the following input at the command line:

```
>javac Client.java
```

This creates the class file, Client.class, containing the Java byte code for the Client class. The Client class uses the CharStack class, and if the file CharStack.class does not already exist, the compiler will also compile the source file CharStack.java.

Compiled classes can be executed by the Java interpreter java, which is also part of the Java 2 SDK. Example 1.4 can be run by giving the following input at the command line:

```
>java Client
```

Note that only the name of the class is specified, resulting in starting the execution of the main() method from the specified class. The application in Example 1.4 terminates when the execution of the main() method is completed.

 ## Review Questions

1.8 What command in the Java 2 SDK should be used to compile the following code contained in a file called SmallProg.java?

```
public class SmallProg {
    public static void main(String[] args) { System.out.println("Good luck!"); }
}
```

Select the one correct answer.

(a) java SmallProg
(b) javac SmallProg
(c) java SmallProg.java
(d) javac SmallProg.java
(e) java SmallProg main

1.9 What command in the Java 2 SDK should be used to execute the main() method of a class named SmallProg?

Select the one correct answer.

(a) java SmallProg
(b) javac SmallProg
(c) java SmallProg.java
(d) java SmallProg.class
(e) java SmallProg.main()

Chapter Summary

The following topics were discussed in this chapter:

- basic concepts in OOP, and how they are supported in Java
- essential elements of a Java application
- compiling and running Java applications

Programming Exercise

1.1 Modify the program from Example 1.4 to use the PrintableCharStack class, rather than the CharStack class. Utilize the printStackElements() method from the PrintableCharStack class. Is the new program behavior-wise any different from Example 1.4?

Language Fundamentals

2

●●●

- Identify correctly constructed package declarations, `import` statements, class declarations (of all forms, including inner classes), interface declarations, method declarations (including the `main` method that is used to start execution of a class), variable declarations, and identifiers.
  - *For defining and using packages, see Section 4.6.*
  - *For class declarations, see Section 4.2.*
  - *For nested classes, see Chapter 7.*
  - *For interface declarations, see Section 6.4.*
  - *For method declarations, see Section 4.3.*
- Identify classes that correctly implement an interface where that interface is either `java.lang.Runnable` or a fully specified interface in the question.
  - *For interface implementation, see Section 6.4.*
  - *For implementation of `java.lang.Runnable`, see Section 9.3.*
- State the correspondence between index values in the argument array passed to a `main` method and command line arguments.
  - *See Section 3.23.*
- Identify all Java programming language keywords. Note: There will not be any questions regarding esoteric distinctions between keywords and manifest constants.
- State the effect of using a variable or array element of any kind, when no explicit assignment has been made to it.
  - *For array elements, see Section 4.1.*
- State the range of all primitive data types, and declare literal values for `String` and all primitive types using all permitted formats, bases and representations.
  - *See also Appendix G.*

- State the wrapper classes for primitive data types.

2.1 Basic Language Elements

Like any other programming language, the Java programming language is defined by *grammar rules* that specify how *syntactically* legal constructs can be formed using the language elements, and by a *semantic definition* that specifies the *meaning* of syntactically legal constructs.

Lexical Tokens

The low-level language elements are called *lexical tokens* (or just *tokens* for short) and are the building blocks for more complex constructs. Identifiers, numbers, operators, and special characters are all examples of tokens that can be used to build high-level constructs like expressions, statements, methods, and classes.

Identifiers

A name in a program is called an *identifier*. Identifiers can be used to denote classes, methods, variables, and labels.

In Java an *identifier* is composed of a sequence of characters, where each character can be either a *letter*, a *digit*, a *connecting punctuation* (such as *underscore _*), or any *currency symbol* (such as $, ¢, ¥, or £). However, the first character in an identifier cannot be a digit. Since Java programs are written in the Unicode character set (see p. 23), the definitions of letter and digit are interpreted according to this character set.

Identifiers in Java are case sensitive, for example, price and Price are two different identifiers.

Examples of Legal Identifiers:

```
number, Number, sum_$, bingo, $$_100, mål, grüß
```

Examples of Illegal Identifiers:

```
48chevy, all@hands, grand-sum
```

The name 48chevy is not a legal identifier as it starts with a digit. The character @ is not a legal character in an identifier. It is also not a legal operator so that all@hands cannot not be interpreted as a legal expression with two operands. The character - is also not a legal character in an identifier. However, it is a legal operator so grand-sum could be interpreted as a legal expression with two operands.

Keywords

Keywords are reserved identifiers that are predefined in the language and cannot be used to denote other entities. All the keywords are in lowercase, and incorrect usage results in compilation errors.

Keywords currently defined in the language are listed in Table 2.1. In addition, three identifiers are reserved as predefined *literals* in the language: the null reference and the Boolean literals true and false (see Table 2.2). Keywords currently reserved, but not in use, are listed in Table 2.3. All these reserved words cannot be used as identifiers. The index contains references to relevant sections where currently defined keywords are explained.

Table 2.1 *Keywords in Java*

abstract	default	implements	protected	throw
assert	do	import	public	throws
boolean	double	instanceof	return	transient
break	else	int	short	try
byte	extends	interface	static	void
case	final	long	strictfp	volatile
catch	finally	native	super	while
char	float	new	switch	
class	for	package	synchronized	
continue	if	private	this	

Table 2.2 *Reserved Literals in Java*

null	true	false

Table 2.3 *Reserved Keywords not Currently in Use*

const	goto

Literals

A *literal* denotes a constant value, that is, the value a literal represents remains unchanged in the program. Literals represent numerical (integer or floating-point), character, boolean or string values. In addition, there is the literal null that represents the null reference.

Table 2.4 *Examples of Literals*

Integer	2000	0	-7			
Floating-point	3.14	-3.14	.5	0.5		
Character	'a'	'A'	'0'	':'	'-'	')'
Boolean	true	false				
String	"abba"	"3.14"	"for"	"a piece of the action"		

Integer Literals

Integer data types are comprised of the following primitive data types: int, long, byte, and short (see Section 2.2).

The default data type of an integer literal is always int, but it can be specified as long by appending the suffix L (or l) to the integer value. Without the suffix, the long literals 2000L and 0l will be interpreted as int literals. There is no direct way to specify a short or a byte literal.

In addition to the decimal number system, integer literals can also be specified in octal (*base* 8) and hexadecimal (*base* 16) number systems. Octal and hexadecimal numbers are specified with 0 and 0x (or 0X) prefix respectively. Examples of decimal, octal and hexadecimal literals are shown in Table 2.5. Note that the leading 0 (zero) digit is not the uppercase letter O. The hexadecimal digits from a to f can also be specified with the corresponding uppercase forms (A to F). Negative integers (e.g. -90) can be specified by prefixing the minus sign (-) to the magnitude of the integer regardless of number system (e.g., -0132 or -0X5A). Number systems and number representation are discussed in Appendix G. Java does not support literals in binary notation.

Table 2.5   *Examples of Decimal, Octal, and Hexadecimal Literals*

Decimal	Octal	Hexadecimal
8	010	0x8
10L	012L	0XaL
16	020	0x10
27	033	0x1B
90L	0132L	0x5aL
-90	-0132	-0X5A
2147483647 (i.e., 2^{31}-1)	017777777777	0x7fffffff
-2147483648 (i.e., -2^{31})	-020000000000	-0x80000000
1125899906842624L (i.e., 2^{50})	040000000000000000L	0x4000000000000L

Floating-point Literals

Floating-point data types come in two flavors: float or double.

The default data type of a floating-point literal is double, but it can be explicitly designated by appending the suffix D (or d) to the value. A floating-point literal can also be specified to be a float by appending the suffix F (or f).

Floating-point literals can also be specified in scientific notation, where E (or e) stands for *Exponent*. For example, the double literal 194.9E-2 in scientific notation is interpreted as $194.9*10^{-2}$ (i.e., 1.949).

Examples of double *Literals*

```
0.0        0.0d       0D
0.49       .49        .49D
49.0       49.        49D
4.9E+1     4.9E+1D    4.9e1d     4900e-2    .49E2
```

Examples of float *Literals*

```
0.0F       0f
0.49F      .49F
49.0F      49.F       49F
4.9E+1F    4900e-2f   .49E2F
```

Note that the decimal point and the exponent are optional and that at least one digit must be specified.

Boolean Literals

The primitive data type boolean represents the truth-values *true* or *false* that are denoted by the reserved literals true or false, respectively.

Character Literals

A character literal is quoted in single-quotes ('). All character literals have the primitive data type char.

Characters in Java are represented by the 16-bit Unicode character set, which subsumes the 8-bit ISO-Latin-1 and the 7-bit ASCII characters. In Table 2.6, note that digits (0 to 9), upper-case letters (A to Z), and lower-case letters (a to z) have contiguous Unicode values. Any Unicode character can be specified as a four-digit hexadecimal number (i.e., 16 bits) with the prefix \u.

Table 2.6   *Examples of Unicode Values*

Character Literal	Character Literal using Unicode value	Character
' '	'\u0020'	Space
'0'	'\u0030'	0
'1'	'\u0031'	1
'9'	'\u0039'	9
'A'	'\u0041'	A
'B'	'\u0042'	B
'Z'	'\u005a'	Z
'a'	'\u0061'	a
'b'	'\u0062'	b

Continues

Table 2.6   *Examples of Unicode Values (Continued)*

Character Literal	Character Literal using Unicode value	Character
'z'	'\u007a'	z
'Ñ'	'\u0084'	Ñ
'à'	'\u008c'	à
'ß'	'\u00a7'	ß

Escape Sequences

Certain *escape sequences* define special character values as shown in Table 2.7. These escape sequences can be single-quoted to define character literals. For example, the character literals '\t' and '\u0009' are equivalent. However, the character literals '\u000a' and '\u000d' should not be used to represent newline and carriage return in the source code. These values are interpreted as line-terminator characters by the compiler, and will cause compile time errors. One should use the escape sequences '\n' and '\r', respectively, for correct interpretation of these characters in the source code.

Table 2.7   *Escape Sequences*

Escape Sequence	Unicode Value	Character
\b	\u0008	Backspace (BS)
\t	\u0009	Horizontal tab (HT or TAB)
\n	\u000a	Linefeed (LF) a.k.a., Newline (NL)
\f	\u000c	Form feed (FF)
\r	\u000d	Carriage return (CR)
\'	\u0027	Apostrophe-quote
\"	\u0022	Quotation mark
\\	\u005c	Backslash

We can also use the escape sequence *ddd* to specify a character literal by octal value, where each digit *d* can be any octal digit (0–7), as shown in Table 2.8. The number of digits must be three or fewer, and the octal value cannot exceed \377, that is, only the first 256 characters can be specified with this notation.

Table 2.8 *Examples of Escape Sequence* \ddd

Escape Sequence \ddd	Character Literal
'\141'	'a'
'\46'	'&'
'\60'	'0'

String Literals

A *string literal* is a sequence of characters, which must be quoted in quotation marks and which must occur on a single line. All string literal are objects of the class String (see Section 10.5, p. 407).

Escape sequences as well as Unicode values can appear in string literals:

```
"Here comes a tab.\t And here comes another one\u0009!        (1)
"What's on the menu?"                                         (2)
"\"String literals are double-quoted.\""                      (3)
"Left!\nRight!"                                               (4)
```

In (1), the tab character is specified using the escape sequence and the Unicode value respectively. In (2), the single apostrophe need not be escaped in strings, but it would be if specified as a character literal('\''). In (3), the double apostrophes in the string must be escaped. In (4), we use the escape sequence \n to insert a newline. Printing these strings would give the following result:

```
Here comes a tab.    And here comes another one    !
What's on the menu?
"String literals are double-quoted."
Left!
Right!
```

One should also use the string literals "\n" and "\r", respectively, for correct interpretation of the characters "\u000a" and "\u000d" in the source code.

White Spaces

A *white space* is a sequence of spaces, tabs, form feeds, and line terminator characters in a Java source file. Line terminators can be newline, carriage return, or carriage return-newline sequence.

A Java program is a free-format sequence of characters that is *tokenized* by the compiler, that is, broken into a stream of tokens for further analysis. Separators and operators help to distinguish tokens, but sometimes white space has to be inserted explicitly as separators. For example, the identifier classRoom will be interpreted as a single token, unless white space is inserted to distinguish the keyword class from the identifier Room.

White space aids not only in separating tokens, but also in formatting the program so that it is easy for humans to read. The compiler ignores the white spaces once the tokens are identified.

Comments

A program can be documented by inserting comments at relevant places. These comments are for documentation purposes and are ignored by the compiler.

Java provides three types of comments to document a program:

- A single-line comment: `// ... to the end of the line`
- A multiple-line comment: `/* ... */`
- A documentation (Javadoc) comment: `/** ... */`

Single-line Comment

All characters after the comment-start sequence `//` through to the end of the line constitute a *single-line comment*.

```
// This comment ends at the end of this line.
int age;        // From comment-start sequence to the end of the line is a comment.
```

Multiple-line Comment

A *multiple-line comment*, as the name suggests, can span several lines. Such a comment starts with `/*` and ends with `*/`.

```
/*  A comment
    on several
    lines.
*/
```

The comment-start sequences (`//`, `/*`, `/**`) are not treated differently from other characters when occurring within comments, and are thus ignored. This means trying to nest multiple-line comments will result in compile time error:

```
/*  Formula for alchemy.
    gold = wizard.makeGold(stone);
    /* But it only works on Sundays. */
*/
```

The second occurrence of the comment-start sequence `/*` is ignored. The last occurrence of the sequence `*/` in the code is now unmatched, resulting in a syntax error.

Documentation Comment

A *documentation comment* is a special-purpose comment that when placed before class or class member declarations can be extracted and used by the javadoc tool to generate HTML documentation for the program. Documentation comments are usually placed in front of classes, interfaces, methods and field definitions. Groups of special tags can be used inside a documentation comment to provide more specific information. Such a comment starts with /** and ends with */:

```
/**
 * This class implements a gizmo.
 * @author K.A.M.
 * @version 2.0
 */
```

For details on the javadoc tool, see the documentation for the tools in the Java 2 SDK.

 ## Review Questions

2.1 Which of the following is not a legal identifier?

Select the one correct answer.

(a) a2z
(b) ödipus
(c) 52pickup
(d) _class
(e) ca$h
(f) total#

2.2 Which statement is true?

Select the one correct answer.

(a) new and delete are keywords in the Java language.
(b) try, catch, and thrown are keywords in the Java language.
(c) static, unsigned, and long are keywords in the Java language.
(d) exit, class, and while are keywords in the Java language.
(e) return, goto, and default are keywords in the Java language.
(f) for, while, and next are keywords in the Java language.

2.3 Is this a complete and legal comment?

```
/* // */
```

Select the one correct answer.

(a) No, the block comment (/* ... */) is not ended since the single-line comment (// ...) comments out the closing part.
(b) It is a completely valid comment. The // part is ignored by the compiler.
(c) This combination of comments is illegal and the compiler will reject it.

2.2 Primitive Data Types

Figure 2.1 gives an overview of the primitive data types in Java.

Primitive data types in Java can be divided into three main categories:

- *Integral types*—represent signed integers (byte, short, int, long) and unsigned character values (char)
- *Floating-point types* (float, double)—represent fractional signed numbers
- *Boolean type* (boolean)—represent logical values

Figure 2.1   *Primitive Data Types in Java*

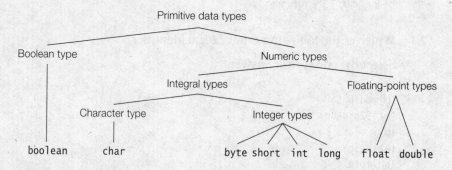

Primitive data values are not objects. Each primitive data type defines the range of values in the data type, and operations on these values are defined by special operators in the language (see Chapter 3).

Each primitive data type also has a corresponding *wrapper* class that can be used to represent a primitive value as an object. Wrapper classes are discussed in Section 10.3.

Integer Types

Table 2.9   *Range of Integer Values*

Data Type	Width (bits)	Minimum value MIN_VALUE	Maximum value MAX_VALUE
byte	8	-2^7 (-128)	2^7-1 (+127)
short	16	-2^{15} (-32768)	$2^{15}-1$ (+32767)
int	32	-2^{31} (-2147483648)	$2^{31}-1$ (+2147483647)
long	64	-2^{63} (-9223372036854775808L)	$2^{63}-1$ (+9223372036854775807L)

Integer data types are byte, short, int, and long (see Table 2.9). Their values are signed integers represented by 2's complement (see Section G.4, p. 598).

Character Type

Table 2.10 *Range of Character Values*

Data Type	Width (bits)	Minimum Unicode value	Maximum Unicode value
char	16	0x0 (\u0000)	uxffff (\uffff)

Characters are represented by the data type char (see Table 2.10). Their values are unsigned integers that denote all the 65536 (2^{16}) characters in the 16-bit Unicode character set. This set includes letters, digits, and special characters.

The first 128 characters of the Unicode set are the same as the 128 characters of the 7-bit ASCII character set, and the first 256 characters of the Unicode set correspond to the 256 characters of the 8-bit ISO Latin-1 character set.

Floating-point Types

Table 2.11 *Range of Floating-point Values*

Data Type	Width (bits)	Minimum Positive Value MIN_VALUE	Maximum Positive Value MAX_VALUE
float	32	1.401298464324817E-45f	3.402823476638528860e+38f
double	64	4.94065645841246544e-324	1.79769313486231570e+308

Floating-point numbers are represented by the float and double data types.

Floating-point numbers conform to the IEEE 754-1985 binary floating-point standard. Table 2.11 shows the range of values for positive floating-point numbers, but these apply equally to negative floating-point numbers with the '-' sign as prefix. Zero can be either 0.0 or -0.0.

Since the size for representation is finite, certain floating-point numbers can only be represented as approximations. For example, the value of the expression (1.0/3.0) is represented as an approximation due to the finite number of bits used.

Boolean Type

Table 2.12   *Boolean Values*

Data Type	Width	True Value Literal	False Value Literal
boolean	not applicable	true	false

The data type `boolean` represents the two logical values denoted by the literals `true` and `false` (see Table 2.12).

Boolean values are produced by all *relational* (see Section 3.9), *conditional* (see Section 3.12) and *boolean logical operators* (see Section 3.11), and are primarily used to govern the flow of control during program execution.

Table 2.13 summarizes the pertinent facts about the primitive data types: their width or size, which indicates the number of the bits required to store a primitive value; their range (of legal values), which is specified by the minimum and the maximum values permissible; and the name of the corresponding wrapper class.

Table 2.13   *Summary of Primitive Data Types*

Data Type	Width (bits)	Minimum Value, Maximum Value	Wrapper Class
boolean	not applicable	true, false (no ordering implied)	Boolean
byte	8	$-2^7, 2^7-1$	Byte
short	16	$-2^{15}, 2^{15}-1$	Short
char	16	0x0, 0xffff	Character
int	32	$-2^{31}, 2^{31}-1$	Integer
long	64	$-2^{63}, 2^{63}-1$	Long
float	32	±1.40129846432481707e-45f, ±3.4028234766385288860e+38f	Float
double	64	±4.94065645841246544e-324, ±1.79769313486231570e+308	Double

 Review Questions

2.4   Which of the following do not denote a primitive data value in Java?

Select the two correct answers.

(a) "t"
(b) 'k'
(c) 50.5F
(d) "hello"
(e) false

2.5   Which of the following primitive data types are not integer types?

Select the three correct answers.

(a) Type `boolean`
(b) Type `byte`
(c) Type `float`
(d) Type `short`
(e) Type `double`

2.6   Which integral type in Java has the exact range from -2147483648 (-2^{31}) to 2147483647 $(2^{31}-1)$, inclusive?

Select the one correct answer.

(a) Type `byte`
(b) Type `short`
(c) Type `int`
(d) Type `long`
(e) Type `char`

2.3 Variable Declarations

A *variable* stores a value of a particular type. A variable has a name, a type, and a value associated with it. In Java, variables can only store values of primitive data types and references to objects. Variables that store references to objects are called *reference variables*.

Declaring and Initializing Variables

Variable declarations are used to specify the type and the name of variables. This implicitly determines their memory allocation and the values that can be stored in them. We show some examples of declaring variables that can store primitive values:

```
char a, b, c;          // a, b and c are character variables.
double area;           // area is a floating-point variable.
boolean flag;          // flag is a boolean variable.
```

The first declaration above is equivalent to the following three declarations:

```
char a;
char b;
char c;
```

A declaration can also include initialization code to specify an appropriate initial value for the variable:

```
int i = 10,            // i is an int variable with initial value 10.
    j = 101;           // j is an int variable with initial value 101.
long big = 2147483648L; // big is a long variable with specified initial value.
```

Object Reference Variables

An *object reference* is a value that denotes an object in Java. Such reference values can be stored in variables and used to manipulate the object denoted by the reference value.

A variable declaration that specifies a *reference type* (i.e., a class, an array, or an interface name) declares an object reference variable. Analogous to the declaration of variables of primitive data types, the simplest form of reference variable declaration only specifies the name and the reference type. The declaration determines what objects a reference variable can denote. Before we can use a reference variable to manipulate an object, it must be declared and initialized with the reference value of the object.

```
Pizza yummyPizza;     // Variable yummyPizza can reference objects of class Pizza.
Hamburger bigOne,     // Variable bigOne can reference objects of class Hamburger,
          smallOne;   // and so can variable smallOne.
```

It is important to note that the declarations above do not create any objects of class Pizza or Hamburger. The declarations only create variables that can store references to objects of these classes.

A declaration can also include an initializer to create an object whose reference can be assigned to the reference variable:

```
Pizza yummyPizza = new Pizza("Hot&Spicy"); // Declaration with initializer.
```

The reference variable yummyPizza can reference objects of class Pizza. The keyword new, together with the *constructor call* Pizza("Hot&Spicy"), creates an object of class Pizza. The reference to this object is assigned to the variable yummyPizza. The newly created object of class Pizza can now be manipulated through the reference stored in this variable.

Initializers for initializing fields in objects, classes, and interfaces are discussed in Section 8.2.

Reference variables for arrays are discussed in Section 4.1.

Lifetime of Variables

Lifetime of a variable, that is, the time a variable is accessible during execution, is determined by the context in which it is declared. We distinguish between lifetime of variables in three contexts:

- *Instance variables*—members of a class and created for each object of the class. In other words, every object of the class will have its own copies of these variables, which are local to the object. The values of these variables at any given time constitute the *state* of the object. Instance variables exist as long as the object they belong to exists.

- *Static variables*—also members of a class, but not created for any object of the class and, therefore, belong only to the class (see Section 4.10, p. 144). They are created when the class is loaded at runtime, and exist as long as the class exists.

- *Local variables* (also called *method automatic variables*)—declared in methods and in blocks and created for each execution of the method or block. After the execution of the method or block completes, local (non-final) variables are no longer accessible.

2.4 Initial Values for Variables

Default Values for Fields

Default values for fields of primitive data types and reference types are listed in Table 2.14. The value assigned depends on the type of the field.

Table 2.14   *Default Values*

Data Type	Default Value
boolean	false
char	'\u0000'
Integer (byte, short, int, long)	0L for long, 0 for others
Floating-point (float, double)	0.0F or 0.0D
Reference types	null

If no initialization is provided for a static variable either in the declaration or in a static initializer block (see Section 8.2, p. 336), it is initialized with the default value of its type when the class is loaded.

Similarly, if no initialization is provided for an instance variable either in the declaration or in an instance initializer block (see Section 8.2, p. 338), it is initialized with the default value of its type when the class is instantiated.

The fields of reference types are always initialized with the null reference value, if no initialization is provided.

Example 2.1 illustrates default initialization of fields. Note that static variables are initialized when the class is loaded the first time, and instance variables are initialized accordingly in *every* object created from the class Light.

Example 2.1   *Default Values for Fields*

```
public class Light {
// Static variable
static int counter;         // Default value 0 when class is loaded.

// Instance variables
int    noOfWatts = 100; // Explicitly set to 100.
boolean indicator;          // Implicitly set to default value false.
String  location;           // Implicitly set to default value null.

public static void main(String[] args) {
    Light bulb = new Light();
    System.out.println("Static variable counter: "      + Light.counter);
    System.out.println("Instance variable noOfWatts: " + bulb.noOfWatts);
    System.out.println("Instance variable indicator: " + bulb.indicator);
    System.out.println("Instance variable location: "  + bulb.location);
    return;
}
}
```

Output from the program:

```
Static variable counter: 0
Instance variable noOfWatts: 100
Instance variable indicator: false
Instance variable location: null
```

Initializing Local Variables of Primitive Data Types

Local variables are *not* initialized when they are created at method invocation, that is, when the execution of a method is started. They must be explicitly initialized before being used. The compiler will report attempts to use uninitialized local variables.

Example 2.2   *Flagging Uninitialized Local Variables of Primitive Data Types*

```
public class TooSmartClass {
    public static void main(String[] args) {
        int weight = 10, thePrice;                          // Local variables

        if (weight <  10) thePrice = 1000;
        if (weight >  50) thePrice = 5000;
        if (weight >= 10) thePrice = weight*10;             // Always executed.
        System.out.println("The price is: " + thePrice);    // (1)
    }
}
```

In Example 2.2, the compiler complains that the local variable thePrice used in the println statement at (1) may not be initialized. However, it can be seen that at runtime the local variable thePrice will get the value 100 in the last if-statement, before it is used in the println statement. The compiler does not perform a rigorous analysis of the program in this regard. It only compiles the body of a conditional statement if it can deduce the condition to be true. The program will compile correctly if the variable is initialized in the declaration, or if an unconditional assignment is made to the variable. Replacing the declaration of the local variables in Example 2.2 with the following declaration solves the problem:

```
int weight = 10, thePrice = 0;          // Both local variables initialized.
```

Initializing Local Reference Variables

Local reference variables are bound by the same initialization rules as local variables of primitive data types.

Example 2.3   *Flagging Uninitialized Local Reference Variables*

```
public class VerySmartClass {
    public static void main(String[] args) {
        String importantMessage;        // Local reference variable

        System.out.println("The message length is: " + importantMessage.length());
    }
}
```

In Example 2.3, the compiler complains that the local variable importantMessage used in the println statement may not be initialized. If the variable importantMessage is set to the value null, the program will compile. However, at runtime, a NullPointerException will be thrown since the variable importantMessage will not denote any object. The golden rule is to ensure that a reference variable, whether local or not, is assigned a reference to an object before it is used, that is, ensure that it does not have the value null. The program compiles and runs if we replace the declaration with the following declaration, which creates a string literal and assigns its reference to the local reference variable importantMessage:

```
String importantMessage = "Initialize before use!";
```

Arrays and their default values are discussed in Section 4.1 on page 101.

Review Questions

2.7   Which of the following lines are valid declarations?

Select the three correct answers.
(a) `char a = '\u0061';`
(b) `char 'a' = 'a';`
(c) `char \u0061 = 'a';`
(d) `ch\u0061r a = 'a';`
(e) `ch'a'r a = 'a';`

2.8   Given the following code within a method, which statement is true?

```
int a, b;
b = 5;
```

Select the one correct answer.
(a) Local variable a is not declared.
(b) Local variable b is not declared.
(c) Local variable a is declared but not initialized.
(d) Local variable b is declared but not initialized.
(e) Local variable b is initialized but not declared.

2.9   In which of these variable declarations will the variable remain uninitialized unless explicitly initialized?

Select the one correct answer.
(a) Declaration of an instance variable of type `int`.
(b) Declaration of a static variable of type `float`.
(c) Declaration of a local variable of type `float`.
(d) Declaration of a static variable of type `Object`.
(e) Declaration of an instance variable of type `int[]`.

2.5 Java Source File Structure

The structure of a skeletal Java source file is depicted in Figure 2.2. A Java source file can have the following elements that, if present, must be specified in the following order:

1.   An optional package declaration to specify a package name. Packages are discussed in Section 4.6.

2. Zero or more import declarations. Since import declarations introduce class and interface names in the source code, they must be placed before any type declarations. The import statement is discussed in Section 4.6.

3. Any number of *top-level* class and interface declarations. Since these declarations belong to the same package, they are said to be defined at the *top level*, which is the package level.

The classes and interfaces can be defined in any order. Class and interface declarations are collectively known as *type declarations*. Technically, a source file need not have any such definitions, but that is hardly useful.

The Java 2 SDK imposes the restriction that at the most one public class definition per source file can be defined. If a public class is defined, the file name must match this public class. If the public class name is NewApp, then the file name must be NewApp.java.

Classes are discussed in Section 4.2, and interfaces are discussed in Section 6.4.

Note that except for the package and the import statements, all code is encapsulated in classes and interfaces. No such restriction applies to comments and white space.

Figure 2.2 *Java Source File Structure*

```
// Filename: NewApp.java
```

```
// PART 1: (OPTIONAL) package declaration
package com.company.project.fragilePackage;
```

```
// PART 2: (ZERO OR MORE) import declarations
import java.io.*;
import java.util.*;
```

```
// PART 3: (ZERO OR MORE) top-level class and interface declarations
public class NewApp { }

class AClass { }

interface IOne { }

class BClass { }

interface ITwo { }
// ...
// end of file
```

Review Questions

2.10 What will be the result of attempting to compile this class?

```
import java.util.*;

package com.acme.toolkit;

public class AClass {
    public Other anInstance;
}

class Other {
    int value;
}
```

Select the one correct answer.

(a) The class will fail to compile, since the class Other has not yet been declared when referenced in class AClass.

(b) The class will fail to compile, since import statements must never be at the very top of a file.

(c) The class will fail to compile, since the package declaration can never occur after an import statement.

(d) The class will fail to compile, since the class Other must be defined in a file called Other.java.

(e) The class will fail to compile, since the class Other must be declared public.

(f) The class will compile without errors.

2.11 Is an empty file a valid source file?

Answer true or false.

2.6 The main() Method

The mechanics of compiling and running Java applications using the Java 2 SDK are outlined in Section 1.10. The Java interpreter executes a method called main in the class specified on the command line. Any class can have a main() method, but only the main() method of the class specified to the Java interpreter is executed to start a Java application.

The main() method must have public accessibility so that the interpreter can call it (see Section 4.9, p. 138). It is a static method belonging to the class, so that no object of the class is required to start the execution (see Section 4.10, p. 144). It does not return a value, that is, it is declared void (see Section 5.4, p. 176). It always has an array of String objects as its only formal parameter. This array contains any arguments passed to the program on the command line (see Section 3.23, p. 95). All this adds up to the following definition of the main() method:

```
public static void main(String[] args) {
    // ...
}
```

The above requirements do not exclude specification of additional modifiers (see Section 4.10, p. 144) or any throws clause (see Section 5.9, p. 201). The main() method can also be overloaded like any other method (see p. 116). The Java interpreter ensures that the main() method, that complies with the above definition is the starting point of the program execution.

 ## Review Questions

2.12   Which of these are valid declarations of the main() method in order to start the execution of a Java application?

Select the two correct answers.
(a) `static void main(String[] args) { /* ... */ }`
(b) `public static int main(String[] args) { /* ... */ }`
(c) `public static void main(String args) { /* ... */ }`
(d) `final public static void main(String[] arguments) { /* ... */ }`
(e) `public int main(Strings[] args, int argc) { /* ... */ }`
(f) `static public void main(String args[]) { /* ... */ }`

2.13   Which of the following are reserved keywords?

Select the three correct answers.
(a) `public`
(b) `static`
(c) `void`
(d) `main`
(e) `String`
(f) `args`

 ## Chapter Summary

The following topics were discussed in this chapter:

- basic language elements: identifiers, keywords, literals, white spaces, and comments

- primitive data types: integral, floating-point, and Boolean

- converting numbers between decimal, octal, and hexadecimal systems

- lifetime of fields and local variables

- declaration and initialization of variables, including reference variables

- usage of default values for fields

- structure of a valid Java source file
- declaration of the main() method whose execution starts the application

    Programming Exercises

2.1   The following program has several errors. Modify it so that it will compile and
run without errors. (See Section 4.6 on page 129 for compiling and running code
from packages.)

```java
import java.util.*;

package com.acme;

public class Exercise1 {
    int counter;

    void main(String[] args) {
        Exercise1 instance = new Exercise1();
        instance.go();
    }

    public void go() {
        int sum;
        int i = 0;
        while (i<100) {
            if (i == 0) sum = 100;
            sum = sum + i;
            i++;
        }
        System.out.println(sum);
    }
}
```

2.2   The following program has several errors. Modify it so that it will compile and
run without errors.

```java
// Filename: Temperature.java
PUBLIC CLASS temperature {
    PUBLIC void main(string args) {
        double fahrenheit = 62.5;
        */ Convert /*
        double celsius = f2c(fahrenheit);
        System.out.println(fahrenheit + 'F = ' + celsius + 'C');
    }

    double f2c(float fahr) {
        RETURN (fahr - 32) * 5 / 9;
    }
}
```

Operators and Assignments

3

- Determine the result of applying any operator (including assignment operators and the `instanceof` operator) to operands of any type, class, scope, or accessibility, or any combination of these.
  - *See also Section 6.6.*
- Determine the result of applying the boolean `equals(Object)` method to objects of any combination of the classes `java.lang.String`, `java.lang.Boolean` and `java.lang.Object`.
- In an expression involving the operators &, |, &&, ||, and variables of known values, state which operands are evaluated and the value of the expression.
- Determine the effect on objects and primitive values of passing variables into methods and performing assignments or other modifying operations in that method.

Supplementary Objectives

- Understand the operator precedence and associativity rules.
- Distinguish between conversions involving casting, widening numeric conversions, and narrowing numeric conversions.
- State unary numeric promotion and binary numeric promotion rules and the contexts in which they are applied.
- Understand type conversions for primitive data types on assignment, string concatenation, arithmetic expression evaluation, and method invocation.

3.1 Precedence and Associativity Rules for Operators

Precedence and associativity rules are necessary for deterministic evaluation of expressions. The operators are summarized in Table 3.1. They are discussed in subsequent sections in this chapter.

The following remarks apply to Table 3.1:

- The operators are shown with decreasing precedence from the top of the table.
- Operators within the same row have the same precedence.
- Parentheses, ( ), can be used to override precedence and associativity.
- The *unary operators*, which require one operand, include the postfix increment (++) and decrement (--) operators from the first row, all the prefix operators (+, -, ++, --, ~, !) in the second row, and the prefix operators (object creation operator new, cast operator (*type*)) in the third row.
- The conditional operator (? :) is *ternary*, that is, requires three operands.
- All operators not listed above as unary or ternary, are *binary*, that is, require two operands.
- All binary operators, except for the relational and assignment operators, associate from left to right. The relational operators are nonassociative.
- Except for unary postfix increment and decrement operators, all unary operators, all assignment operators, and the ternary conditional operator associate from right to left.

Table 3.1 *Operator Summary*

Postfix operators	[] . (*parameters*) expression++ expression--
Unary prefix operators	++expression --expression +expression -expression ~ !
Unary prefix creation and cast	new (*type*)
Multiplicative	* / %
Additive	+ -
Shift	<< >> >>>
Relational	< <= > >= instanceof
Equality	== !=
Bitwise/logical AND	&
Bitwise/logical XOR	^
Bitwise/logical OR	|
Conditional AND	&&
Conditional OR	||
Conditional	?:
Assignment	= += -= *= /= %= <<= >>= >>>= &= ^= |=

Precedence rules are used to determine which operator should be applied first if there are two operators with different precedence, and these follow each other in the expression. In such a case, the operator with the highest precedence is applied first.

2 + 3 * 4 is evaluated as 2 + (3 * 4) (with the result 14) since * has higher precedence than +.

Associativity rules are used to determine which operator should be applied first if there are two operators with the same precedence, and these follow each other in the expression.

Left associativity implies grouping from left to right:

1 + 2 - 3 is interpreted as ((1 + 2) - 3), since the binary operators + and - both have same precedence and left associativity.

Right associativity implies grouping from right to left:

- - 4 is interpreted as (- (- 4)) (with the result 4), since the unary operator - has right associativity.

The precedence and associativity rules together determine the *evaluation order of the operators.*

3.2 Evaluation Order of Operands

In order to understand the result returned by an operator, it is important to understand the *evaluation order of its operands*. Java states that the operands of operators are evaluated from left to right.

Java guarantees that *all* operands of an operator are fully evaluated *before* the operator is applied. The only exceptions are the short-circuit conditional operators &&, ||, and ?:.

In the case of a binary operator, if the left-hand operand causes an exception (see Section 5.5, p. 181), the right-hand operand is not evaluated. The evaluation of the left-hand operand can have side effects that can influence the value of the right-hand operand. For example, in the following code:

```
int b = 10;
System.out.println((b=3) + b);
```

the value printed will be 6 and not 13. The evaluation proceeds as follows:

```
(b=3) + b
   3    + b      b is assigned the value 3
   3    + 3
   6
```

The evaluation order also respects any parentheses, and the precedence and associativity rules of operators.

Examples illustrating how the operand evaluation order influences the result returned by an operator, can be found in Sections 3.4 and 3.7.

3.3 Conversions

In this section we discuss the different kinds of type conversions and list the contexts in which these can occur. Some type conversions must be explicitly stated in the program, while others are done implicitly. Some type conversions can be checked at compile time to guarantee their validity at runtime, while others will require an extra check at runtime.

Unary Cast Operator: (*type*)

Java, being a *strongly typed* language, checks for *type compatibility* (i.e., checks if a type can substitute for another type in a given context) at compile time. However, some checks are only possible at runtime (for example, which type of object a reference actually denotes during execution). In cases where an operator would have incompatible operands (for example, assigning a double to an int), Java demands that a *cast* be used to explicitly indicate the type conversion. The cast construct has the following syntax:

   (*<type>*) *<expression>*

The cast (*<type>*) is applied to the value of the *<expression>*. At runtime, a cast results in a new value of *<type>*, which best represents the value of the *<expression>* in the old type. We use the term *casting* to mean applying the cast operator for explicit type conversion.

Casting can be applied to primitive values as well as references. Casting between primitive data types and reference types is not permitted. Boolean values cannot be cast to other data values, and vice versa. The reference literal null can be cast to any reference type.

Examples of casting between primitive data types are provided in this chapter. Casting between references is discussed in Section 6.6 on page 264.

Narrowing and Widening Conversions

For the primitive data types, the value of a *narrower* data type can be converted to a value of a *broader* data type without loss of information. This is called a *widening primitive conversion*. Widening conversions to the next broader type for primitive data types are summarized in Figure 3.1. The conversions shown are transitive. For example, an int can be directly converted to a double without first having to convert it to a long and a float.

Figure 3.1   *Widening Numeric Conversions*

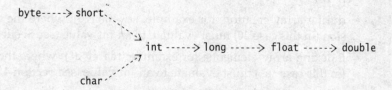

Converting from a broader data type to a narrower data type is called a *narrowing primitive conversion*, which can result in loss of magnitude information. Any conversion which is not a widening conversion according to Figure 3.1 is a narrowing conversion. Note that all conversions between char and the two integer types byte and short are considered narrowing conversions: the reason being that the conversions between the unsigned type char and the signed types byte or short can result in loss of information.

Widening and *narrowing conversions* are also defined for reference types and are discussed in Section 6.6. Conversions *up* the *inheritance hierarchy* are called *widening reference conversions* (a.k.a. *upcasting*). Conversions *down* the inheritance hierarchy are called *narrowing reference conversions* (a.k.a. *downcasting*).

Both narrowing and widening conversions can be either explicit (requiring a cast) or implicit. Widening conversions are usually done implicitly, whereas narrowing conversions typically require a cast. It is not illegal to use a cast for a widening conversion. However, the compiler will flag any conversions that require a cast.

Numeric Promotions

Numeric operators only allow operands of certain types. Numeric promotion is implicitly applied on the operands to convert them to permissible types. Distinction is made between unary and binary numeric promotion.

Unary Numeric Promotion

Unary numeric promotion states that

> If the single operand of the operator has a type narrower than int, it is converted to int by an implicit widening primitive conversion; otherwise, it is not converted.

In other words, unary numeric promotion converts operands of byte, short, and char to int by applying an implicit widening conversion, but operands of other numeric types are not affected.

Unary numeric promotion is applied in the following contexts:

- operand of the unary arithmetic operators + and - (see Section 3.5, p. 51)
- operand of the unary integer bitwise complement operator ~ (see Section 3.13, p. 75)
- during array creation; for example, new int[20], where the dimension expression (in this case 20) must evaluate to an int value (see Section 4.1, p. 101)
- indexing array elements; for example, table['a'], where the index expression (in this case 'a') must evaluate to an int value (see Section 4.1, p. 103)
- individual operands of the shift operators <<, >> and >>> (see Section 3.14, p. 79)

Binary Numeric Promotion

Binary numeric promotion implicitly applies appropriate widening primitive conversions so that a pair of operands have the broadest numeric type of the two, which is always at least int. Given T to be the broadest numeric type of the two operands, the operands are promoted as follows under binary numeric promotion.

If T is broader than int, both operands are converted to T; otherwise, both operands are converted to int.

This means that byte, short, and char are always converted to int at least.

Binary numeric promotion is applied in the following contexts:

- operands of the arithmetic operators *, /, %, +, and - (see Section 3.5, p. 51)
- operands of the relational operators <, <=, >, and >= (see Section 3.9, p. 67)
- operands of the numerical equality operators == and != (see Section 3.10, p. 67)
- operands of the integer bitwise operators &, ^, and | (see Section 3.13, p. 75)

Type Conversion Contexts

Type conversions can occur in the following contexts:

- *assignments* involving primitive data types (see Section 3.4, p. 48) and reference types (see Section 6.6, p. 260)
- *method invocation* involving parameters of primitive data types (see Section 3.17, p. 86) and reference types (see Section 6.6, p. 260)
- *arithmetic expression evaluation* involving numeric types (see Section 3.5, p. 57)
- *string concatenation* involving objects of class String and other data types (see Section 3.6, p. 62)

3.4 Simple Assignment Operator =

The assignment statement has the following syntax:

<variable> = *<expression>*

which can be read as *"the destination, <variable>, gets the value of the source, <expression>"*. The previous value of the destination variable is overwritten by the assignment operator = .

The destination *<variable>* and the source *<expression>* must be type compatible. The destination variable must also have been declared. Since variables can store either primitive data values or object references, *<expression>* evaluates to either a primitive data value or an object reference.

Assigning Primitive Values

The following examples illustrate assignment of primitive values:

```
int j, k;
j = 10;          // j gets the value 10.
j = 5;           // j gets the value 5. Previous value is overwritten.
k = j;           // k gets the value 5.
```

The assignment operator has the lowest precedence, allowing the expression on the right-hand side to be evaluated before assignment.

```
int i;
i = 5;           // i gets the value 5.
i = i + 1;       // i gets the value 6. + has higher precedence than =.
i = 20 - i * 2;  // i gets the value 8: (20 - (i * 2))
```

Assigning References

Copying references by assignment creates aliases, which is discussed in Section 1.3 on page 5. The following example recapitulates that discussion:

```
Pizza pizza1 = new Pizza("Hot&Spicy");
Pizza pizza2 = new Pizza("Sweet&Sour");

pizza2 = pizza1;
```

Variable pizza1 is a reference to a pizza that is hot and spicy, and pizza2 is a reference to a pizza which is sweet and sour. Assigning pizza1 to pizza2 means that pizza2 now references the same pizza as pizza1, that is, the hot and spicy one. After assignment these variables are aliases, and either one can be used to manipulate the hot and spicy Pizza object.

Assigning a reference does not create a copy of the source object denoted by the reference variable on the right-hand side. Reference assignment also does not copy the *state* of the source object to any object denoted by the reference variable on the left-hand side. It merely assigns the reference value to the variable on the right-hand side to the variable on the left-hand side, so that they denote the same object.

A more detailed discussion of reference assignment can be found in Section 6.6.

Multiple Assignments

The assignment statement is an *expression statement,* which means that application of the binary assignment operator returns the value of the expression on the right-hand side.

```
int j, k;
j = 10;          // j gets the value 10 which is returned
k = j;           // k gets the value of j, which is 10, and this value is returned
```

The last two assignments can be written as multiple assignments, illustrating the right associativity of the assignment operator.

```
k = j = 10;        // (k = (j = 10))
```

Multiple assignments are equally valid with references.

```
Pizza pizzaOne, pizzaTwo;
pizzaOne = pizzaTwo = new Pizza("Supreme"); // Aliases.
```

The following example shows the effect of operand evaluation order:

```
int[] a = {10, 20, 30, 40, 50}; // an array of int
int index = 4;
a[index] = index = 2;
```

What is the value of index, and which array element a[index] is assigned a value in the multiple assignment statement? The evaluation proceeds as follows:

```
a[index] = index = 2;
a[4]     = index = 2;
a[4]     = (index = 2);      // index gets the value 2. = is right associative.
a[4]     =       2;          // The value of a[4] is changed from 50 to 2.
```

Numeric Type Conversions on Assignment

If the destination and source have the same type in an assignment, then, obviously, the source and the destination are type compatible, and the source value need not be converted. Otherwise, if a widening primitive conversion is permissible, then the widening conversion is applied implicitly, that is, the source type is promoted to the destination type in an assignment context.

```
// Implicit Widening Primitive Conversions
int    smallOne = 1234;
long   bigOne   = 2000;            // Implicit widening: int to long.
double largeOne = bigOne;          // Implicit widening: long to double.
double hugeOne  = (double) bigOne; // Cast redundant but allowed.
```

Integer values widened to floating-point values can result in loss of *precision*. Precision relates to the number of significant bits in the value, and must not be confused with *magnitude,* which relates how big a value can be represented. In the next

example, the precision of the least significant bits of the long value may be lost
when converting to a float value.

```
long bigInteger = 98765432112345678L;
float realNo = bigInteger;  // Widening but loss of precision: 9.8765436E16
```

Additionally, implicit narrowing primitive conversions on assignment can occur in
cases where all of the following conditions are fulfilled:

- the source is a *constant expression* of either byte, short, char, or int type
- the destination type is either byte, short, or char type
- the value of the source is determined to be in the range of the destination type
  at compile time

```
// Above conditions fulfilled for implicit narrowing primitive conversions.
short s1 = 10;        // int value in range.
short s2 = 'a';       // char value in range.
char c1 = 32;         // int value in range.
char c2 = (byte)35;   // byte value in range. int value in range, without cast.
byte b1 = 40;         // int value in range.
byte b2 = (short)40;  // short value in range. int value in range, without cast.
final int i1 = 20;
byte b3 = i1;         // final value of i1 in range.

// Above conditions not fulfilled for implicit narrowing primitive conversions.
// Explicit cast required.
int i2 = -20;
final int i3 = i2;
final int i4 = 200;
short s3 = (short) i2;    // Not constant expression.
char c3 = (char) i3;      // final value of i3 not determinable.
char c4 = (char) i2;      // Not constant expression.
byte b4 = (byte) 128;     // int value not in range.
byte b5 = (byte) i4;      // final value of i4 not in range.
```

All other narrowing primitive conversions will produce a compile-time error on
assignment, and will explicitly require a cast.

Floating-point values are truncated when converted to integral values.

```
// Explicit narrowing primitive conversions requiring cast.
// The value is truncated to fit the size of the destination type.
float huge   = (float) 1.7976931348623157d; // double to float.
long  giant  = (long) 4415961481999.03D;    // (1) double to long.
int   big    = (int) giant;                  // (2) long to int.
short small  = (short) big;                  // (3) int to short.
byte  minute = (byte) small;                 // (4) short to byte.
char  symbol = (char) 112.5F;                // (5) float to char.
```

Table 3.2 shows how the values are truncated for lines marked (1) to (5) in the previous code.

Table 3.2 *Examples of Truncated Values*

Binary	Decimal	
0000000000000000000001000000010000101011110100001100001100001111	4415961481999	(1)
00101011110100001100001100001111	735101711	(2)
1100001100001111	-15601	(3)
00001111	15	(4)
0000000001110000	'p'	(5)

The discussion on numeric assignment conversions also applies to numeric parameter values at method invocation (see Section 3.18, p. 88), except for the narrowing conversions, which always require a cast.

Review Questions

3.1 Given `char c = 'A';`

What is the simplest way to convert the character value in c into an `int`?

Select the one correct answer.

(a) `int i = c;`
(b) `int i = (int) c;`
(c) `int i = Character.getNumericValue(c);`

3.2 What will be the result of attempting to compile and run the following class?

```java
public class Assignment {
    public static void main(String[] args) {
        int a, b, c;
        b = 10;
        a = b = c = 20;
        System.out.println(a);
    }
}
```

Select the one correct answer.

(a) The code will fail to compile, since the compiler will recognize that the variable c in the assignment statement a = b = c = 20; has not been initialized.
(b) The code will fail to compile because the assignment statement a = b = c = 20; is illegal.
(c) The code will compile correctly and will display 10 when run.
(d) The code will compile correctly and will display 20 when run.

3.3 What will be the result of attempting to compile and run the following program?

```java
public class MyClass {
    public static void main(String[] args) {
        String a, b, c;
        c = new String("mouse");
```

```
        a = new String("cat");
        b = a;
        a = new String("dog");
        c = b;

        System.out.println(c);
    }
}
```

Select the one correct answer.

(a) The program will fail to compile.
(b) The program will print mouse when run.
(c) The program will print cat when run.
(d) The program will print dog when run.
(e) The program will randomly print either cat or dog when run.

3.5 Arithmetic Operators: *, /, %, +, -

The arithmetic operators are used to construct mathematical expressions as in algebra. Their operands are of numeric type (which includes the char type).

Arithmetic Operator Precedence and Associativity

In Table 3.3, the precedence of the operators is in decreasing order, starting from the top row, which has the highest precedence. Unary subtraction has higher precedence than multiplication. The operators in the same row have the same precedence. Binary multiplication, division, and remainder operators have the same precedence. The unary operators have right associativity, and the binary operators have left associativity.

Table 3.3 *Arithmetic Operators*

Unary	+ Addition	- Subtraction	
Binary	* Multiplication	/ Division	% Remainder
	+ Addition	- Subtraction	

Evaluation Order in Arithmetic Expressions

Java guarantees that the operands are fully evaluated from left to right before an arithmetic binary operator is applied. Of course, if evaluation of an operand causes an exception, the subsequent operands will not be evaluated.

In the expression a + b * c, the operand a will always be fully evaluated before the operand b, which will always be fully evaluated before the operand c. However, the multiplication operator * will be applied before the addition operator +, respecting the precedence rules. Note that a, b, and c can be arbitrary arithmetic expressions that have been determined to be the operands of the operators.

Range of Numeric Values

As we have seen, all numeric types have a range of valid values (Section 2.2, p. 28). This range is given by the constants named MAX_VALUE and MIN_VALUE, which are defined in each numeric wrapper class.

The arithmetic operators are overloaded, meaning that the operation of an operator varies depending on the type of its operands. Floating-point arithmetic is performed if any operand of an operator is of floating-point type, otherwise, integer arithmetic is performed.

Values that are out-of-range or are results of invalid expressions, are handled differently depending on whether integer or floating-point arithmetic is performed.

Integer Arithmetic

Integer arithmetic always returns a value that is in range, except in the case of integer division by zero and remainder by zero, which causes an ArithmeticException (see the division operator / and the remainder operator % below). A valid value does not necessarily mean that the result is correct, as demonstrated by the following examples:

```
int tooBig   = Integer.MAX_VALUE + 1;   // -2147483648 which is Integer.MIN_VALUE.
int tooSmall = Integer.MIN_VALUE - 1;   //  2147483647 which is Integer.MAX_VALUE.
```

The results above should be values that are out-of-range. However, integer arithmetic *wraps* if the result is out-of-range, that is, the result is reduced modulo in the range. In order to avoid wrapping of out-of-range values, programs should either use explicit checks or a wider type. If the type long is used in the examples above, the results would be correct in the long range:

```
long notTooBig   = Integer.MAX_VALUE + 1L;   //  2147483648L in range.
long notTooSmall = Integer.MIN_VALUE - 1L;   // -2147483649L in range.
```

Floating-point Arithmetic

Certain floating-point operations result in values that are out-of-range. Typically, adding or multiplying two very large floating-point numbers can result in an out-of-range value which is represented by *Infinity* (see Figure 3.2). Attempting floating-point division by zero also returns infinity. The examples below show how this value is printed as signed infinity.

```
System.out.println( 4.0 / 0.0);       // Prints:  Infinity
System.out.println(-4.0 / 0.0);       // Prints: -Infinity
```

Both positive and negative infinity represent *overflow* to infinity, that is, the value is too large to be represented as a double or float (see Figure 3.2). Signed infinity is represented by named constants POSITIVE_INFINITY and NEGATIVE_INFINITY, in the wrapper classes java.lang.Float and java.lang.Double. A value can be compared with these constants to detect overflow.

Figure 3.2 *Overflow and Underflow in Floating-point Arithmetic*

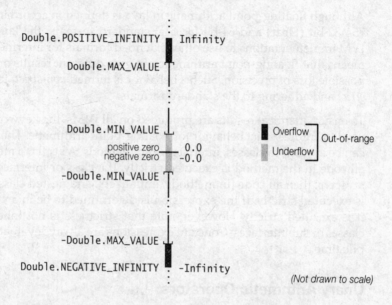

(Not drawn to scale)

Floating-point arithmetic can also result in *underflow* to zero, that is, the value is too small to be represented as a double or float (see Figure 3.2). Underflow occurs in the following situations:

- the result is between Double.MIN_VALUE (or Float.MIN_VALUE) and zero; for example, the result of (5.1E-324 - 4.9E-324). Underflow then returns positive zero 0.0 (or 0.0F).

- the result is between -Double.MIN_VALUE (or -Float.MIN_VALUE) and zero; for example, the result of (-Double.MIN_VALUE * 1E-1). Underflow then returns negative zero -0.0 (or -0.0F).

Negative zero compares equal to positive zero, i.e. (-0.0 == 0.0) is true.

Certain operations have no mathematical result, and are represented by *NaN* (Not a Number), for example calculating the square root of -1. Another example is (floating-point) dividing zero by zero:

```
System.out.println(0.0 / 0.0);          // Prints: NaN
```

NaN is represented by the constant named NaN in the wrapper classes java.lang.Float and java.lang.Double. Any operation involving NaN produces NaN. Any comparison (except inequality !=) involving NaN and any other value (including NaN) returns false. An inequality comparison of NaN with another value (including NaN) always returns true. However, the recommended way of checking a value for NaN is to use the static method isNaN() defined in both wrapper classes, java.lang.Float and java.lang.Double.

Strict Floating-Point Arithmetic: `strictfp`

Although floating-point arithmetic in Java is defined in accordance with the IEEE-754 32-bit (`float`) and 64-bit (`double`) standard formats, the language does allow JVM implementations to use other extended formats for intermediate results. This means that floating-point arithmetic can give different results on such JVMs, with possible loss of precision. Such a behavior is termed *non-strict*, in contrast to being *strict* and adhering to the standard formats.

To ensure identical results are produced on all JVMs, the keyword `strictfp` can be used to enforce strict behavior for floating-point arithmetic. The modifier `strictfp` can be applied to classes, interfaces, and methods. A `strictfp` method ensures that all code in the method is executed strictly. If a class or interface is declared to be `strictfp`, then all code (in methods, initializers, and nested classes and interfaces) is executed strictly. If the expression is determined to be in a `strictfp` construct, it is executed strictly. However, note that strictness is not inherited by the subclasses or subinterfaces. Constant expressions are always evaluated strictly at compile time.

Unary Arithmetic Operators: -, +

The unary operators have the highest precedence of all the arithmetic operators. The unary operator - negates the numeric value of its operand. The following example illustrates the right associativity of the unary operators:

```
int value = - -10;              // (-(-10)) is 10
```

Notice the blank needed to separate the unary operators; otherwise, these would be interpreted as the decrement operator -- (see Section 3.7, p. 63). The unary operator + has no effect on the evaluation of the operand value.

How negative integers are represented using 2's complement, is discussed in Section G.4 on page 598.

Multiplicative Binary Operators: *, /, %

*Multiplication Operator: **

Multiplication operator * multiplies two numbers.

```
int    sameSigns     = -4   * -8;        // result:  32
double oppositeSigns = 4.0  * -8.0;      // result: -32.0
int    zero          = 0    * -0;        // result:  0
```

Division Operator: /

The division operator / is overloaded. If its operands are integral, the operation results in *integer division*.

```
int    i1 = 4  / 5;    // result: 0
int    i2 = 8  / 8;    // result: 1
double d1 = 12 / 8;    // result: 1 by integer division. d1 gets the value 1.0.
```

Integer division always returns the quotient as an integer value, i.e. the result is truncated toward zero. Note that the division performed is integer division if the operands have integral values, even if the result will be stored in a floating-point type.

An `ArithmeticException` is thrown when attempting integer division with zero, meaning that integer division by zero is an illegal operation.

If any of the operands is a floating-point type, the operation performs *floating-point division*.

```
double d2 = 4.0 / 8;       // result: 0.5
double d3 = 8 / 8.0;       // result: 1.0
double d4 = 12.0F / 8;     // result: 1.5F

double result1 = 12.0 / 4.0 * 3.0;     // ((12.0 / 4.0) * 3.0) which is 9
double result2 = 12.0 * 3.0 / 4.0;     // ((12.0 * 3.0) / 4.0) which is 9
```

Remainder Operator: %

In mathematics, when we divide a number (the dividend) by a another number (the divisor), the result can be expressed in terms of a quotient and a remainder. For example, dividing 7 by 5, the quotient is 1 and the remainder is 2. The remainder operator % returns the remainder of the division performed on the operands.

```
int quotient  = 7 / 5;    // Integer division operation: 1
int remainder = 7 % 5;    // Integer remainder operation: 2
```

For *integer remainder operation*, where only integer operands are involved, evaluation of the expression (x % y) always satisfies the following relation:

$$x == (x \ / \ y) * y + (x \% y)$$

In other words, the right-hand side yields a value that is always equal to the value of the dividend. The following examples show how we can calculate the remainder so that the above relation is satisfied:

Calculating (7 % 5):
```
7 == (7 / 5) * 5 + (7 % 5)
  == (  1  ) * 5 + (7 % 5)
  ==             5 + (7 % 5)
2 ==                 (7 % 5)        i.e., (7 % 5) is equal to 2
```

Calculating (7 % -5):
```
7 == (7 / -5) * -5 + (7 % -5)
  == (  -1  ) * -5 + (7 % -5)
  ==             5 + (7 % -5)
2 ==                 (7 % -5)        i.e., (7 % -5) is equal to 2
```

Calculating (-7 % 5):
```
-7 == (-7 / 5) * 5 + (-7 % 5)
   == (  -1  ) * 5 + (-7 % 5)
   ==              -5 + (-7 % 5)
-2 ==                   (-7 % 5)        i.e., (-7 % 5) is equal to -2
```

Calculating (-7 % -5):
```
-7 == (-7 / -5) * -5 + (-7 % -5)
   == (   1   ) * -5 + (-7 % -5)
   ==                -5 + (-7 % -5)
-2 ==                     (-7 % -5)      i.e., (-7 % -5) is equal to -2
```

The above relation shows that the remainder can only be negative if the dividend is negative, the sign of the divisor is irrelevant. A short-cut to evaluating the remainder involving negative operands is the following: ignore the signs of the operands, calculate the remainder, and negate the remainder if the dividend is negative.

```
int  r0 = 7 % 7;      // 0
int  r1 = 7 % 5;      // 2
long r2 = 7L % -5L;   // 2L
int  r3 = -7 % 5;     // -2
long r4 = -7L % -5L;  // -2L
boolean relation = -7L == (-7L / -5L) * -5L + r4;  // true
```

An ArithmeticException is thrown when attempting integer remainder operation with zero.

Note that the remainder operator not only accepts integral operands, but floating-point operands as well. The *floating-point remainder* r is defined by the relation:

$$r == a - (b * q)$$

where a and b are the dividend and the divisor, respectively, and q is the integer quotient of (a/b). The following examples illustrate a floating-point remainder operation:

```
double  dr0 = 7.0 % 7.0;     // 0.0
float   fr1 = 7.0F % 5.0F;   // 2.0F
double  dr1 = 7.0 % -5.0;    // 2.0
float   fr2 = -7.0F % 5.0F;  // -2.0F
double  dr2 = -7.0 % -5.0;   // -2.0
boolean fpRelation = dr2  == (-7.0) - (-5.0) * (long)(-7.0 / -5.0);  // true
float   fr3 = -7.0F % 0.0F;  // NaN
```

Additive Binary Operators: +, -

The addition operator + and the subtraction operator - behave as their names imply: add or subtract values. The binary operator + also acts as *string concatenation* if any of the operands is a string (see Section 3.6, p. 62).

Additive operators have lower precedence than all the other arithmetic operators. Table 3.4 includes examples that show how precedence and associativity are used in arithmetic expression evaluation.

Table 3.4 *Examples of Arithmetic Expression Evaluation*

Arithmetic Expression	Evaluation	Result When Printed
3 + 2 - 1	((3 + 2) - 1)	4
2 + 6 * 7	(2 + (6 * 7))	44
-5+7- -6	(((-5)+7)-(-6))	8
2+4/5	(2+(4/5))	2
13 % 5	(13 % 5)	3
11.5 % 2.5	(11.5 % 2.5)	1.5
10 / 0	ArithmeticException	
2+4.0/5	(2.0+(4.0/5.0))	2.8
4.0 / 0.0	(4.0 / 0.0)	Infinity
-4.0 / 0.0	((-4.0) / 0.0)	-Infinity
0.0 / 0.0	(0.0 / 0.0)	NaN

Numeric Promotions in Arithmetic Expressions

Unary numeric promotion is applied to the single operand of unary arithmetic operators - and +. In other words, when a unary operator is applied to an operand of byte, short or char type, the operand is first promoted to a value of type int, with the evaluation resulting in an int value. If the conditions for implicit narrowing conversion are not fulfilled (p. 48), assigning the int result to a variable of these types will require an explicit cast. This is demonstrated by the following example, where the byte operand b is promoted to an int in the expression (-b):

```
byte b = 3;         // int literal in range. Implicit narrowing.
b = (byte) -b;      // Explicit narrowing on assignment required.
```

Binary numeric promotion is applied to operands of binary arithmetic operators. Its application leads to automatic type promotion for the operands. The result is of the promoted type, which is always type int or wider. For the expression at (1) in Example 3.1, numeric promotions proceed as shown in Figure 3.3. Note the integer division performed in evaluating the subexpression (c / s).

Example 3.1 *Numeric Promotion in Arithmetic Expressions*

```
public class NumPromotion {
    public static void main(String[] args) {
        byte   b = 32;
        char   c = 'z';  // Unicode value 122 (\u007a)
        short  s = 256;
        int    i = 10000;
        float  f = 3.5F;
        double d = 0.5;
        double v = (d * i) + (f * - b) - (c / s);    // (1) 4888.0D
        System.out.println("Value of v: " + v);
    }
}
```

Output from the program:

```
Value of v: 4888.0
```

Figure 3.3 *Numeric Promotion in Arithmetic Expressions*

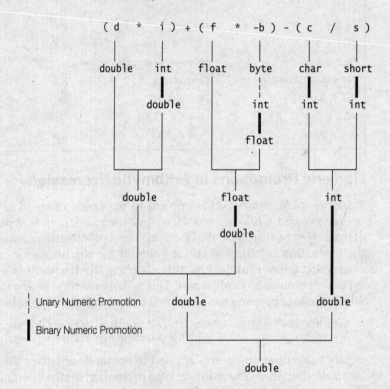

In addition to the binary numeric promotions in arithmetic expression evaluation, the resulting value can undergo an implicit widening conversion if assigned to a variable.

```
byte   b = 10;
short  s = 20;
char   c = 'z';      // 122 (\u007a)
int    i = s * b;    // Values in s and b converted to int.
long   n = 20L + s;  // Value in s converted to long.
float  r = s + c;    // Values in s and c promoted to int, followed by implicit
                     // widening conversion of int to float on assignment.
double d = r + i;    // value in i promoted to float, followed by implicit
                     // widening conversion of float to double on assignment.
```

Binary numeric promotion for operands of binary operators implies that each byte, short, or char operand of a binary operator is promoted to type int or broader numeric type, if necessary. As with unary operators, care must be exercised in assigning the value resulting from applying a binary operator to operands of these types.

```
short h = 40;          // OK: int converted to short. Implicit narrowing.
h = h + 2;             // Error: cannot assign an int to short.
```

The value of expression h + 2 is of type int. Although the result of the expression is in the range of short, this cannot be determined at compile time. The assignment requires an explicit cast.

```
h = (short) (h + 2);   // OK
```

Notice that applying the cast to the int value 2 only does not work:

```
h = h + (short) 2;     // Requires an additional cast.
```

In this case, binary numeric promotion leads to an int value as the result of evaluating the expression on the right-hand side and, therefore, requires an additional cast to narrow it to a short value.

Arithmetic Compound Assignment Operators: *=, /=, %=, +=, -=

A compound assignment operator has the following syntax:

    <variable> <op>= <expression>

and the following semantics:

    <variable> = (<type>) (<variable> <op> (<expression>))

The type of the *<variable>* is *<type>*, and the *<variable>* is evaluated only once. Note the cast and the parentheses implied in the semantics. Here *<op>=* can be any of the compound assignment operators specified in Table 3.1. The compound assignment operators have the lowest precedence of all the operators in Java, allowing the expression on the right-hand side to be evaluated before the assignment. Table 3.5 defines the arithmetic compound assignment operators.

Table 3.5 *Arithmetic Compound Assignment Operators*

Expression:	Given T as the Numeric Type of x, the Expression Is Evaluated as:
x *= a	x = (T) ((x) * (a))
x /= a	x = (T) ((x) / (a))
x %= a	x = (T) ((x) % (a))
x += a	x = (T) ((x) + (a))
x -= a	x = (T) ((x) - (a))

The implied cast, (T), in the compound assignments becomes necessary when the result must be narrowed to the destination type. This is illustrated by the following examples:

```
int i = 2;
i *= i + 4;               // (1) Evaluated as i = (int) (i * (i + 4)).

byte b = 2;
b += 10;                  // (2) Evaluated as b = (byte) ((int) b + 10).
b = b + 10;               // (3) Will not compile. Explicit cast required.
```

At (1) the source int value is assigned to the destination int variable, and the cast in this case is an *identity conversion* (i.e., conversion from a type to the same type). Such casts are permitted. However, at (2), the source value is an int value because the byte value in b is promoted to int to carry out the addition, and to assign it to a destination byte variable requires an implicit narrowing conversion. The situation at (3) with simple assignment will not compile, because implicit narrowing is not applicable.

The <*variable*> is only evaluated once in the expression, not twice, as one might infer from the definition of the compound assignment operator. In the following assignment, a[i] is only evaluated once:

```
a[i] += 1;
```

Implicit narrowing conversions are also applied for increment and decrement operators (see Section 3.7, p. 63).

Other compound assignment operators include boolean logical (see Section 3.11, p. 71), bitwise (see Section 3.13, p. 78), and shift (see Section 3.14, p. 83) operators.

Review Questions

3.4 Which of the following expressions will be evaluated using floating-point arithmetic?

Select the three correct answers.
(a) 2.0 * 3.0
(b) 2 * 3
(c) 2/3 + 5/7
(d) 2.4 + 1.6
(e) 0x10 * 1L * 300.0

3.5 What is the value of the expression (1 / 2 + 3 / 2 + 0.1)?

Select the one correct answer.
(a) 1
(b) 1.1
(c) 1.6
(d) 2
(e) 2.1

3.6   What will be the result of attempting to compile and run the following program?

```java
public class Integers {
    public static void main(String[] args) {
        System.out.println(0x10 + 10 + 010);
    }
}
```

Select the one correct answer.

(a) The program will not compile. The compiler will complain about the expression 0x10 + 10 + 010.
(b) When run, the program will print 28.
(c) When run, the program will print 30.
(d) When run, the program will print 34.
(e) When run, the program will print 36.
(f) When run, the program will print 101010.

3.7   Which of the following expressions are valid?

Select the three correct answers.

(a) (- 1 -)
(b) (+ + 1)
(c) (+-+-+-1)
(d) (--1)
(e) (1 * * 1)
(f) (- -1)

3.8   What is the value of evaluating the following expression (- -1-3 * 10 / 5-1)?

Select the one correct answer.

(a) -8
(b) -6
(c) 7
(d) 8
(e) 10
(f) None of the above.

3.9   Which of these assignments are valid?

Select the four correct answers.

(a) short s = 12;
(b) long l = 012;
(c) int other = (int) true;
(d) float f = -123;
(e) double d = 0x12345678;

3.6 The Binary String Concatenation Operator +

The binary operator + is overloaded in the sense that the operation performed is determined by the type of the operands. When one of the operands is a String object, the other operand is implicitly converted to its string representation and string concatenation is performed. Non-String operands are converted as follows:

- For a operand of a primitive data type, its value is converted to a String object with the string representation of the value.

- Values like true, false, and null are represented by string representations of these literals. A reference variable with the value null also has the string representation "null" in this context.

- For all reference value operands, a string representation is constructed by calling the toString() method on the referred object. Most classes override this method from the Object class in order to provide a more meaningful string representation of their objects. Discussion of the toString() method can be found in Section 10.2.

The result of the concatenation is always a new String object. The String class is discussed in Section 10.5.

```
String theName = " Uranium";
theName = " Pure" + theName;             // " Pure Uranium"
String trademark1 = 100 + "%" + theName;  // "100% Pure Uranium"      (1)
```

The integer literal 100 is implicitly converted to the string "100" before concatenation. This conversion is corresponds to first creating an object of the wrapper class Integer, which represents the integer 100, and then creating a string from this object by using the toString() method supplied by this class:

```
new Integer(100).toString();
```

Note that using the character literal '%', instead of the string literal "%" in line (1) above, does not give the same result:

```
String trademark2 = 100 + '%' + theName;    // "137 Pure Uranium"
```

Integer addition is performed by the first + operator: 100 + '%', that is, (100 + 37). Caution should be exercised as the + operator might not be applied as intended, as shown by the following example:

```
System.out.println("We put two and two together and get " + 2 + 2);
```

The above statement prints "We put two and two together and get 22" and not "We put two and two together and get 4". The first integer literal 2 is promoted to a String literal "2" for the first concatenation, resulting in the String literal "We put two and two together and get 2". This result is then concatenated with the String literal "2". The whole process proceeds as follows:

```
"We put two and two together and get " + 2 + 2
"We put two and two together and get " + "2" + 2
"We put two and two together and get 2" + 2
```

```
"We put two and two together and get 2" + "2"
"We put two and two together and get 22"
```

Both occurrences of the + operator are treated as string concatenation. A pair of parentheses might be in order to perform arithmetic addition, to convey the intended meaning of the sentence

```
System.out.println("We put two and two together and get " + (2 + 2));
```

The compiler uses a *string buffer* to avoid the overhead of temporary String objects when applying the string concatenation operator (+), as explained in Section 10.6 on page 424.

3.7 Variable Increment and Decrement Operators: ++, --

Variable increment (++) and decrement (--) operators come in two flavors: *prefix* and *postfix*. These unary operators have the side effect of changing the value of the arithmetic operand, which must evaluate to a variable. Depending on the operator used, the variable is either incremented or decremented by 1.

These operators are very useful for updating variables in loops where only the side effect of the operator is of interest.

Increment Operator ++

Prefix increment operator has the following semantics:

++i adds 1 to i first, then uses the new value of i as the value of the expression. It is equivalent to the following statements.

```
i += 1;
result = i;
return result;
```

Postfix increment operator has the following semantics:

j++ uses the current value of j as the value of the expression first, then adds 1 to j. It is equivalent to the following statements:

```
result = j;
j += 1;.
return result;
```

Decrement Operator --

Prefix decrement operator has the following semantics:

--i subtracts 1 from i first, then uses the new value of i as the value of the expression.

Postfix decrement operator has the following semantics:

j-- uses the current value of j as the value of the expression first, then subtracts 1 from j.

Examples of Increment and Decrement Operators

```
// (1) Prefix order: increment operand before use.
int i = 10;
int k = ++i + --i;  // ((++i) + (--i)). k gets the value 21 and i becomes 10.
--i;                // Only side effect utilized. i is 9. (expression statement)

// (2) Postfix order: increment operand after use.
long i = 10;
long k = i++ + i--;  // ((i++) + (i--)). k gets the value 21L and i becomes 10L.
i++;                 // Only side effect utilized. i is 11L. (expression statement)
```

An increment or decrement operator, together with its operand can be used as an expression statement (see Section 4.3, p. 113).

Execution of the assignment in the second declaration in (1) proceeds as follows :

```
k = ((++i) + (--i))        Operands are determined.
k = ( 11   + (--i))        i now has the value 11.
k = ( 11   + 10)           i now has the value 10.
k = 21
```

Expressions where variables are modified multiple times during the evaluation should be avoided, because the order of evaluation is not always immediately apparent.

We cannot associate increment and decrement operators. Given that a is a variable, we cannot write (++(++a)). The reason is that any operand to ++ must evaluate to a variable, but the evaluation of (++a) results in a value.

In the case where the operand is of type char, byte, or short, both binary numeric promotion and an implicit narrowing conversion are performed to achieve the side effect of modifying the value of the operand. In the example below, the int value of (++b) (i.e., 11), is assigned to int variable i. The side effect of incrementing the value of byte variable b requires binary numeric promotion to perform int addition, followed by an implicit narrowing conversion of the int value to byte.

```
byte b = 10;
int  i = ++b;        // i is 11, and so is b.
```

The increment and decrement operators can also be applied to floating-point operands. In the example below, the side effect of the ++ operator is overwritten by the assignment.

```
double x = 4.5;
x = x + ++x;         // x gets the value 10.0.
```

Review Questions

3.10   Which statements are true?

Select the three correct answers.

(a) The result of the expression (1 + 2 + "3") would be the string "33".
(b) The result of the expression ("1" + 2 + 3) would be the string "15".
(c) The result of the expression (4 + 1.0f) would be the float value 5.0f.
(d) The result of the expression (10/9) would be the int value 1.
(e) The result of the expression ('a' + 1) would be the char value 'b'.

3.11   What happens when you try to compile and run the following program?

```
public class Prog1 {
    public static void main(String[] args) {
        int k = 1;
        int i = ++k + k++ + + k;
        System.out.println(i);
    }
}
```

Select the one correct answer.

(a) The program will not compile. The compiler will complain about the expression ++k + k++ + + k.
(b) The program will compile and will print the value 3 when run.
(c) The program will compile and will print the value 4 when run.
(d) The program will compile and will print the value 7 when run.
(e) The program will compile and will print the value 8 when run.

3.12   Which is the first incorrect line that will cause a compile time error in the following program?

```
public class MyClass {
    public static void main(String[] args) {
        char c;
        int i;
        c = 'a'; // (1)
        i = c;   // (2)
        i++;     // (3)
        c = i;   // (4)
        c++;     // (5)
    }
}
```

Select the one correct answer.

(a) The line labeled (1)
(b) The line labeled (2)
(c) The line labeled (3)
(d) The line labeled (4)
(e) The line labeled (5)
(f) None of the lines are incorrect. The program will compile just fine.

3.13   What happens when you try to compile and run the following program?

```
public class Cast {
    public static void main(String[] args) {
        byte b = 128;
        int  i = b;
        System.out.println(i);
    }
}
```

Select the one correct answer.

(a) The compiler will refuse to compile it, since you cannot assign a byte to an int without a cast.

(b) The program will compile and will print 128 when run.

(c) The compiler will refuse to compile it, since 128 is outside the legal range of values for a byte.

(d) The program will compile, but will throw a ClassCastException when run.

(e) The program will compile and will print 255 when run.

3.14   What will the following program print when run?

```
public class EvaluationOrder {
    public static void main(String[] args) {
        int[] array = { 4, 8, 16 };
        int i=1;
        array[++i] = --i;
        System.out.println(array[0] + array[1] + array[2]);
    }
}
```

Select the one correct answer.

(a) 13

(b) 14

(c) 20

(d) 21

(e) 24

3.8 Boolean Expressions

Boolean expressions have boolean data type and can only evaluate to the values true or false.

Boolean expressions, when used as conditionals in control statements, allow the program flow to be controlled during execution.

Boolean expressions can be formed using *relational operators* (see Section 3.9, p. 67), *equality operators* (see Section 3.10, p. 67), *logical operators* (see Section 3.11, p. 70), *conditional operators* (see Section 3.12, p. 72), the *assignment operator* (see Section 3.4, p. 47), and the instanceof operator (see Section 6.6, p. 264).

3.9 Relational Operators: <, <=, >, >=

Given that a and b represent numeric expressions, the relational (also called *comparison*) operators are defined as shown in Table 3.6.

Table 3.6 *Relational Operators*

a < b	a less than b?
a <= b	a less than or equal to b?
a > b	a greater than b?
a >= b	a greater than or equal to b?

All relational operators are binary operators, and their operands are numeric expressions. Binary numeric promotion is applied to the operands of these operators. The evaluation results in a boolean value. Relational operators have precedence lower than arithmetic operators, but higher than that of the assignment operators.

```
double  hours = 45.5;
boolean overtime = hours >= 35.0;    // true.
boolean order = 'A' < 'a';           // true. Binary numeric promotion applied.
```

Relational operators are nonassociative. Mathematical expressions like $a \leq b \leq c$ must be written using relational and boolean logical/conditional operators.

```
int a = 1, b = 7, c = 10;
boolean valid1 = a <= b <= c;        // (1) Illegal.
boolean valid2 = a <= b && b <= c;   // (2) OK.
```

Since relational operators have left associativity, the evaluation of the expression a <= b <= c at (1) in the examples above would proceed as follows: ((a <= b) <= c). Evaluation of (a <= b) would yield a boolean value that is not permitted as an operand of a relational operator, that is, (*<boolean value>* <= c) would be illegal.

3.10 Equality

Primitive Data Value Equality: ==, !=

Given that a and b represent operands of primitive data types, the primitive data value equality operators are defined as shown in Table 3.7.

Table 3.7 *Primitive Data Value Equality Operators*

a == b	a and b are equal? That is, have the same primitive value? (Equality)
a != b	a and b are not equal? That is, do not have the same primitive value? (Inequality)

The equality operator == and the inequality operator != can be used to compare primitive data values, including boolean values. Binary numeric promotion is applied to the nonboolean operands of these equality operators.

```
int year = 2002;
boolean isEven  = year % 2 == 0;     // true.
boolean compare = '1' == 1;          // false. Binary numeric promotion applied.
boolean test    = compare == false;  // true.
```

Care must be exercised in comparing floating-point numbers for equality, as an infinite number of floating-point values can be stored in a finite number of bits only as approximations. For example, the expression (1.0 - 2.0/3.0 == 1.0/3.0) returns false, although mathematically the result should be true.

Analogous to the discussion for relational operators, mathematical expressions like $a = b = c$ must be written using relational and logical/conditional operators. Since equality operators have left associativity, the evaluation of the expression a == b == c would proceed as follows: ((a == b) == c). Evaluation of (a == b) would yield a boolean value that *is* permitted as an operand of a data value equality operator, but (*<boolean value>* == c) would be illegal if c had a numeric type. This is illustrated in the examples below. The expression at (1) is illegal, but those at (2) and (3) are legal.

```
int a, b, c;
a = b = c = 5;
boolean valid1 = a == b == c;        // (1) Illegal.
boolean valid2 = a == b && b == c;   // (2) Legal.
boolean valid3 = a == b == true;     // (3) Legal.
```

Object Reference Equality: ==, !=

The equality operator == and the inequality operator != can be applied to object references to test whether they denote the same object. Given that r and s are reference variables, the reference equality operators are defined as shown in Table 3.8.

Table 3.8 *Reference Equality Operators*

r == s	r and s are equal? That is, have the same reference value? (Equality)
r != s	r and s are not equal? That is, do not have the same reference value? (Inequality)

The operands must be type compatible: it must be possible to cast one into the other's type; otherwise, it is a compile-time error. Type compatibility of references is discussed in Section 6.6.

```
Pizza pizza_A = new Pizza("Sweet&Sour");    // new object
Pizza pizza_B = new Pizza("Sweet&Sour");    // new object
Pizza pizza_C = new Pizza("Hot&Spicy");     // new object

String banner = "Come and get it!";         // new object
```

```
boolean test  = banner  == pizza_A;      // (1) Compile-time error.
boolean test1 = pizza_A == pizza_B;       // false
boolean test2 = pizza_A == pizza_C;       // false

pizza_A = pizza_B;                        // Denote the same object, are aliases.
boolean test3 = pizza_A == pizza_B;       // true
```

The comparison banner == pizza_A in (1) is illegal, because String and Pizza types are not type compatible. The values of test1 and test2 are false, because the three references denote different objects, regardless of the fact that pizza_A and pizza_B are both sweet and sour pizzas. The value of test3 is true, because now both pizza_A and pizza_B denote the same object.

The equality and inequality operators are applied to object references to check whether two references denote the same object or not. The state of the objects that the references denote is not compared. This is the same as testing whether the references are aliases, that is, denoting the same object.

The null reference can be assigned to any reference variable, and an object reference in a reference variable can be compared for equality with the null reference. The comparison can be used to avoid inadvertent use of a reference variable that does not denote any object.

```
if (objRef != null) {
    // ... use objRef ...
}
```

Object Value Equality

The Object class provides the method public boolean equals(Object obj), which can be *overridden* (see Section 6.2, p. 233) to give the right semantics of *object value equality*. The default implementation of this method in the Object class returns true only if the object is compared with itself, that is, as if the equality operator == had been used to compare aliases to the object. This means that if a class does not override the semantics of the equals() method from the Object class, then object value equality is the same as object reference equality. For a detailed discussion on implementing the equals() method, see Section 11.7 on page 461.

Certain classes in the standard API override the equals() method, for example, java.lang.String, java.util.BitSet, java.util.Date, java.io.File and the wrapper classes for the primitive data types. For two String objects, value equality means they contain the same character sequence. For the wrapper classes, value equality means that the primitive values in the two wrapper objects are equal.

```
// Equality for String objects means same character sequence.
String movie1 = new String("The Revenge of the Exception Handler");
String movie2 = new String("High Noon at the Java Corral");
String movie3 = new String("The Revenge of the Exception Handler");
boolean test0 = movie1.equals(movie2);        // false
boolean test1 = movie1.equals(movie3);        // true

// Equality for Boolean objects means same primitive value
```

```
Boolean flag1 = new Boolean(true);
Boolean flag2 = new Boolean(true);
boolean test2 = flag1.equals(flag2);                     // true

// Pizza class does not override the equals() method,
// can use either equals (inherited from Object) or ==.
Pizza pizza1 = new Pizza("VeggiesDelight");
Pizza pizza2 = new Pizza("VeggiesDelight");
Pizza pizza3 = new Pizza("CheeseDelight");
boolean test3 = pizza1.equals(pizza2);                   // false
boolean test4 = pizza1.equals(pizza3);                   // false
boolean test5 = pizza1 == pizza2;                        // false
pizza1 = pizza2;                                         // Aliases
boolean test7 = pizza1.equals(pizza2);                   // true
boolean test6 = pizza1 == pizza2;                        // true
```

3.11 Boolean Logical Operators: !, ∧, &, |

Boolean logical operators include the unary operator ! (*logical complement*) and the binary operators & (*logical* AND), | (*logical inclusive* OR), and ∧ (*logical exclusive* OR, a.k.a. *logical* XOR). Boolean logical operators can be applied to boolean operands, returning a boolean value. The operators &, |, and ∧ can also be applied to integral operands to perform *bitwise* logical operations (see Section 3.13, p. 75).

Given that *x* and *y* represent boolean expressions, the boolean logical operators are defined in Table 3.9. In the table, the operators are ranked, with the operator having the highest precedence first.

Table 3.9 *Boolean Logical Operators*

Logical complement	!x	Returns the complement of the truth-value of x.
Logical AND	x & y	true if both operands are true; otherwise, false.
Logical OR	x | y	true if either or both operands are true; otherwise, false.
Logical XOR	x ∧ y	true if and only if one operand is true; otherwise, false.

These operators always evaluate both the operands, unlike their counterpart conditional operators && and || (see Section 3.12, p. 72). Truth-values for boolean logical operators are shown in Table 3.10.

Table 3.10 *Truth-values for Boolean Logical Operators*

x	y	!x	x & y	x | y	x ∧ y
true	true	false	true	true	false
true	false	false	false	true	true
false	true	true	false	true	true
false	false	true	false	false	false

Operand Evaluation for Boolean Logical Operators

In evaluation of boolean expressions involving boolean logical AND, XOR, and OR operators, both the operands are evaluated. The order of operand evaluation is always from left to right.

```
if (i > 0 & i++ < 10) {/*...*/} // i will be incremented, regardless of value in i.
```

The binary boolean logical operators have precedence lower than arithmetic and relational operators, but higher than assignment, conditional AND, and OR operators (see Section 3.12, p. 72). This is illustrated in the following examples:

```
boolean b1, b2, b3 = false, b4 = false;
b1 = 4 == 2 & 1 < 4;              // false, evaluated as (b1 = ((4 == 2) & (1 < 4)))
b2 = b1 | !(2.5 >= 8);            // true
b3 = b3 ∧ b2;                     // true
b4 = b4 | b1 & b2;               // false
```

Order of evaluation is illustrated for the last example:

```
    (b4 = (b4 | (b1 & b2)))
⟹ (b4 = (false | (b1 & b2)))
⟹ (b4 = (false | (false & b2)))
⟹ (b4 = (false | (false & true)))
⟹ (b4 = (false | false))
⟹ (b4 = false)
```

Note that b2 was evaluated although, strictly speaking, it was not necessary. This behavior is guaranteed for boolean logical operators.

Boolean Logical Compound Assignment Operators: &=, ∧=, |=

Compound assignment operators for the boolean logical operators are defined in Table 3.11. The left-hand operand must be a boolean variable, and the right-hand operand must be a boolean expression. An identity conversion is applied implicitly on assignment. These operators can also be applied to integral operands to perform *bitwise* compound assignments (see Section 3.13, p. 78).

Table 3.11 *Boolean Logical Compound Assignment Operators*

Expression:	Given b and a Are of Type Boolean, the Expression Is Evaluated as:
b &= a	b = (b & (a))
b ∧= a	b = (b ∧ (a))
b |= a	b = (b | (a))

Examples of Boolean Logical Compound Assignment

```
boolean b1 = false, b2 = false, b3 = false;
b1 |= true;                          // true
b2 ^= b1;                            // true
b3 &= b1 | b2;                       // (1) false. b3 = (b3 & (b1 | b2)).
b3 = b3 & b1 | b2;                   // (2) true.  b3 = ((b3 & b1) | b2).
```

It is instructive to note how the assignments at (1) and (2) above are performed, giving different results for the same value of the operands.

3.12 Conditional Operators: &&, ||

Conditional operators && and || are similar to their counterpart logical operators & and |, except that their evaluation is *short-circuited*. Given that x and y represent values of boolean expressions, the conditional operators are defined in Table 3.12. In the table, the operators are listed in decreasing precedence order.

Table 3.12 *Conditional Operators*

Conditional AND	x && y	true if both operands are true; otherwise, false.
Conditional OR	x || y	true if either or both operands are true; otherwise, false.

Unlike their logical counterparts & and |, which can also be applied to integral operands for bitwise operations, the conditional operators && and || can only be applied to boolean operands. Their evaluation results in a boolean value. Truth-values for conditional operators are shown in Table 3.13. Not surprisingly, they have the same truth-values as their counterpart logical operators.

Note that, unlike their logical counterparts, there are no compound assignment operators for the conditional operators.

Table 3.13 *Truth-values for Conditional Operators*

x	y	x && y	x || y
true	true	true	true
true	false	false	true
false	true	false	true
false	false	false	false

Short-circuit Evaluation

In evaluation of boolean expressions involving conditional AND and OR, the left-hand operand is evaluated before the right one, and the evaluation is short-circuited (i.e., if the result of the boolean expression can be determined from the left-hand operand, the right-hand operand is not evaluated). In other words, the right-hand operand is evaluated conditionally.

The binary conditional operators have precedence lower than either arithmetic, relational, or logical operators, but higher than assignment operators. The following examples illustrate usage of conditional operators:

```
boolean b1 = 4 == 2 && 1 < 4;    // false, short-circuit evaluated as
                                 // (b1 = ((4 == 2) && (1 < 4)))
boolean b2 = !b1 || 2.5 > 8;     // true, short-circuit evaluated as
                                 // (b2 = ((!b1) || (2.5 > 8)))
boolean b3 = !(b1 && b2);        // true
boolean b4 = b1 || !b3 && b2;    // false, short-circuit evaluated as
                                 // (b4 = (b1 || ((!b3) && b2)))
```

Order of evaluation for computing the value of boolean variable b4 proceeds as follows:

```
      (b4 = (b1 || ((!b3) && b2)))
  ⟹  (b4 = (false || ((!b3) && b2)))
  ⟹  (b4 = (false || ((!true) && b2)))
  ⟹  (b4 = (false || ((false) && b2)))
  ⟹  (b4 = (false || false))
  ⟹  (b4 = false)
```

Note that b2 is not evaluated, short-circuiting the evaluation.

Short-circuit evaluation can be used to ensure that a reference variable denotes an object before it is used.

```
if (objRef != null && objRef.doIt()) { /*...*/ }
```

The method call is now conditionally dependent on the left-hand operand and will not be executed if the variable objRef has the null reference. If we use the logical & operator and the variable objRef has the null reference, evaluation of the right-hand operand will cause a NullPointerException.

In summary, we employ the conditional operators && and || if the evaluation of the right-hand operand is conditionally dependent on the left-hand operand. We use the logical operators & and | if both operands must be evaluated. The subtlety of conditional operators is illustrated by the following examples:

```
if (i > 0 && i++ < 10) {/*...*/}    // i is not incremented if i > 0 is false.
if (i > 0 || i++ < 10) {/*...*/}    // i is not incremented if i > 0 is true.
```

Review Questions

3.15 Which of the following expressions evaluates to true?

Select the two correct answers.

(a) `(false | true)`
(b) `(null != null)`
(c) `(4 <= 4)`
(d) `(!true)`
(e) `(true & false)`

3.16 Which statements are true?

Select the two correct answers.

(a) The remainder operator % can only be used with integral operands.
(b) Identifiers in Java are case insensitive.
(c) The arithmetic operators *, /, and % have the same level of precedence.
(d) A short value ranges from -128 to +127 inclusive.
(e) (+15) is a legal expression.

3.17 Which statements are true about the lines of output printed by the following program?

```java
public class BoolOp {
    static void op(boolean a, boolean b) {
        boolean c = a != b;
        boolean d = a ^ b;
        boolean e = c == d;
        System.out.println(e);
    }

    public static void main(String[] args) {
        op(false, false);
        op(true, false);
        op(false, true);
        op(true, true);
    }
}
```

Select the three correct answers.

(a) All lines printed are the same.
(b) At least one line contains false.
(c) At least one line contains true.
(d) The first line contains false.
(e) The last line contains true.

3.18 What happens during execution of the following program?

```java
public class OperandOrder {
    public static void main(String[] args) {
        int i = 0;
```

```
            int[] a = {3,6};
            a[i] = i = 9;
            System.out.println(i + " " + a[0] + " " + a[1]);
        }
    }
```

Select the one correct answer.

(a) Throws an exception of type ArrayIndexOutOfBoundsException
(b) Prints "9 9 6"
(c) Prints "9 0 6"
(d) Prints "9 3 6"
(e) Prints "9 3 9"

3.19   Which statements are true about the output of the following program?

```
public class Logic {
    public static void main(String[] args) {
        int i = 0;
        int j = 0;

        boolean t = true;
        boolean r;

        r = (t &  0<(i+=1));
        r = (t && 0<(i+=2));
        r = (t |  0<(j+=1));
        r = (t || 0<(j+=2));
        System.out.println(i + " " + j);
    }
}
```

Select the two correct answers.

(a) The first digit printed is 1.
(b) The first digit printed is 2.
(c) The first digit printed is 3.
(d) The second digit printed is 1.
(e) The second digit printed is 2.
(f) The second digit printed is 3.

3.13   Integer Bitwise Operators: ~, &, |, ∧

A review of number representation (see Section G.4, p. 598) is recommended before continuing with this section on how integer bitwise operators can be applied to values of *integral* data types.

Integer bitwise operators include the unary operator ~ (*bitwise complement*) and the binary operators & (*bitwise* AND), | (*bitwise inclusive* OR), and ∧ (*bitwise exclusive* OR, a.k.a. *bitwise* XOR).

The binary bitwise operators perform bitwise operations between corresponding individual bit values in the operands. Unary numeric promotion is applied to the operand of the unary bitwise complement operator ~, and binary numeric promotion is applied to the operands of the binary bitwise operators. The result is a new integer value of the promoted type, which can only be either int or long.

Given that A and B are corresponding bit values (either 0 or 1) in the left-hand and right-hand operands, respectively, these bitwise operators are defined as shown in Table 3.14. The operators are listed in decreasing precedence order.

The operators &, |, and ^ can also be applied to boolean operands to perform *boolean logical operations* (see Section 3.11, p. 70).

Table 3.14 *Integer Bitwise Operators*

Operator Name	Notation	Effect on Each Bit of the Binary Representation
Bitwise complement	~A	Invert the bit value: 1 to 0, 0 to 1.
Bitwise AND	A & B	1 if both bits are 1; otherwise, 0.
Bitwise OR	A | B	1 if either or both bits are 1; otherwise, 0.
Bitwise XOR	A ^ B	1 if and only if one of the bits is 1; otherwise, 0.

The result of applying bitwise operators between two corresponding bits in the operands is shown in Table 3.15, where A and B are corresponding bit values in left-hand and right-hand operands, respectively. Table 3.15 is analogous to Table 3.10 for boolean logical operators, if we consider bit value 1 to represent true and bit value 0 to represent false.

Table 3.15 *Result Table for Bitwise Operators*

A	B	~A	A & B	A | B	A ^ B
1	1	0	1	1	0
1	0	0	0	1	1
0	1	1	0	1	1
0	0	1	0	0	0

Examples of Bitwise Operator Application

```
char v1 = ')';          // Unicode value 41
byte v2 = 13;

int result1 = ~v1;      // -42
int result2 = v1 & v2;  // 9
int result3 = v1 | v2;  // 45
int result4 = v1 ^ v2;  // 36
```

Table 3.16 shows how the result is calculated. Unary and binary numeric promotions are applied first, converting the operands to int in these cases. Note that the operator semantics is applied to corresponding individual bits, that is, first bit of left-hand operand and first bit of right-hand operand, second bit of left-hand operand, and second bit of right-hand operand, and so on.

Table 3.16 *Examples of Bitwise Operations*

~v1	v1 & v2	v1 | v2	v1 ^ v2
~ 0...0010 1001	0...0010 1001	0...0010 1001	0...0010 1001
	& 0...0000 1101	| 0...0000 1101	^ 0...0000 1101
= 1...1101 0110	= 0...0000 1001	= 0...0010 1101	= 0...0010 0100
= 0xffffffd6	= 0x00000009	= 0x0000002d	= 0x00000024
= -42	= 9	= 45	= 36

It is instructive to run examples and print the result of a bitwise operation in different notations, as shown in Example 3.2. Converting integers to different notations is discussed in Section 10.3 on page 398.

Example 3.2 *Bitwise Operations*

```
public class BitOperations {
    public static void main(String[] args) {
        char v1 = ')';                           // Unicode value 41
        byte v2 = 13;
        printIntToStr("v1:", v1);                // 41
        printIntToStr("v2:", v2);                // 13
        printIntToStr("~v1:", ~v1);              // -42
        printIntToStr("v1 & v2:", v1 & v2);      // 9
        printIntToStr("v1 | v2:", v1 | v2);      // 45
        printIntToStr("v1 ^ v2:", v1 ^ v2);      // 36
    }

    public static void printIntToStr(String label, int result) {
        System.out.println(label);
        System.out.println("    Binary:  " + Integer.toBinaryString(result));
        System.out.println("    Hex:     " + Integer.toHexString(result));
        System.out.println("    Decimal: " + result);
    }
}
```

Output from the program:

```
v1:
    Binary:  101001
    Hex:     29
    Decimal: 41
```

```
v2:
    Binary:  1101
    Hex:     d
    Decimal: 13
~v1:
    Binary:  11111111111111111111111111010110
    Hex:     ffffffd6
    Decimal: -42
v1 & v2:
    Binary:  1001
    Hex:     9
    Decimal: 9
v1 | v2:
    Binary:  101101
    Hex:     2d
    Decimal: 45
v1 ^ v2:
    Binary:  100100
    Hex:     24
    Decimal: 36
```

Bitwise Compound Assignment Operators: &=, ^=, |=

Bitwise compound assignment operators for the bitwise operators are defined in
Table 3.17. Type conversions for these operators, when applied to integral
operands, are the same as for other compound assignment operators: an implicit
narrowing conversion is performed on assignment when the destination data type
is either byte, short, or char. These operators can also be applied to boolean
operands to perform logical compound assignments (see Section 3.11, p. 71).

Table 3.17 *Bitwise Compound Assignment Operators*

Expression:	Given T Is the Integral Type of b, the Expression Is Evaluated as:
b &= a	b = (T) ((b) & (a))
b ^= a	b = (T) ((b) ^ (a))
b |= a	b = (T) ((b) | (a))

Examples of Bitwise Compound Assignment

```
int  v0 = -42;
char v1 = ')';     // 41
byte v2 = 13;

v0 &= 15;          //     1...1101 0110 & 0...0000 1111 => 0...0000 0110 (= 6)
v1 |= v2;          // (1) 0...0010 1001 | 0...0000 1101 => 0...0010 1101 (= 45)
```

At (1) in the examples above, both the char value in v1 and the byte value in v2 are first promoted to int. The result is implicitly narrowed to the destination type char on assignment.

3.14 Shift Operators: <<, >>, >>>

The binary shift operators form a new value by shifting bits either left or right a specified number of times in a given integral value. The number of shifts (also called the *shift distance*) is given by the right-hand operand, and the value that is to be shifted is given by the left-hand operand. Note that *unary* numeric promotion is applied to each operand *individually*. The value returned has the promoted type of the left-hand operand. Also, the value of the left-hand operand is *not* affected by applying the shift operator.

The shift distance is calculated by AND-ing the value of the right-hand operand with a mask value of 0x1f (31) if the left-hand has the promoted type int, or using a mask value of 0x3f (63) if the left-hand has the promoted type long. This effectively means masking the five lower bits of the right-hand operand in the case of an int left-hand operand, and masking the six lower bits of the right-hand operand in the case of a long left-hand operand. Thus, the shift distance is always in the range 0 to 31 when the promoted type of left-hand operand is int, and in the range 0 to 63 when the promoted type of left-hand operand is long.

Given that a contains the value whose bits are to be shifted and n specifies the number of bits to shift, the bitwise operators are defined in Table 3.18. It is implied that the value n in Table 3.18 is subject to the shift distance calculation outlined above, and that the shift operations are always performed on the value of the left-hand operand represented in 2's complement.

Table 3.18 *Shift Operators*

Shift left	a << n	Shift all bits in a left n times, filling with 0 from the right.
Shift right with sign bit	a >> n	Shift all bits in a right n times, filling with the sign bit from the left.
Shift right with zero fill	a >>> n	Shift all bits in a right n times, filling with 0 from the left.

Since char, byte and short operands are promoted to int, the result of applying these bitwise operators is always either an int or a long value. Care must be taken in employing a cast to narrow the resulting value, as this can result in loss of information as the upper bits are chopped off during conversion.

Note that regardless of the promotion of the values in the operands or determination of the shift distance, the operands a and n are not affected by these three shift operators. However, the shift compound assignment operators, discussed in this section, can change the value of the left-hand operand a.

Bit values shifted out (*falling off*) from bit 0 or the most significant bit are lost. Since bits can be shifted both left and right, a positive value when shifted can result in a negative value and vice versa.

The Shift-left Operator <<

As the bits are shifted left, zeros are always filled in from the right.

```
int i = 12;
int result = i << 4;      // 192
```

The bits in the int value for i are shifted left four places as follows:

```
i << 4
= 0000 0000 0000 0000 0000 0000 0000 1100 << 4
= 0000 0000 0000 0000 0000 0000 1100 0000
= 0x000000c0
= 192
```

Each left-shift corresponds to multiplication of the value by 2. In the above example, $12*2^4$ is 192.

The sign bit of a byte or short value is extended to fill the higher bits when the value is promoted, as illustrated by the example below:

```
byte  b = -42;            // 11010110
short n = 4;
int   result = b << n;    // -672
```

The values of the two operands, b and n, in the previous example are promoted individually. The short value in n is promoted to int. The byte value in b, after promotion to int, is shifted left 4 places:

```
b << n
= 1101 0110 << 0000 0000 0000 0100
= 1111 1111 1111 1111 1111 1111 1101 0110 <<0000 0000 0000 0000 0000 0000 0000 0100
= 1111 1111 1111 1111 1111 1111 1101 0110 << 4
= 1111 1111 1111 1111 1111 1101 0110 0000
= 0xfffffd60
= -672
```

In the above example, $-42*2^4$ is -672.

Care must also be taken when assigning the result of a shift operator to a narrower data type.

```
byte a = 32, b;
int j;

j = a << 3;               // 256
b = (byte) (a << 3);      // 0. Cast mandatory.
```

The result of (a << 3) is 256.

```
a << 3
= 0000 0000 0000 0000 0000 0000 0010 0000 << 3
= 0000 0000 0000 0000 0000 0001 0000 0000
= 0x00000100
= 256
```

The value j gets is 256, but the value b gets is 0, as the higher bits are discarded in the explicit narrowing conversion.

The examples above do not show how the shift distance is determined. It is obvious from the value of the right-hand operand, which is within the range 0 to 31, inclusive. An example with the shift-left operator, where the value of the right-hand operand is out-of-range, is shown below.

```
12 << 36
= 0000 0000 0000 0000 0000 0000 0000 1100 << (0...0010 0100 & 0001 1111)
= 0000 0000 0000 0000 0000 0000 0000 1100 << 0...0000 0100
= 0000 0000 0000 0000 0000 0000 0000 1100 << 4
= 0000 0000 0000 0000 0000 0000 1100 0000
= 0x000000c0
= 192
```

The value of the right-hand operand, 36, is AND-ed with the mask 11111 (i.e., 31, 0x1f) giving the shift distance 4. This is the same as (36 % 32). It is not surprising that (12 << 36) is equal to (12 << 4) (i.e., 192).

The Shift-right-with-sign-fill Operator >>

As the bits are shifted right, the sign bit (the most significant bit) is used to fill in from the left. So, if the left-hand operand is a positive value, zeros are filled in from the left, but if the operand is a negative value, ones are filled in from the left.

```
int i = 12;
int result = i >> 2;     // 3
```

The value for i is shifted right with sign-fill two places.

```
i >> 2
= 0000 0000 0000 0000 0000 0000 0000 1100 >> 2
= 0000 0000 0000 0000 0000 0000 0000 0011
= 0x00000003
= 3
```

Each right-shift corresponds to integer division of the value being shifted by two, but this can give unexpected results if care is not exercised, as bits start falling off. In the above example, $12/2^2$ is 3.

Similarly, when a negative value is shifted right, ones are filled in from the left.

```
byte b = -42;            // 11010110
int result = b >> 4;     //, -3
```

The byte value for b, after promotion to int, is shifted right with sign-fill four places.

```
b >> 4
= 1111 1111 1111 1111 1111 1111 1101 0110 >> 4
= 1111 1111 1111 1111 1111 1111 1111 1101
= 0xfffffffd
= -3
```

In the following example, the right-hand operand has a negative value:

```
-42 >> -4
= 1111 1111 1111 1111 1111 1111 1101 0110 >> (1...1111 1100 & 0001 1111)
= 1111 1111 1111 1111 1111 1111 1101 0110 >> 0...0001 1100
= 1111 1111 1111 1111 1111 1111 1101 0110 >> 28
= 1111 1111 1111 1111 1111 1111 1111 1111
= 0xffffffff
= -1
```

The value of the right-hand operand, -4, is AND-ed with the mask 11111 (i.e., 31, 0x1f) giving the shift distance 28. This is the same as (-4 % 32). The value of (-42 >> -4) is equivalent to (-42 >> 28).

The Shift-right-with-zero-fill Operator >>>

As the bits are shifted right, zeros are filled in from the left, regardless of whether the operand has a positive or a negative value.

Obviously, for positive values, the shift-right-with-zero-fill >>> and shift-right-with-sign-fill >> operators are equivalent. The expression (12 >> 2) and the expression (12 >>> 2) return the same value:

```
12 >>> 2
= 0000 0000 0000 0000 0000 0000 0000 1100 >>> 2
= 0000 0000 0000 0000 0000 0000 0000 0011
= 0x00000003
= 3
```

Individual unary numeric promotion of the left-hand operand is shown in the following example:

```
byte b = -42;            // 1101 0110
int result = b >>> 4;    // 268435453
```

It is instructive to compare the value of the expression (-42 >>> 4) with that of the expression (-42 >> 4), which has the value -3. The byte value for b, after unary numeric promotion to int, is shifted right with zero-fill four places.

```
b >>> 4
= 1111 1111 1111 1111 1111 1111 1101 0110 >>> 4
= 0000 1111 1111 1111 1111 1111 1111 1101
= 0x0fffffffd
= 268435453
```

In the following example, the value of the right-hand operand is out-of-range, resulting in a shift distance of 28 (as we have seen before):

```
-42 >>> -4
= 1111 1111 1111 1111 1111 1111 1101 0110 >>> 28
= 0000 0000 0000 0000 0000 0000 0000 1111
= 0x0000000f
= 15
```

Shift Compound Assignment Operators: <<=, >>=, >>>=

Table 3.19 lists shift compound assignment operators. Type conversions for these operators, when applied to integral operands, are the same as for other compound assignment operators: An implicit narrowing conversion is performed on assignment when the destination data type is either byte, short, or char.

Table 3.19 *Shift Compound Assignment Operators*

Expression	Given T as the Integral Type of x, the Expression Is Evaluated as:
x <<= a	x = (T) ((x) << (a))
x >>= a	x = (T) ((x) >> (a))
x >>>= a	x = (T) ((x) >>> (a))

Examples of Shift Compound Assignment Operators

```
int i = -42;
i >>= 4;                 // 1...1101 0110 >> 4 => 1...1111 1101 (= -3).

byte a = 12;
a <<= 5;                 // (1) -128. Evaluated as a = (byte)((int)a << 5)
a = a << 5;              // Compile-time error. Needs explicit cast.
```

The example at (1) illustrates the truncation that takes place on narrowing to destination type. The byte value in a is first promoted to int (by applying unary numeric promotion in this case), shifted left five places, followed by implicit narrowing to byte:

```
a = (byte) (a << 5)
  = (byte) (0000 0000 0000 0000 0000 0000 0000 1100 << 5)
  = (byte)  0000 0000 0000 0000 0000 0001 1000 0000
  = 1000 0000
  = 0x80
  = -128
```

3.15 The Conditional Operator: ?

The ternary conditional operator allows conditional expressions to be defined. The operator has the following syntax:

<condition> ? *<expression₁>* : *<expression₂>*

If the boolean expression *<condition>* is true then *<expression₁>* is evaluated; otherwise, *<expression₂>* is evaluated. Of course, *<expression₁>* and *<expression₂>* must evaluate to values of compatible types. The value of the expression evaluated is returned by the conditional expression.

```
boolean leapYear = false;
int daysInFebruary = leapYear ? 29 : 28;    // 28
```

The conditional operator is the expression equivalent of the `if-else` statement. The conditional expression can be nested and the conditional operator associates from right to left:

```
(a?b?c?d:e:f:g) evaluates as (a?(b?(c?d:e):f):g)
```

3.16 Other Operators: `new`, `[]`, `instanceof`

The `new` operator is used to create objects, that is, instances of classes and arrays. It is used with a constructor call to instantiate classes (see Section 4.4, p. 117), and with the `[]` notation to create arrays (see Section 4.1, p. 100). It is also used to instantiate anonymous arrays (see Section 4.1, p. 104), and anonymous classes (see Section 7.5, p. 308).

```
Pizza onePizza = new Pizza();        // Create an instance of Pizza class.
```

The `[]` notation is used to declare and construct arrays and also to access array elements (see Section 4.1, p. 100).

```
int[] anArray = new int[5];// Declare and construct an int array of 5 elements.
anArray[4] = anArray[3];   // Element at index 4 gets value of element at index 3.
```

The boolean, binary, and infix operator `instanceof` is used to test an object's type (see Section 6.6, p. 264).

```
Pizza myPizza = new Pizza();
boolean test1 = myPizza instanceof Pizza;   // True.
boolean test2 = "Pizza" instanceof Pizza;   // Compile error. String is not Pizza.
boolean test3 = null instanceof Pizza;      // Always false. null not an instance.
```

 Review Questions

3.20 What would be printed during execution of the following program?

```
public class MyClass {
    public static void main(String[] args) {
        test(1<<32, "1<<32");
        test(1<<31, "1<<31");
        test(1<<30, "1<<30");
        test(1,     "1"   );
        test(0,     "0"   );
        test(-1,    "-1"  );
    }
```

```
            public static void test(int i, String exp) {
                if ((i >> 1) != (i >>> 1)) System.out.println(exp);
            }
        }
```

Select the two correct answers.

(a) "1<<32"
(b) "1<<31"
(c) "1<<30"
(d) "1"
(e) "0"
(f) "-1"

3.21 Which of the following are not operators in Java?

Select the two correct answers.

(a) %
(b) <<<
(c) &
(d) %=
(e) >>>
(f) <=
(g) &&=

3.22 Given a variable x of type int (which may contain a negative value), which are correct ways of doubling the value of x, barring any wrapping of out-of-range intermediate values?

Select the four correct answers.

(a) x << 1;
(b) x = x * 2;
(c) x *= 2;
(d) x += x;
(e) x <<= 1;

3.23 Which of the following operators can be used both as an integer bitwise operator and a boolean logical operator?

Select the three correct answers.

(a) ^
(b) !
(c) &
(d) |
(e) ~

3.24   Given these declarations, which of the following expressions are valid?

```
byte  b = 1;
char  c = 1;
short s = 1;
int   i = 1;
```

Select the three correct answers.

(a) s = b * 2;
(b) i = b << s;
(c) b <<= s;
(d) c = c + b;
(e) s += i;

3.17 Parameter Passing

Objects communicate by passing *messages* (see Section 1.4, p. 7). A message is implemented as a *method call* to invoke a particular method on an object. Static methods can be invoked on classes in Java. Parameters in the method call provide one way of exchanging information between the caller object and the callee object (which need not be different). Defining methods is discussed in Section 4.3.

The syntax of a method call can be any one of the following:

> *<object reference>*.*<method name>* (*<actual parameter list>*)
>
> *<class name>*.*<static method name>* (*<actual parameter list>*)
>
> *<method name>* (*<actual parameter list>*)

The *<object reference>* must be an expression that evaluates to an object reference. If the caller and the callee are the same, then *<object reference>* can be omitted (see discussion on this reference in Section 4.3 on page 114). The *<class name>* can be the *fully qualified name* (see Section 4.6, p. 126) of the class. The *<actual parameter list>* is *comma-separated* if there is more than one parameter. The parentheses are mandatory even if the actual parameter list is empty. This distinguishes the method call from the construct for accessing fields, specifying fully qualified names for classes and packages using the dot operator.

```
objRef.doIt(time, place);          // Explicit object reference
int i = java.lang.Math.abs(-1);    // Fully qualified class name
int j = Math.abs(-1);              // Class name
someMethod(ofValue);               // Object or class implicitly implied
someObjRef.make().make().make();   // make() returns an object reference
```

The dot operator . has left associativity. In the last code line, the first call of the make() method returns an object reference that indicates the object to execute the next call, and so on. This is an example of *call chaining*.

Actual parameters are parameters passed to the method when the method is invoked by a method call, and can vary from call to call. *Formal parameters* are parameters defined in the *method definition* (see Section 4.3, p. 112) and are local to the method (see *Local variables*, p. 33).

Actual and formal parameters must be compatible in the following respects:

- The number of actual parameters must equal the number of formal parameters in the method definition.

- Corresponding individual actual and formal parameters must be *type compatible*. Method invocation conversions for primitive values are discussed in Section 3.18, and those for reference types are discussed in Section 6.6.

In Java, all parameters are passed by value, that is, an actual parameter is evaluated and its value is assigned to the corresponding formal parameter. Table 3.20 summarizes what value is passed depending on the type of the formal parameter. In the case of primitive data types, the data value of the actual parameter is passed. If the actual parameter is a reference to an object (i.e., instantiation of a class or an array), then the reference value is passed and not the object itself. If the actual parameter is an array element of a primitive data type, then its data value is passed, and if the array element is a reference to an object, then its reference value is passed.

Table 3.20 *Parameter Passing*

Data Type of the Formal Parameters	Value Passed
Primitive data types	Primitive data value
Class type	Reference value
Array type	Reference value

It should also be stressed that each invocation of a method has its own copies of the formal parameters, as is the case for any local variable in the method.

The order of evaluation in the actual parameter list is always from left to right. Given the following declaration:

```
int i = 4;
```

the method call

```
leftRight(i++, i);
```

is effectively the same as

```
leftRight(4, 5);
```

and not as

```
leftRight(4, 4);
```

For expositional purposes, the examples in subsequent sections primarily show method invocation on the same object or the same class. The parameter passing mechanism is no different when different objects or classes are involved.

3.18 Passing Primitive Data Values

When the actual parameter is a variable of a primitive data type, the value of the variable is copied to the formal parameter at method invocation. Since formal parameters are local to the method, any changes made to the formal parameter will not be reflected in the actual parameter after the call completes.

Note that the actual parameter can be an expression that is evaluated first, and the resulting value is then passed.

Type conversions between actual and formal parameters of primitive data types are similar to those for numeric assignment conversions (i.e., widening primitive conversions are implicitly applied). However, for parameter passing there are no implicit narrowing conversions (see Section 3.4, p. 49).

Example 3.3 *Passing Primitive Values*

```
public class CustomerOne {
    public static void main (String[] args) {
        PizzaFactory pizzaHouse = new PizzaFactory();
        int pricePrPizza = 15;
        double totPrice = pizzaHouse.calcPrice(4, pricePrPizza);        // (1)
        System.out.println("Value of pricePrPizza: " + pricePrPizza); // Unchanged.
    }
}

class PizzaFactory {
    public double calcPrice(int numberOfPizzas, double pizzaPrice) {  // (2)
        pizzaPrice = pizzaPrice/2.0; // Change price.
        return numberOfPizzas * pizzaPrice;
    }
}
```

Output from the program:

```
Value of pricePrPizza: 15
```

In Example 3.3, the method calcPrice() is defined in class PizzaFactory at (2). It is called from the CustomerOne.main() method at (1). The value of the first actual parameter, 4, is copied to the int formal parameter numberOfPizzas. Note that the second actual parameter pricePrPizza is of type int, while the corresponding formal parameter pizzaPrice is of type double. Before the value of the actual parameter pricePrPizza is copied to the formal parameter pizzaPrice, it is implicitly widened to a double. Passing of primitive values is illustrated in Figure 3.4.

Figure 3.4   *Parameter Passing: Primitive Data Values*

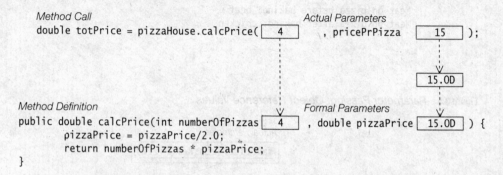

The value of the formal parameter `pizzaPrice` is changed in the `calcPrice()` method, but this does not affect the value of the actual parameter `pricePrPizza` on return. It still has the value 15. The bottom line is that the formal parameter is a local variable, and change of its value does not affect the value of the actual parameter.

3.19   Passing Object Reference Values

If an actual parameter is a reference to an object, then the reference value is passed. This means that both the actual parameter and the formal parameter are aliases to the object denoted by this reference value during the invocation of the method. In particular, this implies that changes made to the object via the formal parameter *will* be apparent after the call returns. The actual parameter expression must evaluate to an object reference before the reference value can be passed.

Type conversions between actual and formal parameters of reference types are discussed in Section 6.6.

Example 3.4   *Passing Object Reference Values*

```
public class CustomerTwo {
    public static void main (String[] args) {
        Pizza favoritePizza = new Pizza();              // (1)
        System.out.println("Meat on pizza before baking: " + favoritePizza.meat);
        bake(favoritePizza);                            // (2)
        System.out.println("Meat on pizza after baking: " + favoritePizza.meat);
    }
    public static void bake(Pizza pizzaToBeBaked) { // (3)
        pizzaToBeBaked.meat = "chicken";  // Change the meat on the pizza.
        pizzaToBeBaked = null;                          // (4)
    }
}

class Pizza {                                           // (5)
    String meat = "beef";
}
```

Output from the program:

```
Meat on pizza before baking: beef
Meat on pizza after baking: chicken
```

Figure 3.5 *Parameter Passing: Object Reference Values*

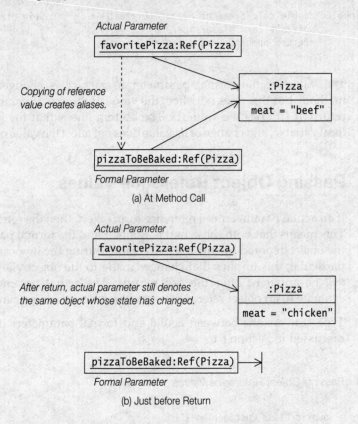

In Example 3.4, a Pizza object is created at (1). Any object of the class Pizza created using the class definition at (5) always results in a beef pizza. In the call to the bake() method at (2), the value of the object reference in the actual parameter favoritePizza is assigned to the formal parameter pizzaToBeBaked in the definition of the bake() method at (3).

One particular consequence of passing reference values to formal parameters is that any changes made to the object via formal parameters will be reflected back in the calling method when the call returns. In this case, the reference favoritePizza will show that chicken has been substituted for beef on the pizza. Setting the formal parameter pizzaToBeBaked to null at (4) does not change the reference value in the actual parameter favoritePizza. The situation at method invocation, and just before return from method bake(), is illustrated in Figure 3.5.

In summary, the formal parameter can only change the *state* of the object whose reference value was passed to the method.

The parameter passing strategy in Java is *call-by-value* and not *call-by-reference*, regardless of the type of the parameter. Call-by-reference would have allowed values in the actual parameters to be changed via formal parameters; that is, the value in pricePrPizza to be halved in Example 3.3 and favoritePizza to be set to null in Example 3.4. However, this cannot be directly implemented in Java.

3.20 Passing Array References

Arrays are objects in Java (see Section 4.1, p. 100). A review of arrays is recommended before continuing with this section.

The discussion on passing object reference values in the previous section is equally valid for arrays. Method invocation conversions for array types are discussed along with those for other reference types in Section 6.6.

Example 3.5 *Passing Arrays*

```java
public class Percolate {

    public static void main (String[] args) {
        int[] dataSeq = {6,4,8,2,1};   // Create and initialize an array.

        // Write array before percolation.
        for (int i = 0; i < dataSeq.length; ++i)
            System.out.print(" " + dataSeq[i]);
        System.out.println();

        // Percolate.
        for (int index = 1; index < dataSeq.length; ++index)
            if (dataSeq[index-1] > dataSeq[index])
                swap(dataSeq, index-1, index);                    // (1)

        // Write array after percolation.
        for (int i = 0; i < dataSeq.length; ++i)
            System.out.print(" " + dataSeq[i]);
        System.out.println();
    }

    public static void swap(int[] table, int i, int j) {         // (2)
        int tmp = table[i]; table[i] = table[j]; table[j] = tmp;
    }

    public static void swap(int v1, int v2) {                    // (3)
        int tmp = v1; v1 = v2; v2 = tmp;
    }
}
```

Output from the program:

```
6 4 8 2 1
4 6 2 1 8
```

In Example 3.5, the idea is to repeatedly swap neighboring elements in an integer array until the largest element in the array *percolates* to the last position of the array.

Note that in the definition of the method swap() at (2), the formal parameter table is of array type. The swap() method is called in the main() method at (1), where one of the actual parameters is the array variable dataSeq. The reference value of the array variable dataSeq is assigned to the array variable table at method invocation. After return from the call to the swap() method, the array variable dataSeq will reflect the changes made to the array via the corresponding formal parameter. This situation is depicted in Figure 3.6 at the first call and return from the swap() method, indicating how values of elements at index 0 and 1 in the array have been swapped.

However, the definition of the swap() method at (3) will *not* swap two values. The method call

```
swap(dataSeq[index-1], dataSeq[index]);
```

will have no effect on the array elements, as the swapping is done on the values of the formal parameters.

Figure 3.6 *Parameter Passing: Arrays*

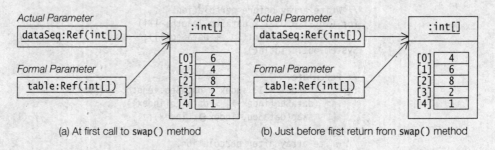

(a) At first call to swap() method   (b) Just before first return from swap() method

3.21 Array Elements as Actual Parameters

Array elements, like other variables, can store values of primitive data types or references to objects. In the latter case it means they can also be arrays, that is, array of arrays (see Section 4.1, p. 104). If an array element is of a primitive data type, then its data value is passed, and if it is a reference to an object, then the reference value is passed.

Example 3.6   *Array Elements as Primitive Data Values*

```
public class FindMinimum {

    public static void main(String[] args) {
        int[] dataSeq = {6,4,8,2,1};

        int minValue = dataSeq[0];
        for (int index = 1; index < dataSeq.length; ++index)
            minValue = minimum(minValue, dataSeq[index]);          // (1)

        System.out.println("Minimum value: " + minValue);
    }

    public static int minimum(int i, int j) {                      // (2)
        return (i <= j) ? i : j;
    }
}
```

Output from the program:

```
Minimum value: 1
```

In Example 3.6, note that the value of all but one element of the array dataSeq is retrieved and passed consecutively at (1) to the formal parameter j of the minimum() method defined at (2). The discussion in Section 3.18 on call-by-value also applies to array elements that have primitive values.

Example 3.7   *Array Elements as Object Reference Values*

```
public class FindMinimumMxN {

    public static void main(String[] args) {
        int[][] matrix = { {8,4},{6,3,2},{7} };                    // (1)

        int min = findMinimum(matrix[0]);                          // (2)
        for (int i = 1; i < matrix.length; ++i) {
            int minInRow = findMinimum(matrix[i]);                 // (3)
            if (min > minInRow) min = minInRow;
        }
        System.out.println("Minimum value in matrix: " + min);
    }

    public static int findMinimum(int[] seq) {                     // (4)
        int min = seq[0];
        for (int i = 1; i < seq.length; ++i)
            min = Math.min(min, seq[i]);
        return min;
    }
}
```

Output from the program:

```
Minimum value in matrix: 2
```

In Example 3.7, note that the formal parameter seq of the findMinimum() method defined at (4) is an array variable. The variable matrix denotes an array of arrays declared at (1), simulating a multidimensional array, which has three rows, where each row is an array. The first row, denoted by matrix[0], is passed to the findMinimum() method in the call at (2). Each remaining row is passed by reference value in the call to the findMinimum() method at (3).

3.22 final **Parameters**

A formal parameter can be declared with the keyword final preceding the parameter declaration in the method definition. A final parameter is also known as a *blank final variable*; that is, it is blank (uninitialized) until a value is assigned to it, (for example, at method invocation) and then the value in the variable cannot be changed during the lifetime of the variable (see also the discussion in Section 4.10, p. 146). The compiler can treat such blank final variables as constants for code optimization purposes. Whether a formal parameter is declared as final, does not affect the caller's code.

The definition of method calcPrice() from Example 3.3 is shown below, with the formal parameter pizzaPrice declared as final.

```
public double calcPrice(int numberOfPizzas, final double pizzaPrice) {  // (2)
    pizzaPrice = pizzaPrice/2.0;                                        // (3)
    return numberOfPizzas * pizzaPrice;
}
```

If this definition of the calcPrice() method is compiled, the compiler will not allow the value of the final parameter pizzaPrice to be changed at (3) in the body of the method.

As another example, the definition of the method bake() from Example 3.4 is shown below, with the formal parameter pizzaToBeBaked declared as final.

```
public static void bake(final Pizza pizzaToBeBaked) { // (3)
    pizzaToBeBaked.meat = "chicken";                  // (3a) Allowed.
    pizzaToBeBaked = null;                            // (4) Not allowed.
}
```

If this definition of the bake() method is compiled, the compiler will not allow the reference value of the final parameter pizzaToBeBaked to be changed at (4) in the body of the method. Note that this applies to the reference value in the final parameter, not the object denoted by this parameter. The state of the object can be changed as before, as shown at (3a).

3.23   Program Arguments

Any arguments passed to the program on the command line can be accessed in the main() method of the class specified on the command line:

```
java Colors red green blue
```

These arguments are called *program arguments*. Note that the command name, java, and the class name Colors are not passed to the main() method of the class Colors.

Since the formal parameter of the main() method is an array of String objects, individual String elements in the array can be accessed by using the [] operator.

In Example 3.8, the three arguments "red", "green", and "blue" can be accessed in the main() method of the Colors class as args[0], args[1], and args[2], respectively. The total number of arguments is given by the field length of the String array args. Note that program arguments can only be passed as a list of character strings and must be explicitly converted to other data types by the program, if necessary.

When no arguments are specified on the command line, an array of zero String elements is created and passed to the main() method. This means that the value of the formal parameter in the main() method is never null.

Program arguments supply information to the application, which can be used to tailor the runtime behavior of the application according to user requirements.

Example 3.8   *Passing Program Arguments*

```
public class Colors {
    public static void main(String[] args) {
        for (int i = 0; i < args.length; i++)
            System.out.println("Argument no. " + i + " (" + args[i] + ") has " +
                               args[i].length() + " characters.");
    }
}
```

Running the program:

```
>java Colors red green blue
Argument no. 0 (red) has 3 characters.
Argument no. 1 (green) has 5 characters.
Argument no. 2 (blue) has 4 characters.
```

 Review Questions

3.25   What will be printed when the following program is run?

```
public class ParameterPass {
    public static void main(String[] args) {
        int i = 0;
```

```
        addTwo(i++);
        System.out.println(i);
    }

    static void addTwo(int i) {
        i += 2;
    }
}
```

Select the one correct answer.

(a) 0
(b) 1
(c) 2
(d) 3

3.26   What will be the result of attempting to compile and run the following class?

```
public class Passing {
    public static void main(String[] args) {
        int a = 0; int b = 0;
        int[] bArr = new int[1]; bArr[0] = b;

        inc1(a); inc2(bArr);

        System.out.println("a=" + a + " b=" + b + " bArr[0]=" + bArr[0]);
    }

    public static void inc1(int x) { x++; }

    public static void inc2(int[] x) { x[0]++; }
}
```

Select the one correct answer.

(a) The code will fail to compile, since x[0]++; is not a legal statement.
(b) The code will compile and will print "a=1 b=1 bArr[0]=1" when run.
(c) The code will compile and will print "a=0 b=1 bArr[0]=1" when run.
(d) The code will compile and will print "a=0 b=0 bArr[0]=1" when run.
(e) The code will compile and will print "a=0 b=0 bArr[0]=0" when run.

3.27   Given the class

```
// Filename: Args.java
public class Args {
    public static void main(String[] args) {
        System.out.println(args[0] + " " + args[args.length-1]);
    }
}
```

what would be the result of executing the following on the command line?

```
java Args In politics stupidity is not a handicap
```

Select the one correct answer.

(a) The program will throw ArrayIndexOutOfBoundsException.
(b) The program will print "java handicap".
(c) The program will print "Args handicap".
(d) The program will print "In handicap".
(e) The program will print "Args a".
(f) The program will print "In a".

3.28 Which statements would cause a compilation error if inserted in the location indicated in the following program?

```
public class ParameterUse {
    static void main(String[] args) {
        int a = 0;
        final int b = 1;
        int[] c = { 2 };
        final int[] d = { 3 };
        useArgs(a, b, c, d);
    }

    static void useArgs(final int a, int b, final int[] c, int[] d) {
        // INSERT STATEMENT HERE.
    }
}
```

Select the two correct answers.

(a) a++;
(b) b++;
(c) b = a;
(d) c[0]++;
(e) d[0]++;
(f) c = d;

Chapter Summary

The following topics were explained in this chapter:

- operators in Java, including precedence and associativity rules
- type conversions: casting, narrowing and widening: in addition, the unary and binary numeric promotions are stated, and the context under which they are applied discussed
- defining and evaluating arithmetic and boolean expressions
- assigning values and assigning references
- object value equality and object reference equality
- parameter passing, both primitive values and object references, including arrays and array elements: in addition, final parameters are also discussed
- passing program arguments

Programming Exercises

3.1 The program below is supposed to calculate and show the time it takes for light to travel from the sun to the earth. It contains some logical errors. Fix the program so that it will compile and show the intended value when run.

```java
// Filename: Sunlight.java
public class Sunlight {
    public static void main(String[] args) {
        // Distance from sun (150 million kilometers)
        int kmFromSun = 150000000;

        int lightSpeed = 299792458; // meters per second

        // Convert distance to meters.
        int mFromSun = kmFromSun * 1000;

        int seconds = mFromSun / lightSpeed;

        System.out.print("Light will use ");
        printTime(seconds);
        System.out.println(" to travel from the sun to the earth.");
    }

    public static void printTime(int sec) {
        int min = sec / 60;
        sec = sec - (min*60);
        System.out.print(min + " minute(s) and " + sec + " second(s)");
    }
}
```

3.2 Create two method that both takes an int as an argument and returns a String object representing the binary representation of the integer. Given the argument 42, it should return "101010". The first method should calculate the binary representation manually, and the other should use the functionality available in the Java class libraries.

3.3 Create a program that will print every other argument given on the command line. If the program was executed with the following on the command line,

```
java ArgumentSkipper one two three a b c d
```

the program would print

```
one
three
b
d
```

Consider how your program would operate when no arguments are given.

Declarations and Access Control

4

- Write code that declares, constructs, and initializes arrays of any base type using any of the permitted forms, both for declaration and for initialization.
- Declare classes, inner classes, methods, instance variables, static variables and automatic (method local) variables, making appropriate use of all permitted modifiers (such as public, final, static, abstract). State the significance of each of these modifiers both singly and in combination, and state the effect of package relationships on declared items qualified by these modifiers.

  o *For nested classes, see Chapter 7.*

- For a given class, determine if a default constructor will be created, and if so, state the prototype of that constructor.
- Identify the legal return types for any method, given the declarations of all related methods in this or parent classes.

  o *For method overriding, see Section 6.2.*

- Define and use anonymous arrays.
- Understand usage of this reference in instance methods.
- Understand the term *method signature* and state the circumstances under which methods can be overloaded.
- Identify a non-default constructor, and understand how constructors can be overloaded.
- State how the package and import statements are used to define packages and import from packages.

4.1 Arrays

An *array* is a data structure that defines an indexed collection of a fixed number of homogeneous data elements. This means that all elements in the array have the same data type. A position in the array is indicated by a non-negative integer value called the *index*. An element at a given position in the array is accessed using the index. The size of an array is fixed and cannot increase to accommodate more elements.

In Java, arrays are objects. Arrays can be of primitive data types or reference types. In the former case, all elements in the array are of a specific primitive data type. In the latter case, all elements are references of a specific reference type. References in the array can then denote objects of this reference type or its subtypes. Each array object has a final field called `length`, which specifies the array size, that is, the number of elements the array can accommodate. The first element is always at index 0 and the last element at index *n*-1, where *n* is the value of the `length` field in the array.

Simple arrays are *one-dimensional arrays*, that is, a simple sequence of values. Since arrays can store object references, the objects referenced can also be array objects. This allows implementation of *array of arrays*.

Passing array references as parameters is discussed in Section 3.20. Type conversions for array references on assignment and method invocation are discussed in Section 6.6.

Declaring Array Variables

An array variable declaration has either the following syntax:

> *<element type>*`[]` *<array name>*`;`

or

> *<element type>* *<array name>*`[]`;

where *<element type>* can be a primitive data type or a reference type. The array variable *<array name>* has the type *<element type>*`[]`. Note that the array size is not specified. This means that the array variable *<array name>* can be assigned an array of any length, as long as its elements have *<element type>*.

It is important to understand that the declaration does not actually create an array. It only declares a reference that can denote an array object.

```
int anIntArray[], oneInteger;
Pizza[] mediumPizzas, largePizzas;
```

These two declarations declare `anIntArray` and `mediumPizzas` to be reference variables that can denote arrays of `int` values and arrays of `Pizza` objects, respectively. The variable `largePizzas` can denote an array of pizzas, but the variable `oneInteger` cannot denote an array of `int` values—it is simply an `int` variable.

When the [] notation follows the type, all variables in the declaration are arrays. Otherwise the [] notation must follow each individual array name in the declaration.

An array variable that is declared as a member of a class, but is not initialized to denote an array, will be initialized to the default reference value null. This default initialization does *not* apply to local reference variables and, therefore, does not apply to local array variables either (see Section 2.4, p. 33). This should not be confused with initialization of the elements of an array during array construction.

Constructing an Array

An array can be constructed for a specific number of elements of the element type, using the new operator. The resulting array reference can be assigned to an array variable of the corresponding type.

<array name> = new *<element type>* [*<array size>*];

The minimum value of *<array size>* is 0 (i.e., arrays with zero elements can be constructed in Java). If the array size is negative, a NegativeArraySizeException is thrown.

Given the following array declarations:

```
int anIntArray[], oneInteger;
Pizza[] mediumPizzas, largePizzas;
```

the arrays can be constructed as follows:

```
anIntArray = new int[10];          // array for 10 integers
mediumPizzas = new Pizza[5];       // array of 5 pizzas
largePizzas = new Pizza[3];        // array of 3 pizzas
```

The array declaration and construction can be combined.

<element type₁>[] *<array name>* = new *<element type₂>*[*<array size>*];

However, here array type *<element type₂>*[] must be *assignable* to array type *<element type₁>*[] (see Section 6.6, p. 260). When the array is constructed, all its elements are initialized to the default value for *<element type₂>*. This is true for both member and local arrays when they are constructed.

In all the examples below, the code constructs the array and the array elements are implicitly initialized to their default value. For example, the element at index 2 in array anIntArray gets the value 0, and the element at index 3 in array mediumPizzas gets the value null when the arrays are constructed.

```
int[] anIntArray = new int[10];                  // Default element value: 0.

Pizza[] mediumPizzas = new Pizza[5];             // Default element value: null.

// Pizza class extends Object class
Object objArray = new Pizza[3];                  // Default element value: null.

// Pizza class implements Eatable interface
Eatable[] eatables = new Pizza[2];               // Default element value: null.
```

The value of the field length in each array is set to the number of elements specified during the construction of the array; for example, medium Pizzas.length has the value 5.

Once an array has been constructed, its elements can also be explicitly initialized individually; for example, in a loop. Examples in the rest of this section make heavy use of a loop to traverse through the elements of an array for various purposes.

Initializing an Array

Java provides the means of declaring, constructing, and explicitly initializing an array in one declaration statement:

<element type>[] *<array name>* = { *<array initialize list>* };

This form of initialization applies to member as well as local arrays. The *<array initialize list>* is a comma-separated list of zero or more expressions. Such an array initialization block results in the construction and initialization of the array.

```
int[] anIntArray = {1, 3, 49, 2, 6, 7, 15, 2, 1, 5};
```

The array anIntArray is declared as an array of ints. It is constructed to hold 10 elements (equal to the length of the list of expressions in the block), where the first element is initialized to the value of the first expression (1), the second element to the value of the second expression (3), and so on.

```
// Pizza class extends Object class
Object[] objArray = { new Pizza(), new Pizza(), null };
```

The array objArray is declared as an array of the Object class, constructed to hold three elements. The initialization code sets the first two elements of the array to refer to two Pizza objects, while the last element is initialized to the null reference. Note that the number of objects created in the above declaration statement is actually three: the array object with three references and the two Pizza objects.

The expressions in the *<array initialize list>* are evaluated from left to right, and the array name obviously cannot occur in any of the expressions in the list. In the examples above, the *<array initialize list>* is terminated by the right curly bracket, }, of the block. The list can also be legally terminated by a comma. The following array has length two, not three:

```
Topping[] pizzaToppings = { new Topping("cheese"), new Topping("tomato"), };
```

The declaration statement at (1) in the following code defines an array of four String objects, while the declaration statement at (2) should make it clear that a String object is not the same as an array of char.

```
// Array with 4 String objects
String[] pets = {"crocodiles", "elephants", "crocophants", "elediles"}; // (1)

// Array of 3 characters
char[] charArray = {'a', 'h', 'a'};    // (2) Not the same as "aha".
```

Using an Array

The whole array is referenced by the array name, but individual array elements are accessed by specifying an index with the [] operator. The array element access expression has the following syntax:

<array name> [*<index expression>*]

Each individual element is treated as a simple variable of the element type. The *index* is specified by the *<index expression>*, which can be any expression that evaluates to an non-negative int value. Since the lower bound of an array is always 0, the upper bound is one less than the array size, that is, (*<array name>*.length-1). The ith element in the array has index (i-1). At runtime, the index value is automatically checked to ensure that it is within the array index bounds. If the index value is less than 0 or greater than or equal to *<array name>*.length in an array element access expression, an ArrayIndexOutOfBoundsException is thrown. A program can either check the index explicitly or catch the exception (see Section 5.5, p. 181), but an illegal index is typically an indication of a program bug.

In the array element access expression, the *<array name>* can, in fact, be any expression that returns a reference to an array. For example, the following expression accesses the element with the index 1 in the character array returned by a call to the toCharArray() method of the String class: "AHA".toCharArray()[1].

The array operator [] is used to declare array types (Topping[]), specify array size (new Toppings[3]), and to access array elements (toppings[1]). This operator is not used when the array reference is manipulated, for example in an array reference assignment (see Section 6.6, p. 260) or when the array reference is passed as an actual parameter in a method call (see Section 3.20, p. 91).

Example 4.1 shows traversal of arrays. The loop at (3) initializes the local array trialArray declared at (2) five times with pseudo-random numbers (from 0.0 to 100.0), by calling the method randomize() at (5). The minimum value in the array is found by calling the method findMinimum() at (6), and is stored in the array storeMinimum declared at (1). The loop at (4) prints the minimum values from the trials. The start value of the loop variable is initially set to 0. The loop condition tests whether the loop variable is less than the length of the array; this guarantees that the index will not go out of bounds.

Example 4.1 *Using Arrays*

```
class Trials {
    public static void main(String[] args) {
        // Declare and construct the local arrays
        double[] storeMinimum = new double[5];                // (1)
        double[] trialArray = new double[15];                 // (2)
        for (int i = 0; i < storeMinimum.length; ++i) {       // (3)
            // Initialize the array
            randomize(trialArray);
            // Find and store the minimum value
            storeMinimum[i] = findMinimum(trialArray);
        }
```

```java
        // Print the minimum values                              (4)
        for (int i = 0; i < storeMinimum.length; ++i)
            System.out.println(storeMinimum[i]);
    }

    public static void randomize(double[] valArray) {        // (5)
        for (int i = 0; i < valArray.length; ++i)
            valArray[i] = Math.random() * 100.0;
    }

    public static double findMinimum(double[] valArray) {  // (6)
        // Assume the array has at least one element.
        double minValue = valArray[0];
        for (int i = 1; i < valArray.length; ++i)
            minValue = Math.min(minValue, valArray[i]);
        return minValue;
    }
}
```

Possible output from the program:

```
6.756931310985048
5.364063199341363
8.359410202984296
8.858272848258109
9.759950059619849
```

Anonymous Arrays

As shown earlier in this section, the following declaration statement

<element type₁>[] *<array name>* = new *<element type₂>*[*<array size>*]; // (1)

```java
int[] intArray = new int[5];
```

can be used to construct arrays using an array creation expression. The size of the array is specified in the array creation expression, which creates the array and initializes the array elements to their default values. On the other hand, the following declaration statement

<element type>[] *<array name>* = { *<array initialize list>* };   // (2)

```java
int[] intArray = {3, 5, 2, 8, 6};
```

both creates the array and initializes the array elements to specific values given in the array initializer block. However, the array initialization block is *not* an expression.

Java has another array creation expression, called *anonymous array*, which allows the concept of the array creation expression from (1) and the array initializer block from (2) to be combined, to create and initialize an array object:

new *<element type>*[] { *<array initialize list>* }

```java
new int[] {3, 5, 2, 8, 6}
```

The construct has enough information to create a nameless array of a specific type. Neither the name of the array nor the size of the array is specified. The construct returns an array reference that can be assigned and passed as parameter. In particular, the following two examples of declaration statements are equivalent.

```
int[] intArray = {3, 5, 2, 8, 6};           // (1)

int[] intArray = new int[] {3, 5, 2, 8, 6}; // (2)
```

In (1), an array initializer block is used to create and initialize the elements. In (2), an anonymous array expression is used. It is tempting to use the array initialization block as an expression; for example, in an assignment statement as a short cut for assigning values to array elements in one go. However, this is illegal—instead, an anonymous array expression should be used.

```
int[] daysInMonth;
daysInMonth = {31, 28, 31, 30, 31, 30, 31, 31, 30, 31, 30, 31}; // Not ok.
daysInMonth = new int[] {31, 28, 31, 30, 31, 30, 31, 31, 30, 31, 30, 31}; // ok.
```

The concept of anonymous arrays is similar to that of *anonymous classes* (see Section 7.5, p. 308): they both combine the definition and instantiation of classes into one process.

In Example 4.2, an anonymous array is constructed at (1) and passed as parameter to the static method findMinimum() defined at (2). Note that no array name or array size is specified for the anonymous array.

Example 4.2 *Using Anonymous Arrays*

```
class AnonArray {
    public static void main(String[] args) {
        System.out.println("Minimum value: " +
                findMinimum(new int[] {3, 5, 2, 8, 6}));          // (1)
    }

    public static int findMinimum(int[] dataSeq) {               // (2)
        // Assume the array has at least one element.
        int min = dataSeq[0];
        for (int index = 1; index < dataSeq.length; ++index)
            if (dataSeq[index] < min)
                min = dataSeq[index];
        return min;
    }
}
```

Output from the program:

```
Minimum value: 2
```

Multidimensional Arrays

Since an array element can be an object reference and arrays are objects, array elements can themselves reference other arrays. In Java, an array of arrays can be defined as follows:

<element type>[][]...[] *<array name>*;

or

<element type> *<array name>*[][]...[];

In fact, the sequence of square bracket pairs, [], indicating the number of dimensions, can be distributed as a postfix to both the element type and the array name. Arrays of arrays are also sometimes called *multidimensional arrays*.

The following declarations are all equivalent:

```
int[][] mXnArray;       // 2-dimensional array
int[]   mXnArray[];     // 2-dimensional array
int     mXnArray[][];   // 2-dimensional array
```

It is customary to combine the declaration with the construction of the multidimensional array.

```
int[][] mXnArray = new int[4][5];     // 4 x 5 matrix of ints
```

The previous declaration constructs an array mXnArray of four elements, where each element is an array (row) of 5 int values. The concept of rows and columns is often used to describe the dimensions of a 2-dimensional array, which is often called a *matrix*. However, such an interpretation is not dictated by the Java language.

Each row in the previous matrix is denoted by mXnArray[i], where $0 \le i < 4$. Each element in the ith row, mXnArray[i], is accessed by mXnArray[i][j], where $0 \le j < 5$. The number of rows is given by mXnArray.length, in this case 4, and the number of values in the ith row is given by mXnArray[i].length, in this case 5 for all the rows, where $0 \le i < 4$.

Multidimensional arrays can also be constructed and explicitly initialized using array initializer blocks discussed for simple arrays. Note that each row is an array which uses an array initializer block to specify its values:

```
double[][] identityMatrix = {
    {1.0, 0.0, 0.0, 0.0 }, // 1. row
    {0.0, 1.0, 0.0, 0.0 }, // 2. row
    {0.0, 0.0, 1.0, 0.0 }, // 3. row
    {0.0, 0.0, 0.0, 1.0 }  // 4. row
}; // 4 x 4 Floating-point matrix
```

Arrays in a multidimensional array need not have the same length. The array of arrays pizzaGalore in the code below will have five rows, the first four rows have different lengths but the fifth row is left unconstructed.

```
Pizza[][] pizzaGalore = {
{ new Pizza(), null, new Pizza() },      // 1. row is an array of 3 elements.
{ null, new Pizza()},                    // 2. row is an array of 2 elements.
new Pizza[1],                            // 3. row is an array of 1 element.
{},                                      // 4. row is an array of 0 elements.
null                                     // 5. row is not constructed.
};
```

When constructing multidimensional arrays with the new operator, the length of
the deeply nested arrays may be omitted. In this case, these arrays are left unconstructed. For example an array of arrays to represent a room on a floor in a hotel
on a street in a city can have the type HotelRoom[][][][]. From left to right, the
square brackets represent indices for street, hotel, floor, and room, respectively.
This 4-dimensional array of arrays can be constructed piecemeal, starting with the
leftmost dimension and proceeding to the rightmost.

```
HotelRoom[][][][] rooms = new HotelRoom[10][5][][];  // Just streets and hotels.
```

The above declaration constructs the array of arrays rooms partially with ten streets,
where each street has five hotels. Floors and rooms can be added to a particular
hotel on a particular street:

```
rooms[0][0]       = new HotelRoom[3][]; // 3 floors in 1st. hotel on 1st. street.
rooms[0][0][0]    = new HotelRoom[8];   // 8 rooms on 1st. floor in this hotel.
rooms[0][0][0][0] = new HotelRoom();    // Initialize 1st. room on this floor.
```

The code below constructs an array of arrays matrix, where the first row has one
element, the second row has two elements, and the third row has three elements.
Note that the outer array is constructed first. The second dimension is constructed
in a loop that constructs the array in each row. The elements in the multidimensional array will be implicitly initialized to the default double value (0.0D). In Figure
4.1, the array of arrays matrix is depicted after the elements have been explicitly
initialized.

```
double[][] matrix = new double[3][];        // No. of rows.

for (int i = 0; i < matrix.length; ++i)
   matrix[i] = new double[i + 1];           // Construct a row.
```

Two other ways of initializing such an array of arrays, the first one using array initializer blocks and the second one using an anonymous array of arrays are shown
as follows:

```
double[][] matrix2 = {
   {0.0},                    // 1. row
   {0.0, 0.0},               // 2. row
   {0.0, 0.0, 0.0}           // 3. row
}

double[][] matrix3 = new double[][] {
   {0.0},                    // 1. row
   {0.0, 0.0},               // 2. row
   {0.0, 0.0, 0.0}           // 3. row
}
```

The type of variable matrix is double[][] (i.e., a two-dimensional array of double values). The type of variable matrix[i] (where $0 \leq i <$ matrix.length) is double[] (i.e., a one-dimensional array of double values). The type of variable matrix[i][j] (where $0 \leq i <$ matrix.length and $0 \leq j <$ matrix[i].length) is double (i.e., a simple variable of type double).

Figure 4.1 *Array of Arrays*

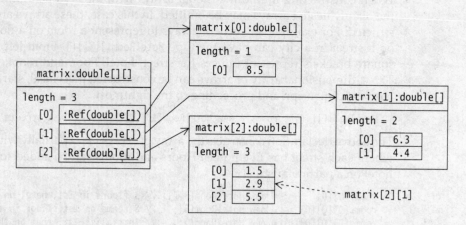

Nested loops are a natural match for manipulating multidimensional arrays. In Example 4.3, a rectangular 4×3 int matrix is declared and constructed at (1). The program finds the minimum value in the matrix. The outer loop at (2) traverses the rows (mXnArray[i], $0 \leq i <$ mXnArray.length), and the inner loop at (3) traverses the elements in each row in turn (mXnArray[i][j], $0 \leq j <$ mXnArray[i].length). The outer loop is executed mXnArray.length times, or 4 times, and the inner loop is executed (mXn-Array.length) $\times$ (mXnArray[i].length), or 12 times, since all rows have the same length, 3.

Example 4.3 *Using Multidimensional Arrays*

```
class MultiArrays {

    public static void main(String[] args) {
        // Declare and construct the M X N matrix.
        int[][] mXnArray = {                                    // (1)
            {16,  7, 12}, // 1. row
            { 9, 20, 18}, // 2. row
            {14, 11,  5}, // 3. row
            { 8,  5, 10}  // 4. row
        }; // 4 x 3 int matrix

        // Find the minimum value in a M X N matrix
        int min = mXnArray[0][0];
        for (int i = 0; i < mXnArray.length; ++i)               // (2)
            // Find min in mXnArray[i], i.e. in the row given by index i.
```

```
                    for (int j = 0; j < mXnArray[i].length; ++j)          // (3)
                        min = Math.min(min, mXnArray[i][j]);
                    System.out.println("Minimum value: " + min);
            }
        }
```

Output from the program:

```
Minimum value: 5
```

 ## Review Questions

4.1 Given the following declaration, which expression returns the size of the array, assuming the array has been initialized?

```
int[] array;
```

Select the one correct answer.
(a) `array[].length()`
(b) `array.length()`
(c) `array[].length`
(d) `array.length`
(e) `array[].size()`
(f) `array.size()`

4.2 Is it possible to create arrays of length zero?

Select the one correct answer.

(a) Yes, you can create arrays of any type with length zero.
(b) Yes, but only for primitive data types.
(c) Yes, but only for arrays of object references.
(d) No, you cannot create zero-length arrays, but the `main()` method may be passed a zero-length array of `String` references when no program arguments are specified.
(e) No, it is not possible to create arrays of length zero in Java.

4.3 Which one of the following array declaration statements is not legal?

Select the one correct answer.
(a) `int []a[] = new int [4][4];`
(b) `int a[][] = new int [4][4];`
(c) `int a[][] = new int [][4];`
(d) `int []a[] = new int [4][];`
(e) `int [][]a = new int [4][4];`

4.4   Which of these array declaration statements are not legal?

Select the two correct answers.

(a) `int[] i[] = { { 1, 2 }, { 1 }, {}, { 1, 2, 3 } };`
(b) `int i[] = new int[2] {1, 2};`
(c) `int i[][] = new int[][] { {1, 2, 3}, {4, 5, 6} };`
(d) `int i[][] = { { 1, 2 }, new int[ 2 ] };`
(e) `int i[4] = { 1, 2, 3, 4 };`

4.5   What would be the result of attempting to compile and run the following program?

```
// Filename: MyClass.java
class MyClass {
    public static void main(String[] args) {
        int size = 20;
        int[] arr = new int[ size ];

        for (int i = 0; i < size; ++i) {
                System.out.println(arr[i]};
        }
    }
}
```

Select the one correct answer.

(a) The code will fail to compile because the array type `int[]` is incorrect.
(b) The program will compile, but will throw an `ArrayIndexOutOfBoundsException` when run.
(c) The program will compile and run without error, but will produce no output.
(d) The program will compile and run without error and will print the numbers 0 through 19.
(e) The program will compile and run without error and will print 0 twenty times.
(f) The program will compile and run without error and will print `null` twenty times.

4.6   Given the following program, which statement is true?

```
class MyClass {
    public static void main(String[] args) {
        String[] numbers = { "one", "two", "three", "four" };

        if (args.length == 0) {
            System.out.println("no arguments");
        } else {
            System.out.println(numbers[ args.length ] + " arguments");
        }
    }
}
```

Select the one correct answer.

(a) The program will fail to compile.

(b) The program will throw a `NullPointerException` when run with zero program arguments.

(c) The program will print "no arguments" and "two arguments" when called with zero and three program arguments, respectively.

(d) The program will print "no arguments" and "three arguments" when called with zero and three program arguments, respectively.

(e) The program will print "no arguments" and "four arguments" when called with zero and three program arguments, respectively.

(f) The program will print "one arguments" and "four arguments" when called with zero and three program arguments, respectively.

4.7 What would be the result of trying to compile and run the following program?

```
public class DefaultValuesTest {
    int[] ia = new int[1];
    boolean b;
    int i;
    Object o;

    public static void main(String[] args) {
        DefaultValuesTest instance = new DefaultValuesTest();
        instance.print();
    }

    public void print() {
        System.out.println(ia[0] + " " + b + " " + i + " " + o);
    }
}
```

Select the one correct answer.

(a) The program will fail to compile because of uninitialized variables.

(b) The program will throw a `java.lang.NullPointerException` when run.

(c) The program will print "0 false NaN null".

(d) The program will print "0 false 0 null".

(e) The program will print "null 0 0 null".

(f) The program will print "null false 0 null".

4.2 Defining Classes

A class declaration introduces a new reference type. It has the following general syntax:

```
<class modifiers> class <class name>
            <extends clause> <implements clause>   // Class header
{ // Class body
    <field declarations>
    <method declarations>
```

```
        <nested class declarations>
        <nested interface declarations>
        <constructor declarations>
        <initializer blocks>
}
```

In the class header, the name of the class is preceded by the keyword class. In addition, the class header can specify the following information:

- scope or *accessibility modifier* (see Section 4.7, p. 131)
- additional *class modifiers* (see Section 4.8, p. 134)
- any class it *extends* (see Section 6.1, p. 226)
- any interfaces it *implements* (see Section 6.4, p. 251)

The class body can contain *member declarations* which comprise

- *field declarations* (see Section 2.3, p. 31)
- *method declarations* (see Section 4.3, p. 112)
- *nested class and interface declarations* (see Section 7.1, p. 284)

Members declared static belong to the class and are called *static members*, and non-static members belong to the objects of the class and are called *instance members*. In addition, the following can be declared in a class body:

- *constructor declarations* (see Section 4.4, p. 117)
- *static and instance initializer blocks* (see Section 8.2, p. 331)

The member declarations, constructor declarations and initializer blocks can appear in any order in the class body.

In order to understand what code is legal to declare in a class, we distinguish between *static context* and *non-static context*. A static context is defined by static methods, static field initializers, and static initializer blocks. A non-static context is defined by instance methods, constructors, non-static field initializers, and instance initializer blocks. By *static code* we mean expressions and statements in a static context, and similarly by *non-static code* we mean expressions and statements in a non-static context. One crucial difference between the two contexts is that static code cannot refer to non-static members.

4.3 Defining Methods

The general syntax of a method declaration is

```
<method modifiers> <return type> <method name> (<formal parameter list>)
        <throws clause> // Method prototype
```

```
{ // Method body
    <local variable declarations>
    <nested local class declarations>
    <statements>
}
```

In addition to the name of the method, the method prototype can specify the following information:

- scope or *accessibility modifier* (see Section 4.5, p. 121)

- additional *method modifiers* (see Section 4.10, p. 144)

- the *type* of the *return value,* or void if the method does not return any value (see Section 5.4, p. 176)

- a *formal parameter list*

- *checked exceptions* thrown by the method in a throws clause (see Section 5.9, p. 201)

The *formal parameter list* is a comma-separated list of parameters for passing information to the method when the method is invoked by a *method call* (see Section 3.17, p. 86). An empty parameter list must be specified by ( ). Each parameter is a simple variable declaration consisting of its type and name:

    <parameter modifier> <type> <parameter name>

The parameter names are local to the method (see Section 4.5, p. 123). The parameter modifier final is discussed in Section 3.22 on page 94.

The *signature* of a method comprises the method name and the formal parameter list only.

The method body is a *block* containing the *local declarations* and the *statements* of the method. *Local variable declarations* are discussed in Section 2.3 on page 31, and *nested local class declarations* in Section 7.4 on page 302.

Like member variables, member methods can be characterized as:

- *instance methods*, which are discussed later in this chapter

- *static methods*, (see Section 4.10, p. 144) which are discussed later in this chapter

Statements

Statements in Java can be grouped into various categories. Variable declarations with explicit initialization of the variables are called *declaration statements* (see Section 2.3, p. 31, and Section 4.1, p. 102). Other basic forms of statements are *control flow statements* (see Section 5.1, p. 158) and *expression statements*.

An *expression statement* is an expression terminated by a semicolon. The expression is evaluated for its side effect and its value discarded. Only certain types of expressions have meaning as statements. They include the following:

- assignments (see Section 3.4, p. 47)
- increment and decrement operators (see Section 3.7, p. 63)
- method calls (see Section 3.17, p. 86)
- object creation expression with the new operator (see Section 3.16, p. 84)

A solitary semicolon denotes the *empty statement* that does nothing.

A block, {}, is a *compound* statement which can be used to group zero or more local declarations and statements (see Section 4.5, p. 123). Blocks can be nested, since a block is a statement that can contain other statements. A block can be used in any context where a simple statement is permitted. The compound statement which is embodied in a block, begins at the left brace, {, and ends with a matching right brace, }. Such a block must not be confused with an array initialization block in declaration statements (see Section 4.1, p. 102).

Labeled statements are discussed in Section 5.4 on page 171.

Instance Methods and Object Reference this

Instance methods belong to every object of the class and can only be invoked on objects. All members defined in the class, both static and non-static, are accessible in the context of an instance method. The reason is that all instance methods are passed an implicit reference to the *current object*, that is, the object on which the method is being invoked. The current object can be referenced in the body of the instance method by the keyword this. In the body of the method, the this reference can be used like any other object reference to access members of the object. In fact, the keyword this can be used in any non-static context. The this reference can be used as a normal reference to reference the current object, but the reference cannot be modified.

The this reference to the current object is useful in situations where a local variable hides, or *shadows*, a field with the same name. In Example 4.4, the two parameters noOfWatts and indicator in the constructor of the Light class have the same names as the fields in the class. The example also declares a local variable location, which has the same name as one of the fields. The reference this can be used to distinguish the fields from the local variables. At (1), the this reference is used to identify the field noOfWatts, which is assigned the value of the parameter noOfWatts. Without the this reference at (2), the value of the parameter indicator is assigned back to this parameter and not to the field by the same name, resulting in a logical error. Similarly at (3), without the this reference it is the local variable location that is assigned the value of the parameter site, and not the field by the same name.

Example 4.4 *Using* this *Reference*

```
class Light {
    // Fields
    int     noOfWatts;      // wattage
    boolean indicator;      // on or off
    String  location;       // placement

    // Constructor
    public Light(int noOfWatts, boolean indicator, String site) {
        String location;

        this.noOfWatts = noOfWatts;   // (1) Assignment to field.
        indicator = indicator;        // (2) Assignment to parameter.
        location = site;              // (3) Assignment to local variable.
        this.superfluous();           // (4)
        superfluous();                // equivalent to call at (4)
    }

    public void superfluous() { System.out.println(this); }  // (5)

    public static void main(String[] args) {
        Light light = new Light(100, true, "loft");
        System.out.println("No. of watts: " + light.noOfWatts);
        System.out.println("Indicator: "    + light.indicator);
        System.out.println("Location: "     + light.location);
    }
}
```

Output from the program:

```
Light@df6ccd
Light@df6ccd
No. of watts: 100
Indicator: false
Location: null
```

If a member is not shadowed by a local declarations, then the simple name member is considered a short-hand notation for this.member. In particular, the this reference can be used explicitly to invoke other methods in the class. This is illustrated at (4) in Example 4.4, where the method superfluous() is called.

If, for some reason, a method needs to pass the current object to another method, it can do so using the this reference. This is illustrated at (5) in Example 4.4, where the current object is passed to the println() method.

Note that the this reference cannot be used in a static context, as static code is not executed in the context of any object.

Method Overloading

Each method has a *signature*, which comprises the name of the method and the types and order of the parameters in the formal parameter list. Several method implementations may have the same name, as long as the method signatures differ. This is called *method overloading*. Since overloaded methods have the same name, their parameter lists must be different.

Rather than inventing new method names, method overloading can be used when the same logical operation requires multiple implementations. The Java 2 SDK APIs make heavy use of method overloading. For example, the class java.lang.Math contains an overloaded method min(), which returns the minimum of two numeric values.

```
public static double min(double a, double b)
public static float min(float a, float b)
public static int min(int a, int b)
public static long min(long a, long b)
```

In the following examples, five implementations of the method methodA are shown:

```
void methodA(int a, double b) { /* ... */ }        // (1)
int  methodA(int a)           { return a; }        // (2)
int  methodA()                { return 1; }        // (3)
long methodA(double a, int b) { return b; }        // (4)
long methodA(int x, double y) { return x; }        // (5) Not OK.
```

The corresponding signatures of the five methods are as follows:

```
methodA(int, double)          1'
methodA(int)                  2': Number of parameters.
methodA()                     3': Number of parameters.
methodA(double, int)          4': Order of parameters.
methodA(int, double)          5': Same as 1'.
```

The first four implementations of the method named methodA are overloaded correctly, each time with a different parameter list and, therefore, different signatures. The declaration at (5) has the same signature methodA(int, double) as the declaration at (1) and is, therefore, not a valid overloading of this method.

```
void bake(Cake k) { /* ... */ }          // (1)
void bake(Pizza p) { /* ... */ }         // (2)

int    halfIt(int a) { return a/2; }     // (3)
double halfIt(int a) { return a/2.0; }   // (4) Not OK. Same signature.
```

The method named bake is correctly overloaded at (1) and (2), with two different signatures. In the implementation, changing just the return type (as shown at (3) and (4)), is not enough to overload a method, and will be flagged as a compile-time error. The parameter list in the definitions must be different. Overloaded methods should be considered as individual methods that just happen to have the same name. Methods with the same name are allowed since methods are identified by their signature. At compile time, the right implementation is chosen based on the signature of the method call. Details of method overloading resolution can be found in Section 6.2 on page 237. Only methods declared in the same class and those that are inherited by the class can be overloaded. Method overloading should not be confused with *method overriding* (see Section 6.2, p. 233).

4.4 Constructors

The main purpose of constructors is to set the initial state of an object when the object is created by using the new operator.

A constructor has the following general syntax:

<accessibility modifier> <class name> (<formal parameter list>)
     <throws clause> // Constructor header

    { // Constructor body
      <local variable declarations>
      <nested local class declarations>
      <statements>
    }

Constructor declarations are very much like method declarations. However, the following restrictions on constructors should be noted:

- Modifiers other than an accessibility modifier are not permitted in the constructor header. Accessibility modifiers for constructors are discussed in Section 4.7 on page 131.

- Constructors cannot return a value and, hence, cannot specify a return type, not even void, in the constructor header, but they can contain the simple form of the return statement in the constructor body.

- Constructor name must be the same as the class name.

Class names and method names exist in different *namespaces*. Thus, there are no name conflicts in Example 4.5, where a method declared at (2) has the same name as the constructor declared at (1). However, using such naming schemes is strongly discouraged.

Example 4.5 *Namespaces*

```
public class Name {

    Name() {                    // (1)
        System.out.println("Constructor");
    }

    void Name() {               // (2)
        System.out.println("Method");
    }
```

```
    public static void main(String[] args) {
        new Name().Name();      // (3) Constructor call followed by method call.
    }
}
```

Output from the program:

```
Constructor
Method
```

Default Constructor

A *default constructor* is a constructor without any parameters. In other words, it has the following signature:

<class name>()

If a class does not specify *any* constructors, then an *implicit* default constructor is supplied for the class. The implicit default constructor is equivalent to the following implementation:

<class name>() { super(); }   // No parameters. Calls superclass constructor.

The only action taken by the implicit default constructor is to call the superclass constructor. This ensures that the inherited state of the object is initialized properly (see Section 6.3, p. 243). In addition, all instance variables in the object are set to the default value of their type.

In the following code, the class Light does not specify any constructors.

```
class Light {
    // Fields
    int     noOfWatts;      // wattage
    boolean indicator;      // on or off
    String  location;       // placement

    // No constructors
    //...
}

class Greenhouse {
    // ...
    Light oneLight = new Light();      // (1) Call of implicit default constructor.
}
```

In the previous code, the following implicit default constructor is employed when a Light object is created at (1):

```
Light() { super(); }
```

Creating an object using the new operator with the implicit default constructor, as at (1), will initialize the fields of the object to their default values (i.e., the fields noOfWatts, indicator, and location in a Light object will be initialized to 0, false, and null, respectively).

A class can choose to provide an implementation of the default constructor. In the following example, the class Light provides an explicit default constructor at (1). Note that it has the same name as the class, and that it does not take any parameters.

```
class Light {
    // ...
    // Explicit Default Constructor
    Light() {                            // (1)
        noOfWatts = 50;
        indicator = true;
        location  = "X";
    }
    //...
}

class Greenhouse {
    // ...
    Light extraLight = new Light();   // (2) Call of explicit default constructor.
}
```

The explicit default constructor ensures that any object created with the expression new Light(), as at (2), will have its fields noOfWatts, indicator and location initialized to 50, true and "X", respectively.

If a class defines any explicit constructors, it can no longer rely on the implicit default constructor to set the state of the objects. If such a class requires a default constructor, its implementation must be provided. In the example below, class Light only provides a non-default constructor at (1). It is called at (2) when an object of class Light is created with the new operator. Any attempt to call the default constructor will be flagged as a compile time error as shown at (3).

```
class Light {
    // ...
    // Only non-default Constructor
    Light(int noOfWatts, boolean indicator, String location) {          // (1)
        this.noOfWatts = noOfWatts;
        this.indicator = indicator;
        this.location  = location;
    }
    //...
}

class Greenhouse {
    // ...
    Light moreLight  = new Light(100, true, "Greenhouse");   // (2) OK.
//  Light firstLight = new Light();                          // (3) Compile time error.
}
```

Overloaded Constructors

Like methods, constructors can also be overloaded. Since the constructors in a class all have the same name as the class, their signatures are differentiated by their parameter lists. In the following example, the class Light now provides both an explicit implementation of the default constructor at (1) and a non-default constructor at (2). The constructors are overloaded, as is evident by their signatures. The non-default constructor is called when an object of class Light is created at (3), and the default constructor is likewise called at (4). Overloading of constructors allows appropriate initialization of objects on creation, depending on the constructor invoked (see also chaining of constructors in Section 6.3, p. 243.)

```
class Light {
    // ...
    // Explicit Default Constructor
    Light() {                                                      // (1)
        noOfWatts = 50;
        indicator = true;
        location  = "X";
    }
    // Non-default Constructor
    Light(int noOfWatts, boolean indicator, String location) { // (2)
        this.noOfWatts = noOfWatts;
        this.indicator = indicator;
        this.location  = location;
    }
    //...
}
class Greenhouse {
    // ...
    Light moreLight  = new Light(100, true, "Greenhouse");     // (3) OK.
    Light firstLight = new Light();                            // (4) OK.
}
```

4.5 Scope Rules

Java provides explicit accessibility modifiers to control the accessibility of members in a class by external clients (see Section 4.9, p. 137), but in two areas access is governed by specific scope rules:

- Class scope for members: how member declarations are accessed within the class.

- Block scope for local variables: how local variable declarations are accessed within a block.

Class Scope for Members

Class scope concerns accessing members (including inherited ones) from code within a class. Table 4.1 gives an overview of how static and non-static code in a class can access members of the class, including those that are inherited. Table 4.1 assumes the following declarations:

```
class SuperName {
    int instanceVarInSuper;
    static int staticVarInSuper;

    void instanceMethodInSuper()   { /* ... */ }
    static void staticMethodInSuper() { /* ... */ }
    // ...
}

class ClassName extends SuperName {
    int instanceVar;
    static int staticVar;

    void instanceMethod()     { /* ... */ }
    static void staticMethod() { /* ... */ }
    // ...
}
```

The golden rule is that static code cannot access non-static members by their simple names. Static code is not executed in the context of an object, therefore the references this and super are not available. An object has knowledge of its class, therefore, static members are always accessible in a non-static context.

Note that using the class name to access static members within the class is no different from how external clients access these static members.

Some factors that can influence the scope of a member declaration are

- shadowing of a field declaration, either by local variables (see Section 4.3, p. 114) or by declarations in the subclass (see Section 6.2, p. 233)

- initializers preceding the field declaration (see Section 8.2, p. 331)

- overriding an instance method from a superclass (see Section 6.2, p. 233)

- hiding a static method declared in a superclass (see Section 6.2, p. 233)

Accessing members within nested classes is discussed in Chapter 7.

Table 4.1   *Accessing Members within a Class*

Member declarations	Non-static Code in the Class `ClassName` Can Refer to the Member as	Static Code in the Class `ClassName` Can Refer to the Member as

Instance variables	`instanceVar`
	`this.instanceVar`
	`instanceVarInSuper`
	`this.instanceVarInSuper`
	`super.instanceVarInSuper`
		Not possible

Instance methods	`instanceMethod()`
	`this.instanceMethod()`
	`instanceMethodInSuper()`
	`this.instanceMethodInSuper()`
	`super.instanceMethodInSuper()`
		Not possible

Static variables	`staticVar`
	`this.staticVar`
	`ClassName.staticVar`
	`staticVarInSuper`
	`this.staticVarInSuper`
	`super.staticVarInSuper`
	`ClassName.staticVarInSuper`
	`SuperName.staticVarInSuper`
		`staticVar`
		
		`ClassName.staticVar`
		`staticVarInSuper`
		
		`ClassName.staticVarInSuper`
		`SuperName.staticVarInSuper`

Static methods	`staticMethod()`
	`this.staticMethod()`
	`ClassName.staticMethod()`
	`staticMethodInSuper()`
	`this.staticMethodInSuper()`
	`super.staticMethodInSuper()`
	`ClassName.staticMethodInSuper()`
	`SuperName.staticMethodInSuper()`
		`staticMethod()`
		
		`ClassName.staticMethod()`
		`staticMethodInSuper()`
		
		`ClassName.staticMethodInSuper()`
		`SuperName.staticMethodInSuper()`

Within a class `C`, reference variables of type `C` can be used to access *all* members in the class `C`, regardless of their accessibility modifiers. In Example 4.6, the method `duplicateLight` at (1) in class `Light` has a parameter `oldLight` and a local variable `newLight` that are references to `Light` objects. Even though the fields of the class are private, they are accessible through the two references (`oldLight` and `newLight`) in the method `duplicateLight()` as shown at (2), (3), and (4).

Example 4.6   *Class Scope*

```
class Light {
    // Instance variables
    private int     noOfWatts;        // wattage
    private boolean indicator;        // on or off
```

```
        private String  location;          // placement

        // Instance methods
        public void switchOn()  { indicator = true; }
        public void switchOff() { indicator = false; }
        public boolean isOn()   { return indicator; }

        public static Light duplicateLight(Light oldLight) {       // (1)
            Light newLight = new Light();
            newLight.noOfWatts = oldLight.noOfWatts;               // (2)
            newLight.indicator = oldLight.indicator;               // (3)
            newLight.location  = oldLight.location;                // (4)
            return newLight;
        }
    }
}
```

Block Scope for Local Variables

Declarations and statements can be grouped into a *block* using braces, {}. Blocks can be nested, and certain scope rules apply to local variable declarations in such blocks. A local declaration can appear anywhere in a block. The general rule is that a variable declared in a block is *in scope* inside the block in which it is declared, but it is not accessible outside of this block. It is not possible to redeclare a variable if a local variable of the same name is already declared in the current scope.

Local variables of a method are comprised of formal parameters of the method and variables that are declared in the method body. The local variables in a method are distinct for each invocation, and have their own storage.

A method body is a block. Parameters cannot be redeclared in the method body, as shown at (1) in Block 1 (see Figure 4.2).

A local variable—already declared in an enclosing block and, therefore, visible in a nested block—cannot be redeclared in the nested block. These cases are shown at (3), (5), and (6).

A local variable in a block can be redeclared in another block if the blocks are *disjoint*, that is, they do not overlap. This is the case for variable i at (2) in Block 3 and at (4) in Block 4, as these two blocks are disjoint.

The scope of a declaration begins from where it is declared in the block and ends where this block terminates. The scope of the loop variable index is Block 2. Even though Block 2 is nested in Block 1, the declaration of the variable index at (7) in Block 1 is valid. Its scope spans from its declaration to the end of this block, and it does not overlap with that of the loop variable index in Block 2.

Figure 4.2 *Block Scope*

```
public static void main(String args[]) {            // Block 1
//   String args = "";        // (1) Cannot redeclare parameters.
     char digit = 'z';

     for (int index = 0; index < 10; ++index) {     // Block 2
         switch(digit) {                            // Block 3
             case 'a':
                 int i;       // (2)
             default:
//           int i;       // (3) Already declared in the same block.
         } // switch

         if (true) {                                // Block 4
             int i;           // (4) OK
//           int digit;       // (5) Already declared in enclosing block 1.
//           int index;       // (6) Already declared in enclosing block 2.
         } //if

     } // for

     int index;              // (7) OK

} // main
```

Review Questions

4.8   Which one of these is a valid method declaration?

Select the one correct answer.

```
(a)  void method1        { /* ... */ }
(b)  void method2()      { /* ... */ }
(c)  void method3(void)  { /* ... */ }
(d)  method4()           { /* ... */ }
(e)  method5(void)       { /* ... */ }
```

4.9   Given the following code, which statements can be placed at the indicated position without causing compilation errors?

```
public class ThisUsage {
    int planets;
    static int suns;

    public void gaze() {
        int i;
        // ... insert statements here ...
    }
}
```

Select the three correct answers.
(a) `i = this.planets;`
(b) `i = this.suns;`
(c) `this = new ThisUsage();`
(d) `this.i = 4;`
(e) `this.suns = planets;`

4.10 Given the following pairs of method declarations, which statements are true?

```
void fly(int distance) {}
int  fly(int time, int speed) { return time*speed; }

void fall(int time) {}
int  fall(int distance) { return distance; }

void glide(int time) {}
void Glide(int time) {}
```

Select the two correct answers.

(a) The first pair of methods will compile correctly and overload the method name fly.
(b) The second pair of methods will compile correctly and overload the method name fall.
(c) The third pair of methods will compile correctly and overload the method name glide.
(d) The second pair of methods will not compile correctly.
(e) The third pair of methods will not compile correctly.

4.11 Given a class named Book, which one of these is a valid constructor declaration for the class?

Select the one correct answer.
(a) `Book(Book b) {}`
(b) `Book Book() {}`
(c) `private final Book() {}`
(d) `void Book() {}`
(e) `public static void Book(String[] args) {}`
(f) `abstract Book() {}`

4.12 Which statements are true?

Select the two correct answers.

(a) All classes must define a constructor.
(b) A constructor can be declared private.
(c) A constructor can return a value.
(d) A constructor must initialize all the fields of a class.
(e) A constructor can access the non-static members of a class.

4.13   What will be the result of attempting to compile the following program?

```java
public class MyClass {
    long var;

    public void MyClass(long param) { var = param; }  // (1)

    public static void main(String[] args) {
        MyClass a, b;
        a = new MyClass();                            // (2)
        b = new MyClass(5);                           // (3)
    }
}
```

Select the one correct answer.

(a) A compilation error will occur at (1), since constructors cannot specify a
     return value.
(b) A compilation error will occur at (2), since the class does not have a default
     constructor.
(c) A compilation error will occur at (3), since the class does not have a construc-
     tor which takes one argument of type int.
(d) The program will compile correctly.

4.6 Packages

A package in Java is an encapsulation mechanism that can be used to group related
classes, interfaces, and subpackages.

Figure 4.3 shows an example of a package hierarchy, comprising of a package
called wizard that contains two other packages: pandorasBox and spells. The package pandorasBox has a class called Clown that implements an interface called Magic,
also found in the same package. In addition, the package pandorasBox has a class
called LovePotion and a subpackage called artifacts containing a class called Ailment. The package spells has two classes: Baldness and LovePotion. The class Baldness is a subclass of class Ailment found in the subpackage artifacts in the package
pandorasBox.

The dot (.) notation is used to uniquely identify package members in the package
hierarchy. The class wizard.pandorasBox.LovePotion is different from the class
wizard.spells.LovePotion. The Ailment class can be easily identified by the name
wizard.pandorasBox.artifacts.Ailment. This is called the *fully qualified name* of the
package member. It is not surprising that most Java programming environments
map the fully qualified name of packages on the underlying (hierarchical) file
system. For example, on a Unix system, the class file LovePotion.class corresponding to the class wizard.pandorasBox.LovePotion would be found under the directory
wizard/pandorasBox.

Figure 4.3 *Package Hierarchy*

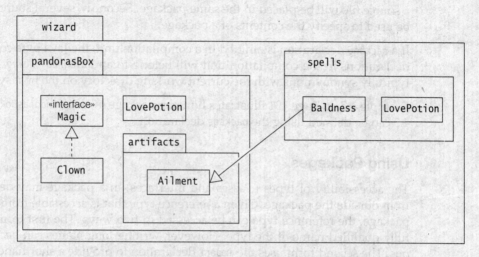

A global naming scheme has been proposed to use the Internet domain names to uniquely identify packages. If the above package `wizard` was implemented by a company called Sorcerers Limited that owns the domain `sorcerersltd.com`, its fully qualified name would be:

```
com.sorcerersltd.wizard
```

The subpackage `wizard.pandorasBox.artifacts` could easily have been placed elsewhere, as long as it was uniquely identified. Subpackages do not affect the accessibility of the members. For all intent and purposes, subpackages are more an *organizational* feature rather than a language feature. Accessibility of members in a package is discussed in Section 4.7. Accessibility of members in classes and interfaces is discussed in Section 4.9.

Defining Packages

A package hierarchy represents an organization of the Java classes and interfaces. It does *not* represent the source code organization of the classes and interfaces. The source code is of no consequence in this regard. Each Java source file (also called *compilation unit*) can contain zero or more definitions of classes and interfaces, but the compiler produces a separate *class* file containing the Java byte code for each of them. A class or interface can indicate that its Java byte code be placed in a particular package, using a package declaration.

The package statement has the following syntax:

```
package <fully qualified package name>;
```

At most one package declaration can appear in a source file, and it must be the first statement in the unit. The package name is saved in the Java byte code for the types contained in the package.

Note that this scheme has two consequences. First, all the classes and interfaces in a source file will be placed in the same package. Secondly, several source files can be used to specify the contents of a package.

If a package declaration is omitted in a compilation unit, the Java byte code for the declarations in the compilation unit will belong to an *unnamed package*, which is typically synonymous with the current working directory on the host system.

Example 4.7 on page 131 illustrates how the package wizard.pandorasBox in Figure 4.3 can be defined using the package declaration.

Using Packages

The accessibility of types (classes and interfaces) in a package may deny access from outside the package. Given a reference type that is accessible from outside a package, the reference type can be accessed in two ways. The first form uses the fully qualified name of the type. However, writing long names can become tedious. The second form uses the import declaration to provide a shorthand notation for specifying the name of the type.

The import declarations must be the first statement after any package declaration in a source file. The simple form of the import declaration has the following syntax:

    import <fully qualified type name>;

This is called *single type import*. As the name implies, such an import declaration provides a shorthand notation for a single class or interface. The *simple* name of the type (i.e., its identifier) can be used to access this particular type. Given the following import declaration:

    import wizard.pandorasBox.Clown;

the name Clown can be used in the source file to refer to this class.

Alternatively, the following form of the import declaration can be used:

    import <fully qualified package name>.*;

This is called *type import on demand*. It allows any type from the specified package to be accessed by its simple name.

An import declaration does not recursively import subpackages. The declaration does not result in inclusion of the source code of the types. The declaration only imports type names (i.e., it makes type names available to the code in a compilation unit).

All compilation units implicitly import the java.lang package (see Section 10.1, p. 388). This is the reason why we can refer to the class String by its simple name, and not need to use its fully qualified name java.lang.String all the time.

Example 4.7 shows several usages of the import declaration. Here we will draw attention to the class Baldness in the file Baldness.java. This class relies on two classes that have the same simple name LovePotion but are in different packages: wizard.pandorasBox and wizard.spells, respectively. To distinguish between the two classes, we can use their fully qualified names. However, since one of them is in the same package as the class Baldness, it is enough to fully qualify the class from the other package. This solution is used in the following code. Such name conflicts can usually be resolved by using variations of the import declaration together with fully qualified names.

```
// File: Baldness.java
package wizard.spells;                      // (1)Package declaration
...
import wizard.pandorasBox.artifacts.*;      // (3) Import from subpackage
...
public class Baldness extends Ailment {     // (4) Abbreviated name for Ailment
    wizard.pandorasBox.LovePotion tlcOne;   // (5) Fully qualified name
    LovePotion tlcTwo;                      // (6) Class in same package
    ...
    }
}
...
```

The class Baldness extends the class Ailment, which is in the subpackage artifacts of the wizard.pandorasBox package. A new import declaration at (3) is used to import the types from the subpackage artifacts.

The following example shows how single type import can be used to disambiguate a class name when access to the class is ambiguous by simple name. The following import declaration allows the simple name List as shorthand for the java.awt.List class as expected:

```
import java.awt.*;          // imports all class names from java.awt
```

Given the following two import declarations:

```
import java.awt.*;          // imports all class names from java.awt
import java.util.*;         // imports all class names from java.util
```

the simple name List is now ambiguous as both the classes java.util.List and java.awt.List match.

Adding a single type import for the java.awt.List class explicitly allows the simple name List as a shorthand notation for this class:

```
import java.awt.*;          // imports all class names from java.awt
import java.util.*;         // imports all class names from java.util
import java.awt.List;       // imports the class name List from java.awt
```

Compiling and Running Code from Packages

As mentioned earlier, a package hierarchy can be mapped on a hierarchical file system. We can think of a package name as a path in the file system. Referring to Example 4.7, the package name wizard.pandorasBox corresponds to the path name wizard/pandorasBox. The javac compiler can place the byte code in a directory that corresponds to the package declaration of the compilation unit. The Java byte code for all the classes (and interfaces) specified in the source files Clown.java and Love-Potion.java will be placed in the directory named wizard/pandorasBox, as these source files have the following package declaration:

```
package wizard.pandorasBox;
```

The absolute path of the wizard/pandorasBox directory is specified by using the -d option (d for destination) when compiling with the javac compiler. Assuming that the current directory is called /pgjc/work, and all the source code files are to be found here, the command

```
>javac -d . Clown.java Ailment.java Baldness.java
```

issued in the work directory, will create ./wizard/pandorasBox (and any other subdirectories required) under the current directory, and place the Java byte code for all the classes (and interfaces) in the directories corresponding to the package names. The dot (.) after the -d option denotes the current directory. After compiling the code in Example 4.7 using the javac command above, the file hierarchy under the /pgjc/work directory should mirror the package hierarchy in Figure 4.3. Without the -d option, the default behavior of the javac compiler is to place all class files directly under the current directory, rather than in the appropriate subdirectories.

How do we run the program? Since the current directory is /pgjc/work and we want to run Clown.class, the fully qualified name of the Clown class must be specified in the java command

```
>java wizard.pandorasBox.Clown
```

This will load the class Clown from the byte code in the file ./wizard/pandorasBox/Clown.class, and start the execution of its main() method.

The tools documentation for the Java 2 SDK explains how to organize packages in more elaborate schemes. In particular, the CLASSPATH environment variable can be used to specify multiple locations where Java tools should search when loading classes and resources.

The JAR Utility

The JAR (Java ARchive) utility provides a convenient way of bundling and deploying Java programs. A JAR file is created by using the jar tool. A typical JAR file for an application will contain the class files and any other resources needed by the application (for example image and audio files). In addition, a special *manifest file* is also created and included in the archive. The manifest file contains pertinent information, such as which class contains the main() method for starting the application.

The jar command has many options (akin to the Unix tar command). A typical command for making a JAR file for an application (for example, Example 4.7) has the following syntax:

```
>jar cmf whereismain.txt bundledApp.jar wizard
```

Option c tells the jar tool to create an archive. Option m is used to create and include a manifest file. Information to be included in the manifest file comes from a text file specified on the command line (whereismain.txt). Option f specifies the name of the archive to be created (bundledApp.jar). The JAR file name can be any valid file name. Files to be included in the archive are listed on the command line after the JAR file name. In the command line above, the contents under the wizard directory will be archived. If the order of the options m and f is switched in the command line, the order of the respective file names for these options must also be switched.

Information to be included in the manifest file is specified as name-value pairs. In Example 4.7, program execution should start in the main() method of the wizard.pandorasBox.Clown class. The file whereismain.txt has the following single text line:

```
Main-Class: wizard.pandorasBox.Clown
```

The value of the predefined header named Main-Class specifies the execution entry point of the application. The last text line in the file must be terminated by a newline as well, in order to be processed by the jar tool. This is also true even if the file only has a single line.

The application in an archive can be run by issuing the following command:

```
>java -jar bundledApp.jar
```

Program arguments can be specified after the JAR file name.

4.7 Accessibility Modifiers for Top-level Classes and Interfaces

Top-level classes and interfaces within a package can be declared as public. This means that they are accessible from everywhere, both inside and outside of their package. If the accessibility modifier is omitted, then they are only accessible in the package and not in any other packages or subpackages. This is called *package* or *default accessibility*.

Accessibility modifiers for nested classes and interfaces are discussed in Section 7.1 on page 284.

Example 4.7 *Accessibility Modifiers for Classes and Interfaces*

```java
// File: Clown.java
package wizard.pandorasBox;                        // (1) Package declaration

import wizard.pandorasBox.artifacts.Ailment;       // (2) Importing class

public class Clown implements Magic {
    LovePotion tlc;                                // (3) Class in same package
    wizard.pandorasBox.artifacts.Ailment problem;  // (4) Fully qualified class name
    Clown() {
        tlc = new LovePotion("passion");
        problem = new Ailment("flu");              // (5) Abbreviated class name
```

```java
    }
    public void levitate()  { System.out.println("Levitating"); }
    public void mixPotion() { System.out.println("Mixing " + tlc); }
    public void healAilment() { System.out.println("Healing " + problem); }

    public static void main(String[] args) {        // (6)
        Clown joker = new Clown();
        joker.levitate();
        joker.mixPotion();
        joker.healAilment();
    }
}

interface Magic { void levitate(); }                // (7)
```

```java
// File: LovePotion.java
package wizard.pandorasBox;                          // (1) Package declaration

public class LovePotion {                            // (2) Accessible outside package
    String potionName;
    public LovePotion(String name) { potionName = name; }
    public String toString() { return potionName; }
}
```

```java
// File: Ailment.java
package wizard.pandorasBox.artifacts;                // (1) Package declaration

public class Ailment {                               // (2) Accessible outside package
    String ailmentName;
    public Ailment(String name) { ailmentName = name; }
    public String toString() { return ailmentName; }
}
```

```java
// File: Baldness.java
package wizard.spells;                               // (1)Package declaration

import wizard.pandorasBox.*;                         // (2) Import of classes/interface
import wizard.pandorasBox.artifacts.*;               // (3) Import from subpackage

public class Baldness extends Ailment {              // (4) Abbreviated name for Ailment
    wizard.pandorasBox.LovePotion tlcOne;            // (5) Fully qualified name
    LovePotion tlcTwo;                               // (6) Class in same package
    Baldness(String name) {
        super(name);
        tlcOne = new wizard.pandorasBox.            // (7) Fully qualified name
                    LovePotion("romance");
        tlcTwo = new LovePotion();                   // (8) Class in same package
    }
}

class LovePotion // implements Magic                 // (9) Not accessible
    { public void levitate(){} }
```

Compiling and running the program from the current working directory results in the following:

```
>javac -d . Clown.java Ailment.java Baldness.java
>java wizard.pandorasBox.Clown
Levitating
Mixing passion
Healing flu
```

In Example 4.7, the class Clown and the interface Magic are placed in a package called wizard.pandorasBox. The public class Clown is accessible from everywhere. The Magic interface has default accessibility, and can only be accessed within the package wizard.pandorasBox. It is not accessible from other packages, not even in any packages nested in this package.

The class LovePotion is also placed in the package called wizard.pandorasBox. The class has public accessibility and is, therefore, accessible from other packages. The two files Clown.java and LovePotion.java demonstrate how several compilation units can be used to group classes in the same package.

The class Clown, from the file Clown.java, uses the class Ailment. The example shows two ways in which a class can access classes from other packages:

1. Denote the class by its fully qualified class name, as shown at (4) (wizard.pandorasBox.artifacts.Ailment).

2. Import the class explicitly from the package wizard.pandorasBox.artifacts as shown at (2) and use the simple class name Ailment as shown at (5).

In the file Baldness.java at (9), the class LovePotion wishes to implement the interface Magic from the package wizard.pandorasBox, but cannot do so, although the file imports from this package. The reason is that the interface Magic has default accessibility and can, therefore, only be accessed within the package wizard.pandorasBox.

Just because the class is accessible, it does not necessarily mean that members of the class are also accessible. Member accessibility is governed separately from class accessibility, as explained in Section 4.5.

Table 4.2 *Summary of Accessibility Modifiers for Classes and Interfaces*

Modifiers	Top-level Classes and Interfaces
default (no modifier)	Accessible in its package (package accessibility)
public	Accessible anywhere

4.8 Other Modifiers for Classes

Modifiers abstract and final can be applied to top-level and nested classes.

abstract Classes

A class can be specified with the keyword abstract to indicate that it cannot be instantiated. A class might choose to do this if the abstraction it represents is so general that it needs to be specialized in order to be of practical use. A class Vehicle might be specified as abstract to represent the general abstraction of a vehicle, as creating instances of the class would not make much sense. Creating instances of non-abstract subclasses, like Car and Bus, would make more sense, as this would make the abstraction more concrete.

A class that has one or more abstract methods (see Section 4.10, p. 147) must be declared abstract. Obviously such classes cannot be instantiated, as their implementation is only partial. A class might choose this strategy to dictate certain behavior, but allow its subclasses the freedom to provide the relevant implementation. In other words, subclasses of the abstract class have to take a stand and provide implementations of inherited abstract methods before they can be instantiated. A subclass that does not provide an implementation of its inherited abstract methods must also be declared abstract.

In Example 4.8, the definition of abstract class Light has an abstract method kwh-Price at (1). This forces its subclasses to provide the implementation for this method. The subclass TubeLight provides an implementation for the method kwh-Price at (2). The class Factory creates an instance of class TubeLight at (3). Reference variables of an abstract class can be declared, as shown at (4), but an abstract class cannot be instantiated, as shown at (5). References of an abstract class can denote objects of the subclasses, as shown at (6).

- -

Example 4.8 *Abstract Classes*

```
abstract class Light {
    // Fields
    int     noOfWatts;      // wattage
    boolean indicator;      // on or off
    String  location;       // placement

    // Instance methods
    public void switchOn()  { indicator = true; }
    public void switchOff() { indicator = false; }
    public boolean isOn()   { return indicator; }

    // Abstract Instance Method
    abstract public double kwhPrice();                    // (1) No method body
}
```

```
class TubeLight extends Light {
    // Fields
    int tubeLength;

    // Implementation of inherited abstract metnod.
    public double kwhPrice() { return 2.75; }          // (2)
}

public class Factory {
    public static void main(String[] args) {
        TubeLight cellarLight = new TubeLight();       // (3) OK
        Light nightLight;                              // (4) OK
    //  Light tableLight = new Light();                // (5) Compile time error
        nightLight = cellarLight;                      // (6) OK
        System.out.println("KWH price: " + nightLight.kwhPrice());
    }
}
```

Output from the program:

```
KWH price: 2.75
```

Interfaces just specify the method prototypes and not any implementation; they are, by their nature, implicitly abstract (i.e., they cannot be instantiated). Though it is legal, it is redundant to declare an interface with the keyword abstract.

final **Classes**

A class can be declared final to indicate that it cannot be extended; that is, one cannot declare subclasses of a final class. This implies that one cannot override any methods declared in such a class. In other words, the class behavior cannot be changed by subclassing. The class marks the lower boundary of its *implementation inheritance hierarchy*. Only a class whose definition is *complete* (i.e., has implementations of all its methods) can be declared final.

A final class must be complete, whereas an abstract class is considered incomplete. Classes, therefore, cannot be both final and abstract at the same time. Interfaces, which are inherently abstract, thus cannot be declared final. A final class and an interface represent two extremes when it comes to providing implementation. An abstract class represents a compromise between these two extremes.

The Java API includes many final classes; for example, java.lang.String which cannot be specialized any further by subclassing.

If it is decided that the class TubeLight in Example 4.8 cannot, or should not, be extended, it can be declared final:

```
final class TubeLight extends Light {
    // Fields
    int tubeLength;

    // Implementation of inherited abstract method.
    public double kwhPrice() { return 2.75; }
}
```

Discussion of final methods, fields and local variables can be found in Section 4.10, p. 146.

Table 4.3 *Summary of Other Modifiers for Classes and Interfaces*

Modifiers	Classes	Interfaces
abstract	Class may contain abstract methods and thus, cannot be instantiated.	Implied.
final	The class cannot be extended (i.e., it cannot be subclassed).	Not possible.

Review Questions

4.14 Given the following class, which of these are valid ways of referring to the class from outside of the package net.basemaster?

```
package net.basemaster;

public class Base {
    // ...
}
```

Select the two correct answers.

(a) By simply referring to the class as Base.
(b) By simply referring to the class as basemaster.Base.
(c) By simply referring to the class as net.basemaster.Base.
(d) By importing with net.basemaster.* and referring to the class as Base.
(e) By importing with net.* and referring to the class as basemaster.Base.

4.15 Which one of the following class definitions is a valid definition of a class that cannot be instantiated?

Select the one correct answer.

(a)
```
class Ghost {
        abstract void haunt();
}
```
(b)
```
abstract class Ghost {
        void haunt();
}
```
(c)
```
abstract class Ghost {
        void haunt() {};
}
```
(d)
```
abstract Ghost {
        abstract void haunt();
}
```

```
(e) static class Ghost {
        abstract haunt();
    }
```

4.16 Which one of the following class definitions is a valid definition of a class that cannot be extended?

Select the one correct answer.

(a) `class Link { }`
(b) `abstract class Link { }`
(c) `native class Link { }`
(d) `static class Link { }`
(e) `final class Link { }`
(f) `private class Link { }`
(g) `abstract final class Link { }`

4.9 Member Accessibility Modifiers

By specifying member accessibility modifiers, a class can control what information is accessible to clients (i.e., other classes). These modifiers help a class to define a *contract* so that clients know exactly what services are offered by the class.

Accessibility of members can be one of the following:

- `public`
- `protected`
- default (also called *package accessibility*)
- `private`

A member has package or default accessibility when no accessibility modifier is specified.

In the following discussion on accessibility modifiers for members of a class, keep in mind that the member accessibility modifier only has meaning if the class (or one of its subclasses) is accessible to the client. Also, note that only one accessibility modifier can be specified for a member. The discussion in this section applies to both instance and static members of top-level classes. Discussion of member accessibility for nested classes is deferred to Chapter 7.

In UML notation the prefixes + , #, and -, when applied to a member name, indicate `public`, `protected`, and `private` member accessibility, respectively. No prefix indicates default or package accessibility.

public **Members**

Public accessibility is the least restrictive of all the accessibility modifiers. A public member is accessible from anywhere, both in the package containing its class and in other packages where this class is visible. This is true for both instance and static members.

Example 4.9 contains two source files, shown at (1) and (6). The package hierarchy defined by the source files is depicted in Figure 4.4, showing the two packages packageA and packageB containing their respective classes. Classes in package packageB use classes from package packageA. SuperclassA in packageA has two subclasses: SubclassA in packageA and SubclassB in packageB.

Example 4.9   *Public Accessibility of Members*

```java
// Filename: SuperclassA.java                          (1)
package packageA;

public class SuperclassA {
    public int superclassVarA;                         // (2)
    public void superclassMethodA() {/*...*/}          // (3)
}

class SubclassA extends SuperclassA {
    void subclassMethodA() { superclassVarA = 10; }  // (4) OK.
}

class AnyClassA {
    SuperclassA obj = new SuperclassA();
    void anyClassMethodA() {
        obj.superclassMethodA();                       // (5) OK.
    }
}
```

```java
// Filename: SubclassB.java                             (6)
package packageB;
import packageA.*;

public class SubclassB extends SuperclassA {
    void subclassMethodB() { superclassMethodA(); }  // (7) OK.
}

class AnyClassB {
    SuperclassA obj = new SuperclassA();
    void anyClassMethodB() {
        obj.superclassVarA = 20;                       // (8) OK.
    }
}
```

Accessibility is illustrated in Example 4.9 by the accessibility modifiers for the field superclassVarA and the method superclassMethodA at (2) and (3), respectively, defined in class SuperclassA. These members are accessed from four different clients in Example 4.9.

- Client 1: From a subclass in the same package, which accesses an inherited field. SubclassA at (4) is such a client.

- Client 2: From a non-subclass in the same package, which invokes a method on an instance of the class. AnyClassA at (5) is such a client.

- Client 3: From a subclass in another package, which invokes an inherited method. SubclassB at (7) is such a client.

- Client 4: From a non-subclass in another package, which accesses a field in an instance of the class. AnyClassB at (8) is such a client.

In Example 4.9, the field superclassVarA and the method superclass MethodA have public accessibility, and are accessible by all the four clients listed above. Subclasses can access their inherited public members by their simple name, and all clients can access public members through an instance of the class. Public accessibility is depicted in Figure 4.4.

Figure 4.4 *Public Accessibility*

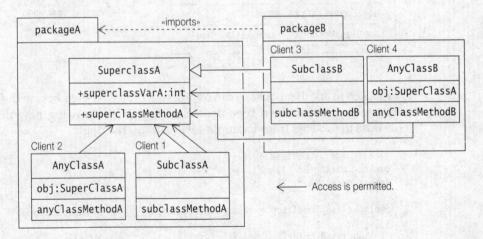

protected **Members**

A protected member is accessible in all classes in the package containing its class, and by all subclasses of its class in any package where this class is visible. In other words, non-subclasses in other packages cannot access protected members from other packages. It is less restrictive than the default accessibility.

In Example 4.9, if the field superclassVarA and the method superclass MethodA have protected accessibility, then they are accessible within package packageA, and only accessible by subclasses in any other packages.

```
public class SuperclassA {
    protected int superclassVarA;                    // (2)
    protected void superclassMethodA() {/*...*/}      // (3)
}
```

Client 4 in package packageB cannot access these members, as shown in Figure 4.5.

Figure 4.5 *Protected Accessibility*

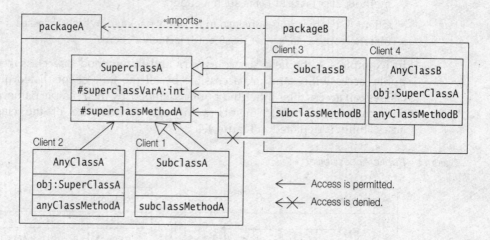

A subclass in another package can only access protected members in the superclass via references of its own type or its subtypes. The following new definition of SubclassB in packageB from Example 4.9 illustrates the point:

```
// Filename: SubclassB.java
package packageB;
import packageA.*;

public class SubclassB extends SuperclassA {          // In packageB.

    SubclassB objRefB = new SubclassB();              // (1)

    void subclassMethodB(SuperclassA objRefA) {
        objRefB.superclassMethodA();                  // (2) OK.
        objRefB.superclassVarA = 5;                   // (3) OK.
        objRefA.superclassMethodA();                  // (4) Not OK.
        objRefA.superclassVarA = 10;                  // (5) Not OK.
    }
}
```

The class SubclassB defines a field of type SubclassB (objRefB). The method subclass-MethodB() has a formal parameter objRefA of type SuperclassA. Access is permitted to a protected member of the SuperclassA in packageA by a reference of the subclass, as shown at (2) and (3), but not by a reference of its superclass, as shown at (4) and (5). References to the field superclassVarA and the call to superclassMethodA() occur in SubclassB. These members are declared in SuperclassA. SubclassB is not involved in the implementation of a SuperclassA, which is the type of objRefA. Hence access to protected members at lines (4) and (5) is not permitted as these are not members of an object that can be guaranteed to be implemented by the code accessing them.

Accessibility to protected members of the superclass would be permitted via any references of subclasses of SubclassB. The above restriction helps to ensure that subclasses in packages different from their superclass can only access protected members of the superclass in their part of the implementation inheritance hierarchy.

Default Accessibility for Members

When no member accessibility modifier is specified, the member is only accessible by other classes in its class's package. Even if its class is visible in another (possibly nested) package, the member is not accessible there. Default member accessibility is more restrictive than protected member accessibility.

In Example 4.9, if the field superclassVarA and the method superclass MethodA are defined with no accessibility modifier, then they are only accessible within package packageA, but not in any other (possibly nested) packages.

```
public class SuperclassA {
    int superclassVarA;                          // (2)
    void superclassMethodA() {/*...*/}           // (3)
}
```

The clients in package packageB (i.e. Clients 3 and 4) cannot access these members. This situation is depicted in Figure 4.6.

Figure 4.6   *Default Accessibility*

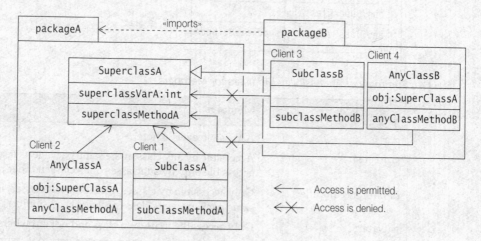

private **Members**

This is the most restrictive of all the accessibility modifiers. Private members are not accessible from any other class. This also applies to subclasses, whether they are in the same package or not. Since they are not accessible by simple name in a subclass, they are also not inherited by the subclass. This is not to be confused with the existence of such a member in the state of an object of the subclass (see Section 8.2, p. 342). A standard design strategy is to make all fields private, and provide public accessor methods for them. Auxiliary methods are often declared private, as they do not concern any client.

In Example 4.9, if the field superclassVarA and the method superclass MethodA have private accessibility, then they are not accessible by any other clients.

```
public class SuperclassA {
    private int superclassVarA;                    // (2)
    private void superclassMethodA() {/*...*/}      // (3)
}
```

None of the clients in Figure 4.7 can access these members.

Figure 4.7 *Private Accessibility*

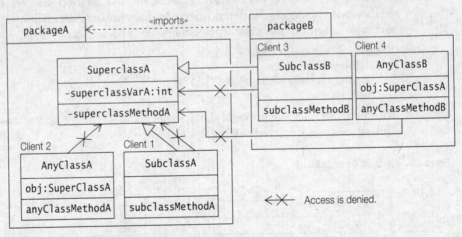

Table 4.4 *Summary of Accessibility Modifiers for Members*

Modifiers	Members
public	Accessible everywhere.
protected	Accessible by any class in the same package as its class, and accessible only by subclasses of its class in other packages.
default (no modifier)	Only accessible by classes, including subclasses, in the same package as its class (package accessibility).
private	Only accessible in its own class and not anywhere else.

Review Questions

4.17 Given the following definition of a class, which fields are accessible from outside the package com.corporation.project?

```
package com.corporation.project;

public class MyClass {
              int i;
    public    int j;
    protected int k;
    private   int l;
}
```

Select the two correct answers.

(a) Field i is accessible in all classes in other packages.
(b) Field j is accessible in all classes in other packages.
(c) Field k is accessible in all classes in other packages.
(d) Field k is accessible in subclasses only in other packages.
(e) Field l is accessible in all classes in other packages.
(f) Field l is accessible in subclasses only in other packages.

4.18 How restrictive is the default accessibility compared to public, protected, and private accessibility?

Select the one correct answer.

(a) Less restrictive than public.
(b) More restrictive than public, but less restrictive than protected.
(c) More restrictive than protected, but less restrictive than private.
(d) More restrictive than private.
(e) Less restrictive than protected from within a package, and more restrictive than protected from outside a package.

4.19 Which statement is true about accessibility of members?

Select the one correct answer.

(a) Private members are always accessible from within the same package.
(b) Private members can only be accessed by code from within the class of the member.
(c) A member with default accessibility can be accessed by any subclass of the class in which it is defined.
(d) Private members cannot be accessed at all.
(e) Package/default accessibility for a member can be declared using the keyword default.

4.10   Other Modifiers for Members

Certain characteristics of fields and/or methods can be specified in their declarations by the following keywords:

- `static`
- `final`
- `abstract`
- `synchronized`
- `native`
- `transient`
- `volatile`

`static` Members

The declaration of static members is prefixed by the keyword `static` to distinguish them from instance members.

Static members belong to the class in which they are declared, and are not part of any instance of the class. Depending on the accessibility modifiers of the static members in a class, clients can access these by using the class name, or through object references of the class. The class need not be instantiated to access its static members.

Static variables (also called *class variables*) only exist in the class they are defined in. They are not instantiated when an instance of the class is created. In other words, the values of these variables are not a part of the state of any object. When the class is loaded, static variables are initialized to their default values if no explicit initialization expression is specified (see Section 8.2, p. 336).

Static methods are also known as *class methods*. A static method in a class can directly access other static members in the class. It cannot access instance (i.e., non-static) members of the class, as there is no notion of an object associated with a static method. However, note that a static method in a class can always use a reference of the class's type to access its members, regardless of whether these members are static or not.

A typical static method might perform some task on behalf of the whole class and/or for objects of the class. In Example 4.10, the static variable counter keeps track of the number of instances of the Light class created. The example shows that the static method writeCount can only access static members directly, as shown at (2), but not non-static members, as shown at (3). The static variable counter will be initialized to the value 0 when the class is loaded at runtime. The main() method at (4) in class Warehouse shows how static members of class Light can be accessed using the class name, and via object references having the class type.

A summary of how static members are accessed in static and non-static code is given in Table 4.1.

Example 4.10   *Accessing Static Members*

```java
class Light {
    // Fields
    int    noOfWatts;      // wattage
    boolean indicator;     // on or off
    String  location;      // placement

    // Static variable
    static int counter;    // No. of Light objects created.          (1)

    // Explicit Default Constructor
    Light() {
        noOfWatts = 50;
        indicator = true;
        location  = "X";
        ++counter;         // Increment counter.
    }

    // Static method
    public static void writeCount() {
        System.out.println("Number of lights: " + counter);     // (2)
        // Compile error. Field noOfWatts is not accessible:
        // System.out.println("Number of Watts: " + noOfWatts);  // (3)
    }
}
public class Warehouse {
    public static void main(String[] args) {                    // (4)

        Light.writeCount();                          // Invoked using class name
        Light aLight = new Light();                  // Create an object
        System.out.println(
            "Value of counter: " + Light.counter     // Accessed via class name
        );
        Light bLight = new Light();                  // Create another object
        bLight.writeCount();                         // Invoked using reference
        Light cLight = new Light();                  // Create another object
        System.out.println(
            "Value of counter: " + cLight.counter // Accessed via reference
        );
    }
}
```

Output from the program:

```
Number of lights: 0
Value of counter: 1
Number of lights: 2
Value of counter: 3
```

`final` **Members**

A `final` variable is a constant, despite being called a variable. Its value cannot be changed once it has been initialized. This applies to instance, static and local variables, including parameters that are declared `final`.

- A `final` variable of a primitive data type cannot change its value once it has been initialized.

- A `final` variable of a reference type cannot change its reference value once it has been initialized, but the state of the object it denotes can still be changed.

These variables are also known as *blank final variables*. Final static variables are commonly used to define *manifest constants* (also called *named constants*), for example `Integer.MAX_VALUE`, which is the maximum `int` value. Variables defined in an interface are implicitly `final` (see Section 6.4, p. 251). Note that a `final` variable need not be initialized at its declaration, but it must be initialized once before it is used. For a discussion on `final` parameters, see Section 3.22, p. 94.

A `final` method in a class is *complete* (i.e., has an implementation) and cannot be overridden in any subclass (see Section 6.2, p. 233). Subclasses are then restricted in changing the behavior of the method.

Final variables ensure that values cannot be changed, and `final` methods ensure that behavior cannot be changed. Final classes are discussed in Section 4.8.

The compiler is able to perform certain code optimizations for `final` members, because certain assumptions can be made about such members.

In Example 4.11, the class `Light` defines a `final` static variable at (1) and a `final` method at (2). An attempt to change the value of the `final` variable at (3) results in a compile-time error. The subclass `TubeLight` attempts to override the `final` method `setWatts()` from the superclass `Light` at (4), which is not permitted. The class `Warehouse` defines a `final` local reference `aLight` at (5). The state of the object denoted by `aLight` can be changed at (6), but its reference value cannot be changed as attempted at (7).

- -

Example 4.11   *Accessing Final Members*

```
class Light {
    // Final static variable               (1)
    final public static double KWH_PRICE = 3.25;

    int noOfWatts;

    // Final instance method               (2)
    final public void setWatts(int watt) {
        noOfWatts = watt;
    }
```

```
        public void setKWH() {
          // KWH_PRICE = 4.10;              // (3) Not OK. Cannot be changed.
        }
    }

    class TubeLight extends Light {
        // Final method in superclass cannot be overridden.
        // This method will not compile.
        /*
        public void setWatts(int watt) {      // (4) Attempt to override.
            noOfWatts = 2*watt;
        }
        */
    }

    public class Warehouse {
        public static void main(String[] args) {

            final Light aLight = new Light();// (5) Final local variable.
            aLight.noOfWatts = 100;          // (6) OK. Changing object state.
        //  aLight = new Light();            // (7) Not OK. Changing final reference.
        }
    }
```

abstract **Methods**

An abstract method has the following syntax:

> abstract *<accessibility modifier> <return type> <method name> (<parameter list>)*
>   *<throws clause>*;

An abstract method does not have an implementation; that is, no method body is defined for an abstract method, only the *method prototype* is provided in the class definition. Its class is then abstract (i.e., incomplete) and must be explicitly declared as such (see Section 4.8, p. 134). Subclasses of an abstract class must then provide the method implementation; otherwise, they are also abstract. See Section 4.8, where Example 4.8 also illustrates the usage of abstract methods.

Only an instance method can be declared abstract. Since static methods cannot be overridden, declaring an abstract static method would make no sense. A final method cannot be abstract (i.e., cannot be incomplete) and vice versa. The keyword abstract cannot be combined with any nonaccessibility modifiers for methods. Methods specified in an interface are implicitly abstract, as only the method prototypes are defined in an interface (see Section 6.4, p. 251).

synchronized **Methods**

Several threads can be executing in a program (see Section 9.4, p. 359). They might try to execute several methods on the same object simultaneously. If it is desired that only one thread at a time can execute a method in the object, the methods can be declared synchronized. Their execution is then mutually exclusive among all threads. At any given time, at the most one thread can be executing a synchronized method on an object. This discussion also applies to static synchronized methods of a class.

In Example 4.12, both the push() and the pop() methods are synchronized in class StackImpl. Now, only one thread at a time can execute a synchronized method in an object of the class StackImpl. This means that it is not possible for the state of an object of the class StackImpl to be corrupted, for example, while one thread is pushing an element and another is popping the stack.

Example 4.12   *Synchronized Methods*

```
class StackImpl {
    private Object[] stackArray;
    private int topOfStack;
    // ...
    synchronized public void push(Object elem) { // (1)
        stackArray[++topOfStack] = elem;
    }

    synchronized public Object pop() {              // (2)
        Object obj = stackArray[topOfStack];
        stackArray[topOfStack] = null;
        topOfStack--;
        return obj;
    }

    // Other methods, etc.
    public Object peek() { return stackArray[topOfStack]; }
}
```

native **Methods**

Native methods are also called *foreign methods*. Their implementation is not defined in Java but in another programming language, for example, C or C++. Such a method can be declared as a member in a Java class definition. Since its implementation appears elsewhere, only the method prototype is specified in the class definition. The method prototype is prefixed with the keyword native. It can also specify checked exceptions in a throws clause, which cannot be checked by the compiler since the method is not implemented in Java. The next example shows how native methods are used.

The Java Native Interface (JNI) is a special API that allows Java methods to invoke native functions implemented in C.

In the following example, a native method in class Native is declared at (2). The class also uses a static initializer block (see Section 8.2, p. 336) at (1) to load the native library when the class is loaded. Clients of the Native class can call the native method like any another method, as at (3).

```
class Native {

    /*
     * The static block ensures that the native method library
     * is loaded before the native method is called.
     */
    static {
        System.loadLibrary("NativeMethodLib");  // (1) Load native library.
    }

    native void nativeMethod();                 // (2) Native method prototype.
    // ...

}

class Client {
    //...
    public static void main(String[] args) {
        Native aNative = new Native();
        aNative.nativeMethod();                 // (3) Native method call.
    }
    //...
}
```

transient **Fields**

Objects can be stored using serialization. Serialization transforms objects into an output format that is conducive for storing objects. Objects can later be retrieved in the same state as when they were serialized, meaning that all fields included in the serialization will have the same values as at the time of serialization. Such objects are said to be *persistent*.

A field can be specified as transient in the class declaration, indicating that its value should not be saved when objects of the class are written to persistent storage. In the following example, the field currentTemperature is declared transient at (1), because the current temperature is most likely to have changed when the object is restored at a later date. However, the value of the field mass, declared at (2), is likely to remain unchanged. When objects of the class Experiment are serialized, the value of the field currentTemperature will not be saved, but that of the field mass will be as part of the state of the serialized object.

```
class Experiment implements Serializable {
    // ...

    // The value of currentTemperature will not persist
    transient int currentTemperature;       // (1) Transient value.

    double mass;                            // (2) Persistent value.

}
```

Specifying the transient modifier for static variables is redundant and, therefore, discouraged. Static variables are not part of the persistent state of a serialized object.

volatile **Fields**

During execution, compiled code might cache the values of fields for efficiency reasons. Since multiple threads can access the same field, it is vital that caching is not allowed to cause inconsistencies when reading and writing the value in the field. The volatile modifier can be used to inform the compiler that it should not attempt to perform optimizations on the field, which could cause unpredictable results when the field is accessed by multiple threads.

In the simple example that follows, the value of the field clockReading might be changed unexpectedly by another thread while one thread is performing a task that involves always using the current value of the field clockReading. Declaring the field as volatile ensures that a write operation will always be performed on the master field variable, and a read operation will always return the correct current value.

```
class VitalControl {
    // ...
    volatile long clockReading;
    // Two successive reads might give different results.

}
```

Table 4.5 *Summary of Other Modifiers for Members*

Modifiers	Fields	Methods
static	Defines a class variable.	Defines a class method.
final	Defines a constant.	The method cannot be overridden.
abstract	Not relevant.	No method body is defined. Its class must also be designated abstract.
synchronized	Not relevant.	Only one thread at a time can execute the method.
native	Not relevant.	Declares that the method is implemented in another language.
transient	The value in the field will not be included when the object is serialized.	Not applicable.
volatile	The compiler will not attempt to optimize access to the value in the field.	Not applicable.

Review Questions

4.20 Which statements are true about the use of modifiers?

Select the two correct answers.

(a) If no accessibility modifier (public, protected, and private) is specified for a member declaration, the member is only accessible for classes in the package of its class and subclasses of its class anywhere.

(b) You cannot specify accessibility of local variables. They are only accessible within the block in which they are declared.

(c) Subclasses of a class must reside in the same package as the class they extend.

(d) Local variables can be declared static.

(e) Objects themselves do not have any accessibility modifiers, only the object references do.

4.21 Given the following source code, which comment line can be uncommented without introducing errors?

```
abstract class MyClass {
    abstract void f();
    final   void g() {}
//  final   void h() {}                          // (1)

    protected static int i;
    private          int j;
}

final class MyOtherClass extends MyClass {
//  MyOtherClass(int n) { m = n; }               // (2)

    public static void main(String[] args) {
        MyClass mc = new MyOtherClass();
    }

    void f() {}
    void h() {}
//  void k() { i++; }                            // (3)
//  void l() { j++; }                            // (4)

    int m;
}
```

Select the one correct answer.

(a) final void h() {}   // (1)
(b) MyOtherClass(int n) { m = n; }   // (2)
(c) void k() { i++; }   // (3)
(d) void l() { j++; }   // (4)

4.22 What would be the result of attempting to compile and run the following program?

```
class MyClass {
    static MyClass ref;
    String[] arguments;

    public static void main(String[] args) {
        ref = new MyClass();
        ref.func(args);
    }

    public void func(String[] args) {
        ref.arguments = args;
    }
}
```

Select the one correct answer.

(a) The program will fail to compile, since the static method main() cannot have a call to the non-static method func().

(b) The program will fail to compile, since the non-static method func() cannot access the static variable ref.

(c) The program will fail to compile, since the argument args passed to the static method main() cannot be passed on to the non-static method func().

(d) The program will fail to compile, since the method func() cannot assign the value of the static variable ref to the non-static variable arguments.

(e) The program will compile, but will throw an exception when run.

(f) The program will compile and run successfully.

4.23 Given the following member declarations, which statement is true?

```
int a;                          // (1)
static int a;                   // (2)
int f() { return a; }           // (3)
static int f() { return a; }    // (4)
```

Select the one correct answer.

(a) Declarations (1) and (3) cannot occur in the same class definition.

(b) Declarations (2) and (4) cannot occur in the same class definition.

(c) Declarations (1) and (4) cannot occur in the same class definition.

(d) Declarations (2) and (3) cannot occur in the same class definition.

4.24 Which statement is true?

Select the one correct answer.

(a) A static method can call other non-static methods in the same class by using the this keyword.

(b) A class may contain both static and non-static variables and both static and non-static methods.

(c) Each object of a class has its own instance of each static variable.

(d) Instance methods may access local variables of static methods.

(e) All methods in a class are implicitly passed a this parameter when called.

4.25 What, if anything, is wrong with the following code?

```
abstract class MyClass {
    transient int j;
    synchronized int k;

    final void MyClass() {}

    static void f() {}
}
```

Select the one correct answer.

(a) The class MyClass cannot be declared abstract.
(b) The field j cannot be declared transient.
(c) The field k cannot be declared synchronized.
(d) The method MyClass() cannot be declared final.
(e) The method f() cannot be declared static.
(f) Nothing is wrong with the code; it will compile without errors.

4.26 Which one of these is not a legal member declaration within a class?

Select the one correct answer.

(a) static int a;
(b) final Object[] fudge = { null };
(c) abstract int t;
(d) native void sneeze();
(e) final static private double PI = 3.14159265358979323846;

4.27 Which statements are true about modifiers?

Select the two correct answers.

(a) Abstract classes can contain final methods.
(b) Fields can be declared native.
(c) Non-abstract methods can be declared in abstract classes.
(d) Classes can be declared native.
(e) Abstract classes can be declared final.

4.28 Which statement is true?

Select the one correct answer.

(a) Transient fields will not be saved during serialization.
(b) Constructors can be declared abstract.
(c) The initial state of an array object constructed with the statement int[] a = new int[10] will depend on whether the array variable a is a local variable or a field.
(d) A subclass of a class with an abstract method must provide an implementation for the abstract method.
(e) Only static methods can access static members.

Chapter Summary

The following information was included in this chapter:

- explanation of declaration, construction, initialization, and usage of both one- and multi-dimensional arrays, including anonymous arrays
- defining classes
- defining methods, usage of the this reference in an instance method, and method overloading
- defining constructors, usage of the default constructor, and overloading of constructors
- defining and using packages
- discussion of accessibility (default, public) and other modifiers (abstract, final) for classes and interfaces
- explanation of class scope for members, and block scope for local variables
- applicability of member accessibility (default, public, protected, private) and other member modifiers (static, final, abstract, synchronized, native, transient, volatile)

 Programming Exercises

4.1 Imagine you are creating an application that has a number of different tools a user may invoke. These tools need a special context to work in. The context describes the current active selection in the application. The selection consists of a reference to an arbitrary object. We wish to create a class representing an editing context that the tools may use. This class should contain the aforementioned selection reference. We do not want to allow direct manipulation of the reference, but want to have methods in the context class that allow anyone to get and set the current selection.

Write such a class. Be sure to get the accessibility right.

4.2 A wide variety of tools can exist in an application, as described in Exercise 4.1. What they all have in common is that they can all be given an instance of an editing context, and that they are in either an active or an inactive state.

Write an interface that contains methods for giving the tool an editing context instance and querying the tool whether it is active or not.

4.3 Design a class for a bank database. The database should support the following operations:

- depositing a certain amount into an account
- withdrawing a certain amount from an account

- looking up the current amount (i.e. the balance) in an account

- transferring an amount from one account to another

The amount in the transactions is a value of type long. The accounts are identified by instances of the class Account that resides in a package called com.megabankcorp. records. The database object should reside in a package called com.megabankcorp. system.

The depositing, withdrawing, and balancing operations should not have any implementation, but allow subclasses to provide the implementation. The transferring operation should use the depositing and withdrawing operations to implement the transfer. It should not be possible to alter this operation in any subclass, and only classes within the package com.megabankcorp.system should be allowed to use this operation. The depositing and withdrawing operations should be available from anywhere. The balancing operation should only be available from subclasses and classes within the package com.megabankcorp.system.

Control Flow, Exception Handling, and Assertions

5

- Write code using if and switch statements, and identify legal argument types for these statements.
- Write code using all forms of loops, including labeled and unlabeled use of break and continue, and state the values taken by loop counter variables during and after loop execution.
- Write code that makes proper use of exceptions and exception handling clauses (try-catch-finally), and declares methods and overriding methods that throw exceptions.
- Recognize the effect of an exception arising at a specified point in a code fragment. Note: The exception may be a runtime exception, a checked exception, or an error (the code may include try, catch, or finally clauses in any legitimate combination).
- Write code that makes proper use of assertions, and distinguish appropriate from inappropriate uses of assertions.
- Identify correct statements about the assertion mechanism.

Supplementary Objectives

- State the names of the major classes in the inheritance hierarchy of exception classes.
- Distinguish between checked and unchecked exceptions.
- Understand exception propagation through the runtime stack.

5.1 Overview of Control Flow Statements

Control flow statements govern *the flow of control* in a program during execution, that is, the order in which statements are executed in a running program. There are three main categories of control flow statements that are discussed in this chapter:

- *Selection* statements: if, if-else and switch.
- *Iteration* statements: while, do-while and for.
- *Transfer* statements: break, continue, return, try-catch-finally and assert.

5.2 Selection Statements

Java provides selection statements that allow the program to choose between alternative actions during execution. The choice is based on criteria specified in the selection statement. These selection statements are

- simple if Statement
- if-else Statement
- switch Statement

Simple if Statement

The simple if statement has the following syntax:

```
if (<conditional expression>)
     <statement>
```

It is used to decide whether an action is to be performed or not, based on a condition. The condition is specified by *<conditional expression>* and the action to be performed is specified by *<statement>*.

The semantics of the simple if statement are straightforward. The *<conditional expression>* is evaluated first. If its value is true, then *<statement>* (called the if block) is executed and execution continues with the rest of the program. If the value is false, then the if block is skipped and execution continues with the rest of the program. The semantics are illustrated by the activity diagram in Figure 5.1a.

Figure 5.1 *Activity Diagram for* if *Statements*

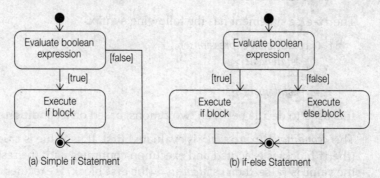

(a) Simple if Statement   (b) if-else Statement

In the following examples of the if statement, it is assumed that the variables and the methods have been defined appropriately:

```
if (emergency)              // emergency is a boolean variable
    operate();

if (temperature > critical)
    soundAlarm();

if (isLeapYear() && endOfCentury())
    celebrate();

if (catIsAway()) {          // Block
    getFishingRod();
    goFishing();
}
```

Note that *<statement>* can be a *block,* and the block notation is necessary if more that one statement is to be executed when the *<conditional expression>* is true.

Since the *<conditional expression>* must be a boolean expression, it avoids a common programming error: using an expression of the form (a=b) as the condition, where inadvertently an assignment operator is used instead of a relational operator. The compiler will flag this as an error, unless both a and b are boolean.

Note that the if block can be any valid statement. In particular, it can be the empty statement (;) or the empty block ({}). A common programming error is an inadvertent use of the empty statement.

```
if (emergency); // Empty if block
    operate();  // Executed regardless of whether it was an emergency or not.
```

if-else **Statement**

The if-else statement has the following syntax:

```
if (<conditional expression>)
        <statement₁>
    else
        <statement₂>
```

It is used to decide between two actions, based on a condition.

The *<conditional expression>* is evaluated first. If its value is true, then *<statement₁>* (the if block) is executed and execution continues with the rest of the program. If the value is false, then *<statement₂>* (the else block) is executed and execution continues with the rest of the program. In other words, one of two mutually exclusive actions is performed. The else clause is optional; if omitted, the construct reduces to the simple if statement. The semantics are illustrated by the activity diagram in Figure 5.1b.

In the following examples of the if-else statement, it is assumed that all variables and methods have been defined appropriately:

```
if (emergency)
    operate();
else
    joinQueue();

if (temperature > critical)
    soundAlarm();
else
    businessAsUsual();

if (catIsAway()) {
    getFishingRod();
    goFishing();
} else
    playWithCat();
```

Since actions can be arbitrary statements, the if statements can be nested.

```
if (temperature >= upperLimit) {        // (1)
    if (danger)                         // (2) Simple if.
        soundAlarm();
    if (critical)                       // (3)
        evacuate();
    else                                // Goes with if at (3).
        turnHeaterOff();
} else                                  // Goes with if at (1).
        turnHeaterOn();
```

The use of the block notation, {}, can be critical to the execution of if statements. The if statements (A) and (B) in the following examples do *not* have the same meaning. The if statements (B) and (C) are the same, with extra indentation used in (C) to make the meaning evident. Leaving out the block notation in this case could have catastrophic consequences: the heater could be turned on when the temperature is above the upper limit.

```
// (A)
if (temperature > upperLimit) {          // (1) Block notation.
    if (danger) soundAlarm();            // (2)
} else                                   // Goes with if at (1).
    turnHeaterOn();

// (B)
if (temperature > upperLimit)            // (1) Without block notation.
    if (danger) soundAlarm();            // (2)
else turnHeaterOn();                     // Goes with if at (2).

// (C)
if (temperature > upperLimit)            // (1)
    if (danger)                          // (2)
        soundAlarm();
    else                                 // Goes with if at (2).
        turnHeaterOn();
```

The rule for matching an else clause is that an else clause always refers to the nearest if that is not already associated with another else clause. Block notation and proper indentation can be used to make the meaning obvious.

Cascading if-else statements are a sequence of nested if-else statements where the if of the next if-else statement is joined to the else clause of the previous one. The decision to execute a block is then based on all the conditions evaluated so far.

```
if (temperature >= upperLimit) {                         // (1)
    soundAlarm();
    turnHeaterOff();
} else if (temperature < lowerLimit) {                   // (2)
    soundAlarm();
    turnHeaterOn();
} else if (temperature == (upperLimit-lowerLimit)/2) {   // (3)
    doingFine();
} else                                                   // (4)
    noCauseToWorry();
```

The block corresponding to the first if condition that evaluates to true is executed, and the remaining ifs are skipped. In the example given above, the block at (3) will execute only if the conditions at (1) and (2) are false and the condition at (3) is true. If none of the conditions are true, the block associated with the last else clause is executed. If there is no last else clause, no actions are performed.

switch **Statement**

Conceptually the switch statement can be used to choose one among many alternative actions, based on the value of an expression. Its general form is as follows:

```
switch (<non-long integral expression>) {
    case label₁: <statement₁>
    case label₂: <statement₂>
    ...
    case labelₙ: <statementₙ>
    default:    <statement>
} // end switch
```

The syntax of the switch statement comprises a switch expression followed by the switch body, which is a block of statements. The type of the switch expression is non-long integral (i.e., char, byte, short, or int). The statements in the switch body can be labeled, defining entry points in the switch body where control can be transferred depending on the value of the switch expression. The semantics of the switch statement are as follows:

- The switch expression is evaluated first.
- The value of the switch expression is compared with the case labels. Control is transferred to the <*statement_i*> associated with the case label that is equal to the value of the switch expression. After execution of the associated statement, control *falls through* to the *next* statement unless appropriate action is taken.
- If no case label is equal to the value of the switch expression, the statement associated with the default label is executed.

Figure 5.2 illustrates the flow of control through a switch statement.

Figure 5.2   *Activity Diagram for* switch *Statement*

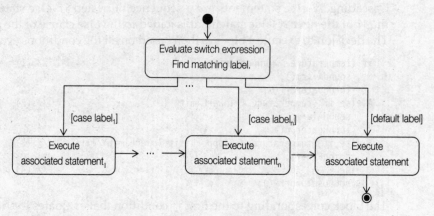

All labels (including the default label) are optional and can be defined in any order in the switch body. There can be at most one default label in a switch statement. If it is left out and no valid case labels are found, the whole switch statement is skipped.

The case labels are constant expressions whose values must be unique, meaning no duplicate values are allowed. The case label values must be *assignable* to the type of the switch expression (see Section 3.4, p. 48). In particular, the case label values must be in the range of the type of the switch expression. Note that the type of the case label cannot be boolean, long, or floating-point.

Example 5.1   *Fall Through in* switch *Statement*

```
public class Advice {

    public final static int LITTLE_ADVICE   = 0;
    public final static int MORE_ADVICE     = 1;
    public final static int LOTS_OF_ADVICE  = 2;

    public static void main(String[] args) {
        dispenseAdvice(LOTS_OF_ADVICE);
    }

    public static void dispenseAdvice(int howMuchAdvice) {
        switch(howMuchAdvice) {                              // (1)
            case LOTS_OF_ADVICE:
                System.out.println("See no evil.");          // (2)
            case MORE_ADVICE:
                System.out.println("Speak no evil.");        // (3)
            case LITTLE_ADVICE:
                System.out.println("Hear no evil.");         // (4)
                break;                                       // (5)
            default:
                System.out.println("No advice.");            // (6)
        }
    }
}
```

Output from the program:

```
See no evil.
Speak no evil.
Hear no evil.
```

In Example 5.1, depending on the value of the howMuchAdvice parameter, different advice is printed in the switch statement at (1) in the method dispenseAdvice(). The example shows the output when the value of the howMuchAdvice parameter is LOTS_OF_ADVICE. In the switch statement, the associated statement at (2) is executed, giving one advice. Control then falls through to the statement at (3), giving the second advice. Control falls through to (4), dispensing the third advice, and finally executing the break statement at (5) causes control to exit the switch statement. Without the break statement at (5), control would continue to fall through the remaining statements if there were any. Execution of the break statement in a switch body transfers control out of the switch statement (see Section 5.4, p. 172). If the parameter howMuchAdvice has the value MORE_ADVICE, then the advice at (3) and (4) is given. The value LITTLE_ADVICE results in only one advice at (4) being given. Any other value results in the default action, which announces that there is no advice.

The associated statement of a case label can be a *list* of statements (which need *not* be a statement block). The case label is prefixed to the first statement in each case. This is illustrated by the associated statement for the case label LITTLE_ADVICE in Example 5.1, which comprises statements (4) and (5).

Example 5.2 makes use of a break statement inside a switch statement to convert a char value representing a digit to its corresponding word in English. Note that the break statement is the last statement in the list of statements associated with each case label. It is easy to think that the break statement is a part of the switch statement syntax, but technically it is not.

Example 5.2 *Using* break *in* switch *Statement*

```java
public class Digits {

    public static void main(String[] args) {
        System.out.println(digitToString('7') + " " +
                           digitToString('8') + " " +
                           digitToString('6'));
    }

    public static String digitToString(char digit) {
        String str = "";
        switch(digit) {
            case '1': str = "one";   break;
            case '2': str = "two";   break;
            case '3': str = "three"; break;
            case '4': str = "four";  break;
            case '5': str = "five";  break;
            case '6': str = "six";   break;
            case '7': str = "seven"; break;
            case '8': str = "eight"; break;
            case '9': str = "nine";  break;
            case '0': str = "zero";  break;
            default:  System.out.println(digit + " is not a digit!");
        }
        return str;
    }
}
```

Output from the program:

```
seven eight six
```

Several case labels can prefix the same statement. They will all result in the associated statement being executed. This is illustrated in Example 5.3 for the switch statement at (1).

The first statement in the switch body must have a case label, or it is unreachable. This statement will never be executed since control can never be transferred to it. The compiler will flag this as an error.

Since each action associated with a case label can be an arbitrary statement, it can be another switch statement. In other words, switch statements can be nested. Since a switch statement defines its own local block, the case labels in an inner block do not conflict with any case labels in an outer block. Labels can be redefined in nested blocks, unlike variables which cannot be redeclared in nested blocks (see Section 4.5, p. 123). In Example 5.3, an inner switch statement is defined at (2). This allows further refinement of the action to take on the value of the switch expression, in cases where multiple labels are used in the outer switch statement. A break statement terminates the innermost switch statement in which it is executed.

Example 5.3   *Nested* switch *Statement*

```
public class Seasons {

    public static void main(String[] args) {
        int monthNumber = 11;
        switch(monthNumber) {                                    // (1) Outer
            case 12: case 1: case 2:
                System.out.println("Snow in the winter.");
                break;
            case 3: case 4: case 5:
                System.out.println("Green grass in spring.");
                break;
            case 6: case 7: case 8:
                System.out.println("Sunshine in the summer.");
                break;
            case 9: case 10: case 11:                            // (2)
                switch(monthNumber) { // Nested switch              (3) Inner
                    case 10:
                        System.out.println("Halloween.");
                        break;
                    case 11:
                        System.out.println("Thanksgiving.");
                        break;
                } // end nested switch
                // Always printed for case labels 9, 10, 11
                System.out.println("Yellow leaves in the fall."); // (4)
                break;
            default:
                System.out.println(monthNumber + " is not a valid month.");
        }
    }
}
```

Output from the program:

```
Thanksgiving.
Yellow leaves in the fall.
```

 Review Questions

5.1　What will be the result of attempting to compile and run the following class?

```
public class IfTest {
    public static void main(String[] args) {
        if (true)
        if (false)
        System.out.println("a");
        else
        System.out.println("b");
    }
}
```

Select the one correct answer.

(a)　The code will fail to compile because the syntax of the if statement is incorrect.

(b)　The code will fail to compile because the compiler will not be able to determine which if statement the else clause belongs to.

(c)　The code will compile correctly and display the letter a when run.

(d)　The code will compile correctly and display the letter b when run.

(e)　The code will compile correctly, but will not display any output.

5.2　Which statements are true?

Select the three correct answers.

(a)　The conditional expression in an if statement can have method calls.

(b)　If a and b are of type boolean, the expression (a = b) can be the conditional expression of an if statement.

(c)　An if statement can have either an if clause or an else clause.

(d)　The statement if (false) ; else ; is illegal.

(e)　Only expressions which evaluate to a boolean value can be used as the condition in an if statement.

5.3　What, if anything, is wrong with the following code?

```
void test(int x) {
    switch (x) {
        case 1:
        case 2:
        case 0:
        default:
        case 4:
    }
}
```

Select the one correct answer.

(a) The variable x does not have the right type for a `switch` expression.
(b) The `case` label 0 must precede case label 1.
(c) Each case section must end with a break statement.
(d) The `default` label must be the last label in the `switch` statement.
(e) The body of the `switch` statement must contain at least one statement.
(f) There is nothing wrong with the code.

5.4 Which of these combinations of `switch` expression types and `case` label value types are legal within a `switch` statement?

Select the one correct answer.

(a) `switch` expression of type `int` and case label value of type `char`.
(b) `switch` expression of type `float` and case label value of type `int`.
(c) `switch` expression of type `byte` and case label value of type `float`.
(d) `switch` expression of type `char` and case label value of type `long`.
(e) `switch` expression of type `boolean` and case value of type `boolean`.

5.3 Iteration Statements

Loops allow a block of statements to be executed repeatedly (i.e., iterated). A boolean condition (called the *loop condition*) is commonly used to determine when to terminate the loop. The statements executed in the loop constitute the *loop body*. The loop body can be a single statement or a block.

Java provides three language constructs for constructing loops:

• `while` statement
• `do-while` statement
• `for` statement

These loops differ in the order in which they execute the loop body and test the loop condition. The `while` and the `for` loops test the loop condition before executing the loop body, while the `do-while` loop tests the loop condition after execution of the loop body.

`while` Statement

The syntax of the `while` loop is

```
while (<loop condition>)
     <loop body>
```

The loop condition is evaluated before executing the loop body. The `while` statement executes the loop body as long as the loop condition is `true`. When the loop condition becomes `false`, the loop is terminated and execution continues with the statement immediately following the loop. If the loop condition is `false` to begin with, the loop body is not executed at all. In other words, a `while` loop can execute zero or more times. The loop condition must be a `boolean` expression. The flow of control in a `while` statement is shown in Figure 5.3.

Figure 5.3   *Activity Diagram for* `while` *Statement*

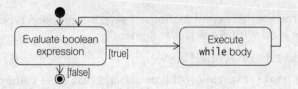

The `while` statement is normally used when the number of iterations is not known *a priori*.

```
while (noSignOfLife())
    keepLooking();
```

Since the loop body can be any valid statement, inadvertently terminating each line with the empty statement (;) can give unintended results.

```
while (noSignOfLife());         // Empty statement as loop body!
    keepLooking();              // Statement not in the loop body.
```

do-while **Statement**

The syntax of the do-while loop is

```
do
    <loop body>
while (<loop condition>);
```

The loop condition is evaluated after executing the loop body. The do-while statement executes the loop body until the loop condition becomes `false`. When the loop condition becomes `false`, the loop is terminated and execution continues with the statement immediately following the loop. Note that the loop body is executed at least once. Figure 5.4 illustrates the flow of control in a do-while statement.

Figure 5.4   *Activity Diagram for* do-while *Statement*

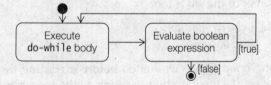

The loop body in a do-while loop is invariably a statement block. It is instructive to compare the while and the do-while loops. In the examples below, the mice might never get to play if the cat is not away, as in the loop at (1). The mice do get to play at least once (at the peril of losing their life) in the loop at (2).

```
while (cat.isAway()) {        // (1)
    mice.play();
}

do {                          // (2)
    mice.play();
} while (cat.isAway());
```

for Statement

The for loop is the most general of all the loops. It is mostly used for counter-controlled loops, that is, when the number of iterations is known beforehand.

The syntax of the loop is as follows:

for (*<initialization>*; *<loop condition>*; *<increment expression>*)
    <loop body>

The *<initialization>* usually declares and initializes a loop variable that controls the execution of the *<loop body>*. The *<loop condition>* is a boolean expression, usually involving the loop variable, such that if the loop condition is true, the loop body is executed; otherwise, execution continues with the statement following the for loop. After each iteration (i.e., execution of the loop body), the *<increment expression>* is executed. This usually modifies the value of the loop variable to ensure eventual loop termination. The loop condition is then tested to determine if the loop body should be executed again. Note that the *<initialization>* is only executed once on entry to the loop. The semantics of the for loop are illustrated in Figure 5.5, and can be summarized by the following equivalent while loop code template:

<initialization>
while (*<loop condition>*) {
    <loop body>
    <increment expression>
}

Figure 5.5 *Activity Diagram for the* for *Statement*

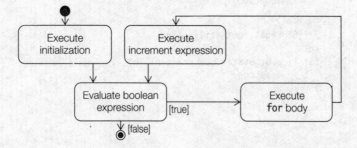

The following code creates an int array and sums the elements in the array.

```
int sum = 0;
int[] array = {12, 23, 5, 7, 19};
for (int index = 0; index < array.length; index++)    // (1)
    sum += array[index];.
```

The loop variable index is declared and initialized in the *<initialization>* section of the loop. It is incremented in the *<increment expression>* section. The for loop defines a local block such that the scope of this declaration is the for block, which comprises the *<initialization>*, the *<loop condition>*, the *<loop body>* and the *<increment expression>* sections.

The loop at (1) showed how a declaration statement can be specified in the *<initialization>* section. Such a declaration statement can also specify a comma-separated list of variables.

```
for (int i = 0, j = 1, k = 2; ... ; ...) ...;        // (2)
```

The variables i, j, and k in the declaration statement all have type int. All variables declared in the *<initialization>* section are local variables in the for block and obey the scope rules for local blocks. However, note that the following code will not compile, as variable declarations of different types (in this case, int and String) require declaration statements that are terminated by semicolons.

```
for (int i = 0, String str = "@"; ... ; ...) ...;  // (3) Compile time error.
```

The *<initialization>* section can also be a comma-separated list of *expression* statements (see Section 4.3, p. 113). For example, the loop at (2) can be rewritten by factoring out the variable declaration.

```
int i, j, k;  // Variable declaration
for (i = 0, j = 1, k = 2; ... ; ...) ...;        // (4) Just initialization
```

The *<initialization>* section is now a comma-separated list of three expressions. The expressions in such a list are always evaluated from left to right. Note that the variables i, j, and k are now obviously not local to the loop.

Declaration statements cannot be mixed with expression statements in the *<initialization>* section, as is the case at (5) in the following example. Factoring out the variable declaration, as at (6), leaves a legal comma-separated list of expression statements only.

```
// (5) Not legal and ugly.
for (int i = 0, System.out.println("This won't do!"); flag; i++) {
    // loop body
}

// (6) Legal, but still ugly.
int i;
for (i = 0, System.out.println("This is legal!"); flag; i++) {
    // loop body
}
```

The *<increment expression>* can also be a comma-separated list of expression statements. The following code specifies a for loop that has a comma-separated list of three variables in the *<initialization>* section, and a comma-separated list of two expressions in the *<increment expression>* section.

```
// Legal usage but not recommended.
int[][] sqMatrix = { {3, 4, 6}, {5, 7, 4}, {5, 8, 9} };
for (int i = 0, j = sqMatrix[0].length - 1, asymDiagonal = 0;  // initialization
     i < sqMatrix.length;                                      // loop condition
     i++, j--)                                                 // increment expression
    asymDiagonal += sqMatrix[i][j];                            // loop body
```

All the sections in the for-header are optional. Any one of them can be left empty, but the two semicolons are mandatory. In particular, leaving out the *<loop condition>* signifies that the loop condition is true. The "crab", (;;), is commonly used to construct an infinite loop, where termination is presumably achieved through code in the loop body (see next section on transfer statements):

```
for (;;) Java.programming();        // Infinite loop
```

5.4 Transfer Statements

Java provides six language constructs for transferring control in a program:

- break
- continue
- return
- try-catch-finally
- throw
- assert

This section discusses the first three statements, and the remaining statements are discussed in subsequent sections.

Note that Java does not have a goto statement, although goto is a reserved word.

Labeled Statements

A statement may have a *label*.

<label> : *<statement>*

A label is any valid identifier and it always immediately proceeds the statement. Label names exist in their own name space, so that they do not conflict with names of packages, classes, interfaces, methods, fields, and local variables. The scope of a label is the statement prefixed by the label, meaning that it cannot be redeclared as a label inside the labeled statement—analogous to the scope of local variables.

```
L1: if (i > 0) {
    L1: System.out.println(i);  // (1) Not OK. Label redeclared.
}

L1: while (i < 0) {              // (2) OK.
    L2: System.out.println(i);
}

L1: {                            // (3) OK. Labeled block.
    int j = 10;
    System.out.println(j);
}

L1: try {                        // (4) OK. Labeled try-catch-finally block.
    int j = 10, k = 0;
    L2: System.out.println(j/k);
} catch (ArithmeticException ae) {
    L3: ae.printStackTrace();
} finally {
    L4: System.out.println("Finally done.");
}
```

A statement can have multiple labels:

```
LabelA: LabelB: System.out.println("Mutliple labels. Use judiciously.");
```

A declaration statement cannot have a label:

```
L0: int i = 0;                  // Compile time error.
```

A labeled statement is executed like it was non-labeled, unless it contains the break or continue statements. This is discussed in the next two subsections.

break **Statement**

The break statement comes in two forms: the *unlabeled* and the *labeled* form.

```
break;            // the unlabeled form

break <label>;    // the labeled form
```

The unlabeled break statement terminates loops (for, while, do-while) and switch statements which contain the break statement, and transfers control out of the current context (i.e., the closest enclosing block). The rest of the statement body is skipped, terminating the enclosing statement, with execution continuing after this statement.

In Example 5.4, the break statement at (1) is used to terminate a for loop. Control is transferred to (2) when the value of i is equal to 4 at (1), skipping the rest of the loop body and terminating the loop.

Example 5.4 also shows that the unlabeled break statement only terminates the innermost loop or switch statement that contains the break statement. The break statement at (3) terminates the inner for loop when j is equal to 2, and execution continues in the outer switch statement at (4) after the for loop.

Example 5.4 break *Statement*

```
class BreakOut {

    public static void main(String[] args) {

        for (int i = 1; i <= 5; ++i) {
            if (i == 4) break;          // (1) Terminate loop. Control to (2).
            // Rest of loop body skipped when i gets the value 4.
            System.out.println(i + "\t" + Math.sqrt(i));
        } // end for
        // (2) Continue here.

        int n = 2;
        switch (n) {
            case 1: System.out.println(n); break;
            case 2: System.out.println("Inner for loop: ");
                    for (int j = 0; j < n; j++)
                        if (j == 2)
                            break;   // (3) Terminate loop. Control to (4).
                        else
                            System.out.println(j);
            default: System.out.println("default: " + n); // (4) Continue here.
        }
    }
}
```

Output from the program:

```
1    1.0
2    1.4142135623730951
3    1.7320508075688772
Inner for loop:
0
1
default: 2
```

A labeled break statement can be used to terminate *any* labeled statement that contains the break statement. Control is then transferred to the statement following the enclosing labeled statement. In the case of a labeled block, the rest of the block is skipped and execution continues with the statement following the block:

```
out:
{                              // (1) Labeled block
    // ...
    if (j == 10) break out; // (2) Terminate block. Control to (3).
    System.out.println(j);  // Rest of the block not executed if j == 10.
    // ...
}
// (3) Continue here.
```

In Example 5.5, the program continues to add the elements below the diagonal of a square matrix until the sum is greater than 10. Two nested for loops are defined at (1) and (2). The outer loop is labeled outer at (1). The unlabeled break statement at (3) transfers control to (5) when it is executed, that is, it terminates the inner loop and control is transferred to the statement after the inner loop. The labeled break statement at (4) transfers control to (6) when it is executed (i.e., it terminates both the inner and the outer loop, transferring control to the statement after the loop labeled outer).

Example 5.5 *Labeled* break *Statement*

```
class LabeledBreakOut {
    public static void main(String[] args) {
        int[][] squareMatrix = {{4, 3, 5}, {2, 1, 6}, {9, 7, 8}};
        int sum = 0;
        outer:                                            // label
        for (int i = 0; i < squareMatrix.length; ++i){          // (1)
            for (int j = 0; j < squareMatrix[i].length; ++j) {  // (2)
                if (j == i) break;        // (3) Terminate this loop.
                                          //     Control to (5).
                System.out.println("Element[" + i + ", " + j + "]: " +
                                    squareMatrix[i][j]);
                sum += squareMatrix[i][j];
                if (sum > 10) break outer;// (4) Terminate both loops.
                                          //     Control to (6).
            } // end inner loop
            // (5) Continue with outer loop.
        } // end outer loop
        // (6) Continue here.
        System.out.println("sum: " + sum);
    }
}
```

Output from the program:

```
Element[1, 0]: 2
Element[2, 0]: 9
sum: 11
```

continue **Statement**

Like the break statement, the continue statement also comes in two forms: the *unlabeled* and the *labeled* form.

```
continue;              // the unlabeled form
continue <label>;      // the labeled form
```

The continue statement can only be used in a for, while, or do-while loop to prematurely stop the current iteration of the loop body and proceed with the next iteration, if possible. In the case of the while and do-while loops, the rest of the loop body is skipped, that is, stopping the current iteration, with execution continuing with the *<loop condition>*. In the case of the for loop, the rest of the loop body is skipped, with execution continuing with the *<increment expression>*.

In Example 5.6, an unlabeled continue statement is used to skip an iteration in a for loop. Control is transferred to (2) when the value of i is equal to 4 at (1), skipping the rest of the loop body and continuing with the *<increment expression>* in the for statement.

Example 5.6 continue *Statement*

```java
class Skip {
    public static void main(String[] args) {
        for (int i = 1; i <= 5; ++i) {
            if (i == 4) continue;                   // (1) Control to (2).
            // Rest of loop body skipped when i has the value 4.
            System.out.println(i + "\t" + Math.sqrt(i));
            // (2). Continue with increment expression.
        } // end for
    }
}
```

Output from the program:

```
1       1.0
2       1.4142135623730951
3       1.7320508075688772
5       2.23606797749979
```

A labeled continue statement must occur within a labeled loop that has the same label. Execution of the labeled continue statement then transfers control to the end of that enclosing labeled loop. In Example 5.7, the unlabeled continue statement at (3) transfers control to (5) when it is executed; that is, the rest of the loop body is skipped and execution continues with the next iteration of the inner loop. The labeled continue statement at (4) transfers control to (6) when it is executed (i.e., it terminates the inner loop but execution continues with the next iteration of the loop labeled outer). It is instructive to compare the output from Example 5.5 (labeled break) and Example 5.7 (labeled continue).

Example 5.7 *Labeled* continue *Statement*

```java
class LabeledSkip {
    public static void main(String[] args) {
        int[][] squareMatrix = {{4, 3, 5}, {2, 1, 6}, {9, 7, 8}};
        int sum = 0;
        outer:                                                  // label
        for (int i = 0; i < squareMatrix.length; ++i){          // (1)
            for (int j = 0; j < squareMatrix[i].length; ++j) {  // (2)
                if (j == i) continue;                  // (3) Control to (5).
                System.out.println("Element[" + i + ", " + j + "]: " +
                        squareMatrix[i][j]);
```

```
                    sum += squareMatrix[i][j];
                    if (sum > 10) continue outer;          // (4) Control to (6).
                    // (5) Continue with inner loop.
            } // end inner loop
            // (6) Continue with outer loop.
        } // end outer loop
        System.out.println("sum: " + sum);
    }
}
```

Output from the program:

```
Element[0, 1]: 3
Element[0, 2]: 5
Element[1, 0]: 2
Element[1, 2]: 6
Element[2, 0]: 9
sum: 25
```

return **Statement**

The return statement is used to stop execution of a method and transfer control back to the calling code (a.k.a. the *caller*). The usage of the two forms of the return statement is dictated by whether it is used in a void or a non-void method. The first form does not return any value to the calling code, but the second form does. Note that the keyword void does not represent any type.

The *<expression>* must evaluate to a primitive value or a reference value, and its type must be *assignable* to the *return type* in the method prototype (see Sections 3.4 and 6.6). As can be seen from Table 5.1, non-void methods must specify a return value using the return statement. A void method need not have a return statement —in which case control normally returns to the caller after the last statement in the method's body has been executed. The first form of the return statement can also be used in constructors, as these also do not return a value. Example 5.8 illustrates the usage of the return statement summarized in Table 5.1.

Table 5.1   return *Statement*

Form of return Statement	In void Method	In Non-void Method
return;	optional	not allowed
return *<expression>*;	not allowed	mandatory

Example 5.8   *The* return *Statement*

```
public class ReturnDemo {

    public static void main (String[] args) { // (1) void method can use return.
        if (args.length == 0) return;
        output(checkValue(args.length));
    }

    static void output(int value) { // (2) void method need not use return.
        System.out.println(value);
        return 'a';                      // Not OK. Cannot return a value.
    }

    static int checkValue(int i) {  // (3) non-void method must return a value.
        if (i > 3)
            return i;                    // OK.
        else
            return 2.0;                  // Not OK. double not assignable to int.
    }
}
```

 Review Questions

5.5   What will be the result of attempting to compile and run the following code?

```
class MyClass {
    public static void main(String[] args) {
        boolean b = false;
        int i = 1;
        do {
            i++;
            b = ! b;
        } while (b);
        System.out.println(i);
    }
}
```

Select the one correct answer.

(a) The code will fail to compile, since b is an invalid conditional expression for the do-while statement.

(b) The code will fail to compile, since the assignment b = ! b is not allowed.

(c) The code will compile without error and will print 1 when run.

(d) The code will compile without error and will print 2 when run.

(e) The code will compile without error and will print 3 when run.

5.6 What will be the output when running the following program?

```
public class MyClass {
    public static void main(String[] args) {
        int i=0;
        int j;
        for (j=0; j<10; ++j) { i++; }
        System.out.println(i + " " + j);
    }
}
```

Select the two correct answers.

(a) The first number printed will be 9.
(b) The first number printed will be 10.
(c) The first number printed will be 11.
(d) The second number printed will be 9.
(e) The second number printed will be 10.
(f) The second number printed will be 11.

5.7 Which one of these for statements is valid?

Select the one correct answer.

(a) `int j=10; for (int i=0, j+=90; i<j; i++) { j--; }`
(b) `for (int i=10; i=0; i--) {}`
(c) `for (int i=0, j=100; i<j; i++, --j) {;}`
(d) `int i, j; for (j=100; i<j; j--) { i += 2; }`
(e) `int i=100; for ((i>0); i--) {}`

5.8 What will be the result of attempting to compile and run the following program?

```
class MyClass {
    public static void main(String[] args) {
        int i = 0;
        for (  ; i<10; i++) ;        // (1)
        for (i=0;    ; i++) break;   // (2)
        for (i=0; i<10;   ) i++;     // (3)
        for (  ;    ;   ) ;          // (4)
    }
}
```

Select the one correct answer.

(a) The code will fail to compile, since the for statement (1) is missing the expression in the first section.
(b) The code will fail to compile, since the for statement (2) is missing the expression in the middle section.
(c) The code will fail to compile, since the for statement (3) is missing the expression in the last section.
(d) The code will fail to compile, since the for statement (4) is invalid.
(e) The code will compile without error, and the program will run and terminate without any output.
(f) The code will compile without error, but will never terminate when run.

5.9 Which statements are valid when occurring on their own?

Select the three correct answers.

(a) `while () break;`
(b) `do { break; } while (true);`
(c) `if (true) { break; }`
(d) `switch (1) { default: break; }`
(e) `for (;true;) break;`

5.10 Given the following code fragment, which of the following lines will be a part of the output?

```
outer:
for (int i = 0; i < 3; i++) {
    for (int j = 0; j < 2; j++) {
        if (i == j) {
            continue outer;
        }
        System.out.println("i=" + i + ", j=" + j);
    }
}
```

Select the two correct answers.

(a) `i=1, j=0`
(b) `i=0, j=1`
(c) `i=1, j=2`
(d) `i=2, j=1`
(e) `i=2, j=2`
(f) `i=3, j=3`
(g) `i=3, j=2`

5.11 What will be the result of attempting to compile and run the following code?

```
class MyClass {
    public static void main(String[] args) {
        for (int i = 0; i<10; i++) {
            switch(i) {
                case 0:
                    System.out.println(i);
            }
            if (i) {
                System.out.println(i);
            }
        }
    }
}
```

Select the one correct answer.

(a) The code will fail to compile, owing to an illegal `switch` expression in the `switch` statement.

(b) The code will fail to compile, owing to an illegal conditional expression in the `if` statement.

(c) The code will compile without error and will print the numbers 0 through 10 when run.

(d) The code will compile without error and will print the number 0 when run.

(e) The code will compile without error and will print the number 0 twice when run.

(f) The code will compile without error and will print the numbers 1 through 10 when run.

5.12 Which of the following implementations of a max() method will correctly return the largest value?

```
// (1)
int max(int x, int y) {
    return (if (x > y) { x; } else { y; });
}

// (2)
int max(int x, int y) {
    return (if (x > y) { return x; } else { return y; });
}

// (3)
int max(int x, int y) {
    switch (x < y) {
        case true:
            return y;
        default:
            return x;
    };
}

// (4)
int max(int x, int y) {
    if (x>y) return x;
    return y;
}
```

Select the one correct answer.

(a) Implementation labeled (1).

(b) Implementation labeled (2).

(c) Implementation labeled (3).

(d) Implementation labeled (4).

5.13 Given the following code, which statement is true?

```
class MyClass {
    public static void main(String[] args) {
        int k=0;
        int l=0;
        for (int i=0; i <= 3; i++) {
            k++;
            if (i == 2) break;
            l++;
```

```
        }
        System.out.println(k + ", " + l);
    }
}
```

Select the one correct answer.

(a) The program will fail to compile.

(b) The program will print 3, 3 when run.

(c) The program will print 4, 3 when run if break is replaced by continue.

(d) The program will fail to compile if break is replaced by return.

(e) The program will fail to compile if break is simply removed.

5.14 Which statements are true?

Select the two correct answers.

(a) {{}} is a valid statement block.

(b) { continue; } is a valid statement block.

(c) block: { break block; } is a valid statement block.

(d) block: { continue block; } is a valid statement block.

(e) The break statement can only be used in a loop (while, do-while or for) or a switch statement.

5.5 Stack-based Execution and Exception Propagation

An exception in Java is a signal that indicates the occurrence of some important or unexpected condition during execution. For example, a requested file cannot be found, or an array index is out of bounds, or a network link failed. Explicit checks in the code for such conditions can easily result in incomprehensible code. Java provides an exception handling mechanism for systematically dealing with such error conditions.

The exception mechanism is built around the throw-and-catch paradigm. To *throw* an exception is to signal that an unexpected error condition has occurred. To *catch* an exception is to take appropriate action to deal with the exception. An exception is caught by an *exception handler*, and the exception need not be caught in the same context that it was thrown in. The runtime behavior of the program determines which exceptions are thrown and how they are caught. The throw-and-catch principle is embedded in the try-catch-finally construct.

Several threads can be executing in the JVM (see Chapter 9). Each thread has its own *runtime stack* (also called the *call stack* or the *invocation stack*) that is used to handle execution of methods. Each element on the stack (called an *activation record* or a *stack frame*) corresponds to a method call. Each new call results in a new activation record being pushed on the stack, which stores all the pertinent information such as storage for the local variables. The method with the activation record on top of the stack is the one currently executing. When this method finishes executing, its record is popped from the stack. Execution then continues in the method corresponding to the activation record which is now uncovered on top of the stack. The methods on the stack are said to be *active*, as their execution has not completed. At any given time, the active methods on a runtime stack comprise what is called the *stack trace* of a thread's execution.

Example 5.9 is a simple program to illustrate method execution. It calculates the average for a list of integers, given the sum of all the integers and the number of integers. It uses three methods:

* The method main() which calls the method printAverage() with parameters giving the total sum of the integers and the total number of integers, (1).

* The method printAverage() in its turn calls the method computeAverage(), (3).

* The method computeAverage() uses integer division to calculate the average and returns the result, (7).

Example 5.9 *Method Execution*

```java
public class Average1 {

    public static void main(String[] args) {
        printAverage(100,0);                              // (1)
        System.out.println("Exit main().");               // (2)
    }

    public static void printAverage(int totalSum, int totalNumber) {
        int average = computeAverage(totalSum, totalNumber);  // (3)
        System.out.println("Average = " +                 // (4)
            totalSum + " / " + totalNumber + " = " + average);
        System.out.println("Exit printAverage().");       // (5)
    }

    public static int computeAverage(int sum, int number) {
        System.out.println("Computing average.");         // (6)
        return sum/number;                                // (7)
    }
}
```

Output of program execution:
```
Computing average.
Average = 100 / 20 = 5
Exit printAverage().
Exit main().
```

Execution of Example 5.9 is illustrated in Figure 5.6. Each method execution is shown as a box with the local variables. The box height indicates how long a method is active. Before the call to the method System.out.println() at (6) in Figure 5.6, the stack trace comprises of the three active methods: main(), printAverage() and computeAverage(). The result 5 from the method computeAverage() is returned at

(7) in Figure 5.6. The output from the program is in correspondence with the sequence of method calls in Figure 5.6.

Figure 5.6 *Method Execution*

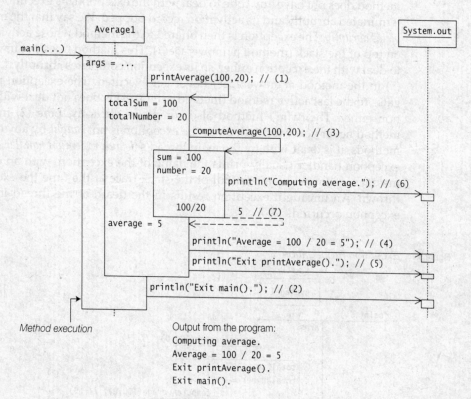

Method execution

Output from the program:
Computing average.
Average = 100 / 20 = 5
Exit printAverage().
Exit main().

If the method call at (1) in Example 5.9

```
printAverage(100, 20);                              // (1)
```

is replaced with

```
printAverage(100,  0);                              // (1)
```

and the program is run again, the output is as follows:

```
Computing average.
Exception in thread "main" java.lang.ArithmeticException: / by zero
        at Average1.computeAverage(Average1.java:18)
        at Average1.printAverage(Average1.java:10)
        at Average1.main(Average1.java:5)
```

Figure 5.7 illustrates the program execution. All goes well until the return statement at (7) in the method computeAverage() is executed. An error condition occurs in calculating the expression sum/number, because integer division by 0 is an illegal operation. This error condition is signalled by the JVM by *throwing* an ArithmeticException (see "Exception Types" on page 185). This exception is *propagated* by the JVM through the runtime stack as explained on the next page.

Figure 5.7 illustrates the case where an exception is thrown and the program does not take any explicit action to deal with the exception. In Figure 5.7, execution of the computeAverage() method is stopped at the point where the exception is thrown. The execution of the return statement at (7) never gets completed. Since this method does not have any code to deal with the exception, its execution is likewise terminated abruptly and its activation record popped. We say that the method *completes abruptly*. The exception is then offered to the method whose activation is now on top of the stack (method printAverage()). This method does not have any code to deal with the exception either, so its execution completes abruptly. Lines (4) and (5) in the method printAverage() never get executed. The exception now propagates to the last active method (method main()). This does not deal with the exception either. The main() method also completes abruptly. Line (2) in the main() method never gets executed. Since the exception is not *caught* by any of the active methods, it is dealt with by the main thread's *default exception handler*. The default exception handler usually prints the name of the exception, with an explanatory message, followed by a printout of the stack trace at the time the exception was thrown. An uncaught exception results in the death of the thread in which the exception occurred.

Figure 5.7   *Exception Propagation*

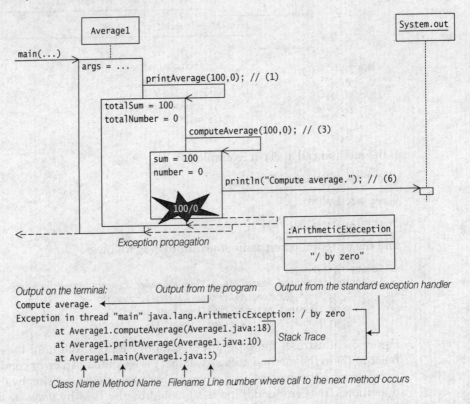

If an exception is thrown during the evaluation of the left-hand operand of a binary expression, then the right operand is not evaluated. Similarly if an exception is thrown during the evaluation of a list of expressions (for example, a list of actual parameters in a method call), then evaluation of the rest of the list is skipped.

If the line numbers in the stack trace are not printed in the output as shown previously, it is advisable to turn off the JIT (Just-in-Time) compilation feature of the JVM in the Java 2 SDK:

```
>java -Djava.compiler=NONE Average1
```

5.6 Exception Types

Exceptions in Java are objects. All exceptions are derived from the java.lang. Throwable class. Figure 5.8 shows a partial hierarchy of classes derived from the Throwable class. The two main subclasses Exception and Error constitute the main categories of *throwables*, the term used to refer to both exceptions and errors. Figure 5.8 also shows that not all exception classes are found in the same package.

The Throwable class provides a String variable that can be set by the subclasses to provide a *detail message*. The purpose of the detail message is to provide more information about the actual exception. All classes of throwables define a one-parameter constructor that takes a string as the detail message.

The class Throwable provides the following common methods to query an exeception:

String getMessage()

Returns the detail message.

void printStackTrace()

Prints the stack trace on the standard error stream. The stack trace comprises the method invocation sequence on the runtime stack when the exception was thrown. The stack trace can also be written to a PrintStream or a PrintWriter by supplying such a destination as an argument to one of the two overloaded printStackTrace() methods.

String toString()

Returns a short description of the exception, which typically comprises the class name of the exception together with the string returned by the getMessage() method.

Figure 5.8   *Partial Exception Inheritance Hierarchy*

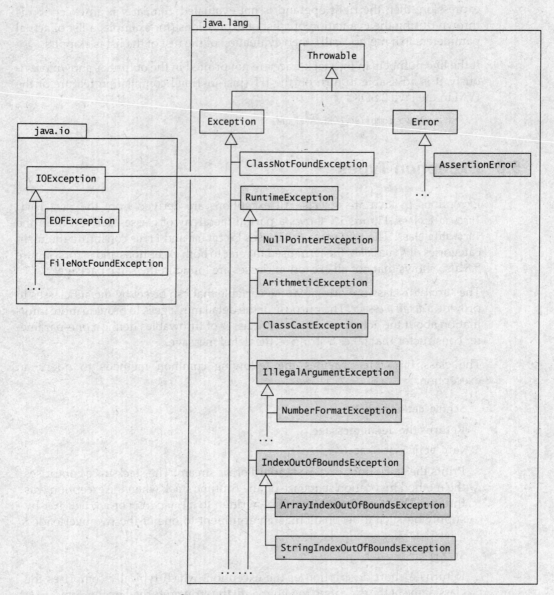

Classes that are shaded (and their subclasses) represent unchecked exceptions.

Class Exception

The class Exception represents exceptions that a program would want to be made aware of during execution. Its subclass RuntimeException represents many common programming errors that manifest at runtime (see the next subsection). Other subclasses of the Exception class define other categories of exceptions, for example, I/O-related exceptions (IOException, FileNotFoundException, EOFException) and GUI-related exceptions (AWTException).

Class RuntimeException

Runtime exceptions, like out-of-bound array indices (ArrayIndexOutOfBounds Exception), uninitialized references (NullPointerException), illegal casting of references (ClassCastException), illegal parameters (IllegalArgumentException), division by zero (ArithmeticException), and number format problems (NumberFormatException) are all subclasses of the java.lang.RuntimeException class, which is a subclass of the Exception class. As these runtime exceptions are usually caused by program bugs that should not occur in the first place, it is more appropriate to treat them as faults in the program design, rather than merely catching them during program execution.

Class Error

The subclass AssertionError of the java.lang.Error class is used by the Java assertion facility (see Section 5.10, p. 208). Other subclasses of the java.lang.Error class define exceptions that indicate class linkage (LinkageError), thread (ThreadDeath), and virtual machine (VirtualMachineError) related problems. These are invariably never explicitly caught and are usually irrecoverable.

Checked and Unchecked Exceptions

Except for RuntimeException, Error, and their subclasses, all exceptions are called *checked* exceptions. The compiler ensures that if a method can throw a checked exception, directly or indirectly, then the method must explicitly deal with it. The method must either catch the exception and take the appropriate action, or pass the exception on to its caller (see Section 5.9, p. 201).

Exceptions defined by Error and RuntimeException classes and their subclasses are known as *unchecked* exceptions, meaning that a method is not obliged to deal with these kinds of exceptions (shown with grey color in Figure 5.8). They are either irrecoverable (exemplified by the Error class) and the program should not attempt to deal with them, or they are programming errors (examplified by the RuntimeException class) and should be dealt with as such and not as exceptions.

Defining New Exceptions

New exceptions are usually defined to provide fine-grained categorization of exceptional conditions, instead of using existing exception classes with descriptive detail messages to differentiate between the conditions. New exceptions usually extend the Exception class directly or one of its checked subclasses, thereby making the new exceptions checked.

As exceptions are defined by classes, they can declare fields and methods, thus providing more information as to their cause and remedy when they are thrown and caught. The super() call can be used to set a detail message in the throwable. Note that the exception class must be instantiated to create an exception object that can be thrown and subsequently caught and dealt with. The code below sketches a class definition for an exception that can include all pertinent information about the exception.

```java
public class EvacuateException extends Exception {
    // Data
    Date date;
    Zone zone;
    TransportMode transport;

    // Constructor
    public EvacuateException(Date d, Zone z, TransportMode t) {
        // Call the constructor of the superclass
        super("Evacuation of zone " + z);
        // ...
    }
    // Methods
    // ...
}
```

Several examples illustrate exception handling in the subsequent sections.

5.7 Exception Handling: try, catch, and finally

The mechanism for handling execeptions is embedded in the try-catch-finally construct, which has the following general form:

```java
try {                                     // try block
    <statements>
} catch (<exception type₁> <parameter₁>) { // catch block
    <statements>
}
...
  catch (<exception typeₙ> <parameterₙ>) { // catch block
    <statements>
} finally {                               // finally block
    <statements>
}
```

Exceptions thrown during execution of the try block can be caught and handled in a catch block. A finally block is guaranteed to be executed, regardless of the cause of exit from the try block, or whether any catch block was executed. Figure 5.9 shows three typical scenarios of control flow through the try-catch-finally construct.

A few aspects about the syntax of this construct should be noted. The block notation is mandatory. For each try block there can be zero or more catch blocks, but only one finally block. The catch blocks and finally block must always appear in conjunction with a try block, and in the above order. A try block must be followed by either at least one catch block or one finally block. Each catch block defines an exception handler. The header of the catch block takes exactly one argument, which is the exception its block is willing to handle. The exception must be of the Throwable class or one of its subclasses.

Each block (try, catch, or finally) of a try-catch-finally construct can contain arbitrary code, which means that a try-catch-finally construct can also be nested in any such block. However, such nesting can easily make the code difficult to read and is best avoided.

Figure 5.9   try-catch-finally *Block*

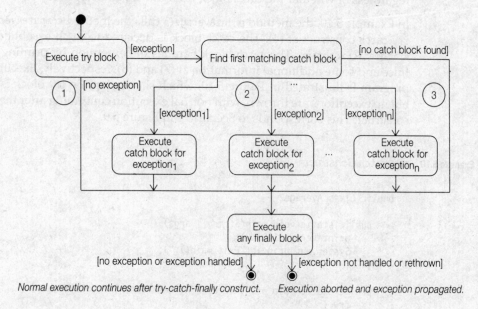

Normal execution continues after try-catch-finally construct.   Execution aborted and exception propagated.

try **Block**

The try block establishes a context that wants its termination to be handled. Termination occurs as a result of encountering an exception, or from successful execution of the code in the try block.

For all exits from the try block, except those due to exceptions, the catch blocks are skipped and control is transferred to the finally block, if one is specified (see (1) in Figure 5.9).

For all exits from the try block resulting from exceptions, control is transferred to the catch blocks—if any such blocks are specified—to find a matching catch block ((2) in Figure 5.9). If no catch block matches the thrown exception, control is transferred to the finally block, if one is specified (see (3) in Figure 5.9).

catch **Block**

Only an exit from a try block resulting from an exception can transfer control to a catch block. A catch block can only *catch* the thrown exception if the exception is assignable to the parameter in the catch block (see Section 6.6, p. 260). The code of the first such catch block is executed and all other catch blocks are ignored.

On exit from a catch block, normal execution continues unless there is any pending exception that has been thrown and not handled. If this is the case, the method is aborted and the exception is propagated up the runtime stack as explained earlier.

After a catch block has been executed, control is always transferred to the finally block, if one is specified. This is always true as long as there is a finally block, regardless of whether the catch block itself throws an exception.

In Example 5.10, the method printAverage() calls the method computeAverage() in a try-catch construct at (4). The catch block is declared to catch exceptions of type ArithmeticException. The catch block handles the exception by printing the stack trace and some additional information at (7) and (8), respectively. Execution of the program is illustrated in Figure 5.10, which shows that the try block is executed but no exceptions are thrown, with normal execution continuing after the try-catch construct. This corresponds to Scenario 1 in Figure 5.9.

Example 5.10   try-catch *Construct*

```java
public class Average2 {

    public static void main(String[] args) {
        printAverage(100, 0);                                   // (1)
        System.out.println("Exit main().");                     // (2)
    }

    public static void printAverage(int totalSum, int totalNumber) {
        try {                                                   // (3)
            int average = computeAverage(totalSum, totalNumber);  // (4)
            System.out.println("Average = " +                  // (5)
                totalSum + " / " + totalNumber + " = " + average);
        } catch (ArithmeticException ae) {                     // (6)
            ae.printStackTrace();                              // (7)
            System.out.println("Exception handled in " +
                                "printAverage().");            // (8)
        }
        System.out.println("Exit printAverage().");            // (9)
    }

    public static int computeAverage(int sum, int number) {
        System.out.println("Computing average.");              // (10)
        return sum/number;                                     // (11)
    }
}
```

Output from the program, with call printAverage(100, 20) at (1):

```
Computing average.
Average = 100 / 20 = 5
Exit printAverage().
Exit main().
```

Output from the program, with call printAverage(100, 0) at (1):

```
Computing average.
java.lang.ArithmeticException: / by zero
        at Average2.computeAverage(Average2.java:24)
        at Average2.printAverage(Average2.java:11)
        at Average2.main(Average2.java:5)
Exception handled in printAverage().
Exit printAverage().
Exit main().
```

Figure 5.10 *Exception Handling (Scenario 1)*

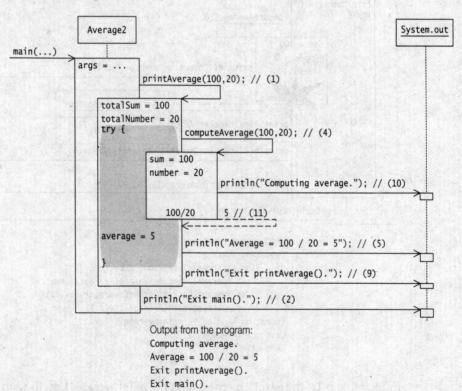

Output from the program:
Computing average.
Average = 100 / 20 = 5
Exit printAverage().
Exit main().

However, if we run the program in Example 5.10 with the following call in (1):

```
printAverage(100, 0)
```

an ArithmeticException is thrown by the integer division in method computeAver-age(). From Figure 5.11 we see that the execution of the method computeAverage() is stopped and the exception propagated to method printAverage(), where it is handled by the catch block at (6). Normal execution of the method continues at (9) after the try-catch construct, as witnessed by the output from the statements at (9) and (2). This corresponds to Scenario 2 in Figure 5.9.

Figure 5.11 *Exception Handling (Scenario 2)*

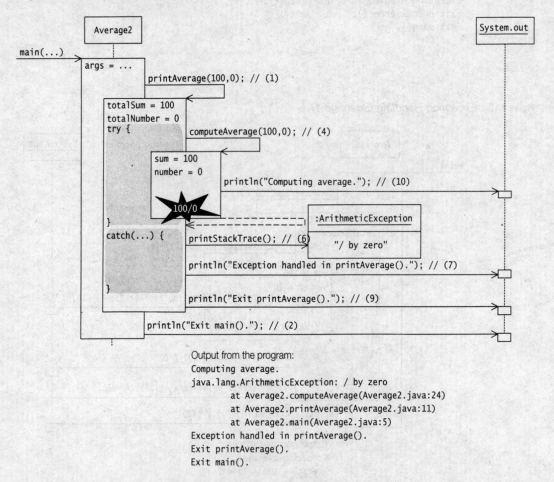

In Example 5.11, the main() method calls the printAverage() method in a try-catch construct at (1). The catch block at (3) is declared to catch exceptions of type ArithmeticException. The printAverage() method calls the computeAverage() method in a try-catch construct at (7), but here the catch block is declared to catch exceptions of type IllegalArgumentException. Execution of the program is illustrated in Figure 5.12, which shows that the ArithmeticException is first propagated to the catch block in the printAverage() method. But since this catch block cannot handle this exception, it is propagated further to the catch block in the main() method, where it is caught and handled. Normal execution continues at (6) after the exception is handled.

Note that the execution of try block at (7) in the printAverage() method is never completed: the statment at (9) is never executed. The catch block at (10) is skipped. The execution of the printAverage() method is aborted: the statment at (13) is never executed, and the exception is propagated. This corresponds to Scenario 3 in Figure 5.9.

Example 5.11 *Exception Propagation*

```java
public class Average3 {

    public static void main(String[] args) {
        try {                                              // (1)
            printAverage(100, 0);                          // (2)
        } catch (ArithmeticException ae) {                 // (3)
            ae.printStackTrace();                          // (4)
            System.out.println("Exception handled in " +
                               "main().");                 // (5)
        }
        System.out.println("Exit main().");                // (6)
    }

    public static void printAverage(int totalSum, int totalNumber) {
        try {                                              // (7)
            int average = computeAverage(totalSum, totalNumber);  // (8)
            System.out.println("Average = " +              // (9)
                totalSum + " / " + totalNumber + " = " + average);
        } catch (IllegalArgumentException iae) {           // (10)
            iae.printStackTrace();                         // (11)
            System.out.println("Exception handled in " +
                               "printAverage().");         // (12)
        }
        System.out.println("Exit printAverage().");        // (13)
    }

    public static int computeAverage(int sum, int number) {
        System.out.println("Computing average.");          // (14)
        return sum/number;                                 // (15)
    }
}
```

Output from the program:

```
Computing average.
java.lang.ArithmeticException: / by zero
        at Average3.computeAverage(Average3.java:30)
```

```
        at Average3.printAverage(Average3.java:17)
        at Average3.main(Average3.java:6)
Exception handled in main().
Exit main().
```

Figure 5.12 *Exception Handling (Scenario 3)*

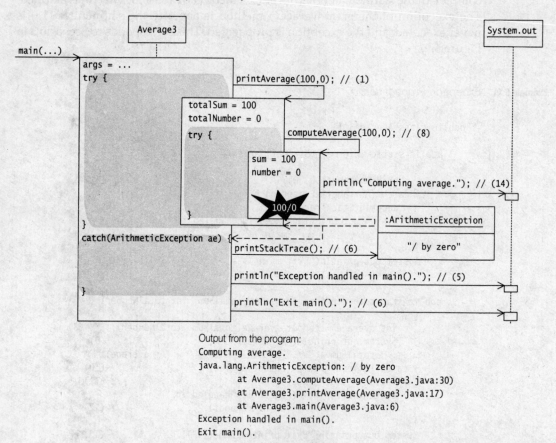

```
Output from the program:
Computing average.
java.lang.ArithmeticException: / by zero
        at Average3.computeAverage(Average3.java:30)
        at Average3.printAverage(Average3.java:17)
        at Average3.main(Average3.java:6)
Exception handled in main().
Exit main().
```

The scope of the argument name in the catch block is the block itself. As mentioned earlier, the type of the exception object must be *assignable* to the type of the argument in the catch block (see Section 6.6, p. 260). In the body of the catch block, the exception object can be queried like any other object by using the argument name. The javac compiler also complains if a catch block for a superclass exception shadows the catch block for a subclass exception, as the catch block of the subclass exception will never be executed. The following example shows incorrect order of the catch blocks at (1) and (2), which will result in a compile time error: the superclass Exception will shadow the subclass ArithmeticException.

```
    ...
    // Compiler complains
    catch (Exception e) {                      // (1) superclass
        System.out.println(e);
    } catch (ArithmeticException e) {          // (2) subclass
        System.out.println(e);
    }
    ...
```

finally **Block**

If the try block is executed, then the finally block is guaranteed to be executed, regardless of whether any catch block was executed. Since the finally block is always executed before control transfers to its final destination, it can be used to specify any clean-up code (for example, to free resources such as, files, net connections).

A try-finally construct can be used to control the interplay between two actions that must be executed in the right order, possibly with other intervening actions.

```
int sum = -1;
try {
    sum = sumNumbers();
    // other actions
} finally {
    if (sum >= 0) calculateAverage();
}
```

The code above guarantees that if the try block is entered sumNumbers() will be executed first and then later calculateAverage() will be executed in the finally block, regardless of how execution proceeds in the try block. As the operation in calculateAverage() is dependent on the success of sumNumbers(), this is checked by the value of the sum variable before calling calculateAverage(). catch blocks can, of course, be included to handle any exceptions.

If the finally block neither throws an exception nor executes a control transfer statement like a return or a labeled break, then the execution of the try block or any catch block determines how execution proceeds after the finally block (see Figure 5.9, p. 189).

- If there is no exception thrown during execution of the try block or the exception has been handled in a catch block, then normal execution continues after the finally block.

- If there is any pending exception that has been thrown and not handled (either due to the fact that no catch block was found or the catch block threw an exception), the method is aborted and the exception is propagated after the execution of the finally block.

If the finally block throws an exception, then this exception is propagated with all its ramifications—regardless of how the try block or any catch block were executed. In particular, the new exception overrules any previously unhandled exception.

If the finally block executes a control transfer statement such as, a return or a labeled break, then this control transfer statement determines how the execution will proceed—regardless of how the try block or any catch block were executed. In particular, a value returned by a return statement in the finally block will supersede any value returned by a return statement in the try block or a catch block.

Output of Example 5.12 shows that the finally block at (9) is executed, regardless of whether an exception is thrown in the try block at (3) or not. If an exception is thrown, it is caught and handled by the catch block at (6). After the execution of the finally block at (9), normal execution continues at (10).

Example 5.12   try-catch-finally *Construct*

```java
public class Average4 {

    public static void main(String[] args) {
        printAverage(100, 20);                              // (1)
        System.out.println("Exit main().");                // (2)
    }

    public static void printAverage(int totalSum, int totalNumber) {
        try {                                              // (3)
            int average = computeAverage(totalSum, totalNumber);  // (4)
            System.out.println("Average = " +             // (5)
                totalSum + " / " + totalNumber + " = " + average);
        } catch (ArithmeticException ae) {                 // (6)
            ae.printStackTrace();                          // (7)
            System.out.println("Exception handled in " +
                               "printAverage().");          // (8)
        } finally {                                        // (9)
            System.out.println("Finally done.");
        }
        System.out.println("Exit printAverage().");        // (10)
    }

    public static int computeAverage(int sum, int number) {
        System.out.println("Computing average.");          // (11)
        return sum/number;                                 // (12)
    }
}
```

Output from the program, with call printAverage(100, 20) at (1):

```
Computing average.
Average = 100 / 20 = 5
Finally done.
Exit printAverage().
Exit main().
```

Output from the program, with call printAverage(100, 0) at (1):

```
Computing average.
java.lang.ArithmeticException: / by zero
        at Average4.computeAverage(Average4.java:26)
        at Average4.printAverage(Average4.java:11)
        at Average4.main(Average4.java:5)
Exception handled in printAverage().
Finally done.
Exit printAverage().
Exit main().
```

On exiting from the finally block, if there is any pending exception, the method is aborted and the exception propagated as explained earlier. This is illustrated in Example 5.13. The method printAverage() is aborted after the finally block at (6) has been executed, as the ArithmeticException thrown at (9) is not handled by any method. In this case, the exception is handled by the default exception handler. Notice the difference in the output from Example 5.12 and Example 5.13.

Example 5.13   try-finally *Construct*

```
public class Average5 {

    public static void main(String[] args) {
        printAverage(100, 0);                                 // (1)
        System.out.println("Exit main().");                   // (2)
    }

    public static void printAverage(int totalSum, int totalNumber) {
        try {                                                 // (3)
            int average = computeAverage(totalSum, totalNumber);  // (4)
            System.out.println("Average = " +                 // (5)
                totalSum + " / " + totalNumber + " = " + average);
        } finally {                                           // (6)
            System.out.println("Finally done.");
        }
        System.out.println("Exit printAverage().");           // (7)
    }

    public static int computeAverage(int sum, int number) {
        System.out.println("Computing average.");             // (8)
        return sum/number;                                    // (9)
    }
}
```

Output from the program:

```
Computing average.
Finally done.
Exception in thread "main" java.lang.ArithmeticException: / by zero
        at Average5.computeAverage(Average5.java:21)
        at Average5.printAverage(Average5.java:10)
        at Average5.main(Average5.java:4)
```

Example 5.14 shows how the execution of a control transfer statement such as a return in the finally block affects the program execution. The first output from the program shows that the average is computed, but the value returned is from the return statement at (8) in the finally block, not from the return statement at (6) in the try block. The second output shows that the ArithmeticException thrown in the computeAverage() method and propagated to the printAverage() method, is nullified by the return statement in the finally block. Normal execution continues after the return statement at (8), with the value 0 being returned from the printAverage() method.

Example 5.14   finally *Block and the* return *Statement*

```java
public class Average6 {

    public static void main(String[] args) {
        System.out.println("Average: " + printAverage(100, 20));  // (1)
        System.out.println("Exit main().");                       // (2)
    }

    public static int printAverage(int totalSum, int totalNumber) {
        int average = 0;
        try {                                                     // (3)
            average = computeAverage(totalSum, totalNumber);      // (4)
            System.out.println("Average = " +                    // (5)
                totalSum + " / " + totalNumber + " = " + average);
            return average;                                       // (6)
        } finally {                                               // (7)
            System.out.println("Finally done.");
            return average*2;                                     // (8)
        }
    }

    public static int computeAverage(int sum, int number) {
        System.out.println("Computing average.");                // (9)
        return sum/number;                                       // (10)
    }
}
```

Output from the program, with call `printAverage(100, 20)` in (1):

```
Computing average.
Average = 100 / 20 = 5
Finally done.
Average: 10
Exit main().
```

Output from the program, with call `printAverage(100, 0)` in (1):

```
Computing average.
Finally done.
Average: 0
Exit main().
```

5.8 `throw` **Statement**

Earlier examples in this chapter have shown how an exception is thrown implicitly during execution. A program can explicitly throw an exception using the `throw` statement. The general format of the `throw` statement is as follows:

`throw <object reference expression>;`

The compiler ensures that the *<object reference expression>* is of type `Throwable` class or one of its subclasses. At runtime a `NullPointerException` is thrown if the *<object reference expression>* is `null`. This ensure that a `Throwable` will always be propagated. A detail message is often passed to the constructor when the exception object is created.

`throw new ArithmeticException("Integer division by 0");`

When an exception is thrown, normal execution is suspended. The runtime system proceeds to find a `catch` block that can handle the exception. The search starts in the context of the current `try` block, propagating to any enclosing `try` blocks and through the runtime stack to find a handler for the exception. Any associated `finally` block of a `try` block encountered along the search path is executed. If no handler is found, then the exception is dealt with by the default exception handler at the top level. If a handler is found, execution resumes with the code in its `catch` block.

In Example 5.15, an exception is thrown using a `throw` statement at (17). This exception is propagated to the `main()` method where it is caught and handled by the catch block at (3). Note that the `finally` blocks at (6) and (14) are executed. Execution continues normally from (7).

Example 5.15   *Throwing Exceptions*

```java
public class Average7 {

    public static void main(String[] args) {
        try {                                                    // (1)
            printAverage(100, 0);                                // (2)
        } catch (ArithmeticException ae) {                       // (3)
            ae.printStackTrace();                                // (4)
            System.out.println("Exception handled in " +         // (5)
                               "main().");
        } finally {
            System.out.println("Finally in main().");            // (6)
        }
        System.out.println("Exit main().");                      // (7)
    }

    public static void printAverage(int totalSum, int totalNumber) {
        try {                                                    // (8)
            int average = computeAverage(totalSum, totalNumber); // (9)
            System.out.println("Average = " +                    // (10)
                totalSum + " / " + totalNumber + " = " + average);
        } catch (IllegalArgumentException iae) {                 // (11)
            iae.printStackTrace();                               // (12)
            System.out.println("Exception handled in " +         // (13)
                               "printAverage().");
        } finally {
            System.out.println("Finally in printAverage().");    // (14)
        }
        System.out.println("Exit printAverage().");              // (15)
    }

    public static int computeAverage(int sum, int number) {
        System.out.println("Computing average.");
        if (number == 0)                                         // (16)
            throw new ArithmeticException("Integer division by 0");// (17)
        return sum/number;                                       // (18)
    }
}
```

Output from the program:

```
Computing average.
Finally in printAverage().
java.lang.ArithmeticException: Integer division by 0
        at Average7.computeAverage(Average7.java:35)
        at Average7.printAverage(Average7.java:19)
        at Average7.main(Average7.java:6)
Exception handled in main().
Finally in main().
Exit main().
```

5.9 throws **Clause**

A throws clause can be specified in the method protoype.

```
... someMethod(...)
    throws <ExceptionType₁>, <ExceptionType₂>,..., <ExceptionTypeₙ> { ... }
```

Each $<ExceptionType_i>$ declares a checked exception. The compiler enforces that the checked exceptions thrown by a method are limited to those specified in its throws clause. Of course, the method can throw exceptions that are subclasses of the checked exceptions in the throws clause. This is permissable since exceptions are objects, and a subclass object can polymorphically act as an object of its superclass (see Section 6.1, p. 226). The throws clause can have unchecked exceptions specified, but this is seldom used and the compiler does not check them.

Handling of checked exceptions in initializers is covered in Section 8.2 on page 331.

Any method that can cause a checked exception to be thrown, either directly by using the throw statement or indirectly by invoking other methods that can throw such an exception, must deal with the exception in one of three ways. It can

- use a try block and catch the exception in a handler and deal with it
- use a try block and catch the exception in a handler, but throw another exception that is either unchecked or declared in its throws clause
- explicitly allow propagation of the exception to its caller by declaring it in the throws clause of its method protoype

This mechanism ensures that, regardless of the path of execution, a checked exception will be dealt with in some way. It aids development of robust programs, as allowance can be made for many contingencies. Native methods can also declare checked exceptions in their throws clause, but the compiler is not able to check them for consistency.

A new checked exception is defined in Example 5.16. The checked exception class IntegerDivisionByZero is defined at (11) by extending the Exception class.

In Example 5.16, the method main() calls the method printAverage() in a try block at (1). In the if statement at (9), the method computeAverage() throws the checked exception IntegerDivisionByZero defined at (11). Neither the computeAverage() method nor the printAverage() method catch the exception, but instead throw it to their caller, as declared in the throws clause in their headers at (6) and (8). The exception propagates to the main() method. Since the printAverage() method was called from the context of the try block at (1) in the main() method, the exception is successfully matched with its catch block at (3). The exception is handled and the finally block at (4) executed, with normal execution proceeding at (5). If the method main() did not catch the exception, it would have to declare this exception in a throws clause. In that case, the exception would end up being taken care of by the default exception handler.

Example 5.16   throws *Clause*

```java
public class Average8 {
    public static void main(String[] args) {
        try {                                              // (1)
            printAverage(100, 0);                          // (2)
        } catch (IntegerDivisionByZero idbze) {            // (3)
            idbze.printStackTrace();
            System.out.println("Exception handled in " +
                               "main().");
        } finally {                                        // (4)
            System.out.println("Finally done in main().");
        }

        System.out.println("Exit main().");               // (5)
    }

    public static void printAverage(int totalSum, int totalNumber)
            throws IntegerDivisionByZero {                 // (6)

        int average = computeAverage(totalSum, totalNumber);
        System.out.println("Average = " +
            totalSum + " / " + totalNumber + " = " + average);
        System.out.println("Exit printAverage().");        // (7)
    }

    public static int computeAverage(int sum, int number)
            throws IntegerDivisionByZero {                 // (8)

        System.out.println("Computing average.");
        if (number == 0)                                   // (9)
            throw new IntegerDivisionByZero("Integer Division By Zero");
        return sum/number;                                 // (10)
    }
}

class IntegerDivisionByZero extends Exception {            // (11)
    IntegerDivisionByZero(String str) { super(str); }     // (12)
}
```

Output from the program:

```
Computing average.
IntegerDivisionByZero: Integer Division By Zero
        at Average8.computeAverage(Average8.java:33)
        at Average8.printAverage(Average8.java:22)
        at Average8.main(Average8.java:7)
Exception handled in main().
Finally done in main().
Exit main().
```

The exception type specified in the throws clause in the method protoype can be a superclass type of the actual exceptions thrown, that is, the exceptions thrown must be assignable to the type of the exceptions specified in the throws clause. If a method can throw exceptions of the type A, B, and C where these are subclasses of type D, then the throws clause can either specify A, B, and C or just specify D. In the printAverage() method, the method protoype could specify the superclass Exception of the subclass IntegerDivisionByZero in a throws clause.

```
public static void printAverage(int totalSum, int totalNumber)
        throws Exception { /* ... */ }
```

It is generally a bad programming style to specify exception superclasses in the throws clause of the method protoype, when the actual exceptions thrown in the method are instances of their subclasses. Programmers will be deprived of information about which specific subclass exceptions can be thrown, unless they have access to the source code.

A subclass can *override* a method defined in its superclass by providing a new implementation (see Section 6.2, p. 233). What happens when an inherited method with a list of exceptions in its throws clause is overridden in a subclass? The method definition in the subclass can only specify a *subset* of the *checked* exception classes (including their subclasses) from the throws clause of the inherited method in the superclass. This means that an overriding method cannot allow more checked exceptions in its throws clause than the inherited method does. Allowing more checked exceptions in the overriding method would create problems for clients who already deal with the exceptions specified in the inherited method. Such clients would be ill prepared if an object of the subclass (under the guise of polymorphism) threw a checked exception they were not prepared for.

```
class A {
    // ...
    protected void superclassMethodX()
        throws FirstException, SecondException, ThirdException {/* ... */} // (1)
    // ...
}

class B extends A {
    // ...
    protected void superclassMethodX()
        throws FirstException, ThirdException { /* ... */ }                // (2)
    // ...

}
```

In the previous code, the method superclassMethodX in superclass A is overridden in subclass B. The throws clause of the method in subclass B at (2) is a subset of the exceptions specified for the method in the superclass at (1).

Review Questions

5.15 Which digits, and in which order, will be printed when the following program is run?

```java
public class MyClass {
    public static void main(String[] args) {
        int k=0;
        try {
            int i = 5/k;
        } catch (ArithmeticException e) {
            System.out.println("1");
        } catch (RuntimeException e) {
            System.out.println("2");
            return;
        } catch (Exception e) {
            System.out.println("3");
        } finally {
            System.out.println("4");
        }
        System.out.println("5");
    }
}
```

Select the one correct answer.

(a) The program will only print 5.

(b) The program will only print 1 and 4, in that order.

(c) The program will only print 1, 2, and 4, in that order.

(d) The program will only print 1, 4, and 5, in that order.

(e) The program will only print 1, 2, 4, and 5, in that order.

(f) The program will only print 3 and 5, in that order.

5.16 Given the following program, which statements are true?

```java
public class Exceptions {
    public static void main(String[] args) {
        try {
            if (args.length == 0) return;
            System.out.println(args[0]);
        } finally {
            System.out.println("The end");
        }
    }
}
```

Select the two correct answers.

(a) If run with no arguments, the program will produce no output.

(b) If run with no arguments, the program will print "The end".

(c) The program will throw an ArrayIndexOutOfBoundsException.

(d) If run with one argument, the program will simply print the given argument.

(e) If run with one argument, the program will print the given argument followed by "The end".

5.17 What will be the result of attempting to compile and run the following program?

```
public class MyClass {
    public static void main(String[] args) {
        RuntimeException re = null;
        throw re;
    }
}
```

Select the one correct answer.

(a) The code will fail to compile, since the main() method does not declare that it throws RuntimeException in its declaration.

(b) The program will fail to compile, since it cannot throw re.

(c) The program will compile without error and will throw java.lang.Runtime-Exception when run.

(d) The program will compile without error and will throw java.lang.Null-pointerException when run.

(e) The program will compile without error and will run and terminate without any output.

5.18 Which statements are true?

Select the two correct answers.

(a) If an exception is uncaught in a method, the method will terminate and normal execution will resume.

(b) An overriding method must declare that it throws the same exception classes as the method it overrides.

(c) The main() method of a program can declare that it throws checked exceptions.

(d) A method declaring that it throws a certain exception class may throw instances of any subclass of that exception class.

(e) finally blocks are executed if, and only if, an exception gets thrown while inside the corresponding try block.

5.19 Which digits, and in which order, will be printed when the following program is compiled and run?

```
public class MyClass {
    public static void main(String[] args) {
        try {
            f();
        } catch (InterruptedException e) {
            System.out.println("1");
            throw new RuntimeException();
        } catch (RuntimeException e) {
            System.out.println("2");
            return;
        } catch (Exception e) {
            System.out.println("3");
        } finally {
            System.out.println("4");
        }
```

```
            System.out.println("5");
        }

        // InterruptedException is a direct subclass of Exception.
        static void f() throws InterruptedException {
            throw new InterruptedException("Time for lunch.");
        }
    }
```

Select the one correct answer.

(a) The program will print 5.
(b) The program will print 1 and 4, in that order.
(c) The program will print 1, 2, and 4, in that order.
(d) The program will print 1, 4, and 5, in that order.
(e) The program will print 1, 2, 4, and 5, in that order.
(f) The program will print 3 and 5, in that order.

5.20   Which digits, and in which order, will be printed when the following program is run?

```
public class MyClass {
    public static void main(String[] args) throws InterruptedException {
        try {
            f();
            System.out.println("1");
        } finally {
            System.out.println("2");
        }
        System.out.println("3");
    }

    // InterruptedException is a direct subclass of Exception.
    static void f() throws InterruptedException {
        throw new InterruptedException("Time to go home.");
    }
}
```

Select the one correct answer.

(a) The program will print 2 and throw InterruptedException.
(b) The program will print 1 and 2, in that order.
(c) The program will print 1, 2, and 3, in that order.
(d) The program will print 2 and 3, in that order.
(e) The program will print 3 and 2, in that order.
(f) The program will print 1 and 3, in that order.

5.21   What is wrong with the following code?

```
public class MyClass {
    public static void main(String[] args) throws A {
        try {
            f();
        } finally {
            System.out.println("Done.");
```

```
            } catch (A e) {
                throw e;
            }
        }

        public static void f() throws B {
            throw new B();
        }
    }

    class A extends Throwable {}

    class B extends A {}
```

Select the one correct answer.

(a) The main() method must declare that it throws B.
(b) The finally block must follow the catch block in the main() method.
(c) The catch block in the main() method must declare that it catches B rather than A.
(d) A single try block cannot be followed by both a finally and a catch block.
(e) The declaration of class A is illegal.

5.22 What is the minimal list of exception classes that the overriding method f() in the following code must declare in its throws clause before the code will compile correctly?

```
    class A {
        // InterruptedException is a direct subclass of Exception.
        void f() throws ArithmeticException, InterruptedException {
            div(5, 5);
        }

        int div(int i, int j) throws ArithmeticException {
            return i/j;
        }
    }

    public class MyClass extends A {
        void f() /* throws [...list of exceptions...] */ {
            try {
                div(5, 0);
            } catch (ArithmeticException e) {
                return;
            }
            throw new RuntimeException("ArithmeticException was expected.");
        }
    }
```

Select the one correct answer.

(a) Does not need to specify any exceptions.
(b) Needs to specify that it throws ArithmeticException.
(c) Needs to specify that it throws InterruptedException.
(d) Needs to specify that it throws RuntimeException.
(e) Needs to specify that it throws both ArithmeticException and Interrupted-Exception.

5.23   What, if anything, would cause the following code not to compile?

```
class A {
    void f() throws ArithmeticException {
        //...
    }
}

public class MyClass extends A {
    public static void main(String[] args) {
        A obj = new MyClass();

        try {
            obj.f();
        } catch (ArithmeticException e) {
            return;
        } catch (Exception e) {
            System.out.println(e);
            throw new RuntimeException("Something wrong here");
        }
    }

    // InterruptedException is a direct subclass of Exception.
    void f() throws InterruptedException {
        //...
    }
}
```

Select the one correct answer.

(a) The main() method must declare that it throws RuntimeException.

(b) The overriding f() method in MyClass must declare that it throws Arithmetic-Exception, since the f() method in class A declares that it does.

(c) The overriding f() method in MyClass is not allowed to throw Interrupted-Exception, since the f() method in class A does not throw this exception.

(d) The compiler will complain that the catch(ArithmeticException) block shadows the catch(Exception) block.

(e) You cannot throw exceptions from a catch block.

(f) Nothing is wrong with the code, it will compile without errors.

5.10 Assertions

Assertions in Java can be used to document and validate assumptions made about the state of the program at designated locations in the code. Each assertion contains a boolean expression that is expected to be true when the assertion is executed. If this assumption is false, the system throws a special assertion error. The assertion facility uses the exception handling mechanism to propagate the error. The assertion facility can be enabled or disabled at runtime.

The assertion facility is an invaluable aid in implementing *correct* programs (i.e., programs that adhere to their specification). It should not be confused with the exception handling mechanism that aids in developing *robust* programs (i.e., programs that handle unexpected conditions gracefully). Used judiciously, the two mechanisms facilitate programs that are *reliable*.

assert **Statement and** AssertionError **Class**

The following two forms of the assert statement can be used to specify assertions:

```
assert <boolean expression> ;                          // the simple form

assert <boolean expression> : <message expression> ;   // the augmented form
```

If assertions are enabled (see p. 212), the execution of an assert statement proceeds as shown in Figure 5.13. The two forms are essentially equivalent to the following code, respectively:

```
if (<assertions enabled> && !<boolean expression>)    // the simple form
    throw new AssertionError();

if (<assertions enabled> && !<boolean expression>)    // the augmented form
    throw new AssertionError(<message expression>);
```

If assertions are enabled, then *<boolean expression>* is evaluated. If its value is true, execution continues normally after the assert statement. However, if it is false, an AssertionError is thrown and propagated. In the simple form, the AssertionError does not provide any detailed message about the assertion failure.

Figure 5.13 *Execution of the Simple* assert *Statement (When Assertions Are Enabled)*

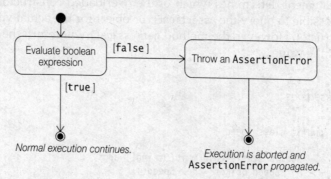

The augmented form provides a *<message expression>* that can be used to provide a detailed error message. In the augmented form, if the assertion is false, the *<message expression>* is evaluated and its value passed to the appropriate AssertionError constructor. The *<message expression>* must evaluate to a value (i.e., either a primitive or a reference value). The AssertionError constructor invoked converts the value to a textual representation. In particular, the *<message expression>* cannot call a method that is declared void. The compiler will flag this as an error.

Lines (2), (3), and (4) in class Speed (see Example 5.17) are assertion statements. In this particular context of calculating the speed, it is required that the values fulfill the criteria in lines (2), (3) and (4) in the private method calcSpeed(). Lines (2) and (4) use the simple form.

```
assert distance >= 0.0;                                         // (2)
...
assert speed >= 0.0;                                            // (4)
```

Line (3) uses the augmented form.

```
assert time > 0.0 : "Time is not a positive value: " + time;  // (3)
```

Line (3) is equivalent to the following line of code, assuming assertions have been enabled at runtime:

```
if (time <= 0.0) throw new AssertionError("Time is not a positive value: " + time);
```

The java.lang.AssertionError class is a subclass of java.lang.Error (see Figure 5.8). This makes AssertionError exceptions unchecked. They could be explicitly caught and handled using the try-catch construct. The execution would then continue normally, as one would expect. However, since Error exceptions are seldom caught and handled by the program, the same applies to AssertionError exceptions. Catching these exceptions would defeat the whole purpose of the assertion facility.

In addition to the default constructor (invoked by the simple assert form), the AssertionError class provides seven single-parameter constructors: six for the primitive data types (byte and short being promoted to int) and one for object references. The type of the *<message expression>* used in the augmented assertion statement determines which of the overloaded constructors is invoked. It is not possible to query the AssertionError object for the actual value passed to the constructor. However, the method getMessage() will return the textual representation of the value.

Example 5.17 *Assertions*

```
public class Speed {

    public static void main(String[] args) {
        Speed objRef = new Speed();.
        double speed = objRef.calcSpeed(-12.0, 3.0);              // (1a)
        // double speed = objRef.calcSpeed(12.0, -3.0);            // (1b)
        // double speed = objRef.calcSpeed(12.0, 2.0);             // (1c)
        // double speed = objRef.calcSpeed(12.0, 0.0);             // (1d)
        System.out.println("Speed (km/h): " + speed);
    }

    /** Requires distance >= 0.0 and time > 0.0 */
    private double calcSpeed(double distance, double time) {
        assert distance >= 0.0;                                   // (2)
        assert time >0.0 : "Time is not a positive value: " + time; // (3)
        double speed = distance / time;
```

```
                    assert speed >= 0.0;                                    // (4)
                    return speed;
                }
            }
```

- -

Compiling Assertions

The assertion facility was introduced in J2SE 1.4. At the same time, two new options for the javac compiler were introduced for dealing with assertions in the source code.

Option -source 1.4

The javac compiler distributed with the Java SDK v1.4 will only compile assertions if the option -source 1.4 is used on the command-line:

```
>javac -source 1.4 Speed.java
```

This also means that incorrect use of the keyword assert will be flagged as an *error*, for example, if assert is used as an identifier. The following program

```
public class Legacy {
    public static void main(String[] args) {
        int assert = 2003;
        System.out.println("The year is: " + assert);
    }
}
```

when compiled, results in two errors:

```
>javac -source 1.4 Legacy.java
Legacy.java:4: as of release 1.4, assert is a keyword, and may not be used as an
  identifier
        int assert = 2003;
            ^
Legacy.java:5: as of release 1.4, assert is a keyword, and may not be used as an
  identifier
        System.out.println("The year is: " + assert);
                                              ^
2 errors
```

Option -source 1.3

The default behavior of the javac compiler is equivalent to using the option -source 1.3 on the command-line.

```
>javac -speed 1.3 Speed.java
Speed.java:14: warning: as of release 1.4, assert is a keyword, and may not be used
as an identifier
        assert distance >= 0.0;                                 // (2)
        ^
Speed.java:15: ';' expected
        assert distance >= 0.0;                                 // (2)
             ^
```

```
...
9 errors
3 warnings
```

The compiler will reject assert statements. It will also warn about the use of the keyword assert as an identifier. In other words, source code that contains the keyword assert as an identifier will compile (barring any other errors), but it will also result in a *warning*. Compiling and running the Legacy class above gives the following results:

```
>javac -source 1.3 Legacy.java
Legacy.java:4: as of release 1.4, assert is a keyword, and may not be used as an
 identifier
        int assert = 2003;
            ^
Legacy.java:5: as of release 1.4, assert is a keyword, and may not be used as an
 identifier
        System.out.println("The year is: " + assert);
                                              ^
2 warnings
>java Legacy
The year is: 2003
```

Runtime Enabling and Disabling of Assertions

Enabling assertions means they will be executed at runtime. By default, assertions are disabled. Their execution is then effectively equivalent to empty statements. This means that disabled assertions carry an insignificant performance penalty, although they add storage overhead to the byte code of a class. Typically, assertions are enabled during development and left disabled once the program is deployed.

Two command switches are provided by the java tool to enable and disable assertions with various granularities. The switch -enableassertions, or its short form -ea, enables assertions, and the switch -disableassertions, or its short form -da, disables assertions at various granularities. The granularities that can be specified are shown in Table 5.2.

Table 5.2 *Granularities for Enabling and Disabling Assertions at Runtime*

Argument	Granularity
-ea -da	Applies to all non-system classes.
-ea:*<package name>*... -da:*<package name>*...	Applies to the named package and its subpackages.
-ea:... -da:...	Applies to the unnamed package in the current working directory.
-ea:*<class name>* -da:*<class name>*	Applies to the named class.

Assertion Execution for All Non-system Classes

The -ea option means that *all non-system* classes loaded during the execution of the program have their assertions enabled. A *system class* is a class that is in the Java platform libraries. For example, classes in the java.* packages are system classes. A system class is loaded directly by the JVM.

Note that class files not compiled with a J2SE 1.4-compatible compiler are not affected, whether assertions are enabled or disabled. Also, once a class has been loaded and initialized at runtime, its assertion status cannot be changed.

Assuming that the file Speed.java has been compiled with the -source 1.4 option, all assertions in non-system classes required for execution (of which Speed class is one) can be enabled, and the program run as follows:

```
>java -ea Speed
java.lang.AssertionError
        at Speed.calcSpeed(Speed.java:14)
        at Speed.main(Speed.java:6)
Exception in thread "main"
```

Since the distance is negative in line (1a), the assertion in line (2) fails in Example 5.17. An AssertionError is thrown, which is propagated, being finally caught by the default exception handler and resulting in the stack trace being printed on the terminal.

All assertions (in all non-system classes) can be disabled during the execution of the Speed class.

```
>java -da Speed
Speed (km/h): -4.0
```

In this case, this is effectively equivalent to running the program with neither the -ea nor the -da options.

```
>java Speed
Speed (km/h): -4.0
```

If we comment-out line (1a) and uncomment line (1b) in Example 5.17 and run the program with the options enabled, we get the following behavior from the program.

```
>java -ea Speed
java.lang.AssertionError: Time is not a positive value: -3.0
        at Speed.calcSpeed(Speed.java:15)
        at Speed.main(Speed.java:7)
Exception in thread "main"
```

We see that the value of the *<message expression>* in the augmented assertion in line (3) is written on the terminal, together with the stack trace, because this assertion failed. The augmented form is recommended, as it allows a detailed error message to be included in reporting the assertion failure.

Assertion Execution at the Package Level

Assume that we have a program called `Trickster` in the unnamed package, that uses the package hierarchy for the `wizard` package shown in Figure 4.3 on page 127.

The following command-line will only enable assertions for all classes in the package `wizard.pandorasBox` and its subpackage `wizard.pandorasBox.artifacts`. The assertions in the class `Trickster` are not enabled.

```
>java -ea:wizard.pandorasBox... Trickster
```

Without the `...` notation, the package name will be interpreted as a class name. Non-existent package names specified in the command line are silently accepted, but simply have no consequences under execution.

The following command-line will only enable assertions in the unnamed package, and, thereby, the assertions in the class `Trickster` since this class resides in the unnamed package.

```
>java -ea:... Trickster
```

Note that the package switch applies to the package specified and all its subpackages, recursively.

Assertion Execution at the Class Level

The following command line will only enable assertions in the `Trickster` class.

```
>java -ea:Trickster Trickster
```

The following command line will only enable assertions in the named class `wizard.pandorasBox.artifacts.Ailment` and no other class.

```
>java -ea:wizard.pandorasBox.artifacts.Ailment Trickster
```

A java command can contain multiple instances of the switches, each specifying its own granularity. The switches are then processed in order of their specification from left to right, before any classes are loaded. The latter switches take priority over former switches. This allows a fine-grained control of what assertions are enabled at runtime. The following command line will enable assertions for all classes in the package `wizard.pandorasBox` and its subpackage `wizard.pandorasBox.artifacts`, but disable them in the class `wizard.pandorasBox.artifacts.Ailment`.

```
>java -ea:wizard.pandorasBox... -da:wizard.pandorasBox.artifacts.Ailment Trickster
```

The following switches all enable assertions in the class `wizard.spells.Baldness`.

```
>java -ea                             Trickster
>java -ea:wizard...                   Trickster
>java -ea:wizard.spells...            Trickster
>java -ea:wizard.spells.Baldness      Trickster
```

It is worth noting that inheritance (see Section 6.1, p. 226) has no affect on the execution of assertions. Assertions are enabled or disabled on per-class basis. Whether assertions in the superclass will be executed through code inherited by the subclass, depends entirely on the superclass. In the following command line, assertions from the superclass wizard.pandorasBox.artifacts.Ailment will not be executed, although assertions for the subclass wizard.spells.Baldness are enabled:

```
>java -ea -da:wizard.pandorasBox.artifacts.Ailment Trickster
```

Assertion Execution for All System Classes

In order to enable or disable assertions in *all system classes*, we can use the switches shown in Table 5.3. Enabling assertions in system classes can be useful to shed light on internal errors reported by the JVM. In the following command line, the first switch will enable assertions for all system classes. The second switch will enable assertions in the package wizard and its subpackages wizard.pandorasBox, wizard.pandorasBox.artifacts and wizard.spells, but the third switch will disable them in the package wizard.pandorasBox.artifacts.

```
>java -esa -ea:wizard... -da:wizard.pandorasBox.artifacts... Trickster
```

Table 5.3   *Enabling and Disabling Assertions in All System Classes at Runtime*

Option	Short Form	Description
-enablesystemassertions	-esa	Enable assertions in *all* system classes.
-disablesystemassertions	-dsa	Disable assertions in *all* system classes.

Using Assertions

Assertions should have no side effects that can produce adverse behavior in the code, whether enabled or not. The assertion facility is a defensive mechanism, meaning that it should only be used to test the code, and should not be employed after the code is delivered. The program should exhibit the same behavior whether assertions are enabled or disabled. The program should not rely on any computations done within an assertion statement. With assertions enabled, the following statement would be executed, but if assertions were disabled, it could have dire consequences.

```
assert reactor.controlCoreTemperature();
```

Assertions should also not be used to validate information supplied by a client. A typical example is argument checking in public methods. Argument checking is part of such a method's contract, which could be violated if the assertions were disabled. Another drawback is that assertion failures can only provide limited information, in the form of an AssertionError, about the cause of any failure. Appropriate argument checking can provide more suitable information about erroneous arguments, in the form of specific exceptions such as IllegalArgumentException, IndexOutOfBoundsException, or NullPointerException.

The rest of this section illustrates useful idioms that employ assertions.

Internal Invariants

Very often assumptions about the program are documented as comments in the code. The following code makes the assumption in line (1) that variable `status` must be negative for the `else` clause to be executed.

```
int status = ref1.compareTo(ref2);
if (status == 0) {
    ...
} else if (status > 0) {
    ...
} else { // (1) status must be negative.
    ...
}
```

This assumption is an *internal invariant* and can be verified using an assertion, as shown in line (2) below.

```
int status = ref1.compareTo(ref2);
if (status == 0) {
    ...
} else if (status > 0) {
    ...
} else {
    assert status < 0 : status; // (2)
    ...
}
```

Often an alternative action is chosen, based on a value that is guaranteed to be one of a small set of predefined values. A `switch` statement with no `default` clause is a typical example. The value of the `switch` expression is guaranteed to be one of the case labels and the `default` case is omitted, as the following code shows.

```
switch (trinityMember) {
    case Housefather:
        ...
        break;
    case THE_SON:
        ...
        break;
    case THE_HOLY_GHOST:
        ...
        break;
}
```

A `default` clause that executes an assertion can be used to formulate this invariant.

```
    default:
        assert false : trinityMember;
```

If assertions are enabled, an `AssertionError` will signal the failure in case the trinity no longer holds.

However, the previous code causes a compile-time error in a non-void method if all case labels return a value and no return statement follows the switch statement.

```
switch (trinityMember) {
    case THE_FATHER:
        return psalm101;
    case THE_SON:
        return psalm102;
    case THE_HOLY_GHOST:
        return psalm103;
    default:
        assert false: trinityMember;
}
return psalm100;          // (3) Compile time error if commented out.
```

Without line (3) and with assertions disabled, the method could return without a value, violating the fact that it is a non-void method. Explicitly throwing an AssertionError rather than using an assert statement in the default clause, would be a better option in this case.

```
default:
    throw new AssertionError(trinityMember);
```

Control Flow Invariants

Control flow invariants can be used to test assumptions about the flow of control in the program. The following idiom can be employed to explicitly test that certain locations in the code will never be reached.

```
assert false : "This line should never be reached.";
```

If program control does reach this statement, assertion failure will detect it.

In the following code, the assumption is that execution never reaches the end of the method declaration indicated by line (1).

```
private void securityMonitor() {
    // ...
    while (alwaysOnDuty) {
        // ...
        if (needMaintenance)
            return;
        // ...
    }
    // (1) This line should never be reached.
}
```

The previous assertion can be inserted after the comment at line (1) to check the assumption.

Care should be taken in using this idiom, as the compiler can flag the assert statement at this location as being unreachable. For example, if the compiler can deduce that the while condition will always be true, it will flag the assert statement as being unreachable.

Preconditions and Postconditions

The assertion facility can be used to practice a limited form of *programming-by-contract*. For example, the assertion facility can be used to check that methods comply with their contract.

Preconditions define assumptions for the proper execution of a method when it is invoked. As discussed earlier, assertions should not be used to check arguments in public methods. For non-public methods, preconditions can be checked at the start of method execution.

```
private void adjustReactorThroughput(int increment) {
    // Precondition:
    assert isValid(increment) : "Throughput increment invalid.";
    // Proceed with the adjustment.
    // ...
}
```

Section 9.4 (p. 359) provides an example of a *lock-status* precondition in a non-synchronized method, where an assertion is used to check whether the current thread holds a lock on a certain object.

Postconditions define assumptions about the successful completion of a method. Postconditions in any method can be checked by assertions executed just before returning from the method. For example, if the method adjustReactorThroughPut() guarantees that the reactor core is in a stable state after its completion, we can check this postcondition using an assertion.

```
private void adjustReactorThroughput(int increment) {
    // Precondition:
    assert isValid(increment) : "Throughput increment invalid.";
    // Proceed with the adjustment.
    // ...
    // Postcondition -- the last action performed before returning.
    assert isCoreStable() : "Reactor core not stable.";
}
```

Section 7.4 (p. 302) provides an example using a *local class* where data can be saved before doing a computation, so that it can later be used to check a postcondition.

Other Uses

If minimizing the size of the class file is crucial, then the following conditional compilation idiom should be used to insert assertions in the source code:

```
final static boolean COMPILE_ASSERTS = false;
...
if (COMPILE_ASSERTS)
    assert whatEverYouWant;        // Not compiled if COMPILE_ASSERTS is false.
...
```

It is possible to enforce that a class be loaded and initialized only if its assertions are enabled. The idiom for this purpose uses a *static initializer* (see Section 8.2, p. 331).

```
static {  // Static initializer
    boolean assertsAreEnabled = false;   // (1)
    assert assertsAreEnabled = true;     // (2) utilizing side effect
    if (!assertsAreEnabled)              // (3)
        throw new AssertionError("Enable assertions!");
}
```

Line (1) sets the local variable assertsAreEnabled to false. If assertions are enabled, line (2) is executed. The assignment operator sets the variable assertsAreEnabled to true as a side effect of evaluating the boolean expression that has the value true. The assertion in line (2) is, of course, true. No exception is thrown by the if statement in line (3). However, if assertions are disabled, line (2) is never executed. As the variable assertsAreEnabled is false, the if statement in line (3) throws an exception. The static initializer is placed first in the class declaration, so that it is executed first during class initialization.

Review Questions

5.24 Assuming assertions are enabled, which of these assertion statements will throw an error?

Select the two correct answers.

(a) assert true : true;
(b) assert true : false;
(c) assert false : true;
(d) assert false : false;

5.25 Which of the following are valid runtime options?

Select the two correct answers.

(a) -ae
(b) -enableassertions
(c) -source 1.4
(d) -disablesystemassertions
(e) -dea

5.26 What is the class name of the exception thrown by an assertion statement?

Select the one correct answer.

(a) Depends on the assertion statement.
(b) FailedAssertion
(c) AssertionException
(d) RuntimeException
(e) AssertionError
(f) Error

5.27   What can cause an assertion statement to be ignored?

Select the one correct answer.

(a) Nothing.
(b) Using appropriate compiler options.
(c) Using appropriate runtime options.
(d) Using both appropriate compiler and runtime options.

5.28   Given the following method, which statements will throw an exception, assuming assertions are enabled?

```
static int inv(int value) {
    assert value > -50 : value < 100;
    return 100/value;
}
```

Select the two correct answers.

(a) `inv(-50);`
(b) `inv(0);`
(c) `inv(50);`
(d) `inv(100);`
(e) `inv(150);`

5.29   Which runtime options would cause assertions to be enabled for the class org.example.ttp.Bottle?

Select the two correct answers.

(a) `-ea`
(b) `-ea:Bottle`
(c) `-ea:org.example`
(d) `-ea:org...`
(e) `-enableexceptions:org.example.ttp.Bottle`
(f) `-ea:org.example.ttp`

5.30   What will be the result of compiling and running the following code with assertions enabled?

```
public class TernaryAssertion {
    public static void assertBounds(int low, int high, int value) {
        assert ( value > low ? value < high : false )
            : (value < high ? "too low" : "too high" );
    }
    public static void main(String[] args) {
        assertBounds(100, 200, 150);
    }
}
```

Select the one correct answer.

(a) The compilation fails because the method name assertBounds cannot begin with the keyword assert.

(b) The compilation fails because the assert statement is invalid.

(c) The compilation succeeds and the program runs without errors.

(d) The compilation succeeds and an AssertionError with the error message "too low" is thrown.

(e) The compilation succeeds and an AssertionError with the error message "too high" is thrown.

5.31 Which statements are true about the AssertionError class?

Select the two correct answers.
(a) It is a checked exception.
(b) It has a method named toString().
(c) It has a method named getErrorMessage().
(d) It can be caught by a try-catch construct.

5.32 Which of these classes is the direct superclass of AssertionError?

Select the one correct answer.
(a) Object
(b) Throwable
(c) Exception
(d) Error
(e) RuntimeError

5.33 Given the following command, which classes would have assertions enabled?

```
java -ea -da:com... net.example.LaunchTranslator
```

Select the two correct answers.
(a) com.example.Translator
(b) java.lang.String
(c) dot.com.Boom
(d) net.example.LaunchTranslator
(e) java.lang.AssertionError

 Chapter Summary

The following information was included in this chapter:

• explanation of the selection statements: if, if-else, switch

• explanation of the iteration statements: for, while, do-while

• explanation of the transfer statements: break, continue, return

- discussion of exception handling and exception classes in the core APIs
- defining new exception types
- explanation of the try-catch-finally construct and control flow paths through the construct
- throwing explicit exceptions with the throw statement
- using the throws clause to specify checked exceptions
- explanation of the assert statement
- using, compiling, and executing assertions

 Programming Exercises

5.1   Create different versions of a program that finds all the primes below 100. Create one version that uses only the for loop (i.e., no while or do-while). Create another version that uses only the while loop.

5.2   Here is a skeleton of a system for simulating a nuclear power plant. Implement the methods in the class named Control. Modify the method declarations if necessary. The Javadoc comments for each method give a description of what the implementation should do. Some of the methods in the other classes have unspecified implementations. Assume that these methods have been properly implemented and provide hooks to the rest of the system.

```
/** A PowerPlant with a reactor core. */
public class PowerPlant {
    /** Each power plant has a reactor core. This has package
        accessibility so that the Control class that is defined in
        the same package can access it. */
    Reactor core;

    /** Initializes the power plant, creates a reactor core. */
    PowerPlant() {
        core = new Reactor();
    }

    /** Sound the alarm to evacuate the power plant. */
    public void soundEvacuateAlarm() {
        // ... implementation unspecified ...
    }

    /** Get the level of reactor output that is most desirable at this time.
        (Units are unspecified.) */
    public int getOptimalThroughput() {
        // ... implementation unspecified ...
        return 0;
    }

    /** The main entry point of the program: sets up a PowerPlant
        object and a Control object and lets the Control object run the
        power plant. */
```

```java
        public static void main(String[] args) {
            PowerPlant plant = new PowerPlant();
            Control ctrl = new Control(plant);
            ctrl.runSystem();
        }
    }

/** A reactor core that has a throughput that can be either decreased or
    increased. */
class Reactor {
    /** Get the current throughput of the reactor. (Units are unspecified.) */
    public int getThroughput() {
        // ... implementation unspecified ...
        return 0;
    }

    /** @returns true if the reactor status is critical, false otherwise. */
    public boolean isCritical() {
        // ... implementation unspecified ...
        return false;
    }

    /** Ask the reactor to increase throughput. */
    void increaseThroughput() throws ReactorCritical {
        // ... implementation unspecified ...
    }

    /** Ask the reactor to decrease throughput. */
    void decreaseThroughput() {
        // ... implementation unspecified ...
    }
}

/** This exception class should be used to report that the reactor status is
    critical. */
class ReactorCritical extends Exception {}

/** A controller that will manage the power plant and make sure that the reactor
    runs with optimal throughput. */
class Control {
    PowerPlant thePlant;

    public Control(PowerPlant p) {
        thePlant = p;
    }

    /** Run the power plant by continuously monitoring the
        optimalThroughput and the actual throughput of the reactor. If
        the throughputs differ by more than 10 units, adjust the reactor
        throughput. If the reactor status becomes critical, the evacuate alarm is
        sounded and the reactor is shut down.
        <p>The runSystem() method can handle the reactor core directly
        but calls methods needAdjustment(), adjustThroughput(), and shutdown()
        instead. */
    public void runSystem() {
        // ... provide implementation here ...
    }
```

```java
/** Reports whether the throughput of the reactor needs adjusting.
    This method should also monitor and report if the reactor status becomes
    critical.
    @return true if the optimal and actual throughput values
    differ by more than 10 units. */
public boolean needAdjustment() {
    // ... provide implementation here ...
}

/** Adjust the throughput of the reactor by calling increaseThroughput() and
    decreaseThroughput() methods until the actual throughput is within 10
    units of the target throughput. */
public void adjustThroughput(int target) {
    // ... provide implementation here ...
}

/** Shut down the reactor by lowering the throughput to 0. */
public void shutdown() {
    // ... provide implementation here ...
}
}
```

Object-oriented Programming

6

- State the benefits of encapsulation in object-oriented design and write code that implements tightly encapsulated classes and the relationships *is-a* and *has-a*.
- Write code to invoke overridden or overloaded methods and parental or overloaded constructors; describe the effect of invoking these methods.
- Write code to construct instances of any concrete class, including normal top-level classes and nested classes.
  - *For nested classes, see Chapter 7.*

- Understand the concepts single implementation inheritance, multiple interface inheritance, subtype-supertype relationship, and their implications for object-oriented programming (OOP).
- Understand constructor chaining involving this() and super() constructs.
- State conversion rules for assigning, casting, and passing references.
- Determine at runtime if an object is an instance of a specified reference type (or of this type's subtypes), using the instanceof operator.
- Understand polymorphism and dynamic method lookup.

6.1 Single Implementation Inheritance

One of the fundamental mechanisms for code reuse in OOP, is *inheritance*. It allows new classes to be derived from an existing class. The new class (a.k.a. *subclass, subtype, derived class, child class*) can inherit members from the old class (a.k.a. *superclass, supertype, base class, parent class*). The subclass can add new behavior and properties, and under certain circumstances, modify its inherited behavior.

In Java, *implementation inheritance* is achieved by extending classes (i.e., adding new fields and methods) and modifying inherited members (see Section 6.2, p. 233). Inheritance of members is closely tied to their declared accessibility. If a superclass member is accessible by its simple name in the subclass (without the use of any extra syntax like super), then that member is considered inherited. This means that private, overridden, and hidden members of the superclass are *not* inherited (see Section 6.2, p. 233). Inheritance should not be confused with the *existence* of such members in the state of a subclass object (see Example 6.1).

The superclass is specified using the extends clause in the header of the subclass declaration. The subclass only specifies the additional new and modified members in its class body. The rest of its declaration is made up of its inherited members. If no extends clause is specified in the header of a class declaration, then the class implicitly inherits from the java.lang.Object class. This implicit inheritance is assumed in the declaration of the Light class at (1) in Example 6.1. Also in Example 6.1, the subclass TubeLight at (2) explicitly uses the extends clause and only specifies additional members to what it already inherits from the superclass Light (which, in turn, inherits from the Object class). Members of the superclass Light that are accessible by their simple names in the subclass TubeLight, are inherited by the subclass.

Private members of the superclass are not inherited by the subclass and can only be indirectly accessed. The private field indicator of the superclass Light is not inherited, but exists in the subclass object and is indirectly accessible.

Using appropriate accessibility modifiers, the superclass can limit which members can be accessed directly and, thereby, inherited by its subclasses (see Section 4.9, p. 137). As shown in Example 6.1, the subclass can use the inherited members as if they were declared in its own class body. This is not the case for members that are declared private in the superclass. Members that have package accessibility in the superclass are also not inherited by subclasses in other packages, as these members are only accessible by their simple names in subclasses within the same package as the superclass.

Since constructors (see Section 6.3, p. 243) and initializer blocks (see Section 8.2, p. 331) are not members of a class, they are not inherited by a subclass.

Example 6.1   *Extending Classes: Inheritance and Accessibility*

```
class Light {                      // (1)
    // Instance fields
             int      noOfWatts;   // wattage
    private  boolean indicator;    // on or off
    protected String  location;    // placement

    // Static fields
    private static int counter;        // no. of Light objects created

    // Constructor
    Light() {
        noOfWatts = 50;
        indicator = true;
        location  = "X";
        counter++;
    }

    // Instance methods
    public  void    switchOn()  { indicator = true; }
    public  void    switchOff() { indicator = false; }
    public  boolean isOn()      { return indicator; }
    private void    printLocation() {
        System.out.println("Location: " + location);
    }

    // Static methods
    public static void writeCount() {
        System.out.println("Number of lights: " + counter);
    }
    //...
}

class TubeLight extends Light {     // (2) Subclass uses the extends clause.
    // Instance fields
    private int tubeLength = 54;
    private int colorNo    = 10;

    // Instance methods
    public int getTubeLength() { return tubeLength; }

    public void printInfo() {
        System.out.println("Tube length: "  + getTubeLength());
        System.out.println("Color number: " + colorNo);
        System.out.println("Wattage: "       + noOfWatts); // Inherited.
    //  System.out.println("Indicator: "     + indicator); // Not Inherited.
        System.out.println("Indicator: "     + isOn());    // Inherited.
        System.out.println("Location: "      + location);  // Inherited.
    //  printLocation();                                   // Not Inherited.
    //  System.out.println("Counter: "     + counter);     // Not Inherited.
        writeCount();                                      // Inherited.
    }
    // ...
}
```

```
public class Utility {                    // (3)
    public static void main(String[] args) {
        new TubeLight().printInfo();
    }
}
```

Output from the program:

```
Tube length: 54
Color number: 10
Wattage: 50
Indicator: true
Location: X
Number of lights: 1
```

A class in Java can only extend one other class; that is, it can only have one immediate superclass. This kind of inheritance is sometimes called *single* or *linear implementation inheritance*. The name is appropriate, as the subclass inherits the *implementations* of its superclass members. The inheritance relationship can be depicted as an *inheritance hierarchy* (also called *class hierarchy*). Classes higher up in the hierarchy are more *generalized*, as they abstract the class behavior. Classes lower down in the hierarchy are more *specialized*, as they customize the inherited behavior by additional properties and behavior. Figure 6.1 illustrates the inheritance relationship between the class Light, which represents the more general abstraction, and its more specialized subclasses. The java.lang.Object class is always at the top of any Java inheritance hierarchy, as all classes, with the exception of the Object class itself, inherit (either directly or indirectly) from this class.

Figure 6.1 *Inheritance Hierarchy*

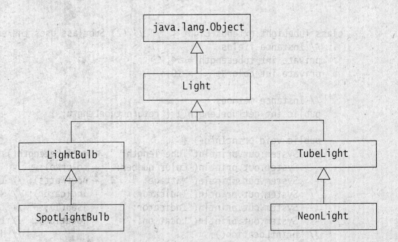

Inheritance defines the relationship *is-a* (also called the *superclass–subclass* relationship) between a superclass and its subclasses. This means that an object of a subclass can be used wherever an object of the superclass can be used. This is often employed as a litmus test for using inheritance. It has particular consequences on how objects can be used. An object of the TubeLight class can be used wherever an object of the superclass Light can be used. An object of the TubeLight class *is-an* object of the superclass Light. The inheritance relationship is transitive: if class B extends class A, then a class C, which extends class B, will also inherit from class A via class B. An object of the SpotLightBulb class *is-a* object of the class Light. The *is-a* relationship does not hold between peer classes: an object of the LightBulb class is not an object of the class TubeLight and vice versa.

Whereas inheritance defines the relationship *is-a* between a superclass and its subclasses, *aggregation* defines the relationship *has-a* (a.k.a. *whole–part* relationship) between an instance of a class and its constituents (a.k.a. *parts*). An instance of class Light *has* the following parts: a field to store its wattage (noOfWatts), a field to store whether it is on or off (indicator), and a String object to store its location (denoted by the field reference location). In Java, a composite object cannot contain other objects. It can only have *references* to its constituent objects. This relationship defines an *aggregation hierarchy* that embodies the *has-a* relationship. Constituent objects can be shared between objects and their lifetimes can be independent of the lifetime of the composite object. Inheritance and aggregation are compared in Section 6.8.

Object-oriented Programming Concepts

The example in this section illustrates basic OOP concepts, and subsequent sections in this chapter will elaborate on the concepts introduced here.

Figure 6.2 shows the inheritance relationship between the class String and its superclass Object. A client that uses a String object is defined in Example 6.2. During the execution of the main() method, the String object created at (1) is denoted by two references: stringRef of the subclass String and objRef of the superclass Object. Walking through the code for the main() method reveals salient features of OOP.

Figure 6.2   *Inheritance Relationship between* String *and* Object *Classes*

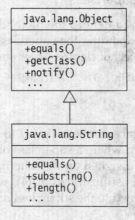

Example 6.2 *Illustrating Inheritance*

```
// String class is a subclass of Object class
class Client {
    public static void main(String[] args) {
        String stringRef = new String("Java");                      // (1)

        System.out.println("(2): " + stringRef.getClass());         // (2)
        System.out.println("(3): " + stringRef.length());           // (3)
        Object objRef = stringRef;                                  // (4)
//      System.out.println("(5): " + objRef.length());              // (5) Not OK.
        System.out.println("(6): " + objRef.equals("Java"));        // (6)
        System.out.println("(7): " + objRef.getClass());            // (7)

        stringRef = (String) objRef;                                // (8)
        System.out.println("(9): " + stringRef.equals("C++"));      // (9)
    }
}
```

Output from the program:

```
(2): class java.lang.String
(3): 4
(6): true
(7): class java.lang.String
(9): false
```

Inheriting from the Superclass

The subclass String inherits the method getClass() from the superclass Object. A client of the String class can directly invoke this inherited method on objects of the String class in the same way as if the method had been defined in the String class itself. In Example 6.2, this is illustrated at (2).

```
System.out.println("(2): " + stringRef.getClass());    // (2)
```

Extending the Superclass

The subclass String defines the method length(), which is not in the superclass Object, thereby extending the superclass. In Example 6.2, invocation of this new method on an object of class String is shown at (3).

```
System.out.println("(3): " + stringRef.length());      // (3)
```

Upcasting

A subclass reference can be assigned to a superclass reference because a subclass object can be used where a superclass object can be used. This is called *upcasting*, as references are assigned up the inheritance hierarchy (see Section 6.6, p. 260). In Example 6.2, this is illustrated at (4), where the value of the subclass reference stringRef is assigned to the superclass reference objRef.

```
Object objRef = stringRef;                               // (4)
```

Both references denote the same String object after the assignment. One might be tempted to invoke methods exclusive to the String subclass via the superclass reference objRef, as illustrated at (5).

```
System.out.println("(5): " + objRef.length());          // (5) Not OK.
```

However, this will not work as the compiler does not know what object the reference objRef is denoting. It only knows the class of the reference. As the declaration of the Object class does not have a method called length(), this invocation of length() at (5) would be flagged as a compile-time error.

Method Overriding

In contrast to the situation at (5), the invocation of the equals() method at (6) using the superclass reference objRef is legal because the compiler can check that the Object class does define a method named equals.

```
System.out.println("(6): " + objRef.equals("Java"));    // (6)
```

Note that this method is redefined in the String class with the same signature (i.e., method name and parameters) and the same return type. This is called *method overriding* (see Section 6.2, p. 233).

Polymorphism and Dynamic Method Binding

The invocation of the equals() method at (6), using the superclass reference objRef, does not necessarily invoke the equals() method from the Object class at runtime. The method invoked is dependent on the type of the actual object denoted by the reference at runtime. The actual method is determined by *dynamic method lookup*. The ability of a superclass reference to denote objects of its own class and its subclasses at runtime is called *polymorphism*. Section 6.7 provides a discussion on how polymorphism and dynamic method lookup can be employed to achieve code reuse.

Under normal program execution, the reference objRef will refer to an object of the String class at (6), resulting in the equals() method from the String class being executed, and not the one in the Object class.

The situation at (7), where the getClass() method is invoked using the superclass reference objRef, is allowed at compile time because the Object class defines a method named getClass.

```
System.out.println("(7): " + objRef.getClass());        // (7)
```

In this case, under normal program execution, the reference objRef will refer to an object of the String class at (7). Dynamic method lookup determines which method implementation binds to the method signature getClass(). Since no getClass() method is defined in the String class, the method getClass() inherited from the Object class is thus executed.

Downcasting

Casting the value of a superclass reference to a subclass type is called *downcasting* (see Section 6.6, p. 260). This is illustrated in Example 6.2 by assigning references down the inheritance hierarchy, which requires explicit casting.

```
stringRef = (String) objRef;                                    // (8)
System.out.println("(9): " + stringRef.equals("C++"));  // (9)
```

At (8), the source reference objRef is of type Object, which is the superclass of the class of the destination reference stringRef. If the reference objRef actually denoted an object of class String at runtime, the cast would convert it to the proper subclass type, so that the assignment to the reference stringRef would be legal at (8). The reference stringRef could then be used to invoke the equals() method on this String object, as at (9). Not surprisingly, the equals() method from the String class would be executed.

The compiler verifies that an inheritance relationship exists between the source reference type and the reference type specified in the cast. However, the cast can be invalid at runtime. If, at runtime, the reference objRef denotes an object of class Object or some unrelated subclass of class Object, then obviously casting the reference value to that of subclass String would be illegal. In such a case, a ClassCast-Exception would be thrown at runtime. The instanceof operator (see Section 6.6, p. 264) can be used to determine the runtime type of an object before any cast is applied.

 Review Questions

6.1 Which statements are true?

Select the two correct answers.

(a) In Java the extends clause is used to specify inheritance.
(b) The subclass of a non-abstract class can be declared abstract.
(c) All the members of the superclass are inherited by the subclass.
(d) A final class can be abstract.
(e) A class in which all the members are declared private, cannot be declared public.

6.2 Which statements are true?

Select the two correct answers.

(a) Inheritance defines a *has-a* relationship between a superclass and its subclasses.
(b) Every Java object has a public method named equals.
(c) Every Java object has a public method named length.
(d) A class can extend any number of other classes.
(e) A non-final class can be extended by any number of classes.

6.2 Overriding and Hiding Members

Instance Method Overriding

Under certain circumstances, a subclass may *override* non-static methods defined in the superclass that would otherwise be inherited. When the method is invoked on an object of the subclass, it is the new method implementation in the subclass that is executed. The overridden method in the superclass is not inherited by the subclass, and the new method in the subclass must uphold the following rules of method overriding:

- The new method definition must have the same *method signature* (i.e., method name and parameters) and the same return type.

  Whether parameters in the overriding method should be `final` is at the discretion of the subclass (see Section 3.22, p. 94). A method's signature does not encompass the `final` modifier of parameters, only their types and order.

- The new method definition cannot *narrow* the accessibility of the method, but it can *widen* it (see Section 4.9, p. 137).

- The new method definition can only specify all or none, or a subset of the exception classes (including their subclasses) specified in the throws clause of the overridden method in the superclass (see Section 5.9, p. 201).

These requirements also apply to interfaces, where a subinterface can override method prototypes from its superinterfaces (see Section 6.4, p. 251).

In Example 6.3, the new definition of the `getBill()` method at (5) in the subclass `TubeLight` has the same signature and the same return type as the method at (2) in the superclass `Light`. The new definition specifies a subset of the exceptions (`ZeroHoursException`) thrown by the overridden method (exception class `Invalid HoursException` is a superclass of `NegativeHoursException` and `ZeroHoursException`). The new definition also widens the accessibility (`public`) from what it was in the overridden definition (`protected`). The overriding method also declares the parameter to be `final`. Invocation of the method `getBill()` on an object of subclass `Tube-Light` using references of the subclass and the superclass at (12) and (13) respectively, results in the new definition at (5) being executed. Invocation of the method `getBill()` on an object of superclass `Light` using a reference of the superclass at (14), results in the overridden definition at (2) being executed.

Example 6.3 *Overriding, Overloading, and Hiding*

```
// Exceptions
class InvalidHoursException extends Exception {}
class NegativeHoursException extends InvalidHoursException {}
class ZeroHoursException extends InvalidHoursException {}
```

```java
class Light {

    protected String billType = "Small bill";       // (1)

    protected double getBill(int noOfHours)
            throws InvalidHoursException {           // (2)
        if (noOfHours < 0)
            throw new NegativeHoursException();
        double smallAmount = 10.0,
               smallBill = smallAmount * noOfHours;
        System.out.println(billType + ": " + smallBill);
        return smallBill;
    }

    public static void printBillType() {            // (3)
        System.out.println("Small bill");
    }

}

class TubeLight extends Light {

    public static String billType = "Large bill"; // (4) Hiding static field.

    public double getBill(final int noOfHours)
            throws ZeroHoursException {      // (5) Overriding instance method.
        if (noOfHours == 0)
            throw new ZeroHoursException();
        double largeAmount = 100.0,
               largeBill = largeAmount * noOfHours;
        System.out.println(billType + ": " + largeBill);
        return largeBill;
    }

    public static void printBillType() {            // (6) Hiding static method.
        System.out.println(billType);
    }

    public double getBill() {                       // (7) Overloading method.
        System.out.println("No bill");
        return 0.0;
    }
}

public class Client {
    public static void main(String[] args)
            throws InvalidHoursException {           // (8)

        TubeLight tubeLight = new TubeLight();       // (9)
        Light     light1    = tubeLight;             // (10) Aliases.
        Light     light2    = new Light();           // (11)

        System.out.println("Invoke overridden instance method:");
        tubeLight.getBill(5);                        // (12) Invokes method at (5)
        light1.getBill(5);                           // (13) Invokes method at (5)
        light2.getBill(5);                           // (14) Invokes method at (2)
```

```
                    System.out.println("Access hidden field:");
                    System.out.println(tubeLight.billType);     // (15) Accesses field at (4)
                    System.out.println(light1.billType);        // (16) Accesses field at (1)
                    System.out.println(light2.billType);        // (17) Accesses field at (1)

                    System.out.println("Invoke hidden static method:");
                    tubeLight.printBillType();                  // (18) Invokes method at (6)
                    light1.printBillType();                     // (19) Invokes method at (3)
                    light2.printBillType();                     // (20) Invokes method at (3)

                    System.out.println("Invoke overloaded method:");
                    tubeLight.getBill();                        // (21) Invokes method at (7)
            }
    }
```

Output from the program:

```
Invoke overridden instance method:
Large bill: 500.0
Large bill: 500.0
Small bill: 50.0
Access hidden field:
Large bill
Small bill
Small bill
Invoke hidden static method:
Large bill
Small bill
Small bill
Invoke overloaded method:
No bill
```

A subclass must use the keyword super in order to invoke an overridden method in the superclass (see p. 238).

An instance method in a sublass cannot override a static method in the superclass. The compiler will flag this as an error. A static method is class-specific and not part of any object, while overriding methods are invoked on behalf of objects of the subclass. However, a static method in a subclass can *hide* a static method in the superclass (see below).

A final method cannot be overridden because the modifier final prevents method overriding. An attempt to override a final method will result in a compile-time error. However, an abstract method requires the non-abstract subclasses to override the method, in order to provide an implementation.

Accessibility modifier private for a method means that the method is not accessible outside the class in which it is defined; therefore, a subclass cannot override it. However, a subclass can give its own definition of such a method, which may have the same signature as the method in its superclass.

Field Hiding

A subclass cannot override fields of the superclass, but it can *hide* them. The subclass can define fields with the same name as in the superclass. If this is the case, the fields in the superclass cannot be accessed in the subclass by their simple names; therefore, they are not inherited by the subclass. Code in the subclass can use the keyword super to access such members, including hidden fields. A client can use a reference of the *superclass* to access members that are hidden in the subclass, as explained below. Of course, if the hidden field is static, it can also be accessed by the superclass name.

The following distinction between invoking instance methods on an object and accessing fields of an object must be noted. When an instance method is invoked on an object using a reference, it is the *class of the current object* denoted by the reference, not the type of the reference, that determines which method implementation will be executed. In Example 6.3 at (12), (13), and (14), this is evident from invoking the overridden method getBill(): the method from the class corresponding to the current object is executed, regardless of the reference type. When a field of an object is accessed using a reference, it is the *type of the reference*, not the class of the current object denoted by the reference, that determines which field will actually be accessed. In Example 6.3 at (15), (16), and (17), this is evident from accessing the hidden field billType: the field accessed is declared in the class corresponding to the reference type, regardless of the object denoted by the reference.

In contrast to method overriding where an instance method cannot override a static method, there are no such restrictions on the hiding of fields. The field billType is static in the subclass, but not in the superclass. The type of the fields need not be the same either, it is only the field name that matters in the hiding of fields.

Static Method Hiding

A static method cannot override an inherited instance method, but it can *hide* a static method if the exact requirements for overriding instance methods are fulfilled. A hidden superclass static method is not inherited. The compiler will flag an error if the signatures are the same but the other requirements regarding return type, throws clause, and accessibility are not met. If the signatures are different, the method name is overloaded, not hidden.

The binding of a method call to a method implementation is done at compile time if the method is static or final (private methods are implicitly final). Example 6.3 illustrates invocation of static methods. Analogous to accessing fields, the method invoked in (18), (19), and (20) is determined by the *class* of the reference. In (18) the class type is TubeLight, therefore, the static method printBillType() at (6) in this class is invoked. In (19) and (20) the class type is Light and the hidden static method printBillType() at (3) in that class is invoked. This is borne out by the output from the program.

A hidden static method can, of course, be invoked by using the superclass name in the subclass declaration. Additionally, the keyword super can be used in non-static code in the subclass declaration to invoke hidden static methods (see p. 238).

Overriding vs. Overloading

Method overriding should not be confused with *method overloading* (see Section 4.3, p. 116). Method overriding requires the same method signature (name and parameters) and the same return type. Only non-final instance methods in the superclass that are directly accessible from the subclass are eligible for overriding. Overloading occurs when the method names are the same, but the parameter lists differ. Therefore, to overload methods, the parameters must differ in type, order, or number. As the return type is not a part of the signature, having different return types is not enough to overload methods.

A method can be overloaded in the class it is defined in or in a subclass of its class. Invoking an overridden method in the superclass from a subclass requires special syntax (e.g., the keyword super). This is not necessary for invoking an overloaded method in the superclass from a subclass. If the right kinds of arguments are passed in the method call occurring in the subclass, the overloaded method in the superclass will be invoked. In Example 6.3, the method getBill() at (2) in class Light is overridden in class TubeLight at (5) and overloaded at (7). When invoked at (21), the definition at (7) is executed.

Method Overloading Resolution

Example 6.4 illustrates how parameter resolution is done to choose the right implementation for an overloaded method. The method testIfOn() is overloaded at (1) and (2) in class OverloadResolution. The call client.testIfOn(tubeLight) at (3) *satisfies* the parameter lists in both the implementations given at (1) and (2), as the reference tubeLight, which denotes an object of class TubeLight, can also be assigned to a reference of its superclass Light. The *most specific* method, (2), is chosen, resulting in false being written on the terminal. The call client.testIfOn(light) at (4) only satisfies the parameter list in the implementation given at (1), resulting in true being written on the terminal.

Example 6.4   *Overloaded Method Resolution*

```
class Light { /* ... */ }

class TubeLight extends Light { /* ... */ }

public class OverloadResolution {
    boolean testIfOn(Light aLight)          { return true; }    // (1)
    boolean testIfOn(TubeLight aTubeLight) { return false; }   // (2)
```

```java
    public static void main(String[] args) {

        TubeLight tubeLight = new TubeLight();
        Light     light     = new Light();

        OverloadResolution client = new OverloadResolution();
        System.out.println(client.testIfOn(tubeLight));// (3) ==> method at (2)
        System.out.println(client.testIfOn(light));    // (4) ==> method at (1)

    }
}
```

Output from the program:

```
false
true
```

- -

Object Reference super

The this reference is available in non-static code and refers to the current object. When an instance method is invoked, the this reference denotes the object on which the method is called (see Section 4.3, p. 114). The keyword super can also be used in non-static code (e.g., in the body of an instance method), but only in a subclass, to access fields and invoke methods from the superclass (see Table 4.1, p.122). The keyword super provides a reference to the current object as an instance of its superclass. In method invocations with super, the method from the superclass is simply invoked regardless of the actual type of the object or whether the current class overrides the method. It is typically used to invoke methods that are overridden and to access members that are hidden in the subclass. Unlike the this keyword, the super keyword cannot be used as an ordinary reference. For example, it cannot be assigned to other references or cast to other reference types.

In Example 6.5, the method demonstrate() at (9) in class NeonLight makes use of the super keyword to access members higher up in its inheritance hierarchy. This is the case when the banner() method is invoked at (10). This method is defined at (4) in class Light and not in the immediate superclass of subclass NeonLight. The overridden method getBill() and its overloaded version at (6) and (8) in class TubeLight are invoked, using super at (12) and (11), respectively.

Class NeonLight is a subclass of class TubeLight, which is a subclass of class Light, which has a field named billType and a method named getBill defined at (1) and (2), respectively. One might be tempted to use the syntax super.super.getBill(20) in subclass NeonLight to invoke this method, but this is not a valid construct. One might also be tempted to cast the this reference to the class Light and try again as shown at (13). The output shows that the method getBill() at (6) in class TubeLight was executed, not the one from class Light. The reason is that a cast only changes the type of the reference (in this case to Light), not the class of the object (which is still NeonLight). Method invocation is determined by the class of the current object, resulting in the inherited method getBill() in class TubeLight being executed. There is no way to invoke the method getBill() in class Light from the subclass NeonLight.

At (14) the keyword super is used to access the field billType at (5) in class Tube-Light. At (15) the field billType from class Light is accessed successfully by casting the this reference, because it is the type of the reference that determines the field accessed. From non-static code in a subclass, it is possible to directly access fields in a class higher up the inheritance hierarchy, by casting the this reference. However, it is futile to cast the this reference to invoke instance methods in a class higher up the inheritance hierarchy, as illustrated above in the case of the overridden method getBill().

Finally, calls to static methods at (16) and (17) using super and this references, exhibit runtime behavior analagous to accessing fields as discussed earlier.

Example 6.5   *Using* super *Keyword*

```
// Exceptions
class InvalidHoursException extends Exception {}
class NegativeHoursException extends InvalidHoursException {}
class ZeroHoursException extends InvalidHoursException {}

class Light {

    protected String billType  = "Small bill";      // (1)

    protected double getBill(int noOfHours)
            throws InvalidHoursException {           // (2)
        if (noOfHours < 0)
            throw new NegativeHoursException();
        double smallAmount = 10.0,
            smallBill = smallAmount * noOfHours;
        System.out.println(billType + ": " + smallBill);
        return smallBill;
    }

    public static void printBillType() {            // (3)
        System.out.println("Small bill");
    }

    public void banner() {                          // (4)
        System.out.println("Let there be light!");
    }
}

class TubeLight extends Light {

    public static String billType = "Large bill";   // (5) Hiding static field.

    public double getBill(final int noOfHours)
            throws ZeroHoursException {              // (6) Overriding instance method.
        if (noOfHours == 0)
            throw new ZeroHoursException();
```

```
                    double largeAmount = 100.0,
                        largeBill = largeAmount * noOfHours;
                    System.out.println(billType + ": " + largeBill);
                    return largeBill;
            }

            public static void printBillType() {              // (7) Hiding static method.
                System.out.println(billType);
            }

            public double getBill() {                          // (8) Overloading method.
                System.out.println("No bill");
                return 0.0;
            }
        }

        class NeonLight extends TubeLight {
            // ...
            public void demonstrate()
                    throws InvalidHoursException {              // (9)

                super.banner();                                // (10) Invokes method at (4)
                super.getBill();                               // (11) Invokes method at (8)
                super.getBill(20);                             // (12) Invokes method at (6)
                ((Light) this).getBill(20);                    // (13) Invokes method at (6)
                System.out.println(super.billType);            // (14) Accesses field at (5)
                System.out.println(((Light) this).billType);   // (15) Accesses field at (1)
                super.printBillType();                         // (16) Invokes method at (7)
                ((Light) this).printBillType();                // (17) Invokes method at (3)
            }
        }

        public class Client {
            public static void main(String[] args)
                            throws InvalidHoursException {
                NeonLight neonRef = new NeonLight();
                neonRef.demonstrate();
            }
        }
```

Output from the program:

```
Let there be light!
No bill
Large bill: 2000.0
Large bill: 2000.0
Large bill
Small bill
Large bill
Small bill
```

Review Questions

6.3 Which statements are true?

Select the two correct answers.

(a) A subclass must define all the methods from the superclass.

(b) It is possible for a subclass to define a method with the same name and parameters as a method defined by the superclass.

(c) It is possible for a subclass to define a field with the same name as a field defined by the superclass.

(d) It is possible for two classes to be the superclass of each other.

6.4 Given the following classes and declarations, which statements are true?

```
// Classes
class Foo {
    private int i;
    public void f() { /* ... */ }
    public void g() { /* ... */ }
}

class Bar extends Foo {
    public int j;
    public void g() { /* ... */ }
}

// Declarations:
// ...
    Foo a = new Foo();
    Bar b = new Bar();
// ...
```

Select the three correct answers.

(a) The Bar class is a legal subclass of Foo.

(b) The statement b.f(); is legal.

(c) The statement a.j = 5; is legal.

(d) The statement a.g(); is legal.

(e) The statement b.i = 3; is legal.

6.5 Which statement is true?

Select the one correct answer.

(a) Private methods cannot be overridden in subclasses.

(b) A subclass can override any method in a superclass.

(c) An overriding method can declare that it throws more exceptions than the method it is overriding.

(d) The parameter list of an overriding method must be a subset of the parameter list of the method that it is overriding.

(e) The overriding method can have a different return type than the overridden method.

6.6 Given classes A, B, and C, where B extends A, and C extends B, and where all classes implement the instance method void doIt(). How can the doIt() method in A be called from an instance method in C?

Select the one correct answer.

(a) doIt();
(b) super.doIt();
(c) super.super.doIt();
(d) this.super.doIt();
(e) A.this.doIt();
(f) ((A) this).doIt();
(g) It is not possible.

6.7 What would be the result of attempting to compile and run the following code?

```java
// Filename: MyClass.java
public class MyClass {
    public static void main(String[] args) {
        C c = new C();
        System.out.println(c.max(13, 29));
    }
}

class A {
    int max(int x, int y) { if (x>y) return x; else return y; }
}

class B extends A{
    int max(int x, int y) { return super.max(y, x) - 10; }
}

class C extends B {
    int max(int x, int y) { return super.max(x+10, y+10); }
}
```

Select the one correct answer.

(a) The code will fail to compile because the max() method in B passes the arguments in the call super.max(y, x) in the wrong order.
(b) The code will fail to compile because a call to a max() method is ambiguous.
(c) The code will compile without errors and will print 13 when run.
(d) The code will compile without errors and will print 23 when run.
(e) The code will compile without errors and will print 29 when run.
(f) The code will compile without errors and will print 39 when run.

6.8 Given the following code, which is the simplest print statement that can be inserted into the print() method?

```java
// Filename: MyClass.java
public class MyClass extends MySuperclass {
    public static void main(String[] args) {
        MyClass object = new MyClass();
        object.print();
    }
```

```
            public void print() {
                // INSERT CODE HERE THAT WILL PRINT
                // THE "Hello, world!" STRING FROM THE Message
                // CLASS.
            }
        }

        class MySuperclass {
            Message msg = new Message();
        }

        class Message {
            // The message that should be printed:
            String text = "Hello, world!";
        }
```

Select the one correct answer.

(a) `System.out.println(text);`
(b) `System.out.println(Message.text);`
(c) `System.out.println(msg.text);`
(d) `System.out.println(object.msg.text);`
(e) `System.out.println(super.msg.text);`
(f) `System.out.println(object.super.msg.text);`

6.3 Chaining Constructors Using `this()` and `super()`

Constructors are discussed in Section 4.4 on page 117. Other uses of the keywords this and super can be found in Section 6.2 on page 233.

`this()` Constructor Call

Constructors cannot be inherited or overridden. They can be overloaded, but only in the same class. Since a constructor always has the same name as the class, each parameter list must be different when defining more than one constructor for a class. In Example 6.6, the class Light has three overloaded constructors. In the non-default constructor at (3), the this reference is used to access the fields shadowed by the parameters. In the main() method at (4), the appropriate constructor is invoked depending on the arguments in the constructor call, as illustrated by the program output.

Example 6.6   *Constructor Overloading*

```
        class Light {

            // Fields
            private int     noOfWatts;    // wattage
            private boolean indicator;    // on or off
            private String  location;     // placement
```

```java
    // Constructors
    Light() {                                    // (1) Explicit default constructor
        noOfWatts = 0;
        indicator = false;
        location  = "X";
        System.out.println("Returning from default constructor no. 1.");
    }
    Light(int watts, boolean onOffState) {                      // (2) Non-default
        noOfWatts = watts;
        indicator = onOffState;
        location  = "X";
        System.out.println("Returning from non-default constructor no. 2.");
    }
    Light(int noOfWatts, boolean indicator, String location) {  // (3) Non-default
        this.noOfWatts = noOfWatts;
        this.indicator = indicator;
        this.location  = location;
        System.out.println("Returning from non-default constructor no. 3.");
    }
}

public class DemoConstructorCall {
    public static void main(String[] args) {                        // (4)
        System.out.println("Creating Light object no. 1.");
        Light light1 = new Light();
        System.out.println("Creating Light object no. 2.");
        Light light2 = new Light(250, true);
        System.out.println("Creating Light object no. 3.");
        Light light3 = new Light(250, true, "attic");
    }
}
```

Output from the program:

```
Creating Light object no. 1.
Returning from default constructor no. 1.
Creating Light object no. 2.
Returning from non-default constructor no. 2.
Creating Light object no. 3.
Returning from non-default constructor no. 3.
```

Example 6.7 illustrates the use of the this() construct, which is used to implement *local chaining* of constructors in the class when an instance of the class is created. The first two constructors at (1) and (2) from Example 6.6 have been rewritten using the this() construct. The this() construct can be regarded as being locally overloaded, since its parameters (and hence its signature) can vary, as shown in the body of the constructors at (1) and (2). The this() call invokes the constructor with the corresponding parameter list. In the main() method at (4), the appropriate constructor is invoked depending on the arguments in the constructor call when each of the three Light objects are created. Calling the default constructor to create a Light object results in the second and third constructors being executed as well.

This is confirmed by the output from the program. In this case, the output shows that the third constructor completed first, followed by the second, and finally the default constructor that was called first. Bearing in mind the definition of the constructors, the constructors are invoked in the *reverse* order; that is, invocation of the default constructor immediately leads to invocation of the second constructor by the call this(0, false), and its invocation leads to the third constructor being called immediately by the call this(watt, ind, "X"), with the completion of the execution in the reverse order of their invocation. Similarly, calling the second constructor to create an instance of the Light class results in the third constructor being executed as well.

Java requires that any this() call must occur as the *first* statement in a constructor. The this() call can be followed by any other relevant code. This restriction is due to Java's handling of constructor invocation in the superclass when an object of the subclass is created. This mechanism is explained in the next subsection.

Example 6.7   this() *Constructor Call*

```java
class Light {
    // Fields
    private int     noOfWatts;
    private boolean indicator;
    private String  location;

    // Constructors
    Light() {                                          // (1) Explicit default constructor
        this(0, false);
        System.out.println("Returning from default constructor no. 1.");
    }
    Light(int watt, boolean ind) {                     // (2) Non-default
        this(watt, ind, "X");
        System.out.println("Returning from non-default constructor no. 2.");
    }
    Light(int noOfWatts, boolean indicator, String location) {   // (3) Non-default
        this.noOfWatts = noOfWatts;
        this.indicator = indicator;
        this.location  = location;
        System.out.println("Returning from non-default constructor no. 3.");
    }
}

public class DemoThisCall {
    public static void main(String[] args) {                        // (4)
        System.out.println("Creating Light object no. 1.");
        Light light1 = new Light();                                 // (5)
        System.out.println("Creating Light object no. 2.");
        Light light2 = new Light(250, true);                        // (6)
        System.out.println("Creating Light object no. 3.");
        Light light3 = new Light(250, true, "attic");               // (7)
    }
}
```

Output from the program:

```
Creating Light object no. 1.
Returning from non-default constructor no. 3.
Returning from non-default constructor no. 2.
Returning from default constructor no. 1.
Creating Light object no. 2.
Returning from non-default constructor no. 3.
Returning from non-default constructor no. 2.
Creating Light object no. 3.
Returning from non-default constructor no. 3.
```

super() Constructor Call

The super() construct is used in a subclass constructor to invoke a constructor in the *immediate* superclass. This allows the subclass to influence the initialization of its inherited state when an object of the subclass is created. A super() call in the constructor of a subclass will result in the execution of the relevant constructor from the superclass, based on the signature of the call. Since the superclass name is known in the subclass declaration, the superclass constructor invoked is determined by the signature of the parameter list.

A constructor in a subclass can access the class's inherited members directly (i.e., by their simple name). The keyword super can also be used in a subclass constructor to access inherited members via its superclass. One might be tempted to use the super keyword in a constructor to specify initial values of inherited fields. However, the super() construct provides a better solution, using superclass constructors to initialize the inherited state.

In Example 6.8, the non-default constructor at (3) of the class Light has a super() call (with no arguments) at (4). Although the constructor is not strictly necessary, as the compiler will insert one—as explained below—it is included for expositional purposes. The non-default constructor at (6) of class TubeLight has a super() call (with three arguments) at (7). This super() call will match the non-default constructor at (3) of superclass Light. This is evident from the program output.

Example 6.8 super() *Constructor Call*

```
class Light {
    // Fields
    private int     noOfWatts;
    private boolean indicator;
    private String  location;

    // Constructors
    Light() {                                // (1) Explicit default constructor
        this(0, false);
        System.out.println(
```

```
                    "Returning from default constructor no. 1 in class Light");
        }
        Light(int watt, boolean ind) {                          // (2) Non-default
            this(watt, ind, "X");
            System.out.println(
                "Returning from non-default constructor no. 2 in class Light");
        }
        Light(int noOfWatts, boolean indicator, String location) {  // (3) Non-default
            super();                                            // (4)
            this.noOfWatts = noOfWatts;
            this.indicator = indicator;
            this.location  = location;
            System.out.println(
                "Returning from non-default constructor no. 3 in class Light");
        }
    }
    class TubeLight extends Light {
        // Instance variables
        private int tubeLength;
        private int colorNo;

        TubeLight(int tubeLength, int colorNo) {                // (5) Non-default
            this(tubeLength, colorNo, 100, true, "Unknown");
            System.out.println(
                "Returning from non-default constructor no. 1 in class TubeLight");
        }

        TubeLight(int tubeLength, int colorNo, int noOfWatts,
                    boolean indicator, String location) {       // (6) Non-default
            super(noOfWatts, indicator, location);              // (7)
            this.tubeLength = tubeLength;
            this.colorNo    = colorNo;
            System.out.println(
                "Returning from non-default constructor no. 2 in class TubeLight");
        }
    }
    public class Chaining {
        public static void main(String[] args) {
            System.out.println("Creating a TubeLight object.");
            TubeLight tubeLightRef = new TubeLight(20, 5);      // (8)
        }
    }
```

Output from the program:

```
    Creating a TubeLight object.
    Returning from non-default constructor no. 3 in class Light
    Returning from non-default constructor no. 2 in class TubeLight
    Returning from non-default constructor no. 1 in class TubeLight
```

The super() construct has the same restrictions as the this() construct: if used, the super() call must occur as the *first* statement in a constructor, and it can only be used in a constructor declaration. This implies that this() and super() calls cannot both occur in the same constructor. The this() construct is used to *chain* constructors in the *same* class, and the constructor at the end of such a chain can invoke a superclass constructor using the super() construct. Just as the this() construct leads to chaining of constructors in the same class, the super() construct leads to chaining of subclass constructors to superclass constructors. This chaining behavior guarantees that all superclass constructors are called, starting with the constructor of the class being instantiated, all the way to the top of the inheritance hierarchy, which is always the Object class. Note that the body of the constructors is executed in the reverse order to the call order, as super() can only occur as the first statement in a constructor. This ensures that the constructor from the Object class is completed first, followed by the constructors in the other classes down to the class being instantiated in the inheritance hierarchy. This is called (subclass– superclass) *constructor chaining*. The output from Example 6.8 clearly illustrates this chain of events when an object of class TubeLight is created.

If a constructor at the end of a this()-chain (which may not be a chain at all if no this() call is invoked) does not have an explicit call to super(), then the call super() (without the parameters) is implicitly inserted to invoke the default constructor of the superclass. In other words, if a constructor has neither a this() nor a super() call as its first statement, then a super() call to the default constructor in the superclass is inserted. The code

```
class A {
    public A() {}
    // ...
}
class B extends A {
    // no constructors
    // ...
}
```

is equivalent to

```
class A {
    public A() { super(); }      // (1)
    // ...
}
class B extends A {
    public B() { super(); }      // (2)
    // ...
}
```

where the default constructors with calls to the default superclass constructor are inserted in the code.

If a class only defines non-default constructors (i.e., only constructors with parameters), then its subclasses cannot rely on the implicit super() call being inserted. This will be flagged as a compile-time error. The subclasses must then explicitly call a superclass constructor, using the super() construct with the right arguments.

```
class NeonLight extends TubeLight {
    // Field
    String sign;

    NeonLight() {                               // (1)
        super(10, 2, 100, true, "Roof-top");    // (2) Cannot be commented out.
        sign = "All will be revealed!";
    }
    // ...
}
```

The previous declaration of the subclass NeonLight provides a constructor at (1). The call at (2) of the constructor in the superclass TubeLight cannot be omitted. If it is omitted, any insertion of a super() call (with no arguments) in this constructor will not match any default constructor in the superclass TubeLight, as this superclass does not provide one. The superclass TubeLight only provides non-default constructors. The class NeonLight will not compile unless an explicit super() call (with valid arguments) is inserted at (2).

If the superclass provides non-default constructors only (i.e., does not have a default constructor), then this has implications for its subclasses. A subclass that relies on its implicit default constructor will fail to compile. This is because the implicit default constructor of the subclass will attempt to call the non-existent default constructor in the superclass. Any constructor in a subclass must explicitly use the super() call, with the appropriate arguments, to invoke a non-default constructor in the superclass. This is because the constructor in the subclass cannot rely on an implicit super() call to the default constructor in the superclass.

 Review Questions

6.9 Given the following code, which of these constructors can be added to MySubclass without causing a compile-time error?

```
class MySuper {
    int number;
    MySuper(int i) { number = i; }
}

class MySub extends MySuper {
    int count;
    MySub(int cnt, int num) {
        super(num);
        count=cnt;
    }

    // INSERT ADDITIONAL CONSTRUCTOR HERE
}
```

Select the one correct answer.

(a) MySub() {}
(b) MySub(int cnt) { count = cnt; }
(c) MySub(int cnt) { super(); count = cnt; }
(d) MySub(int cnt) { count = cnt; super(cnt); }
(e) MySub(int cnt) { this(cnt, cnt); }
(f) MySub(int cnt) { super(cnt); this(cnt, 0); }

6.10 Which statement is true?

Select the one correct answer.

(a) A super() or this() call must always be provided explicitly as the first statement in the body of a constructor.
(b) If both a subclass and its superclass do not have any declared constructors, the implicit default constructor of the subclass will call super() when run.
(c) If neither super() nor this() is declared as the first statement in the body of a constructor, then this() will implicitly be inserted as the first statement.
(d) If super() is the first statement in the body of a constructor, then this() can be declared as the second statement.
(e) Calling super() as the first statement in the body of a constructor of a subclass will always work, since all superclasses have a default constructor.

6.11 What will the following program print when run?

```java
// Filename: MyClass.java
public class MyClass {
    public static void main(String[] args) {
        B b = new B("Test");
    }
}

class A {
    A() { this("1", "2"); }

    A(String s, String t) { this(s + t); }

    A(String s) { System.out.println(s); }
}

class B extends A {
    B(String s) { System.out.println(s); }

    B(String s, String t) { this(t + s + "3"); }

    B() { super("4"); };
}
```

Select the one correct answer.

(a) It will simply print Test.
(b) It will print Test followed by Test.
(c) It will print 123 followed by Test.
(d) It will print 12 followed by Test.
(e) It will print 4 followed by Test.

6.4 Interfaces

Extending classes using *single implementation inheritance* creates new class types. A superclass reference can denote objects of its own type and its subclasses strictly according to the inheritance hierarchy. Because this relationship is linear, it rules out *multiple implementation inheritance*, that is, a subclass inheriting from more than one superclass. Instead Java provides *interfaces*, which not only allow new named reference types to be introduced, but also permit *multiple interface inheritance*.

Defining Interfaces

A top-level interface has the following general syntax:

```
<accessibility modifier> interface <interface name>
                        <extends interface clause> // Interface header

{ // Interface body
    <constant declarations>
    <method prototype declarations>
    <nested class declarations>
    <nested interface declarations>
}
```

In the interface header, the name of the interface is preceded by the keyword inter- face. In addition, the interface header can specify the following information:

- scope or *accessibility modifier* (see Section 4.7, p. 131)

- any interfaces it *extends* (see Section 6.4, p. 254)

The interface body can contain *member declarations* which comprise

- *constant declarations* (see Section 6.4, p. 255)
- *method prototype declarations* (see Section 6.4, p. 254)
- *nested class and interface declarations* (see Section 7.1, p. 284)

An interface does not provide any implementation and is, therefore, abstract by definition. This means that it cannot be instantiated, but classes can implement it by providing implementations for its method prototypes. Declaring an interface abstract is superfluous and seldom done.

The member declarations can appear in any order in the interface body. Since interfaces are meant to be implemented by classes, interface members implicitly have public accessibility and the public modifier is omitted.

Interfaces with empty bodies are often used as *markers* to *tag* classes as having a certain property or behavior. Such interfaces are also called *ability* interfaces. Java APIs provide several examples of such marker interfaces: java.lang.Cloneable, java.io.Serializable, java.util.EventListener.

Method Prototype Declarations

An interface defines a *contract* by specifying a set of method prototypes, but no implementation. The methods in an interface are all implicitly abstract and public by virtue of their definition. A *method prototype* has the same syntax as an abstract method (see Section 4.10, p. 147). However, only the modifiers abstract and public are allowed, but these are invariably omitted.

<return type> <method name> (<parameter list>) <throws clause>;

Example 6.9 declares two interfaces: IStack at (1) and ISafeStack at (5). These interfaces are discussed in the subsequent subsections.

Example 6.9   *Interfaces*

```
interface IStack {                                                    // (1)
    void    push(Object item);
    Object pop();
}

class StackImpl implements IStack {                                    // (2)
    protected Object[] stackArray;
    protected int      tos;  // top of stack

    public StackImpl(int capacity) {
        stackArray = new Object[capacity];
        tos        = -1;
    }

    public void push(Object item)                                     // (3)
        { stackArray[++tos] = item; }

    public Object pop() {                                             // (4)
        Object objRef = stackArray[tos];
        stackArray[tos] = null;
        tos--;
        return objRef;
    }

    public Object peek() { return stackArray[tos]; }
}

interface ISafeStack extends IStack {                                 // (5)
    boolean isEmpty();
    boolean isFull();
}

class SafeStackImpl extends StackImpl implements ISafeStack {         // (6)

    public SafeStackImpl(int capacity) { super(capacity); }
    public boolean isEmpty() { return tos < 0; }                      // (7)
    public boolean isFull() { return tos >= stackArray.length-1; }// (8)
}
```

```
    public class StackUser {

        public static void main(String[] args) {                    // (9)
            SafeStackImpl safeStackRef  = new SafeStackImpl(10);
            StackImpl     stackRef      = safeStackRef;
            ISafeStack    isafeStackRef = safeStackRef;
            IStack        istackRef     = safeStackRef;
            Object        objRef        = safeStackRef;

            safeStackRef.push("Dollars");                            // (10)
            stackRef.push("Kroner");
            System.out.println(isafeStackRef.pop());
            System.out.println(istackRef.pop());
            System.out.println(objRef.getClass());
        }
    }
```

Output from the program:

```
Kroner
Dollars
class SafeStackImpl
```

Implementing Interfaces

Any class can elect to implement, wholly or partially, zero or more interfaces. A class specifies the interfaces it implements as a comma-separated list of unique interface names in an implements clause in the class header. The interface methods must all have public accessibility when implemented in the class (or its subclasses). A class can neither narrow the accessibility of an interface method nor specify new exceptions in the method's throws clause, as attempting to do so would amount to altering the interface's contract, which is illegal. The criteria for overriding methods also apply when implementing interface methods.

A class can provide implementations of methods declared in an interface, but it does not reap the benefits of interfaces unless the interface name is explicitly specified in its implements clause.

In Example 6.9, the class StackImpl implements the interface IStack by both specifying the interface name using the implements clause in its class header at (2) and providing the implementation for the methods in the interface at (3) and (4). Changing the public accessibility of these methods in the class will result in a compile-time error, as this would narrow their accessibility.

A class can choose to implement only some of the methods of its interfaces, (i.e., give a partial implementation of its interfaces). The class must then be declared as abstract (see Section 4.8, p. 134). Note that interface methods cannot be declared static, because they comprise the contract fulfilled by the *objects* of the class implementing the interface. Interface methods are always implemented as instance methods.

The interfaces a class implements and the classes it extends (directly or indirectly) are called *supertypes* of the class. Conversely, the class is a *subtype* of its supertypes. Classes implementing interfaces introduce multiple interface inheritance into their linear implementation inheritance hierarchy. However, note that regardless of how many interfaces a class implements directly or indirectly, it only provides a single implementation of a member that might have multiple declarations in the interfaces.

Extending Interfaces

An interface can extend other interfaces, using the extends clause. Unlike extending classes, an interface can extend several interfaces. The interfaces extended by an interface (directly or indirectly), are called *superinterfaces*. Conversely, the interface is a *subinterface* of its superinterfaces. Since interfaces define new reference types, superinterfaces and subinterfaces are also supertypes and subtypes, respectively.

A subinterface inherits all methods from its superinterfaces, as their method declarations are all implicitly public. A subinterface can override method prototype declarations from its superinterfaces. Overridden methods are not inherited. Method prototype declarations can also be overloaded, analogous to method overloading in classes.

Example 6.9 provides an example of multiple inheritance in Java. In Example 6.9, the interface ISafeStack extends the interface IStack at (5). The class SafeStackImpl both extends the StackImpl class and implements the ISafeStack interface at (6). Both the implementation and interface inheritance hierarchies for classes and interfaces defined in Example 6.9 are shown in Figure 6.3.

In UML, an interface resembles a class. One way to differentiate between them is to use an «*interface*» stereotype as in Figure 6.3. Interface inheritance is shown similar to implementation inheritance, but with a dotted inheritance arrow. Thinking in terms of types, every reference type in Java is a subtype of Object type. This means that any interface type is also a subtype of Object type. We have augmented Figure 6.3 with an extra inheritance arrow to show this subtype relation.

It is instructive to note how class SafeStackImpl implements the ISafeStack interface: it inherits implementations of the push() and pop() methods from its superclass StackImpl, and provides its own implementation of the isFull() and isEmpty() methods from the ISafeStack interface. The interface ISafeStack inherits two method prototypes from its superinterface IStack. All its methods are implemented by the SafeStackImpl class. The class SafeStackImpl implicitly implements the IStack interface: it implements the ISafeStack interface that inherits from the IStack interface. This is readily evident from the diamond shape of the inheritance hierarchy in Figure 6.3. There is only one single *implementation* inheritance into the class SafeStackImpl.

Figure 6.3 *Inheritance Relations*

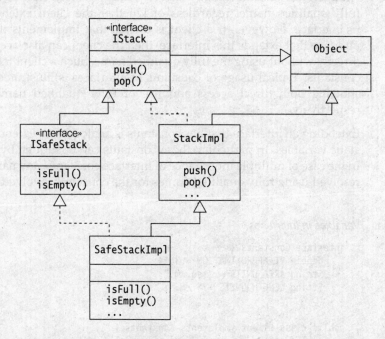

Note that there are three different inheritance relations at work when defining inheritance among classes and interfaces:

1. Linear implementation inheritance hierarchy between classes: a class extends another class (subclasses–superclasses).

2. Multiple inheritance hierarchy between interfaces: an interface extends other interfaces (subinterfaces–superinterfaces).

3. Multiple interface inheritance hierarchy between interfaces and classes: a class implements interfaces.

Although interfaces cannot be instantiated, references of an interface type can be declared. References to objects of a class can be assigned to references of the class' supertypes. In Example 6.9, an object of the class SafeStackImpl is created in the main() method of the class StackUser at (9). The reference value of the object is assigned to references of all the object's supertypes, which are used to manipulate the object. Polymorphic behavior of supertype references is discussed in Section 6.7.

Constants in Interfaces

An interface can also define named constants. Such constants are defined by field declarations and are considered to be public, static and final. These modifiers are usually omitted from the declaration. Such a constant must be initialized with an initializer expression (see Section 8.2, p. 331).

An interface constant can be accessed by any client (a class or interface) using its fully qualified name, regardless of whether the client extends or implements its interface. However, if a client is a class that implements this interface or an interface that extends this interface, then the client can also access such constants directly without using the fully qualified name. Such a client inherits the interface constants. Typical usage of constants in interfaces is illustrated in Example 6.10, showing both direct access and use of fully qualified names at (1) and (2), respectively.

Extending an interface that has constants is analogous to extending a class having static variables. In particular, these constants can be hidden by the subinterfaces. In the case of multiple inheritance of interface constants, any name conflicts can be resolved using fully qualified names for the constants involved.

Example 6.10   *Variables in Interfaces*

```
interface Constants {
    double PI_APPROXIMATION = 3.14;
    String AREA_UNITS = " sq.cm.";
    String LENGTH_UNITS = " cm.";
}

public class Client implements Constants {
    public static void main(String[] args) {
        double radius = 1.5;
        System.out.println("Area of circle is " +
                          (PI_APPROXIMATION*radius*radius) +
                          AREA_UNITS);              // (1) Direct access.
        System.out.println("Circumference of circle is " +
                          (2*Constants.PI_APPROXIMATION*radius) +
                          Constants.LENGTH_UNITS); // (2) Fully qualified name.
    }
}
```

Output from the program:

```
Area of circle is 7.0649999999999995 sq.cm.
Circumference of circle is 9.42 cm.
```

 Review Questions

6.12   Which statements are true about interfaces?

Select the two correct answers.

(a) Interfaces allow multiple implementation inheritance.
(b) Interfaces can be extended by any number of other interfaces.
(c) Interfaces can extend any number of other interfaces.
(d) Members of an interface are never static.
(e) Members of an interface can always be declared static.

6.13 Which of these field declarations are legal within the body of an interface?

Select the three correct answers.

(a) `public static int answer = 42;`
(b) `int answer;`
(c) `final static int answer = 42;`
(d) `public int answer = 42;`
(e) `private final static int answer = 42;`

6.14 Which statements are true about interfaces?

Select the two correct answers.

(a) The keyword extends is used to specify that an interface inherits from another interface.
(b) The keyword extends is used to specify that a class inherits from an interface.
(c) The keyword `implements` is used to specify that an interface inherits from another interface.
(d) The keyword `implements` is used to specify that a class inherits from an interface.
(e) The keyword `implements` is used to specify that a class inherits from another class.

6.15 Which statement is true about the following code?

```
// Filename: MyClass.java
abstract class MyClass implements Interface1, Interface2 {
    public void f() { }
    public void g() { }
}

interface Interface1 {
    int VAL_A = 1;
    int VAL_B = 2;

    void f();
    void g();
}

interface Interface2 {
    int VAL_B = 3;
    int VAL_C = 4;

    void g();
    void h();
}
```

Select the one correct answer.

(a) `Interface1` and `Interface2` do not match, therefore, `MyClass` cannot implement them both.
(b) `MyClass` only implements `Interface1`. Implementation for void `h()` from Interface2 is missing.
(c) The declarations of void `g()` in the two interfaces conflict, therefore, the code will not compile.

(d) The declarations of int VAL_B in the two interfaces conflict, therefore, the code
will not compile.

(e) Nothing is wrong with the code, it will compile without errors.

6.16 Given the following code, which declaration can be inserted at the indicated line
without causing a compilation error?

```
interface MyConstants {
    int r = 42;
    int s = 69;
    // INSERT CODE HERE
}
```

Select the two correct answers.

(a) final double circumference = 2*Math.PI*r;

(b) int total = total + r + s;

(c) int AREA = r*s;

(d) public static MAIN = 15;

(e) protected int CODE = 31337;

6.5 Completing the Type Hierarchy

Table 6.1 summarizes the types found in Java. Only primitive data and reference
values can be stored in variables. Only class and array types can be instantiated to
create objects.

Table 6.1 *Types and Values*

Types	Values
Primitive data types	Primitive data values
Class, interface, and array types (*reference types*)	Reference values

Arrays are objects in Java. Array types (boolean[], Object[], StackImpl[]) implicitly
augment the inheritance hierarchy. The inheritance hierarchy depicted in Figure
6.3 can be augmented by the corresponding array types. The resulting *type hierar-*
chy is shown in Figure 6.4. An array type is shown as a "class" with the [] notation
appended to the name of the element type. The class SafeStackImpl is a subclass
of the class StackImpl. The corresponding array types, SafeStackImpl[] and
StackImpl[], are shown as subtype and supertype, respectively, in the type hierarchy. Figure 6.4 also shows array types corresponding to some of the primitive data
types.

Figure 6.4 *Reference Type Hierarchy*

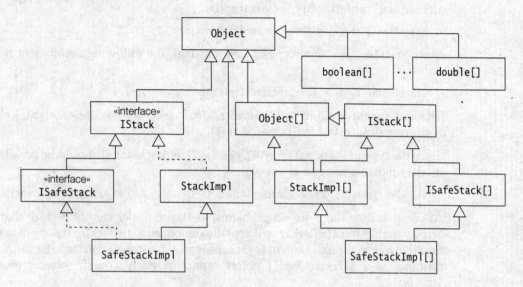

From the type hierarchy in Figure 6.4, we can summarize the following:

- *All* reference types are subtypes of Object type. This applies to classes, interfaces, and array types, as these comprise all reference types.

- All arrays of reference types are also subtypes of the array type Object[], but arrays of primitive data types are not. Note that the array type Object[] is also a subtype of Object type.

- If a reference type is a subtype of another reference type, then the corresponding array types also have an analogous subtype-supertype relationship.

- There is no subtype-supertype relationship between a type and its corresponding array type.

We can create an array of an interface type, but we cannot instantiate an interface (as is the case with abstract classes). In the declaration statement below, the reference iSafeStackArray has type ISafeStack[], (i.e., array of interface type ISafeStack). The array creation expression creates an array whose element type is ISafeStack. The array object can accommodate five references of type ISafeStack. The following statement does not initialize these references to denote any objects:

```
ISafeStack[] iSafeStackArray = new ISafeStack[5];
```

An array reference exhibits polymorphic behavior like any other reference, subject to its location in the type hierarchy (see Section 6.7, p. 272). However, a runtime check can be necessary when objects are inserted in an array, as the following example illustrates.

The following assignment is valid, as a supertype reference (StackImpl[]) can denote objects of its subtype (SafeStackImpl[]):

```
StackImpl[] stackImplArray = new SafeStackImpl[2]; // (1)
```

Since StackImpl is a supertype of SafeStackImpl, the following assignment is also valid:

```
stackImplArray[0] = new SafeStackImpl(10);          // (2)
```

The assignment at (2) inserts a SafeStackImpl object in the SafeStackImpl[] object (i.e., array of SafeStackImpl) created at (1).

Since the type of stackImplArray[i], $(0 \leq i < 2)$, is StackImpl, it should be possible to do the following assignment as well:

```
stackImplArray[1] = new StackImpl(20);              // (3) ArrayStoreException
```

At compile time there are no problems, as the compiler cannot deduce that the array variable stackImplArray will actually denote an SafeStackImpl[] object at runtime. However, the assignment at (3) causes an ArrayStoreException to be thrown at runtime, as a SafeStackImpl[] object cannot possibly contain objects of type StackImpl.

6.6 Assigning, Passing, and Casting Reference Values

Reference values, like primitive values, can be assigned, cast, and passed as arguments. For values of the primitive data types and reference types, conversions can occur during

- assignment
- parameter passing
- explicit casting

The rule of thumb for the primitive data types is that widening conversions are permitted, but narrowing conversions require an explicit cast. The rule of thumb for reference values is that conversions up the type hierarchy are permitted (*upcasting*), but conversions down the hierarchy require explicit casting (*downcasting*). In other words, conversions that are from a subtype to its supertypes are allowed, other conversions require an explicit cast or are illegal. There is no notion of promotion for reference values.

Reference Value Assignment Conversions

Reference value assignments are generally permitted *up* the type hierarchy, with implicit conversion of the source reference value to that of the destination reference type.

Example 6.11 *Assigning and Passing Reference Values*

```java
interface IStack                      { /* From Example 6.9 */ }
interface ISafeStack extends IStack   { /* From Example 6.9 */ }
class StackImpl implements IStack     { /* From Example 6.9 */ }
class SafeStackImpl extends StackImpl
            implements ISafeStack     { /* From Example 6.9 */ }

public class ReferenceConversion {

    public static void main(String[] args) {
        // Reference declarations
        Object        objRef;
        StackImpl     stackRef;
        SafeStackImpl safeStackRef;
        IStack        iStackRef;
        ISafeStack    iSafeStackRef;

        // SourceType is a class type
        safeStackRef  = new SafeStackImpl(10);
        objRef        = safeStackRef;// (1) Always possible
        stackRef      = safeStackRef;// (2) Subclass to superclass assignment
        iStackRef     = stackRef;    // (3) StackImpl implements IStack
        iSafeStackRef = safeStackRef;// (4) SafeStackImpl implements ISafeStack

        // SourceType is an interface type
        objRef    = iStackRef;     // (5) Always possible
        iStackRef = iSafeStackRef; // (6) Sub- to super-interface assignment

        // SourceType is an array type.
        Object[]        objArray       = new Object[3];
        StackImpl[]     stackArray     = new StackImpl[3];
        SafeStackImpl[] safeStackArray = new SafeStackImpl[5];
        ISafeStack[]    iSafeStackArray = new ISafeStack[5];
        int[]           intArray       = new int[10];

        // Reference value assignments
        objRef    = objArray;       // (7) Always possible
        objRef    = stackArray;     // (8) Always possible
        objArray  = stackArray;     // (9) Always possible
        objArray  = iSafeStackArray;// (10) Always possible
        objRef    = intArray;       // (11) Always possible
//      objArray  = intArray;       // (12) Compile-time error
        stackArray = safeStackArray; // (13) Subclass array to superclass array
        iSafeStackArray =
                safeStackArray;      // (14) SafeStackImpl implements ISafeStack

        // Parameter Conversion
        System.out.println("First call:");
        sendParams(stackRef, safeStackRef, iStackRef,
                safeStackArray, iSafeStackArray);           // (15)
```

```
    // Call Signature: sendParams(StackImpl, SafeStackImpl, IStack,
    //                            SafeStackImpl[], ISafeStack[]);

        System.out.println("Second call:");
        sendParams(iSafeStackArray, stackRef, iSafeStackRef,
                stackArray, safeStackArray);                              // (16)
    // Call Signature: sendParams(ISafeStack[], StackImpl, ISafeStack,
    //                            StackImpl[], SafeStackImpl[]);
    }

    public static void sendParams(Object objRefParam, StackImpl stackRefParam,
            IStack iStackRefParam, StackImpl[] stackArrayParam,
            final IStack[] iStackArrayParam) {                            // (17)
    // Signature: sendParams(Object, StackImpl, IStack, StackImpl[], IStack[])
    // Print class name of object denoted by the reference at runtime.
        System.out.println(objRefParam.getClass());
        System.out.println(stackRefParam.getClass());
        System.out.println(iStackRefParam.getClass());
        System.out.println(stackArrayParam.getClass());
        System.out.println(iStackArrayParam.getClass());
    }
}
```

Output from the program:

```
First call:
class SafeStackImpl
class SafeStackImpl
class SafeStackImpl
class [LSafeStackImpl;
class [LSafeStackImpl;
Second call:
class [LSafeStackImpl;
class SafeStackImpl
class SafeStackImpl
class [LSafeStackImpl;
class [LSafeStackImpl;
```

The rules for reference value assignment are stated, based on the following code:

```
SourceType srcRef;
// srcRef is appropriately initialized.
DestinationType destRef = srcRef;
```

If an assignment is legal, then the reference value of srcRef is said to be *assignable* (or *assignment compatible*) to the reference of DestinationType. The rules are illustrated by concrete cases from Example 6.11.

- If SourceType is a *class type*, then the reference value in srcRef may be assigned to the destRef reference, provided DestinationType is one of the following:
  - o DestinationType is a superclass of the subclass SourceType.
  - o DestinationType is an interface type that is implemented by the class SourceType.

```
           objRef       = safeStackRef;  // (1) Always possible
           stackRef     = safeStackRef;  // (2) Subclass to superclass assignment
           iStackRef    = stackRef;      // (3) StackImpl implements IStack
           iSafeStackRef = safeStackRef; // (4) SafeStackImpl implements ISafeStack
```

- If SourceType is an *interface type*, then. the reference value in srcRef may be assigned to the destRef reference, provided DestinationType is one of the following:

  o DestinationType is Object.

  o DestinationType is a superinterface of subinterface SourceType.

```
           objRef    = iStackRef;     // (5) Always possible
           iStackRef = iSafeStackRef; // (6) Subinterface to superinterface assignment
```

- If SourceType is an *array type*, then the reference value in srcRef may be assigned to the destRef reference, provided DestinationType is one of the following:

  o DestinationType is Object.

  o DestinationType is an array type, where the element type of SourceType is assignable to the element type of DestinationType.

```
           objRef     = objArray;       // (7) Always possible
           objRef     = stackArray;     // (8) Always possible
           objArray   = stackArray;     // (9) Always possible
           objArray   = iSafeStackArray;// (10) Always possible
           objRef     = intArray;       // (11) Always possible
        // objArray   = intArray;       // (12) Compile-time error
           stackArray = safeStackArray; // (13) Subclass array to superclass array
           iSafeStackArray =
                      safeStackArray;    // (14) SafeStackImpl implements ISafeStack
```

The rules for assignment are enforced at compile time, guaranteeing that no type conversion error will occur during assignment at runtime. Such conversions are *type safe*. The reason the rules can be enforced at compile time is that they concern the type of the reference (which is always known at compile time) rather than the actual type of the object being referenced (which is known at runtime).

Parameter Passing Conversions

The rules for reference value assignment conversion also apply for *parameter passing conversions*. This is reasonable, as parameters in Java are passed by value (see Section 3.19, p. 89), requiring that values of actual parameters must be assignable to formal parameters of compatible types.

In Example 6.11, the method sendParams() at (17) has the following signature, showing the types of the formal parameters:

```
   sendParams(Object, StackImpl, IStack, StackImpl[], IStack[])
```

The method call at (15) has the following signature, showing the types of the actual parameters:

```
   sendParams(StackImpl, SafeStackImpl, IStack, SafeStackImpl[], ISafeStack[]);
```

Note that the assignment of the values of the actual parameters to the corresponding formal parameters is legal, according to the rules for assignment discussed earlier. The method call at (16) provides another example of parameter passing conversion. It has the following signature:

```
sendParams(ISafeStack[], StackImpl, ISafeStack, StackImpl[], SafeStackImpl[]);
```

Analogous to assignment, the rules for parameter passing conversions are based on the reference type of the parameters and are enforced at compile time. The output in Example 6.11 shows the class of the actual objects referenced by the formal parameters at runtime, which in this case turns out to be either SafeStackImpl or SafeStackImpl[]. The characters [L in the output indicate a one-dimensional array of a class or interface type (see the Class.getName() method in the API documentation).

The parameter passing conversion rules are useful in creating *generic data types* that can handle objects of arbitrary types. The classes in the java.util package make heavy use of Object as parameter type in their methods, to implement *collections* that can hold arbitrary objects (see Chapter 11).

Reference Casting and instanceof Operator

The expression to cast a *<reference>* of *<source type>* to *<destination type>* has the following syntax:

(*<destination type>*) *<reference>*

A cast expression checks that the reference value of the object denoted by the *<reference>* is assignable to a reference of the *<destination type>*, that is, that the *<source type>* is compatible to the *<destination type>*. If this is not the case, a ClassCastException is thrown. The null reference value can be cast to any reference type.

The binary instanceof operator has the following syntax (note that the keyword is composed of only lowercase letters):

<reference> instanceof *<destination type>*

The instanceof operator returns true if the left-hand operand (*<reference>*) can be *cast* to the right-hand operand (*<destination type>*), but always returns false if the left-hand operand is null. If the instanceof operator returns true, then the corresponding cast expression will always be valid. Both the cast and the instanceof operators require a compile-time check and a runtime check as explained below.

The compile-time check determines whether a reference of *<source type>* and a reference of *<destination type>* can denote objects of a reference type that is a common subtype of both *<source type>* and *<destination type>* in the type hierarchy. If this is not the case, then obviously there is no relationship between the types, and neither the cast nor the instanceof operator application would be valid. At runtime, it is the type of the actual object denoted by the *<reference>* that determines the outcome of the operation.

With *<source type>* and *<destination type>* as classes Light and String, respectively, there is no subtype-supertype relationship between the *<source type>* and *<destination type>*. The compiler would reject casting a reference of type Light to type String or applying the instanceof operator, as shown at (2) and (3) in Example 6.12. With *<source type>* and *<destination type>* as classes Light and TubeLight, respectively, references of Light and TubeLight can denote objects of class TubeLight (or its subclasses) in the inheritance hierarchy depicted in Figure 6.3. Therefore, it makes sense to apply the instanceof operator or cast a reference of type Light to type TubeLight, as shown at (4) and (5), respectively, in Example 6.12.

At runtime, the result of applying the instanceof operator at (4) is false because the reference light1 of class Light will actually denote an object of subclass LightBulb, and this object cannot be denoted by a reference of the peer class TubeLight. Applying the cast at (5) results in a ClassCastException for the same reason. This is the reason why cast conversions are said to be *unsafe*, as they may throw a ClassCastException at runtime. Note that if the result of the instanceof operator is false, then the cast involving the operands will throw a ClassCastException.

In Example 6.12, the result of applying the instanceof operator at (6) is also false, because the reference light1 will still denote an object of class LightBulb, whose objects cannot be denoted by a reference of its subclass SpotLightBulb. Thus applying the cast at (7) causes a ClassCastException to be thrown at runtime.

The situation shown at (8), (9), and (10) illustrates typical usage of the instanceof operator to determine what object a reference is denoting so that it can be cast for the purpose of carrying out some special action. The reference light1 of class Light is initialized to an object of subclass NeonLight at (8). The result of the instanceof operator at (9) is true, because the reference light1 will denote an object of subclass NeonLight, whose objects can also be denoted by a reference of its superclass TubeLight. By the same token, the cast at (10) is also valid. If the result of the instanceof operator is true, then the cast involving the operands will always be valid.

- -

Example 6.12   instanceof *and Cast Operator*

```
class Light { /* ... */ }
class LightBulb extends Light { /* ... */ }
class SpotLightBulb extends LightBulb { /* ... */ }
class TubeLight extends Light { /* ... */ }
class NeonLight extends TubeLight { /* ... */ }

public class WhoAmI {
    public static void main(String[] args) {
        boolean result1, result2, result3, result4, result5;
        Light light1 = new LightBulb();                // (1)
    //  String str = (String) light1;                  // (2) Compile-time error.
    //  result1 = light1 instanceof String;            // (3) Compile-time error.
```

```
        result2 = light1 instanceof TubeLight;        // (4) false. Peer class.
//      TubeLight tubeLight1 = (TubeLight) light1;     // (5) ClassCastException.

        result3 = light1 instanceof SpotLightBulb;     // (6) false: Superclass
//      SpotLightBulb spotRef = (SpotLightBulb) light1;// (7) ClassCastException

        light1 = new NeonLight();                      // (8)
        if (light1 instanceof TubeLight) {             // (9) true
            TubeLight tubeLight2 = (TubeLight) light1; // (10) OK
            // Can now use tubeLight2 to access object of class NeonLight.
        }
    }
}
```

As we have seen, the instanceof operator effectively determines whether the reference value of the object denoted by the reference on the left-hand side is assignable to a reference of the type that is specified on the right-hand side. Note that an instance of a subtype *is-an* instance of its supertypes. At runtime, it is the type of the actual object denoted by the reference on the left-hand side that is compared with the type specified on the right-hand side. In other words, what matters is the type of the actual object denoted by the reference at runtime, not the type of the reference.

Example 6.13 provides more examples of the instanceof operator. It is instructive to go through the print statements and understand the results printed out. The literal null is not an instance of any reference type, as shown in the print statements (1), (2), and (16). An instance of a superclass is not an instance of its subclass, as shown in the print statement (4). An instance of a class is not an instance of a totally unrelated class, as shown in the print statement (10). An instance of a class is not an instance of an interface type that the class does not implement, as shown in the print statement (6). Any array of non-primitive type is an instance of both Object and Object[] types, as shown in the print statements (14) and (15), respectively.

Example 6.13   *Using* instanceof *Operator*

```
interface IStack                       { /* From Example 6.9 */ }
interface ISafeStack extends IStack    { /* From Example 6.9 */ }
class StackImpl implements IStack      { /* From Example 6.9 */ }
class SafeStackImpl extends StackImpl
            implements ISafeStack      { /* From Example 6.9 */ }

public class Identification {
    public static void main(String[] args) {
        Object obj = new Object();
        StackImpl stack = new StackImpl(10);
        SafeStackImpl safeStack = new SafeStackImpl(5);
        IStack iStack;
```

```
            System.out.println("(1): " +
                (null instanceof Object));         // Always false.
            System.out.println("(2): " +
                (null instanceof IStack));         // Always false.

            System.out.println("(3): " +          // true: instance of subclass of
                (stack instanceof Object));        //       Object.
            System.out.println("(4): " +
                (obj instanceof StackImpl));       // false: Downcasting.
            System.out.println("(5): " +
                (stack instanceof StackImpl));     // true: instance of StackImpl.

            System.out.println("(6): " +          // false: Object does not implement
                (obj instanceof IStack));          //        IStack.
            System.out.println("(7): " +          // true: SafeStackImpl implements
                (safeStack instanceof IStack));    //        IStack.

            obj = stack;                           // Assigning subclass to superclass.
            System.out.println("(8): " +
                (obj instanceof StackImpl));       // true: instance of StackImpl.
            System.out.println("(9): " +          // true: StackImpl implements
                (obj instanceof IStack));          //        IStack.
            System.out.println("(10): " +
                (obj instanceof String));          // false: No relationship.

            iStack = (IStack) obj; // Cast required: superclass assigned subclass.
            System.out.println("(11): " +          // true: instance of subclass
                (iStack instanceof Object));       //         of Object.
            System.out.println("(12): " +
                (iStack instanceof StackImpl));    // true: instance of StackImpl.

            String[] strArray = new String[10];
//          System.out.println("(13): " +          // Compile-time error,
//              (strArray instanceof String);      // no relationship.
            System.out.println("(14): " +
                (strArray instanceof Object));     // true: array subclass of Object.
            System.out.println("(15): " +
                (strArray instanceof Object[]));   // true: array subclass of Object[].
            System.out.println("(16): " +
                (strArray[0] instanceof Object));  // false: strArray[0] is null.
            strArray[0] = "Amoeba strip";
            System.out.println("(17): " +
                (strArray[0] instanceof String));  // true: instance of String.
        }
    }
```

Output from the program:

```
    (1): false
    (2): false
    (3): true
    (4): false
    (5): true
    (6): false
```

```
(7): true
(8): true
(9): true
(10): false
(11): true
(12): true
(14): true
(15): true
(16): false
(17): true
```

Converting References of Class and Interface Types

References of an interface type can be declared and these can denote objects of classes that implement this interface. This is another example of upcasting. Note that converting a reference value of interface type to the type of the class implementing the interface, requires explicit casting. This is an example of downcasting. The following code illustrates these cases:·

```
IStack    istackOne = new StackImpl(5);          // Upcasting
StackImpl stackTwo  = (StackImpl) istackOne;      // Downcasting
```

Using the reference istackOne of interface type IStack, methods of the IStack interface can be invoked on objects of the StackImpl class that implements this interface. However, the additional members of the StackImpl class cannot be accessed via this reference without first casting it to the StackImpl class:

```
Object obj1 = istackOne.pop();      // OK. Method in IStack interface.
Object obj2 = istackOne.peek();     // Not OK. Method not in IStack interface.
Object obj3 = ((StackImpl) istackOne).peek(); // OK. Method in StackImpl class.
```

 ## Review Questions

6.17   Given the following program, which statement is true?

```
// Filename: MyClass.java
public class MyClass {
    public static void main(String[] args) {
        A[] arrA;
        B[] arrB;

        arrA = new A[10];
        arrB = new B[20];
        arrA = arrB;       // (1)
        arrB = (B[]) arrA; // (2)
        arrA = new A[10];
        arrB = (B[]) arrA; // (3)
    }
}

class A {}

class B extends A {}
```

Select the one correct answer.

(a) The program will fail to compile because of the assignment at (1).

(b) The program will throw a java.lang.ClassCastException in the assignment at (2) when run.

(c) The program will throw a java.lang.ClassCastException in the assignment at (3) when run.

(d) The program will compile and run without errors, even if the (B[]) cast in the statements at (2) and (3) is removed.

(e) The program will compile and run without errors, but will not do so if the (B[]) cast in statements at (2) and (3) is removed.

6.18 Which is the first line that will cause compilation to fail in the following program?

```java
// Filename: MyClass.java
class MyClass {
    public static void main(String[] args) {
        MyClass a;
        MySubclass b;

        a = new MyClass();           // (1)
        b = new MySubclass();        // (2)

        a = b;                       // (3)
        b = a;                       // (4)

        a = new MySubclass();        // (5)
        b = new MyClass();           // (6)
    }
}

class MySubclass extends MyClass {}
```

Select the one correct answer.

(a) Line labeled (1).

(b) Line labeled (2).

(c) Line labeled (3).

(d) Line labeled (4).

(e) Line labeled (5).

(f) Line labeled (6).

6.19 Given the following definitions and reference declarations, which one of the following assignments is legal?

```java
// Definitions:
interface I1 {}
interface I2 {}
class C1 implements I1 {}
class C2 implements I2 {}
class C3 extends C1 implements I2 {}
```

```
// Reference declarations:
// ...
    C1 obj1;
    C2 obj2;
    C3 obj3;
// ...
```

Select the one correct answer.

(a) obj2 = obj1;
(b) obj3 = obj1;
(c) obj3 = obj2;
(d) I1 a = obj2;
(e) I1 b = obj3;
(f) I2 c = obj1;

6.20 Given the following class definitions and the reference declarations, what can be said about the statement y = (Sub) x?

```
// Class definitions:
class Super {}
class Sub extends Super {}
```

```
// Reference declarations
// ...
    Super x;
    Sub y;
// ...
```

Select the one correct answer.

(a) Illegal at compile time.
(b) Legal at compile time, but might be illegal at runtime.
(c) Definitely legal at runtime, but the (Sub) cast is not strictly needed.
(d) Definitely legal at runtime, and the (Sub) cast is needed.

6.21 Given the following class definitions and declaration statements, which one of these assignments is legal at compile time?

```
// Definitions:
interface A {}
class B {}
class C extends B implements A {}
class D implements A {}
```

```
// Declaration statements:
// [...]
    B b = new B();
    C c = new C();
    D d = new D();
// [...]
```

Select the one correct answer.

(a) `c = d;`
(b) `d = c;`
(c) `A a = d;`
(d) `d = (D) c;`
(e) `c = b;`

6.22 Which letters will be printed when the following program is run?

```java
// Filename: MyClass.java
public class MyClass {
    public static void main(String[] args) {
        B b = new C();
        A a = b;
        if (a instanceof A) System.out.println("A");
        if (a instanceof B) System.out.println("B");
        if (a instanceof C) System.out.println("C");
        if (a instanceof D) System.out.println("D");
    }
}

class A {}
class B extends A {}
class C extends B {}
class D extends C {}
```

Select the three correct answers.

(a) A will be printed.
(b) B will be printed.
(c) C will be printed.
(d) D will be printed.

6.23 Given three classes A, B, and C, where B is a subclass of A and C is a subclass of B, which one of these boolean expressions is true when an object denoted by reference o has actually been instantiated from class B as opposed to from A or C?

Select the one correct answer.

(a) `(o instanceof B) && (!(o instanceof A))`
(b) `(o instanceof B) && (!(o instanceof C))`
(c) `!((o instanceof A) || (o instanceof B))`
(d) `(o instanceof B)`
(e) `(o instanceof B) && !((o instanceof A) || (o instanceof C))`

6.24 When the following program is run, it will print all the letters I, J, C, and D. Is this statement true or false?

```java
public class MyClass {
    public static void main(String[] args) {
        I x = new D();
        if (x instanceof I) System.out.println("I");
```

```
        if (x instanceof J) System.out.println("J");
        if (x instanceof C) System.out.println("C");
        if (x instanceof D) System.out.println("D");
    }
}

interface I{}
interface J{}
class C implements I {}
class D extends C implements J {}
```

Select the one correct answer.

(a) True.
(b) False.

6.7 Polymorphism and Dynamic Method Lookup

Which object a reference will actually denote during runtime, cannot always be determined at compile time. Polymorphism allows a reference to denote objects of different types at different times during execution. A supertype reference exhibits polymorphic behavior, since it can denote objects of its subtypes.

When a non-private instance method is invoked on an object, the method definition actually executed is determined both by the type of the object at runtime and the method signature. Dynamic method lookup is the process of determining which method definition a method signature denotes during runtime, based on the type of the object. However, a call to a private instance method is not polymorphic. Such a call can only occur within the class, and gets bound to the private method implementation at compile time.

The inheritance hierarchy depicted in Figure 6.5 is implemented in Example 6.14. The implementation of the method draw() is overridden in all subclasses of the class Shape. The invocation of the draw() method in the two loops at (3) and (4) in Example 6.14, relies on the polymorphic behavior of references and dynamic method lookup. The array shapes holds Shape references denoting a Circle, a Rectangle and a Square, as shown at (1). At runtime, dynamic lookup determines the draw() implementation to execute, based on the type of the object denoted by each element in the array. This is also the case for the elements of the array drawables at (2), which holds IDrawable references that can be assigned any object of a class that implements the IDrawable interface. The first loop will still work without any change if objects of new subclasses of the class Shape are added to the array shapes. If they did not override the draw() method, then an inherited version of the method would be executed. This polymorphic behavior applies to the array drawables, where the subtype objects are guaranteed to have implemented the IDrawable interface.

Figure 6.5 *Polymorphic Methods*

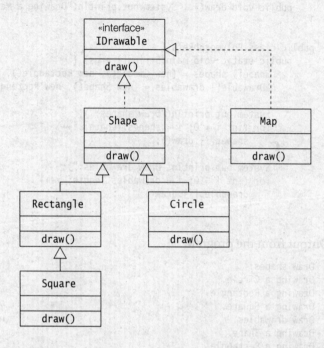

Polymorphism and dynamic method lookup form a powerful programming paradigm that simplifies client definitions, encourages object decoupling, and supports dynamically changing relationships between objects at runtime.

Example 6.14 *Polymorphism and Dynamic Method Lookup*

```
interface IDrawable {
    void draw();
}

class Shape implements IDrawable {
    public void draw() { System.out.println("Drawing a Shape."); }
}

class Circle extends Shape {
    public void draw() { System.out.println("Drawing a Circle."); }
}

class Rectangle extends Shape {
    public void draw() { System.out.println("Drawing a Rectangle."); }
}

class Square extends Rectangle {
    public void draw() { System.out.println("Drawing a Square."); }
}
```

```java
class Map implements IDrawable {
    public void draw() { System.out.println("Drawing a Map."); }
}

public class PolymorphRefs {
    public static void main(String[] args) {
        Shape[] shapes = {new Circle(), new Rectangle(), new Square()};   // (1)
        IDrawable[] drawables = {new Shape(), new Rectangle(), new Map()};// (2)

        System.out.println("Draw shapes:");
        for (int i = 0; i < shapes.length; i++)                          // (3)
            shapes[i].draw();

        System.out.println("Draw drawables:");
        for (int i = 0; i < drawables.length; i++)                       // (4)
            drawables[i].draw();
    }
}
```

Output from the program:

```
Draw shapes:
Drawing a Circle.
Drawing a Rectangle.
Drawing a Square.
Draw drawables:
Drawing a Shape.
Drawing a Rectangle.
Drawing a Map.
```

 Review Questions

6.25 What will be the result of attempting to compile and run the following program?

```java
public class Polymorphism {
    public static void main(String[] args) {
        A ref1 = new C();
        B ref2 = (B) ref1;
        System.out.println(ref2.f());
    }
}

class A            { int f() { return 0; } }
class B extends A { int f() { return 1; } }
class C extends B { int f() { return 2; } }
```

Select the one correct answer.

(a) The program will fail to compile.
(b) The program will compile without error, but will throw a ClassCastException when run.
(c) The program will compile without error and print 0 when run.
(d) The program will compile without error and print 1 when run.
(e) The program will compile without error and print 2 when run.

6.26 What will be the result of attempting to compile and run the following program?

```
public class Polymorphism2 {
    public static void main(String[] args) {
        A ref1 = new C();
        B ref2 = (B) ref1;
        System.out.println(ref2.g());
    }
}
class A {
    private int f() { return 0; }
    public int g() { return 3; }
}
class B extends A {
    private int f() { return 1; }
    public int g() { return f(); }
}
class C extends B {
    public int f() { return 2; }
}
```

Select the one correct answer.

(a) The program will fail to compile.
(b) The program will compile without error and print 0 when run.
(c) The program will compile without error and print 1 when run.
(d) The program will compile without error and print 2 when run.
(e) The program will compile without error and print 3 when run.

6.8 Inheritance vs. Aggregation

Encapsulation

An object has properties and behaviors that are *encapsulated* inside the object. The services it offers to its clients comprises its *contract*. Only the *contract* defined by the object is available to the clients. The *implementation* of its properties and behavior is not a concern of the clients. Encapsulation helps to make clear the distinction between an object's contract and implementation. This has major consequences for program development. The implementation of an object can change without implications for the clients. Encapsulation also reduces complexity, as the internals of an object are hidden from the clients, who cannot influence its implementation.

Choosing between Inheritance and Aggregation

Figure 6.6 is a UML class diagram, showing several aggregation relationships and one inheritance relationship. The class diagram shows a queue defined by aggregation, and a stack defined by inheritance. Both are based on linked lists. A linked list is defined by aggregation. The implementation of these data structures is shown in Example 6.15. The purpose of the example is to illustrate inheritance and aggregation, not industrial-strength implementation of queues and stacks. The class Node at (1) is straightforward, defining two fields: one denoting the data and the other denoting the next node in the list. The class LinkedList at (2) keeps track of the list by managing a head and a tail reference. Nodes can be inserted in the front or back, but deleted only from the front of the list.

Figure 6.6 *Implementing Data Structures by Inheritance and Aggregation*

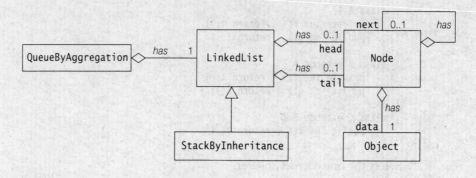

Example 6.15 *Implementing Data Structures by Inheritance and Aggregation*

```
class Node {                                                    // (1)
    private Object data;        // Data
    private Node   next;        // Next node

    // Constructor for initializing data and reference to the next node.
    Node(Object data, Node next) {
        this.data = data;
        this.next = next;
    }

    // Methods
    public void    setData(Object obj) { data = obj; }
    public Object  getData()           { return data; }
    public void    setNext(Node node)  { next = node; }
    public Node    getNext()           { return next; }
}

class LinkedList {                                              // (2)
    protected Node head = null;
    protected Node tail = null;

    // Methods
    public boolean isEmpty() { return head == null; }
    public void insertInFront(Object dataObj) {
        if (isEmpty()) head = tail = new Node(dataObj, null);
        else head = new Node(dataObj, head);
    }
}
```

```
            public void insertAtBack(Object dataObj) {
                if (isEmpty())
                    head = tail = new Node(dataObj, null);
                else {
                    tail.setNext(new Node(dataObj, null));
                    tail = tail.getNext();
                }
            }
            public Object deleteFromFront() {
                if (isEmpty()) return null;
                Node removed = head;
                if (head == tail) head = tail = null;
                else head = head.getNext();
                return removed.getData();
            }
    }

    class QueueByAggregation {                              // (3)
        private LinkedList qList;

        // Constructor
        QueueByAggregation() {
            qList = new LinkedList();
        }

        // Methods
        public boolean isEmpty() { return qList.isEmpty(); }
        public void enqueue(Object item) { qList.insertAtBack(item); }
        public Object dequeue() {
            if (qList.isEmpty()) return null;
            else return qList.deleteFromFront();
        }
        public Object peek() {
            return (qList.isEmpty() ? null : qList.head.getData());
        }
    }

    class StackByInheritance extends LinkedList {           // (4)
        public void push(Object item) { insertInFront(item); }
        public Object pop() {
            if (isEmpty()) return null;
            else return deleteFromFront();
        }
        public Object peek() {
            return (isEmpty() ? null : head.getData());
        }
    }

    public class Client {                                  // (5)
        public static void main(String[] args) {
            String string1 = "Queues are boring to stand in!";
            int length1 = string1.length();
            QueueByAggregation queue = new QueueByAggregation();
```

```
        for (int i = 0; i<length1; i++)
            queue.enqueue(new Character(string1.charAt(i)));
        while (!queue.isEmpty())
            System.out.print((Character) queue.dequeue());
        System.out.println();

        String string2 = "!no tis ot nuf era skcatS";
        int length2 = string2.length();
        StackByInheritance stack = new StackByInheritance();
        for (int i = 0; i<length2; i++)
            stack.push(new Character(string2.charAt(i)));
        stack.insertAtBack(new Character('!'));              // (6)
        while (!stack.isEmpty())
            System.out.print((Character) stack.pop());
        System.out.println();
    }
}
```

Output from the program:

```
Queues are boring to stand in!
Stacks are fun to sit on!!
```

Choosing between inheritance and aggregation to model relationships can be a crucial design decision. A good design strategy advocates that inheritance should be used only if the relationship *is-a* is unequivocally maintained throughout the lifetime of the objects involved; otherwise, aggregation is the best choice. A *role* is often confused with an *is-a* relationship. For example, given the class Employee, it would not be a good idea to model the roles an employee can play (such as a manager or a cashier) by inheritance if these roles change intermittently. Changing roles would involve a new object to represent the new role every time this happens.

Code reuse is also best achieved by aggregation when there is no *is-a* relationship. Enforcing an artificial *is-a* relationship that is not naturally present, is usually not a good idea. This is illustrated in Example 6.15 at (6). Since the class StackByInheritance at (4) is a subclass of the class LinkedList at (2), any inherited method from the superclass can be invoked on an instance of the subclass. Also, methods that contradict the abstraction represented by the subclass can be invoked, as shown at (6). Using aggregation in such a case results in a better solution, as demonstrated by the class QueueByAggregation at (3). The class defines the operations of a queue by *delegating* such requests to the underlying class LinkedList. Clients implementing a queue in this manner do not have access to the underlying class and, therefore, cannot break the abstraction.

Both inheritance and aggregation promote encapsulation of *implementation*, as changes to the implementation are localized to the class. Changing the *contract* of a superclass can have consequences for the subclasses (called the *ripple effect*) and also for clients who are dependent on a particular behavior of the subclasses.

Polymorphism is achieved through inheritance and interface implementation. Code relying on polymorphic behavior will still work without any change if new subclasses or new classes implementing the interface are added. If no obvious *is-a* relationship is present, then polymorphism is best achieved by using aggregation with interface implementation.

 Review Questions

6.27   Given the following code, which statements are true?

```java
public interface HeavenlyBody { String describe(); }

class Star {
    String starName;
    public String describe() { return "star " + starName; }
}

class Planet extends Star {
    String name;
    public String describe() {
        return "planet " + name + " orbiting star " + starName;
    }
}
```

Select the two correct answers:

(a) The code will fail to compile.
(b) The use of inheritance is justified, since Planet *is-a* Star.
(c) The code will fail to compile if the name starName is replaced with the name bodyName throughout the declaration of the Star class.
(d) The code will fail to compile if the name starName is replaced with the name name throughout the declaration of the Star class.
(e) An instance of Planet is a valid instance of HeavenlyBody.

6.28   Given the following code, which statement is true?

```java
public interface HeavenlyBody { String describe(); }

class Star implements HeavenlyBody {
    String starName;
    public String describe() { return "star " + starName; }
}

class Planet {
    String name;
    Star orbiting;
    public String describe() {
        return "planet " + name + " orbiting " + orbiting.describe();
    }
}
```

Select the one correct answer:

(a) The code will fail to compile.

(b) The use of aggregation is justified, since Planet *has-a* Star.

(c) The code will fail to compile if the name starName is replaced with the name bodyName throughout the declaration of the Star class.

(d) The code will fail to compile if the name starName is replaced with the name name throughout the declaration of the Star class.

(e) An instance of Planet is a valid instance of a HeavenlyBody.

Chapter Summary

The following information was included in this chapter:

- inheritance and its implications in OOP
- overriding and hiding of superclass members
- method overriding vs. method overloading
- usage of super reference to access superclass members
- usage of this() and super() calls, including constructor chaining
- interfaces and multiple interface inheritance
- subtype-supertype relationship
- conversions due to assigning, casting, and passing reference values
- identifying the type of objects using the instanceof operator
- polymorphism and dynamic method lookup
- inheritance (*is-a*) vs. aggregation (*has-a*)

Programming Exercises

6.1 Declare an interface called Function that has a method named evaluate that takes an int parameter and returns an int value.

Create a class Half that implements Function. Make the implementation of the method evaluate() return the value obtained by dividing the int argument by 2.

In a client, create a method that takes an arbitrary array of int values as parameter and returns an array that has the same length, but the value of an element in the new array is half that of the value in the corresponding element in the array passed as parameter. Let the implementation of this method create an instance of Half and use this instance to calculate the values in the array to be returned.

6.2   Rewrite the method that operated on arrays from the previous exercise: the method should now also take a Function reference as an argument and use this instead of creating an instance of Half.

Create a class called Print that implements Function, has a method that simply prints the int value given as an argument, and returns the value.

Now, write a program that creates an array of the int values from 1 to 10 and does the following:

1. Prints the array using an instance of the Print class and the method described earlier.

2. Halves the values in the array and prints the values again, using the Half and Print classes and the method described above.

Nested Classes and Interfaces

7

Exam Objectives

- Write code to construct instances of any concrete class, including normal top-level classes and nested classes.

Supplementary Objectives

- State the kinds of nested classes and interfaces that can be defined.
- Identify the context in which a nested class or interface can be defined.
- State which accessibility modifiers are allowed for each category of nested classes.
- State which nested classes create instances that are associated with instances of the enclosing context.
- State the access rules that govern accessing entities in the enclosing context of nested classes, and write code that uses the augmented syntax involving the this keyword for this purpose.
- State whether a definition of a nested class can contain static and non-static members.
- Write code to instantiate nested classes, using the augmented syntax of the new operator.
- Write code to show how nested classes can be imported and used.
- Distinguish between the inheritance hierarchy and the enclosing context of any nested class or interface.
- Write code to implement anonymous classes by extending an existing class or by implementing an interface.

7.1 Overview of Nested Classes and Interfaces

A class that is declared within another class or interface, is called a *nested class*. Similarly, an interface that is declared within another class or interface, is called a *nested interface*. A *top-level class* or *a top-level interface* is one that is not nested.

In addition to the top-level classes and interfaces, there are four categories of *nested classes* and one of *nested interfaces*, defined by the context these classes and interfaces are declared in:

- static member classes and interfaces
- non-static member classes
- local classes
- anonymous classes

The last three categories are collectively known as *inner classes*. They differ from non-inner classes in one important aspect: that an instance of an inner class may be associated with an instance of the enclosing class. The instance of the enclosing class is called the *immediately enclosing instance*. An instance of an inner class can access the members of its immediately enclosing instance by their simple name.

A *static member class or interface* is defined as a static member in a class or an interface. Such a nested class can be instantiated like any ordinary top-level class, using its full name. No enclosing instance is required to instantiate a static member class. Note that there are no non-static member, local, or anonymous interfaces. Interfaces are always defined either at the top level or as static members.

Non-static member classes are defined as instance members of other classes, just like fields and instance methods are defined in a class. An instance of a non-static member class always has an enclosing instance associated with it.

Local classes can be defined in the context of a block as in a method body or a local block, just as local variables can be defined in a method body or a local block.

Anonymous classes can be defined as expressions and instantiated *on the fly*. An instance of a local (or an anonymous) class has an enclosing instance associated with it, if the local (or anonymous) class is declared in a non-static context.

A nested class or interface cannot have the same name as any of its enclosing classes or interfaces.

Skeletal code for nested classes is shown Example 7.1. Table 7.1 presents a summary of various aspects relating to nested classes and interfaces. The *Entity* column lists the different kinds of classes and interfaces that can be declared. The *Declaration Context* column lists the lexical context in which the class or interface can be defined. The *Accessibility Modifiers* column indicates what accessibility can be specified for the class or interface. The *Enclosing Instance* column specifies whether an enclosing instance is associated with an instance of the class. The *Direct Access to Enclosing Context* column lists what is directly accessible in the enclosing context from within the class or interface. The *Declarations in Entity Body* column refers to what can be declared in the class or interface body. Subsequent sections on each nested class elaborate on the summary presented in Table 7.1. (N/A in the table means not applicable.)

Example 7.1 *Overview of Nested Classes and Interfaces*

```
class TLC {                      // (1) Top level class

    static class SMC {/*...*/} // (2) Static member class

    interface SMI {/*...*/}    // (3) Static member interface

    class NSMC {/*...*/}        // (4) Non-static member (inner) class

    void nsm() {
        class NSLC {/*...*/}   // (5) Local (inner) class in non-static context
    }

    static void sm() {
        class SLC {/*...*/}    // (6) Local (inner) class in static context
    }

    SMC nsf = new SMC()
             {/*...*/};        // (7) Annonymous (inner) class in non-static context

    static SMI sf = new SMI()
             {/*...*/};        // (8) Annonymous (inner) class in static context
}
```

Nested type (i.e., nested classes and interfaces) can be regarded as a form of encapsulation, enforcing relationships between types by greater proximity. They allow structuring of types and a special binding relationship between a nested object and its enclosing instance. Used judiciously, they can be beneficial, but unrestrained use of nested classes can easily result in unreadable code.

Table 7.1 *Overview of Classes and Interfaces*

Entity	Declaration Context	Accessibility Modifiers	Enclosing Instance	Direct Access to Enclosing Context	Declarations in Entity Body
Top-level Class (or Interface)	Package	public or default	No	N/A	All that are valid in a class (or interface) body
Static Member Class (or Interface)	As static member of enclosing class or interface	All	No	Static members in enclosing context	All that are valid in a class (or interface) body
Non-static Member Class	As non-static member of enclosing class or interface	All	Yes	All members in enclosing context	Only non-static declarations + final static fields
Local Class	In block with non-static context	None	Yes	All members in enclosing context + final local variables	Only non-static declarations + final static fields
	In block with static context	None	No	Static members in enclosing context + final local variables	Only non-static declarations + final static fields
Anonymous Class	As expression in non-static context	None	Yes	All members in enclosing context + final local variables	Only non-static declarations + final static fields
	As expression in static context	None	No	Static members in enclosing context + final local variables	Only non-static declarations + final static fields

7.2 Static Member Classes and Interfaces

Declaring and Using Static Member Classes and Interfaces

A *static member class* or *a static member interface* comprises the same declarations as those allowed in an ordinary top-level class or interface. A static member class must be declared as a static member of an enclosing class or interface. Nested interfaces are considered implicitly static, the keyword static can, therefore, be omitted. Since static member classes and interfaces are members of an enclosing class or interface, they can have any member accessibility.

Static member classes and interfaces can only be nested within other static member or top-level classes and interfaces.

In Example 7.2, the top-level class TopLevelClass at (1) contains a static member class StaticMemberClass_1 at (2), which in turn defines a static member interface StaticMemberInterface_1_1 at (3) and a static member class StaticMemberClass_1_1 at (4). The static member class StaticMemberClass_1_1 at (4) implements the static member interface StaticMemberInterface_1 at (5). Note that each static member class is defined as static, just like static variables and methods in a top-level class.

Example 7.2 *Static Member Classes and Interfaces*

```
// Filename: TopLevelClass.java
package express;

public class TopLevelClass {                                  // (1)
    // ...
    public static class StaticMemberClass_1 {          // (2)
        // ...
        private interface StaticMemberInterface_1_1 { // (3)
            // ...
        }
        public static class StaticMemberClass_1_1
            implements StaticMemberInterface_1 {        // (4)
            // ...
        }
    }
    interface StaticMemberInterface_1
        extends StaticMemberClass_1.StaticMemberInterface_1_1 {        // (5)
        // ...
    }
}
```

```
class AnotherTopLevelClass
       implements TopLevelClass.StaticMemberInterface_1 {                    // (6)

    TopLevelClass.StaticMemberClass_1.StaticMemberClass_1_1 objRef1 =
        new TopLevelClass.StaticMemberClass_1.StaticMemberClass_1_1(); // (7)

    //TopLevelClass.StaticMemberClass_1.StaticMemberInterface_1_1 ref; // (8)
    // ...
}
```

The *full name* of a (static or non-static) member class or interface includes the names of the classes and interfaces it is lexically nested in. For example, the full name of the member class StaticMemberClass_1_1 at (4) is TopLevelClass.StaticMemberClass_1.StaticMemberClass_1_1. The full name of the member interface StaticMemberInterface_1 at (5) is TopLevelClass.Static-MemberInterface_1. Each member class or interface is uniquely identified by this naming syntax, which is a generalization of the naming scheme for packages. The full name can be used in exactly the same way as any other top-level class or interface name, as shown at (6) and (7). Such a member's fully qualified name is its full name prefixed by the name of its package. For example, the fully qualified name of the member class at (4) is express.TopLevelClass.StaticMember-Class_1.StaticMemberClass_1_1. Note that a member class or interface, cannot have the same name as an enclosing class, interface, or package.

For all intents and purposes, a static member class or interface is very much like any other top-level class or interface. Static variables and methods belong to a class, and not to instances of the class. The same is true for static member classes and interfaces.

Within the scope of its top-level class or interface, a member class or interface can be referenced regardless of its accessibility modifier and lexical nesting, as shown at (5) in Example 7.2. Its accessibility modifier (and that of the types making up its full name) come into play when it is referenced in an external client. The declaration at (8) in Example 7.2 will not compile because the member interface TopLevel-Class.StaticMemberClass_1.StaticMemberInterface_1_1 has private accessibility.

A static member class can be instantiated without any reference to any instance of the enclosing context, as is the case for instantiating top-level classes. An example of creating an instance of a static member class is shown at (7) in Example 7.2, using the new operator.

If the file TopLevelClass.java containing the declarations in Example 7.2 is compiled, it will result in the generation of the following class files, where each file corresponds to a class or interface definition:

```
TopLevelClass$StaticMemberClass_1$StaticMemberClass_1_1.class
TopLevelClass$StaticMemberClass_1$StaticMemberInterface_1_1.class
TopLevelClass$StaticMemberClass_1.class
TopLevelClass$StaticMemberInterface_1.class
TopLevelClass.class
AnotherTopLevelClass.class
```

Note how the full class name corresponds to the class file name (minus the extension), with the dollar sign ($) replaced by the dot sign (.).

There is seldom any reason to import member classes or interfaces from packages. It would undermine the encapsulation achieved by such classes or interfaces. However, a compilation unit for a named package can use the import declaration to provide a short cut for the names of member classes and interfaces. (Java does not allow imports from the unnamed package.) Some variations on usage of the import declaration for member classes are shown in Example 7.3.

Example 7.3 *Importing Member Classes*

```java
// Filename: Client1.java
package express;
import express.TopLevelClass.*;                                    // (1)

public class Client1 {
    StaticMemberClass_1.StaticMemberClass_1_1 objRef1 =
            new StaticMemberClass_1.StaticMemberClass_1_1();       // (2)
}
```

```java
// Filename: Client2.java
package express;
import express.TopLevelClass.StaticMemberClass_1.*;                // (3)

public class Client2 {
    StaticMemberClass_1_1 objRef2 = new StaticMemberClass_1_1();   // (4)
}
class SomeClass implements
    express.TopLevelClass.StaticMemberInterface_1 {                // (5)
    /* ... */
}
```

In the file Client1.java, the import statement at (1) allows the static member class StaticMemberClass_1_1 to be referenced as StaticMemberClass_1.StaticMemberClass-_1_1 as at (2), whereas in the file Client2.java, the import statement at (3) will allow the same class to be referenced using its simple name, as at (4). At (5) the fully qualified name of the static member interface is used in an implements clause.

Accessing Members in Enclosing Context

Static code does not have a this reference and can, therefore, only directly access other members that are declared static within the same class. Since static member classes are static, they do not have any notion of an enclosing instance of the enclosing context. This means that any code in a static member class can only directly access static members in its enclosing context, not instance members in its enclosing context.

Figure 7.1 is a class diagram that illustrates static member classes and interfaces. These are shown as members of the enclosing context, with the {static} tag to indicate that they are static, that is, they can be instantiated without regard to any object of the enclosing context. Since they are members of a class or an interface, their accessibility can be specified exactly like that of any other member of a class or interface. The classes from the diagram are implemented in Example 7.4.

Figure 7.1   *Static Member Classes and Interfaces*

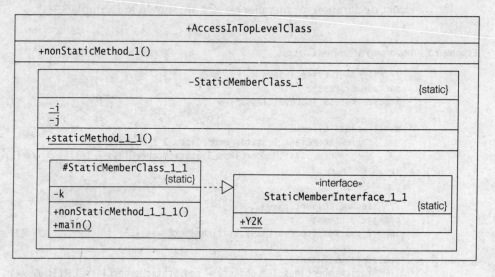

- -

Example 7.4   *Accessing Members in Enclosing Context*

```java
// Filename: AccessInTopLevelClass.java
public class AccessInTopLevelClass {                              // (1)

    public void nonStaticMethod_1() {                            // (2)
        System.out.println("nonstaticMethod_1 in AccessInTopLevelClass");
    }

    private static class StaticMemberClass_1 {                   // (3)
        private static int i;                                    // (4)
        private int j;                                           // (5)

        public static void staticMethod_1_1() {                  // (6)
            System.out.println("staticMethod_1_1 in StaticMemberClass_1");
        }

        interface StaticMemberInterface_1_1 { int Y2K = 2000; } // (7)

        protected static class StaticMemberClass_1_1
                implements StaticMemberInterface_1_1 {           // (8)

            private int k = Y2K;                                 // (9)
```

```
                    public void nonStaticMethod_1_1_1() {                // (10)
                //  int jj = j;                // (11) Not OK.
                    int ii = i;                // (12)
                    int kk = k;                // (13)

                //  nonStaticMethod_1();       // (14) Not OK.
                    staticMethod_1_1();        // (15)
                }

                public static void main (String[] args) {
                    int ii = i;                // (16)
                //  int kk = k;                // (17) Not OK.
                    staticMethod_1_1();        // (18)
                }
            }
        }
    }
```

Output from the program:

```
staticMethod_1_1 in StaticMemberClass_1
```

Example 7.4 demonstrates accessing members directly in the enclosing context of class StaticMemberClass_1_1 defined at (8). The initialization of the field k at (9) is valid, since the field Y2K, defined in the outer interface StaticMemberInterface_1_1 at (7), is implicitly static. The compiler will flag an error at (11) and (14) in the method nonStaticMethod_1_1_1(), because direct access to non-static members in the enclosing class is not permitted by *any* method in a static member class. It will also flag an error at (17) in the method main(), because a static method cannot access directly other non-static fields in its own class. Statements at (16) and (18) access static members only in the enclosing context. The references in these statements can also be specified using full names.

```
int ii = AccessInTopLevelClass.StaticMemberClass_1.i;
AccessInTopLevelClass.StaticMemberClass_1.staticMethod_1_1();
```

Note that a static member class can define both static and instance members, like any other top-level class. However, its code can only directly access static members in its enclosing context.

A static member class, being a member of the enclosing class or interface, can have any accessibility (public, protected, package/default, private), like any other member of a class. The class StaticMemberClass_1 at (3) has private accessibility, whereas its nested class StaticMemberClass_1_1 at (8) has protected accessibility. The class StaticMemberClass_1_1 defines the method main(), which can be executed by the command

```
>java AccessInTopLevelClass$StaticMemberClass_1$StaticMemberClass_1_1
```

Note that the class StaticMemberClass_1_1 is specified using the full name of the class file, minus the extension.

7.3 Non-static Member Classes

Non-static member classes are inner classes that are defined without the keyword static, as members of an enclosing class or interface. Non-static member classes are on par with other non-static members defined in a class. The following aspects about non-static member classes should be noted:

- An instance of a non-static member class can only exist with an instance of its enclosing class. This means that an instance of a non-static member class must be created in the context of an instance of the enclosing class. This also means that a non-static member class cannot have static members. In other words, the non-static member class does not provide any services, only instances of the class do. However, final static variables are allowed, as these are constants.

- Code in a non-static member class can directly refer to any member (including nested) of any enclosing class or interface, including private members. No explicit reference is required.

- Since a non-static member class is a member of an enclosing class, it can have any accessibility: public, package/default, protected, or private.

A typical application of non-static member classes is implementing data structures. Code below outlines implementing a linked list, where the Node class is nested in the LinkedList class. Since the non-static member class Node is declared private, it is not accessible outside of class LinkedList. Nesting promotes encapsulation, and the close proximity allows classes to exploit each others capabilities.

```
class LinkedList {                                          // (1)
    private class Node {                                    // (2)
        private Object data;       // Data
        private Node next;         // Next node
        // ...
    }

    protected Node head;
    protected Node tail;
    // ...
}
```

Instantiating Non-static Member Classes

In Example 7.5, the class ToplevelClass at (1) defines a non-static member class at (5). Declaration of a static variable at (6) in class NonStaticMemberClass is flagged as a compile-time error, but defining a final static variable at (7) is allowed.

Example 7.5 *Defining Non-static Member Classes*

```
class ToplevelClass {                                       // (1)
    private String headlines = "Shine the inner light";    // (2)
    public NonStaticMemberClass makeInstance() {           // (3)
        return new NonStaticMemberClass();                 // (4)
```

```
            }
            public class NonStaticMemberClass {              // (5) NSMC
            //   static int sf = 2003;                       // (6) Not OK.
                 final static int fsf = 2003;                // (7) OK.
                 private String banner;                      // (8)
                 public NonStaticMemberClass() { banner = headlines; }  // (9)
                 public void print(String prefix) {
                     System.out.println(prefix + banner + " in " + fsf);}// (10)
            }
        }

        public class Client {                                // (11)
            public static void main(String[] args) {         // (12)
            ToplevelClass topRef = new ToplevelClass();      // (13)
            ToplevelClass.NonStaticMemberClass innerRef1 =
                        topRef.makeInstance();               // (14)
            innerRef1.print("innerRef1: ");                  // (15)
        //  ToplevelClass.NonStaticMemberClass innerRef2 =
        //              new ToplevelClass.NonStaticMemberClass(); // (16) Not OK.
            ToplevelClass.NonStaticMemberClass innerRef3 =
                        topRef.new NonStaticMemberClass();   // (17)
            innerRef3.print("innerRef3: ");                  // (18)
            }
        }
```

Output from the program:

```
    innerRef1: Shine the inner light in 2003
    innerRef3: Shine the inner light in 2003
```

A special form of the new operator is used to instantiate a non-static member class.

<enclosing object reference>.new *<non-static member class constructor call>*

The *<enclosing object reference>* in the object creation expression evaluates to an instance of the enclosing class in which the designated non-static member class is defined. A new instance of the non-static member class is created and associated with the indicated instance of the enclosing class. Note that the expression returns a reference value that denotes a new instance of the non-static member class. It is illegal to specify the full name of the non-static member class in the constructor call, as the enclosing context is already given by the *<enclosing object reference>*.

The non-static method makeInstance() at (3) in the class ToplevelClass creates an instance of the NonStaticMemberClass using the new operator, as shown at (4):

```
        return new NonStaticMemberClass();                   // (4)
```

This creates an instance of a non-static member class in the context of the instance of the enclosing class on which the makeInstance() method is invoked. The new operator in the statement at (4) has an implicit this reference as the *<enclosing object reference>*, since the non-static member class is directly defined in the context of the object denoted by the this reference:

```
        return this.new NonStaticMemberClass();              // (4')
```

The makeInstance() method is called at (14). This associates a new object of the Non-StaticMemberClass with the object denoted by the reference topRef. This object of the NonStaticMemberClass is denoted by the reference innerRef1. The reference innerRef1 can then be used in the normal way to access members of this object of the non-static member class as shown at (15).

An attempt to create an instance of the non-static member class without an outer instance, using the new operator with the full name of the inner class, as shown at (16), results in a compile-time error.

The special form of the new operator is also used in the object creation expression at (17).

```
Top1evelClass.NonStaticMemberClass innerRef3 =
                   topRef.new NonStaticMemberClass();              // (17)
```

The reference topRef denotes an object of the class ToplevelClass. After the execution of the statement at (17), the ToplevelClass object has two instances of the non-static member class NonStaticInnerClass associated with it. This is depicted in Figure 7.2, where the outer object (denoted by topRef) of class ToplevelClass is shown with its two associated inner objects (denoted by references innerRef1 and innerRef3, respectively) right after the execution of the statement at (17). In other words, multiple objects of the non-static member classes can be associated with an object of an enclosing class at runtime.

Figure 7.2 *Outer Object with Associated Inner Objects*

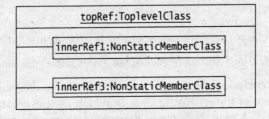

Accessing Members in Enclosing Context

An implicit reference to the enclosing object is always available in every method and constructor of a non-static member class. A method can explicitly use this reference with a special form of the this construct, as explained in the next example.

From within a non-static member class, it is possible to refer to all members in the enclosing class directly. An example is shown at (9), where the field headlines from the enclosing class is accessed in the non-static member class. It is also possible to explicitly refer to members in the enclosing class, but this requires special usage of the this reference. One might be tempted to define the constructor at (9) as follows:

```
public NonStaticMemberClass() { this.banner = this.headlines; }
```

The reference this.banner is correct, because the field banner certainly belongs to the current object (denoted by this) of NonStaticMemberClass, but this.headlines cannot possibly work, as the current object (indicated by this) of NonStaticMember Class has no field headlines. The correct syntax is the following:

```
public NonStaticMemberClass() { this.banner = ToplevelClass.this.headlines; }
```

The expression

<enclosing class name>.this

evaluates to a reference that denotes the enclosing object (of class *<enclosing class name>*) of the current instance of a non-static member class.

Accessing Hidden Members

Fields and methods in the enclosing context can be *hidden* by fields and methods with the same names in the non-static member class. The special form of the this syntax can be used to access members in the enclosing context, somewhat analogous to using the keyword super in subclasses to access hidden superclass members.

Example 7.6   *Special Form of* this *and* new *Constructs in Non-static Member Classes*

```
// Filename: Client2.java
class TLClass {                                                   // (1) TLC
    private String id = "TLClass object ";                        // (2)
    public TLClass(String objId) { id = id + objId; }            // (3)
    public void printId() {                                       // (4)
        System.out.println(id);
    }

    class InnerB {                                                // (5) NSMC
        private String id = "InnerB object ";                     // (6)
        public InnerB(String objId) { id = id + objId; }         // (7)
        public void printId() {                                   // (8)
            System.out.print(TLClass.this.id + " : ");            // (9)
            System.out.println(id);                               // (10)
        }

        class InnerC {                                            // (11) NSMC
            private String id = "InnerC object ";                 // (12)
            public InnerC(String objId) { id = id + objId; }     // (13)
            public void printId() {                               // (14)
                System.out.print(TLClass.this.id + " : ");        // (15)
                System.out.print(InnerB.this.id + " : ");         // (16)
                System.out.println(id);                           // (17)
            }
            public void printIndividualIds() {                    // (18)
                TLClass.this.printId();                           // (19)
                InnerB.this.printId();                            // (20)
                printId();                                        // (21)
            }
        }
    }
}
```

```
public class OuterInstances {                                           // (22)
    public static void main(String[] args) {                            // (23)
        TLClass a = new TLClass("a");                                   // (24)
        TLClass.InnerB b = a.new InnerB("b");                           // (25)
        b.printId();                                                    // (26)
        TLClass.InnerB.InnerC c = b.new InnerC("c");                    // (27)
        c.printId();                                                    // (28)
        TLClass.InnerB.InnerC d = b.new InnerC("d");                    // (29)
        d.printId();                                                    // (30)
        TLClass.InnerB bb = new TLClass("aa").new InnerB("bb");         // (31)
        bb.printId();                                                   // (32)
        TLClass.InnerB.InnerC cc = bb.new InnerC("cc");                 // (33)
        cc.printId();                                                   // (34)
        TLClass.InnerB.InnerC ccc =
            new TLClass("aaa").new InnerB("bbb").new InnerC("ccc");     // (35)
        ccc.printId();                                                  // (36)
        System.out.println("------------");
        ccc.printIndividualIds();                                       // (37)
    }
}
```

Output from the program:

```
TLClass object a : InnerB object b
TLClass object a : InnerB object b : InnerC object c
TLClass object a : InnerB object b : InnerC object d
TLClass object aa : InnerB object bb
TLClass object aa : InnerB object bb : InnerC object cc
TLClass object aaa : InnerB object bbb : InnerC object ccc
------------
TLClass object aaa
TLClass object aaa : InnerB object bbb
TLClass object aaa : InnerB object bbb : InnerC object ccc
```

Example 7.6 illustrates the special form of the this construct employed to access members in the enclosing context, and also demonstrates the special form of the new construct employed to create instances of non-static member classes. The example shows the non-static member class InnerC at (11), which is nested in the non-static member class InnerB at (5), which in turn is nested in the top-level class TLClass at (1). All three classes have a private non-static String field named id and a non-static method named printId. The member name in the nested class *hides* the name in the enclosing context. These members are *not* overridden in the nested classes, as no inheritance is involved. In order to refer to the hidden members, the nested class can use the special this construct, as shown at (9), (15), (16), (19), and (20). Within the nested class InnerC, the three forms used in the following statements to access its field id are equivalent:

```
System.out.println(id);                        // (17)
System.out.println(this.id);                    // (17a)
System.out.println(InnerC.this.id);             // (17b)
```

The main() method at (23) uses the special syntax of the new operator to create objects of non-static member classes and associate them with enclosing objects. An instance of class InnerC (denoted by c) is created at (27) in the context of an instance of class InnerB (denoted by b), which was created at (25) in the context of an instance of class TLClassA (denoted by a), which in turn was created at (24). The reference c is used at (28) to invoke the method printId() declared at (14) in the nested class InnerC. This method prints the field id from all the objects associated with an instance of the nested class InnerC.

When the intervening references to an instance of a non-static member class are of no interest (i.e., if the reference values need not be stored in variables), then the new operator can be chained as shown at (31) and (35).

Note that the (outer) objects associated with the instances denoted by the references c, cc, and ccc are distinct, as evident from the program output. However, the instances denoted by references c and d have the same outer objects associated with them.

Inheritance Hierarchy and Enclosing Context

Inner classes can extend other classes, and vice versa. An inherited field (or method) in an inner subclass can hide a field (or method) with the same name in the enclosing context. Using the simple name to access this member will access the inherited member, not the one in the enclosing context.

Example 7.7 illustrates the situation outlined earlier. The standard form of the this reference is used to access the inherited member as shown at (4). The keyword super would be another alternative. To access the member from the enclosing context, the special form of the this reference together with the enclosing class name is used as shown at (5).

Example 7.7 *Inheritance Hierarchy and Enclosing Context*

```
class Superclass {
    protected double x = 3.0e+8;
}

class TopLevelClass {                          // (1) Top-level Class
    private double x = 3.14;

    class Inner extends Superclass {           // (2) Non-static member Class
        public void printHidden() {            // (3)

            // (4) x from superclass:
            System.out.println("this.x: " + this.x);

            // (5) x from enclosing context:
            System.out.println("TopLevelClass.this.x: "+TopLevelClass.this.x);
```

```
            }
          }
        }

        public class HiddenAndInheritedAccess {
            public static void main(String[] args) {
                TopLevelClass.Inner ref = new TopLevelClass().new Inner();
                ref.printHidden();
            }
        }
```

Output from the program:

```
this.x: 3.0E8
TopLevelClass.this.x: 3.14
```

Some caution should be exercised when extending an inner class. Some of the subtleties involved are illustrated by Example 7.8.

The non-static member class InnerA, declared at (2) in class OuterA, is extended by the subclass SomeUnrelatedClass at (3). Note that SomeUnrelatedClass and class OuterA are not related in any way. An instance of subclass SomeUnrelatedClass is created at (8). An instance of class OuterA is explicitly passed as argument in the constructor call to SomeUnrelatedClass. The constructor at (4) for SomeUnrelatedClass has a special super() call in its body at (5). This call ensures that the constructor of the superclass InnerA has an outer object (denoted by the reference outerRef) to bind to. Using the standard super() call in the subclass constructor is not adequate, because it does not provide an outer instance for the superclass constructor to bind to. The non-default constructor at (4) and the outerRef.super() expression at (5) are mandatory to set up the proper relationships between the objects involved.

The outer object problem mentioned above does not arise if the subclass that extends an inner class is also declared within an outer class that extends the outer class of the superclass. This situation is illustrated at (6) and (7): classes InnerB and OuterB extend classes InnerA and OuterA, respectively. The type InnerA is inherited by class OuterB from its superclass OuterA. Thus an object of class OuterB can act as an outer object for an instance of class InnerA. The object creation expression at (9)

```
        new OuterB().new InnerB();
```

creates an OuterB object and implicitly passes its reference to the default constructor of class InnerB. The default constructor of class InnerB invokes the default constructor of its superclass InnerA by calling super() and passing it the reference of the OuterB object, which the superclass constructor can readily bind to.

Example 7.8 *Extending Inner Classes*

```
        class OuterA {                                      // (1)
            class InnerA { }                                // (2)
        }
```

```
    class SomeUnrelatedClass extends OuterA.InnerA { // (3) Extends NSMC at (2)

        // (4) Mandatory non-default constructor
        SomeUnrelatedClass(OuterA outerRef) {
            outerRef.super();                          // (5) Explicit super() call
        }
    }

    class OuterB extends OuterA {                      // (6) Extends class at (1)
        class InnerB extends OuterB.InnerA { }         // (7) Extends NSMC at (2)
    }

    public class Extending {
        public static void main(String[] args) {

            // (8) Outer instance passed explicitly in constructor call:
            new SomeUnrelatedClass(new OuterA());

            // (9) No outer instance passed explicitly in constructor call to InnerB:
            new OuterB().new InnerB();
        }
    }
```

 Review Questions

7.1 What will be the result of attempting to compile and run the following code?

```
public class MyClass {
    public static void main(String[] args) {
        Outer objRef = new Outer();
        System.out.println(objRef.createInner().getSecret());
    }
}

class Outer {
    private int secret;
    Outer() { secret = 123; }

    class Inner {
        int getSecret() { return secret; }
    }

    Inner createInner() { return new Inner(); }
}
```

Select the one correct answer.

(a) The code will fail to compile because the class Inner cannot be declared within the class Outer.

(b) The code will fail to compile because the method createInner() cannot be allowed to pass objects of the class Inner to methods outside of the class Outer.

(c) The code will fail to compile because the secret field is not accessible from the method getSecret().

(d) The code will fail to compile because the method getSecret() is not visible from the main() method in the class MyClass.

(e) The code will compile without error and will print 123 when run.

7.2 Which statements are true about nested classes?

Select the two correct answers.

(a) An instance of a static member class has an inherent outer instance.

(b) A static member class can contain non-static fields.

(c) A static member interface can contain non-static fields.

(d) A static member interface has an inherent outer instance.

(e) For each instance of the outer class, there can exist many instances of a non-static member class.

7.3 What will be the result of attempting to compile and run the following code?

```
public class MyClass {
    public static void main(String[] args) {
        State st = new State();
        System.out.println(st.getValue());
        State.Memento mem = st.memento();
        st.alterValue();
        System.out.println(st.getValue());
        mem.restore();
        System.out.println(st.getValue());
    }

    public static class State {
        protected int val = 11;

        int getValue() { return val; }
        void alterValue() { val = (val + 7) % 31; }
        Memento memento() { return new Memento(); }

        class Memento {
            int val;

            Memento() { this.val = State.this.val; }
            void restore() { ((State) this).val = this.val; }
        }
    }
}
```

Select the one correct answer.

(a) The code will fail to compile since the static main() method tries to create a new instance of the static member class State.

(b) The code will fail to compile since the declaration of class State.Memento is not accessible from the main() method.

(c) The code will fail to compile since the non-static member class Memento declares a field with the same name as a field in the outer class State.

(d) The code will fail to compile since the State.this.val expression in the Memento constructor is invalid.

(e) The code will fail to compile since the `((State) this).val` expression in the method `restore()` of the class `Memento` is invalid.

(f) The program compiles without error and prints 11, 18, and 11 when run.

7.4 What will be the result of attempting to compile and run the following program?

```
public class Nesting {
    public static void main(String[] args) {
        B.C obj = new B().new C();
    }
}

class A {
    int val;
    A(int v) { val = v; }
}

class B extends A {
    int val = 1;
    B() { super(2); }

    class C extends A {
        int val = 3;
        C() {
            super(4);
            System.out.println(B.this.val);
            System.out.println(C.this.val);
            System.out.println(super.val);
        }
    }
}
```

Select the one correct answer.

(a) The program will fail to compile.

(b) The program will compile without error and print 2, 3, and 4, in that order, when run.

(c) The program will compile without error and print 1, 4, and 2, in that order, when run.

(d) The program will compile without error and print 1, 3, and 4, in that order, when run.

(e) The program will compile without error and print 3, 2, and 1, in that order, when run.

7.5 Which statements are true about the following program?

```
public class Outer {
    public void doIt() {
    }
    public class Inner {
        public void doIt() {
        }
    }
}
```

```
public static void main(String[] args) {
    new Outer().new Inner().doIt();
}
}
```

Select the two correct answers.

(a) The doIt() method in the Inner class overrides the doIt() method in the Outer class.

(b) The doIt() method in the Inner class overloads the doIt() method in the Outer class.

(c) The doIt() method in the Inner class hides the doIt() method in the Outer class.

(d) The full name of the Inner class is Outer.Inner.

(e) The program will fail to compile.

7.4 Local Classes

A local class is an inner class that is defined in a block. This could be a method body, a constructor, a local block, a static initializer, or an instance initializer.

Blocks in a non-static context have a this reference available, which denotes an instance of the class containing the block. An instance of a local class, which is declared in such a non-static block, has an instance of the enclosing class associated with it. This gives such a non-static local class much of the same capability as a non-static member class.

However, if the block containing a local class declaration is defined in a static context (i.e., a static method or a static initializer), then the local class is implicitly static in the sense that its instantiation does not require any outer object. This aspect of local classes is reminiscent of static member classes. However, note that a local class cannot be specified with the keyword static.

Some restrictions that apply to local classes are

- Local classes cannot have static members, as they cannot provide class-specific services. However, final static fields are allowed, as these are constants. This is illustrated in Example 7.9 at (1) and (2) in the NonStaticLocal class, and also by the StaticLocal class at (11) and (12).

- Local classes cannot have any accessibility modifier. The declaration of the class is only accessible in the context of the block in which it is defined, subject to the same scope rules as for local variable declarations.

Example 7.9 *Access in Enclosing Context*

```
class Base {
    protected int nsf1;
}
```

```
class TLCWithLocalClasses {             // Top level Class
    private double nsf1;                 // Non-static field
    private int    nsf2;                 // Non-static field
    private static int sf;               // Static field

    void nonStaticMethod(final int fp) { // Non-static Method
        final int flv  = 10;            // final local variable
        final int hlv  = 30;            // final (hidden) local variable
              int nflv = 20;            // non-final local variable

        class NonStaticLocal extends Base { // Non-static local class
//            static int f1;            // (1) Not OK. Static members not allowed.
            final static int f2 = 10;   // (2) final static members allowed.
            int    f3  = fp;            // (3) final param from enclosing method.
            int    f4  = flv;           // (4) final local var from enclosing method.
//          double f5  = nflv;          // (5) Not OK. Only finals from enclosing method.
            double f6  = nsf1;          // (6) Inherited from superclass.
            double f6a = this.nsf1;     // (6a) Inherited from superclass.
            double f6b = super.nsf1;    // (6b) Inherited from superclass.
            double f7  = TLCWithLocalClasses.this.nsf1;// (7) In enclosing object.
            int    f8  = nsf2;          // (8)  In enclosing object.
            int    f9  = sf;            // (9)  static from enclosing class.
            int    hlv;                 // (10) Hides local variable.
        }
    }

    static void staticMethod(final int fp) { // Static Method
        final int flv  = 10;            // final local variable
        final int hlv  = 30;            // final (hidden) local variable
              int nflv = 20;            // non-final local variable

        class StaticLocal extends Base { // Static local class
//            static int f1;            // (11) Not OK. Static members not allowed.
            final static int f2 = 10;   // (12) final static members allowed.
            int    f3  = fp;            // (13) final param from enclosing method.
            int    f4  = flv;           // (14) final local var from enclosing method.
//          double f5  = nflv;          // (15) Not OK. Only finals from enclosing method.
            double f6  = nsf1;          // (16) Inherited from superclass.
            double f6a = this.nsf1;     // (16a) Inherited from superclass.
            double f6b = super.nsf1;    // (16a) Inherited from superclass.
//          double f7  = TLCWithLocalClasses.this.nsf1;//(17) No enclosing object.
//          int    f8  = nsf2;          // (18)  No enclosing object.
            int    f9  = sf;            // (19)  static from enclosing class.
            int    hlv;                 // (20) Hides local variable.
        }
    }
}
```

Accessing Declarations in Enclosing Context

Example 7.9 illustrates how a local class can access declarations in its enclosing context. Declaring a local class in a static or a non-static block, influences what the class can access in the enclosing context.

Accessing Local Declarations in the Enclosing Block

A local class can access final local variables, final method parameters, and final catch-block parameters in the scope of the local context. Such final variables are also read-only in the local class. This situation is shown at (3) and (4), where the final parameter fp and the final local variable flv of the method nonStaticMethod() in the NonStaticLocal class are accessed. This also applies to static local classes, as shown at (13) and (14) in the StaticLocal class.

Access to non-final local variables is not permitted from local classes, as shown at (5) and (15).

Declarations in the enclosing block of a local class can be hidden by declarations in the local class. At (10) and (20), the field hlv hides the local variable by the same name in the enclosing method. There is no way for the local class to refer to such hidden declarations.

Accessing Members in the Enclosing Class

A local class can access members inherited from its superclass in the usual way. The field nsf1 in the superclass Base is inherited by the local subclass NonStatic-Local. This inherited field is accessed in the NonStaticLocal class as shown at (6), (6a), and (6b) by using the field's simple name, the standard this reference, and the super keyword, respectively. This also applies for static local classes as shown at (16), (16a), and (16b).

Fields and methods in the enclosing class can be hidden by member declarations in the local class. The non-static field nsf1, inherited by the local classes, hides the field by the same name in the TLCWithLocalClasses class. The special form of the this construct can be used in non-static local classes for *explicit* referencing of members in the enclosing class, regardless of whether these members are hidden or not.

```
double f7 = TLCWithLocalClasses.this.nsf1; // (7)
```

However, the special form of the this construct cannot be used in a static local class, as shown at (17), since it does not have any notion of an outer object. The static local class cannot refer to such hidden declarations.

A non-static local class can access both static and non-static members defined in the enclosing class. The non-static field nsf2 and static field sf are defined in the enclosing TLCWithLocalClasses class. They are accessed in the NonStaticLocal class at (8) and (9), respectively. The special form of the this construct can also be used in non-static local classes, as previously mentioned.

However, a static local class can only directly access members defined in the enclosing class that are static. The static field sf in the TLCWithLocalClasses class is accessed in the StaticLocal class at (19), but the non-static field nsf1 cannot be accessed, as shown at (18).

Instantiating Local Classes

Clients outside the scope of a local class cannot instantiate the class directly because such classes are, after all, local. A local class can be instantiated in the block in which it is defined. Like a local variable, a local class must be declared before being used in the block.

A method can return instances of any local class it declares. The local class type must then be assignable to the return type of the method. The return type cannot be the same as the local class type, since this type is not accessible outside of the method. A supertype of the local class must be specified as the return type. This also means that, in order for the objects of the local class to be useful outside the method, a local class should implement an interface or override the behavior of its supertypes.

Example 7.10 illustrates how clients can instantiate local classes. The non-static local class Circle at (5) is defined in the non-static method createCircle() at (4), which has the return type Shape. The static local class Map at (8) is defined in the static method createMap() at (7), which has the return type IDrawable. The inheritance hierarchy of the local classes and their supertypes Shape and IDrawable is depicted in Figure 6.5, p. 273. The main() method creates a polymorphic array drawables of type IDrawable[] at (10), which is initialized at lines (10) through (13) with instances of the local classes.

Example 7.10 *Instantiating Local Classes*

```java
interface IDrawable {                    // (1)
    void draw();
}
class Shape implements IDrawable {       // (2)
    public void draw() { System.out.println("Drawing a Shape."); }
}

class Painter {                          // (3) Top-level Class
    public Shape createCircle(final double radius) { // (4) Non-static Method
        class Circle extends Shape {     // (5) Non-static local class
            public void draw() {
                System.out.println("Drawing a Circle of radius: " + radius);
            }
        }
        return new Circle();             // (6) Object of non-static local class
    }
```

```
    public static IDrawable createMap() {  // (7) Static Method
        class Map implements IDrawable {   // (8) Static local class
            public void draw() { System.out.println("Drawing a Map."); }
        }
        return new Map();                  // (9) Object of static local class
    }
}

public class LocalClassClient {
    public static void main(String[] args) {
        IDrawable[] drawables = {           // (10)
          new Painter().createCircle(5),// (11) Object of non-static local class
          Painter.createMap(),          // (12) Object of static local class
          new Painter().createMap()     // (13) Object of static local class
        };
        for (int i = 0; i < drawables.length; i++)      // (14)
            drawables[i].draw();

        System.out.println("Local Class Names:");
        System.out.println(drawables[0].getClass());   // (15)
        System.out.println(drawables[1].getClass());   // (16)
    }
}
```

Output from the program:

```
Drawing a Circle of radius: 5.0
Drawing a Map.
Drawing a Map.
Local Class Names:
class Painter$1$Circle
class Painter$1$Map
```

- -

Creating an instance of a non-static local class requires an instance of the enclosing class. The non-static method createCircle() is invoked on the instance of the enclosing class to create an instance of the non-static local class, as shown at (11). In the non-static method, the reference to the instance of the enclosing context is passed implicitly in the constructor call of the non-static local class at (6).

A static method can be invoked either through the class name or through a reference of the class type. An instance of a static local class can be created either way by calling the createMap() method as shown at (12) and (13). As might be expected, no outer object is involved.

As references to a local class cannot be declared outside of the local context, the functionality of the class is only available through supertype references. The method draw() is invoked on objects in the array at (14). The program output indicates which objects were created. In particular, note that the final parameter radius of the method createCircle() at (4) is accessed by the draw() method of the local class Circle at (5). An instance of the local class Circle is created at (11) by a call to the method createCircle(). The draw() method is invoked on this instance of the local class Circle in the loop at (14). The value of the final parameter radius is still accessible to the draw() method invoked on this instance, although the call to the method createCircle(), which created the instance in the first place, has completed. Values of final local variables continue to be available to instances of local classes whenever these values are needed.

The output in Example 7.10 also shows the actual names of the local classes. In fact, the local class names are reflected in the class filenames.

Another use of local classes is shown in the following example. The code shows how local classes can be used, together with assertions, to implement certain kinds of postconditions (see Section 5.10, p. 218). The basic idea is that a computation wants to save some data that is later required when checking a postconditon. For example, a deposit is made into an account, and we want to check that the transaction is valid after it is done. The computation can save the old balance before the transaction, so that the new balance can be correlated with the old balance after the transaction.

The local class Auditor at (2) acts as a repository for data that needs to be retrieved later to check the postconditon. Note that it accesses the final parameter, but declarations that follow its declaration would not be accessible. The assertion in the method check() at (4) ensures that the postcondition is checked, utilizing the data that was saved when the Auditor object was constructed at (5).

```
class Account {
    int balance;

    /** (1) Method makes a deposit into an account. */
    void deposit(final int amount) {

        /** (2) Local class to save the necessary data and to check
            that the transaction was valid. */
        class Auditor {

            /** (3) Stores the old balance. */
            private int balanceAtStartOfTransaction = balance;

            /** (4) Checks the postcondition. */
            void check() {
                assert balance - balanceAtStartOfTransaction == amount;
            }
        }

        Auditor auditor = new Auditor();    // (5) Save the data.
        balance += amount;                  // (6) Do the transaction.
        auditor.check();                    // (7) Check the postcondition.
    }

    public static void main(String[] args) {
        Account ac = new Account();
        ac.deposit(250);
    }
}
```

7.5 Anonymous Classes

Classes are usually first defined and then instantiated using the new operator. Anonymous classes combine the process of definition and instantiation into a single step. Anonymous classes are defined at the location they are instantiated, using additional syntax with the new operator. As these classes do not have a name, an instance of the class can only be created together with the definition.

An anonymous class can be defined and instantiated in contexts where a reference can be used (i.e., as expressions that evaluate to a reference denoting an object). Anonymous classes are typically used for creating objects *on the fly* in contexts such as the value in a return statement, an argument in a method call, or in initialization of variables. Anonymous classes are heavily used to implement *event listeners* in GUI-based applications.

Like local classes, anonymous classes can be defined in static or non-static context. The keyword static is never used.

Extending an Existing Class

The following syntax can be used for defining and instantiating an anonymous class that extends an existing class specified by *<superclass name>*:

new *<superclass name>* (*<optional argument list>*) { *<member declarations>* }

Optional arguments can be specified, which are passed to the superclass constructor. Thus, the superclass must provide a constructor corresponding to the arguments passed. No extends clause is used in the construct. Since an anonymous class cannot define constructors (as it does not have a name), an instance initializer can be used to achieve the same effect as a constructor. Only non-static members and final static fields can be declared in the class body.

Example 7.11   *Defining Anonymous Classes*

```
interface IDrawable {                            // (1)
    void draw();
}
class Shape implements IDrawable {.              // (2)
    public void draw() { System.out.println("Drawing a Shape."); }
}

class Painter {                                  // (3) Top-level Class

    public Shape createShape() {                 // (4) Non-static Method
        return new Shape(){                       // (5) Extends superclass at (2)
            public void draw() { System.out.println("Drawing a new Shape."); }
        };
    }
    public static IDrawable createIDrawable() { // (7) Static Method
        return new IDrawable(){                   // (8) Implements interface at (1)
            public void draw() {
```

```
                        System.out.println("Drawing a new IDrawable.");
                }
            };
        }
    }

    public class AnonClassClient {
        public static void main(String[] args) { // (9)
            IDrawable[] drawables = {                 // (10)
                new Painter().createShape(),      // (11) non-static anonymous class
                Painter.createIDrawable(),        // (12) static anonymous class
                new Painter().createIDrawable()   // (13) static anonymous class
            };
            for (int i = 0; i < drawables.length; i++)      // (14)
                drawables[i].draw();

            System.out.println("Anonymous Class Names:");
            System.out.println(drawables[0].getClass());  // (15)
            System.out.println(drawables[1].getClass());  // (16)
        }
    }
```

Output from the program:

```
Drawing a new Shape.
Drawing a new IDrawable.
Drawing a new IDrawable.
Anonymous Class Names:
class Painter$1
class Painter$2
```

Class definitions from Example 7.11, an adaptation of Example 7.10 to anonymous classes, are shown below. The non-static method createShape() at (4) defines a non-static anonymous class at (5), which extends the superclass Shape. The anonymous class overrides the inherited method draw(). As references to an anonymous class cannot be declared, the functionality of the class is only available through superclass references. Usually it makes sense to override methods from the superclass. Any other members declared in an anonymous class cannot be accessed by an external client.

```
// ...
class Shape implements IDrawable {          // (2)
    public void draw() { System.out.println("Drawing a Shape."); }
}

class Painter {                              // (3) Top-level Class

    public Shape createShape() {             // (4) Non-static Method
        return new Shape() {                 // (5) Extends superclass at (2)
            public void draw() { System.out.println("Drawing a new Shape."); }
        };
    }
    // ...

}
// ...
```

Implementing an Interface

The following syntax can be used for defining and instantiating an anonymous class that implements an interface specified by *<interface name>*:

new *<interface name>*() { *<member declarations>* }

An anonymous class provides a single interface implementation, and no arguments are passed. The anonymous class implicitly extends the Object class. Note that no implements clause is used in the construct. The class body has the same restrictions as previously noted for anonymous classes extending an existing class.

An anonymous class implementing an interface is shown below. Details can be found in Example 7.11. The static method createIDrawable() at (7) defines a static anonymous class at (8), which implements the interface IDrawable, by providing an implementation of the method draw(). The functionality of objects of an anonymous class that implements an interface is available through references of the interface type and the Object type, (i.e., the supertypes).

```java
interface IDrawable {                          // (1) Interface
    void draw();
}
// ...
class Painter {                                // (3) Top-level Class
    // ...
    public static IDrawable createIDrawable() { // (7) Static Method
        return new IDrawable(){                 // (8) Implements interface at (1)
            public void draw() {
                System.out.println("Drawing a new IDrawable.");
            }
        };
    }
}
// ...
```

The following code is an example of a typical use of anonymous classes in building GUI-application. The anonymous class at (1) implements the ActionListener interface that has the method actionPerformed(). When the addActionListener() method is called on the GUI-button denoted by the reference quitButton, the anonymous class is instantiated and the object reference value passed as a parameter to the method. The method addActionListener() of the GUI-button can use the reference value to invoke the method actionPerformed() in the ActionListener object.

```java
quitButton.addActionListener(
        new ActionListener() {     // (1) Anonymous class implements interface.
            // Invoked when the user clicks the quit button.
            public void actionPerformed(ActionEvent evt) {
                System.exit(0);    // (2) Terminates the program.
            }
        }
);
```

Instantiating Anonymous Classes

The discussion on instantiating local classes (see Example 7.10) is also valid for instantiating anonymous classes. The class AnonClassClient in Example 7.11 creates one instance at (11) of the non-static anonymous class defined at (5), and two instances at (12) and (13) of the static anonymous class defined at (8). The program output shows the polymorphic behavior and the runtime types of the objects. Similar to a non-static local class, an instance of a non-static anonymous class has an instance of its enclosing class at (11). An enclosing instance is not mandatory for creating objects of a static anonymous class, as shown at (12).

The names of the anonymous classes at runtime are also shown in the program output in Example 7.11. They are also the names used to designate their respective class files. Anonymous classes are not so anonymous after all.

Accessing Declarations in Enclosing Context

Access rules for local classes (see Section 7.4, p. 304) also apply to anonymous classes. Example 7.12 is an adaptation of Example 7.9 and illustrates the access rules for anonymous classes. The local classes in Example 7.9 have been adapted to anonymous classes in Example 7.12. The TLCWithAnonClasses class has two methods: one non-static and the other static, which return an instance of a non-static and a static anonymous class, respectively. Both anonymous classes extend the Base class.

Anonymous classes can access final variables only in the enclosing context. Inside the definition of a non-static anonymous class, members of the enclosing context can be referenced using the *<enclosing class name>*.this construct. Non-static anonymous classes can also access any non-hidden members by their simple names in the enclosing context, whereas static anonymous classes can only access non-hidden static members.

- -

Example 7.12 *Accessing Declarations in Enclosing Context*

```
class Base {
    protected int nsf1;
}

class TLCWithAnonClasses {            // Top level Class
    private double nsf1;              // Non-static field
    private int    nsf2;             // Non-static field
    private static int sf;           // Static field

    Base nonStaticMethod(final int fp) { // Non-static Method
        final int flv  = 10;          // final local variable
        final int hlv  = 30;          // final (hidden) local variable
              int nflv = 20;          // non-final local variable
```

```
        return new Base() {              // Non-static anonymous class
//           static int f1;              // (1) Not OK. Static members not allowed.
             final static int f2 = 10;   // (2) final static members allowed.
             int     f3   = fp;     // (3) final param from enclosing method.
             int     f4   = flv;    // (4) final local var from enclosing method.
//           double f5   = nflv;   // (5) Not OK. Only finals from enclosing method.
             double f6   = nsf1;          // (6) Inherited from superclass.
             double f6a  = this.nsf1;    // (6a) Inherited from superclass.
             double f6b  = super.nsf1;   // (6b) Inherited from superclass.
             double f7   = TLCWithAnonClasses.this.nsf1; // (7) In enclosing object.
             int     f8   = nsf2;         // (8)  In enclosing object.
             int     f9   = sf;           // (9)  static from enclosing class.
             int     hlv;                 // (10) Hides local variable.
        };
    }

    static Base staticMethod(final int fp) { // Static Method
        final int flv  = 10;                      // final local variable
        final int hlv  = 30;                      // final (hidden) local variable
              int nflv = 20;                      // non-final local variable

        return new Base() {              // Static anonymous class
//           static int f1;              // (11) Not OK. Static members not allowed.
             final static int f2 = 10;   // (12) final static members allowed.
             int     f3   = fp;     // (13) final param from enclosing method.
             int     f4   = flv;    // (14) final local var from enclosing method.
//           double f5   = nflv;   // (15) Not OK. Only finals from enclosing method.
             double f6   = nsf1;          // (16 ) Inherited from superclass.
             double f6a  = this.nsf1;    // (16a) Inherited from superclass.
             double f6b  = super.nsf1;   // (16b) Inherited from superclass.
//           double f7   = TLCWithAnonClasses.this.nsf1; //(17) No enclosing object.
//           int     f8   = nsf2;         // (18)  No enclosing object.
             int     f9   = sf;           // (19)  static from enclosing class.
             int     hlv;                 // (20) Hides local variable.
        };
    }
}
```

 Review Questions

7.6   Which statement is true?

Select the one correct answer.

(a) Non-static member classes must have either default or public accessibility.
(b) All nested classes can declare static member classes.
(c) Methods in all nested classes can be declared static.
(d) All nested classes can be declared static.
(e) Static member classes can contain non-static methods.

7.7 Given the declaration

```
interface IntHolder { int getInt(); }
```

which of the following methods are valid?

```
//----(1)----
    IntHolder makeIntHolder(int i) {
        return new IntHolder() {
            public int getInt() { return i; }
        };
    }
//----(2)----
    IntHolder makeIntHolder(final int i) {
        return new IntHolder {
            public int getInt() { return i; }
        };
    }
//----(3)----
    IntHolder makeIntHolder(int i) {
        class MyIH implements IntHolder {
            public int getInt() { return i; }
        }
        return new MyIH();
    }
//----(4)----
    IntHolder makeIntHolder(final int i) {
        class MyIH implements IntHolder {
            public int getInt() { return i; }
        }
        return new MyIH();
    }
//----(5)----
    IntHolder makeIntHolder(int i) {
        return new MyIH(i);
    }
    static class MyIH implements IntHolder {
        final int j;
        MyIH(int i) { j = i; }
        public int getInt() { return j; }
    }
```

Select the two correct answers.

(a) The method labeled (1).
(b) The method labeled (2).
(c) The method labeled (3).
(d) The method labeled (4).
(e) The method labeled (5).

7.8   Which statements are true?

Select the two correct answers.

(a) No other static members, except final static fields, can be declared within a non-static member class.

(b) If a non-static member class is nested within a class named Outer, then methods within the non-static member class must use the prefix Outer.this to access the members of the class Outer.

(c) All fields in any nested class must be declared final.

(d) Anonymous classes cannot have constructors.

(e) If objRef is an instance of any nested class within the class Outer, then the expression (objRef instanceof Outer) will evaluate to true.

7.9   Which statement is true?

Select the one correct answer.

(a) Top-level classes can be declared static.

(b) Classes declared as members of top-level classes can be declared static.

(c) Local classes can be declared static.

(d) Anonymous classes can be declared static.

(e) No classes can be declared static.

Chapter Summary

The following information was included in this chapter:

- categories of nested classes: static member classes and interfaces, non-static member classes, local classes, anonymous classes

- discussion of salient aspects of nested classes and interfaces:
    - the context in which they can be defined
    - which accessibility modifiers are valid for such classes and interfaces
    - whether an instance of the enclosing context is associated with an instance of the nested class
    - which entities a nested class or interface can access in its enclosing contexts
    - whether both static and non-static members can be defined in a nested class

- importing and using nested classes and interfaces

- instantiating non-static member classes using *<enclosing object reference>*.new syntax

- accessing members in the enclosing context of inner classes using *<enclosing class name>*.this syntax

- accessing members both in the inheritance hierarchy and the enclosing context of nested classes

- implementing anonymous classes by extending an existing class or by implementing an interface

 Programming Exercise

7.1   Create a new program with a nested class named PrintFunc that extends class Print from Exercise 6.2. In addition to just printing the value, class PrintFunc should first apply a Function object on the value. Class PrintFunc should have a constructor that takes an instance of Function type as a parameter. The evaluate() method of class PrintFunc should use the Function object on its argument. The evaluate() method should print and return the result. The evaluate() method in superclass Print should be used to print the value.

The program should behave like the one in Exercise 6.2, but this time use the nested class PrintFunc instead of class Print.

Object Lifetime

8

- State the behavior that is guaranteed by the garbage collection system.
- Write code that explicitly makes objects eligible for garbage collection.
- Recognize the point in a piece of source code at which an object becomes eligible for garbage collection.

Supplementary Objectives

- Write code that makes proper use of the finalization mechanism to free resources before an object is garbage collected.
- Distinguish between static and instance initializer expressions and initializer blocks, and how they are used for object initialization and class initialization.
- State the phases involved in initializing the object state when an object is created using the new operator.

8.1 Garbage Collection

Efficient memory management is essential in a runtime system. Storage for objects is allocated in a designated part of memory called the *heap*. The size of the heap is finite. Garbage collection is a process of managing the heap efficiently; that is, reclaiming memory occupied by objects that are no longer needed and making it available for new objects. Java provides automatic garbage collection, meaning that the runtime environment can take care of memory management concerning objects without the program having to take any special action. Storage allocated on the heap through the new operator is administered by the automatic garbage collector. The automatic garbage collection scheme guarantees that a reference to an object is always valid while the object is needed in the program. The object will not be reclaimed, leaving the reference dangling.

Having an automatic garbage collector frees the programmer from the responsibility of providing code for deleting objects. In relying on the automatic garbage collector, a Java program also forfeits any significant influence on the garbage collection of its objects (see p. 327). However, this price is insignificant when compared to the cost of putting the code for object management in place and plugging all the memory leaks. Time-critical applications should bear in mind that the automatic garbage collector runs as a background task and may prove detrimental to their performance.

Reachable References

An automatic garbage collector essentially performs two tasks:

- decide if and when memory needs to be reclaimed
- find objects that are no longer needed by the program and reclaim their storage

A program has no guarantees that the automatic garbage collector will be run during its execution. A program should not rely on the scheduling of the automatic garbage collector for its behavior (see p. 327).

In order to understand how the automatic garbage collector finds objects whose storage should be reclaimed, we need to look at the activity going on in the JVM. Java provides thread-based multitasking, meaning there can be several threads executing in the JVM, each doing its own task (see Chapter 9). A thread is an independent path of execution through the program code. A thread is alive if it has not completed its execution. Each live thread has its own runtime stack, as explained in Section 5.5 on page 181. The runtime stack contains activation records of methods that are currently active. Local references declared in a method can always be found in the method's activation record, on the runtime stack associated with the thread in which the method is called. Objects, on the other hand, are always created in the heap. If an object has a field reference, then the field is to be found inside the object in the heap, and the object denoted by the field reference is also to be found in the heap.

An example of how memory is organized during execution is depicted in Figure 8.1. It shows two live threads (t_1 and t_2) and their respective runtime stacks with the activation records. The diagram shows which objects in the heap are referenced by local references in the method activation records. The diagram also shows field references in objects, which denote other objects in the heap. Some objects have several aliases.

An object in the heap is said to be *reachable* if it is denoted by any local reference in a runtime stack. Additionally, any object that is denoted by a reference in a reachable object is also said to be reachable. Reachability is a transitive relation. Thus, a reachable object has at least one chain of reachable references from the runtime stack. Any reference that makes an object reachable is called a *reachable reference*. An object that is not reachable is said to be *unreachable*.

A reachable object is *alive*. It is *accessible* by the live thread that owns the runtime stack. Note that an object can be accessible by more than one thread. Any object that is *not* accessible by a live thread is a candidate for garbage collection. When an object becomes unreachable and is waiting for its memory to be reclaimed, it is said to be *eligible* for garbage collection. An object is eligible for garbage collection if all references denoting it are in eligible objects. Eligible objects do not affect the future course of program execution. When the garbage collector runs, it finds and reclaims the storage of eligible objects. However, garbage collection does not necessarily occur as soon as an object becomes unreachable.

From Figure 8.1 we see that objects o4, o5, o11, o12, o14, and o15 all have reachable references. Objects o13 and o16 have no reachable references and are, therefore, eligible for garbage collection.

From the discussion above we can conclude that if a composite object becomes unreachable, then its constituent objects also become unreachable, barring any reachable references to the constituent objects. Although objects o1, o2, and o3 form a circular list, they do not have any reachable references. Thus, these objects are all eligible. On the other hand, objects o5, o6, and o7 form a linear list, but they are all reachable, as the first object in the list, o5, is reachable. Objects o8, o10, o11, and o9 also form a linear list (in that order), but not all objects in the list are reachable. Only objects o9 and o11 are reachable, as object o11 has a reachable reference. Objects o8 and o10 are eligible for garbage collection.

The lifetime of an object is the time from when it is created to the time it is garbage collected. Under normal circumstances, an object is accessible from the time when it is created to the time when it is unreachable. The lifetime of an object can also include a period when it is eligible for garbage collection, waiting for its storage to be reclaimed. The finalization mechanism (see p. 324) in Java does provide a means for *resurrecting* an object after it is eligible for garbage collection, but the finalization mechanism is rarely used for this purpose.

Figure 8.1 *Memory Organization at Runtime*

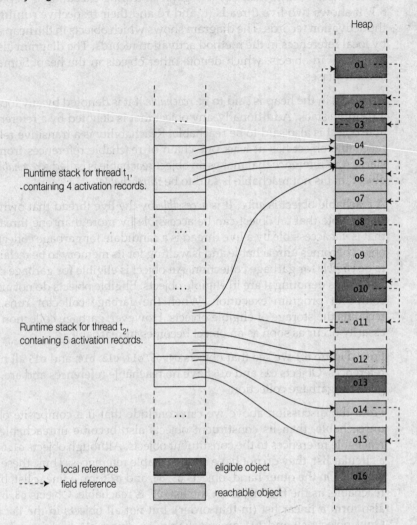

Runtime stack for thread t₁,
containing 4 activation records.

Runtime stack for thread t₂,
containing 5 activation records.

Heap

o1
o2
o3
o4
o5
o6
o7
o8
o9
o10
o11
o12
o13
o14
o15
o16

→ local reference   ▮ eligible object
----▶ field reference   ▯ reachable object

In the garbage collection scheme discussed above, an object remains reachable as long as there is a reference to it from running code. Using *strong references* (the technical name for the normal kind of references) can prove to be a handicap in certain situations. An application that uses a clipboard would most likely want its clipboard accessible at all times, but it would not mind if the contents of the clipboard were garbage collected when memory became low. This would not be possible if strong references were used to refer to the clipboard's contents.

The abstract class java.lang.ref.Reference and its concrete subclasses (SoftReference, WeakReference, PhantomReference) provide *reference objects* that can be used to maintain more sophisticated kinds of references to another object (called the *referent*). A reference object introduces an extra level of indirection, so that the program does not access the referent directly. The automatic garbage collector knows about reference objects and can reclaim the referent if it is only reachable through reference objects. The concrete subclasses implement references of various strength and reachability, which the garbage collector takes into consideration.

Facilitating Garbage Collection

The automatic garbage collector figures out which objects are not reachable and, therefore, eligible for garbage collection. It will certainly go to work if there is a danger of running out of memory. Although the automatic garbage collector tries to run unobtrusively, certain programming practices can nevertheless help in minimizing the overhead associated with garbage collection during program execution. Automatic garbage collection should not be perceived as a license for uninhibited creation of objects and forgetting about them.

Certain objects, such as files and net connections, can tie up other resources and should be disposed of properly when they are no longer needed. In most cases, the finally block in the try-catch-finally construct (see Section 5.7, p. 188) provides a convenient facility for such purposes, as it will always be executed, thereby ensuring proper disposal of any unwanted resources.

To optimize its memory footprint, a live thread should only retain access to an object as long as the object is needed for its execution. The program can make objects become eligible for garbage collection as early as possible by removing all references to the object when it is no longer needed.

Objects that are created and accessed by local references in a method are eligible for garbage collection when the method terminates, unless reference values to these objects are exported out of the method. This can occur if a reference value is returned from the method, passed as argument to another method that records the reference, or thrown as an exception. However, a method need not always leave objects to be garbage collected after its termination. It can facilitate garbage collection by taking suitable action, for example, by nulling references.

```java
import java.io.*;

class WellbehavedClass {
    // ...
    void wellbehavedMethod() {

        File aFile;
        long[] bigArray = new long[20000];

        // ... uses local variables ...

        // Does cleanup (before starting something extensive)
        aFile = null;                     // (1)
        bigArray = null;                  // (2)

        // Start some other extensive activity
        // ...
    }
    // ...
```

In the previous code, the local variables are set to null after use at (1) and (2), before starting some other extensive activity. This makes the objects denoted by the local variables eligible for garbage collection from this point onward, rather than after the method terminates. This optimization technique of nulling references need only be used as a last resort when resources are scarce.

When a method returns a reference value and the object denoted by the value is not needed, not assigning this value to a reference also facilitates garbage collection.

If a reference is assigned a new reference value, the object denoted by the reference prior to the assignment can become eligible for garbage collection.

Removing reachable references to a composite object can make the constituent objects become eligible for garbage collection, as explained earlier.

Example 8.1 illustrates how the program can influence garbage collection eligibility. Class HeavyItem represents objects with a large memory footprint, on which we want to monitor garbage collection. Each composite HeavyItem object has a reference to a large array. The class overrides the finalize() method from the Object class to print out an ID, when the object is finalized. This method is always called on an eligible object before it is destroyed (see finalizers, p. 324). We use it to indicate in the output if and when a HeavyItem is reclaimed. To illustrate the effect of garbage collection on object hierarchies, each object may also have a reference to another HeavyItem.

In Example 8.1, the class RecyclingBin defines a method createHeavyItem() at (4). In this method, the HeavyItem created at (5) is eligible for garbage collection after the reassignment of reference itemA at (6), as this object will have no references. The HeavyItem created at (6) is accessible on return from the method. Its fate depends on the code that calls this method.

In Example 8.1, the class RecyclingBin also defines a method createList() at (7). It returns the reference value in the reference item1, which denotes the first item in a list of three HeavyItems. Because of the list structure, none of the HeavyItems in the list are eligible for garbage collection on return from the method. Again, the fate of the objects in the list is decided by the code that calls this method. It is enough for the first item in the list to become unreachable, in order for all objects in the list to become eligible for garbage collection (barring any reachable references).

Example 8.1   *Garbage Collection Eligibility*

```
class HeavyItem {                              // (1)
    int[]     itemBody;
    String    itemID;
    HeavyItem nextItem;

    HeavyItem(String ID, HeavyItem itemRef) {  // (2)
        itemBody = new int[100000];
        itemID   = ID;
        nextItem = itemRef;
    }
```

```
                    protected void finalize() throws Throwable {     // (3)
                        System.out.println(itemID + ": recycled.");
                        super.finalize();
                    }
                }

                public class RecyclingBin {

                    public static HeavyItem createHeavyItem(String itemID) {          // (4)
                        HeavyItem itemA = new HeavyItem(itemID + " local item", null); // (5)
                        itemA = new HeavyItem(itemID, null);                           // (6)
                        System.out.println("Return from creating HeavyItem " + itemID);
                        return itemA;                                                  // (7)
                    }

                    public static HeavyItem createList(String listID) {               // (8)
                        HeavyItem item3 = new HeavyItem(listID + ": item3", null);     // (9)
                        HeavyItem item2 = new HeavyItem(listID + ": item2", item3);    // (10)
                        HeavyItem item1 = new HeavyItem(listID + ": item1", item2);    // (11)
                        System.out.println("Return from creating list " + listID);
                        return item1;                                                  // (12)
                    }

                    public static void main(String[] args) {                          // (13)
                        HeavyItem list = createList("X");                             // (14)
                        list = createList("Y");                                       // (15)

                        HeavyItem itemOne = createHeavyItem("One");                   // (16)
                        HeavyItem itemTwo = createHeavyItem("Two");                   // (17)
                        itemOne = null;                                               // (18)
                        createHeavyItem("Three");                                     // (19)
                        createHeavyItem("Four");                                      // (20)
                        System.out.println("Return from main().");
                    }
                }
```

Possible output from the program:

```
        Return from creating list X
        Return from creating list Y
        X: item3: recycled.
        X: item2: recycled.
        X: item1: recycled.
        Return from creating HeavyItem One
        Return from creating HeavyItem Two
        Return from creating HeavyItem Three
        Three local item: recycled.
        Three: recycled.
        Two local item: recycled.
        Return from creating HeavyItem Four
        One local item: recycled.
        One: recycled.
        Return from main().
```

In Example 8.1, the main() method at (13) in the class RecyclingBin uses the methods createHeavyItem() and createList(). It creates a list X at (14), but the reference to its first item is reassigned at (15), making objects in list X eligible for garbage collection after (15). The first item of list Y is stored in the reference list, making this list non-eligible for garbage collection during the execution of the main() method.

The main() method creates two items at (16) and (17), storing their reference values in references itemOne and itemTwo, respectively. The reference itemOne is nulled at (18), making HeavyItem with identity One eligible for garbage collection. The two calls to the createHeavyItem() method at (19) and (20) return reference values to HeavyItems, which are not stored, making each object eligible for garbage collection right after the respective method call returns.

The output from the program bears out the observations made above. Objects in list Y (accessible through reference list) and HeavyItem with identity Two (accessible through reference itemTwo) remain non-eligible while the main() method executes. Although the output shows that HeavyItems with identities Four and Five were never garbage collected, they are not accessible once they become eligible for garbage collection at (19) and (20), respectively. Any objects in the heap after the program terminates are reclaimed by the operating system.

Object Finalization

Object finalization provides an object a last resort to undertake any action before its storage is reclaimed. The automatic garbage collector calls the finalize() method in an object that is eligible for garbage collection before actually destroying the object. The finalize() method is defined in the Object class.

```
protected void finalize() throws Throwable
```

An implementation of the finalize() method is called a *finalizer*. A subclass can override the finalizer from the Object class in order to take more specific and appropriate action before an object of the subclass is destroyed.

A finalizer can, like any other method, catch and throw exceptions (see Section 5.7, p. 188). However, any exception thrown but not caught by a finalizer invoked by the garbage collector is ignored. The finalizer is only called once on an object, regardless of whether any exception is thrown during its execution. In case of finalization failure, the object still remains eligible for disposal at the discretion of the garbage collector (unless it has been resurrected, as explained in the next subsection). Since there is no guarantee that the garbage collector will ever run, there is also no guarantee that the finalizer will ever be called.

In the following code, the finalizer at (1) will take appropriate action if and when called on objects of the class before they are garbage collected, ensuring that the resource is freed. Since it is not guaranteed that the finalizer will ever be called at all, a program should not rely on the finalization to do any critical operations.

```
    public class AnotherWellbehavedClass {
        SomeResource objRef;
        // ...
        protected void finalize() throws Throwable {     // (1)
            try {                                         // (2)
                if (objRef != null) objRef.close();
            } finally {                                   // (3)
                super.finalize();                         // (4)
            }
        }
    }
```

Finalizer Chaining

Unlike subclass constructors, overridden finalizers are not implicitly chained (see Section 6.3, p. 243). Therefore, a finalizer in a subclass should explicitly call the finalizer in its superclass as its last action, as shown at (4) in the previous code. The call to the finalizer of the superclass is in a finally block at (3), guaranteed to be executed regardless of any exceptions thrown by the code in the try block at (2).

A finalizer may make the object accessible again (i.e., *resurrect* it), thus avoiding it being garbage collected. One simple technique is to assign its this reference to a static field, from which it can later be retrieved. Since a finalizer is called only once on an object before being garbage collected, an object can only be resurrected once. In other words, if the object again becomes eligible for garbage collection and the garbage collector runs, the finalizer will not be called. Such object resurrections are not recommended, as they only undermine the purpose of the finalization mechanism.

Example 8.2 illustrates chaining of finalizers. It creates a user-specified number of large objects of a user-specified size. The number and size are provided through command-line program arguments. The loop at (7) in the main() method creates Blob objects, but does not store any references to them. Objects created are instances of the class Blob defined at (3). The Blob constructor at (4) initializes the field fat by constructing a large array of integers. The Blob class extends the BasicBlob class that assigns each blob a unique number (blobId) and keeps track of the number of blobs (population) not yet garbage collected. Creation of each Blob object by the constructor at (4) prints the ID number of the object and the message "Hello". The finalize() method at (5) is called before a Blob object is garbage collected. It prints the message "Bye" and calls the finalize() method in the class BasicBlob at (2), which decrements the population count. The program output shows that two blobs were not garbage collected at the time the print statement at (8) was executed. It is evident from the number of "Bye" messages that three blobs were garbage collected before all the five blobs had been created in the loop at (7).

Example 8.2   *Using Finalizers*

```
class BasicBlob {                                        // (1)
    static    int idCounter;
    static    int population;
    protected int blobId;

    BasicBlob() {
        blobId = idCounter++;
        ++population;
    }
    protected void finalize() throws Throwable {         // (2)
        --population;
        super.finalize();
    }
}

class Blob extends BasicBlob {                            // (3)
    int[] fat;

    Blob(int bloatedness) {                               // (4)
        fat = new int[bloatedness];
        System.out.println(blobId + ": Hello");
    }

    protected void finalize() throws Throwable {          // (5)
        System.out.println(blobId + ": Bye");
        super.finalize();
    }
}

public class Finalizers {
    public static void main(String[] args) {             // (6)
        int blobsRequired, blobSize;
        try {
            blobsRequired = Integer.parseInt(args[0]);
            blobSize      = Integer.parseInt(args[1]);
        } catch(IndexOutOfBoundsException e) {
            System.err.println(
                "Usage: Finalizers <number of blobs> <blob size>");
            return;
        }
        for (int i=0; i<blobsRequired; ++i) {            // (7)
            new Blob(blobSize);
        }
        System.out.println(BasicBlob.population + " blobs alive"); // (8)
    }
}
```

Running the program with the command

```
>java Finalizers 5 500000
```

might result in the following output:

```
0: Hello
1: Hello
2: Hello
0: Bye
1: Bye
2: Bye
3: Hello
4: Hello
2 blobs alive
```

Invoking Garbage Collection

Although Java provides facilities to invoke the garbage collection explicitly, there are no guarantees that it will be run. The program can only request that garbage collection be performed, but there is no way that garbage collection can be forced.

The System.gc() method can be used to request garbage collection, and the System.runFinalization() method can be called to suggest that any pending finalizers be run for objects eligible for garbage collection. Alternatively, corresponding methods in the Runtime class can be used. A Java application has a unique Runtime object that can be used by the application to interact with the JVM. An application can obtain this object by calling the method Runtime.getRuntime(). The Runtime class provides various methods related to memory issues.

static Runtime getRuntime()
Returns the Runtime object associated with the current application.

void gc()
Requests that garbage collection be run. However, it is recommended to use the more convenient static method System.gc().

void runFinalization()
Requests that any pending finalizers be run for objects eligible for garbage collection. Again, it is more convenient to use the static method System.runFinalization().

long freeMemory()
Returns the amount of free memory (bytes) in the JVM, that is available for new objects.

long totalMemory()
Returns the total amount of memory (bytes) available in the JVM. This includes both memory occupied by current objects and that which is available for new objects.

Example 8.3 illustrates invoking garbage collection. The class MemoryCheck is an adaptation of the class Finalizers from Example 8.2. The RunTime object for the application is obtained at (7). This object is used to get information regarding total memory and free memory in the JVM at (8) and (9), respectively. Blobs are created in the loop at (10). The amount of free memory after blob creation is printed at (11). We see from the program output that some blobs were already garbage collected before the execution got to (11). A request for garbage collection is made at (12). Checking free memory after the request shows that more memory has become available, indicating that the request was honoured. It is instructive to run the program without the method call System.gc() at (12), in order to compare the results.

Example 8.3   *Invoking Garbage Collection*

```
class BasicBlob {  /* See Example 8.2. */ }
class Blob extends BasicBlob { /* See Example 8.2.*/ }

public class MemoryCheck {
    public static void main(String[] args) {              // (6)
        int blobsRequired, blobSize;
        try {
            blobsRequired = Integer.parseInt(args[0]);
            blobSize      = Integer.parseInt(args[1]);
        } catch(IndexOutOfBoundsException e) {
            System.err.println(
                "Usage: MemoryCheck <number of blobs> <blob size>");
            return;
        }
        Runtime environment = Runtime.getRuntime();                       // (7)
        System.out.println("Total memory: " + environment.totalMemory());// (8)
        System.out.println("Free memory before blob creation: "
                        + environment.freeMemory());                      // (9)
        for (int i=0; i<blobsRequired; ++i) {                             // (10)
            new Blob(blobSize);
        }
        System.out.println("Free memory after blob creation: "
                        + environment.freeMemory());                      // (11)
        System.gc();                                                      // (12)
        System.out.println("Free memory after requesting GC: "
                        + environment.freeMemory());                      // (13)
        System.out.println(BasicBlob.population + " blobs alive");        // (14)
    }
}
```

Running the program with the command

```
>java MemoryCheck 5 100000
```

gave the following output:

```
Total memory: 2031616
Free memory before blob creation: 1773192
```

```
0: Hello
1: Hello
2: Hello
1: Bye
2: Bye
3: Hello
0: Bye
3: Bye
4: Hello
Free memory after blob creation: 818760
4: Bye
Free memory after requesting GC: 1619656
0 blobs alive
```

Certain aspects regarding automatic garbage collection should be noted:

- There are no guarantees that objects that are eligible for garbage collection will have their finalizers executed. Garbage collection might not even be run if the program execution does not warrant it. Thus, any memory allocated during program execution might remain allocated after program termination, but will be reclaimed by the operating system.

- There are also no guarantees about the order in which the objects will be garbage collected, or the order in which their finalizers will be executed. Therefore, the program should not make any assumptions based on these aspects.

- Garbage collection does not guarantee that there is enough memory for the program to run. A program can rely on the garbage collector to run when memory gets very low and it can expect an OutOfMemoryException to be thrown if its memory demands cannot be met.

 Review Questions

8.1 Which statement is true?

Select the one correct answer.

(a) Objects can be explicitly destroyed using the keyword delete.
(b) An object will be garbage collected immediately after it becomes unreachable.
(c) If object obj1 is accessible from object obj2, and object obj2 is accessible from obj1, then obj1 and obj2 are not eligible for garbage collection.
(d) Once an object has become eligible for garbage collection, it will remain eligible until it is destroyed.
(e) If object obj1 can access object obj2 that is eligible for garbage collection, then obj1 is also eligible for garbage collection.

8.2   Identify the location in the following program where the object, initially referenced with arg1, is eligible for garbage collection.

```
public class MyClass {
    public static void main(String[] args) {
        String msg;
        String pre = "This program was called with ";
        String post = " as first argument.";

        String arg1 = new String((args.length > 0) ?
                        "'" + args[ 0 ] + "'" :
                        "<no argument>");
        msg = arg1;
        arg1 = null;               // (1)
        msg = pre + msg + post;    // (2)
        pre = null;                // (3)

        System.out.println(msg);

        msg = null;                // (4)
        post = null;               // (5)
        args = null;               // (6)
    }
}
```

Select the one correct answer.

(a) After the line labeled (1).
(b) After the line labeled (2).
(c) After the line labeled (3).
(d) After the line labeled (4).
(e) After the line labeled (5).
(f) After the line labeled (6).

8.3   Which statement is true?

Select the one correct answer.

(a) If an exception is thrown during the execution of the finalize() method of an eligible object, then the exception is ignored and the object is destroyed.
(b) All objects have a finalize() method.
(c) Objects can be destroyed by explicitly calling the finalize() method.
(d) The finalize() method can be declared with any accessibility.
(e) The compiler will fail to compile code that defines an overriding finalize() method that does not explicitly call the overridden finalize() method from the superclass.

8.4   Which statement is true?

Select the one correct answer.

(a) The compiler will fail to compile code that explicitly tries to call the finalize() method.
(b) The finalize() method must be declared with protected accessibility.

(c) An overriding finalize() method in any class can always throw checked exceptions.

(d) The finalize() method can be overloaded.

(e) The body of the finalize() method can only access other objects that are eligible for garbage collection.

8.5 Which statement describes guaranteed behavior of the garbage collection and finalization mechanisms?

Select the one correct answer.

(a) Objects will not be destroyed until they have no references to them.

(b) The finalize() method will never be called more than once on an object.

(c) An object eligible for garbage collection will eventually be destroyed by the garbage collector.

(d) If object A became eligible for garbage collection before object B, then object A will be destroyed before object B.

(e) An object, once eligible for garbage collection, can never become accessible by a live thread.

8.2 Initializers

Initializers can be employed for initialization of fields in objects and classes, resulting in the fields being assigned initial values. These initializers are

- *field initializer expressions*
- *static initializer blocks*
- *instance initializer blocks*

The rest of this section provides details on these initializers, concluding with a discussion on the phases involved in constructing the state of an object, when the object is created by using the new operator.

Field Initializer Expressions

Initialization of fields can be explicitly specified in field declaration statements using initializer expressions. The value of the initializer expression must be assignment compatible to the declared field (see Section 3.4, p. 47 and Section 6.6, p. 260). We distinguish between static and non-static field initializers.

```
class ConstantInitializers {
    int minAge = 12;                    // (1) Non-static
    static double pensionPoints = 10.5; // (2) Static
    // ...
}
```

The fields of an object are initialized with the values of initializer expressions when the object is created by using the new operator. In the previous example, the declaration at (1) will result in the field minAge being initialized to 12 in every object of the class ConstantInitializers created with the new operator. If no explicit initializer expressions are specified, default values (see Section 2.4, p. 33) are assigned to the fields.

Class initialization results in the static fields of a class being initialized with the values of the initializer expressions. The declaration at (2) will result in the static field pensionPoints being initialized to 10.5 when the class is initialized. Again, if no explicit initializers are specified, default values are assigned to the static fields.

An initializer expression for a static field cannot refer to non-static members by their simple names. The keywords this and super cannot occur in a static initializer expression.

Since a class is always initialized before it can be instantiated, an instance initializer expression can always refer to any static member of a class, regardless of the member declaration order. In the following code, the instance initializer expression at (1) refers to the static field NO_OF_WEEKS declared and initialized at (2). Such a *forward reference* is legal. More examples of forward references are given in the next subsection.

```
class MoreInitializers {
        int noOfDays    = 7 * NO_OF_WEEKS;    // (1) Non-static
    static int NO_OF_WEEKS = 52;              // (2) Static
    // ...
}
```

Initializer expressions can also be used to define constants in interfaces (see Section 6.4, p. 255). Such initializer expressions are implicitly static, as they define values of final static fields.

Initializer expressions are also used to initialize local variables (see Section 2.3, p. 31). A local variable is initialized with the value of the initializer expression every time the local variable declaration is executed.

Initializer Expression Execution in Textual Order

When an object is created using the new operator, instance initializer expressions are executed in the order in which the instance fields are declared in the class.

Java requires that the declaration of a field must occur before its usage in any initializer expression, if the field is *used on the right-hand side of an assignment* in the initializer expression. This essentially means that the declaration of a field must occur before the value of the field is *read* in an initializer expression. Using the field on the left-hand side of an assignment in the initializer expression does not violate the declaration-before-read rule, as this constitutes a write operation. This rule applies when the usage of the field is by its simple name.

There is one caveat to the declaration-before-read rule: it does not apply if the initializer expression defines an anonymous class, as the usage then occurs in a different class, which has its own accessibility rules in the enclosing context. Restrictions outlined earlier help to detect initialization anomalies at compile time.

In the next example, the initialization at (2) generates a compile-time error, because the field width in the initializer expression violates the declaration-before-read rule. The usage of the field width in the initializer expression at (2) does not occur on the left-hand side of the assignment. This is an illegal forward reference. To remedy the situation, the declaration of the field width at (4) can be moved in front of the declaration at (2). In any case, we can use the keyword this as shown at (3), but this will read the default value 0 in the field width.

```
class NonStaticInitializers {
    int length  = 10;                    // (1)
//  double area = length * width;        // (2) Not Ok. Illegal forward reference.
    double area = length * this.width;   // (3) Ok, but width has default value 0.
    int width   = 10;                    // (4)

    int sqSide = height = 20;            // (5) OK. Legal forward reference.
    int height;                          // (6)
}
```

The forward reference at (5) is legal. The usage of field height in the initializer expression at (5) occurs on the left-hand side of the assignment. The initializer expression at (5) is evaluated as (sqSide = (height = 20)). Every object of class NonStaticInitializers will have the field height set to the value 20.

The declaration-before-read rule is equally applicable to static initializer expressions when static fields are referenced by their simple name.

Example 8.4 shows why the order of field initializer expressions can be important. The initializer expressions in Example 8.4 are calls to methods defined in the class. Methods are not subject to the same access rules as initializer expressions. The call at (2) to the method initMaxGuests() defined at (4) is expected to return the maximum number of guests. However, the field occupancyPerRoom at (3) will not have been explicitly initialized; therefore, its default value (0) will be used in the method initMaxGuests(), which will return an incorrect value. The program output shows that after object creation the occupancy per room is correct, but the maximum number of guests is wrong.

Example 8.4 *Initializer Expression Order and Method Calls*

```
class Hotel {
    private int noOfRooms       = 12;               // (1)
    private int maxNoOfGuests   = initMaxGuests();  // (2) Bug
    private int occupancyPerRoom = 2;               // (3)

    public int initMaxGuests() {                    // (4)
        System.out.println("occupancyPerRoom: " +
                          occupancyPerRoom);
```

```
        System.out.println("maxNoOfGuests: " +
                         noOfRooms * occupancyPerRoom);
        return noOfRooms * occupancyPerRoom;
    }

    public int getMaxGuests() {                          // (5)
        return maxNoOfGuests;
    }

    public int getOccupancy() {                          // (6)
        return occupancyPerRoom;
    }
}

public class TestOrder {
    public static void main(String[] args) {
        Hotel hotel = new Hotel();                       // (7)
        System.out.println("After object creation: ");
        System.out.println("occupancyPerRoom: " +
                         hotel.getOccupancy());           // (8)
        System.out.println("maxNoOfGuests: " +
                         hotel.getMaxGuests());           // (9)
    }
}
```

Output from the program:

```
occupancyPerRoom: 0
maxNoOfGuests: 0
After object creation:
occupancyPerRoom: 2
maxNoOfGuests: 0
```

Initializer Expressions and Checked Exceptions

Initializer expressions in named classes and interfaces must not result in any uncaught checked exception (see Section 5.9, p. 201). If any checked exception is thrown during execution of an initializer expression, it must be caught and handled by code called from the initializer expression. This restriction does not apply to instance initializer expressions in anonymous classes.

Example 8.5 illustrates exception handling for initializer expressions in named classes. The static initializer expression at (3) calls the static method createHotel-Pool() at (4), which can catch and handle the checked TooManyHotelsException defined at (2). If the method createHotelPool() uses the throws clause to specify the checked exception, instead of catching and handling it within a try-catch block, then the initializer expression at (3), which called the method, must handle the exception. However, the syntax of the initializer expression does not allow any exception handling to be specified, and the compiler complains that the checked exception is not handled.

The instance initializer expression at (5) calls the method initMaxGuests() at (6), which can throw the unchecked RoomOccupancyTooHighException. If thrown, this exception will be caught and handled in the main() method. Program output confirms that an unchecked RoomOccupancyTooHighException was thrown during program execution.

Example 8.5 *Exceptions in Initializer Expressions*

```
class RoomOccupancyTooHighException
    extends RuntimeException {}               // (1) Unchecked Exception
class TooManyHotelsException
    extends Exception {}                      // (2) Checked Exception

class Hotel {
    // Static Members
    private static int noOfHotels = 12;
    private static Hotel[] hotelPool = createHotelPool();   // (3)

    private static Hotel[] createHotelPool() {              // (4)
        try {
            if (noOfHotels > 10)
                throw new TooManyHotelsException();
        } catch (TooManyHotelsException e) {
            noOfHotels = 10;
            System.out.println("No. of hotels adjusted to " +
                                noOfHotels);
        }
        return new Hotel[noOfHotels];
    }
    // Instance Members
    private int noOfRooms        = 215;
    private int occupancyPerRoom = 5;
    private int maxNoOfGuests    = initMaxGuests();          // (5)

    private int initMaxGuests() {                           // (6)
        if (occupancyPerRoom > 4)
                throw new RoomOccupancyTooHighException();
        return noOfRooms * occupancyPerRoom;
    }
}

public class ExceptionsInInitializers {
    public static void main(String[] args) {
        try { new Hotel();}
        catch (RoomOccupancyTooHighException exception) {
            exception.printStackTrace();
        }
    }
}
```

Output from the program:

```
No. of hotels adjusted to 10
RoomOccupancyTooHighException
        at Hotel.initMaxGuests(ExceptionsInInitializers.java:29)
        at Hotel.<init>(ExceptionsInInitializers.java:25)
        at ExceptionsInInitializers.main(ExceptionsInInitializers.java:36)
```

Static Initializer Blocks

Java allows static initializer blocks to be defined in a class. Although such blocks can include arbitrary code, they are primarily used for initializing static fields. The code in a static initializer block is executed once only when the class is initialized.

The syntax of a static initializer block consists of the keyword static followed by a local block that can contain arbitrary code as shown at (3).

```
class StaticInitializers {

    final static int ROWS = 12, COLUMNS = 10;          // (1)
    static long[][] matrix = new long[ROWS][COLUMNS];  // (2)
    // ...
    static {                                           // (3) Static Initializer
        for (int i = 0; i < matrix.length; i++)
            for (int j = 0; j < matrix[i].length; j++)
                matrix[i][j] = 2*i + j;
    }
    // ...
}
```

When the class StaticInitializers is first loaded in the previous example, the final static fields at (1) are initialized. Then the array of arrays matrix of specified size is created at (2), followed by the execution of the static block at (3) .

If a class relies on native method implementations, a static initializer can be used to load any external libraries that the class needs (see Section 4.10, p. 148).

Note that the static initializer block is not contained in any method. A class can have more than one static initializer block. Initializer blocks are *not* members of a class nor can they have a return statement, as they cannot be called directly.

When a class is initialized, the initializer expressions in static field declarations and static initializer blocks are executed in the order they are specified in the class. In the previous example, the initializer expressions at (1) and (2) are executed before the static initializer block at (3).

Similar restrictions apply to static initializer blocks as for static initializer expressions: the keywords this and super cannot occur in a static initializer block.

When making forward references using simple names, code in a static initializer block is also subject to the declaration-before-read rule discussed in the previous subsection. Example 8.6 illustrates forward references and the order of execution for static initializer expressions and static initializer blocks. An illegal forward reference occurs at (4), where an attempt is made to read the value of the field sf1 before its declaration. At (11) the read operation is after the declaration and, therefore, allowed. Forward reference made on the left-hand side of the assignment is always allowed, as shown at (2), (5), and (7). The initializers are executed in their textual order. A static field has the value it was last assigned in an initializer. If there is no explicit assignment, the field has the default value of its type.

Example 8.6 *Static Initializers and Forward References*

```
class StaticForwardReferences {

    static {                  // (1) Static initializer block
        sf1 = 10;             // (2) OK. Assignment to sf1 allowed
//      sf1 = if1;            // (3) Not OK. Non-static field access in static context
//      int a = 2 * sf1;      // (4) Not OK. Read operation before declaration
        int b = sf1 = 20;     // (5) OK. Assignment to sf1 allowed
        int c = StaticForwardReferences.sf1;// (6) OK. Not accessed by simple name
    }

    static int sf1 = sf2 = 30;  // (7) Static field. Assignment to sf2 allowed
    static int sf2;             // (8) Static field
    int if1 = 5;                // (9) Non-static field

    static {                  // (10) Static initializer block
        int d = 2 * sf1;      // (11) OK. Read operation after declaration
        int e = sf1 = 50;     // (12)
    }

    public static void main(String[] args) {
        System.out.println("sf1: " + StaticForwardReferences.sf1);
        System.out.println("sf2: " + StaticForwardReferences.sf2);
    }
}
```

Output from the program:

```
sf1: 50
sf2: 30
```

Exception handling in static initializer blocks is no different from that in static initializer expressions: execution cannot allow an uncaught checked exception. Example 8.7 shows a static initializer block at (3) that catches and handles a checked exception in the try-catch block at (4). A static initializer block cannot be called directly, therefore, any checked exceptions must be caught and handled in the body of the static initializer block.

Example 8.7 also shows a static initializer block at (5) that throws an unchecked exception at (6) during class initialization. As the program output shows, this exception is handled by the default exception handler, resulting in termination of the program.

Example 8.7   *Static Initializer Blocks and Exceptions*

```
class BankrupcyException
       extends RuntimeException {}              // (1) Unchecked Exception
class TooManyHotelsException
       extends Exception {}                     // (2) Checked Exception

class Hotel {
    // Static Members
    private static boolean bankrupt   = true;
    private static int     noOfHotels = 11;
    private static Hotel[] hotelPool;

    static {                                     // (3) Static block
        try {                                    // (4) Handles checked exception
            if (noOfHotels > 10)
                throw new TooManyHotelsException();
        } catch (TooManyHotelsException e) {
            noOfHotels = 10;
            System.out.println("No. of hotels adjusted to " +
                              noOfHotels);
        }
        hotelPool = new Hotel[noOfHotels];
    }

    static {                                     // (5) Static block
        if (bankrupt)
            throw new BankrupcyException();      // (6) Throws unchecked exception
    }
    // ...
}

public class ExceptionInStaticInitBlocks {
    public static void main(String[] args) {
        new Hotel();
    }
} .
```

Output from the program:

```
No. of hotels adjusted to 10
Exception in thread "main" java.lang.ExceptionInInitializerError
        at ExceptionInStaticInitBlocks.main(ExceptionInStaticInitBlocks.java:33)
Caused by: BankrupcyException
        at Hotel.<clinit>(ExceptionInStaticInitBlocks.java:26)
```

Instance Initializer Blocks

Just as static initializer blocks can be used to initialize static fields in a named class, Java provides the ability to initialize fields during object creation using instance initializer blocks. In this respect, such blocks serve the same purpose as constructors during object creation. The syntax of an instance initializer block is the same as that of a local block, as shown at (2) in the following code. The code in the local block is executed every time an instance of the class is created.

```
class InstanceInitializers {

    long[] squares = new long[10];    // (1)
    // ...
    {                                 // (2) Instance Initializer
        for (int i = 0; i < squares.length; i++)
            squares[i] = i*i;
    }
    // ...
}
```

The array squares of specified size is created first at (1), followed by the execution of the instance initializer block at (2) every time an instance of the class InstanceIn-itializers is created. Note that the instance initializer block is not contained in any method. A class can have more than one instance initializer block, and these (and any instance initializer expressions in instance field declarations) are executed in the order they are specified in the class.

Analogous to other initializers discussed so far, an instance initializer block cannot make a forward reference to a field that violates the declaration-before-read rule. In Example 8.8, an illegal forward reference occurs in the code at (4), which attempts to read the value of the field nsf1 before it is declared. The read operation at (11) is after the declaration and is, therefore, allowed. Forward reference made on the left-hand side of the assignment is always allowed, as shown at (2), (3), (5), and (7).

Example 8.8 *Instance Initializers and Forward References*

```
class NonStaticForwardReferences {

    {                        // (1) Instance initializer block
        nsf1 = 10;           // (2) OK. Assignment to nsf1 allowed
        nsf1 = sf1;          // (3) OK. Static field access in non-static context
    //  int a = 2 * nsf1;    // (4) Not OK. Read operation before declaration
        int b = nsf1 = 20;   // (5) OK. Assignment to nsf1 allowed
        int c = this.nsf1;   // (6) OK. Not accessed by simple name
    }

    int nsf1 = nsf2 = 30;    // (7) Non-static field. Assignment to nsf2 allowed
    int nsf2;                // (8) Non-static field
    static int sf1 = 5;      // (9) Static field

    {                        // (10) Instance initializer block
        int d = 2 * nsf1;    // (11) OK. Read operation after declaration
        int e = nsf1 = 50;   // (12)
    }

    public static void main(String[] args) {
        NonStaticForwardReferences objRef = new NonStaticForwardReferences();
        System.out.println("nsf1: " + objRef.nsf1);
        System.out.println("nsf2: " + objRef.nsf2);
    }
}
```

Output from the program:

```
nsf1: 50
nsf2: 30
```

Similar to instance initializer expressions, the keywords this and super can be used to refer to the current object in an instance initializer block. As with static initializer blocks, the return statement is also not allowed in instance initializer blocks.

An instance initializer block can be used to factor out common initialization code that will be executed regardless of which constructor is invoked.

A typical use of an instance initializer block is in anonymous classes (see Section 7.5, p. 308), which cannot declare constructors, and instead can use instance initializer blocks to initialize fields. In Example 8.9, the anonymous class defined at (1) uses an instance initializer block defined at (2) to initialize its fields.

Example 8.9   *Instance Initializer Block in Anonymous Class*

```
class Base {
    protected int a;
    protected int b;
    void print() {
        System.out.println("a: " + a);
    }
}

class AnonymousClassMaker {
    Base createAnonymous() {
        return new Base() {                    // (1) Anonymous class
            {                                  // (2) Instance initializer
                a = 5; b = 10;
            }
            void print() {
                super.print();
                System.out.println("b: " + b);
            }
        }; // end anonymous class
    }
}

public class InstanceInitBlock {
    public static void main(String[] args) {
        new AnonymousClassMaker().createAnonymous().print();
    }
}
```

Output from the program:

```
a: 5
b: 10
```

Exception handling in instance initializer blocks is similar to that in static initializer blocks. Example 8.10 shows an instance initializer block at (3) that catches and handles a checked exception in the try-catch block at (4). Another instance initializer block at (5) throws an unchecked exception at (6). The runtime system handles the exception, printing the stack trace and terminating the program.

Exception handling in instance initializer blocks differs from that in static initializer blocks in the following respect: the execution of an instance initializer block can result in an uncaught checked exception, provided the exception is declared in the throws clause of *every* constructor in the class. Static initializer blocks cannot allow this, since no constructors are involved in class initialization. Instance initializer blocks in anonymous classes have greater freedom: they can throw any exception.

Example 8.10 *Exception Handling in Instance Initializer Blocks*

```
class RoomOccupancyTooHighException
    extends Exception {}                          // (1) Checked exception
class BankrupcyException
    extends RuntimeException {}                   // (2) Unchecked exception

class Hotel {
    // Instance Members
    private boolean bankrupt       = true;
    private int     noOfRooms      = 215;
    private int     occupancyPerRoom = 5;
    private int     maxNoOfGuests;

    {                                             // (3) Instance block
        try {
            if (occupancyPerRoom > 4)             // (4) Handles checked exception
                throw new RoomOccupancyTooHighException();
        } catch (RoomOccupancyTooHighException exception) {
            System.out.println("ROOM OCCUPANCY TOO HIGH: " + occupancyPerRoom);
            occupancyPerRoom = 4;
        }
        maxNoOfGuests = noOfRooms * occupancyPerRoom;
    }

    {                                             // (5) Instance initializer block
        if (bankrupt)
            throw new BankrupcyException();       // (6) Throws unchecked exception
    } // ...
}

public class ExceptionsInInstBlocks {
    public static void main(String[] args) {
        new Hotel();
    }
}
```

342

Output from the program:

```
ROOM OCCUPANCY TOO HIGH: 5
Exception in thread "main" BankrupcyException
        at Hotel.<init>(ExceptionsInInstBlocks.java:26)
        at ExceptionsInInstBlocks.main(ExceptionsInInstBlocks.java:32)
```

Constructing Initial Object State

Object initialization involves constructing the initial state of an object when it is created by using the new operator. First, the fields are initialized to their default values (see Section 2.4, p. 33)—whether they are subsequently given non-default initial values or not—then the constructor is invoked. This can lead to *local* chaining of constructors. The invocation of the constructor at the end of the local chain of constructor invocations results in the following actions, before the constructor's execution resumes:

- Implicit or explicit invocation of the superclass constructor. Constructor chaining ensures that the inherited state of the object is constructed first (see Section 6.3, p. 243).

- Initialization of the instance fields by executing their instance initializer expressions and any instance initializer blocks in the order they are specified in the class declaration.

Example 8.11 illustrates object initialization. The new operator is used at (8) to create an object of class SubclassB. The default constructor SubclassB() at (2) uses the this() construct to locally chain to the non-default constructor at (3). It is this constructor that leads to an implicit call of the superclass constructor. As can be seen from the program output, the execution of the superclass's constructor at (1) reaches completion first. This is followed by the execution of the instance initializer block at (4) and instance initializer expression at (6). Then the execution of the body of the non-default constructor at (3) is resumed. Finally, the default constructor completes its execution, thereby completing the construction of the object state.

Note that the instance initializers are executed in the order they are specified in the class declaration. The forward reference to the field value at (5) is legal because the usage of the field value is on the left-hand side of the assignment. The default value of the field value is overwritten by the instance initializer block at (5). The field value is again overwritten by the instance initializer expression at (6), and finally by the non-default constructor at (3).

Example 8.11 *Object State Construction*

```
class SuperclassA {
    public SuperclassA() {                              // (1)
        System.out.println("Constructor in SuperclassA");
    }
}
```

```
class SubclassB extends SuperclassA {

    SubclassB() {                              // (2)
        this(3);
        System.out.println("Default constructor in SubclassB");
    }

    SubclassB(int i) {                         // (3)
        System.out.println("Non-default constructor in SubclassB");
        value = i;
    }

    {                                          // (4)
        System.out.println("Instance initializer block in SubclassB");
        value = 2;                             // (5)
    }

    int value = initializerExpression();       // (6)

    private int initializerExpression() {      // (7)
        System.out.println("Instance initializer expression in SubclassB");
        return 1;
    }
}

public class ObjectConstruction {
    public static void main(String[] args) {
        SubclassB objRef = new SubclassB();    // (8)
        System.out.println("value: " + objRef.value);
    }
}
```

Output from the program:

```
Constructor in SuperclassA
Instance initializer block in SubclassB
Instance initializer expression in SubclassB
Non-default constructor in SubclassB
Default constructor in SubclassB
value: 3
```

Some care should be exercised when writing constructors for non-final classes, since the object that is constructed might be a subclass instance. Example 8.12 shows a situation where use of overridden methods in *superclass* initializers and constructors can give unexpected results. The example intentionally uses the this reference to underline the fact that the instance methods and constructors are invoked on the current object, and that the constructor call results in the initialization of the object state as we would expect.

The program output shows that the field superValue at (1) in class SuperclassA never gets initialized explicitly when an object of the SubclassB is created at (8). The SuperclassA constructor at (2) does have a call to a method called doValue() at (3). A method with such a name is defined in class SuperclassA at (4), but is also overridden in SubclassB at (7). The program output indicates that the method doValue() from the SubclassB is called at (3) in the SuperclassA constructor. The implementation of the method doValue() at (4) never gets executed when an object of the SubclassB is created. Method invocation always determines the implementation of the method to be executed, based on the *actual* type of the object. Keeping in mind that it is an object of SubclassB that is being initialized, it is not surprising that the call to the method named doValue at (3) results in the method from SubclassB being executed. This can lead to unintended results. The overriding method doValue() at (7) in class SubclassB can access the field value declared at (5) before its initializer expression has been executed; that is, the method invoked can access the state of the object *before* this has been completely initialized.

Example 8.12   *Initialization under Object State Construction*

```
class SuperclassA {
    protected int superValue;                            // (1)
    SuperclassA() {                                      // (2)
        System.out.println("Constructor in SuperclassA");
        this.doValue();                                  // (3)
    }
    void doValue() {                                     // (4)
        this.superValue = 911;
        System.out.println("superValue: " + this.superValue);
    }
}

class SubclassB extends SuperclassA {
    private int value = 800;                             // (5)
    SubclassB() {                                        // (6)
        System.out.println("Constructor in SubclassB");
        this.doValue();
        System.out.println("superValue: " + this.superValue);
    }
    void doValue() {                                     // (7)
        System.out.println("value: " + this.value);
    }
}

public class ObjectInitialization {
    public static void main(String[] args) {
        System.out.println("Creating an object of SubclassB.");
        new SubclassB();                                 // (8)
    }
}
```

Output from the program:

```
Creating an object of SubclassB.
Constructor in SuperclassA
value: 0
Constructor in SubclassB
value: 800
superValue: 0
```

Class initialization takes place before any instance of the class can be created or a static method of the class can be invoked. A superclass is initialized before its subclasses are initialized. Initializing a class involves initialization of the static fields by executing their static initializer expressions and execution of any static initializer blocks.

Initialization of an interface only involves execution of any static initializer expressions for the static fields declared in the interface. An interface cannot specify instance initializer expressions as it has no instance fields, and neither can it specify instance initializer blocks as it cannot be instantiated.

 ## Review Questions

8.6 Given the following class, which of these static initializer blocks can be inserted after the comment?

```java
public class MyClass {
    private static int count = 5;
    final static int STEP = 10;
    boolean alive;

    // INSERT STATIC INITIALIZER BLOCK HERE
}
```

Select the three correct answers.

(a) static { alive = true; count = 0; }
(b) static { STEP = count; }
(c) static { count += STEP; }
(d) static ;
(e) static {;}
(f) static { count = 1; }

8.7 What will be the result of attempting to compile and run the following code?

```java
public class MyClass {
    public static void main(String[] args) {
        MyClass obj = new MyClass(1);
    }

    static int i = 5;
    static int l;
    int j = 7;
    int k;

    public MyClass(int m) {
        System.out.println(i + ", " + j + ", " + k + ", " + l + ", " + m);
    }

    { j = 70; l = 20; } // Instance Initializer Block

    static { i = 50; }  // Static Initializer Block
}
```

Select the one correct answer.

(a) The code will fail to compile, since the instance initializer block tries to assign a value to a static field.
(b) The code will fail to compile, since the field k will be uninitialized when it is used.
(c) The code will compile without error and will print 50, 70, 0, 20, 0 when run.
(d) The code will compile without error and will print 50, 70, 0, 20, 20 when run.
(e) The code will compile without error and will print 5, 70, 0, 20, 0 when run.
(f) The code will compile without error and will print 5, 7, 0, 20, 0 when run.

8.8 Given the following class, which instance initializer block inserted at the indicated location will allow the class to compile without errors?

```
public class MyClass {
    static int gap = 10;
    double length;
    final boolean active;

    // INSERT CODE HERE
}
```

Select the one correct answer.

(a) `instance { active = true; }`
(b) `MyClass { gap += 5; }`
(c) `{ gap = 5; length = (active ? 100 : 200) + gap; }`
(d) `{ ; }`
(e) `{ length = 4.2; }`
(f) `{ active = (gap > 5); length = 5.5 + gap;}`

8.9 What will be the result of attempting to compile and run the following program?

```
public class Initialization {
    private static String msg(String msg) {
        System.out.println(msg); return msg;
    }

    public Initialization() { m = msg("1"); }

    { m = msg("2"); }

    String m = msg("3");

    public static void main(String[] args) {
        Object obj = new Initialization();
    }
}
```

Select the one correct answer.

(a) The program will fail to compile.
(b) The program will compile without error and will print 1, 2, and 3 when run.
(c) The program will compile without error and will print 2, 3, and 1 when run.
(d) The program will compile without error and will print 3, 1, and 2 when run.
(e) The program will compile without error and will print 1, 3, and 2 when run.

8.10 What will be the result of attempting to compile and run the following program?

```
public class Initialization {
    private static String msg(String msg) {
        System.out.println(msg); return msg;
    }

    static String m = msg("1");

    { m = msg("2"); }

    static { m = msg("3"); }

    public static void main(String[] args) {
        Object obj = new Initialization();
    }
}
```

Select the one correct answer.

(a) The program will fail to compile.
(b) The program will compile without error and will print 1, 2, and 3 when run.
(c) The program will compile without error and will print 2, 3, and 1 when run.
(d) The program will compile without error and will print 3, 1, and 2 when run.
(e) The program will compile without error and will print 1, 3, and 2 when run.

8.11 Which of the labeled lines in the following code can be *uncommented* by removing the // characters and still allow the code to compile correctly?

```
class GeomInit {
//   int width = 14;              /* Line A */
     {
//       area = width * height;  /* Line B */
     }
     int width = 37;
     {
//       height = 11;             /* Line C */
     }
     . int height, area;
//   area = width * height;       /* Line D */
     {
//       int width = 15;          /* Line E */
         area = 100;
     }
};
```

Select the two correct answers.

(a) Line A
(b) Line B
(c) Line C
(d) Line D
(e) Line E

Chapter Summary

The following information was included in this chapter:

- discussion of automatic garbage collection, including the workings of the garbage collector and guidelines for facilitating garbage collection
- discussion of object finalization and chaining as part of garbage collection
- discussion of static and instance initializers, both as initializer expressions and as initializer blocks
- the role played by initializers in initializing objects, classes, and interfaces

Threads

9

● ●

Exam Objectives

- Write code to define, instantiate, and start new threads using both `java.lang.Thread` and `java.lang.Runnable`.
- Recognize conditions that might prevent a thread from executing.
- Write code using `synchronized`, `wait()`, `notify()`, and `notifyAll()` to protect against concurrent access problems and to communicate between threads.
- Define the interaction among threads and object locks when executing synchronized `wait()`, `notify()`, or `notifyAll()`.

Supplementary Objectives

- Understand thread states and the transitions between them.

9.1 Multitasking

Multitasking allows several activities to occur concurrently on the computer. A distinction is usually made between:

- Process-based multitasking
- Thread-based multitasking

At the coarse-grain level there is *process-based* multitasking, which allows processes (i.e., programs) to run concurrently on the computer. A familiar example is running the spreadsheet program while also working with the word-processor. At the fine-grain level there is *thread-based* multitasking, which allows parts of the *same* program to run concurrently on the computer. A familiar example is a word-processor that is printing and formatting text at the same time. This is only feasible if the two tasks are performed by two independent paths of execution at runtime. The two tasks would correspond to executing parts of the program concurrently. The sequence of code executed for each task defines a separate path of execution, and is called a *thread (of execution)*.

In a single-threaded environment only one task at a time can be performed. CPU cycles are wasted, for example, when waiting for user input. Multitasking allows idle CPU time to be put to good use.

Some advantages of thread-based multitasking as compared to process-based multitasking are

- threads share the same address space
- context switching between threads is usually less expensive than between processes
- cost of communication between threads is relatively low

Java supports thread-based multitasking and provides high-level facilities for multithreaded programming. *Thread safety* is the term used to describe the design of classes that ensure that the state of their objects is always consistent, even when the objects are used concurrently by multiple threads.

9.2 Overview of Threads

A thread is an independent sequential path of execution within a program. Many threads can run concurrently within a program. At runtime, threads in a program exist in a common memory space and can, therefore, share both data and code, that is, they are *lightweight* compared to processes. They also share the process running the program.

Every thread in Java is created and controlled by a unique object of the java.lang.Thread class. Often the thread and its associated Thread object are thought of as being synonymous.

Threads make the runtime environment asynchronous, allowing different tasks to be performed concurrently. Using this powerful paradigm in Java centers around understanding the following aspects of multithreaded programming:

- creating threads and providing the code that gets executed by a thread (see Section 9.3, p. 351)
- accessing common data and code through synchronization (see Section 9.4, p. 359).
- transitioning between thread states (see Section 9.5, p. 366).

The Main Thread

The runtime environment distinguishes between *user threads* and *daemon threads*. As long as a user thread is alive, the JVM does not terminate. A daemon thread is at the mercy of the runtime system: it is stopped if there are no more user threads running, thus terminating the program. Daemon threads exist only to serve user threads.

When a standalone application is run, a user thread is automatically created to execute the main() method. This thread is called the *main thread*. If no other user threads are spawned, the program terminates when the main() method finishes executing. All other threads, called *child* threads, are spawned from the main thread, inheriting its user-thread status. The main() method can then finish, but the program will keep running until all the user threads have finished. Calling the set-Daemon(boolean) method in the Thread class marks the status of the thread as either daemon or user, but this must be done before the thread is *started*. Any attempt to change the status after the thread has been started, throws an IllegalThreadState-Exception. Marking all spawned threads as daemon threads ensures that the application terminates when the main thread dies.

When a GUI application is started, a special thread is automatically created to monitor the user–GUI interaction. This user thread keeps the program running, allowing interaction between the user and the GUI, even though the main thread might have died after the main() method finished executing.

9.3 Thread Creation

A thread in Java is represented by an object of the Thread class. Implementing threads is achieved in one of two ways:

- implementing the java.lang.Runnable interface
- extending the java.lang.Thread class

Implementing the Runnable Interface

The Runnable interface has the following specification, comprising one method prototype declaration:

```
public interface Runnable {
    void run();
}
```

A thread, which is created based on an object that implements the Runnable interface, will execute the code defined in the public method run(). In other words, the code in the run() method defines an independent path of execution and thereby the entry and the exits for the thread. The thread ends when the run() method ends, either by normal completion or by throwing an uncaught exception.

The procedure for creating threads based on the Runnable interface is as follows:

1. A class implements the Runnable interface, providing the run() method that will be executed by the thread. An object of this class is a Runnable object.

2. An object of Thread class is created by passing a Runnable object as argument to the Thread constructor. The Thread object now has a Runnable object that implements the run() method.

3. The start() method is invoked on the Thread object created in the previous step. The start() method returns immediately after a thread has been spawned.

The run() method of the Runnable object is eventually executed by the thread represented by the Thread object on which the start() method was invoked. This sequence of events is illustrated in Figure 9.1.

Figure 9.1   *Spawning Threads Using a Runnable Object*

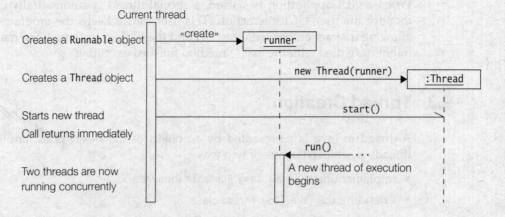

The following is a summary of important constructors and methods from the java.lang.Thread class:

```
Thread(Runnable threadTarget)
Thread(Runnable threadTarget, String threadName)
```

The argument threadTarget is the object whose run() method will be executed when the thread is started. The argument threadName can be specified to give an explicit name for the thread, rather than an automatically generated one. A thread's name can be retrieved by using the getName() method.

```
static Thread currentThread()
```

This method returns a reference to the Thread object of the currently executing thread.

```
final String getName()
final void setName(String name)
```

The first method returns the name of the thread. The second one sets the thread's name to the argument.

```
void run()
```

The Thread class implements the Runnable interface by providing an implementation of the run() method. This implementation does nothing. Subclasses of the Thread class should override this method.

If the current thread is created using a separate Runnable object, then the Runnable object's run() method is called.

```
final void setDaemon(boolean flag)
final boolean isDaemon()
```

The first method sets the status of the thread either as a daemon thread or as a user thread, depending on whether the argument is true or false, respectively. The status should be set before the thread is started. The second method returns true if the thread is a daemon thread, otherwise, false.

```
void start()
```

This method spawns a new thread, that is, the new thread will begin execution as a child thread of the current thread. The spawning is done asynchronously as the call to this method returns immediately. It throws an IllegalThread-StateException if the thread was already started.

In Example 9.1, the class Counter implements the Runnable interface. The constructor for the Counter class ensures that each object of the Counter class will create a new thread by passing the Counter instance to the Thread constructor, as shown at (1). In addition, the thread is enabled for execution by the call to its start() method, as shown at (2). At (3), the class defines the run() method that constitutes the code executed by the thread. In each iteration the thread will sleep for 250 milliseconds after writing the current value of the counter, as shown at (4). While it is sleeping, other threads may run (see Section 9.5, p. 370).

Example 9.1   *Implementing the* Runnable *Interface*

```java
class Counter implements Runnable {

    private int currentValue;

    private Thread worker;

    public Counter(String threadName) {
        currentValue = 0;
        worker = new Thread(this, threadName);   // (1) Create a new thread.
        System.out.println(worker);
        worker.start();                          // (2) Start the thread.
    }

    public int getValue() { return currentValue; }

    public void run() {                          // (3) Thread entry point
        try {
            while (currentValue < 5) {
                System.out.println(worker.getName() + ": " + (currentValue++));
                Thread.sleep(250);               // (4) Current thread sleeps.
            }
        } catch (InterruptedException e) {
            System.out.println(worker.getName() + " interrupted.");
        }
        System.out.println("Exit from thread: " + worker.getName());
    }
}

public class Client {
    public static void main(String[] args) {
        Counter counterA = new Counter("Counter A"); // (5) Create a thread.

        try {
            int val;
            do {
                val = counterA.getValue();       // (6) Access the counter value.
                System.out.println("Counter value read by main thread: " + val);
                Thread.sleep(1000);              // (7) Current thread sleeps.
            } while (val < 5);
        } catch (InterruptedException e) {
            System.out.println("main thread interrupted.");
        }

        System.out.println("Exit from main(), method.");
    }
}
```

Possible output from the program:

```
Thread[Counter A,5,main]
Counter value read by main thread: 0
Counter A: 0
Counter A: 1
```

```
Counter A: 2
Counter A: 3
Counter value read by main thread: 4
Counter A: 4
Exit from thread: Counter A
Counter value read by main thread: 5
Exit from main() method.
```

The Client class uses the Counter class. It creates an object of class Counter at (5) and retrieves its value in a loop at (6). After each retrieval, it sleeps for 1,000 milliseconds at (7), allowing other threads to run.

Note that the main thread executing in the Client class sleeps for a longer time between iterations than the Counter thread, giving the Counter thread the opportunity to run as well. The Counter thread is a *child* thread of the main thread. It inherits the user-thread status from the main thread. If the code after statement at (5) in the main() method was removed, the main thread would finish executing before the child thread. However, the program would continue running until the child thread completed.

Since thread scheduling is not predictable and Example 9.1 does not enforce any synchronization between the two threads in accessing the counter value, the output shown may vary. The first line of the output shows the string representation of a Thread object: its name (Counter A), its priority (5), and its parent thread (main). The output from the main thread and the Counter A thread is interleaved. Not surprisingly, it also shows that the value in the Counter A thread was incremented faster than the main thread could access the counter's value after each increment.

Extending the Thread Class

A class can also extend the Thread class to create a thread. A typical procedure for doing this is as follows (see Figure 9.2):

1. A class extending the Thread class overrides the run() method from the Thread class to define the code executed by the thread.

2. This subclass may call a Thread constructor explicitly in its constructors to initialize the thread, using the super() call.

3. The start() method inherited from the Thread class is invoked on the object of the class to make the thread eligible for running.

In Example 9.2, the Counter class from Example 9.1 has been modified to illustrate extending the Thread class. Note the call to the constructor of the superclass Thread at (1) and the invocation of the inherited start() method at (2) in the constructor of the Counter class. The program output shows that the Client class creates two threads and exits, but the program continues running until the child threads have completed. The two child threads are independent, each having its own counter and executing its own run() method.

Figure 9.2   *Spawning Threads—Extending the* Thread *Class*

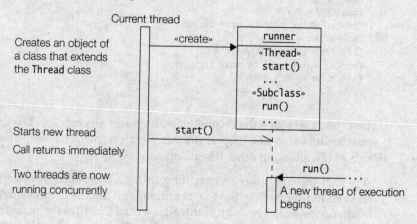

The Thread class implements the Runnable interface, which means that this approach is not much different from implementing the Runnable interface directly. The only difference is that the roles of the Runnable object and the Thread object are combined in a single object.

The static method currentThread() in the Thread class can be used to obtain a reference to the Thread object associated with the current thread. An example of its usage is shown at (5) in Example 9.2:

```
Thread.currentThread().getName());   // (5) Current thread
```

Adding the following statement before the call to the start() method at (2) in Example 9.2:

```
setDaemon(true);
```

illustrates the daemon nature of threads. The program execution will now terminate after the main thread has completed, without waiting for the daemon Counter threads to finish normally.

Example 9.2   *Extending the* Thread *Class*

```
class Counter extends Thread {

    private int currentValue;

    public Counter(String threadName) {
        super(threadName);                          // (1) Initialize thread.
        currentValue = 0;
        System.out.println(this);
        start();                                    // (2) Start this thread.
    }

    public int getValue() { return currentValue; }
```

```
        public void run() {                           // (3) Override from superclass.
            try {
                while (currentValue < 5) {
                    System.out.println(getName() + ": " + (currentValue++));
                    Thread.sleep(250);                 // (4) Current thread sleeps.
                }
            } catch (InterruptedException e) {
                System.out.println(getName() + " interrupted.");
            }
            System.out.println("Exit from thread: " + getName());
        }
    }

    public class Client {
        public static void main(String[] args) {

            System.out.println("Method main() runs in thread " +
                    Thread.currentThread().getName());    // (5) Current thread

            Counter counterA = new Counter("Counter A"); // (6) Create a thread.
            Counter counterB = new Counter("Counter B"); // (7) Create a thread.

            System.out.println("Exit from main() method.");
        }
    }
```

Possible output from the program:

```
Method main() runs in thread main
Thread[Counter A,5,main]
Thread[Counter B,5,main]
Exit from main() method.
Counter A: 0
Counter B: 0
Counter A: 1
Counter B: 1
Counter A: 2
Counter B: 2
Counter A: 3
Counter B: 3
Counter A: 4
Counter B: 4
Exit from thread: Counter A
Exit from thread: Counter B
```

When creating threads, there are two reasons why implementing the Runnable interface may be preferable to extending the Thread class:

- Extending the Thread class means that the subclass cannot extend any other class, whereas a class implementing the Runnable interface has this option.

- A class might only be interested in being runnable, and therefore, inheriting the full overhead of the Thread class would be excessive.

In Examples 9.1 and 9.2, the Thread object was created and the start() method called immediately to initiate the thread execution, as shown at (2). There are other ways of starting a thread. The call to the start() method can be factored out of the constructor, and the method can be called later, using a reference that denotes the thread object.

Inner classes are useful for implementing threads that do simple tasks. The anonymous class below will create a thread and start it:

```
(   new Thread() {
        public void run() {
            for(;;) System.out.println("Stop the world!");
        }
    }
).start();
```

Review Questions

9.1   Which is the correct way to start a new thread?

Select the one correct answer.

(a) Just create a new Thread object. The thread will start automatically.
(b) Create a new Thread object and call the method begin().
(c) Create a new Thread object and call the method start().
(d) Create a new Thread object and call the method run().
(e) Create a new Thread object and call the method resume().

9.2   When extending the Thread class to provide a thread's behavior, which method should be overridden?

Select the one correct answer.

(a) begin()
(b) start()
(c) run()
(d) resume()
(e) behavior()

9.3   Which statements are true?

Select the two correct answers.

(a) The class Thread is abstract.
(b) The class Thread implements Runnable.
(c) Classes implementing the Runnable interface must define a method named start.
(d) Calling the method run() on an object implementing Runnable will create a new thread.
(e) A program terminates when the last non-daemon thread ends.

9.4 What will be the result of attempting to compile and run the following program?

```
public class MyClass extends Thread {
    public MyClass(String s) { msg = s; }
    String msg;
    public void run() {
        System.out.println(msg);
    }

    public static void main(String[] args) {
        new MyClass("Hello");
        new MyClass("World");
    }
}
```

Select the one correct answer.

(a) The program will fail to compile.

(b) The program will compile without errors and will print Hello and World, in that order, every time the program is run.

(c) The program will compile without errors and will print a never-ending stream of Hello and World.

(d) The program will compile without errors and will print Hello and World when run, but the order is unpredictable.

(e) The program will compile without errors and will simply terminate without any output when run.

9.4 Synchronization

Threads share the same memory space, that is, they can share resources. However, there are critical situations where it is desirable that only one thread at a time has access to a shared resource. For example, crediting and debiting a shared bank account concurrently amongst several users without proper discipline, will jeopardize the integrity of the account data. Java provides high-level concepts for *synchronization* in order to control access to shared resources.

Locks

A *lock* (a.k.a. *monitor*) is used to synchronize access to a shared resource. A lock can be associated with a shared resource. Threads gain access to a shared resource by first acquiring the lock associated with the resource. At any given time, at the most one thread can hold the lock (i.e., own the monitor) and thereby have access to the shared resource. A lock thus implements *mutual exclusion* (a.k.a. *mutex*).

In Java, *all* objects have a lock—including arrays. This means that the lock from any Java object can be used to implement mutual exclusion. By associating a shared resource with a Java object and its lock, the object can act as a *guard*, ensuring synchronized access to the resource. Only one thread at a time can access the shared resource guarded by the *object lock*.

The object lock mechanism enforces the following rules of synchronization:

- A thread must *acquire* the object lock associated with a shared resource, before it can *enter* the shared resource. The runtime system ensures that no other thread can enter a shared resource if another thread already holds the object lock associated with the shared resource. If a thread cannot immediately acquire the object lock, it is *blocked*, that is, it must wait for the lock to become available.

- When a thread *exits* a shared resource, the runtime system ensures that the object lock is also relinquished. If another thread is waiting for this object lock, it can proceed to acquire the lock in order to gain access to the shared resource.

Classes also have a class-specific lock that is analogous to the object lock. Such a lock is actually a lock on the java.lang.Class object associated with the class. Given a class A, the reference A.class denotes this unique Class object. The class lock can be used in much the same way as an object lock to implement mutual exclusion.

The keyword synchronized and the lock form the basis for implementing synchronized execution of code. There are two ways in which execution of code can be synchronized:

- synchronized methods
- synchronized blocks

Synchronized Methods

If the methods of an object should only be executed by one thread at a time, then the declaration of all such methods should be specified with the keyword synchronized. A thread wishing to execute a synchronized method must first obtain the object's lock (i.e., hold the lock) before it can enter the object to execute the method. This is simply achieved by calling the method. If the lock is already held by another thread, the calling thread waits. No particular action on the part of the program is necessary. A thread relinquishes the lock simply by returning from the synchronized method, allowing the next thread waiting for this lock to proceed.

Synchronized methods are useful in situations where methods can manipulate the state of an object in ways that can corrupt the state if executed concurrently. A stack implementation usually defines the two operations push and pop as synchronized, so that pushing and popping of elements are mutually exclusive operations. If several threads were to share a stack, then one thread would, for example, not be able to push an element on the stack while another thread was popping the stack. The integrity of the stack is maintained in the face of several threads accessing the state of the same stack. This situation is illustrated by Example 9.3.

In Example 9.3, the main() method in class Mutex creates a stack at (6), which is used by the two threads created at (7) and (8). The two threads continually push and pop the stack, respectively. The non-synchronized push() and pop() methods at (2a) and

(4a) intentionally sleep at (3) and (5), respectively, between an update and the use of the value in the field topOfStack. This setup exaggerates the chances for the state of the stack being corrupted by one of the threads, while the other one is sleeping. The output from the program bears this out, when the methods are not declared synchronized. Non-synchronized updating of the value in the field topOfStack between the two threads is a disaster waiting to happen. This is an example of what is called a *race condition*. It occurs when two or more threads simultaneously update the same value, and as a consequence, leave the value in an undefined or inconsistent state.

From the output shown in Example 9.3, we can see that the main thread exits right after creating and starting the threads. The threads push and pop the stack. The stack state eventually gets corrupted, resulting in an ArrayOutOfBoundsException in the Pusher thread. The uncaught exception results in the demise of the Pusher thread, but the Popper thread continues.

Running the program in Example 9.3 with the synchronized version of the push() and pop() methods at (2b) and (4b), respectively, avoids the race condition. The method sleep() does not relinquish any lock that the thread might have on the current object. It is only relinquished when the synchronized method exits, guaranteeing mutually exclusive push-and-pop operations on the stack.

Example 9.3   *Mutual Exclusion*

```
class StackImpl {                                          // (1)
    private Object[] stackArray;
    private int topOfStack;

    public StackImpl(int capacity) {
        stackArray = new Object[capacity];
        topOfStack = -1;
    }

    public boolean push(Object element) {                  // (2a) non-synchronized
//  public synchronized boolean push(Object element) {     // (2b) synchronized
        if (isFull()) return false;
        ++topOfStack;
        try { Thread.sleep(1000); } catch (Exception ex) { } // (3) Sleep a little.
        stackArray[topOfStack] = element;
        return true;
    }

    public Object pop() {                                  // (4a) non-synchronized
//  public synchronized Object pop() {                     // (4b) synchronized
        if (isEmpty()) return null;
        Object obj = stackArray[topOfStack];
        stackArray[topOfStack] = null;
        try { Thread.sleep(1000); } catch (Exception ex) { } // (5) Sleep a little.
        topOfStack--;
        return obj;
    }
```

```
            public boolean isEmpty() { return topOfStack < 0; }
            public boolean isFull()  { return topOfStack >= stackArray.length - 1; }
        }

    public class Mutex {
        public static void main(String[] args) {

            final StackImpl stack = new StackImpl(20);  // (6) Shared by the threads.

            (new Thread("Pusher") {                     // (7) Thread no. 1
                public void run() {
                    for(;;) {
                        System.out.println("Pushed: " +
                            stack.push(new Integer(2003)));
                    }
                }
            }).start();

            (new Thread("Popper") {                     // (8) Thread no. 2
                public void run() {
                    for(;;) {
                        System.out.println("Popped: " + stack.pop());
                    }
                }
            }).start();

            System.out.println("Exit from main().");
        }
    }
```

Possible output from the program:

```
Exit from main().
...
Pushed: true
Popped: 2003
Popped: 2003
Popped: null
...
Popped: null
java.lang.ArrayIndexOutOfBoundsException: -1
        at StackImpl.push(Mutex.java:15)
        at Mutex$1.run(Mutex.java:41)
Popped: null
Popped: null
...
```

While a thread is inside a synchronized method of an object, all other threads that wish to execute this synchronized method or any other synchronized method of the object will have to wait. This restriction does not apply to the thread that already has the lock and is executing a synchronized method of the object. Such a method can invoke other synchronized methods of the object without being blocked. The non-synchronized methods of the object can of course be called at any time by any thread.

Not surprisingly, static methods synchronize on the class lock. Acquiring and relinquishing a class lock by a thread in order to execute a static synchronized method, proceeds analogous to that of an object lock for a synchronized instance method. A thread acquires the class lock before it can proceed with the execution of any static synchronized method in the class, blocking other threads wishing to execute any such methods in the same class. This, of course, does not apply to static, non-synchronized methods, which can be invoked at any time. A thread acquiring the lock of a class to execute a static synchronized method, has no bearing on any thread acquiring the lock on any object of the class to execute a synchronized instance method. In other words, synchronization of static methods in a class is independent from the synchronization of instance methods on objects of the class.

A subclass decides whether the new definition of an inherited synchronized method will remain synchronized in the subclass.

Synchronized Blocks

Whereas execution of synchronized methods of an object is synchronized on the lock of the object, the synchronized block allows execution of arbitrary code to be synchronized on the lock of an arbitrary object. The general form of the synchronized statement is as follows:

```
synchronized (<object reference expression>) { <code block> }
```

The *<object reference expression>* must evaluate to a non-null reference value, otherwise, a NullPointerException is thrown. The code block is usually related to the object on which the synchronization is being done. This is the case with synchronized methods, where the execution of the method is synchronized on the lock of the current object:

```
public Object pop() {
    synchronized (this) {              // Synchronized block on current object
        // ...
    }
}
```

Once a thread has entered the code block after acquiring the lock on the specified object, no other thread will be able to execute the code block, or any other code requiring the same object lock, until the lock is relinquished. This happens when the execution of the code block completes normally or an uncaught exception is thrown. In contrast to synchronized methods, this mechanism allows fine-grained synchronization of code on arbitrary objects.

Object specification in the synchronized statement is mandatory. A class can choose to synchronize the execution of a part of a method, by using the this reference and putting the relevant part of the method in the synchronized block. The braces of the block cannot be left out, even if the code block has just one statement.

```
class SmartClient {
    BankAccount account;
    // ...
    public void updateTransaction() {
        synchronized (account) {        // (1) synchronized block
            account.update();            // (2)
        }
    }
}
```

In the previous example, the code at (2) in the synchronized block at (1) is synchronized on the BankAccount object. If several threads were to concurrently execute the method updateTransaction() on an object of SmartClient, the statement at (2) would be executed by one thread at a time, only after synchronizing on the BankAccount object associated with this particular instance of SmartClient.

Inner classes can access data in their enclosing context (see Section 7.1, p. 284). An inner object might need to synchronize on its associated outer object, in order to ensure integrity of data in the latter. This is illustrated in the following code where the synchronized block at (5) uses the special form of the this reference to synchronize on the outer object associated with an object of the inner class. This setup ensures that a thread executing the method setPi() in an inner object can only access the private double field myPi at (2) in the synchronized block at (5), by first acquiring the lock on the associated outer object. If another thread has the lock of the associated outer object, the thread in the inner object has to wait for the lock to be relinquished before it can proceed with the execution of the synchronized block at (5). However, synchronizing on an inner object and on its associated outer object are independent of each other, unless enforced explicitly, as in the following code:

```
class Outer {                              // (1) Top-level Class
    private double myPi;                   // (2)

    protected class Inner {                // (3) Non-static member Class
        public void setPi() {              // (4)
            synchronized(Outer.this) {     // (5) Synchronized block on outer object
                myPi = Math.PI;            // (6)
            }
        }
    }
}
```

Synchronized blocks can also be specified on a class lock:

```
synchronized (<class name>.class) { <code block> }
```

The block synchronizes on the lock of the object denoted by the reference *<class name>*.class. A static synchronized method classAction() in class A is equivalent to the following declaration:

```
static void classAction() {
    synchronized (A.class) {              // Synchronized block on class A
        // ...
    }
}
```

— night 9pm ki Sanagalu nanu
                          pettali
— Cooker lo Senagulu munige
vavaku Vesi — 1 whistle
ayyaaka → pressure Koddiga vunelo
theeyali
— popu → pachi mirchi + onion
+ ginger garlic paste + karam +
kampu + salt
                    vegali → then
→ batani veyyali → water from
batani

○○○○○○○○○○
① Osi vikayn venchali in oil
② mirchi, Jillakarra, vellilu, uppu, Chintapendu
                                    Koncham
③ popu — chanaga pappu, inguva

వంటకి పనవచ్చే
Ghee
నువ్వులనూనె
Almond oil

In summary, a thread can hold a lock on an object

- by executing a synchronized instance method of the object
- by executing the body of a synchronized block that synchronizes on the object
- by executing a synchronized static method of a class

 Review Questions

9.5 Given the following program, which statements are guaranteed to be true?

```
public class ThreadedPrint {
    static Thread makeThread(final String id, boolean daemon) {
        Thread t = new Thread(id) {
            public void run() {
                System.out.println(id);
            }
        };
        t.setDaemon(daemon);
        t.start();
        return t;
    }

    public static void main(String[] args) {
        Thread a = makeThread("A", false);
        Thread b = makeThread("B", true);
        System.out.print("End\n");
    }
}
```

Select the two correct answers.

(a) The letter A is always printed.

(b) The letter B is always printed.

(c) The letter A is never printed after End.

(d) The letter B is never printed after End.

(e) The program might print B, End and A, in that order.

9.6 Which statement is true?

Select the one correct answer.

(a) No two threads can concurrently execute synchronized methods on the same object.

(b) Methods declared synchronized should not be recursive, since the object lock will not allow new invocations of the method.

(c) Synchronized methods can only call other synchronized methods directly.

(d) Inside a synchronized method, one can assume that no other threads are currently executing any other methods in the same class.

9.7   Given the following program, which statement is true?

```java
public class MyClass extends Thread {
    static Object lock1 = new Object();
    static Object lock2 = new Object();

    static volatile int i1, i2, j1, j2, k1, k2;

    public void run() { while (true) { doit(); check(); } }

    void doit() {
        synchronized(lock1) { i1++; }
        j1++;
        synchronized(lock2) { k1++; k2++; }
        j2++;
        synchronized(lock1) { i2++; }
    }

    void check() {
        if (i1 != i2) System.out.println("i");
        if (j1 != j2) System.out.println("j");
        if (k1 != k2) System.out.println("k");
    }

    public static void main(String[] args) {
        new MyClass().start();
        new MyClass().start();
    }
}
```

Select the one correct answer.

(a) The program will fail to compile.

(b) One cannot be certain whether any of the letters i, j, and k will be printed during execution.

(c) One can be certain that none of the letters i, j, and k will ever be printed during execution.

(d) One can be certain that the letters i and k will never be printed during execution.

(e) One can be certain that the letter k will never be printed during execution.

9.5 Thread Transitions

Thread States

Understanding the life cycle of a thread is valuable when programming with threads. Threads can exist in different states. Just because a thread's start() method has been called, it does not mean that the thread has access to the CPU and can start executing straight away. Several factors determine how it will proceed.

Figure 9.3 shows the states and the transitions in the life cycle of a thread.

- *Ready-to-run state*

  A thread starts life in the Ready-to-run state (see p. 369).

- *Running state*

  If a thread is in the Running state, it m ... he thread is currently executing (see p. 369).

... see p. 380).

... le states, depending on ... le state until a special ... Running state from a ... n state.

... s:

... ime (see p. 370).

... tion to complete (see

... n of another thread

... om another thread

... e lock of an object

Figure 9.3 Thre...

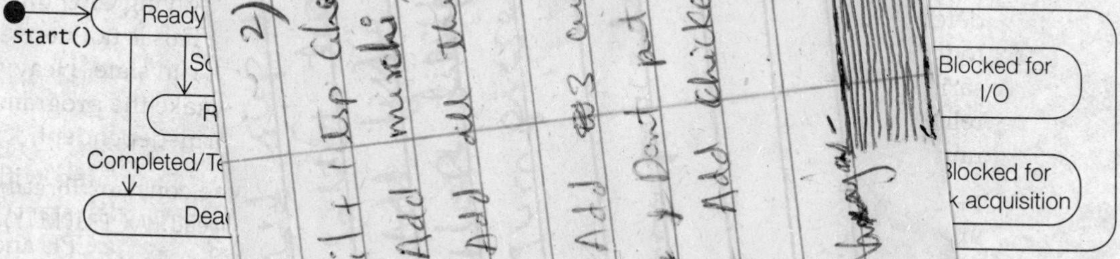

start() Ready

Sc...

R...

Completed/Te...

Dea...

Blocked for I/O

Blocked for ... k acquisition

Various ... presented next. Examples of their usage are prese... ...quent sections.

```
final boolean isAlive()
```

This method can be used to find out if a thread is alive or dead. A thread is *alive* if it has been started but not yet terminated, that is, it is not in the Dead state.

```
final int getPriority()
final void setPriority(int newPriority)
```

The first method returns the priority of the current thread. The second method changes its priority. The priority set will be the minimum of the two values: the specified newPriority and the maximum priority permitted for this thread.

```
static void yield()
```

This method causes the current thread to temporarily pause its execution and, thereby, allow other threads to execute.

```
static void sleep (long millisec) throws InterruptedException
```

The current thread sleeps for the specified time before it takes its turn at running again.

```
final void join() throws InterruptedException
final void join(long millisec) throws InterruptedException
```

A call to any of these two methods invoked on a thread will wait and not return until either the thread has completed or it is timed out after the specified time, respectively.

```
void interrupt()
```

The method interrupts the thread on which it is invoked. In the Waiting-for-notification, Sleeping, or Blocked-for-join-completion states, the thread will receive an InterruptedException.

Thread Priorities

Threads are assigned priorities that the thread scheduler *can* use to determine how the threads will be scheduled. The thread scheduler can use thread priorities to determine which thread gets to run. The thread scheduler favors giving CPU time to the thread with the highest priority in the Ready-to-run state. This is not necessarily the thread that has been the longest time in the Ready-to-run state. Heavy reliance on thread priorities for the behavior of a program can make the program unportable across platforms, as thread scheduling is host platform–dependent.

Priorities are integer values from 1 (lowest priority given by the constant Thread. MIN_PRIORITY) to 10 (highest priority given by the constant Thread.MAX_PRIORITY). The default priority is 5 (Thread.NORM_PRIORITY).

A thread inherits the priority of its parent thread. Priority of a thread can be set using the setPriority() method and read using the getPriority() method, both of which are defined in the Thread class. The following code sets the priority of the thread myThread to the minimum of two values: maximum priority and current priority incremented to the next level:

```
myThread.setPriority(Math.min(Thread.MAX_PRIORITY, myThread.getPriority()+1));
```

Thread Scheduler

Schedulers in JVM implementations usually employ one of the two following strategies:

- Preemptive scheduling.

  If a thread with a higher priority than the current running thread moves to the Ready-to-run state, then the current running thread can be *preempted* (moved to the Ready-to-run state) to let the higher priority thread execute.

- Time-Sliced or Round-Robin scheduling.

  A running thread is allowed to execute for a fixed length of time, after which it moves to the Ready-to-run state to await its turn to run again.

It should be pointed out that thread schedulers are implementation- and platform-dependent; therefore, how threads will be scheduled is unpredictable, at least from platform to platform.

Running and Yielding

After its start() method has been called, the thread starts life in the Ready-to-run state. Once in the Ready-to-run state, the thread is eligible for running, that is, it waits for its turn to get CPU time. The thread scheduler decides which thread gets to run and for how long.

Figure 9.4 illustrates the transitions between the Ready-to-Run and Running states. A call to the static method yield(), defined in the Thread class, will cause the current thread in the Running state to transit to the Ready-to-run state, thus relinquishing the CPU. The thread is then at the mercy of the thread scheduler as to when it will run again. If there are no threads waiting in the Ready-to-run state, this thread continues execution. If there are other threads in the Ready-to-run state, their priorities determine which thread gets to execute.

Figure 9.4 *Running and Yielding*

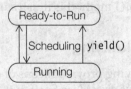

By calling the static method yield(), the running thread gives other threads in the Ready-to-run state a chance to run. A typical example where this can be useful is when a user has given some command to start a CPU-intensive computation, and has the option of canceling it by clicking on a Cancel button. If the computation thread hogs the CPU and the user clicks the Cancel button, chances are that it might take a while before the thread monitoring the user input gets a chance to run and take appropriate action to stop the computation. A thread running such a computation should do the computation in increments, yielding between increments to allow other threads to run. This is illustrated by the following run() method:

```
public void run() {
    try {
        while (!done()) {
            doLittleBitMore();
            Thread.yield();                // Current thread yields
        }
    } catch (InterruptedException e) {
        doCleaningUp();
    }
}
```

Sleeping and Waking up

Figure 9.5   *Sleeping and Waking up*

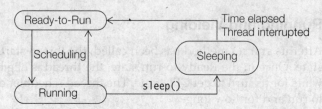

A call to the static method sleep() in the Thread class will cause the currently running thread to pause its execution and transit to the Sleeping state. The method does not relinquish any lock that the thread might have. The thread will sleep for at least the time specified in its argument, before transitioning to the Ready-to-run state where it takes its turn to run again. If a thread is interrupted while sleeping, it will throw an InterruptedException when it awakes and gets to execute.

There are serveral overloaded versions of the sleep() method in the Thread class.

Usage of the sleep() method is illustrated in Examples 9.1, 9.2, and 9.3.

Waiting and Notifying

Waiting and notifying provide means of communication between threads that *synchronize on the same object* (see Section 9.4, p. 359). The threads execute wait() and notify() (or notifyAll()) methods on the shared object for this purpose. These final methods are defined in the Object class, and therefore, inherited by all objects.

These methods can only be executed on an object whose lock the thread holds, otherwise, the call will result in an IllegalMonitorStateException.

```
final void wait(long timeout) throws InterruptedException
final void wait(long timeout, int nanos) throws InterruptedException
final void wait() throws InterruptedException
```

A thread invokes the wait() method on the object whose lock it holds. The thread is added to the *wait set* of the object.

```
final void notify()
final void notifyAll()
```

A thread invokes a notification method on the object whose lock it holds to notify thread(s) that are in the wait set of the object.

Communication between threads is facilitated by waiting and notifying, as illustrated by Figures 9.6 and 9.7. A thread usually calls the wait() method on the object whose lock it holds because a condition for its continued execution was not met. The thread leaves the Running state and transits to the Waiting-for-notification state. There it waits for this condition to occur. The thread relinquishes ownership of the object lock.

Figure 9.6 *Waiting and Notifying*

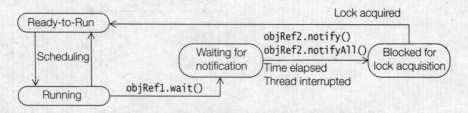

Transition to the Waiting-for-notification state and relinquishing the object lock are completed as one *atomic* (non-interruptable) operation. The releasing of the lock of the shared object by the thread allows other threads to run and execute synchronized code on the same object after acquiring its lock.

Note that the waiting thread does not relinquish any other object locks that it might hold, only that of the object on which the wait() method was invoked. Objects that have these other locks remain locked while the thread is waiting.

Each object has a *wait set* containing threads waiting for notification. Threads in the Waiting-for-notification state are grouped according to the object whose wait() method they invoked.

Figure 9.7 shows a thread t_1 that first acquires a lock on the shared object, and afterwards invokes the wait() method on the shared object. This relinquishes the object lock and the thread t_1 awaits to be notified. While the thread t_1 is waiting, another thread t_2 can acquire the lock on the shared object for its own purpose.

Figure 9.7   *Thread Communication*

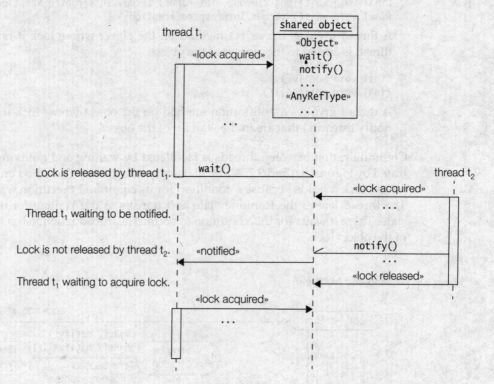

A thread in the Waiting-for-notification state can be awakened by the occurrence of any one of these three incidents:

1.   Another thread invokes the notify() method on the object of the waiting thread, and the waiting thread is selected as the thread to be awakened.

2.   The waiting thread times out.

3.   Another thread interrupts the waiting thread.

Notify

Invoking the notify() method on an object wakes up a single thread that is waiting on the lock of this object. The selection of a thread to awaken is dependent on the thread policies implemented by the JVM. On being *notified*, a waiting thread first transits to the Blocked-for-lock-acquisition state to acquire the lock on the object, and not directly to the Ready-to-run state. The thread is also removed from the wait set of the object. Note that the object lock is not relinquished when the notifying thread invokes the notify() method. The notifying thread relinquishes the lock at its own discretion, and the awakened thread will not be able to run until the notifying thread relinquishes the object lock.

When the notified thread obtains the object lock, it is enabled for execution, waiting in the Ready-to-run state for its turn to execute again. Finally, when it does get to execute, the call to the `wait()` method returns and the thread can continue with its execution.

From Figure 9.7 we see that thread t_2 does not relinquish the object lock when it invokes the `notify()` method. Thread t_1 is forced to wait in the Blocked-for-lock-acquisition state. It is shown no privileges and must compete with any other threads waiting for lock acquisition.

A call to the `notify()` method has no consequences if there are no threads in the wait set of the object.

In contrast to the `notify()` method, the `notifyAll()` method wakes up *all* threads in the wait set of the shared object. They will all transit to the Blocked-for-lock-acquisition state and contend for the object lock as explained earlier.

Time-out

The `wait()` call specified the time the thread should wait before being timed out, if it was not awakened as explained earlier. The awakened thread competes in the usual manner to execute again. Note that the awakened thread has no way of knowing whether it was timed out or awakened by one of the notification methods.

Interrupt

This means that another thread invoked the `interrupt()` method on the waiting thread. The awakened thread is enabled as previously explained, but if and when the awakened thread finally gets a chance to run, the return from the `wait()` call will result in an `InterruptedException`. This is the reason why the code invoking the `wait()` method must be prepared to handle this checked exception.

Figure 9.8 *Stack Users*

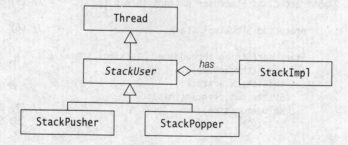

Example 9.4 *Waiting and Notifying*

```
class StackImpl {
    private Object[] stackArray;
    private volatile int topOfStack;

    StackImpl (int capacity) {
        stackArray = new Object[capacity];
        topOfStack = -1;
    }

    public synchronized Object pop() {
        System.out.println(Thread.currentThread() + ": popping");
        while (isEmpty())
            try {
                System.out.println(Thread.currentThread() + ": waiting to pop");
                wait();                                    // (1)
            } catch (InterruptedException e) { }
        Object obj = stackArray[topOfStack];
        stackArray[topOfStack--] = null;
        System.out.println(Thread.currentThread() + ": notifying after pop");
        notify();                                          // (2)
        return obj;
    }

    public synchronized void push(Object element) {
        System.out.println(Thread.currentThread() + ": pushing");
        while (isFull())
            try {
                System.out.println(Thread.currentThread() + ": waiting to push");
                wait();                                    // (3)
            } catch (InterruptedException e) { }
        stackArray[++topOfStack] = element;
        System.out.println(Thread.currentThread() + ": notifying after push");
        notify();                                          // (4)
    }

    public boolean isFull() { return topOfStack >= stackArray.length -1; }
    public boolean isEmpty() { return topOfStack < 0; }
}

abstract class StackUser extends Thread {                  // (5) Stack user

    protected StackImpl stack;                             // (6)

    StackUser(String threadName, StackImpl stack) {
        super(threadName);
        this.stack = stack;
        System.out.println(this);
        setDaemon(true);                                   // (7) Daemon thread
        start();                                           // (8) Start this thread.
    }
}
```

```
class StackPopper extends StackUser {                // (9) Popper
    StackPopper(String threadName, StackImpl stack) {
        super(threadName, stack);
    }
    public void run() { while (true) stack.pop(); }
}

class StackPusher extends StackUser {                // (10) Pusher
    StackPusher(String threadName, StackImpl stack) {
        super(threadName, stack);
    }
    public void run() { while (true) stack.push(new Integer(1)); }
}

public class WaitAndNotifyClient {
    public static void main(String[] args)
        throws InterruptedException {                // (11)

        StackImpl stack = new StackImpl(5);

        new StackPusher("A", stack);
        new StackPusher("B", stack);
        new StackPopper("C", stack);
        System.out.println("Main Thread sleeping.");
        Thread.sleep(1000);
        System.out.println("Exit from Main Thread.");
    }
}
```

Possible output from the program:

```
Thread[A,5,main]
Thread[B,5,main]
Thread[C,5,main]
Main Thread sleeping.
...
Thread[A,5,main]: pushing
Thread[A,5,main]: waiting to push
Thread[B,5,main]: pushing
Thread[B,5,main]: waiting to push
Thread[C,5,main]: popping
Thread[C,5,main]: notifying after pop
Thread[A,5,main]: notifying after push
Thread[A,5,main]: pushing
Thread[A,5,main]: waiting to push
Thread[B,5,main]: waiting to push
Thread[C,5,main]: popping
Thread[C,5,main]: notifying after pop
Thread[A,5,main]: notifying after push
...
Thread[B,5,main]: notifying after push
...
Exit from Main Thread.
...
```

In Example 9.4, three threads are manipulating the same stack. Two of them are pushing elements on the stack, while the third one is popping elements off the stack. The class diagram for Example 9.4 is shown in Figure 9.8.

- The subclasses StackPopper at (9) and StackPusher at (10) extend the abstract superclass StackUser at (5).

- Class StackUser, which extends the Thread class, creates and starts each thread.

- Class StackImpl implements the synchronized methods pop() and push().

The field topOfStack in class StackImpl is declared volatile, so that read and write operations on this variable will access the *master* value of this variable, and not any copies, during runtime (see Section 4.10, p. 150).

Since the threads manipulate the same stack object and the push() and pop() methods in the class StackImpl are synchronized, it means that the threads synchronize on the same object. In other words, the mutual exclusion of these operations is guaranteed on the same stack object.

Example 9.4 illustrates how a thread waiting as a result of calling the wait() method on an object, is notified by another thread calling the notify() method on the same object, in order for the first thread to start running again.

One usage of the wait() call is shown in Example 9.4 at (1) in the synchronized pop() method. When a thread executing this method on the StackImpl object finds that the stack is empty, it invokes the wait() method in order to wait for some thread to push something on this stack first.

Another use of the wait() call is shown at (3) in the synchronized push() method. When a thread executing this method on the StackImpl object finds that the stack is full, it invokes the wait() method to await some thread removing an element first, in order to make room for a push operation on the stack.

When a thread executing the synchronized method push() on the StackImpl object successfully pushes an element on the stack, it calls the notify() method at (4). The wait set of the StackImpl object contains all waiting threads that had earlier called the wait() method at either (1) or (3) on this StackImpl object. A single thread from the wait set is enabled for running. If this thread was executing a pop operation, it now has a chance of being successful because the stack is not empty at the moment. If this thread was executing a push operation, it can try again to see if there is room on the stack.

When a thread executing the synchronized method pop() on the StackImpl object successfully pops an element off the stack, it calls the notify() method at (2). Again assuming that the wait set of the StackImpl object is not empty, one thread from the set is arbitrarily chosen and enabled. If the notified thread was executing a pop operation, it can proceed to see if the stack still has an element to pop. If the notified thread was executing a push operation, it now has a chance of succeeding because the stack is not full at the moment.

Note that the waiting condition at (1) for the pop operation is executed in a loop. A waiting thread that has been notified is not guaranteed to run straight away. Before it gets to run, another thread may synchronize on the stack and empty it. If the notified thread was waiting to pop the stack, it would now incorrectly pop the stack, because the condition was not tested after notification. The loop ensures that the condition is always tested after notification, sending the thread back to the Waiting-on-notification state if the condition is not met. To avert the analogous danger of pushing on a full stack, the waiting condition at (3) for the push operation is also executed in a loop.

The behavior of each thread can be traced in the output from Example 9.4. Each push-and-pop operation can be traced by a sequence consisting of the name of the operation to be performed, followed by zero or more wait messages, and concluding with a notification after the operation is done. For example, thread A performs two pushes as shown in the output from the program:

```
Thread[A,5,main]: pushing
Thread[A,5,main]: waiting to push
...
Thread[A,5,main]: notifying after push
Thread[A,5,main]: pushing
Thread[A,5,main]: waiting to push
...
Thread[A,5,main]: notifying after push
```

Thread B is shown doing one push:

```
Thread[B,5,main]: pushing
Thread[B,5,main]: waiting to push
...
Thread[B,5,main]: notifying after push
```

Whereas thread C pops the stack twice without any waiting:

```
Thread[C,5,main]: popping
Thread[C,5,main]: notifying after pop
...
Thread[C,5,main]: popping
Thread[C,5,main]: notifying after pop
```

When the operations are interweaved, the output clearly shows that the pushers wait when the stack is full, and only push after the stack is popped.

The three threads created are daemon threads. Their status is set at (7). They will be terminated if they have not completed when the main user-thread dies, thereby stopping the execution of the program.

Joining

A thread can invoke the overloaded method join() on another thread in order to wait for the other thread to complete its execution before continuing, that is, the first thread waits for the second thread to *join it after completion*. A running thread

t_1 invokes the method join() on a thread t_2. The join() call has no effect if thread t_2 has already completed. If thread t_2 is still alive, then thread t_1 transits to the Blocked-for-join-completion state. Thread t_1 waits in this state until one of these events occur (see Figure 9.9):

- Thread t_2 completes.

  In this case thread t_1 is enabled and when it gets to run, it will continue normally after the join() method call.

- Thread t_1 is timed out.

  The time specified in the argument in the join() method call has elapsed, without thread t_2 completing. In this case as well, thread t_1 is enabled. When it gets to run, it will continue normally after the join() method call.

- Thread t_1 is interrupted.

  Some thread interrupted thread t_1 while thread t_1 was waiting for join completion. Thread t_1 is enabled, but when it gets to execute, it will now throw an InterruptedException.

Figure 9.9 *Joining of Threads*

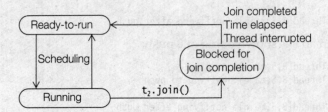

Example 9.5 illustrates joining of threads. The AnotherClient class below uses the Counter class, which extends the Thread class from Example 9.2. It creates two threads that are enabled for execution. The main thread invokes the join() method on the Counter A thread. If the Counter A thread has not already completed, the main thread transits to the Blocked-for-join-completion state. When the Counter A thread completes, the main thread will be enabled for running. Once the main thread is running, it continues with execution after (5). A parent thread can call the isAlive() method to find out whether its child threads are alive, before terminating itself. The call to the isAlive() method on the Counter A thread at (6) correctly reports that the Counter A thread is not alive. A similar scenario transpires between the main thread and the Counter B thread. The main thread passes through the Blocked-for-join-completion state twice at the most.

Example 9.5 *Joining of Threads*

```
class Counter extends Thread { /* See Example 9.2. */ }

public class AnotherClient {
    public static void main(String[] args) {

        Counter counterA = new Counter("Counter A");
        Counter counterB = new Counter("Counter B");

        try {
            System.out.println("Wait for the child threads to finish.");
            counterA.join();                                    // (5)
            if (!counterA.isAlive())                            // (6)
                System.out.println("Counter A not alive.");
            counterB.join();                                    // (7)
            if (!counterB.isAlive())                            // (8)
                System.out.println("Counter B not alive.");
        } catch (InterruptedException e) {
            System.out.println("Main Thread interrupted.");
        }
        System.out.println("Exit from Main Thread.");
    }
}
```

Possible output from the program:

```
Thread[Counter A,5,main]
Thread[Counter B,5,main]
Wait for the child threads to finish.
Counter A: 0
Counter B: 0
Counter A: 1
Counter B: 1
Counter A: 2
Counter B: 2
Counter A: 3
Counter B: 3
Counter A: 4
Counter B: 4
Exit from Counter A.
Counter A not alive.
Exit from Counter B.
Counter B not alive.
Exit from Main Thread.
```

Blocking for I/O

A running thread, on executing a *blocking operation* requiring a resource (like a call to an I/O method), will transit to the Blocked-for-I/O state. The blocking operation must complete before the thread can proceed to the Ready-to-run state. An example is a thread reading from the standard input terminal, which blocks until input is provided:

```
int input = System.in.read();
```

Thread Termination

A thread can transit to the Dead state from the Running or the Ready-to-run states. The thread dies when it completes its run() method, either by returning normally or by throwing an exception. Once in this state, the thread cannot be resurrected. There is no way the thread can be enabled for running again, not even by calling the start() method once more on the thread object.

Example 9.6 illustrates a typical scenario where a thread can be controlled by one or more threads. Work is performed by a loop body, which the thread executes continually. It should be possible for other threads to start and stop the *worker* thread. This functionality is implemented by the class Worker at (1), which has a private field theThread declared at (2) to keep track of the Thread object executing its run() method.

The kickStart() method at (3) in class Worker creates and starts a thread if one is not already running. It is not enough to just call the start() method on a thread that has terminated. A new Thread object must be created first. The terminate() method at (4) sets the field theThread to null. Note that this does not affect any Thread object that might have been denoted, by the reference theThread. The runtime system maintains any such Thread object; therefore, changing one of its references does not affect the object.

The run() method at (5) has a loop whose execution is controlled by a special condition. The condition tests to see whether the Thread object denoted by the reference theThread and the Thread object executing now, are one and the same. This is bound to be the case if the reference theThread has the same reference value it was assigned when the thread was created and started in the kickStart() method. The condition will then be true, and the body of the loop will execute. However, if the value in the reference theThread has changed, the condition will be false. In that case, the loop will not execute, the run() method will complete and the thread will terminate.

A client can control the thread implemented by the class Worker, using the kickStart() and the terminate() methods. The client is able to terminate the running thread at the start of the next iteration of the loop body, simply by changing the theThread reference to null.

In Example 9.6, a Worker object is first created at (8) and a thread started on this Worker object at (9). The main thread invokes the yield() method at (10) to temporarily stop its execution, and give the thread of the Worker object a chance to run. The main thread, when it is executing again, terminates the thread of the Worker object at (11), as explained earlier. This simple scenario can be generalized where several threads, sharing a single Worker object, could be starting and stopping the thread of the Worker object.

Example 9.6   *Thread Termination*

```
class Worker implements Runnable {                          // (1)
    private Thread theThread;                               // (2)

    public void kickStart() {                              // (3)
        if (theThread == null) {
            theThread = new Thread(this);
            theThread.start();
        }
    }

    public void terminate() {                              // (4)
        theThread = null;
    }

    public void run() {                                    // (5)
        while (theThread == Thread.currentThread()) {      // (6)
            System.out.println("Going around in loops.");
        }
    }
}

public class Controller {
    public static void main(String[] args) {               // (7)
        Worker worker = new Worker();                      // (8)
        worker.kickStart();                                // (9)
        Thread.yield();                                    // (10)
        worker.terminate();                                // (11)
    }
}
```

Possible output from the program:

```
Going around in loops.
Going around in loops.
Going around in loops.
Going around in loops.
Going around in loops.
```

Deadlocks

A deadlock is a situation where a thread is waiting for an object lock that another thread holds, and this second thread is waiting for an object lock that the first thread holds. Since each thread is waiting for the other thread to relinquish a lock, they both remain waiting forever in the Blocked-for-lock-acquisition state. The threads are said to be *deadlocked*.

A deadlock is depicted in Figure 9.10. Thread t_1 has a lock on object o_1, but cannot acquire the lock on object o_2. Thread t_2 has a lock on object o_2, but cannot acquire the lock on object o_1. They can only proceed if one of them relinquishes a lock the other one wants, which is never going to happen.

Figure 9.10 *Deadlock*

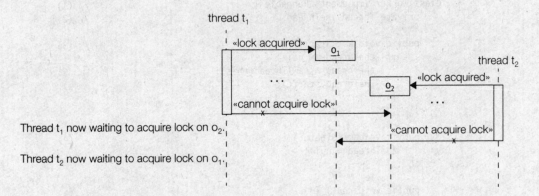

The situation in Figure 9.10 is implemented in Example 9.7. Thread t1 at (3) tries to synchronize at (4) and (5), first on string o1 at (1) then on string o2 at (2), respectively. The thread t2 at (6) does the opposite. It synchronizes at (7) and (8), first on string o2 then on string o1, respectively. A deadlock can occur as explained previously.

However, the potential of deadlock in the situation in Example 9.7 is easy to fix. If the two threads acquire the locks on the objects in the same order, then mutual lock dependency is avoided and a deadlock can never occur. This means having the same locking order at (4) and (5) as at (7) and (8). In general, the cause of a deadlock is not álways easy to discover, let alone easy to fix.

Example 9.7 *Deadlock*

```
public class DeadLockDanger {

    String o1 = "Lock " ;                          // (1)
    String o2 = "Step ";                           // (2)

    Thread t1 = (new Thread("Printer1") {          // (3)
        public void run() {
            while(true) {
                synchronized(o1) {                 // (4)
                    synchronized(o2) {             // (5)
                        System.out.println(o1 + o2);
                }
            }
        }
```

```
                        }
                    }
                });

        Thread t2 = (new Thread("Printer2") {         // (6)
            public void run() {
                while(true) {
                    synchronized(o2) {                 // (7)
                        synchronized(o1) {             // (8)
                            System.out.println(o2 + o1);
                        }
                    }
                }
            }
        });

        public static void main(String[] args) {
            DeadLockDanger dld = new DeadLockDanger();
            dld.t1.start();
            dld.t2.start();
        }
    }
```

Possible output from the program:

```
...
Step Lock
Step Lock
Lock Step
Lock Step
Lock Step
...
```

 Review Questions

9.8 Which one of these events will cause a thread to die?

Select the one correct answer.

(a) The method sleep() is called.
(b) The method wait() is called.
(c) Execution of the start() method ends.
(d) Execution of the run() method ends.
(e) Execution of the thread's constructor ends.

9.9   Which statements are true about the following code?

```
public class Joining {
    static Thread createThread(final int i, final Thread t1) {
        Thread t2 = new Thread() {
            public void run() {
                System.out.println(i+1);
                try {
                    t1.join();
                } catch (InterruptedException e) {
                }
                System.out.println(i+2);
            }
        };
        System.out.println(i+3);
        t2.start();
        System.out.println(i+4);
        return t2;
    }

    public static void main(String[] args) {
        createThread(10, createThread(20, Thread.currentThread()));
    }
}
```

Select the two correct answers.

(a) The first number printed is 13.
(b) The number 14 is printed before the number 22.
(c) The number 24 is printed before the number 21.
(d) The last number printed is 12.
(e) The number 11 is printed before the number 23.

9.10   What can be guaranteed by calling the method yield()?

Select the one correct answer.

(a) All lower priority threads will be granted CPU time.
(b) The current thread will sleep for some time while some other threads run.
(c) The current thread will not continue until other threads have terminated.
(d) The thread will wait until it is notified.
(e) None of the above.

9.11   Where is the notify() method defined?

Select the one correct answer.

(a) Thread
(b) Object
(c) Applet
(d) Runnable

9.12   How can the priority of a thread be set?

Select the one correct answer.

(a) By using the setPriority() method in the class Thread.
(b) By passing the priority as a parameter to the constructor of the thread.
(c) Both of the above.
(d) None of the above.

9.13   Which statements are true about locks?

Select the two correct answers.

(a) A thread can hold more than one lock at a time.
(b) Invoking wait() on a Thread object will relinquish all locks held by the thread.
(c) Invoking wait() on an object whose lock is held by the current thread will relinquish the lock.
(d) Invoking notify() on a object whose lock is held by the current thread will relinquish the lock.
(e) Multiple threads can hold the same lock at the same time.

9.14   What will be the result of invoking the wait() method on an object without ensuring that the current thread holds the lock of the object?

Select the one correct answer.

(a) The code will fail to compile.
(b) Nothing special will happen.
(c) An IllegalMonitorStateException will be thrown if the wait() method is called while the current thread does not hold the lock of the object.
(d) The thread will be blocked until it gains the lock of the object.

9.15   Which of these are plausible reasons why a thread might be alive, but still not be running?

Select the four correct answers.

(a) The thread is waiting for some condition as a result of a wait() call.
(b) The execution has reached the end of the run() method.
(c) The thread is waiting to acquire the lock of an object in order to execute a certain method on that object.
(d) The thread does not have the highest priority and is currently not executing.
(e) The thread is sleeping as a result of a call to the sleep() method.

Chapter Summary

The following information was included in this chapter:

- creating threads by extending the Thread class or implementing the Runnable interface

- writing synchronized code using synchronized methods and synchronized blocks to achieve mutually exclusive access to shared resources

- discussing thread states and the transitions between them, and thread communication

Programming Exercises

9.1 Implement three classes: Storage, Counter, and Printer. The Storage class should store an integer. The Counter class should create a thread that starts counting from 0 (0, 1, 2, 3 ...) and stores each value in the Storage class. The Printer class should create a thread that keeps reading the value in the Storage class and printing it.

Write a program that creates an instance of the Storage class and sets up a Counter and a Printer object to operate on it.

9.2 Modify the program from the previous exercise to ensure that each number is printed exactly once, by adding suitable synchronization.

Fundamental Classes

10

- Write code using the following methods of the java.lang.Math class: abs(), ceil(), floor(), max(), min(), random(), round(), sin(), cos(), tan(), sqrt().
- Describe the significance of the immutability of String objects.
- Describe the significance of wrapper classes, including making appropriate selections in the wrapper classes to suit specified behavior requirements, stating the result of executing a fragment of code that includes an instance of one of the wrapper classes, and writing code using the following methods of the wrapper classes (e.g., Integer, Double, etc.):
  - doubleValue()
  - floatValue()
  - intValue()
  - longValue()
  - parseXxx()
  - getXxx()
  - toString()
  - toHexString()

- Understand the functionality inherited by all classes from the Object class, which is at the top of any class hierarchy.
- Write code for manipulating immutable and dynamic strings, using the facilities provided by the String and StringBuffer classes, respectively.

10.1   Overview of the `java.lang` **Package**

The `java.lang` package is indispensable when programming in Java. It is automatically imported into every source file at compile time. The package contains the `Object` class that is the mother of all classes, and the wrapper classes (`Boolean`, `Character`, `Byte`, `Short`, `Integer`, `Long`, `Float`, `Double`) used to handle primitive values as objects. It provides classes essential for interacting with the JVM (`Runtime`), for security (`SecurityManager`), for loading classes (`ClassLoader`), for dealing with threads (`Thread`), and for exceptions (`Throwable`). The `java.lang` package also contains classes that provide the standard input, output, and error streams (`System`), string handling (`String`, `StringBuffer`), and mathematical functions (`Math`).

Figure 10.1 shows the important classes that are discussed in detail in this chapter.

Figure 10.1   *Partial Inheritance Hierarchy in the* `java.lang` *Package*

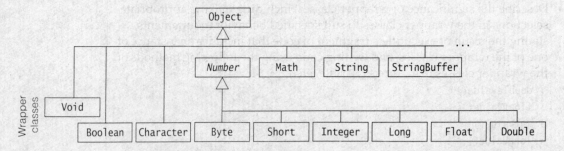

10.2   The `Object` **Class**

All classes extend the `Object` class, either directly or indirectly. A class declaration, without the extends clause, implicitly extends the `Object` class (see Section 6.1, p. 226). Thus, the `Object` class is always at the top of any inheritance hierarchy. The `Object` class defines the basic functionality that all objects exhibit and that all classes inherit. Note that this also applies for arrays, since these are genuine objects in Java.

The `Object` class provides the following general utility methods (see Example 10.1 for usage of some of these methods):

`int hashCode()`

When storing objects in hash tables, this method can be used to get a hash value for an object. This value is guaranteed to be consistent during the execution of the program. For a detailed discussion of the `hashCode()` method, see Section 11.7 on page 461.

```
boolean equals(Object obj)
```

Object reference and value equality are discussed together with the == and != operators (see Section 3.10, p. 68). The equals() method in the Object class returns true only if the two references compared denote the same object. The equals() method is usually overridden to provide the semantics of object value equality, as is the case for the wrapper classes and the String class. For a detailed discussion of the equals() method, see Section 11.7 on page 461.

```
final Class getClass()
```

Returns the *runtime class* of the object, which is represented by an object of the class java.lang.Class at runtime.

```
protected Object clone() throws CloneNotSupportedException
```

New objects that are exactly the same (i.e., have identical states) as the current object can be created by using the clone() method, that is, primitive values and reference values are copied. This is called *shallow copying*. A class can override this method to provide its own notion of cloning. For example, cloning a composite object by recursively cloning the constituent objects is called *deep copying*.

When overridden, the method in the subclass is usually declared public to allow any client to clone objects of the class.

If the overriding clone() method relies on the clone() method in the Object class, then the subclass must implement the Cloneable marker interface to indicate that its objects can be safely cloned. Otherwise, the clone() method in the Object class will throw a checked CloneNotSupportedException.

```
String toString()
```

If a subclass does not override this method, it returns a textual representation of the object, which has the following format:

"*<name of the class>*@*<hash code value of object>*"

This method is usually overridden and used for debugging purposes. The method call System.out.println(objRef) will implicitly convert its argument to a textual representation using the toString() method. See also the binary string concatenation operator +, discussed in Section 3.6 on page 62.

```
protected void finalize() throws Throwable
```

This method is discussed in connection with garbage collection (see Section 8.1, p. 324). It is called on an object just before it is garbage collected, so that any cleaning up can be done. However, the default finalize() method in the Object class does not do anything useful.

In addition, the Object class provides support for thread communication in synchronized code, through the following methods, which are discussed in Section 9.5 on page 370:

```
final void wait(long timeout) throws InterruptedException
final void wait(long timeout, int nanos) throws InterruptedException
final void wait() throws InterruptedException
final void notify()
final void notifyAll()
```

A thread invokes these method on the object whose lock it holds. A thread waits for notification by another thread.

Example 10.1   *Methods in the* Object *class*

```
public class ObjectMethods {
    public static void main(String[] args) {
        // Two objects of MyClass.
        MyClass obj1 = new MyClass();
        MyClass obj2 = new MyClass();

        // Two strings.
        String str1 = new String("WhoAmI");
        String str2 = new String("WhoAmI");

        // Method hashCode() overridden in String class.
        // Strings with same content (i.e., are equal) have the same hash code.
        System.out.println("hash code for str1: " + str1.hashCode());
        System.out.println("hash code for str2: " + str2.hashCode() + "\n");

        // Hash codes are different for different MyClass objects.
        System.out.println("hash code for MyClass obj1: " + obj1.hashCode());
        System.out.println("hash code for MyClass obj2: " + obj2.hashCode()+"\n");

        // Method equals() overridden in the String class.
        System.out.println("str1.equals(str2): " + str1.equals(str2));
        System.out.println("str1 == str2 : " + (str1 == str2) + "\n");

        // Method equals() from the Object class called.
        System.out.println("obj1.equals(obj2): " + obj1.equals(obj2));
        System.out.println("obj1 == obj2 : " + (obj1 == obj2) + "\n");

        // The runtime object that represents the class of an object.
        Class rtStringClass  = str1.getClass();
        Class rtMyClassClass = obj1.getClass();
        // The name of the class represented by the runtime object.
        System.out.println("Class for str1: " + rtStringClass);
        System.out.println("Class for obj1: " + rtMyClassClass + "\n");
```

```
                    // The toString() method is overridden in the String class.
                    String textRepStr = str1.toString();
                    String textRepObj = obj1.toString();
                    System.out.println("Text representation of str1: " + textRepStr);
                    System.out.println("Text representation of obj1: " + textRepObj + "\n");

                    // Shallow copying of arrays.
                    MyClass[] array1 = {new MyClass(), new MyClass(), new MyClass()};
                    MyClass[] array2 = (MyClass[]) array1.clone(); // Cast required.
                    // Array objects are different, but share the element objects.
                    System.out.println("array1 == array2 : " + (array1 == array2));
                    for(int i = 0; i < array1.length; i++) {
                        System.out.println("array1[" + i + "] == array2[" + i + "] : "
                                + (array1[i] == array2[i]));
                    }
                    System.out.println();

                    // Clone an object of MyClass.
                    MyClass obj3 = (MyClass) obj1.clone();
                    System.out.println("hash code for MyClass obj3: " + obj3.hashCode());
                    System.out.println("obj1 == obj3 : " + (obj1 == obj3));
            }
    }

    class MyClass implements Cloneable {

        public Object clone() {
            Object obj = null;
            try { obj = super.clone();}              // Calls overridden method.
            catch (CloneNotSupportedException e) { System.out.println(e);}
            return obj;
        }
    }
```

Output from the program:

```
    hash code for str1: -1704812257
    hash code for str2: -1704812257

    hash code for MyClass obj1: 24216257
    hash code for MyClass obj2: 20929799

    str1.equals(str2): true
    str1 == str2 : false

    obj1.equals(obj2): false
    obj1 == obj2 : false

    Class for str1: class java.lang.String
    Class for obj1: class MyClass

    Text representation of str1: WhoAmI
    Text representation of obj1: MyClass@17182c1
```

```
array1 == array2 : false
array1[0] == array2[0] : true
array1[1] == array2[1] : true
array1[2] == array2[2] : true

hash code for MyClass obj3: 16032330
obj1 == obj3 : false
```

Review Questions

10.1   What is the return type of the `hashCode()` method in the `Object` class?

Select the one correct answer.

(a) `String`
(b) `int`
(c) `long`
(d) `Object`
(e) `Class`

10.2   Which statement is true?

Select the one correct answer.

(a) If the references x and y denote two different objects, then the expression `x.equals(y)` is always `false`.
(b) If the references x and y denote two different objects, then the expression `(x.hashCode() == y.hashCode())` is always `false`.
(c) The `hashCode()` method in the `Object` class is declared `final`.
(d) The `equals()` method in the `Object` class is declared `final`.
(e) All arrays have a method named `clone`.

10.3   Which exception can the `clone()` method of the `Object` class throw?

Select the one correct answer.

(a) `CloneNotSupportedException`
(b) `NotCloneableException`
(c) `IllegalCloneException`
(d) `NoClonesAllowedException`

10.3   The Wrapper Classes

Wrapper classes were introduced with the discussion of the primitive data types (see Section 2.2, p. 28). Primitive values in Java are not objects. In order to manipulate these values as objects, the java.lang package provides a *wrapper* class for each of the primitive data types. All wrapper classes are `final`. The objects of all wrapper classes that can be instantiated are *immutable*, that is, their state cannot be changed.

Although the Void class is considered a wrapper class, it does not wrap any primitive value and is not instantiable (i.e., has no public constructors). It just denotes the Class object representing the keyword void. The Void class will not be discussed further in this section.

In addition to the methods defined for constructing and manipulating objects of primitive values, the wrapper classes also define useful constants, fields, and conversion methods.

Figure 10.2   *Converting Values between Primitive, Wrapper, and String Types*

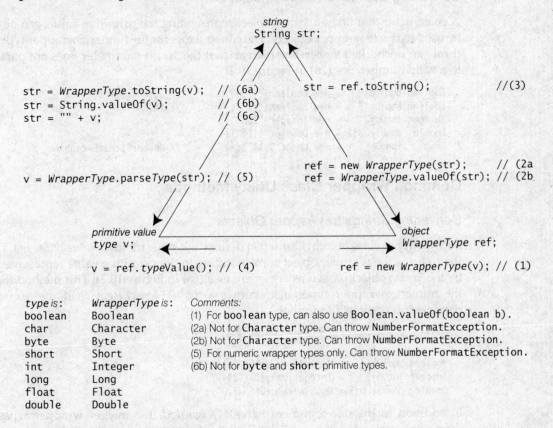

type is:	*WrapperType is:*	*Comments:*
boolean	Boolean	(1) For boolean type, can also use Boolean.valueOf(boolean b).
char	Character	(2a) Not for Character type. Can throw NumberFormatException.
byte	Byte	(2b) Not for Character type. Can throw NumberFormatException.
short	Short	(5) For numeric wrapper types only. Can throw NumberFormatException.
int	Integer	(6b) Not for byte and short primitive types.
long	Long	
float	Float	
double	Double	

Common Wrapper Class Constructors

The Character class has only one public constructor, taking a char value as parameter. The other wrapper classes all have two public one-argument constructors: one takes a primitive value and the other takes a string.

```
WrapperType( type v )
WrapperType( String str )
```

Converting Primitive Values to Wrapper Objects

A constructor that takes a primitive value can be used to create wrapper objects. See (1) in Figure 10.2.

```
Character charObj1  = new Character('\n');
Boolean   boolObj1  = new Boolean(true);
Integer   intObj1   = new Integer(2003);
Double    doubleObj1 = new Double(3.14);
```

Converting Strings to Wrapper Objects

A constructor that takes a String object representing the primitive value, can also be used to create wrapper objects. The constructors for the numeric wrapper types throw an unchecked NumberFormatException if the String parameter does not parse to a valid number. See (2a) in Figure 10.2.

```
Boolean boolObj2  = new Boolean("TrUe");      // case ignored: true
Boolean boolObj3  = new Boolean("XX");        // false
Integer intObj2   = new Integer("2003");
Double  doubleObj2 = new Double("3.14");
Long    longObj1  = new Long("3.14");         // NumberFormatException
```

Common Wrapper Class Utility Methods

Converting Strings to Wrapper Objects

Each wrapper class (except Character) defines the static method valueOf(String s) that returns the wrapper object corresponding to the primitive value represented by the String object passed as argument (see (6a) in Figure 10.2). This method for the numeric wrapper types also throws a NumberFormatException if the String parameter is not a valid number.

```
static WrapperType valueOf( String s )
```

```
Boolean boolObj4   = Boolean.valueOf("false");
Integer intObj3    = Integer.valueOf("1949");
Double  doubleObj3 = Double.valueOf("-3.0");
```

In addition to the one-argument valueOf() method, the integer wrapper types define an overloaded static valueOf() method that can take a second argument. This argument specifies the base (or *radix*) in which to interpret the string representing the signed integer in the first argument:

```
static WrapperType valueOf( String s, int base )
```

```
Byte    byteObj1  = Byte.valueOf("1010", 2);    // Decimal value 10
Short   shortObj2 = Short.valueOf("012", 8);    // Not "\012". Decimal value 10.
Integer intObj4   = Integer.valueOf("-a", 16);  // Not "-0xa". Decimal value -10.
Long    longObj2  = Long.valueOf("-a", 16);     // Not "-0xa". Decimal value -10L.
```

Converting Wrapper Objects to Strings

Each wrapper class overrides the toString() method from the Object class. The overriding method returns a String object containing the string representation of the primitive value in the wrapper object (see (3) in Figure 10.2).

```
String toString()

String charStr   = charObj1.toString();    // "\n"
String boolStr   = boolObj2.toString();    // "true"
String intStr    = intObj1.toString();     // "2003"
String doubleStr = doubleObj1.toString();  // "3.14"
```

Converting Primitive Values to Strings

Each wrapper class defines a static method toString(*type* v) that returns the string corresponding to the primitive value of *type* passed as argument (see (6a) in Figure 10.2).

```
static String toString( type v )

String charStr2   = Character.toString('\n');  // "\n"
String boolStr2   = Boolean.toString(true);    // "true"
String intStr2    = Integer.toString(2003);    // Base 10. "2003"
String doubleStr2 = Double.toString(3.14);     // "3.14"
```

For integer primitive types, the base is assumed to be 10. For floating-point numbers, the textual representation (decimal form or scientific notation) depends on the sign and the magnitude (absolute value) of the number. The NaN value, positive infinity and negative infinity will result in the strings "NaN", "Infinity", and "-Infinity", respectively.

In addition, the wrapper classes Integer and Long define overloaded toString() methods for converting integers to string representation in decimal, binary, octal, and hexadecimal notation (see p. 398).

Converting Wrapper Objects to Primitive Values

Each wrapper class defines a *type*Value() method which returns the primitive value in the wrapper object (see (4) in Figure 10.2).

```
type typeValue()

char    c = charObj1.charValue();        // '\n'
boolean b = boolObj2.booleanValue();     // true
int     i = intObj1.intValue();          // 2003
double  d = doubleObj1.doubleValue();    // 3.14
```

In addition, each numeric wrapper class defines *type*Value() methods for converting the primitive value in the wrapper object to a value of any numeric primitive data type. These methods are discussed below.

Wrapper Comparison, Equality, and Hashcode

Each wrapper class (except `Boolean`) defines the following method:

```
int compareTo(WrapperType obj2)
```

that returns a value which is less than, equal to, or greater than zero, depending on whether the primitive value in the current *WrapperType* object is less than, equal to, or greater than the primitive value in the *WrapperType* object denoted by argument obj2.

Each wrapper class (except `Boolean`) also implements the `Comparable` interface (see Section 11.6, p. 453), which defines the following method:

```
int compareTo(Object obj2)
```

This method is equivalent to the `compareTo(WrapperType)` method when the current object and the object denoted by the argument obj2 have the same *WrapperType*. Otherwise, a `ClassCastException` is thrown.

```
// Comparisons based on objects created above
Character charObj2   = new Character('a');
int result1 = charObj1.compareTo(charObj2);     // < 0
int result2 = intObj1.compareTo(intObj3);       // > 0
int result3 = doubleObj1.compareTo(doubleObj2); // == 0
int result4 = doubleObj1.compareTo(intObj1);    // ClassCastException
```

Each wrapper class overrides the `equals()` method from the `Object` class. The overriding method compares two wrapper objects for object value equality.

```
boolean equals(Object obj2)
```

```
// Comparisons based on objects created above
boolean charTest   = charObj1.equals(charObj2);      // false
boolean boolTest   = boolObj2.equals(Boolean.FALSE); // false
boolean intTest    = intObj1.equals(intObj2);        // true
boolean doubleTest = doubleObj1.equals(doubleObj2);  // true
```

Each wrapper class overrides the `hashCode()` method in the `Object` class. The overriding method returns a hash value based on the primitive value in the wrapper object.

```
int hashCode()
```

```
int index = charObj1.hashCode();
```

Numeric Wrapper Classes

The numeric wrapper classes `Byte`, `Short`, `Integer` `Long`, `Float`, and `Double` are all subclasses of the abstract class `Number` (see Figure 10.1).

Each numeric wrapper class defines an assortment of constants, including the minimum and maximum value of the corresponding primitive data type:

> *<wrapper class name>*.MIN_VALUE
> *<wrapper class name>*.MAX_VALUE

The following code retrieves the minimum and maximum values of various numeric types:

```
byte   minByte   = Byte.MIN_VALUE;      // -128
int    maxInt    = Integer.MAX_VALUE;   // 2147483647
double maxDouble = Double.MAX_VALUE;    // 1.7976931348623157e+308
```

Converting any Numeric Wrapper Object to any Numeric Primitive Type

Each numeric wrapper class defines the following set of *type*Value() methods for converting the primitive value in the wrapper object to a value of any numeric primitive type:

```
byte   byteValue()
short  shortValue()
int    intValue()
long   longValue()
float  floatValue()
double doubleValue()
```

See also (4) in Figure 10.2.

The following code shows converting of values in numeric wrapper objects to any numeric primitive type.

```
Byte    byteObj2   = new Byte((byte) 16);    // Cast mandatory
Integer intObj5    = new Integer(42030);
Double  doubleObj4 = new Double(Math.PI);

short  shortVal  = intObj5.shortValue();     // (1)
long   longVal   = byteObj2.longValue();
int    intVal    = doubleObj4.intValue();    // (2) Truncation
double doubleVal = intObj5.doubleValue();
```

Notice the potential for loss of information at (1) and (2) above, when the primitive value in a wrapper object is converted to a narrower primitive data type.

Converting Strings to Numeric Values

Each numeric wrapper class defines a static method parse*Type*(String s), which returns the primitive numeric value represented by the String object passed as argument. The *Type* in the method name parse*Type* stands for the name of a numeric wrapper class, except for the name of the Integer class which is abbreviated to Int. These methods throw a NumberFormatException if the String parameter is not a valid argument (see (5) in Figure 10.2.)

```
type parseType(String s)
```

```
byte   value1 = Byte.parseByte("16");
int    value2 = Integer.parseInt("2010");        // parseInt, not parseInteger.
int    value3 = Integer.parseInt("7UP");         // NumberFormatException
double value4 = Double.parseDouble("3.14");
```

For the integer wrapper types, the overloaded static method parse*Type*() can, in addition, take a second argument, which can specify the base in which to interpret the string representing the signed integer in the first argument:

```
type parseType(String s, int base)
```

```
byte  value6 = Byte.parseByte("1010", 2);   // Decimal value 10
short value7 = Short.parseShort("012", 8);  // Not "\012". Decimal value 10.
int   value8 = Integer.parseInt("-a", 16);  // Not "-0xa". Decimal value -10.
long  value9 = Long.parseLong("-a", 16);    // Not "-0xa". Decimal value -10L.
```

Converting Integer Values to Strings in different Notations

The wrapper classes Integer and Long provide static methods for converting integers to string representation in decimal, binary, octal, and hexadecimal notation. Some of these methods from the Integer class are listed here, but analogous methods are also defined in the Long class. Example 10.2 demonstrates use of these methods.

```
static String toBinaryString(int i)
static String toHexString(int i)
static String toOctalString(int i)
```

These three methods return a string representation of the integer argument as an *unsigned* integer in base 2, 16, and 8, respectively, with no extra leading zeroes.

```
static String toString(int i, int base)
static String toString(int i)
```

The first method returns the minus sign '-' as the first character if the integer i is negative. In all cases, it returns the string representation of the *magnitude* of the integer i in the specified base.

The last method is equivalent to the method toString(int i, int base), where the base has the value 10, that is, returns the string representation as a signed decimal. (see also (6a) in Figure 10.2).

- -

Example 10.2   *String Representation of Integers*

```
public class IntegerRepresentation {
    public static void main(String[] args) {
        int positiveInt = +41;    // 051, 0x29
        int negativeInt = -41;    // 037777777727, -051, 0xffffffd7, -0x29
```

```
                System.out.println("String representation for decimal value: "
                            + positiveInt);
                integerStringRepresentation(positiveInt);
                System.out.println("String representation for decimal value: "
                            + negativeInt);
                integerStringRepresentation(negativeInt);
    }

    public static void integerStringRepresentation(int i) {
        System.out.println("    Binary:\t\t" + Integer.toBinaryString(i));
        System.out.println("    Hex:\t\t"    + Integer.toHexString(i));
        System.out.println("    Octal:\t\t"  + Integer.toOctalString(i));
        System.out.println("    Decimal:\t"  + Integer.toString(i));

        System.out.println("    Using toString(int i, int base) method:");
        System.out.println("    Base 2:\t\t" + Integer.toString(i, 2));
        System.out.println("    Base 16:\t"  + Integer.toString(i, 16));
        System.out.println("    Base 8:\t\t" + Integer.toString(i, 8));
        System.out.println("    Base 10:\t"  + Integer.toString(i, 10));
    }
}
```

Output from the program:

```
String representation for decimal value: 41
    Binary:     101001
    Hex:        29
    Octal:      51
    Decimal:    41
    Using toString(int i, int base) method:
    Base 2:     101001
    Base 16:    29
    Base 8:     51
    Base 10:    41
String representation for decimal value: -41
    Binary:     11111111111111111111111111010111
    Hex:        ffffffd7
    Octal:      37777777727
    Decimal:    -41
    Using toString(int i, int base) method:
    Base 2:     -101001
    Base 16:    -29
    Base 8:     -51
    Base 10:    -41
```

Character **Class**

The Character class defines a myriad of constants, including the following which represent the minimum and the maximum value of the char type (see Section 2.2, p. 29):

```
Character.MIN_VALUE
Character.MAX_VALUE
```

The Character class also defines a plethora of static methods for handling various attributes of a character, and case issues relating to characters, as defined by Unicode:

```
static int     getNumericValue(char ch)
static boolean isLowerCase(char ch)
static boolean isUpperCase(char ch)
static boolean isTitleCase(char ch)
static boolean isDigit(char ch)
static boolean isLetter(char ch)
static boolean isLetterOrDigit(char ch)
static char    toUpperCase(char ch)
static char    toLowerCase(char ch)
static char    toTitleCase(char ch)
```

The following code converts a lowercase character to an uppercase character:

```
char ch = 'a';
if (Character.isLowerCase(ch)) ch = Character.toUpperCase(ch);
```

Boolean **Class**

The Boolean class defines the following wrapper objects to represent the primitive values true and false, respectively:

```
Boolean.TRUE
Boolean.FALSE
```

 ## Review Questions

10.4 Which of the following are wrapper classes?

Select the three correct answers.

(a) java.lang.Void
(b) java.lang.Int
(c) java.lang.Boolean
(d) java.lang.Long
(e) java.lang.String

10.5 Which of the following classes do not extend the java.lang.Number class?

Select the two correct answers.

(a) java.lang.Float
(b) java.lang.Byte
(c) java.lang.Character
(d) java.lang.Boolean
(e) java.lang.Short

10.6 Which of these classes define immutable objects?

Select the three correct answers.
(a) `Character`
(b) `Byte`
(c) `Thread`
(d) `Short`
(e) `Object`

10.7 Which of these classes have a one-parameter constructor taking a string?

Select the two correct answers.
(a) `Void`
(b) `Integer`
(c) `Boolean`
(d) `Character`
(e) `Object`

10.8 Which of the wrapper classes have a `booleanValue()` method?

Select the one correct answer.
(a) All wrapper classes.
(b) All wrapper classes except `Void`.
(c) All wrapper classes that also implement the `compareTo()` method.
(d) All wrapper classes extending `Number`.
(e) Only the class `Boolean`.

10.9 Which statements are true about wrapper classes?

Select the two correct answers.
(a) `String` is a wrapper class.
(b) `Double` has a `compareTo()` method.
(c) `Character` has a `intValue()` method.
(d) `Byte` extends `Number`.

10.4 The Math Class

The `final` class `Math` defines a set of `static` methods to support common mathematical functions, including functions for rounding numbers, performing trigonometry, generating pseudo random numbers, finding maximum and minimum of two numbers, calculating logarithms and exponentiation. The `Math` class cannot be instantiated. Only the class name `Math` can be used to invoke the static methods.

The final class Math provides constants to represent the value of *e*, the base of the natural logarithms, and the value π (*pi*), the ratio of the circumference of a circle to its diameter:

```
Math.E
Math.PI
```

Miscellaneous Rounding Functions

```
static int     abs(int i)
static long    abs(long l)
static float   abs(float f)
static double  abs(double d)
```

The overloaded method abs() returns the absolute value of the argument. For a non-negative argument, the argument is returned. For a negative argument, the negation of the argument is returned.

```
static int     min(int a, int b)
static long    min(long a, long b)
static float   min(float a, float b)
static double  min(double a, double b)
```

The overloaded method min() returns the smaller of the two values a and b for any numeric type.

```
static int     max(int a, int b)
static long    max(long a, long b)
static float   max(float a, float b)
static double  max(double a, double b)
```

The overloaded method max() returns the greater of the two values a and b for any numeric type.

The following code illustrates the use of these methods from the Math class:

```
long   l1 = Math.abs(2010L);          // 2010L
double dd = Math.abs(-Math.PI);       // 3.141592653589793

double d1 = Math.min(Math.PI, Math.E);  // 2.718281828459045
long   m1 = Math.max(1984L, 2010L);     // 2010L
int    i1 = (int) Math.max(3.0, 4);     // Cast required.
```

Note the cast required in the last example. The method with the signature max(double, double) is executed, with implicit conversion of the int argument to a double. Since this method returns a double, it must be explicitly cast to an int.

```
static double ceil(double d)
```

The method ceil() returns the *smallest* double value that is *greater than or equal* to the argument d, and is equal to a mathematical integer.

```
static double floor(double d)
```

The method floor() returns the *largest* double value that is *less than or equal* to the argument d, and is equal to a mathematical integer.

```
static int  round(float f)
static long round(double d)
```

The overloaded method round() returns the integer closest to the argument. This is equivalent to adding 0.5 to the argument, taking the floor of the result, and casting it to the return type. This is not the same as rounding to a specific number of decimal places, as the name of the method might suggest.

If the fractional part of a *positive* argument is *less than* 0.5, then the result returned is the same as Math.floor(). If the fractional part of a positive argument is *greater than or equal* to 0.5, then the result returned is the same as Math.ceil().

If the fractional part of a *negative* argument is *less than or equal* to 0.5, then the result returned is the same as Math.ceil(). If the fractional part of a negative argument is *greater than* 0.5, then the result returned is the same as Math.floor().

It is important to note the result obtained on negative arguments, keeping in mind that a negative number whose absolute value is less than that of another negative number, is actually greater than the other number (e.g., –3.2 is greater than –4.7). Compare also the results returned by these methods, shown in Table 10.1.

```
double upPI    = Math.ceil(Math.PI);     // 4.0
double downPI  = Math.floor(Math.PI);    // 3.0
long   roundPI = Math.round(Math.PI);    // 3L

double upNegPI    = Math.ceil(-Math.PI);  // -3.0
double downNegPI  = Math.floor(-Math.PI); // -4.0
long   roundNegPI = Math.round(-Math.PI); // -3L
```

Table 10.1 *Applying Rounding Functions*

Argument:	7.0	7.1	7.2	7.3	7.4	7.5	7.6	7.7	7.8	7.9	8.0
ceil:	7.0	8.0	8.0	8.0	8.0	8.0	8.0	8.0	8.0	8.0	8.0
floor:	7.0	7.0	7.0	7.0	7.0	7.0	7.0	7.0	7.0	7.0	8.0
round:	7	7	7	7	7	8	8	8	8	8	8
Argument:	-7.0	-7.1	-7.2	-7.3	-7.4	-7.5	-7.6	-7.7	-7.8	-7.9	-8.0
ceil:	-7.0	-7.0	-7.0	-7.0	-7.0	-7.0	-7.0	-7.0	-7.0	-7.0	-8.0
floor:	-7.0	-8.0	-8.0	-8.0	-8.0	-8.0	-8.0	-8.0	-8.0	-8.0	-8.0
round:	-7	-7	-7	-7	-7	-7	-8	-8	-8	-8	-8

Exponential Functions

```
static double pow(double d1, double d2)
```

The method pow() returns the value of d1 raised to the power of d2 (i.e., d1^{d2}).

```
static double exp(double d)
```

The method exp() returns the exponential number e raised to the power of d (i.e., e^d).

```
static double log(double d)
```

The method log() returns the natural logarithm (base e) of d (i.e., log_ed).

```
static double sqrt(double d)
```

The method sqrt() returns the square root of d (i.e., d$^{0.5}$). For a NaN or a negative argument, the result is a NaN (see Section 3.5, p. 52).

Some examples of exponential functions:

```
double r = Math.pow(2.0, 4.0);          // 16.0
double v = Math.exp(2.0);               // 7.38905609893065
double l = Math.log(Math.E);            // 0.9999999999999981
double c = Math.sqrt(3.0*3.0 + 4.0*4.0); // 5.0
```

Trigonometry Functions

```
static double sin(double d)
```

The method sin() returns the trigonometric sine of an angle d specified in radians.

```
static double cos(double d)
```

The method cos() returns the trigonometric cosine of an angle d specified in radians.

```
static double tan(double d)
```

The method tan() returns the trigonometric tangent of an angle d specified in radians.

```
static double toRadians(double degrees)
```

The method toRadians() converts an angle in degrees to its approximation in radians.

```
static double toDegrees(double radians)
```

The method toRadians() converts an angle in radians to its approximation in degrees.

Some examples of trigonometry functions:

```
double deg1 = Math.toDegrees(Math.PI/4.0);   // 45 degrees
double deg2 = Math.toDegrees(Math.PI/2.0);   // 90 degrees

double rad1 = Math.toRadians(deg1);          // 0.7853981633974483
double rad2 = Math.toRadians(deg2);          // 1.5707963267948966

double r1 = Math.sin(Math.PI/2.0);           // 1.0
double r2 = Math.sin(Math.PI*2);             // -2.4492935982947064E-16 (0.0)

double r3 = Math.cos(Math.PI);               // -1.0
double r4 = Math.cos(Math.toRadians(360.0)); // 1.0

double r5 = Math.tan(Math.toRadians(90.0));  // 1.633123935319537E16 (infinity)
double r6 = Math.tan(Math.toRadians(45.0));  // 0.9999999999999999   (1.0)
```

Expected mathematical values are shown in parentheses.

Pseudorandom Number Generator

```
static double random()
```

The method random() returns a random number greater than or equal to 0.0 and less than 1.0, where the value is selected randomly from the range according to a uniform distribution.

An example of using the pseudorandom number generator is as follows:

```
for (int i = 0; i < 10; i++)
    System.out.println((int)(Math.random()*10));   // int values in range [0 .. 9].
```

The loop will generate a run of ten pseudorandom integers between 0 (inclusive) and 10 (exclusive).

 Review Questions

10.10 Given the following program, which lines will print 11 exactly?

```
class MyClass {
    public static void main(String[] args) {
        double v = 10.5;

        System.out.println(Math.ceil(v));         // (1)
        System.out.println(Math.round(v));        // (2)
        System.out.println(Math.floor(v));        // (3)
        System.out.println((int) Math.ceil(v));   // (4)
        System.out.println((int) Math.floor(v));  // (5)
    }
}
```

Select the two correct answers.

(a) The line labeled (1).
(b) The line labeled (2).
(c) The line labeled (3).
(d) The line labeled (4).
(e) The line labeled (5).

10.11 Which method is not defined in the Math class?

Select the one correct answer.

(a) `double tan2(double)`
(b) `double cos(double)`
(c) `int abs(int a)`
(d) `double ceil(double)`
(e) `float max(float, float)`

10.12 What is the return type of the method `round(float)` from the Math class?

Select the one correct answer.

(a) `int`
(b) `float`
(c) `double`
(d) `Integer`
(e) `Float`

10.13 What is the return type of the method `ceil(double)` from the Math class?

Select the one correct answer.

(a) `int`
(b) `float`
(c) `double`
(d) `Integer`
(e) `Double`

10.14 What will the following program print when run?

```
public class Round {
    public static void main(String[] args) {
        System.out.println(Math.round(-0.5) + " " + Math.round(0.5));
    }
};
```

Select the one correct answer.

(a) 0 0
(b) 0 1
(c) -1 0
(d) -1 1
(e) None of the above.

10.15   Which statements are true about the expression `((int)(Math.random()*4))`?

Select the three correct answers.
(a) It may evaluate to a negative number.
(b) It may evaluate to the number 0.
(c) The probability of it evaluating to the number 1 or the number 2 is the same.
(d) It may evaluate to the number 3.
(e) It may evaluate to the number 4.

10.5 **The** `String` **Class**

Handling character strings is supported through two final classes: `String` and `StringBuffer`. The `String` class implements immutable character strings, which are read-only once the string has been created and initialized, whereas the `String-Buffer` class implements dynamic character strings.

Character strings implemented using these classes are genuine objects, and the characters in such a string are represented using 16-bit characters (see Section 2.1, p. 23).

This section discusses the class `String` that provides facilities for creating, initializing, and manipulating character strings. The next section discusses the `String-Buffer` class.

Creating and Initializing Strings

String Literals Revisited

The easiest way of creating a `String` object is using a string literal:

```
String str1 = "You cannot change me!";
```

A string literal is a reference to a `String` object. The value in the `String` object is the character sequence enclosed in the double quotes of the string literal. Since a string literal is a reference, it can be manipulated like any other `String` reference. The reference value of a string literal can be assigned to another `String` reference: the reference str1 will denote the `String` object with the value `"You cannot change me!"` after the assignment above. A string literal can be used to invoke methods on its `String` object:

```
int len = "You cannot change me!".length(); // 21
```

The compiler optimizes handling of string literals (and compile-time constant expressions that evaluate to strings): only one `String` object is shared by all string-valued constant expressions with the same character sequence. Such strings are said to be *interned*, meaning that they share a unique `String` object if they have the same content. The `String` class maintains a private pool where such strings are interned.

```
String str2 = "You cannot change me!";
```

Both String references str1 and str2 denote the same String object, initialized with the character string: "You cannot change me!". So does the reference str3 in the following code. The compile-time evaluation of the constant expression involving the two string literals, results in a string that is already interned:

```
String str3 = "You cannot" + " change me!"; // Compile-time constant expression
```

In the following code, both the references can1 and can2 denote the same String object that contains the string "7Up":

```
String can1 = 7 + "Up";   // Value of compile-time constant expression: "7Up"
String can2 = "7Up";      // "7Up"
```

However, in the code below, the reference can4 will denote a *new* String object that will have the value "7Up" at runtime:

```
String word = "Up";
String can4 = 7 + word;  // Not a compile-time constant expression.
```

The sharing of String objects between string-valued constant expressions poses no problem, since the String objects are immutable. Any operation performed on one String reference will never have any effect on the usage of other references denoting the same object. The String class is also declared final, so that no subclass can override this behavior.

String Constructors

The String class has numerous constructors to create and initialize String objects based on various types of arguments. The following shows two of them:

```
String(String s)
```

This constructor creates a new String object, whose contents are the same as those of the String object passed as argument.

```
String()
```

This constructor creates a new String object, whose content is the empty string, ""

Note that using a constructor creates a brand new String object, that is, using a constructor does not intern the string. A reference to an interned string can be obtained by calling the intern() method in the String class—in practice, there is usually no reason to do so.

In the following code, the String object denoted by str4 is different from the String object passed as argument:

```
String str4 = new String("You cannot change me!");
```

Constructing String objects can also be done from arrays of bytes, arrays of characters, or string buffers:

```
byte[] bytes = {97, 98, 98, 97};
char[] characters = {'a', 'b', 'b', 'a'};
```

```
                    StringBuffer strBuf = new StringBuffer("abba");
                    //...
                    String byteStr = new String(bytes);        // Using array of bytes: "abba"
                    String charStr = new String(character);     // Using array of chars: "abba"
                    String buffStr = new String(strBuf);        // Using string buffer: "abba"
```

In Example 10.3, note that the reference str1 does not denote the same String object as references str4 and str5. Using the new operator with a String constructor always creates a new String object. The expression "You cannot" + words is not a constant expression and, therefore, results in a new String object. The local references str2 and str3 in the main() method and the static reference str1 in the Auxiliary class all denote the same interned string. Object value equality is hardly surprising between these references. It might be tempting to use the operator == for object value equality of string literals, but this is not advisable.

Example 10.3   *String Construction and Equality*

```
        public class StringConstruction {

            static String str1 = "You cannot change me!";                // Interned

            public static void main(String[] args) {
                String emptyStr = new String();                          // ""
                System.out.println("emptyStr: " + emptyStr);

                String str2 = "You cannot change me!";                   // Interned
                String str3 = "You cannot" + " change me!";              // Interned
                String str4 = new String("You cannot change me!");       // New String object

                String words = " change me!";
                String str5 = "You cannot" + words;                      // New String object

                System.out.println("str1 == str2:          " +
                                   (str1 == str2));                      // (1) true
                System.out.println("str1.equals(str2):     " +
                                   str1.equals(str2));                   // (2) true

                System.out.println("str1 == str3:          " +
                                   (str1 == str3));                      // (3) true
                System.out.println("str1.equals(str3):     " +
                                   str1.equals(str3));                   // (4) true

                System.out.println("str1 == str4:          " +
                                   (str1 == str4));                      // (5) false
                System.out.println("str1.equals(str4):     " +
                                   str1.equals(str4));                   // (6) true

                System.out.println("str1 == str5:          " +
                                   (str1 == str5));                      // (7) false
                System.out.println("str1.equals(str5):     " +
                                   str1.equals(str5));                   // (8) true
```

```
            System.out.println("str1 == Auxiliary.str1:      " +
                          (str1 == Auxiliary.str1));        // (9) true
            System.out.println("str1.equals(Auxiliary.str1): " +
                          str1.equals(Auxiliary.str1));     // (10) true

            System.out.println("\"You cannot change me!\".length(): " +
                          "You cannot change me!".length());// (11) 21
        }
    }

    class Auxiliary {
        static String str1 = "You cannot change me!";          // Interned
    }
```

Output from the program:

```
emptyStr:
str1 == str2:                    true
str1.equals(str2):               true
str1 == str3:                    true
str1.equals(str3):               true
str1 == str4:                    false
str1.equals(str4):               true
str1 == str5:                    false
str1.equals(str5):               true
str1 == Auxiliary.str1:          true
str1.equals(Auxiliary.str1):     true
"You cannot change me!".length(): 21
```

Reading Characters from a String

```
char charAt(int index)
```

A character at a particular index in a string can be read using the charAt() method. The first character is at index 0 and the last one at index one less than the number of characters in the string. If the index value is not valid, a StringIndexOutOfBoundsException is thrown.

```
void getChars(int srcBegin, int srcEnd, char[] dst, int dstBegin)
```

This method copies characters from the current string into the destination character array. Characters from the current string are read from index srcBegin to the index srcEnd-1, inclusive. They are copied into the destination array, starting at index dstBegin and ending at index dstbegin+(srcEnd-srcBegin)-1. The number of characters copied is (srcEnd-srcBegin). An IndexOutOfBoundsException is thrown if the indices do not meet the criteria for the operation.

```
int length()
```

This method returns the number of characters in a string.

Example 10.4 uses these methods at (3), (4), (5), and (6). The program prints the frequency of a character in a string and illustrates copying from a string into a character array.

Example 10.4 *Reading Characters from a String*

```
public class ReadingCharsFromString {
    public static void main(String[] args) {
        int[] frequencyData = new int [Character.MAX_VALUE];// (1)
        String str = "You cannot change me!";                // (2)

        // Count the frequency of each character in the string.
        for (int i = 0; i < str.length(); i++)               // (3)
            try {
                frequencyData[str.charAt(i)]++;              // (4)
            } catch(StringIndexOutOfBoundsException e) {
                System.out.println("Index error detected: "+ i +" not in range.");
            }
        // Print the character frequency.
        System.out.println("Character frequency for string: \"" + str + "\"");
        for (int i = 0; i < frequencyData.length; i++)
            if (frequencyData[i] != 0)
                System.out.println((char)i + " (code "+ i +"): " +
                                    frequencyData[i]);

        System.out.println("Copying into a char array:");
        char[] destination = new char [str.length()];
        str.getChars( 0,            7, destination, 0);     // (5) "You can"
        str.getChars(10, str.length(), destination, 7);     // (6) " change me!"
        // Print the character array.
        for (int i = 0; i < 7 + (str.length() - 10); i++)
            System.out.print(destination[i]);
        System.out.println();
    }
}
```

Output from the program:

```
Character Frequency for string: "You cannot change me!"
  (code 32): 3
! (code 33): 1
Y (code 89): 1
a (code 97): 2
c (code 99): 2
e (code 101): 2
g (code 103): 1
h (code 104): 1
m (code 109): 1
n (code 110): 3
o (code 111): 2
t (code 116): 1
u (code 117): 1
Copying into a char array:
You can change me!
```

In Example 10.4, the frequencyData array at (1) stores the frequency of each character that can occur in a string. The string in question is declared at (2). Since a char value is promoted to an int value in arithmetic expressions, it can be used as an index in an array. Each element in the frequencyData array functions as a frequency counter for the character corresponding to the index value of the element:

```
frequencyData[str.charAt(i)]++;                          // (4)
```

The calls to the getChars() method at (5) and (6) copy particular substrings from the string into designated places in the destination array, before printing the whole character array.

Comparing Strings

Characters are compared based on their integer values.

```
boolean test = 'a' < 'b';      // true since 0x61 < 0x62
```

Two strings are compared *lexicographically*, as in a dictionary or telephone directory, by successively comparing their corresponding characters at each position in the two strings, starting with the characters in the first position. The string "abba" is less than "aha", since the second character 'b' in the string "abba" is less than the second character 'h' in the string "aha". The characters in the first position in each of these strings are equal.

The following public methods can be used for comparing strings:

```
boolean equals(Object obj)
boolean equalsIgnoreCase(String str2)
```

The String class overrides the equals() method from the Object class. The String class equals() method implements String object value equality as two String objects having the same sequence of characters. The equalsIgnoreCase() method does the same, but ignores the case of the characters.

```
int compareTo(String str2)
int compareTo(Object obj)
```

The first compareTo() method compares the two strings and returns a value based on the outcome of the comparison:

- the value 0, if this string is equal to the string argument
- a value less than 0, if this string is lexicographically less than the string argument
- a value greater than 0, if this string is lexicographically greater than the string argument

The second compareTo() method (required by the Comparable interface) behaves like the first method if the argument obj is actually a String object; otherwise, it throws a ClassCastException.

Here are some examples of string comparisons:

```java
String strA = new String("The Case was thrown out of Court");
String strB = new String("the case was thrown out of court");

boolean b1 = strA.equals(strB);                // false
boolean b2 = strA.equalsIgnoreCase(strB);      // true

String str1 = new String("abba");
String str2 = new String("aha");

int compVal1 = str1.compareTo(str2);           // negative value => str1 < str2
```

Character Case in a String

```java
String toUpperCase()
String toUpperCase(Locale locale)
String toLowerCase()
String toLowerCase(Locale locale)
```

Note that the original string is returned if none of the characters need their case changed, but a new String object is returned if any of the characters need their case changed. These methods delegate the character-by-character case conversion to corresponding methods from the Character class.

These methods use the rules of the (default) *locale* (returned by the method Locale.getDefault()), which embodies the *idiosyncrasies* of a specific geographical, political, or cultural region regarding number/date/currency formats, character classification, alphabet (including case idiosyncrasies), and other localizations.

Example of case in strings:

```java
String strA = new String("The Case was thrown out of Court");
String strB = new String("the case was thrown out of court");

String strC = strA.toLowerCase();   // Case conversion => New String object:
                                    // "the case was thrown out of court"
String strD = strB.toLowerCase();   // No case conversion => Same String object
String strE = strA.toUppperCase();  // Case conversion => New String object:
                                    // "THE CASE WAS THROWN OUT OF COURT"

boolean test1 = strC == strA; // false
boolean test2 = strD == strB; // true
boolean test3 = strE == strA; // false
```

Concatenation of Strings

Concatenation of two strings results in a string that consists of the characters of the first string followed by the characters of the second string. The overloaded operator + for string concatenation is discussed in Section 3.6 on page 62. In addition, the following method can be used to concatenate two strings:

```java
String concat(String str)
```

The concat() method does not modify the String object on which it is invoked, as
String objects are immutable. Instead the concat() method returns a reference to a
brand new String object:

```
String billboard = "Just";
billboard.concat(" lost in space.");     // (1) Returned reference value not stored.
System.out.println(billboard);           // (2) "Just"
billboard = billboard.concat(" grooving").concat(" in heap.");  // (3) Chaining.
System.out.println(billboard);           // (4) "Just grooving in heap."
```

At (1), the reference value of the String object returned by the method concat() is
not stored. This String object becomes inaccessible after (1). We see that the reference billboard still denotes the string literal "Just" at (2).

At (3), two method calls to the concat() method are *chained*. The first call returns a
reference value to a new String object whose content is "Just grooving". The second
method call is invoked on this String object using the reference value that was
returned in the first method call. The second call results in yet another String object
whose content is "Just grooving in heap." The reference value of this String object
is assigned to the reference billboard. Because String objects are immutable, the
creation of the temporary String object with the content "Just grooving" is inevita-
ble at (3).

The compiler uses a string buffer to avoid this overhead of temporary String
objects when applying the string concatenation operator (p. 424).

A simple way to convert any primitive value to its string representation is by concatenating it with the empty string (""), using the string concatenation operator (+)
(see also (6c) in Figure 10.2):

```
String strRepresentation = "" + 2003;  // "2003"
```

Some more examples of string concatenation follow:

```
String motto = new String("Program once");     // (1)
motto += ", execute everywhere.";              // (2)
motto = motto.concat(" Don't bet on it!");     // (3)
```

Note that a new String object is assigned to the reference motto each time in the
assignment at (1), (2), and (3). The String object with the contents "Program once"
becomes inaccessible after the assignment at (2). The String object with the contents "Program once, execute everywhere." becomes inaccessible after (3). The reference motto denotes the String object with the following contents after execution of
the assignment at (3):

```
"Program once, execute everywhere. Don't bet on it!"
```

Searching for Characters and Substrings

The following overloaded methods can be used to find the index of a character, or
the start index of a substring in a string. These methods search *forward* toward the
end of the string. In other words, the index of the *first* occurrence of the character
or substring is found. If the search is unsuccessful, the value −1 is returned.

```
int indexOf(int ch)
```

Finds the index of the first occurrence of the argument character in a string.

```
int indexOf(int ch, int fromIndex)
```

Finds the index of the first occurrence of the argument character in a string, starting at the index specified in the second argument. If the index argument is negative, the index is assumed to be 0. If the index argument is greater than the length of the string, it is effectively considered to be equal to the length of the string—returning the value -1.

```
int indexOf(String str)
```

Finds the start index of the first occurrence of the substring argument in a string.

```
int indexOf(String str, int fromIndex)
```

Finds the start index of the first occurrence of the substring argument in a string, starting at the index specified in the second argument.

The String class also defines a set of methods that search for a character or a substring, but the search is *backward* toward the start of the string. In other words, the index of the *last* occurrence of the character or substring is found.

```
int lastIndexOf(int ch)
int lastIndexOf(int ch, int fromIndex)
int lastIndexOf(String str)
int lastIndexOf(String str, int fromIndex)
```

The following method can be used to create a string in which all occurrences of a character in a string have been replaced with another character:

```
String replace(char oldChar, char newChar)
```

Examples of search methods:

```
String funStr = "Java Jives";
//              0123456789
String newStr = funStr.replace('J', 'W');       // "Wava Wives"

int jInd1a = funStr.indexOf('J');               // 0
int jInd1b = funStr.indexOf('J', 1);            // 5
int jInd2a = funStr.lastIndexOf('J');           // 5
int jInd2b = funStr.lastIndexOf('J', 4);        // 0

String banner = "One man, One vote";
//              01234567890123456

int subInd1a = banner.indexOf("One");           // 0
int subInd1b = banner.indexOf("One", 3);        // 9
int subInd2a = banner.lastIndexOf("One");       // 9
int subInd2b = banner.lastIndexOf("One", 10);   // 9
int subInd2c = banner.lastIndexOf("One", 8);    // 0
int subInd2d = banner.lastIndexOf("One", 2);    // 0
```

Extracting Substrings

```
String trim()
```

This method can be used to create a string where white space (in fact all characters with values less than or equal to the space character '\u0020') from the front (leading) and the end (trailing) of a string has been removed.

```
String substring(int startIndex)
String substring(int startIndex, int endIndex)
```

The String class provides these overloaded methods to extract substrings from a string. A new String object containing the substring is created and returned. The first method extracts the string that starts at the given index startIndex and extends to the end of the string. The end of the substring can be specified by using a second argument endIndex that is the index of the first character *after* the substring, that is, the last character in the substring is at index endIndex-1. If the index value is not valid, a StringIndexOutOfBoundsException is thrown.

Examples of extracting substrings:

```
String utopia = "\t\n  Java Nation \n\t  ";
utopia = utopia.trim();                       // "Java Nation"
utopia = utopia.substring(5);                 // "Nation"
String radioactive = utopia.substring(3,6);   // "ion"
```

Converting Primitive Values and Objects to Strings

The String class overrides the toString() method in the Object class and returns the String object itself:

```
String toString()
```

The String class also defines a set of static overloaded valueOf() methods to convert objects and primitive values into strings.

```
static String valueOf(Object obj)
static String valueOf(char[] character)
static String valueOf(boolean b)
static String valueOf(char c)
```

All these methods return a string representing the given parameter value. A call to the method with the parameter obj is equivalent to obj.toString(). The boolean values true and false are converted into the strings "true" and "false". The char parameter is converted to a string consisting of a single character.

```
static String valueOf(int i)
static String valueOf(long l)
static String valueOf(float f)
static String valueOf(double d)
```

The static valueOf() method that accepts a primitive value as argument is equivalent to the static toString() method in the corresponding wrapper class for each of the primitive data types (see also (6a) and (6b) in Figure 10.2 on p. 393).

Note that there are no valueOf() methods that accept a byte or a short.

Examples of string conversions:

```
String anonStr   = String.valueOf("Make me a string.");      // "Make me a string."
String charStr   = String.valueOf(new char[] {'a', 'h', 'a'});// "aha"
String boolTrue  = String.valueOf(true);                      // "true"
String doubleStr = String.valueOf(Math.PI);                   // "3.141592653589793"
```

Other miscellaneous methods exist for reading the string characters into an array of characters (toCharArray()), converting the string into an array of bytes (getBytes()), and searching for prefixes (startsWith()) and suffixes (endsWith()) of the string. The method hashCode() can be used to compute a hash value based on the characters in the string.

 ## Review Questions

10.16 Which of the following operators cannot be used in conjunction with a String object?

Select the two correct answers.

(a) +
(b) -
(c) +=
(d) .
(e) &

10.17 Which expression will extract the substring "kap" from a string defined by String str = "kakapo"?

Select the one correct answer.

(a) str.substring(2, 2)
(b) str.substring(2, 3)
(c) str.substring(2, 4)
(d) str.substring(2, 5)
(e) str.substring(3, 3)

10.18   What will be the result of attempting to compile and run the following code?

```
class MyClass {
    public static void main(String[] args) {
        String str1 = "str1";
        String str2 = "str2";
        String str3 = "str3";

        str1.concat(str2);
        System.out.println(str3.concat(str1));
    }
}
```

Select the one correct answer.

(a) The code will fail to compile since the expression str3.concat(str1) will not result in a valid argument for the println() method.
(b) The program will print str3str1str2 when run.
(c) The program will print str3 when run.
(d) The program will print str3str1 when run.
(e) The program will print str3str2 when run.

10.19   What function does the trim() method of the String class perform?

Select the one correct answer.

(a) It returns a string where the leading white space of the original string has been removed.
(b) It returns a string where the trailing white space of the original string has been removed.
(c) It returns a string where both the leading and trailing white space of the original string has been removed.
(d) It returns a string where all the white space of the original string has been removed.
(e) None of the above.

10.20   Which statements are true?

Select the two correct answers.

(a) String objects are immutable.
(b) Subclasses of the String class can be mutable.
(c) All wrapper classes are declared final.
(d) All objects have a public method named clone().
(e) The expression ((new StringBuffer()) instanceof String) is always true.

10.21   Which of these expressions are legal?

Select the four correct answers.

(a) "co".concat("ol")
(b) ("co" + "ol")

(c) ('c' + 'o' + 'o' + 'l')
(d) ("co" + new String('o' + 'l'))
(e) ("co" + new String("co"))

10.22 What will be the result of attempting to compile and run the following code?

```
public class RefEq {
    public static void main(String[] args) {
        String s = "ab" + "12";
        String t = "ab" + 12;
        String u = new String("ab12");
        System.out.println((s==t) + " " + (s==u));
    }
}
```

Select the one correct answer.

(a) The code will fail to compile.
(b) The program will print false false when run.
(c) The program will print false true when run.
(d) The program will print true false when run.
(e) The program will print true true when run.

10.23 Which of these parameter lists have a corresponding constructor in the String class?

Select the three correct answers.

(a) ()
(b) (int capacity)
(c) (char[] data)
(d) (String str)

10.24 Which method is not defined in the String class?

Select the one correct answer.

(a) trim()
(b) length()
(c) concat(String)
(d) hashCode()
(e) reverse()

10.25 Which statement concerning the charAt() method of the String class is true?

Select the one correct answer.

(a) The charAt() method takes a char value as an argument.
(b) The charAt() method returns a Character object.
(c) The expression ("abcdef").charAt(3) is illegal.
(d) The expression "abcdef".charAt(3) evaluates to the character 'd'.
(e) The index of the first character is 1.

10.26   Which expression will evaluate to true?

Select the one correct answer.
(a) "hello: there!".equals("hello there")
(b) "HELLO THERE".equals("hello there")
(c) ("hello".concat("there")).equals("hello there")
(d) "Hello There".compareTo("hello there") == 0
(e) "Hello there".toLowerCase().equals("hello there")

10.27   What will the following program print when run?

```
public class Search {
    public static void main(String[] args) {
        String s = "Contentment!";
        int middle = s.length()/2;
        String nt = s.substring(middle-1, middle+1);
        System.out.println(s.lastIndexOf(nt, middle));
    }
};
```

Select the one correct answer.
(a) 2
(b) 4
(c) 5
(d) 7
(e) 9
(f) 11

10.6 The StringBuffer Class

In contrast to the String class, which implements immutable character strings, the StringBuffer class implements mutable character strings. Not only can the character string in a string buffer be changed, but the capacity of the string buffer can also change dynamically. The *capacity* of a string buffer is the maximum number of characters that a string buffer can accommodate before its size is automatically augmented.

Although there is a close relationship between objects of the String and StringBuffer classes, these are two independent final classes, both directly extending the Object class. Hence, String references cannot be stored (or cast) to StringBuffer references and vice versa. Both String and StringBuffer are thread-safe. String buffers are preferred when heavy modification of character strings is involved.

The StringBuffer class provides various facilities for manipulating string buffers:

- constructing string buffers
- changing, deleting, and reading characters in string buffers

- constructing strings from string buffers
- appending, inserting, and deleting in string buffers
- controlling string buffer capacity

Constructing String Buffers

The final class StringBuffer provides three constructors that create and initialize StringBuffer objects and set their initial capacity.

StringBuffer(String s)

The contents of the new StringBuffer object are the same as the contents of the String object passed as argument. The initial capacity of the string buffer is set to the length of the argument string, plus room for 16 more characters.

StringBuffer(int length)

The new StringBuffer object has no content. The initial capacity of the string buffer is set to the value of the argument length, which cannot be less than 0.

StringBuffer()

This constructor also creates a new StringBuffer object with no content. The initial capacity of the string buffer is set for 16 characters.

Examples of StringBuffer object creation and initialization:

```
StringBuffer strBuf1 = new StringBuffer("Phew!");      // "Phew!", capacity 21
StringBuffer strBuf2 = new StringBuffer(10);           // "", capacity 10
StringBuffer strBuf3 = new StringBuffer();             // "", capacity 16
```

Reading and Changing Characters in String Buffers

int length()

Returns the number of characters in the string buffer.

char charAt(int index)
void setCharAt(int index, char ch)

These methods read and change the character at a specified index in the string buffer, respectively. The first character is at index 0 and the last one at index one less than the number of characters in the string buffer. A StringIndexOutOf-BoundsException is thrown if the index is not valid.

The following is an example of reading and changing string buffer contents:

```
StringBuffer strBuf = new StringBuffer("Javv");            // "Javv", capacity 20
strBuf.setCharAt(strBuf.length()-1, strBuf.charAt(1));     // "Java"
```

Constructing Strings from String Buffers

The StringBuffer class overrides the toString() method from the Object class. It returns the contents of a string buffer in a String object.

```
String fromBuf = strBuf.toString();                              // "Java"
```

Since the StringBuffer class does not override the equals() method from the Object class, contents of string buffers should be converted to String objects for string comparison.

Appending, Inserting, and Deleting Characters in String Buffers

Appending, inserting, and deleting characters automatically results in adjustment of the string buffer's capacity, if necessary. The indices passed as arguments in the methods must be equal to or greater than 0. A StringIndexOutOfBoundsException is thrown if an index is not valid.

Appending Characters to a String Buffer

The overloaded method append() can be used to append characters at the end of a string buffer.

```
StringBuffer append(Object obj)
```

The obj argument is converted to a string as if by the static method call String.valueOf(obj), and this string is appended to the current string buffer.

```
StringBuffer append(String str)
StringBuffer append(char[] str)
StringBuffer append(char[] str, int offset, int len)
StringBuffer append(char c)
```

These methods allow characters from various sources to be appended at the end of the current string buffer.

```
StringBuffer append(boolean b)
StringBuffer append(int i)
StringBuffer append(long l)
StringBuffer append(float f)
StringBuffer append(double d)
```

These methods convert the primitive value of the argument to a string by applying the static method String.valueOf() to the argument, before appending the result to the string buffer:

Inserting Characters in a String Buffer

The overloaded method insert() can be used to insert characters at a given position in a string buffer.

```
StringBuffer insert(int offset, Object obj)
StringBuffer insert(int offset, String str)
StringBuffer insert(int offset, char[] str)
StringBuffer insert(int offset, char c)
StringBuffer insert(int offset, boolean b)
StringBuffer insert(int offset, int i)
StringBuffer insert(int offset, long l)
StringBuffer insert(int offset, float f)
StringBuffer insert(int offset, double d)
```

The argument is converted, if necessary, by applying the static method String.valueOf(). The offset argument specifies where the characters are to be inserted and must be greater than or equal to 0.

Deleting Characters in a String Buffer

The following methods can be used to delete characters from specific positions in a string buffer:

```
StringBuffer deleteCharAt(int index)
StringBuffer delete(int start, int end)
```

The first method deletes a character at a specified index in the string buffer, contracting the string buffer by one character. The second method deletes a substring, which is specified by the start index (inclusive) and the end index (exclusive).

Among other miscellaneous methods included in the class StringBuffer is the following method, which reverses the contents of a string buffer:

```
StringBuffer reverse()
```

Examples of appending, inserting, and deleting in string buffers:

```
StringBuffer buffer = new StringBuffer("banana split");   // "banana split"
buffer.delete(4,12);                                       // "bana"
buffer.append(42);                                         // "bana42"
buffer.insert(4,"na");                                     // "banana42"
buffer.reverse();                                          // "24ananab"
buffer.deleteCharAt(buffer.length()-1);                    // "24anana"
buffer.append('s');                                        // "24ananas"
```

All the previous methods modify the contents of the string buffer and also return a reference value denoting the string buffer. This allows *chaining* of method calls. The method calls invoked on the string buffer denoted by the reference buffer can be chained as follows, giving the same result:

```
buffer.delete(4,12).append(42).insert(4,"na").reverse().
    deleteCharAt(buffer.length()-1).append('s');          // "24ananas"
```

The method calls in the chain are evaluated from left to right, so that the previous chain of calls is interpreted as follows:

```
(((((buffer.delete(4,12)).append(42)).insert(4,"na")).reverse()).
    deleteCharAt(buffer.length()-1)).append('s');         // "24ananas"
```

Each method call returns the reference value of the modified string buffer. This value is used to invoke the next method. The string buffer remains denoted by the reference buffer.

The compiler uses string buffers to implement the string concatenation, +. The following example code of string concatenation

```
String str1 = 4 + "U" + "Only";                                    // (1) "4UOnly"
```

is equivalent to the following code using one string buffer:

```
String str2 = new StringBuffer().
                append(4).append("U").append("Only").toString(); // (2)
```

The code at (2) does not create any temporary String objects when concatenating several strings, since a single StringBuffer object is modified and finally converted to a String object.

Controlling String Buffer Capacity

```
int capacity()
```

Returns the current capacity of the string buffer, that is, the number of characters the current buffer can accommodate without allocating a new, larger array to hold characters.

```
void ensureCapacity(int minCapacity)
```

Ensures that there is room for at least minCapacity number of characters. It expands the string buffer, depending on the current capacity of the buffer.

```
void setLength(int newLength)
```

This method ensures that the actual number of characters, that is, length of the string buffer, is exactly equal to the value of the newLength argument, which must be greater than or equal to 0. This operation can result in the string being truncated or padded with null characters ('\u0000').

This method only affects the capacity of the string buffer if the value of the parameter newLength is greater than current capacity.

One use of this method is to clear the string buffer:

```
buffer.setLength(0);        // Empty the buffer.
```

 Review Questions

10.28 What will be the result of attempting to compile and run the following program?

```
public class MyClass {
    public static void main(String[] args) {
        String s = "hello";
        StringBuffer sb = new StringBuffer(s);
        sb.reverse();
```

```
                    if (s == sb) System.out.println("a");
                    if (s.equals(sb)) System.out.println("b");
                    if (sb.equals(s)) System.out.println("c");
            }
        }
```

Select the one correct answer.

(a) The code will fail to compile since the constructor of the String class is not called properly.

(b) The code will fail to compile since the expression (s == sb) is illegal.

(c) The code will fail to compile since the expression (s.equals(sb)) is illegal.

(d) The program will print c when run.

(e) The program will throw a ClassCastException when run.

10.29 What will be the result of attempting to compile and run the following program?

```
public class MyClass {
    public static void main(String[] args) {
        StringBuffer sb = new StringBuffer("have a nice day");
        sb.setLength(6);
        System.out.println(sb);
    }
}
```

Select the one correct answer.

(a) The code will fail to compile since there is no method named setLength in the StringBuffer class.

(b) The code will fail to compile since the StringBuffer reference sb is not a legal argument to the println() method.

(c) The program will throw a StringIndexOutOfBoundsException when run.

(d) The program will print have a nice day when run.

(e) The program will print have a when run.

(f) The program will print ce day when run.

10.30 Which of these parameter lists have a corresponding constructor in the StringBuffer class?

Select the three correct answers.

(a) ()

(b) (int capacity)

(c) (char[] data)

(d) (String str)

10.31 Which method is not defined in the StringBuffer class?

Select the one correct answer.

(a) trim()

(b) length()

(c) append(String)

(d) reverse()

(e) setLength(int)

10,32 What will be the result of attempting to compile and run the following code?

```
public class StringMethods {
    public static void main(String[] args) {
        String str = new String("eenny");
        str.concat(" meeny");
        StringBuffer strBuf = new StringBuffer(" miny");
        strBuf.append(" mo");
        System.out.println(str + strBuf);
    }
}
```

Select the one correct answer.

(a) The code will fail to compile.
(b) The program will print eenny meeny miny mo when run.
(c) The program will print meeny miny mo when run.
(d) The program will print eenny miny mo when run.
(e) The program will print eenny meeny miny when run.

 ## Chapter Summary

The following information was included in this chapter:

- discussion of the Object class, which is the most fundamental class in Java

- discussion of the wrapper classes, which not only allow primitive values to be treated as objects, but also contain useful methods for converting values

- discussion of the Math class, which provides an assortment of mathematical functions

- discussion of the String class, showing how immutable strings are created and used

- discussion of the StringBuffer class, showing how dynamic string buffers are created and manipulated

 ## Programming Exercises

10.1 Create a class named Pair, which aggregates two arbitrary objects. Implement the equals() and hashCode() methods in such a way that a Pair object is identical to another Pair object if, and only if, the pair of constituent objects are identical. Make the toString() implementation return the textual representation of both the constituent objects in a Pair object. Objects of the Pair class should be immutable.

10.2 A palindrome is a text phrase that spells the same thing backward and forward. The word *redivider* is a palindrome, since the word would spell the same even if the character sequence were reversed. Write a program that takes a word as an argument and reports whether the word is a palindrome.

Collections and Maps

•••

- Make appropriate selection of collection classes/interfaces to suit specified behavior requirements.
- Distinguish between correct and incorrect implementations of hashCode() (and equals()) methods.

- Identify the core collection interfaces and their inheritance relationships: Collection, Set, SortedSet, List, Map, SortedMap.
- Understand the differences between collections and maps.
- Understand the operations performed by the addAll(), removeAll(), and retainAll() methods in the Collection interface.
- Recognize destructive and non-destructive collection operations.
- Understand how data can be passed between collections.
- Identify the implementations of the core collection interfaces and state their usage: HashSet, TreeSet, LinkedHashSet, ArrayList, Vector, LinkedList, HashMap, Hashtable, TreeMap, LinkedHashMap.
- Write code to create views on collections.
- Use an iterator to traverse all the elements of a collection.
- Distinguish between unordered, ordered, and sorted collections.
- Understand the natural ordering of elements provided by the Comparable interface and the total ordering imposed by the Comparator interface.
- State the conditions under which an UnsupportedOperationException may occur in collections.
- Identify the methods in the Collections class that can be used to produce immutable and thread-safe versions of various types of collections.
- State the major algorithms provided by the Collections class.
- Write code to pass data between arrays and collections.

11.1   The Collections Framework

A *collection* allows a group of objects to be treated as a single unit. Arbitrary objects can be stored, retrieved, and manipulated as *elements* of collections.

Program design often requires handling of groups of objects. The collections framework presents a set of standard utility classes for managing such collections. This framework is provided in the java.util package and comprises three main parts:

- The core *interfaces* that allow collections to be manipulated independently of their implementation (see Figure 11.1 and Table 11.1). These interfaces define the common functionality exhibited by collections and facilitate data exchange between collections.

- A small set of *implementations* (i.e., concrete classes, listed in Table 11.1) that are specific implementations of the core interfaces, providing data structures that a program can use readily.

- An assortment of static *utility methods* that can be used to perform various operations on collections, such as sorting and searching, or creating customized collections.

Figure 11.1   *The Core Interfaces*

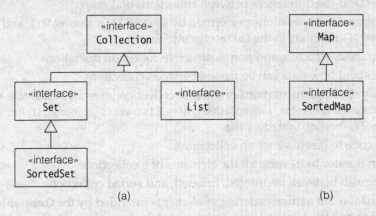

(a)   (b)

Core Interfaces

The Collection interface is a generalized interface for maintaining collections, and is the top of the interface inheritance hierarchy for collections shown in Figure 11.1a. These interfaces are summarized in Table 11.1.

Table 11.1 *Core Interfaces in the Collections Framework*

Interface	Description	Concrete Classes
Collection	A basic interface that defines the normal operations that allow a collection of objects to be maintained or handled as a single unit.	
Set	The Set interface extends the Collection interface to represent its mathematical namesake: a *set* of unique elements.	HashSet LinkedHashSet
SortedSet	The SortedSet interface extends the Set interface to provide the required functionality for maintaining a set in which the elements are stored in some sorted order.	TreeSet
List	The List interface extends the Collection interface to maintain a sequence of elements that need not be unique.	ArrayList Vector LinkedList
Map	A basic interface that defines operations for maintaining mappings of keys to values.	HashMap Hashtable LinkedHashMap
SortedMap	Extends the Map interface for maps that maintain their mappings sorted in key order.	TreeMap

The elements in a Set must be unique, that is, no two elements in the set can be equal. The order of elements in a List is retained, and individual elements can be accessed according to their position in the list.

As can be seen from Figure 11.1b, the Map interface does not extend the Collection interface because conceptually, a map is not a collection. A map does not contain elements. It contains *mappings* (also called *entries*) from a set of *key* objects to a set of *value* objects. A key can, at most, be associated with one value. As the name implies, the SortedMap interface extends the Map interface to maintain its mappings sorted in *key order*.

Implementations

The java.util package provides implementations of a selection of well-known abstract data types, based on the core interfaces. Figures 11.2 and 11.3 show the inheritance relationship between the core interfaces and the corresponding implementations. None of the concrete implementations inherit directly from the Collection interface. The abstract classes provide the basis on which concrete classes are implemented.

Figure 11.2 *The Core Collection Interfaces and Their Implementations*

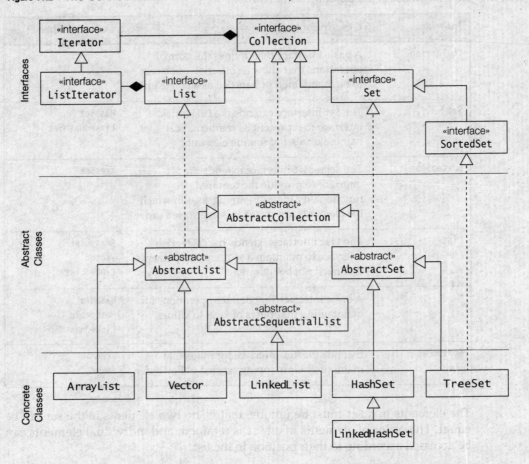

By convention, each of the collection implementation classes provides a constructor for creating a collection based on the elements of another Collection object passed as argument. This allows the implementation of a collection to be changed by merely passing the collection to the constructor of the desired implementation. This interchangeability is also true between Map implementations. But collections and maps are not interchangeable. Note that a collection (or a map) only stores references to objects, and not the actual objects.

The collections framework is *interface-based*, meaning that collections are manipulated according to their interface types, rather than by the implementation types. By using these interfaces wherever collections of objects are used, various implementations can be used interchangeably.

All the concrete classes shown in Figures 11.2 and 11.3 implement the Serializable and the Cloneable interfaces; therefore, the objects of these classes can be serialized and also cloned.

Figure 11.3 *The Core Map Interfaces and Their Implementations*

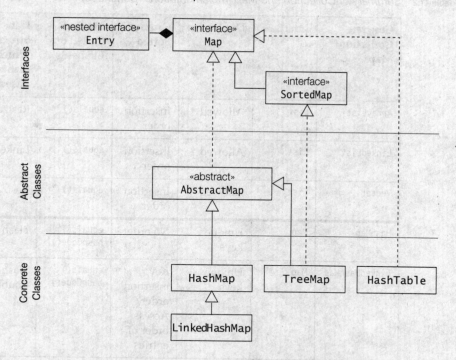

A summary of collection and map implementations is given in Table 11.2. The contents of this table will be the focus as each core interface and its corresponding implementations are discussed in the following sections.

Table 11.2 *Summary of Collection and Map Implementations*

Concrete Collection/ Map	Interface	Duplicates	Ordered/ Sorted	Methods Called on Elements	Data Structures on Which Implementation Is Based
HashSet	Set	Unique elements	No order	equals() hashCode()	Hash table
LinkedHashSet	Set	Unique elements	Insertion order	equals() hashCode()	Hash table and doubly-linked list
TreeSet	SortedSet	Unique elements	Sorted	equals() compareTo()	Balanced tree

Continues

Table 11.2 *Summary of Collection and Map Implementations (Continued)*

Concrete Collection/ Map	Interface	Duplicates	Ordered/ Sorted	Methods Called on Elements	Data Structures on Which Implementation Is Based
ArrayList	List	Allowed	Insertion order	equals()	Resizable array
LinkedList	List	Allowed	Insertion order	equals()	Linked list
Vector	List	Allowed	Insertion order	equals()	Resizable array
HashMap	Map	Unique keys	No order	equals() hashCode()	Hash table
LinkedHashMap	Map	Unique keys	Key insertion order/ Access order of entries	equals() hashCode()	Hash table and doubly-linked list
Hashtable	Map	Unique keys	No order	equals() hashCode()	Hash table
TreeMap	SortedMap	Unique keys	Sorted in key order	equals() compareTo()	Balanced tree

11.2 Collections

The Collection interface specifies the contract that all collections should implement. Some of the operations in the interface are *optional*, meaning that a collection may choose to provide a stub implementation of such an operation that throws an UnsupportedOperationException when invoked. The implementations of collections from the java.util package support all the optional operations in the Collection interface (see Figure 11.2 and Table 11.2).

Many of the methods return a boolean value to indicate whether the collection was modified as a result of the operation.

Basic Operations

The basic operations are used to query a collection about its contents and allow elements to be added and removed from a collection.

```
int size()
boolean isEmpty()
boolean contains(Object element)
boolean add(Object element)        // Optional
boolean remove(Object element)     // Optional
```

The add() and remove() methods return true if the collection was modified as a result of the operation.

By returning the value false, the add() method indicates that the collection excludes duplicates, and that the collection already contains an object equal to the argument object.

The contains() method checks for membership of the argument object in the collection using object value equality.

Bulk Operations

These operations perform on a collection as a single unit.

```
boolean containsAll(Collection c)
boolean addAll(Collection c)       // Optional
boolean removeAll(Collection c)    // Optional
boolean retainAll(Collection c)    // Optional
void clear()                       // Optional
```

These bulk operations can be used to perform the equivalent of set logic on *arbitrary collections* (not just on sets). The containsAll() method returns true if all elements of the specified collection are also contained in the current collection.

The addAll(), removeAll(), and retainAll() methods are *destructive* in the sense that the collection on which they are invoked can be modified. The operations performed by these methods are visualized by Venn diagrams in Figure 11.4.

Figure 11.4 *Bulk Operations on Collections*

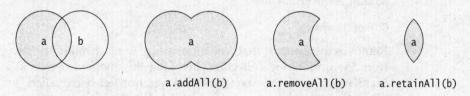

a.addAll(b)   a.removeAll(b)   a.retainAll(b)

Array Operations

These operations convert collections to arrays.

```
Object[] toArray()
Object[] toArray(Object a[])
```

The first toArray() method returns an array with all the elements of the collection. The second method stores the elements of a collection into an array of a specified type.

If the given array is big enough, the elements are stored in this array. If there is room to spare in the array, that is, the length of the array is greater than the number of elements in the collection, the spare room is filled with null values before the array is returned. If the array is too small, a new array of the same runtime type and appropriate size is created. If the runtime type of the specified array is not a supertype of the runtime type of every element in the collection, an ArrayStoreException is thrown.

Iterators

A collection provides an iterator which allows sequential access to the elements of a collection. An iterator can be obtained by calling the following method of the Collection interface:

```
Iterator iterator()
```

Returns an object which implements the Iterator interface.

The Iterator interface is defined as follows:

```
boolean hasNext()
```

Returns true if the underlying collection still has elements left to return. A future call to the next() method will return the next element from the collection.

```
Object next()
```

Moves the iterator to the next element in the underlying collection, and returns the current element. If there are no more elements left to return, it throws a NoSuchElementException.

```
Object remove()
```

Removes the element that was returned by the last call to the next() method, from the underlying collection. Invoking this method results in an IllegalStateException, if the next() method has not yet been called, or when the remove() method has already been called after the last call to the next() method. This method is optional for an iterator, that is, it throws an UnsupportedOperationException if the remove operation is not supported.

After obtaining the iterator for a collection, the methods provided by the Iterator interface can be used to systematically traverse the elements of the underlying collection one by one. Example 11.1 illustrates the use of an iterator.

Example 11.1 *Using an Iterator*

```java
import java.util.*;

public class IteratorUsage {
    public static void main(String[] args) {

        // (1) Create a list of Integers.
        Collection intList = new ArrayList();
        int[] values = { 9, 11, -4, 1, 13, 99, 1, 0 };
        for (int i = 0; i < values.length; i++)
            intList.add(new Integer(values[i]));

        System.out.println("Before: " + intList);             // (2)

        Iterator interator = intList.iterator();              // (3) Get an iterator.
        while (interator.hasNext()) {                         // (4) Loop
            Integer element = (Integer) interator.next();    // (5) The next element
            int value = element.intValue();
            if (value < 1 || value > 10) // (6) Remove the element if
                interator.remove();       //      its value is not between 1 and 10.
        }

        System.out.println("After:  " + intList);     // (7)
    }
}
```

Output from the program:

```
Before: [9, 11, -4, 1, 13, 99, 1, 0]
After:  [9, 1, 1]
```

Example 11.1 creates a list of integers and then removes from the list all integers that are not between 1 and 10, inclusive. The example uses an ArrayList for the list of integers. Since int values are not objects, they cannot be inserted into a collection. Therefore, each int value must be wrapped in an Integer object, which is then added to the collection.

The Collection interface allows arbitrary objects to be added to a collection. When inserting an element, its reference is upcasted to the type Object. On retrieval, it might be necessary to downcast the reference value of the object to invoke subtype-specific behavior.

The concrete collection classes override the toString() method to provide a textual representation of their contents. The standard textual representation generated by the toString() method for a collection is

$$[element_1, \ element_2, \ \dots, \ element_n]$$

where each *element*$_i$ is the textual representation generated by the `toString()` method of the individual elements in the collection. At (2) and at (7) the `toString()` method of the collection class is used implicitly to generate a textual representation for the collection.

In Example 11.1, an iterator is obtained at (3) and used in the loop at (4) to traverse all the elements in the integer list. The reference value of the next element is downcast at (5). It might be advisable to use the `instanceof` operator to check the type of a retrieved object before attempting to downcast the reference. We have not done so in this simple example because we know that the collection is guaranteed to hold only `Integers`.

Note that the methods are invoked on the iterator, not the underlying collection. The three methods of the iterator should be used *in step* inside a loop, as shown in Example 11.1.

The majority of the iterators provided in the `java.util` package are said to be *fail-fast*. When an iterator has already been obtained, structurally modifying the underlying collection by other means will invalidate the iterator. Subsequent use of this iterator will throw a `ConcurrentModificationException`. The `remove()` method of an iterator is the only recommended way to delete elements from the underlying collection during traversal with an iterator.

The order in which the iterator will return the elements from an underlying collection depends on the traversal order supported by the collection. For example, an iterator for a list will traverse the elements in the sequential order they have in the list, whereas the traversal order for the elements in an ordinary set is not predetermined. An iterator for a sorted collection will make the elements available in a given sorted order. Traversal order will be discussed together with the individual concrete classes.

 ## Review Questions

11.1 Which of these are core interfaces in the collections framework?

Select the three correct answers.
- (a) `Set`
- (b) `Bag`
- (c) `LinkedList`
- (d) `Collection`
- (e) `Map`

11.2 Which of these implementations are provided by the `java.util` package?

Select the two correct answers.
- (a) `HashList`
- (b) `HashMap`

(c) ArraySet
(d) ArrayMap
(e) TreeMap

11.3 What is the name of the interface used to represent collections that maintain non-unique elements in order?

Select the one correct answer.
(a) Collection
(b) Set
(c) SortedSet
(d) List
(e) Sequence

11.3 Sets

Unlike other implementations of the Collection interface, implementations of the Set interface do not allow duplicate elements. This also means that a set can contain at most one null value. The Set interface does not define any new methods, and its add() and addAll() methods will not store duplicates. If an element is not currently in the set, two consecutive calls to the add() method to insert the element will first return true, then false. A Set models a mathematical set (see Table 11.3), that is, it is an unordered collection of distinct objects.

Multisets (a.k.a. *bags*) that allow duplicate elements cannot be implemented using the Set interface since this interface requires that elements are unique in the collection.

Table 11.3 *Bulk Operations and Set Logic*

Set Methods (a and b are sets)	Corresponding Mathematical Operations
a.containsAll(b)	$b \subseteq a$ (subset)
a.addAll(b)	$a = a \cup b$ (union)
a.removeAll(b)	$a = a - b$ (difference)
a.retainAll(b)	$a = a \cap b$ (intersection)
a.clear()	$a = \varnothing$ (empty set)

HashSet **and** LinkedHashSet

The HashSet class implements the Set interface. Since this implementation uses a hash table, it offers near constant-time performance for most operations. A HashSet does not guarantee any ordering of the elements. However, the LinkedHashSet subclass of HashSet guarantees insertion-order. The sorted counterpart is TreeSet, which implements the SortedSet interface and has logarithmic time complexity (see Section 11.6, p. 452).

A HashSet relies on the implementation of the hashCode() and equals() methods of its elements (see Section 11.7, p. 461). The hashCode() method is used for hashing the elements, and the equals() method is needed for comparing elements. In fact, the equality and the hash codes of HashSets are defined in terms of the equality and the hash codes of their elements.

As mentioned earlier, the LinkedHashSet implementation is a subclass of the HashSet class. It works similarly to a HashSet, except for one important detail. Unlike a Hash-Set, a LinkedHashSet guarantees that the iterator will access the elements in *insertion order*, that is, in the order in which they were inserted into the LinkedHashSet.

The LinkedHashSet class offers constructors analogous to the ones in the HashSet class. The initial *capacity* (i.e., the number of buckets in the hash table) and its *load factor* (i.e., the ratio of number of elements stored to its current capacity) can be tuned when the set is created. The default values for these parameters will under most circumstances provide acceptable performance.

HashSet()

Constructs a new, empty set.

HashSet(Collection c)

Constructs a new set containing the elements in the specified collection. The new set will not contain any duplicates. This offers a convenient way to remove duplicates from a collection.

HashSet(int initialCapacity)

Constructs a new, empty set with the specified initial capacity.

HashSet(int initialCapacity, float loadFactor)

Constructs a new, empty set with the specified initial capacity and the specified load factor.

- -

Example 11.2 *Using Sets*

```
import java.util.*;

public class CharacterSets {
    public static void main(String[] args) {
        int numArgs = args.length;

        // A set keeping track of all characters previously encountered.
        Set encountered = new HashSet();                           // (1)
```

```
        // For each program argument in the command line ...
        for (int i=0; i<numArgs; i++) {

            // Convert the current argument to a set of characters.
            String argument = args[i];
            Set characters = new HashSet();                          // (2)
            int size = argument.length();
            // For each character in the argument...
            for (int j=0; j<size; j++)
                // add character to the characters set.
                characters.add(new Character(argument.charAt(j)));   // (3)

            // Determine whether a common subset exists.              (4)
            Set commonSubset = new HashSet(encountered);
            commonSubset.retainAll(characters);
            boolean areDisjunct = commonSubset.size()==0;

            if (areDisjunct)
                System.out.println(characters + " and " + encountered +
                    " are disjunct.");
            else {
                // Determine superset and subset relations.           (5)
                boolean isSubset = encountered.containsAll(characters);
                boolean isSuperset = characters.containsAll(encountered);
                if (isSubset && isSuperset)
                    System.out.println(characters + " is equivalent to " +
                        encountered);
                else if (isSubset)
                    System.out.println(characters + " is a subset of " +
                        encountered);
                else if (isSuperset)
                    System.out.println(characters + " is a superset of " +
                        encountered);
                else
                    System.out.println(characters + " and " +
                        encountered + " have " + commonSubset + " in common.");
            }

            // Update the set of characters encountered so far.
            encountered.addAll(characters);                          // (6)
        }
    }
}
```

Running the program with the following arguments:

```
java CharacterSets i said i am maids
```

results in the following output:

```
[i] and [] are disjunct.
[d, a, s, i] is a superset of [i]
[i] is a subset of [d, a, s, i]
[a, m] and [d, a, s, i] have [a] in common.
[d, a, s, m, i] is equivalent to [d, a, s, m, i]
```

Example 11.2 demonstrates set operations. It determines a relationship between two sets of characters:

- whether they are disjunct, that is, have no common elements
- whether they have the same elements, that is, are equivalent
- whether one is a subset of the other
- whether one is a superset of the other
- whether they have a common subset

Given a list of words as program arguments, each argument is turned into a set of characters. This set is compared with the set containing all the characters encountered prior to the current argument in the argument list.

The set keeping track of all the characters encountered prior to the current argument, is called encountered. This set is created at (1). For each argument, a set of characters is created, as shown at (2). This set, called characters, is populated with the characters of the current argument, as shown at (3). The program first determines if there is a common subset for the two sets, as shown at (4):

```
// Determine whether a common subset exists.                    (4)
Set commonSubset = new HashSet(encountered);
commonSubset.retainAll(characters);
boolean areDisjunct = commonSubset.size()==0;
```

Note that the retainAll() operation is destructive. The code at (4) does not affect the encountered and the characters sets. If the size of the common subset is zero, the sets are disjunct; otherwise, the relationship must be narrowed down. The subset and superset relations are determined at (5) using the containsAll() method.

```
// Determine superset and subset relations.                     (5)
boolean isSubset = encountered.containsAll(characters);
boolean isSuperset = characters.containsAll(encountered);
```

The sets are equivalent if both the previous relations are true. If they are both false, that is, no subset or superset relationship exists, they only have the common subset. The set of characters for the current argument is added to the set of all characters previously encountered. The addAll() method is used for this purpose, as shown at (6):

```
encountered.addAll(characters);                                // (6)
```

Textual representation of a set is supplied by the overriding method toString() in the AbstractSet class on which the HashSet implementation is based (see Figure 11.2).

11.4 Lists

Lists are collections that maintain their elements *in order*, and can contain duplicates. The elements in a list are *ordered*. Each element, therefore, has a position in the list. A zero-based index can be used to access the element at the position designated by the index value. The position of an element can change as elements are inserted or deleted from the list.

In addition to the operations inherited from the Collection interface, the List interface also defines operations that work specifically on lists: position-based access of the list elements, searching in a list, creation of customized iterators, and operations on parts of a list (called *open range-view* operations). This additional functionality is provided by the following methods in the List interface:

```
// Element Access by Index
Object get(int index)
```

Returns the element at the specified index.

```
Object set(int index, Object element)              Optional
```

Replaces the element at the specified index with the specified element. It returns the previous element at the specified index.

```
void add(int index, Object element)                Optional
```

Inserts the specified element at the specified index. If necessary, it shifts the element previously at this index and any subsequent elements one position toward the end of the list. The inherited method add(Object) from the Collection interface will append the specified element to the end of the list.

```
Object remove(int index)                           Optional
```

Deletes and returns the element at the specified index, contracting the list accordingly. The inherited method remove(Object) from the Collection interface will remove the first occurrence of the element from the list.

```
boolean addAll(int index, Collection c)            Optional
```

Inserts the elements from the specified collection at the specified index, using the iterator of the specified collection. The method returns true if any elements were added.

In a non-empty list, the first element is at index 0 and the last element is at size()-1. As might be expected, all methods throw an IndexOutOfBoundsException if an illegal index is specified.

```
// Element Search
int indexOf(Object o)
int lastIndexOf(Object o)
```

These methods respectively return the index of the first and the last occurrence of the element in the list if the element is found; otherwise, the value –1 is returned.

```
// List Iterators
ListIterator listIterator()
ListIterator listIterator(int index)
```

The iterator from the first method traverses the elements consecutively, starting with the first element of the list, whereas the iterator from the second method starts traversing the list from the element indicated by the specified index.

```
interface ListIterator extends Iterator {
    boolean hasNext();
    boolean hasPrevious();

    Object next();          // Element after the cursor
    Object previous();      // Element before the cursor

    int nextIndex();        // Index of element after the cursor
    int previousIndex();    // Index of element before the cursor

    void remove();          // Optional
    void set(Object o);     // Optional
    void add(Object o);     // Optional
}
```

The ListIterator interface is a bidirectional iterator for lists. It extends the Iterator interface and allows the list to be traversed in either direction. When traversing lists, it can be helpful to imagine a *cursor* moving forward or backward *between* the elements when calls are made to the next() and the previous() method, respectively. The element that the cursor passes over is returned. When the remove() method is called, the element last passed over is removed from the list.

```
// Open Range-View
List subList(int fromIndex, int toIndex)
```

This method returns a *view* of the list, which consists of the sublist of the elements from the index fromIndex to the index toIndex-1. A view allows the range it represents in the underlying list to be manipulated. Any changes in the view are reflected in the underlying list, and vice versa. Views can be used to perform operations on specific ranges of a list.

ArrayList, LinkedList, and Vector

Three implementations of the List interface are provided in the java.util package: ArrayList, LinkedList, and Vector.

The ArrayList class implements the List interface. The Vector class is a legacy class that has been retrofitted to implement the List interface. The Vector and ArrayList classes are implemented using dynamically resizable arrays, providing fast random access and fast list traversal—very much like using an ordinary array. Unlike the ArrayList class, the Vector class is thread-safe, meaning that concurrent calls to the vector will not compromise its integrity.

The LinkedList implementation uses a doubly-linked list. Insertions and deletions in a doubly-linked list are very efficient—elements are not shifted, as is the case for an array. The LinkedList class provides extra methods that implement operations that add, get, and remove elements at either end of a LinkedList:

```
void addFirst(Object obj)
void addLast(Object obj)
Object getFirst()
Object getLast()
Object removeFirst()
Object removeLast()
```

The ArrayList and Vector classes offer comparable performance, but Vector objects suffer a slight performance penalty due to synchronization. Position-based access has constant-time performance for the ArrayList and Vector classes. However, position-based access is in linear time for a LinkedList, owing to traversal in a doubly-linked list. When frequent insertions and deletions occur inside a list, a LinkedList can be worth considering. In most cases, the ArrayList implementation is the over-all best choice for implementing lists.

The ArrayList class provides the following constructors:

ArrayList()

Constructs a new, empty ArrayList. An analogous constructor is provided by the LinkedList and Vector classes.

ArrayList(Collection c)

Constructs a new ArrayList containing the elements in the specified collection. The new ArrayList will retain any duplicates. The ordering in the ArrayList will be determined by the traversal order of the iterator for the collection passed as argument. An analogous constructor is provided by the LinkedList and Vector classes.

ArrayList(int initialCapacity)

Constructs a new, empty ArrayList with the specified initial capacity. An analogous constructor is provided by the Vector class.

Example 11.3 *Using Lists*

```
import java.util.*;

public class TakeAGuess {
    final static int NUM_DIGITS = 5;

    public static void main(String[] args) {

        // Sanity check on the given data.
        if (args.length != NUM_DIGITS) {
            System.err.println("Guess " + NUM_DIGITS + " digits.");
            return;
        }
```

```
        /* Initialize the solution list. This program has a fixed solution. */
        List secretSolution = new ArrayList();                              // (1)
        secretSolution.add("5");
        secretSolution.add("3");
        secretSolution.add("2");
        secretSolution.add("7");
        secretSolution.add("2");

        // Convert the user's guess from string array to list.              (2)
        List guess = new ArrayList();
        for (int i=0; i<NUM_DIGITS; i++)
            guess.add(args[i]);

        // Find the number of digits that were correctly included.          (3)
        List duplicate = new ArrayList(secretSolution);
        int numIncluded = 0;
        for (int i=0; i<NUM_DIGITS; i++)
            if (duplicate.remove(guess.get(i))) numIncluded++;

        /* Find the number of correctly placed digits by comparing the two
            lists, element by element, counting each correct placement. */
        // Need two iterators to traverse through guess and solution.  (4)
        ListIterator correct = secretSolution.listIterator();
        ListIterator attempt = guess.listIterator();
        int numPlaced = 0;
        while (correct.hasNext())
            if (correct.next().equals(attempt.next())) numPlaced++;

        // Print the results.
        System.out.println(numIncluded + " digit(s) correctly included.");
        System.out.println(numPlaced +   " digit(s) correctly placed.");
    }
}
```

Running the program with the following arguments:

```
java TakeAGuess 3 2 2 2 7
```

gives the following output:

```
4 digit(s) correctly included.
1 digit(s) correctly placed.
```

Example 11.3 illustrates some basic operations on lists. The user gets one shot at guessing a five-digit code. The solution is hard-wired in the example as a list of five elements, where each element represents a digit as a String object. The secretSolution list is created at (1) and populated using the add() method. The guess specified at the command line is placed in a separate list, called guess, at (2).

The number of digits that are correctly guessed is determined at (3). The solution is first duplicated and each digit in the guess is removed from the duplicated solution. The number of deletions corresponds to the number of correct digits in the guess list. A digit at a particular index in the guess list is returned by the get()

method. The remove() method returns true if the duplicate list was modified, that is, the digit from the guess was found and removed from the duplicated solution.

```
// Find the number of digits that were correctly included.     (3)
List duplicate = new ArrayList(secretSolution);
int numIncluded = 0;
for (int i=0; i<NUM_DIGITS; i++)
    if (duplicate.remove(guess.get(i))) numIncluded++;
```

Finding the number of digits that are correctly placed is achieved by using two list iterators, which allow digits in the same position in the guess and the secretSolution lists to be compared:

```
// Need two iterators to traverse through guess and solution.   (4)
ListIterator correct = secretSolution.listIterator();
ListIterator attempt = guess.listIterator();
int numPlaced = 0;
while (correct.hasNext())
    if (correct.next().equals(attempt.next())) numPlaced++;
```

 ## Review Questions

11.4   Which statements are true about collections?

Select the two correct answers.

(a) Some operations on a collection may throw an UnsupportedOperationException.
(b) Methods calling optional operations in a collection must either catch an UnsupportedOperationException or declare it in their throws clause.
(c) A List can have duplicate elements.
(d) An ArrayList can only accommodate a fixed number of elements.
(e) The Collection interface contains a method named get.

11.5   What will be the result of attempting to compile and run the following program?

```java
import java.util.*;

public class Sets {
    public static void main(String[] args) {
        HashSet set1 = new HashSet();
        addRange(set1, 1);
        ArrayList list1 = new ArrayList();
        addRange(list1, 2);
        TreeSet set2 = new TreeSet();
        addRange(set2, 3);
        LinkedList list2 = new LinkedList();
        addRange(list2, 5);

        set1.removeAll(list1);
        list1.addAll(set2);
        list2.addAll(list1);
        set1.removeAll(list2);

        System.out.println(set1);
    }
```

```
        static void addRange(Collection col, int step) {
            for (int i = step*2; i<=25; i+=step)
                col.add(new Integer(i));
        }
    }
```

Select the one correct answer.

(a) The program will fail to compile since operations are performed on incompat-
    ible collection implementations.
(b) The program will fail to compile since the TreeSet denoted by set2 has not
    been given a Comparator to use when sorting its elements.
(c) The program will compile without error, but will throw an UnsupportedOpera-
    tionException when run.
(d) The program will compile without error and will print all primes below 25
    when run.
(e) The program will compile without error and will print some other sequence
    of numbers when run.

11.6   Which of these methods are defined in the Collection interface?

Select the three correct answers.

(a) add(Object o)
(b) retainAll(Collection c)
(c) get(int index)
(d) iterator()
(e) indexOf(Object o)

11.7   What will be the output from the following program?

```
import java.util.*;
public class Iterate {
    public static void main(String[] args) {
        List l = new ArrayList();
        l.add("A"); l.add("B"); l.add("C"); l.add("D"); l.add("E");
        ListIterator i = l.listIterator();
        i.next(); i.next(); i.next(); i.next();
        i.remove();
        i.previous(); i.previous();
        i.remove();
        System.out.println(l);
    };
};
```

Select the one correct answer.

(a) It will print [A, B, C, D, E].
(b) It will print [A, C, E].
(c) It will print [B, D, E].
(d) It will print [A, B, D].
(e) It will print [B, C, E].
(f) It will print throw a NoSuchElementException.

11.8 Which of these methods from the Collection interface will return the value true if the collection was modified during the operation?

Select the two correct answers.

(a) contains()
(b) add()
(c) containsAll()
(d) retainAll()
(e) clear()

11.5 Maps

A Map defines mappings from keys to values. The *<key, value>* pair is called an *entry*. A map does not allow duplicate keys, in other words, the keys are unique. Each key maps to one value at the most, implementing what is called a *single-valued map*. Thus, there is a *many-to-one* relation between keys and values. For example, in a student-grade map, a grade (value) can be awarded to many students (keys), but each student has only one grade.

Both the keys and the values must be objects. This means that primitive values must be wrapped in their respective wrapper objects, if they are to be put in a map.

A map is not a collection and the Map interface does not extend the Collection interface. However, the mappings can be viewed as a collection in various ways: a key set, a value collection, or an entry set. These collection views are the only means of traversing a map.

The Map interface specifies some optional methods. Implementations should throw an UnsupportedOperationException if they do not support such an operation. The implementations of maps from the java.util package support all the optional operations of the Map interface (see Table 11.2 and Figure 11.3).

Basic Operations

These operations constitute the basic functionality provided by a map.

```
Object put(Object key, Object value)     Optional
```

Inserts the <key, value> entry into the map. It returns the *value* previously associated with the specified key, if any. Otherwise, it returns the null value.

```
Object get(Object key)
```

Returns the value to which the specified key is mapped, or null if no entry is found.

```
Object remove(Object key)                    Optional
```

The remove() method deletes the entry for the specified key. It returns the *value* previously associated with the specified key, if any. Otherwise, it returns the null value.

```
boolean containsKey(Object key)
```

Returns true if the specified key is mapped to a value in the map.

```
boolean containsValue(Object value)
```

Returns true if there exists one or more keys that are mapped to the specified value.

```
int size()
boolean isEmpty()
```

These methods return the number of entries (i.e., number of unique keys in the map) and whether the map is empty or not.

Bulk Operations

```
void putAll(Map t)      Optional
void clear()            Optional
```

The first method copies all entries from the specified map to the current map, and the second method deletes all the entries from the current map.

Collection Views

```
Set keySet()
Collection values()
Set entrySet()
```

These methods provide different views of a map. Changes in the map are reflected in the view, and vice versa. These methods return a set view of keys, a collection view of values and a set view of *<key, value>* entries, respectively. Note that the Collection returned by the values() method is not a Set, as several keys can map to the same value, that is, duplicate values can be included in the returned collection. Each *<key, value>* in the entry set view is represented by an object implementing the nested Map.Entry interface. An entry in the entry set view can be manipulated by methods defined in this interface, which are self-explanatory:

```
interface Entry {
    Object getKey();
    Object getValue();
    Object setValue(Object value);
}
```

HashMap, LinkedHashMap, **and** Hashtable

Figure 11.3 shows four implementations of the Map interface in the java.util package: HashMap, LinkedHashMap, TreeMap, and Hashtable.

The classes HashMap and Hashtable implement unordered maps. The class Linked-HashMap implements ordered maps, which are discussed below. The class TreeMap implements sorted maps (see Section 11.6, p. 452).

While the HashMap class is not thread-safe and permits one null key, the Hashtable class is thread-safe and permits non-null keys and values only. The thread-safety the Hashtable class provides has a performance penalty. Thread-safe use of maps is also provided by the methods in the Collections class (see Section 11.8, p. 481). Like the Vector class, the Hashtable class is also a legacy class that has been retrofitted to implement the Map interface.

These map implementations are based on a hashing algorithm. Operations on a map thus rely on the hashCode() and equals() methods of the key objects (see Section 11.7, p. 461).

The LinkedHashMap implementation is a subclass of the HashMap class. The relationship between the map classes LinkedHashMap and HashMap is analogous to the relationship between their counterpart set classes LinkedHashSet and HashSet. Elements of a HashMap (and a HashSet) are unordered. The elements of a LinkedHashMap (and a LinkedHashSet) are ordered. By default, the entries of a LinkedHashMap are in *key insertion order*, that is, the order in which the keys are inserted in the map. This order does not change if a key is re-inserted, because no new entry is created if the key's entry already exists from before. The elements in a LinkedHashSet are in (element) insertion order. However, a LinkedHashMap can also maintain its elements in (element) *access order*, that is, the order in which its entries are accessed, from least-recently accessed to most-recently accessed entries. This *ordering mode* can be specified in one of the constructors of the LinkedHashMap class.

Both the HashMap and LinkedHashMap classes provide comparable performance, but the HashMap class is the natural choice if ordering is not an issue. Operations such as adding, removing, or finding an entry based on a key are constant time, as these hash the key. Operations such as finding the entry with a particular value are in linear time, as these involve searching through the entries.

Adding, removing, and finding entries in a LinkedHashMap can be slightly slower than in a HashMap, as an ordered doubly-linked list has to be maintained. Traversal of a map is through one of its collection-views. For an underlying LinkedHashMap, the traversal time is proportional to the size of the map—regardless of its capacity. However, for an underlying HashMap, it is proportional to the capacity of the map.

The concrete map classes override the toString() method. The standard textual representation generated by the toString() method for a map is

$$\{key_1=value_1,\ key_2=value_2,\ \ldots,\ key_n=value_n\}$$

where each *key*$_i$ and each *value*$_i$ is the textual representation generated by the toString() method of the individual key and value objects in the map, respectively.

As was the case with collections, implementation classes provide a standard constructor that creates a new empty map, and a constructor that creates a new map based on an existing one. These classes also create a new empty map with an initial capacity and/or load factor. The HashMap class provides the following constructors:

```
HashMap()
HashMap(int initialCapacity)
HashMap(int initialCapacity, float loadFactor)
```

Constructs a new, empty HashMap, using either specified or default initial capacity and load factor.

```
HashMap(Map otherMap)
```

Constructs a new map containing the elements in the specified map.

The LinkedHashMap and Hashtable classes have constructors analogous to the four constructors for the HashMap class. In addition, the LinkedHashMap class provides a constructor where the ordering mode can also be specified:

```
LinkedHashMap(int initialCapacity, float loadFactor, boolean accessOrder)
```

Constructs a new, empty LinkedHashMap with the specified initial capacity, the specified load factor, and the specified ordering mode. The ordering mode is true for *access order* and false for *key insertion order*.

- -

Example 11.4   *Using Maps*

```java
import java.util.*;

public class WeightGroups {
    public static void main(String[] args) {

        // Create a map to store the frequency for each group.
        Map groupFreqData = new HashMap();

        int numArgs = args.length;
        for (int i=0; i<numArgs; i++) {
            // Get the value from an argument and group into intervals of 5.(1)
            double weight = Double.parseDouble(args[i]);
            Integer weightGroup = new Integer((int) Math.round(weight/5)*5);
            // Increment count, set to 1 if it's the first value of group.   (2)
            Integer oldCount = (Integer) groupFreqData.get(weightGroup);
            Integer newCount = (oldCount==null) ?
                new Integer(1) :
                new Integer(oldCount.intValue()+1);
            groupFreqData.put(weightGroup, newCount);                         // (3)
        }
```

```
        /* Print by traversing a sorted list of groups (keys),
           and extracting count (values) from the groupFreqData map. */

        /* Create a list of groups (keys), and use the sort algorithm from
           the Collections class to sort the keys. */
        List keys = new ArrayList(groupFreqData.keySet());          // (4)
        Collections.sort(keys);                                     // (5)

        /* Create an iterator on the sorted keys. Traverse the keys,
           looking up the frequency from the frequency map. */
        ListIterator keyIterator = keys.listIterator();             // (6)
        while (keyIterator.hasNext()) {
            // Current key (group).                                     (7)
            Integer group = (Integer) keyIterator.next();
            // Extract count (value) from the map.
            Integer count = (Integer) groupFreqData.get(group);     // (8)
            int intCount = count.intValue();

            /* Use the fill() method from the Arrays class to create a
               string consisting of intCount number of '*'. */
            char[] bar = new char[intCount];
            Arrays.fill(bar, '*');                                  // (9)

            System.out.println(group + ":\t" + new String(bar));
        } // end while
    } // end main()
} // end of class
```

Running the program with the following arguments:

```
>java WeightGroups 74 75 93 75 93 82 61 92 10 185
```

gives the following output:

```
10:     *
60:     *
75:     ***
80:     *
90:     *
95:     **
185:    *
```

Example 11.4 prints a textual histogram for the frequency of weight measurements in a weight group, where a weight group is defined as an interval of five units. The weight measurements are supplied as program arguments. The example illustrates the use of maps, creation of key views, and the use of a list iterator to traverse a map. The program proceeds as follows:

1. It reads the program arguments, converting each weight to its corresponding weight group and updating the frequency of the weight group:

The weight group is determined at (1). The count is incremented, if necessary, as shown at (2), and registered for the group, as shown at (3). Since keys are unique in a map, any previous entry is overwritten.

```
// Increment count, set to 1 if it's the first value of group.    (2)
Integer oldCount = (Integer) groupFreqData.get(weightGroup);
Integer newCount = (oldCount==null) ?
    new Integer(1) :
    new Integer(oldCount.intValue()+1);
groupFreqData.put(weightGroup, newCount);                         // (3)
```

2. It creates a list of keys (which are weight groups) from the groupFreqData map and sorts them. The keySet() method returns a set view of keys, which is converted to a list, as shown at (4). The key list is sorted by the algorithm sort() from the Collections class, as shown at (5).

```
List keys = new ArrayList(groupFreqData.keySet());               // (4)
Collections.sort(keys);                                          // (5)
```

3. It uses an iterator to traverse the keys, looking up the frequency in the groupFreqData map. A map can only be traversed through one of its views.

The list iterator is created at (6).

```
ListIterator keyIterator = keys.listIterator();                 // (6)
```

For each key, the corresponding value (i.e., frequency count) is retrieved, as shown at (7) and (8).

```
// Current key (group).                                          (7)
Integer group = (Integer) keyIterator.next();
// Extract count (value) from the map.
Integer count = (Integer) groupFreqData.get(group);             // (8)
```

A *bar* for each frequency is created using the fill() method from the Arrays class, as shown at (9).

11.6 Sorted Sets and Sorted Maps

Sets and maps have special interfaces, called SortedSet and SortedMap, for implementations that sort their elements in a specific order (see Figures 11.2 and 11.3). Objects can specify their *natural order* by implementing the Comparable interface, or be dictated a *total order* by a *comparator* object that implements the Comparator interface.

We'll first look at the two interfaces Comparable and Comparator, before discussing sorted sets and maps.

The Comparator Interface

Precise control of ordering can be achieved by creating a customized comparator that imposes a specific total ordering on the elements. All comparators implement the Comparator interface, which has the following single-method:

```
int compare(Object o1, Object o2)
```

The compare() method returns a negative integer, zero, or a positive integer if the first object is less than, equal to, or greater than the second object, according to the total order. Since this method tests for equality, it is strongly recommended that its implementation does not contradict the semantics of the equals() method (see Section 11.7).

The Comparable Interface

A class can define the natural order of its instances by implementing the Comparable interface. Many of the standard classes in the Java API, such as the wrapper classes, String, Date, and File, implement this interface. The java.lang.Comparable interface specifies a single method:

```
int compareTo(Object o)
```

This method returns a negative integer, zero, or a positive integer if the current object is less than, equal to, or greater than the specified object, based on the natural order. It throws a ClassCastException if the reference value passed in the argument cannot be cast to the type of the current object. Since this method tests for equality, it is recommended that its implementation does not contradict the semantics of the equals() method (see Section 11.7).

Objects implementing this interface can be used as

- elements in a sorted set
- keys in a sorted map
- elements in lists that are sorted manually using the Collections.sort() method

Note that the natural order for String objects (and Character objects) is lexicographical order (see Section 10.5, p. 412). Strings will be lexicographically maintained as elements in a sorted set or as keys in a sorted map that uses natural ordering. A collection of strings sorted by natural order would be ordered in lexicographical order.

The natural order for objects of a numerical wrapper type is ascending order of the values of the corresponding numerical primitive type (see Section 10.3, p. 396). As elements in a sorted set, or as keys in a sorted map, the objects would be maintained in ascending order.

An alternative ordering to the default natural order can be specified by passing a Comparator to the constructor when the sorted set or map is created. The Collections and Arrays classes provide utility methods for sorting, which also take a Comparator (see Section 11.8, p. 482).

Example 11.5 demonstrates the use of different comparators for strings. The program creates an empty sorted set using the TreeSet class (discussed later in this section). Each program argument is added to the sorted set in the loop at (2). A textual representation of the sorted set is then printed at (3). The output shows the sorting order in which the elements are maintained in the set. The set is traversed according to the sorting order.

The String class implements the Comparable interface, providing an implementation of the compareTo() method. The compareTo() method defines the natural order for strings, which is lexicographical. The natural order is used to maintain the program arguments sorted lexicographically when the sorted set at (1a) is used. If we wish to maintain the strings in a different ordering, we need to provide a customized comparator.

The String class provides a static field (CASE_INSENSITIVE_ORDER) that denotes a comparator object with a compare() method that ignores the case when comparing strings lexicographically. This particular total order is used to maintain the program arguments sorted when the sorted set at (1b) is used. The comparator is passed as argument to the set constructor. The output shows how the elements are maintained sorted in the set by this total order, which is a case-insensitive order.

We can create a string comparator that enforces *rhyming order* on the strings. In rhyming order, two strings are compared by examining their corresponding characters at each position in the two strings, starting with the characters in the *last* position. First the characters in the last position are compared, then those in the last but one position, and so on. For example, given the two strings "report" and "court", the last two characters in both the strings are the same. Continuing backward in the two strings, the character 'o' in the first string is less than the character 'u' in the second string. According to the rhyming order, the string "report" is less than the string "court".

Comparing two strings according to the rhyming order is equivalent to reversing the strings and comparing the reversed strings lexicographically. If we reverse the two strings, "report" and "court", the reversed string "troper" is lexicographically less than the reversed string "truoc".

A rhyming order comparator is implemented by the RhymingStringComparator class in Example 11.5. The compare() method at (4) first creates reversed versions of the strings passed as arguments. A reversed version of a string is created using a string buffer, which is first reversed and then converted back to a string, as shown at (5). The compare() method then calls the compareTo() method at (6) to compare the reversed strings, as the lexicographical order for the reversed strings is equivalent to the rhyming order for the original strings. This particular total order is used to maintain the program arguments sorted when the sorted set at (1c) is used. The comparator is again passed as argument to the set constructor. The output shows how the elements are maintained sorted in the set by this total order, which is rhyming order.

Example 11.5 *Natural Order and Total Order*

```java
import java.util.*;

public class ComparatorUsage {
    public static void main(String[] args) {

        // Choice of comparator.
    //  Set strSet = new TreeSet();                              // (1a)
    //  Set strSet = new TreeSet(String.CASE_INSENSITIVE_ORDER); // (1b)
        Set strSet = new TreeSet(new RhymingStringComparator()); // (1c)

        // Add each command line argument to the set.
        for (int i=0; i < args.length; i++) {                    // (2)
            strSet.add(args[i]);
        }
        System.out.println(strSet);                              // (3)
    }
}

class RhymingStringComparator implements Comparator {
    public int compare(Object obj1, Object obj2) {               // (4)

        // (5) Create reversed versions of the strings.
        String reverseStr1 = new StringBuffer((String) obj1).reverse().toString();
        String reverseStr2 = new StringBuffer((String) obj2).reverse().toString();

        // Compare the reversed strings lexicographically.
        return reverseStr1.compareTo(reverseStr2);               // (6)
    }
}
```

The program is run with the following program arguments on the command line:

```
>java ComparatorUsage court Stuart report Resort assort support transport distort
```

Output from the program using the natural order (1a):

```
[Resort, Stuart, assort, court, distort, report, support, transport]
```

Output from the program using the case insensitive order (1b):

```
[assort, court, distort, report, Resort, Stuart, support, transport]
```

Output from the program using the rhyming order (1c):

```
[Stuart, report, support, transport, Resort, assort, distort, court]
```

The SortedSet **Interface**

The SortedSet interface extends the Set interface to provide the functionality for handling sorted sets.

```
// Range-view operations
SortedSet headSet(Object toElement)
SortedSet tailSet(Object fromElement)
SortedSet subSet(Object fromElement, Object toElement)
```

The headSet() method returns a view of a portion of this sorted set, whose elements are strictly less than the specified element. Similarly, the tailSet() method returns a view of the portion of this sorted set, whose elements are greater than or equal to the specified element. The subSet() method returns a view of the portion of this sorted set, whose elements range from fromElement, inclusive, to toElement, exclusive. Note that the views present the elements sorted in the same order as the underlying sorted map.

```
// First-last elements
Object first()
Object last()
```

The first() method returns the first element currently in this sorted set, and the last() method returns the last element currently in this sorted set. Both throw a NoSuchElementException if the sorted set is empty.

```
// Comparator access
Comparator comparator()
```

This method returns the comparator associated with this sorted set, or null if it uses the natural ordering of its elements. This comparator, if defined, is used by default when a sorted set is constructed, and also used when copying elements into new sorted sets.

The SortedMap **Interface**

The SortedMap interface extends the Map interface to provide the functionality for implementing maps with *sorted keys*. Its operations are analogous to those of the SortedSet interface, applied to maps and keys rather than to sets and elements.

```
// Range-view operations
SortedMap headMap(Object toKey)
SortedMap tailMap(Object fromKey)
SortedMap subMap(Object fromKey, Object toKey)
// First-last keys
Object firstKey()
Object lastKey()
// Comparator access
Comparator comparator()
```

TreeSet **and** TreeMap

The TreeSet and TreeMap classes implement the SortedSet and SortedMap interfaces, respectively. By default, operations on sorted sets or maps rely on the natural ordering of the elements or keys, respectively. However, a total ordering can be specified by passing a customized comparator to the constructor.

These implementations use balanced trees, which deliver excellent performance for all operations. Searching in a HashSet or HashMap can be faster than in a TreeSet or TreeMap, as hashing algorithms usually offer better performance than the search algorithms for balanced trees.

Each class provides four constructors:

```
TreeSet()
TreeMap()
```

A standard constructor to create a new empty sorted set or map, according to the natural order of the elements or the keys, respectively.

```
TreeSet(Comparator c)
TreeMap(Comparator c)
```

A constructor that takes an explicit comparator for ordering the elements or the keys.

```
TreeSet(Collection c)
TreeMap(Map m)
```

A constructor that can create a sorted set or a sorted map based on a collection or a map, according to the natural order of the elements or the keys, respectively.

```
TreeSet(SortedSet s)
TreeMap(SortedMap m)
```

A constructor that creates a new set or map containing the same elements or entries as the specified sorted set or sorted map, with the same ordering.

Example 11.6 *Using SortedMaps*

```
import java.util.*;

public class WeightGroups2 {
    public static void main(String[] args) {

        // Create a map to store the frequency for each group.
        Map groupFreqData = new HashMap();

        int numArgs = args.length;
        for (int i=0; i<numArgs; i++) {
            // Get the value from argument and group into intervals of 5    (1)
            double weight = Double.parseDouble(args[i]);
```

```
        Integer weightGroup = new Integer((int) Math.round(weight/5)*5);
        // Increment count, set to 1 if it's the first value of group.  (2)
        Integer oldCount = (Integer) groupFreqData.get(weightGroup);
        Integer newCount = (oldCount==null) ?
            new Integer(1) :
            new Integer(oldCount.intValue()+1);
        groupFreqData.put(weightGroup, newCount);                    // (3)
    }

    /* Only the histogram for the weight groups between 50 and 150
       is of interest. Print frequency for these groups in a sorted order. */

    // Transfer the data to a sorted map.
    SortedMap sortedGroupFreqData = new TreeMap(groupFreqData);      // (4)

    // Select the relevant sub-map.
    SortedMap selectedGroupFreqData =                               // (5)
            sortedGroupFreqData.subMap(new Integer(50), new Integer(150));

    /** Print by traversing the sorted entries of weight groups (key)
        and count (value). */
    Iterator entryIterator =
            selectedGroupFreqData.entrySet().iterator();            // (6)
    while (entryIterator.hasNext()) {
        Map.Entry entry = (Map.Entry) entryIterator.next();         // (7)

        // Extract groups (key) and count (value) from entry.        (8)
        Integer group = (Integer) entry.getKey();
        Integer count = (Integer) entry.getValue();
        int intCount = count.intValue();

        /* Use the fill() method from the Arrays class to create a
           string consisting of intCount number of '*'. */
        char[] bar = new char[intCount];
        Arrays.fill(bar, '*');                                      // (9)

        System.out.println(group + ":\t" + new String(bar));
    } // end while
  } // end main()
} // end of class
```

Running the program with the following argument:

```
java WeightGroups2 74 75 93 75 93 82 61 92 10 185
```

gives the following output:

```
60:     *
75:     ***
80:     *
90:     *
95:     **
```

Example 11.6 illustrates sorted maps. It also prints a textual histogram like the one in Example 11.4, but now the histogram is limited to a range of weight groups. The program defines the following steps:

1. Read the program arguments, converting each weight to its corresponding weight group and updating the frequency of the weight group. This is the same step as in Example 11.4.

2. Transfer the data to a sorted map, as shown at (4).

    ```
    SortedMap sortedGroupFreqData = new TreeMap(groupFreqData);        // (4)
    ```

3. Create a sorted submap view of the required range of weight groups, as shown at (5).

    ```
    SortedMap selectedGroupFreqData =                                  // (5)
            sortedGroupFreqData.subMap(new Integer(50), new Integer(150));
    ```

4. Set up an iterator on a set view of entries in the submap, as shown at (6). First, a set view of the entries is created using the entrySet() method. The elements (i.e., the entries) in this set view will be sorted, since the underlying submap is sorted. An iterator is then created on this set.

    ```
    Iterator entryIterator =
            selectedGroupFreqData.entrySet().iterator();              // (6)
    ```

5. Use the iterator to traverse the underlying set. Each element in this set is an entry in the underlying sorted submap. Each entry conforms to the Map.Entry interface, which allows the key and the value to be extracted, as shown at (8).

    ```
    // Extract groups (key) and count (value) from entry.            (8)
    Integer group = (Integer) entry.getKey();
    Integer count = (Integer) entry.getValue();
    int intCount = count.intValue();
    ```

 Review Questions

11.9   Which of these methods can be called on objects implementing the Map interface?

Select the two correct answers.

(a) contains(Object o)
(b) addAll(Collection c)
(c) remove(Object o)
(d) values()
(e) toArray()

11.10   Which statements are true about maps?

Select the two correct answers.

(a) The return type of the values() method is Set.
(b) Changes made in the set view returned by keySet() will be reflected in the original map.

(c) The Map interface extends the Collection interface.

(d) All keys in a map are unique.

(e) All Map implementations keep the keys sorted.

11.11 Which sequence of digits will the following program print?

```
import java.util.*;
public class Lists {
    public static void main(String[] args) {
        List list = new ArrayList();
        list.add("1");
        list.add("2");
        list.add(1, "3");
        List list2 = new LinkedList(list);
        list.addAll(list2);
        list2 = list.subList(2, 5);
        list2.clear();
        System.out.println(list);
    }
}
```

Select the one correct answer.

(a) [1, 3, 2]

(b) [1, 3, 3, 2]

(c) [1, 3, 2, 1, 3, 2]

(d) [3, 1, 2]

(e) [3, 1, 1, 2]

(f) None of the above.

11.12 Which of these classes have a comparator() method?

Select the two correct answers.

(a) ArrayList

(b) HashMap

(c) TreeSet

(d) HashSet

(e) TreeMap

11.13 Which method prototypes are defined in the interface java.util.Map.Entry?

Select the two correct answers.

(a) Object getKey()

(b) Object setKey(Object value)

(c) void remove()

(d) Object getValue()

(e) void setValue(Object value)

11.7 Implementing the equals(), hashCode(), and compareTo() Methods

The majority of the non-final methods of the Object class are meant to be overridden. They provide general contracts for objects, which the classes overriding the methods should honor.

It is important to understand how and why a class should override the equals() and hashCode() methods. Implementation of the compareTo() method of the Comparable interface is closely related to the other two methods.

Objects of a class that override the equals() method can be used as elements in a collection. If they override the hashCode() method, they can also be used as elements in a HashSet and as keys in a HashMap. Implementing the Comparable interface allows them to be used as elements in sorted collections and sorted maps. Table 11.2 summarizes the methods that objects should provide if the objects are to be maintained in collections and maps.

As a running example, we will implement different versions of a class for *version numbers*. A version number (VNO) for a software product comprises three pieces of information:

- a release number
- a revision number
- a patch number

The idea is that releases do not happen very often. Revisions take place more frequently than releases, but less frequently than code patches are issued. We can say that the release number is most *significant*. The revision number is less significant than the release number, and the patch number is the least significant of the three fields. This ranking would also be employed when ordering version numbers chronologically.

The equals() Method

If every object is to be considered unique, then it is not necessary to override the equals() method in the Object class. This method implements object reference equality. It implements the most discriminating equivalence relation possible on objects. Each instance of the class is only equal to itself.

The class SimpleVNO in Example 11.7 does not override the equals() method in the Object class. It only overrides the toString() method to generate a meaningful textual representation for a version number.

Example 11.7   *A Simple Class for Version Number*

```java
public class SimpleVNO {
    // Does not override equals() or hashCode().

    private int release;
    private int revision;
    private int patch;

    public SimpleVNO(int release, int revision, int patch) {
        this.release  = release;
        this.revision = revision;
        this.patch    = patch;
    }

    public String toString() {
        return "(" + release + "." + revision + "." + patch + ")";
    }
}
```

The class TestVersionSimple in Example 11.8 uses objects of the class SimpleVNO. It declares three references that denote three different SimpleVNO objects, as shown at (1), (2), and (3), respectively. It also creates an array of SimpleVNO objects, called versions, as shown at (4). The type of these version objects will change in the subsequent examples, as we successively develop new versions of a class for version numbers. All of the examples will use the test() method defined in Example 11.8.

We assume that the integers in the downloads array created at (5), represent the number of downloads for the software versions from the corresponding position in the versions array.

Example 11.8 demonstrates that all SimpleVNO objects are unique, because the class SimpleVNO does not override the equals() method to provide any other equivalence relation. The object denoted by the reference latest is compared with the object denoted by the reference inShops and with the object denoted by the reference older, as shown at (6), (7), (8), and (9). The output from the program shows that the result is false for object reference equality and for the object value equality. These references denote distinct objects, although the object denoted by the reference latest and the object denoted by the reference inShops have identical states.

Not overriding the equals() method appropriately makes it impossible to search for SimpleVNO objects in arrays, collections, or maps. Searching involves specifying a copy object, called the *search key*, which can be compared with objects in the collection. Since all SimpleVNO objects are distinct, the equals() method will always return false, regardless of which object is compared with the search key object. As shown by the output from Example 11.8, searching for the version number (9.1.1) in the versions array will always fail.

The versions array is converted to a List at (14), denoted by the reference vnoList, and the contains() method is called at (15) to check if the search key is in the list. The contains() method of a List relies on the equals() method provided by its elements. The result is, as expected, false.

A HashMap with SimpleVNO objects as keys and Integer objects as values, is created at (17), based on the associative arrays versions and downloads. Hash codes for all the map keys are printed at (19), and the hash code for the search key is printed at (20). Since the hashCode() method is not overridden either, the implementation in the Object class attempts to return distinct integers as hash codes for the objects.

The code attempts to create a sorted set and a sorted map from the list and the map at (22) and (23), respectively. The class SimpleVNO must either implement the compareTo() method of the Comparable interface, or a comparator must be provided, in order to maintain objects in sorted sets or sorted maps (see Section 11.6, p. 452). In this example, the program output shows that an exception is thrown because SimpleVNO objects do not meet this criteria. However, the result is unpredictable when objects that do not meet the criteria are used in sorted sets or sorted maps.

We will run the test() method in Example 11.8 on successive versions of a class for version numbers developed in this section.

Example 11.8 *Implications of Not Overriding the* equals() *Method*

```java
import java.util.*;

public class TestVersionSimple {
    public static void main(String[] args) {
        (new TestVersionSimple()).test();
    }

    protected Object makeVersion(int a, int b, int c) {
        return new SimpleVNO(a, b, c);
    }

    protected void test() {
        // Three individual version numbers.
        Object latest  = makeVersion(9,1,1);           // (1)
        Object inShops = makeVersion(9,1,1);           // (2)
        Object older   = makeVersion(6,6,6);           // (3)

        // An array of version numbers.
        Object[] versions = {                          // (4)
            makeVersion( 3,49, 1), makeVersion( 8,19,81),
            makeVersion( 2,48,28), makeVersion(10,23,78),
            makeVersion( 9, 1, 1)};

        // An array of downloads.
        Integer[] downloads = {                        // (5)
            new Integer(245), new Integer(786),
            new Integer(54), new Integer(1010),
            new Integer(123)};
```

```
                // Various tests.
                System.out.println("Test object reference and value equality:");
                System.out.println("    latest: " + latest + ", inShops: " + inShops
                        + ", older: " + older);
                System.out.println("    latest == inShops: " +
                        (latest == inShops));                          // (6)
                System.out.println("    latest.equals(inShops): " +
                        (latest.equals(inShops)));                     // (7)
                System.out.println("    latest == older: " +
                        (latest == older));                            // (8)
                System.out.println("    latest.equals(older): " +
                        (latest.equals(older)));                       // (9)

                Object searchKey = inShops;
                System.out.println("Search key: " + searchKey);        // (10)

                System.out.print("Array: ");
                for (int i = 0; i < versions.length; i++)              // (11)
                    System.out.print(versions[i] + " ");
                boolean found = false;
                for (int i = 0; i < versions.length && !found; i++)
                    found = searchKey.equals(versions[i]);             // (12)
                System.out.println("\n    Search key found in array: "
                        + found);                                      // (13)

                List vnoList = Arrays.asList(versions);                // (14)
                System.out.println("List: " + vnoList);
                System.out.println("    Search key contained in list: " +
                        vnoList.contains(searchKey));                  // (15)

                Map versionStatistics = new HashMap();                 // (16)
                for (int i = 0; i < versions.length; i++)              // (17)
                    versionStatistics.put(versions[i], downloads[i]);
                System.out.println("Map: " + versionStatistics);       // (18)
                System.out.println("    Hash code for keys in the map:");
                for (int i = 0; i < versions.length; i++)              // (19)
                    System.out.println("        " + versions[i] + ": "
                            + versions[i].hashCode());
                System.out.println("    Search key " + searchKey
                        + " has hash code: " + searchKey.hashCode());  // (20)
                System.out.println("    Map contains search key: " +
                        versionStatistics.containsKey(searchKey));     // (21)

                System.out.println("Sorted list:\n\t"
                        + (new TreeSet(vnoList)));                     // (22)
                System.out.println("Sorted map:\n\t"
                        + (new TreeMap(versionStatistics)));           // (23)

                System.out.println("List before sorting: " + vnoList); // (24)
                Collections.sort(vnoList);
                System.out.println("List after sorting:  " + vnoList);
```

```
                    System.out.println("Binary search in list:");          // (25)
                    int resultIndex = Collections.binarySearch(vnoList, searchKey);
                    System.out.println("\tKey: " + searchKey +
                                        "\tKey index: " + resultIndex);
        }
    }
```

Output from the program:

```
Test object reference and value equality:
    latest: (9.1.1), inShops: (9.1.1), older: (6.6.6)
    latest == inShops: false
    latest.equals(inShops): false
    latest == older: false
    latest.equals(older): false
Search key: (9.1.1)
Array: (3.49.1) (8.19.81) (2.48.28) (10.23.78) (9.1.1)
    Search key found in array: false
List: [(3.49.1), (8.19.81), (2.48.28), (10.23.78), (9.1.1)]
    Search key contained in list: false
Map: {(9.1.1)=123, (10.23.78)=1010, (8.19.81)=786, (3.49.1)=245, (2.48.28)=54}
    Hash code for keys in the map:
        (3.49.1): 13288040
        (8.19.81): 27355241
        (2.48.28): 30269696
        (10.23.78): 24052850
        (9.1.1): 26022015
    Search key (9.1.1) has hash code: 20392474
    Map contains search key: false
Exception in thread "main" java.lang.ClassCastException
...
```

An implementation of the equals() method must satisfy the properties of an *equivalence relation*:

- *Reflexive*: For any reference self, self.equals(self) is always true.

- *Symmetric*: For any references x and y, x.equals(y) is true if and only if y.equals(x) is true.

- *Transitive*: For any references x, y and z, if both x.equals(y) and y.equals(z) are true, then x.equals(z) is true.

- *Consistent*: For any references x and y, multiple invocations of x.equals(y) always return the same result, provided the objects denoted by these references have not been modified to affect the equals comparison.

- null *comparison*: For any non-null reference obj, obj.equals(null) is always false.

The general contract of the equals() method is defined between *objects of arbitrary classes*. Understanding its criteria is important for providing a proper implementation.

Reflexivity

This rule simply states that an object is equal to itself, regardless of how it is modified. It is easy to satisfy: the object passed as argument and the current object are compared for object reference equality (==):

```
if (this == argumentObj)
    return true;
```

Symmetry

The expression x.equals(y) invokes the equals() method on the object denoted by the reference x, whereas the expression y.equals(x) invokes the equals() method on the object denoted by the reference y. Both invocations must return the same result.

If the equals() methods invoked are in different classes, the classes must bilaterally agree whether their objects are equal or not. In other words, symmetry can be violated if the equals() method of a class makes unilateral decisions about which classes it will interoperate with, but the other classes are not aware of this. Avoiding interoperability with other (non-related) classes when implementing the equals() method is strongly recommended.

Transitivity

If two classes, A and B, have a bilateral agreement on their objects being equal, then this rule guarantees that one of them, say B, does not enter into an agreement with a third class C on its own. All classes involved must multilaterally abide by the terms of the contract.

A typical pitfall resulting in broken transitivity is when the equals() method in a subclass calls the equals() method of its superclass, as part of its equals comparison. The equals() method in the subclass usually has code equivalent to the following line:

```
return super.equals(argumentObj) && compareSubclassSpecificAspects();
```

The idea is to compare only the subclass-specific aspects in the subclass equals() method, and to leverage on the superclass equals() method for comparing the superclass-specific aspects. However, this approach should be used with extreme caution. The problem lies in getting the equivalence contract fulfilled bilaterally between the superclass and the subclass equals() methods. If the subclass equals() method does not interoperate with superclass objects, symmetry is easily broken. If the subclass equals() method does interoperate with superclass objects, transitivity is easily broken.

If the superclass is abstract, leveraging on the superclass equals() method works well. There are no superclass objects for the subclass equals() method to consider. In addition, the superclass equals() method cannot be called directly by any other clients than subclasses. The subclass equals() method then has control of how the superclass equals() method is called. It can safely call the superclass equals() method to compare the superclass-specific aspects of subclass objects.

Consistency

This rule enforces that two objects that are equal (or non-equal) remain equal (or non-equal) as long as they are not modified. For mutable objects, the result of the equals comparison can change if one (or both) are modified between method invocations. However, for immutable objects, the result must always be the same. The equals() method should take into consideration whether the class implements immutable objects, and ensure that the consistency rule is not violated.

null *comparison*

This rule states that no object is equal to null. The contract calls for the equals() method to return false. The method must not throw an exception; that would be violating the contract. A check for this rule is necessary in the implementation. Typically, the reference value passed as argument is explicitly compared with the null value:

```
if (argumentObj == null)
    return false;
```

In many cases, it is preferable to use the instanceof operator. It always returns false if its left operand is null:

```
if (!(argumentObj instanceof MyRefType))
    return false;
```

This test has the added advantage that if the condition fails, the argument reference can be safely downcast.

Example 11.9 *Implementing the* equals() *Method*

```
public class UsableVNO {
    // Overrides equals(), but not hashCode().

    private int release;
    private int revision;
    private int patch;

    public UsableVNO(int release, int revision, int patch) {
        this.release  = release;
        this.revision = revision;
        this.patch    = patch;
    }
```

```
    public String toString() {
        return "(" + release + "." + revision + "." + patch + ")";
    }

    public boolean equals(Object obj) {              // (1)
        if (obj == this)                             // (2)
            return true;
        if (!(obj instanceof UsableVNO))             // (3)
            return false;
        UsableVNO vno = (UsableVNO) obj;             // (4)
        return vno.patch    == this.patch    &&      // (5)
               vno.revision == this.revision &&
               vno.release  == this.release;
    }
}
```

Example 11.9 shows an implementation of the equals() method for version numbers. Next, we provide a checklist for implementing the equals() method.

Method overriding signature

The method prototype is

```
    public boolean equals(Object obj)            // (1)
```

The signature of the method requires that the argument passed is of the type Object. The following header will overload the method, not override it:

```
    public boolean equals(MyRefType obj)     // Overloaded.
```

The compiler will not complain. Calls to overloaded methods are resolved at compile time, depending on the type of the argument. Calls to overridden methods are resolved at runtime, depending on the type of the actual object denoted by the argument. Comparing the objects of the class MyRefType that overloads the equals() method for equivalence, can give inconsistent results:

```
    MyRefType ref1 = new MyRefType();
    MyRefType ref2 = new MyRefType();
    Object    ref3 = ref2;
    boolean b1 = ref1.equals(ref2);     // True. Calls equals() in MyRefType.
    boolean b2 = ref1.equals(ref3);     // Always false. Calls equals() in Object.
```

However, if the equals() method is overridden correctly, only the overriding method in MyRefType is called. A class can provide both implementations, but the equals() methods must be consistent.

Reflexivity test

This is usually the first test performed in the equals() method, avoiding further computation if the test is true. The equals() method in Example 11.9 does this test at (2).

Correct argument type

The equals() method in Example 11.9 checks the type of the argument object at (3), using the instanceof operator:

```
if (!(obj instanceof UsableVNO))              // (3)
    return false;
```

This code also does the null comparison correctly, returning false if the argument obj has the value null.

The instanceof operator will also return true if the argument obj denotes a subclass object of the class UsableVNO. If the class is final, this issue does not arise—there are no subclass objects. The test at (3) can also be replaced by the following code in order to exclude all other objects, including subclass objects:

```
if ((obj == null) || (obj.getClass() != this.getClass()))   // (3a)
    return false;
```

The test in (3a) first performs the null comparison explicitly. The expression (obj.getClass() != this.getClass()) determines whether the classes of the two objects have the same runtime object representing them. If this is the case, the objects are instances of the same class.

Argument casting

The argument is only cast after checking that the cast will be successful. The instanceof operator ensures the validity of the cast, as done in Example 11.9. The argument is cast at (4) to allow for class-specific field comparisons:

```
UsableVNO vno = (UsableVNO) obj;              // (4)
```

Field comparisons

Equivalence comparison involves comparing certain fields from both objects to determine if their logical states match. For fields that are of primitive data types, their primitive values can be compared. Instances of the class UsableVNO in Example 11.9 have only fields of primitive data types. Values of corresponding fields are compared to test for equality between two UsableVNO objects:

```
return vno.patch    == this.patch    &&       // (5)
       vno.revision == this.revision &&
       vno.release  == this.release;
```

If all field comparisons evaluate to true, the equals() method returns true.

For fields that are references, the objects denotes by the references can be compared. For example, if the UsableVNO class declares a field called productInfo, which is a reference, the following code could be used:

```
(vno.productInfo  == this.productInfo ||
 (this.productInfo != null && this.productInfo.equals(vno.productInfo)))
```

The expression vno.productInfo == this.productInfo checks for the possibility that the two objects being compared have a common object denoted by both product-Info references. In order to avoid a NullPointerException being thrown, the equals() method is not invoked if the this.productInfo reference is null.

Exact comparison of floating-point values should not be done directly on the values, but on the integer values obtained from their bit patterns (see static methods Float.floatToIntBits() and Double.doubleToLongBits()). This technique eliminates certain anomalies in floating-point comparisons that involve a NAN value or a negative zero (see also the equals() method in Float and Double classes).

Only fields that have significance for the equivalence relation should be considered. Derived fields, whose computation is dependent on other field values in the object, might be redundant to include, or only including the derived fields might be prudent. Computing the equivalence relation should be deterministic, so the equals() method should not depend on unreliable resources, such as network access.

The order in which the comparisons are carried out can influence the performance of the equals comparison. Fields that are most likely to differ should be compared as early as possible in order to short-circuit the computation. In our example, patch numbers evolve faster than revision numbers, which, in turn, evolve faster than release numbers. This order is reflected in the return statement at (5) in Example 11.9.

Above all, an implementation of the equals() method must ensure that the equivalence relation is fulfilled.

Example 11.10 is a client that uses the class UsableVNO from Example 11.9. This client runs the same tests as the client in Example 11.8. The difference is that the class UsableVNO overrides the equals() method.

Example 11.10 *Implications of Overriding the* equals() *Method*

```
public class TestVersionUsable extends TestVersionSimple {
    public static void main(String[] args) {
        (new TestVersionUsable()).test();
    }
    protected Object makeVersion(int a, int b, int c) {
        return new UsableVNO(a, b, c);
    }
}
```

Output from the program:

```
Test object reference and value equality:
    latest: (9.1.1), inShops: (9.1.1), older: (6.6.6)
    latest == inShops: false
    latest.equals(inShops): true
    latest == older: false
    latest.equals(older): false
```

```
Search key: (9.1.1)
Array: (3.49.1) (8.19.81) (2.48.28) (10.23.78) (9.1.1)
    Search key found in array: true
List: [(3.49.1), (8.19.81), (2.48.28), (10.23.78), (9.1.1)]
    Search key contained in list: true
Map: {(10.23.78)=1010, (2.48.28)=54, (3.49.1)=245, (9.1.1)=123, (8.19.81)=786}
    Hash code for keys in the map:
        (3.49.1): 27355241
        (8.19.81): 30269696
        (2.48.28): 24052850
        (10.23.78): 26022015
        (9.1.1): 3541984
    Search key (9.1.1) has hash code: 11352996
    Map contains search key: false
Exception in thread "main" java.lang.ClassCastException
...
```

The output from the program shows that object value equality is compared correctly. Object value equality is now based on identical states, as defined by the equals() method.

The search for an UsableVNO object in an array or a list of UsableVNO objects is now successful, as the equals comparison is based on the states of the objects, and not on their reference values.

However, searching in a map or creating sorted collections, is still not feasible. For searching in a HashMap, we have to look at the relationship between the equals() and the hashCode() methods. For creating sorted collections or sorted maps, we will provide an implementation of the compareTo() method.

The hashCode() **Method**

Hashing is an efficient technique for storing and retrieving data. A common hashing scheme uses an array, where each element is a list of items. The array elements are called *buckets*. Operations in a hashing scheme involve computing an array index from an item. Converting an item to its array index is done by a *hash function*. The array index returned by the hash function is called the *hash value* of the item. The hash value identifies a particular bucket.

Storing an item involves the following steps:

1. Hashing the item to determine the bucket.

2. If the item does not match one already in the bucket, it is stored in the bucket.

Note that no duplicate items are stored. Retrieving an item is based on using a *key*. The key represents the identify the item. Item retrieval is also a two-step process:

1. Hashing the key to determine the bucket.

2. If the key matches an item in the bucket, this item is retrieved from the bucket.

Different items can hash to the same bucket, meaning that the hash function returns the same hash value for these items. This condition is called a *collision*. The list maintained by a bucket contains the items that hash to the bucket.

The hash value only identifies the bucket. Finding an item in the bucket entails a search, and requires an equality function to compare items. The items maintained in a hash-based storage scheme must, therefore, provide two essential functions: a hash and an equality function.

The performance of a hashing scheme is largely affected by how well the hash function distributes a collection of items over the available buckets. A hash function should not be biased toward any particular hash values. An ideal hash function produces a uniform distribution of hash values for a collection of items across all possible hash values. Such a hash function is not an easy task to design. Fortunately, there exist heuristics for constructing adequate hash functions.

A *hash table* contains *key-value entries* as items, and the hashing is done only on the keys to provide efficient lookup of values. Matching a given key with a key in an entry, determines the value.

If objects of a class are to be maintained in hash-based collections and maps of the `java.util` package (see Table 11.2), the class must provide appropriate implementations of the following methods from the `Object` class:

- a `hashCode()` method that produces hash values for the objects

- an `equals()` method that tests objects for equality

As a general rule for implementing these methods, *a class that overrides the* `equals()` *method must override the* `hashCode()` *method*. Consequences of not doing so are illustrated by the class `UsableVNO` in Example 11.9. Elements of this class are used as keys in Example 11.10. The output from the program shows that a map with the following entries is created:

```
Map: {(10.23.78)=1010, (2.48.28)=54, (3.49.1)=245, (9.1.1)=123, (8.19.81)=786}
```

The `hashCode()` method from the `Object` class is not overridden by the `UsableVNO` class and is, therefore, used to compute the hash values of the key objects. The output from the program shows the hash values assigned by this method to the keys in the map:

```
Hash code for keys in the map:
    (3.49.1): 27355241
    (8.19.81): 30269696
    (2.48.28): 24052850
    (10.23.78): 26022015
    (9.1.1): 3541984
```

Attempting to find the search key (9.1.1) is in the map is unsuccessful:

```
Search key (9.1.1) has hash code: 11352996
Map contains search key: false
```

The hash values of two objects, which are equal according to the equals() method, are not equal according to the hashCode() method of the Object class. Therefore, the key object (9.1.1) of the entry <9.1.1, 123> in the map has a different hash value than the search key object (9.1.1). These objects hash to different buckets. The lookup for the search key object is done in one bucket and does not find the entry <9.1.1, 123>, which is to be found in a completely different bucket. Only overriding the equals() method is not enough. The class UsableVNO violates the key tenet of the hashCode() contract: *equal objects must produce equal hash codes.*

General Contract of the hashCode() *method*

The general contract of the hashCode() method stipulates:

- *Consistency during execution*: Multiple invocations of the hashCode() method on an object must consistently return the same hash code during the execution of an application, provided the object is not modified to affect the result returned by the equals() method. The hash code need not remain consistent across different executions of the application. This means that using a pseudorandom number generator to produce hash values is not a valid strategy.

- *Object value equality implies hash value equality*: If two objects are equal according to the equals() method, then the hashCode() method must produce the same hash code for these objects. This tenet ties in with the general contract of the equals() method.

- *Object value inequality places no restrictions on the hash value*: If two objects are unequal according to the equals() method, then the hashCode() method need not produce distinct hash codes for these objects. It is strongly recommended that the hashCode() method produce unequal hash codes for unequal objects.

Note that the hash contract does not imply that objects with equal hash codes are equal. Not producing unequal hash codes for unequal objects can have an adverse effect on performance, as unequal objects will hash to the same bucket.

Heuristics for implementing the hashCode() *method*

In Example 11.11, the computation of the hash value in the hashCode() method of the ReliableVNO class embodies heuristics that can produce fairly reasonable hash functions. The hash value is computed according to the following formula:

```
hashValue = 11 * 31³ + release * 31² + revision * 31¹ + patch
```

This can be verified by back substitution (see Section G.3, p. 596). Each significant field is included in the computation. Only the fields that have bearing on the equals() method are included. This ensures that objects that are equal according to the equals() method, also have equal hash values according to the hashCode() method.

Example 11.11 *Implementing the* hashCode() *Method*

```java
public class ReliableVNO {
    // Overrides both equals() and hashCode().

    private int release;
    private int revision;
    private int patch;

    public ReliableVNO(int release, int revision, int patch) {
        this.release  = release;
        this.revision = revision;
        this.patch    = patch;
    }

    public String toString() {
        return "(" + release + "." + revision + "." + patch + ")";
    }

    public boolean equals(Object obj) {                 // (1)
        if (obj == this)                                // (2)
            return true;
        if (!(obj instanceof ReliableVNO))              // (3)
            return false;
        ReliableVNO vno = (ReliableVNO) obj;            // (4)
        return vno.patch    == this.patch    &&         // (5)
                vno.revision == this.revision &&
                vno.release  == this.release;
    }

    public int hashCode() {                             // (6)
        int hashValue = 11;
        hashValue = 31 * hashValue + release;
        hashValue = 31 * hashValue + revision;
        hashValue = 31 * hashValue + patch;
        return hashValue;
    }
}
```

The basic idea is to compute an int hash value sfVal for each significant field sf, and include an assignment of the form shown at (1) in the computation:

```java
public int hashCode() {
    int sfVal;
    int hashValue = 11;
    ...
    sfVal = ...                     // Compute hash value for each significant field sf.
    hashValue = 31 * hashValue + sfVal;    // (1)
    ...
    return hashValue;
}
```

This setup ensures that the result from incorporating a field value is used to calculate the contribution from the next field value.

Calculating the hash value sfVal for a significant field sf depends on the type of the field:

- Field sf is boolean: sfVal = sf ? 0 : 1
- Field sf is byte, char, short, or int: sfVal = (int)sf
- Field sf is long: sfVal = (int) (sf ^ (sf >>> 32))
- Field sf is float: sfVal = Float.floatToInt(sf)
- Field sf is double: long sfValTemp = Double.doubleToLong(sf);

$$sfVal = (int) (sfValTemp \wedge (sfValTemp >>> 32))$$

- Field sf is a reference that denotes an object. Typically, the hashCode() method is invoked recursively if the equals() method is invoked recursively:

$$sfVal = (sf == null ? 0 : sf.hashCode())$$

- Field sf is an array. Contribution from each element is calculated similarly to a field.

The order in which the fields are incorporated into the hash code computation will influence the hash value. Fields whose values are derived from other fields can be excluded. There is no point in feeding the hash function with redundant information since this is unlikely to improve the value distribution. Fields that are not significant for the equals() method must be excluded; otherwise, the hashCode() method might end up contradicting the equals() method. As with the equals() method, data from unreliable resources (e.g., network access) should not be used.

A legal or correct hash function does not necessarily mean it is appropriate or efficient. The classical example of a legal but inefficient hash function is

```
public int hashCode() {
    return 1949;
}
```

All objects using this method are assigned to the same bucket. The hash table is then no better than a list. For the sake of efficiency, a hash function should strive to produce unequal hash codes for unequal objects.

For numeric wrapper types, the hashCode() implementation returns an int representation of the primitive value, converting the primitive value to an int, if necessary. The Boolean objects for the boolean literals true and false have specific hash values, which are returned by the hashCode() method.

The hashCode() method of the String class returns a hash value that is the value of a polynomial whose variable has the value 31, the coefficients are the characters in the string, and the degree is the string length minus one. For example, the hash value of the string "abc" is computed as follows:

$$hashValue = 'a' * 31^2 + 'b' * 31^1 + 'c' * 31^0 = 97 * 31 * 31 + 98 * 31 + 99 = 96354$$

For immutable objects, the hash code can be cached, that is, calculated once and returned whenever the hashCode() method is called.

The client in Example 11.12 uses objects of the class ReliableVNO in Example 11.11 to create a map and to search for a key in the map. Output from the program shows that the key object (9.1.1) of the entry <9.1.1, 123> in the map has the same hash value as the search key object (9.1.1). The search is successful. These objects hash to the same bucket. Therefore, the search for the key object takes place in the right bucket. It finds the entry <9.1.1, 123> using the equals() method by successfully checking for equality between the search key object (9.1.1) and the key object (9.1.1) of this entry.

Example 11.12 *Implications of Overriding the* hashCode() *Method*

```
public class TestVersionReliable extends TestVersionSimple {
    public static void main(String[] args) {
        (new TestVersionReliable()).test();
    }
    protected Object makeVersion(int a, int b, int c) {
        return new ReliableVNO(a, b, c);
    }
}
```

Output from the program:

```
...
Map: {(10.23.78)=1010, (2.48.28)=54, (3.49.1)=245, (8.19.81)=786, (9.1.1)=123}
    Hash code for keys in the map:
        (3.49.1): 332104
        (8.19.81): 336059
        (2.48.28): 331139
        (10.23.78): 338102
        (9.1.1): 336382
    Search key (9.1.1) has hash code: 336382
    Map contains search key: true
Exception in thread "main" java.lang.ClassCastException
...
```

The compareTo() Method

The Comparable interface is discussed in Section 11.6 on page 452. In this subsection we discuss how to implement its only method: the compareTo() method. This method defines the natural ordering for the instances of the class that implements the Comparable interface. Objects implementing Comparable can be used in sorted collections and sorted maps.

We repeat the general contract for the compareTo() method from Section 11.6 on page 452 :

```
int compareTo(Object o)
```

It returns a negative integer, zero, or a positive integer if the current object is less than, equal to, or greater than the specified object, based on the natural order. It throws a ClassCastException if the reference value passed in the argument cannot be cast to the type of the current object.

An implementation of the compareTo() method for the objects of a class should meet the following criteria:

- For any two objects of the class, if the first object is *less than*, *equal to*, or *greater than* the second object, then the second object must be *greater than*, *equal to*, or *less than* the first object, respectively.

- All three order comparison relations (*less than*, *equal to*, *greater than*) embodied in the compareTo() method must be *transitive*. For example, if obj1.compareTo(obj2) > 0 and obj2.compareTo(obj3) > 0, then obj1.compareTo(obj3) > 0.

- For any two objects of the class, which compare as equal, the compareTo() method must return the same results if these two objects are compared with any other object.

- The compareTo() method must be *consistent with equals*, that is, (obj1.compareTo(obj2) == 0) == (obj1.equals(obj2)). This is recommended if the objects will be maintained in sorted sets or sorted maps.

The magnitude of non-zero values returned by the method is immaterial; the sign indicates the result of the comparison. The general contract of the compareTo() method augments the general contract of the equals() method, providing a natural ordering of the compared objects. The equality test of the compareTo() method has the same provisions as that of the equals() method. A compareTo() method is seldom implemented to interoperate with objects of other classes.

Implementing the compareTo() method is not much different from implementing the equals() method. In fact, given that the functionality of the equals() method is a subset of the functionality of the compareTo() method, the equals() implementation can call the compareTo() method. This guarantees that the two methods are always consistent with each other.

```
public boolean equals(Object other) {
    // ...
    return compareTo(other) == 0;
}
```

An implementation of the compareTo() method for the class of version numbers is shown in Example 11.13. The implementation is also consistent with equals. Following general class design principles, the class is declared final so that it cannot be extended.

Example 11.13 *Implementing the* compareTo() *Method of the* Comparable *Interface*

```
public final class VersionNumber implements Comparable {

    private final int release;
    private final int revision;
    private final int patch;

    public VersionNumber(int release, int revision, int patch) {
        this.release  = release;
        this.revision = revision;
        this.patch    = patch;
    }

    public String toString() {
        return "(" + release + "." + revision + "." + patch + ")";
    }

    public boolean equals(Object obj) {              // (1)
        if (obj == this)                             // (2)
            return true;
        if (!(obj instanceof VersionNumber))         // (3)
            return false;
        VersionNumber vno = (VersionNumber) obj;     // (4)
        return vno.patch    == this.patch    &&      // (5)
               vno.revision == this.revision &&
               vno.release  == this.release;
    }

    public int hashCode() {                          // (6)
        int hashValue = 11;
        hashValue = 31 * hashValue + release;
        hashValue = 31 * hashValue + revision;
        hashValue = 31 * hashValue + patch;
        return hashValue;
    }

    public int compareTo(Object obj) {               // (7)
        VersionNumber vno = (VersionNumber) obj;     // (8)

        // Compare the release numbers.                 (9)
        if (release < vno.release)
            return -1;
        if (release > vno.release)
            return 1;

        // Release numbers are equal,                   (10)
        // must compare revision numbers.
        if (revision < vno.revision)
            return -1;
        if (revision > vno.revision)
            return 1;
```

```
                        // Release and revision numbers are equal,      (11)
                        // must compare patch numbers.
                        if (patch < vno.patch)
                           return -1;
                        if (patch > vno.patch)
                           return 1;

                        // All fields are equal.                        (12)
                        return 0;
                     }
                  }
```

The compareTo() contract requires that an illegal argument type should result in a ClassCastException, and a null argument should result in a NullPointerException. Both these checks are embodied in the cast at (8) in Example 11.13.

The fields are compared with the most significant field first and the least significant field last. In the case of the version numbers, the release numbers are compared first, followed by the revision numbers, with the patch numbers being compared last. Note that the next least significant fields are only compared if the comparison of the previous higher significant fields yielded equality. Inequality between corresponding significant fields short-circuits the computation. If all significant fields are equal, a zero is returned. This approach is shown in the implementation of the compareTo() method at (9) through (12) in Example 11.13.

Comparison of integer values in fields can be optimized. For example, the code for comparing the release numbers at (9) in Example 11.13:

```
if (release < vno.release)
    return -1;
if (release > vno.release)
    return 1;
// Next field comparison
```

can be replaced by the following code for doing the comparison, which relies on the difference between the values:

```
int releaseDiff = release - vno.release;
if (releaseDiff != 0)
    return releaseDiff;
// Next field comparison
```

The above code can break if the difference is a value not in the range of the int type.

Significant fields with non-boolean primitive values are normally compared using the relational operators < and >. For comparing significant fields denoting constituent objects, the main options are to invoke the compareTo() method on them or to use a comparator.

Example 11.14 is a client that uses the class VersionNumber from Example 11.13. This client also runs the same tests as the client in Example 11.8. The difference is that the class VersionNumber overrides both the equals() and hashCode() methods, and implements the compareTo() method. In addition, the compareTo() method is consistent with equals. All the tests run as one would expect. Unlike previous attempts, VersionNumber objects can now be maintained in sorted sets and maps.

```
System.out.println("Sorted list:\n\t"
        + (new TreeSet(vnoList)));                          // (22)
System.out.println("Sorted map:\n\t"
        + (new TreeMap(versionStatistics)));                // (23)
```

By default, the class TreeSet relies on its elements to implement the compareTo() method. The output from the program in Example 11.14 shows that the TreeSet, created at (22), maintains its elements sorted in the natural order dictated by the compareTo() method. Analogously, the output from the program in Example 11.14 shows that the TreeMap, created at (23), maintains its entries sorted on the keys, which are in the natural order dictated by the compareTo() method.

Example 11.14 *Implications of Implementing the* compareTo() *Method*

```
public class TestVersion extends TestVersionSimple {
    public static void main(String[] args) {
        (new TestVersion()).test();
    }
    protected Object makeVersion(int a, int b, int c) {
        return new VersionNumber(a, b, c);
    }
}
```

Output from the program:

```
...
Sorted list:
    [(2.48.28), (3.49.1), (8.19.81), (9.1.1), (10.23.78)]
Sorted map:
    {(2.48.28)=54, (3.49.1)=245, (8.19.81)=786, (9.1.1)=123, (10.23.78)=1010}
...
```

We can run generic algorithms on collections of version numbers. Utility methods provided by the Collections and Arrays classes in the java.util package are discussed in Section 11.8. The following code sorts the elements in the list that was created at (14) in Example 11.14, and denoted by the reference vnoList:

```
System.out.println("List before sorting: " + vnoList);  // (24)
Collections.sort(vnoList);
System.out.println("List after sorting:  " + vnoList);
```

The output from executing this code shows that the elements in the list are now sorted:

```
List before sorting: [(3.49.1), (8.19.81), (2.48.28), (10.23.78), (9.1.1)]
List after sorting:  [(2.48.28), (3.49.1), (8.19.81), (9.1.1), (10.23.78)]
```

A binary search can be run on this sorted list to find the index of the version number (9.1.1), denoted by the reference searchKey in Example 11.14:

```
int resultIndex = Collections.binarySearch(vnoList, searchKey);
System.out.println("\tKey: " + searchKey + "\tKey index: " + resultIndex);
```

Executing the code prints the correct index of the search key in the list:

```
Key: (9.1.1)    Key index: 3
```

11.8 Working with Collections

The collection implementations can be augmented with the following functionality:

- thread-safety
- collection immutability

The collection implementation classes, except for Vector and Hashtable, are not thread-safe, that is, their integrity can be jeopardized by concurrent access. A situation might also demand that a collection be immutable. Java provides solutions to both these requirements through *decorators*. A decorator object *wraps around* a collection, modifying the behavior of the collection.

Instead of providing public decorator classes, Java provides *static factory methods* that return appropriately decorated collection instances. In this regard, these decorators are known as *anonymous implementations*. In addition to being a repository of useful utility methods, the Collections class provides decorators for making collections and maps thread-safe and unmodifiable.

Synchronized Collection Decorators

The following static factory methods from the Collections class can be utilized to create decorators that provide thread-safety for collections:

```
static Collection   synchronizedCollection(Collection c)
static List         synchronizedList(List list)
static Map          synchronizedMap(Map m)
static Set          synchronizedSet(Set s)
static SortedMap    synchronizedSortedMap(SortedMap m)
static SortedSet    synchronizedSortedSet(SortedSet s)
```

All threads must access the underlying collection through the synchronized view, otherwise, non-deterministic behavior may occur.

```
// Create a synchronized decorator.
Collection syncDecorator = Collections.synchronizedCollection(nonsyncCollection);
```

In addition, for traversing a synchronized collection, the code for traversing the collection must be synchronized on the decorator:

```
// Each thread can only traverse when synchronized on the decorator.
synchronized(syncDecorator) {
    for (Iterator iterator = syncDecorator.iterator(); iterator.hasNext();)
        doSomething(iterator.next());
}
```

Unmodifiable Collection Decorators

The following static factory methods from the Collections class create *views* that provide read-only access to the underlying collection:

```
static Collection unmodifiableCollection(Collection c)
static List       unmodifiableList(List list)
static Map        unmodifiableMap(Map m)
static Set        unmodifiableSet(Set s)
static SortedMap  unmodifiableSortedMap(SortedMap m)
static SortedSet  unmodifiableSortedSet(SortedSet s)
```

The unmodifiable views intercept all calls that can modify the underlying collection, and throw an UnsupportedOperationException. If the view is a collection, then this restriction applies for any iterator of this collection. In the case of a map, the restriction also applies to any collections created from this map.

Sorting Collections

The Collections class provides two static methods for sorting lists.

```
static void sort(List list)
static void sort(List list, Comparator comp)
```

The first method sorts the elements in the list according to their natural order. The second method does the sorting according to the total ordering specified by the comparator (see Section 11.6).

Searching in Collections

The Collections class provides two static methods for searching in sorted lists.

```
static int binarySearch(List sortedList, Object obj)
static int binarySearch(List sortedList, Object obj, Comparator comp)
```

The methods use a binary search to find the index of the obj element in the specified sorted list. The first method requires that the list is sorted according to natural order, whereas the second method requires that it is sorted according to the total ordering dictated by the comparator.

The following methods find the minimum and maximum elements in a collection:

```
static Object max(Collection c)
static Object max(Collection c, Comparator comp)
static Object min(Collection c)
static Object min(Collection c, Comparator comp)
```

The one-argument methods require that the elements have a natural ordering. The other methods require that the elements have a total ordering enforced by the comparator.

The time for the search is proportional to the size of the collection. The methods are applicable to any collection, regardless of any ordering.

Calling any of the method with an empty collection as parameter results in an `NoSuchElementException`.

Singleton Collections

A *singleton* set, list or map (i.e., an immutable collection or map containing only one element or one entry, respectively) can be created by calling the following static factory methods of the `Collections` class, respectively:

```
static Set  singleton(Object o)
static List singletonList(Object o)
static Map  singletonMap(Object key, Object value)
```

For example, removing an element from a set can be done by using an immutable singleton set:

```
// Create a singleton set with the element to remove.
Set fishBone = Collections.singleton(bone);      // bone is a fish part.
// Remove the element
fish.removeAll(fishBone);                         // fish is a set of fish parts.
```

The empty set, the empty list, and the empty map are designated by the following constants:

```
Collections.EMPTY_SET
Collections.EMPTY_LIST
Collections.EMPTY_MAP
```

These constants come in handy when a collection or map is needed that cannot be populated.

Other Utility Methods in the Collections Class

Most methods accept a List, while a few operate on arbitrary Collection objects. Practically any operation on a list can be done using these methods.

```
static void copy(List dst, List src)
```

Adds the elements from the src list to the dst list.

```
static void fill(List list, Object o)
```

Replaces all of the elements of the list with the specified element.

```
static List nCopies(int n, Object o)
```

Creates an immutable list with n copies of the specified object.

```
static void reverse(List list)
```

Reverses the order of the elements in the list.

```
static Comparator reverseOrder()
```

Returns a comparator that enforces the reverse of the natural ordering. Useful for maintaining objects in reverse-natural order in sorted collections and arrays.

The following code conjures up a modifiable list initialized with 99 null elements:

```
List itemsList = new ArrayList(Collections.nCopies(99, null));
```

This code would sort a list of Integers and an array of strings in descending order and in inverse-lexicographical order, respectively:

```
Collections.sort(intList, Collections.reverseOrder());
Arrays.sort(strArray, Collections.reverseOrder());
```

The elements in the following set would be maintained sorted in descending order:

```
Collection intSet = new TreeSet(Collections.reverseOrder());
intSet.add(new Integer(9));  intSet.add(new Integer(11));
intSet.add(new Integer(-4)); intSet.add(new Integer(1));
System.out.println(intSet);          // [11, 9, 1, -4]
```

```
static void shuffle(List list)
```

Randomly permutes the list, that is, *shuffles* the elements.

```
boolean replaceAll(List list, Object oldVal, Object newVal)
```

Replaces all elements equal to oldVal with newVal in the list; returns true if the list was modified.

```
static void rotate(List list, int distance)
```

Rotates the elements towards the end of the list by the specified distance. A negative value will rotate toward the start of the list.

```
static void swap(List list, int i, int j)
```

Swaps the elements at indices i and j.

The effect of these utility methods can be limited to a sublist, that is, a segment of the list. The following code illustrates rotation of elements in a list. Note how the rotation in the sublist view is reflected in the original list.

```
// intList denotes the following list:                    [9, 11, -4, 1, 7]
Collections.rotate(intList, 2);        // Two to the right.  [1, 7, 9, 11, -4]
Collections.rotate(intList, -2);       // Two to the left.   [9, 11, -4, 1, 7]
List intSublist = intList.subList(1,4);// Sublist:           [11, -4, 1]
Collections.rotate(intSublist, -1);    // One to the left.   [-4, 1, 11]
                                       // intList is now:    [9, -4, 1, 11, 7]
```

Utility Methods in the Arrays Class

The Arrays class provides useful utility methods that operate on arrays: binary search, sorting, array comparison, array filling.

The Arrays class also provides the static asList() method, which can be used to create List views of arrays. Changes to the List view reflect in the array, and vice versa. The List is said to be *backed* by the array. The List size is equal to the array length and cannot be changed. The asList() method in the Arrays class and the toArray() method in the Collection interface provide the bidirectional bridge between arrays and collections.

```
static List asList(Object[] backingArray)
```

```
String[] jiveArray     = new String[] {"java", "jive", "java", "jive"};
Set   jiveSet          = new HashSet(Arrays.asList(jivearray));      // (1)
String[] uniqueJiveArray = (String[]) jiveSet.toArray(new String[0]); // (2)
```

At (1), the jiveArray is used to create a List, which, in turn, is used to create a Set. At (2) the argument to the toArray() method specifies the type of the array to be created from the set. The final array uniqueJiveArray does not contain duplicates.

Abstract Implementations

The concrete collection implementations in the java.util package are based on *abstract implementations* (see Figures 11.2 and 11.3). For example, the HashSet implementation is based on the AbstractSet implementation, which, in turn, extends the AbstractCollection implementation. These abstract classes already provide most of the machinery by implementing the relevant collection interfaces, and are excellent starting points for implementing customized collections.

Review Questions

11.14 Given that the objects denoted by the parameters override the `equals()` and the `hashCode()` methods appropriately, which return values are possible from the following method?

```
String func(Object x, Object y) {
    return (x == y) + " " + x.equals(y) + " " + (x.hashCode() == y.hashCode());
}
```

Select the two correct answers.

(a) "false false true"
(b) "false true false"
(c) "false true true"
(d) "true false false"
(e) "true false true"

11.15 Insert code into the `equalsImpl()` method in order to provide a correct implementation of the `equals()` method.

```
public class Pair {
    int a, b;
    public Pair(int a, int b) {
        this.a = a;
        this.b = b;
    }

    public boolean equals(Object o) {
        return (this == o) || (o instanceof Pair) && equalsImpl((Pair) o);
    }

    private boolean equalsImpl(Pair o) {
        // ... PROVIDE IMPLEMENTATION HERE ...
    }
}
```

Select the three correct answers.

(a) `return a == o.a || b == o.b;`
(b) `return false;`
(c) `return a >= o.a;`
(d) `return a == o.a;`
(e) `return a == o.a && b == o.b;`

11.16 Which collection implementation is thread-safe?

Select the one correct answer.

(a) ArrayList
(b) HashSet
(c) Vector
(d) TreeSet
(e) LinkedList

11.17   Which code provides a correct implementation of the hashCode() method in the following program?

```java
import java.util.*;
public class Measurement {
    int count;
    int accumulated;
    public Measurement() {}
    public void record(int v) {
        count++;
        accumulated += v;
    }
    public int average() {
        return accumulated/count;
    }
    public boolean equals(Object other) {
        if (this == other)
            return true;
        if (!(other instanceof Measurement))
            return false;
        Measurement o = (Measurement) other;
        if (count != 0 && o.count != 0)
            return average() == o.average();
        return count == o.count;
    }
    public int hashCode() {
        // ... PROVIDE IMPLEMENTATION HERE ...
    }
}
```

Select the two correct answers.

(a) return 31337;

(b) return accumulated / count;

(c) return (count << 16) ^ accumulated;

(d) return ~accumulated;

(e) return count == 0 ? 0 : average();

Chapter Summary

The following information was included in this chapter:

- an overview of the collections framework in the java.util package: core interfaces and their implementations.

- discussion of the functionality specified by the Collection interface and its role in the collections framework.

- discussion of sets, how their functionality is defined by the Set interface and implemented by HashSet and LinkedHashSet.

- discussion of lists, how their functionality is defined by the List interface and implemented by ArrayList, Vector, and LinkedList.

- discussion of maps, how their functionality is defined by the Map interface and implemented by HashMap, LinkedHashMap, and Hashtable.

- the role of the Comparator and Comparable interfaces for ordering of elements.

- discussion of sorted sets and sorted maps, how their functionality is defined by the SortedSet and SortedMap interfaces and implemented by TreeSet and TreeMap.

- customizing collections for synchronization and data immutability.

- an overview of utility methods found in the Collections and Arrays class.

 ## Programming Exercises

11.1   Write a method that takes a string and returns the number of unique characters in the string. It is expected that a string with the same character sequence may be passed several times to the method. Since the counting operation can be time consuming, the method should cache the results, so that when the method is given a string previously encountered, it will simply retrieve the stored result. Use collections and maps where appropriate.

11.2   Write a program which creates a concordance of characters occurring in a string (i.e., which characters occur where in a string). Read the string from the command line.

Running the program:
```
>java Concordance Hello World
{d=[9], o=[4, 6], r=[7], W=[5], H=[0], l=[2, 3, 8], e=[1]}
```

Taking the SCPJ2 1.4 Exam

•••

A.1 Preparing for the Programmer Exam

Sun Educational Services offers three types of certification exams for Java:

- Programmer exam
  Basically a multiple choice exam, testing the candidate's knowledge of the Java language and its usage.

- Developer exam
  Comprising a programming assignment and an essay exam testing comprehension of advanced Java features.

- Web Component Developer exam
  A multiple-choice and short-answer examination, testing the candidate's knowledge of Servlets, JSP pages, and web development.

- Technology Architect exam
  Basically a multiple-choice exam, dealing with the large-scale issues of deploying Java technology. This exam tests the candidate's knowledge regarding Java-related technologies and products, and also the planning and designing involved in Java projects.

The focus of this book is on the Sun Certified Programmer for the Java 2 Platform 1.4 (SCPJ2 1.4) exam, which is a prerequisite for taking the Sun Certified Developer for the Java 2 Platform exam.

The goal of the programmer exam is to test practical knowledge of the Java language. The exam tests for thorough understanding of both the syntax and the semantics of the Java programming language.

The exam covers a wide variety of topics, as defined in the objectives for the programmer exam (see Appendix B, p. 497). It covers everything from the basic syntax of the language to detailed knowledge of threading and the core APIs, such as the java.lang package and the collections framework.

The need for real-world experience for this exam cannot be stressed enough. It is next to impossible to pass the test without having some actual experience programming in Java. Simply reading straight through this book is not recommended. Readers should take time to try out what they have learned every step of the way. Readers are encouraged to gauge their newly acquired knowledge, using the review questions provided after every major topic.

Experimenting with the examples and working through the programming exercises in the book will serve to give the reader a much better chance of passing the test. The exam is considered to be hard, and requires a fair amount of studying on the part of the candidate.

When the reader feels ready for the exam, she should test her skills on the sample exam that is provided in the back of the book (Appendix F). This will give an indication of how well the reader is prepared for the exam, and which topics need further study. The structure of the book should make it easy for the reader to focus on single topics, if necessary.

Even seasoned Java programmers should invest some time in preparing for the exam. Simply having real-world experience is also not enough to pass the exam.

A.2   Registering for the Exam

The exam is administered through a company called *Prometric*. They provide computer-based testing services for a wide variety of clients. Prometric has more than 4,800 testing centers located in 121 countries around the world. The test is paid for through the purchase of vouchers. An exam voucher must be obtained before signing up for the test at a local testing center.

Obtaining an Exam Voucher

Exam vouchers are sold by Sun Educational Services. Some testing centers may be able to help in obtaining a voucher for the exam. If not, you can obtain one by calling Sun Educational Services. The main number for Sun Educational Services in the United States and Canada is (800) 422-8020.

Be sure to obtain the correct voucher for the programmer exam. The test number for the Sun Certified Programmer for the Java 2 Platform 1.4 is *CX-310-035*. Sun will need credit card information to arrange payment. The cost of the voucher vary, depending on the country you live in. For US residents it costs $150.

Sun will send the voucher as soon as the credit information has been verified. The voucher is sent by FedEx, and will normally arrive within one business day.

It is important to take good care of the voucher, as it is needed when signing up for the test at Prometric. Note that your voucher has an expiration date, usually of 6 to 12 months. Neither Sun nor Prometric will replace lost or expired vouchers, nor will they offer refunds for unused vouchers.

Signing up for the Test

After obtaining the exam voucher, Prometric can be called to sign up for the test by making an appointment at one of the local testing centers.

Contact Information

Both Sun and Prometric have offices and associates around the world that can provide information about the exam. They can be contacted to purchase a voucher or sign up for the test.

The best way to find contact information and local testing centers is to visit their Web sites at:

Sun Educational Services

`http://suned.sun.com/`

Prometric

`http://www.prometric.com/`

After taking the Exam

Those passing the exam will immediately receive a temporary certificate. Prometric will inform Sun Educational Services about the passing of the exam, and Sun will send a permanent certificate by mail, which should arrive within a few weeks.

A.3 How the Examination Is Conducted

The Testing Locations

When a candidate shows up at the local testing center at the appointed time, she will be escorted to her own little cubicle with a desktop computer. The test will be conducted in this cubicle, using a testing program on the computer. The program will ask questions, record answers, and tabulate scores.

Candidates will not be allowed to bring personal belongings or food with them to the cubicle. During the exam, candidates will be allowed to make notes on a single piece of paper, but they will not be allowed to take these notes with them after the exam. Quite often the exam area is fitted with security cameras.

Utilizing the Allotted Time

The exam consists of 61 questions, which must be answered within 2 hours. The questions vary in difficulty. Some are easy and some are hard. With about 2 minutes on average to answer each question, the candidate cannot afford to get stuck on the hard questions. If the answer does not become apparent within a reasonable time, it is advisable to move on to the next question. Time permitting, it is possible to return to the unanswered questions later.

An experienced Java programmer used to taking exams should be able to complete the exam well within the allotted time. Any remaining time is best used reviewing the answers.

The Exam Program

The computer program used to conduct the exam will select a set of questions at random, and present them through a graphical user interface. The interface is designed in such a way that candidates are able to move back and forth through the questions for reviewing purposes. Questions can be temporarily left un-answered, and the candidate can return to them later. Before the exam starts, the candidate is allowed a test run with the computer program. A demo test that has nothing to do with the Java exam is used. Its sole purpose is to allow the candidate to get acquainted with the program being used to conduct the exam.

Immediately after the completion of the exam, the program will present the candidate with the following information:

- An indication of whether the candidate passed or failed. A score of 52% (32 of 61) or more correct answers is needed to pass the exam.

- The total score. All the questions are weighted equally, and the score is calculated based on the percentage of correct answers. No credit is given for partially correct answers.

- Indications on how well the candidate did on each of the categories of the objectives. Candidates who fail the exam should pay close attention to this information. If the candidate is planning to retake the exam, it may give a good indication of which topics need closer attention.

However, the program will not divulge which questions were answered correctly.

A.4 The Questions

Types of Questions Asked

Most of the questions follow some common form that requires candidates to apply their knowledge in a special way.

- Analyzing program code.
  The question provides a source code snippet and asks a specific question pertaining to the snippet. Will running the program provide the expected result? What will be written to the standard output when the program is run? Will the code compile?

- Identifying true or false statements.
- Naming specific classes or members.

When analyzing program code, it is useful to try to apply the same rules as the compiler: examining the exact syntax used rather than making assumptions on what the code tries to accomplish.

The wording of the questions is precise, and expects the responses selected in multiple-choice questions to be precise. This often causes the test to be perceived as fastidious. Close attention should be paid to the wording of the responses in a multiple-choice question.

None of the questions are intentionally meant to be trick questions. Exam questions have been reviewed by both Java experts and language experts, to remove as much ambiguity from the wording of the questions as possible.

Since the program used in the exam will select and present the questions in a random fashion, there is no point in trying to guess the form of the questions. The order of the answers in multiple choice questions has been randomized and, thus, has no significance.

Types of Answers Expected

The majority of the questions are multiple choice. All of the appropriate and none of the inappropriate choices must be selected for the question as a whole to be considered correctly answered.

A rarer form of question expects the candidate to type in short answers.

There should be no problem identifying which form of answer each question requires. The wording of the questions will indicate this, and the software used will present the candidate with an input method corresponding to the form of answer expected.

For multiple-choice questions, the program will ask the candidate to select a specific number of answers from a list. Where a single correct answer is expected, radio buttons will allow the selection of only one of the answers. The most appropriate response should be selected.

In questions where all appropriate responses should be selected, checkboxes will allow the selection of each response individually. In this case, all choices should be considered on their own merit. They should not be weighed against each other. It can be helpful to think of each of the choices for the question as an individual true–false question.

Care should be exercised when answering a question requiring all appropriate responses to be selected. A common mistake is to select only one of the appropriate responses, as a result of assuming the question has only one correct answer.

For short-answer type-in questions, the program will present a text field in which the answer should be typed. As with all other answers, these fill-in answers will be judged by the computer. It is, therefore, a common concern that seemingly correct answers can be rejected because of minute differences from the correct answer that the program holds. These concerns are usually unfounded. The program allows the candidate a certain amount of flexibility, and will most often accept several variations of an answer. However, answers should be typed in with extra care. Attention should be paid to correct spelling and capitalization. Some questions describe the exact format of the answer expected.

Topics Covered by the Questions

Topics covered by the exam are basically derived from the set of objectives defined by Sun for the programmer exam. These objectives are included in Appendix B together with study notes that highlight important topics to study for the exam. All the major topics are covered extensively in the relevant chapters of the book.

The ultimate goal of the exam is to differentiate experienced Java programmers from the rest. Some of the questions are, therefore, aimed at topics that new Java programmers usually find difficult. Such topics include:

- casting and conversion
- polymorphism, overriding, and overloading
- exceptions and try-catch-finally blocks
- thread control
- nested classes

Knowledge obtained from studying other languages such as C++ should be used with care. Some of the questions often seem to lead astray C++ programmers who have not grasped the many differences between C++ and Java. Those with a C++ background should pay special attention to the following Java topics:

- use null, not NULL
- use true and false, not 1 and 0.
- signed and unsigned shifts
- widening conversions
- conditional and boolean logic operators
- labeled statements
- accessibility rules
- how polymorphism works

Some of the questions may require intimate knowledge of the core APIs. This book covers the most important classes and methods of the API, but it does not go as far as listing every member of every class. The Java API reference documentation for the Java 2 SDK should be consulted. It is essential that readers familiarize themselves with the relevant parts of API documentation. There are API references readily available from many sources.

A.5 Moving on to the Developer Exam

Those passing the programmer exam may want to go on to take the Sun Certified Developer for the Java 2 Platform exam. This exam tests the ability to put together real-world applications using Java. This book does not focus on the developer exam. The developer exam usually requires writing a working client/server application with an advanced graphical user interface. The exam comprises a programming assignment and five to ten essay questions regarding the assignment. Unlike the programmer exam, this exam will be graded by a person rather than by a program.

The objectives for the developer exam include the following topics:

- I/O streams
- GUI construction
- TCP/IP networking
- databases (JDBC)
- documenting and justifying a design

The programming assignment can be downloaded from the Web site of Sun Educational Services by those who have passed the programmer exam.

Submitting the completed programming assignment costs $250, and the essay exam will cost another $150. More information about the developer exam can be obtained by contacting Sun.

Objectives for the SCPJ2 1.4 Exam

The objectives for the Sun Certified Programmer for Java 2 Platform 1.4 exam (SCPJ2 1.4, code CX-310-035) are defined by Sun, and can be found at

http://suned.sun.com/US/certification/java/java_exam_
objectives.html#programmer1.4

The objectives (Copyright 2003, Sun Microsystems, Inc.) are organized in sections, and each section is *reproduced verbatim* in this appendix. For each section, we have provided study notes, which highlight related topics that are essential for the exam. Each section title provides a reference to the main chapter that covers the objectives in the section.

Section 1: Declarations and Access Control (Chapter 4)

- Write code that declares, constructs and initializes arrays of any base type using any of the permitted forms both for declaration and for initialization.

- Declare classes, nested classes, methods, instance variables, static variables and automatic (method local) variables making appropriate use of all permitted modifiers (such as public, final, static, abstract, etc.). State the significance of each of these modifiers both singly and in combination and state the effect of package relationships on declared items qualified by these modifiers.

- For a given class, determine if a default constructor will be created and if so state the prototype of that constructor.

- Identify legal return types for any method given the declarations of all related methods in this or parent classes.

Study Notes

Arrays are objects. They contain a fixed number of elements of a specific type. The index of the first element is 0. The index of the last element is one less than the length of the array. Note how arrays are declared and constructed. Array size is not specified in the declaration, but is given when the array object is created. Multidimensional arrays are implemented as arrays of arrays.

Modifiers affect classes, methods, and variables and each modifier has a specific significance. Accessibility modifiers specify where classes and methods can be accessed and used. Knowing which modifiers are applicable in a given context is important.

Constructors are not normal methods. They must have the same name as the class. Constructors do not declare a return type, not even void. The implicit default constructor is employed when no constructors are specified. Calls to other constructors from within a constructor must be done as the first statement in the constructor body, using this() or super().

Section 2: Flow Control, Assertions, and Exception Handling (Chapter 5)

- Write code using if and switch statements and identify legal argument types for these statements.
- Write code using all forms of loops including labeled and unlabeled, use of break and continue, and state the values taken by loop counter variables during and after loop execution.
- Write code that makes proper use of exceptions and exception handling clauses (try, catch, finally) and declares methods and overriding methods that throw exceptions.
- Recognize the effect of an exception arising at a specified point in a code fragment. Note: The exception may be a runtime exception, a checked exception, or an error (the code may include try, catch, or finally clauses in any legitimate combination).
- Write code that makes proper use of assertions, and distinguish appropriate from inappropriate uses of assertions.
- Identify correct statements about the assertion mechanism.

Study Notes

The if statement affects control flow based on a boolean expression. The switch statement affects control flow based on a non-long integral expression. The break statement exits the loop or switch statement, and the continue statement skips the rest of the current iteration in a loop. Transfer of control using labeled break and continue statements should be understood.

Exceptions are objects in Java. An exception is either checked or unchecked. Methods must explicitly declare any checked exceptions they throw but do not catch. Declaration of try, catch, and finally blocks must follow certain rules. There are three basic control flow scenarios that may occur in conjunction with exceptions. The control flow for each of these scenarios should be understood:

1. When no exception is generated.
2. When an exception is thrown within a try block, and a catch block handles the exception.

3. When an exception is thrown within a try block, and no catch block handles the exception.

The finally block is always executed.

The boolean expression of an assert statement will be evaluated if assertions are enabled during runtime, and an java.lang.AssertionError will be thrown if the result is false. An augmented form of the assert statement allows a value to be displayed as a detailed error message. AssertionError is a direct subclass of Error. The assertion mechanism should be used to write correct programs, and the exception facility should be used to make them robust.

Section 3: Garbage Collection (Chapter 8)

- State the behavior that is guaranteed by the garbage collection system.
- Write code that explicitly makes objects eligible for garbage collection.
- Recognize the point in a piece of source code at which an object becomes eligible for garbage collection.

Study Notes

There is no guarantee that any object will ever be garbage collected. An object becomes eligible for garbage collection when it has no references from running code. If a reference is reassigned, the object previously denoted by the reference now has one reference less, increasing this object's chances of becoming eligible for garbage collection. It is important to be able to identify where in the code an object will have no references during execution. Objects may override the finalize() method, which is called only once after the object becomes eligible, but before its memory is reclaimed.

Section 4: Language Fundamentals (Chapter 2)

- Identify correctly constructed package declarations, import statements, class declarations (of all forms including inner classes) interface declarations, method declarations (including the main method that is used to start execution of a class), variable declarations, and identifiers.
- Identify classes that correctly implement an interface where that interface is either java.lang.Runnable or a fully specified interface in the question.
- State the correspondence between index values in the argument array passed to a main method and command line arguments.
- Identify all Java programming language keywords. Note: There will not be any questions regarding esoteric distinctions between keywords and manifest constants.
- State the effect of using a variable or array element of any kind when no explicit assignment has been made to it.

- State the range of all primitive formats and data types and declare literal values for String and all primitive types using all permitted formats bases and representations.

Study Notes

The structure of a Java source file containing declarations of package and import statements, interfaces, and classes follows certain rules. Classes, interfaces, methods, and variables can be defined within several contexts, and the contexts influence the meaning of the declaration and the modifiers applicable. The modifiers used also influence the restrictions that apply for the implementation of methods. Certain rules of consistency must be observed when extending classes, and when extending or implementing interfaces. Variables can be shadowed by extending classes, methods can be overridden by extending classes. Methods are distinguished from each other at compile time, based on the method signature.

A method with the signature public static void main(String[] args) serves as the entry point for executing applications. The parameter in the main() method corresponds to the program arguments given on the command line.

It is important to know all the keywords in the Java language and to be able to identify valid identifiers.

Each primitive data type has a range of valid values and a default value. Depending on the context of the declaration, some variables are either initialized to a default value or remain uninitialized until first assigned a value. Code that tries to access uninitialized variables is illegal. Elements of array objects are always initialized. Various notations are used to specify literals.

Section 5: Operators and Assignments (Chapter 3)

- Determine the result of applying any operator (including assignment operators and instance of) to operands of any type class scope or accessibility or any combination of these.

- Determine the result of applying the boolean equals (Object) method to objects of any combination of the classes java.lang.String, java.lang.Boolean and java.lang.Object.

- In an expression involving the operators &, |, &&, || and variables of known values state which operands are evaluated and the value of the expression.

- Determine the effect upon objects and primitive values of passing variables into methods and performing assignments or other modifying operations in that method.

Study Notes

Operators require operands of certain types. The operands used with an operator influence which conversions can occur, and determine the type of the resulting expression. Some operators, such as +, can be applied to non-numeric values. Some operators are related, such as >> and >>>, | and ||, & and &&, but their behaviors are different.

There are several forms of conversions, and all except for casts, occur implicitly depending on the context. The key to casting and conversion is to know the rules for widening numeric promotion, narrowing conversion, and converting references up and down the inheritance hierarchy (upcasting and downcasting). The instanceof operator returns true if an object can be cast to the given reference type.

In addition to the == operator, objects have the equals() method that can be used to compare objects. The == operator and the default equals() method consider every object to be unique. Classes can provide implementations of the equals() method that are less discriminatory. Correct implementation of the equals() must be understood.

Some operators exhibit short-circuit behavior, which means that some operands may never be evaluated.

Parameters are passed by value. Methods get their own copy of the argument values. This holds for values of primitive data types, as well as for reference values denoting objects. Objects themselves are not passed as arguments.

Section 6: Overloading, Overriding, Runtime Type and Object Orientation (Chapter 6, Chapter 11)

- State the benefits of encapsulation in object oriented design and write code that implements tightly encapsulated classes and the relationships "is a" and "has a".

- Write code to invoke overridden or overloaded methods and parental or over-loaded constructors and describe the effect of invoking these methods.

- Write code to construct instances of any concrete class including normal top-level classes and nested classes.

Study Notes

Is-a relationships are implemented through inheritance; *has-a* relationships are implemented through aggregation. Subclass instances may take on the role of super-class instances, but not vice versa. Encapsulation in object-oriented design places the focus on an object's contract and safely hides its implementation from clients.

Pay attention to which casts are allowed between superclasses and subclasses at compile time, and the effect of casts at runtime. Polymorphism is the result of dynamic method binding of overridden methods at runtime, and the binding is based on the actual type of the object, not the type of the reference. It is illegal for overriding methods to contradict the declaration of the overridden methods. Overloaded methods are distinct methods not subject to dynamic method binding. The ability to overload method names is purely a result of methods being identified by the full signature, rather than just by the method name.

Special language constructs allow explicit access to variables and methods in super-classes and in enclosing contexts. Shadowed variables can be accessed, and over-riding methods may call the overridden versions of the methods.

Interface and class definitions can be nested. The exact nature of such definitions and the restrictions placed on the definitions depend on the declaration context. Instances of some nested classes are associated with an outer instance. It is important to understand the correlation between an instance of an inner class and the outer class, and what can be accessed from within an inner class and how. There are several ways of declaring nested classes, and this affects the correlation between an instance of an inner class and its outer class.

Section 7: Threads (Chapter 9)

- Write code to define, instantiate and start new threads using both java.lang.Thread and java.lang.Runnable.
- Recognize conditions that might prevent a thread from executing.
- Write code using synchronized wait, notify and notifyAll to protect against concurrent access problems and to communicate between threads.
- Define the interaction among threads and object locks when executing synchronized wait, notify or notifyAll.

Study Notes

Both java.lang.Thread and java.lang.Runnable can be used to create new threads. A thread can exist in one of several states. Various method calls and events may cause a thread to go from one state to another. Several conditions may prevent a thread from executing.

Most questions related to thread control concern using and implementing threads (through the Thread class or Runnable interface) and the use of the notify() and wait() methods. A good understanding of object locks and synchronized code is required. Note the difference between the notify() and notifyAll() methods.

Section 8: Fundamental Classes in the java.lang Package (Chapter 10)

- Write code using the following methods of the java.lang.Math class: abs, ceil, floor, max, min, random, round, sin, cos, tan, sqrt.
- Describe the significance of the immutability of String objects.
- Describe the significance of wrapper classes, including making appropriate selections in the wrapper classes to suit specified behavior requirements, stating the result of executing a fragment of code that includes an instance of one of the wrapper classes, and writing code using the following methods of the wrapper classes (e.g., Integer, Double, etc.):
  - doubleValue
  - floatValue
  - intValue
  - longValue
  - parseXxx

○ getXxx
○ toString
○ toHexString

Study Notes

The java.lang.Math class defines many useful mathematical functions, whose purpose should be understood. Argument type, result type, and the effect of applying each of these functions should be known.

Strings are immutable objects, that is, their contents cannot be changed. String manipulation operations in the String class return new String objects as the result of the operation. The indexing of characters used by string operations is important.

StringBuffer implements a mutable sequence of characters. Most string buffer operations manipulate the character sequence directly. There is no inheritance relationship between the classes String and StringBuffer, and objects of these classes cannot be compared directly.

Each primitive data type has a corresponding wrapper class that allows you to create immutable objects that represent primitive values. The methods toString() and *type*-Value() can be called on wrapper objects to convert their value to a string or primitive values, respectively. The static wrapper class methods parse*Type*() and valueOf() convert a string to a primitive value or wrapper object, respectively. The static method get*Type*() in the Integer and Long classes can be used to determine values of system properties by name. The static method toHexString() can be used to create a string representation of an int or a long in the hexadecimal notation.

Section 9: The Collections Framework (Chapter 11)

* Make appropriate selection of collection classes/interfaces to suit specified behavior requirements.

* Distinguish between correct and incorrect implementations of hashcode methods.

Study Notes

The collections framework consists of various interfaces, concrete implementations of collections, and utility classes. Familiarity with the methods defined by the interfaces is required. Some collection interfaces are better suited for certain types of information. Knowledge of which collection implementation is best suited for a particular situation is important.

The hashCode() method of two objects must return the same result if the state of the objects are equal according to the equals() method, and must consistently return the same result as long as the state remains the same. Correct implementation of the hash-Code() and its relation to the equals() method must be understood.

Objectives for the Java 2 Platform Upgrade Exam

The objectives for the Sun Certified Programmer for Java 2 Platform Upgrade Exam (code CX-310-036) are defined by Sun, and can be found at:

`http://suned.sun.com/US/certification/java/certification_details.html#upgrade`

This exam can be taken by individuals who have passed a previous version of the programmer exam. The exam consists of 33 multiple-choice questions, which must be answered in 75 minutes. Seventeen questions (51%) must be answered correctly in order to pass. In the United States, the price of the exam is USD 100.

The objectives (Copyright 2003, Sun Microsystems, Inc.) are organized in sections, and each section is *reproduced verbatim* in this appendix. The upgrade exam is a subset of the regular programmer exam. For each section, we have provided references to where the relevant material is covered in the book.

Section 1: Declarations and Access Control

- Declare classes, nested classes, methods, instance variables static variables, and automatic (method local) variables making appropriate use of all permitted modifiers (such as public, final, static, abstract, etc.). State the significance of each of these modifiers both singly and in combination and state the effect of package relationships on declared items qualified by these modifiers.

- Identify legal return types for any method given the declarations of all related methods in this or parent classes.

Relevant Sections

Read Sections 4.2 "Defining Classes" and 4.3 "Defining Methods," and all the sections from 4.5 "Scope Rules" till the end of the chapter. For inner classes, see Chapter 7. For method overriding, see Section 6.2.

Study Notes

Modifiers affect classes, methods, and variables and each modifier has a specific significance. Accessibility modifiers specify where classes and methods can be accessed and used. Knowing which modifiers are applicable in a given context is important.

Section 2: Flow Control, Assertions, and Exception Handling

- Write code using if and switch statements and identify legal argument types for these statements.

- Recognize the effect of an exception arising at a specified point in a code fragment. Note: The exception may be a runtime exception, a checked exception, or an error (the code may include try, catch, or finally clauses in any legitimate combination).

- Write code that makes proper use of assertions, and distinguish appropriate from inappropriate uses of assertions. Identify correct statements about the assertion mechanism.

Relevant Sections

Read Section 5.2 "Selection Statements" and all sections from 5.5 "Stack-based Execution and Exception Propagation" to the end of the chapter.

Study Notes

The if statement affects control flow based on a boolean expression. The switch statement affects control flow based on a non-long integral expression. The break statement exits the loop or switch statement.

There are three basic control flow scenarios that may occur in conjunction with exceptions. The control flow for each of these scenarios should be understood:

1. When no exception is generated.
2. When an exception is thrown within a try block, and a catch block handles the exception.
3. When an exception is thrown within a try block, and no catch block handles the exception.

The finally block is always executed.

The boolean expression of an assert statement will be evaluated if assertions are enabled during runtime, and an java.lang.AssertionError will be thrown if the result is false. An augmented form of the assert statement allows a value to be displayed as a detailed error message. AssertionError is a direct subclass of Error. The assertion mechanism should be used to write correct programs, and the exception facility should be used to make them robust.

Section 3: Garbage Collection

- Recognize the point in a piece of source code at which an object becomes eligible for garbage collection.

  ### Relevant Sections

  Read subsections "Reachable References" and "Facilitating Garbage Collection" in Section 8.1.

  ### Study Notes

  An object becomes eligible for garbage collection when it has no references from running code. If a reference is reassigned, the object previously denoted by the reference now has one less reference, increasing this object's chances of becoming eligible for garbage collection. It is important to be able to identify where in the code an object will have no references during execution.

Section 4: Language Fundamentals

- Identify classes that correctly implement an interface where that interface is either java.lang.Runnable or a fully specified interface in the question.
- State the effect of using a variable or array element of any kind when no explicit assignment has been made to it.

  ### Relevant Sections

  Read Sections 2.3 "Variable Declarations" and 2.4 "Initial Values for Variables." For interface implementation, see Section 6.4 "Interfaces." For implementation of java.lang.Runnable, see Section 9.3 "Thread Creation."

  ### Study Notes

  Interfaces can be defined within several contexts, and the contexts influence the meaning of the declaration and the modifiers applicable. The modifiers used also influence the restrictions that apply for the implementation of methods. Certain rules of consistency must be observed when extending or implementing interfaces. Methods are distinguished from each other at compile time, based on the method signature.

  Each primitive data type has a range of valid values and a default value. Depending on the context of the declaration, some variables are either initialized to a default value or remain uninitialized until first assigned a value. Code that tries to access uninitialized variables is illegal. Elements of array objects are always initialized.

Section 5: Operators and Assignments

- Determine the result of applying any operator (including assignment operators and instance of) to operands of any type class scope or accessibility or any combination of these.

- In an expression involving the operators &, |, &&, || and variables of known values state which operands are evaluated and the value of the expression.
- Determine the effect upon objects and primitive values of passing variables into methods and performing assignments or other modifying operations in that method.

Relevant Sections

Read Chapter 3. The subsection "Object Value Equality" in Section 3.10 is not covered by the objectives. See also subsection "Reference Casting and instanceof Operator" in Section 6.6.

Study Notes

Operators require operands of certain types. The operands used with an operator influence which conversions can occur, and determine the type of the resulting expression. Some operators, such as +, can be applied to non-numeric values. Some operators are related, such as >> and >>>, | and ||, & and &&, but their behaviors are different.

There are several forms of conversions, and all except for casts occur implicitly depending on the context. The key to casting and conversion is to know the rules for widening numeric promotion, narrowing conversion, and conversion of references up and down the inheritance hierarchy (upcasting and downcasting). The instanceof operator returns true if an object can be cast to the given reference type.

Some operators exhibit short-circuit behavior, which means that some operands may never be evaluated.

Parameters are passed by value. Methods get their own copy of the argument values. This holds for values of primitive data types, as well as for reference values denoting objects. Objects themselves are not passed as arguments.

Section 6: Overloading, Overriding, Runtime Type and Object Orientation

- Write code to invoke overridden or overloaded methods and parental or over-loaded constructors; and describe the effect of invoking these methods.
- Write code to construct instances of any concrete class including normal top-level classes and nested classes.

Relevant Sections

Read Sections 6.1 "Single Implementation Inheritance" through 6.3 "Chaining Constructors Using this() and super()." See also Sections 4.4 "Constructors," 7.3 "Non-static Member Classes," and 7.4 "Local Classes" for constructing instances of nested classes.

Study Notes

Pay attention to which casts are allowed between superclasses and subclasses at compile time, and the effect of casts at runtime. Polymorphism is the result of dynamic method binding of overridden methods at runtime, and the binding is based on the actual type of the object, not the type of the reference. It is illegal for overriding methods to contradict the declaration of the overridden methods. Overloaded methods are distinct methods not subject to dynamic method binding. The ability to overload method names is purely a result of methods being identified by the full signature, rather than just by the method name.

Special language constructs allow explicit access to variables and methods in superclasses and in enclosing contexts. Shadowed variables can be accessed, and overriding methods may call the overridden versions of the methods.

Interface and class definitions can be nested. The exact nature of such definitions and the restrictions placed on the definitions depend on the declaration context. Instances of some nested classes are associated with an outer instance. It is important to understand the correlation between an instance of an inner class and the outer class, and what can be accessed from within an inner class and how. There are several ways of declaring nested classes, and this affects the correlation between an instance of an inner class and its outer class.

Section 7: Threads

- Recognize conditions that might prevent a thread from executing. Write code using synchronized wait, notify and notifyAll to protect against concurrent access problems and to communicate between threads.

- Define the interaction among threads and object locks when executing synchronized wait, notify, or notifyAll.

Relevant Sections

Read Sections 9.4 "Synchronization" and 9.5 "Thread Transitions."

Study Notes

Various method calls and events may cause a thread to go from one state to another. Several conditions may prevent a thread from executing.

A good understanding of object locks and synchronized code is required. Note the difference between the `notify()` and `notifyAll()` methods.

Section 8: The Collections Framework

- Make appropriate selection of collection classes/interfaces to suit specified behavior requirements.

- Distinguish between correct and incorrect implementations of hashcode methods.

Relevant Sections

Read Chapter 11.

Study Notes

The collections framework consists of various interfaces, concrete implementations of collections, and utility classes. Familiarity with the methods defined by the interfaces is required. Some collection interfaces are better suited for certain types of information. Knowledge of which collection implementation is best suited for a particular situation is important.

The hashCode() method of two objects must return the same result if the state of the objects are equal according to the equals() method, and must consistently return the same result as long as the state remains the same. Correct implementation of the hash-Code() and its relation to the equals() method must be understood.

Annotated Answers
to Review Questions

●●

1 Basics of Java Programming

1.1 *(d)*

A method is an operation defining the behavior for a particular abstraction. Java implements abstractions, using classes that have properties and behavior. Behavior is dictated by the operations of the abstraction.

1.2 *(b)*

An object is an instance of a class. Objects are created from class definitions that implement abstractions. The objects that are created are concrete realizations of those abstractions.

1.3 *(b)*

The code marked with (2) is a constructor. A constructor in Java is declared like a method, except that the name is identical to the class name and it does not specify a return value.

1.4 *(b) and (f)*

Two objects and three reference variables are created by the code. Objects are typically created by using the new operator. Declaration of a reference variable creates a variable regardless of whether a reference value is assigned to it or not.

1.5 *(d)*

An instance member is a field or an instance method. These members belong to an instance of the class rather than the class as a whole. Members which are not explicitly declared static in a class definition are instance members.

1.6 *(c)*

An object can pass a message to another object by calling an instance method of the other object.

1.7   *(d) and (f)*

Given the declaration class B extends A {...} we can conclude that class B extends class A, class A is the superclass of class B, class B is a subclass of class A, and class B inherits from class A, which means that objects of class B will inherit the field value1 from class A.

1.8   *(d)*

The compiler supplied with the Java 2 SDK is named javac. It requires the names of the source files that should be compiled.

1.9   *(a)*

Java programs are executed by the Java Virtual Machine (JVM). In the Java 2 SDK, the command java is used to start the execution by the JVM. The java command requires the name of a class that has a valid main() method. The JVM starts the program execution by calling the main() method of the given class. The exact name of the class should be specified, and not the name of the class file, that is, the ".class" extension in the class file name should not be specified.

2 Language Fundamentals

2.1   *(c)*

52pickup is not a legal identifier. The first character of an identifier cannot be a digit.

2.2   *(e)*

In Java, the identifiers delete, thrown, exit, unsigned, and next are not keywords. Java has a goto keyword, but it is reserved and not currently used.

2.3   *(b)*

It is a completely valid comment. Comments do not nest. Everything from the start marker of a comment block (/*) until the first occurrence of the end marker of the comment block (*/) is ignored by the compiler.

2.4   *(a) and (d)*

String is a class, and "hello" and "t" denote String objects. Java only has the following primitive data types: boolean, byte, short, char, int, long, float, and double.

2.5   *(a), (c), and (e)*

Type (a) is a boolean data type, while types (c) and (e) are floating-point data types.

2.6   *(c)*

The bit representation of int is 32-bits wide and can hold values in the range -2^{31} through $2^{31}-1$.

2.7   *(a), (c), and (d)*

The \u*xxxx* notation can be used anywhere in the source to represent unicode characters.

2.8   *(c)*

Local variable a is declared but not initialized. The first line of code declares the local variables a and b. The second line of code initializes the local variable b. Local variable a remains uninitialized.

2.9   *(c)*

The local variable of type float will remain uninitialized. Fields receive a default value unless explicitly initialized. Local variables remain uninitialized unless explicitly initialized. The type of the variable does not affect whether a variable is initialized or not.

2.10   *(c)*

The class will fail to compile since the package declaration can never occur after an import statement. The package and import statements, if present, must always precede any class definitions. If a file contains both import statements and a package statement, then the package statement must occur before the import statements.

2.11   *true*

Although nonsensical, an empty file is a valid source file. A source file can contain an optional package declaration, any number of import statements, and any number of class and interface definitions.

2.12   *(d) and (f)*

The main() method must be declared public, static, and void and takes a single array of String objects as argument. The order of the static and public keywords is irrelevant. Also, declaring the method final is irrelevant in this respect.

2.13   *(a), (b), and (c)*

Neither main, string, nor args are reserved keywords, but they are legal identifiers. In the declaration public static void main(String[] args), the identifier main denotes the method that is the main entry point of a program. In all other contexts, the identifier main has no predefined meaning.

3 Operators and Assignments

3.1   *(a)*

A value of type char can be assigned to a variable of type int. An implicit widening conversion will convert the value to an int.

3.2   *(d)*

An assignment statement is an expression statement. The value of the expression statement is the value of the expression on the right hand side. Since the assignment operator is right associative, the statement a = b = c = 20 is evaluated as follows: (a = (b = (c = 20))). This results in the value 20 being assigned to variable c, then the same value being assigned to variable b and finally to variable a. The program will compile correctly and display 20 when run.

3.3   *(c)*

Strings are objects. The variables a, b, and c are references that can denote such objects. Assigning to a reference only changes the reference value. It does not create a copy of the source object or change the object denoted by the old reference value in the destination reference. In other words, assignment to references only affects which object the destination reference denotes. The reference value of the "cat" object is first assigned to variable a, then to variable b, and later to variable c. The program prints the string denoted by the variable c, which is "cat".

3.4   *(a), (d), and (e)*

A binary expression with any floating-point operand will be evaluated using floating-point arithmetic. Expressions such as 2/3, where both operands are integers, will use integer arithmetic and evaluate to an integer value.

3.5   *(b)*

The / operator has higher precedence than the + operator. This means that the expression is evaluated as ((1/2) + (3/2) + 0.1). The associativity of the binary operators is from left to right, giving (((1/2) + (3/2)) + 0.1). Integer division results in ((0 + 1) + 0.1) which evaluates to 1.1.

3.6   *(d)*

0x10 is a hexadecimal literal equivalent to the decimal value 16. 10 is a decimal literal. 010 is an octal literal equivalent to the decimal value 8. The println() method will print the sum of these values, which is 34, in decimal form.

3.7   *(b), (c), and (f)*

The unary + and - operators with right-to-left associativity are used in the valid expressions (b), (c), and (f). Expression (a) tries to use a nonexistent unary - operator with left-to-right associativity, expression (d) tries to use a decrement operator (--) on an expression that does not resolve to a variable, and expression (e) tries to use a nonexistent unary * operator.

3.8   *(b)*

The expression evaluates to –6. The whole expression is evaluated as ((((-(-1)) - ((3 * 10) / 5)) - 1) according to the precedence and associativity rules.

3.9   *(a), (b), (d), and (e)*

In (a) the conditions for implicit narrowing conversion are fulfilled: the source is a constant expression of type int, the destination type is of type short, the value of the source (12) is in the range of the destination type. The assignments in (b), (d), and (e) are valid, since the source type is narrower than the target type and an implicit widening conversion will be applied. The expression (c) is not valid. Values of type boolean cannot be converted to other types.

3.10   *(a), (c), and (d)*

The left associativity of the + operator makes the evaluation of (1 + 2 + "3") proceed as follows: (1 + 2) + "3" → 3 + "3" → "33". Evaluation of the expression ("1" + 2 + 3), however, will proceed as follows: ("1" + 2) + 3 → "12" + 3 → "123". (4 + 1.0f) evaluates as 4.0f + 1.0f → 5.0f and (10/9) performs integer division, resulting in the value 1. The operand 'a' in the expression ('a' + 1) will be promoted to int, and the resulting value will be of type int.

3.11   *(d)*

The expression ++k + k++ + + k is evaluated as ((++k) + (k++)) + (+k) → ((2) + (2) + (3)), resulting in the value 7.

3.12   *(d)*

The types char and int are both integral. A char value can be assigned to an int variable since the int type is wider than the char type and an implicit widening conversion will be done. An int type cannot be assigned to a char variable because the char type is narrower than the int type. The compiler will report an error about a possible loss of precision in the line labeled (4).

3.13   *(c)*

Variables of type byte can store values in the range –128 to 127. The expression on the right-hand side of the first assignment is the int literal 128. Had this literal been in the range of the byte type, an implicit narrowing conversion would have to be applied during assignment to convert it to a byte value. Since 128 is outside the valid range of type byte, the compiler will not compile the code.

3.14   *(a)*

First, the expression ++i is evaluated, resulting in the value 2, Now the variable i also has the value 2. The target of the assignment is now determined to be the element array[2]. Evaluation of the right-hand expression, --i, results in the value 1. The variable i now has the value 1. The value of the right-hand expression 1 is then assigned to the array element array[2], resulting in the array contents to become {4, 8, 1}. The program sums these values and prints 13.

3.15   *(a) and (c)*

The expression (4 <= 4) is true. The null literal can be compared, so (null != null) yields false.

3.16   *(c) and (e)*

The remainder operator is not limited to integral values, but can also be applied to floating-point operands. Identifiers in Java are case sensitive. Operators *, /, and % have the same level of precedence. Type short has the range -32768 to +32767 inclusive. (+15) is a legal expression using the unary + operator.

3.17   *(a), (c), and (e)*

The != and ∧ operators, when used on boolean operands, will return true if and only if one operand is true, and false otherwise. This means that d and e in the program will always be assigned the same value, given any combination of truth values in a and b. The program will, therefore, print true four times.

3.18   *(b)*

The element referenced by a[i] is determined based on the current value of i, which is zero, that is, the element a[0]. The expression i = 9 will evaluate to the value 9, which will be assigned to the variable i. The value 9 is also assigned to the array element a[0]. After the execution of the statement, the variable i will contain the value 9, and the array a will contain the values 9 and 6. The program will print 9 9 6 when run.

3.19   *(c) and (d)*

Unlike the & and | operators, the && and || operators short-circuit the evaluation of their operands if the result of the operation can be determined from the value of the first operand. The second operand of the || operator in the program is never evaluated because of short-circuiting. All the operands of the other operators are evaluated. Variable i ends up with a value of 3, which is the first digit printed, and j ends up with a value of 1, which is the second digit printed.

3.20   *(b) and (f)*

The method test() will print out its second argument if the results of performing a signed and an unsigned 1-bit right shift on its first argument differ. The only difference between these operations is that when performing a signed shift, the leftmost bit will retain its state, rather than being assigned the bit value 0. The operational difference will, therefore, only be apparent when applied on values where the value of the leftmost bit is 1. Of the values being passed to the method test(), only the result of the expression 1<<31 (i.e., 1000 ... 0000) and the value -1 (1111 ... 1111) have the left-most bit set.

3.21   *(b) and (g)*

Java has the operators >> and >>> to perform signed and unsigned right shifts. For left shifts there is no difference between shifting signed and unsigned values. Java, therefore, only has one left-shift operator, which is <<. <<< is not an operator in Java. Java has the boolean AND compound assignment operator &=, but &&= is not an operator in Java.

3.22   *(b), (c), (d), and (e)*

All the expressions will return the same result. All expressions will accommodate negative values, and x can be any value of type int. However, expression (a) will not assign the result back to the variable x.

3.23   *(a), (c), and (d)*

The logical complement operator (!) cannot be used as an integer bitwise operator, and the bitwise complement operator (~) cannot be used as a boolean logical operator.

3.24   *(b), (c), and (e)*

All the values of the expressions on the right-hand side of the assignments are implicitly promoted to type int. For expression (b) this works, since the target type is also int. The compound assignment operators in expressions (c) and (e) ensure that an implicit narrowing conversion makes the result fit back in the target variable. Expressions (a) and (d) are simply invalid, since the type of expression on the right-hand side of the assignment operator is not compatible with the type of the target variable on the left-hand side.

3.25   *(b)*

Evaluation of the actual parameter i++ yields 0, and increments i to 1 in the process. The value 0 is copied into the formal parameter i of the method addTwo() during method invocation. However, the formal parameter is local to the method, and changing its value does not affect the value in the actual parameter. The value of variable i in the main() method remains 1.

3.26   *(d)*

The variables a and b are local variables that contain primitive values. When these variables are passed as parameters to another method, the method receives copies of the primitive values in the variables. The original variables are unaffected by operations performed on the copies of the primitive values within the called method. The variable bArr contains a reference value that denotes an array object containing primitive values. When the variable is passed as a parameter to another method, the method receives a copy of the reference value. Using this reference value, the method can manipulate the object that the reference value denotes. This allows the elements in the array object referenced by bArr to be accessed and modified in the method inc2().

3.27   *(d)*

The length of the array passed to the main() method corresponds exactly to the number of command-line arguments given to the program. Unlike some other programming languages, the element at index 0 does not contain the name of the program. The first argument given is retrieved using args[0], and the last argument given is retrieved using args[args.length-1].

3.28   *(a) and (f)*

Values can only be assigned once to final variables. A final formal parameter is assigned the value of the actual parameter at method invocation. Within the method body, it is illegal to reassign or modify the value of a final parameter. This causes a++ and c = d to.fail. Whether the actual parameter is final does not constrain the client that invoked the method, since the actual parameter values are copied to the formal parameters.

4   Declarations and Access Control

4.1   *(d)*

In Java, arrays are objects. Each array object has a final field named length that stores the size of the array.

4.2   *(a)*

Java allows arrays of length zero. Such an array is passed as an argument to the main() method when a Java program is run without any program arguments.

4.3   *(c)*

The [] notation can be placed both before and after the variable name in an array declaration. Multidimensional arrays are created by constructing arrays that can contain references to other arrays. The expression new int[4][] will create an array of length 4, which can contain references to arrays of int values. The expression new int[4][4] will create the same array, but will in addition create four more arrays, each containing four int values. References to each of these arrays are stored in the first array. The expression int[][4] will not work, because the arrays for the dimensions must be created from left to right.

4.4   *(b) and (e)*

The size of the array cannot be specified as in (b) and (e). The size of the array is given implicitly by the initialization code. The size of the array is never specified in the declaration of an array reference. The size of an array is always associated with the array instance, not the array reference.

4.5   *(e)*

The array declaration is valid and will declare and initialize an array of length 20 containing int values. All the values of the array are initialized to their default value of 0. The for loop will print all the values in the array, that is, it will print 0 twenty times.

4.6   *(e)*

The program will type "no arguments" and "four arguments" when called with 0 and 3 arguments, respectively. When the program is called with no arguments, the args

array will be of length zero. The program will in this case type "no arguments".
When the program is called with three arguments, the args array will have length
3. Using the index 3 on the numbers array will retrieve the string "four", because the
start index is 0.

4.7   (d)

The program will print "0 false 0 null" when run. All the instance variables,
including the array element, will be initialized to their default values. When concatenated with a string, the values are converted to their string representation.
Notice that the null pointer is converted to the string "null" rather than throwing
a NullPointerException.

4.8   (b)

Only (b) is a valid method declaration. Methods must specify a return type or are
declared void. This makes (d) and (e) invalid. Methods must specify a list of zero
or more comma-separated parameters delimited by ( ). The keyword void is not a
valid type for a parameter. This makes (a) and (c) invalid.

4.9   (a), (b), and (e)

Non-static methods have an implicit this object reference. The this reference cannot be changed, as shown in (c). The this reference can be used in a non-static context to refer to both instance and static members. However, it cannot be used to
refer to local variables, as shown in (d).

4.10   (a) and (d)

The first and the third pairs of methods will compile correctly. The second pair of
methods will not compile correctly, since their method signatures do not differ. The
compiler has no way of differentiating between the two methods. Note that return
type and the names of the parameters are not a part of the method signatures. Both
methods in the first pair are named fly and, therefore, overload this method name.
The methods in pair three do not overload the method name glide, since only one
method has that name. The method named Glide is distinct from the method
named glide, as identifiers in Java are case sensitive.

4.11   (a)

A constructor cannot specify any return type, not even void. A constructor cannot
be final, static or abstract.

4.12   (b) and (e)

A constructor can be declared private, but this means that this constructor can only
be used within the class. Constructors need not initialize all the fields of the class.
A field will be assigned a default value if not explicitly initialized. A constructor is
non-static, and as such it can directly access both the static and non-static members
of the class.

4.13   (c)

A compilation error will occur at (3), since the class does not have a constructor accepting a single argument of type int. The declaration at (1) declares a method, not a constructor, since it is declared as void. The method happens to have the same name as the class, but that is irrelevant. The class has an implicit default constructor since the class contains no constructor declarations. This constructor is invoked to create a MyClass object at (2).

4.14   (c) and (d)

A class or interface name can be referred to by using either its fully qualified name or its simple name. Using the fully qualified name will always work, but in order to use the simple name it has to be imported. By importing net.basemaster.* all the type names from the package net.basemaster will be imported and can now be referred to using simple names. Importing net.* will not import the subpackage basemaster.

4.15   (c)

A class is uninstantiable if the class is declared abstract. The declaration of an abstract method cannot provide an implementation. The declaration of a non-abstract method must provide an implementation. If any method in a class is declared abstract, then the class must be declared abstract. Definition (d) is not valid since it omits the class keyword.

4.16   (e)

A class can be extended unless it is declared final. For classes, final means it cannot be extended, while for methods, final means it cannot be overridden in a subclass. A nested static class, (d), can be extended. A private member class, (f), can also be extended. The keyword native can only be used for methods, not for classes and fields.

4.17   (b) and (d)

Outside the package, member j is accessible to any class, whereas member k is only accessible to subclasses of MyClass.

Field i has package accessibility and is only accessible by classes inside the package. Field j has public accessibility and is accessible from anywhere. Field k has protected accessibility and is accessible from any class inside the package and from subclasses anywhere. Field l has private accessibility and is only accessible within its own class.

4.18   (c)

The default accessibility for members is more restrictive than protected accessibility, but less restrictive than private. Members with default accessibility are only accessible within the class itself and from classes in the same package. Protected members are in addition accessible from subclasses anywhere. Members with private accessibility are only accessible within the class itself.

4.19   (b)

A private member is only accessible by code from within the class of the member. If no accessibility modifier has been specified, a member has default accessibility, also known as package accessibility. The keyword default is not an accessibility modifier, and its only use is as a label in a switch statement. Members with package accessibility are only accessible from classes in the same package. Subclasses outside the package cannot access members with default accessibility.

4.20   (b) and (e)

You cannot specify accessibility of local variables. They are accessible only within the block in which they are declared.

Objects themselves do not have any accessibility, only references to objects do. If no accessibility modifier (public, protected, or private) is given in the member declaration of a class, the member is only accessible to classes in the same package. A class does not have access to members with default accessibility declared in a superclass, unless both classes are in the same package. Inheritance has no consequence with respect to accessing members with default accessibility in the same package. Local variables cannot be declared static or given an accessibility modifier.

4.21   (c)

The line void k() { i++; } can be re-inserted without introducing errors. Re-inserting line (1) will cause the compilation to fail, since MyOtherClass will try to override a final method. Re-inserting line (2) will fail, since MyOtherClass will no longer have a default constructor. The main() method needs to call the default constructor. Re-inserting line (3) will work without any problems, but re-inserting line (4) will fail, since the method will try to access a private member of the superclass.

4.22   (f)

An object reference is needed to access non-static members. Static methods do not have the implicit object reference this, and must always supply an explicit object reference when referring to non-static members. The static method main() refers legally to the non-static method func() using the reference variable ref. Static members are accessible both from static and non-static methods, using their simple names.

4.23   (c)

Local variables can have the same name as member variables. The local variables will simply shadow the member variables with the same names. Declaration (4) defines a static method that tries to access a variable named a, which is not locally declared. Since the method is static, this access will only be valid if variable a is declared static within the class. Therefore, declarations (1) and (4) cannot occur in the same class definition, while declarations (2) and (4) can.

4.24   *(b)*

The keyword this can only be used in non-static code, like in non-static methods. Only one occurrence of each static variable of a class is created. This occurrence is shared among all the objects of the class (or for that matter, by other clients). Local variables are only accessible within the local scope, regardless of whether the local scope is defined within a static context.

4.25   *(c)*

The variable k cannot be declared synchronized. Only methods and code blocks can be synchronized.

4.26   *(c)*

The declaration abstract int t; is not legal. Keywords static and final are valid modifiers for both field and method declarations. The modifiers abstract and native are only valid for methods.

4.27   *(a) and (c)*

Abstract classes can contain both final methods and non-abstract methods. Non-abstract classes cannot, however, contain abstract methods. Nor can abstract classes be final. Only methods can be declared native.

4.28   *(a)*

The transient keyword signifies that the fields should not be stored when objects are serialized. Constructors cannot be declared abstract. When an array object is created, as in (c), the elements in the array object are assigned the default value corresponding to the type of the elements. Whether the reference variable denoting the array object is a local or a member variable is irrelevant. Abstract methods from a superclass need not be implemented by a subclass. The subclass must then be declared abstract.

5 Control Flow, Exception Handling, and Assertions

5.1   *(d)*

The program will display the letter b when run. The second if statement is evaluated since the boolean expression of the first if statement is true. The else clause belongs to the second if statement. Since the boolean expression of the second if statement is false, the if block is skipped and the else clause is executed.

5.2   *(a), (b), and (e)*

The conditional expression of an if statement can have any subexpressions, including method calls, as long as the whole expression evaluates to a value of type boolean. The expression (a = b) does not compare the variables a and b, but assigns the value of b to the variable a. The result of the expression is the value being assigned. Since a and b are boolean variables, the value returned by the expression is also boolean. This allows the expression to be used as the condition for an if statement. An if statement must always have an if block, but the else clause is optional. The expression if (false) ; else ; is legal. In this case, both the if block and the else block are simply the empty statement.

5.3   (f)

There is nothing wrong with the code. The case and default labels do not have to be specified in any specific order. The use of the break statement is not mandatory, and without it the control flow will simply fall through the labels of the switch statement.

5.4   (a)

The type of the switch expression must be either byte, char, short, or int. This excludes (b) and (e). The type of the case labels must be assignable to the type of the switch expression. This excludes (c) and (d).

5.5   (e)

The loop body is executed twice and the program will print 3. The first time the loop is executed, the variable i changes from 1 to 2 and the variable b changes from false to true. Then the loop condition is evaluated. Since b is true, the loop body is executed again. This time the variable i changes from 2 to 3 and the variable b changes from true to false. The loop condition is now evaluated again. Since b is now false, the loop terminates and the current value of i is printed.

5.6   (b) and (e)

Both the first and the second number printed will be 10. Both the loop body and the increment expression will be executed exactly 10 times. Each execution of the loop body will be directly followed by an execution of the increment expression. Afterwards, the condition j<10 is evaluated to see whether the loop body should be executed again.

5.7   (c)

Only (c) contains a valid for loop. The initializer in a for statement can contain either declarations or a list of expression statements, but not both as attempted in (a). The loop condition must be of type boolean. (b) tries to use an assignment of an int value (notice the use of = rather than ==) as a loop condition and is, therefore, not valid. The loop condition in the for loop (d) tries to use the uninitialized variable i, and the for loop in (e) is simply syntactically invalid.

5.8   (f)

The code will compile without error, but will never terminate when run. All the sections in the for header are optional and can be omitted (but not the semicolons).

An omitted loop condition is interpreted as being true. Thus, a for loop with an omitted loop condition will never terminate, unless a break statement is encountered in the loop body. The program will enter an infinite loop at (4).

5.9   *(b), (d), and (e)*

The loop condition in a while statement is not optional. It is not possible to break out of the if statement in (c). Notice that if the if statement had been placed within a labeled block, a switch statement, or a loop, the usage of break would be valid.

5.10 *(a) and (d)*

"i=1, j=0" and "i=2, j=1" are part of the output. The variable i iterates through the values 0, 1, and 2 in the outer loop, while j toggles between the values 0 and 1 in the inner loop. If the values of i and j are equal, the printing of the values is skipped and the execution continues with the next iteration of the outer loop. The following can be deduced when the program is run: variables i and j are both 0 and the execution continues with the next iteration of the outer loop. "i=1, j=0" is printed and the next iteration of the inner loop starts. Variables i and j are both 1 and the execution continues with the next iteration of the outer loop. "i=2, j=0" is printed and the next iteration of the inner loop starts. "i=2, j=1" is printed, j is incremented, j < 2 fails, and the inner loop ends. Variable i is incremented, i < 3 fails, and the outer loop ends.

5.11 *(b)*

The code will fail to compile, since the conditional expression of the if statement is not of type boolean. The conditional expression of an if statement must be of type boolean. The variable i is of type int. There is no conversion between boolean and other primitive types.

5.12 *(d)*

Implementation (4) will correctly return the largest value. The if statement does not return any value and, therefore, cannot be used as in implementations (1) and (2). Implementation (3) is invalid since neither the switch expression nor the case label values can be of type boolean.

5.13 *(c)*

As it stands, the program will compile correctly and will print "3, 2" when run. If the break statement is replaced with a continue statement, the loop will perform all four iterations and will print "4, 3". If the break statement is replaced with a return statement, the whole method will end when i equals 2, before anything is printed. If the break statement is simply removed, leaving the empty statement (;), the loop will complete all four iterations and will print "4, 4".

5.14   *(a) and (c)*

The block construct {} is a compound statement. The compound statement can contain zero or more arbitrary statements. Thus, {{}} is a legal compound statement, containing one statement that is also a compound statement, containing no statement. The block { continue; } by itself is not valid, since the continue statement cannot be used outside the context of a loop. (c) is a valid example of breaking out of a labeled block. (d) is not valid for the same reasons (b) was not valid. The statement at (e) is not true, since the break statement can also be used to break out of labeled blocks, as illustrated by (c).

5.15   *(d)*

The program will only print 1, 4, and 5, in that order. The expression 5/k will throw an ArithmeticExecption, since k equals 0. Control is transferred to the first catch block, since it is the first block that can handle arithmetic exceptions. This exception handler simply prints 1. The exception has now been caught and normal execution can resume. Before leaving the try statement, the finally block is executed. This block prints 4. The last statement of the main() method prints 5.

5.16   *(b) and (e)*

If run with one argument, the program will print the given argument followed by "The end". The finally block will always be executed, no matter how control leaves the try block.

5.17   *(d)*

The program will compile without error, but will throw a NullPointerException when run. The throw statement can only throw Throwable objects. A NullPointerException will be thrown if the expression of the throw statement results in a null reference.

5.18   *(c) and (d)*

Normal execution will only resume if the exception is caught by the method. The uncaught exception will propagate up the runtime stack until some method handles it. An overriding method need only declare that it can throw a subset of the checked exceptions the overridden method can throw. The main() method can declare that it throws checked exceptions just like any other method. The finally block will always be executed, no matter how control leaves the try block.

5.19   *(b)*

The program will print 1 and 4, in that order. An InterruptedException is handled in the first catch block. Inside this block a new RuntimeException is thrown. This exception was not thrown inside the try block and will not be handled by the catch blocks, but will be sent to the caller of the main() method. Before this happens, the finally block is executed. The code printing 5 is never reached, since the runtime-Exception remains uncaught after the execution of the finally block.

5.20   (a)

The program will print 2 and throw an InterruptedException. An InterruptedException is thrown in the try block. There is no catch block to handle the exception, so it will be sent to the caller of the main() method, that is, to the default exception handler. Before this happens, the finally block is executed. The code printing 3 is never reached.

5.21   (b)

The only thing that is wrong with the code is the ordering of the catch and finally blocks. If present, the finally block must always appear last in a try-catch-finally construct.

5.22   (a)

Overriding methods can specify all, none, or a subset of the checked exceptions the overridden method declares in its throws clause. The InterruptedException is the only checked exception specified in the throws clause of the overridden method. The overriding method f() need not specify any checked exception from the throws clause of the overridden method.

5.23   (c)

The overriding f() method in MyClass is not permitted to throw the checked InterruptedException, since the f() method in class A does not throw this exception. To avoid compilation errors, either the overriding f() method must not throw an InterruptedException or the overridden f() method must declare that it can throw an InterruptedException.

5.24   (c) and (d)

Statements (c) and (d) will throw an AssertionError because the first expression is false. Statement (c) will report true as the error message, while (d) will report false as the error message.

5.25   (b) and (d)

-ea (enable assertions) is a valid runtime option, not -ae. -source 1.4 is a compile time option -dsa (disable system assertions) is a valid runtime option, not -dea.

5.26   (e)

The class of exceptions thrown by assertion statements is always AssertionError.

5.27   (c)

Assertions can be enabled or disabled at runtime, but the assert statements are always compiled into bytecode.

5.28   *(a) and (b)*

Statement (a) will cause the assert statement to throw an AssertionError since (-50 > -50) evaluates to false. Statement (b) will cause the expression 100/value to throw an ArithmeticException since an integer division by zero is attempted.

5.29   *(a) and (d)*

Option (a) enables assertions for all non-system classes, while (d) enables assertions for all classes in the package org and its subpackages. Options (b), (c), and (f) try to enable assertions in specifically named classes: Bottle, org.example, and org.example.ttp. Option (e) is not a valid runtime option.

5.30   *(c)*

The assert statement correctly asserts that 150 is greater than 100 and less than 200.

5.31   *(b) and (d)*

The AssertionError class, like all other error classes, is not a checked exception, and need not be declared in a throws clause. After an AssertionError is thrown, it is propagated exactly the same way as other exceptions, and can be caught by a try-catch construct.

5.32   *(d)*

The class Error is the direct superclass of AssertionError.

5.33   *(c) and (d)*

The command line enables assertions for all non-system classes, except for those in the com package or one of its subpackages. Assertions are not enabled for the system classes in (b) and (e).

6   Object-oriented Programming

6.1   *(a) and (b)*

The extends clause is used to specify that a class extends another class. A subclass can be declared abstract regardless of whether the superclass was declared abstract. Private, overridden, and hidden members from the superclass are not inherited by the subclass. A class cannot be declared both abstract and final, since an abstract class needs to be extended to be useful and a final class cannot be extended. The accessibility of the class is not limited by the accessibility of its members. A class with all the members declared private can still be declared public.

6.2   *(b) and (e)*

Inheritance defines an *is-a* relation. Aggregation defines a *has-a* relation. The Object class has a public method named equals, but it does not have any method named length. Since all classes are subclasses of the Object class, they all inherit the equals() method. Thus, all Java objects have a public method named equals. In Java, a class can only extend a single superclass, but there is no limit on how many classes can extend a superclass.

6.3 *(b) and (c)*

A subclass need not redefine all the methods defined in the superclass. It is possible for a subclass to define a method with the same name and parameters as a method defined by the superclass, but then the return type should also be the same. This is called method overriding. A subclass can define a field that can hide a field defined in a superclass. Two classes cannot be the superclass of each other.

6.4 *(a), (b), and (d)*

Bar is a legal subclass of Foo that overrides the method g(). The statement a.j = 5 is not legal, since the member j in class Bar cannot be accessed through a Foo reference. The statement b.i = 3 is not legal either, since the private member i cannot be accessed from outside of the class Foo.

6.5 *(a)*

A method can be overridden by defining a method with the same signature (i.e., name and parameter list) and return type as the method in a superclass. Only instance methods that are accessible by their simple name can be overridden. A private method, therefore, cannot be overridden in subclasses, but the subclasses are allowed to define a new method with exactly the same signature. A final method cannot be overridden. An overriding method cannot exhibit behavior that contradicts the declaration of the original method. An overriding method, therefore, cannot return a different type of value or declare that it throws more exceptions than the original method in the superclass.

6.6 *(g)*

It is not possible to invoke the doIt() method in A from an instance method in class C. The method in C needs to call a method in a superclass two levels up in the inheritance hierarchy. The super.super.doIt() strategy will not work, since super is a keyword and cannot be used as an ordinary reference, nor accessed like a field. If the member to be accessed had been a field, the solution would be to cast the this reference to the class of the field and use the resulting reference to access the field. Field access is determined by the declared type of the reference, whereas the instance method to execute is determined by the actual type of the object denoted by the reference.

6.7 *(e)*

The code will compile without errors. None of the calls to a max() method are ambiguous. When the program is run, the main() method will call the max() method in C with the parameters 13 and 29. This method will call the max() method in B with the parameters 23 and 39. The max() method in B will in turn call the max() method in A with the parameters 39 and 23. The max() method in A will return 39 to the max() method in B. The max() method in B will return 29 to the max() method in C. The max() method in C will return 29 to the main() method.

6.8   *(c)*

The simplest way to print the message in the class Message would be to use System. out.println(msg.text). The main() method creates an instance of MyClass, which results in the creation of a Message instance. The field msg denotes this Message object in MySuperclass and is inherited by the MyClass object. Thus, the message in the Message object can be accessed directly by msg.text in the print() method of MyClass.

6.9   *(e)*

The class MySuper does not have a default constructor. This means that constructors in subclasses must explicitly call the superclass constructor to provide the required parameters. The supplied constructor accomplishes this by calling super(num) in its first statement. Additional constructors can accomplish this either by calling the superclass constructor directly using the super() call, or by calling another constructor in the same class using the this() call, which in turn calls the superclass constructor. (a) and (b) are not valid since they do not call the superclass constructor explicitly. (d) fails since the super() call must always be the first statement in the constructor body. (f) fails since the super() and this() calls cannot be combined.

6.10   *(b)*

In a subclass without any declared constructors, the implicit default constructor will call super(). The use of the super() and this() statements are not mandatory as long as the superclass has a default constructor. If neither super() nor this() is declared as the first statement in the body of a constructor, then super() will implicitly be the first statement. A constructor body cannot have both a super() and a this() statement. Calling super() will not always work, since a superclass might not have a default constructor.

6.11   *(d)*

The program will print 12 followed by Test. When the main() method is executed, it will create a new instance of B by giving "Test" as argument. This results in a call to the constructor of class B that has one String parameter. The constructor does not explicitly call any superclass constructor, but instead the default constructor of the superclass A is called implicitly. The default constructor of class A calls the constructor in A that has two String parameters, giving it the arguments "1", "2". This constructor calls the constructor with one String parameter, passing the argument "12". This constructor prints the argument. Now the execution of all the constructors in A is completed, and execution continues in the constructor of B. This constructor now prints the original argument "Test" and returns to the main() method.

6.12   *(b) and (c)*

Interfaces do not have any implementations and only permit multiple interface inheritance. An interface can extend any number of other interfaces and can be extended by any number of interfaces. Fields in interfaces are always static and method prototypes in interfaces are never static.

6.13   *(a), (c), and (d)*

Fields in interfaces declare named constants, and are always public, static, and final. None of these modifiers are mandatory in a constant declaration. All named constants must be explicitly initialized in the declaration.

6.14   *(a) and (d)*

The keyword implements is used when a class inherits from an interface. The keyword extends is used when an interface inherits from another interface or a class inherits from another class.

6.15   *(e)*

The code will compile without errors. The class MyClass declares that it implements the interfaces Interface1 and Interface2. Since the class is declared abstract, it does not need to supply implementations for all the method prototypes defined in these interfaces. Any non-abstract subclasses of MyClass must provide the missing method implementations. The two interfaces share a common method prototype void g(). MyClass provides an implementation for this prototype that satisfies both Interface1 and Interface2. Both interfaces provide declarations of constants named VAL_B. This can lead to an ambiguity when referring to VAL_B by its simple name from MyClass. The ambiguity can be resloved by using fully qualified names: Interface1.VAL_B and Interface2.VAL_B. However, there are no problems with the code as it stands.

6.16   *(a) and (c)*

Declaration (b) fails since it contains an illegal forward reference to its own named constant. The field type is missing in declaration (d). Declaration (e) tries illegally to use the protected modifier, even though named constants always have public accessibility.

6.17   *(c)*

The program will throw a java.lang.ClassCastException in the assignment at (3) when run. The statement at (1) will compile since the assignment is done from a subclass reference to a superclass reference. The cast at (2) assures the compiler that arrA will refer to an object that can be referenced by arrB. This will work when run since arrA will refer to an object of type B[]. The cast at (3) will also assure the compiler that arrA will refer to an object that can be referenced by arrB. This will not work when run since arrA will refer to an object of type A[].

6.18   *(d)*

Line (4) will cause a compile-time error since it attempts to assign a reference value of a supertype object to a reference of a subtype. The type of the source reference value is MyClass and the type of the destination reference is MySubclass. Lines (1) and (2) will compile since the reference is assigned a reference value of the same type. Line (3) will also compile since the reference is assigned a reference value of a subtype.

6.19   *(e)*

Only the assignment I1 b = obj3 is valid. The assignment is allowed since C3 extends C1, which implements I1. Assignment obj2 = obj1 is not legal since C1 is not a subclass of C2. Assignments obj3 = obj1 and obj3 = obj2 are not legal since neither C1 nor C2 is a subclass of C3. Assignment I1 a = obj2 is not legal since C2 does not implement I1. Assignment I2 c = obj1 is not legal since C1 does not implement I2.

6.20   *(b)*

The statement would be legal at compile time, since the reference x might actually refer to an object of the type Sub. The cast tells the compiler to go ahead and allow the assignment. At runtime, the reference x may turn out to denote an object of the type Super instead. If this happens, the assignment will be aborted and a ClassCast-Exception will be thrown.

6.21   *(c)*

Only A a = d is legal. The reference value in d can be assigned to a since D implements A. The statements c = d and d = c are illegal since there is no subtype-supertype relationship between classes C and D. Even though a cast is provided, the statement d = (D) c is illegal. The object referred to by c cannot possibly be of type D, since D is not a subclass of C. The statement c = b is illegal since assigning a reference value of a reference of type B to a reference of type C requires a cast.

6.22   *(a), (b), and (c)*

The program will print A, B, and C when run. The object denoted by reference a is of type C. The object is also an instance of A and B, since C is a subclass of B and B is a subclass of A. The object is not an instance of D.

6.23   *(b)*

The expression (o instanceof B) will return true if the object referred to by o is of type B or a subtype of B. The expression (!(o instanceof C)) will return true unless the object referred to by o is of type C or a subtype of C. Thus, the expression (o instanceof B) && (!(o instanceof C)) will only return true if the object is of type B or a subtype of B that is not C or a subtype of C. Given objects of classes A, B, and C, this expression will only return true for objects of class B.

6.24 *(a)*

The program will print all of I, J, C, and D when run. The object referred to by reference x is of class D. Class D extends class C and class C implements interface I. This makes I, J, and C supertypes of class D. A reference of type D can be cast to any of its supertypes and is, therefore, an instanceof these types.

6.25 *(e)*

The program will print 2 when System.out.println(ref2.f()) is executed. The object referenced by ref2 is of class C, but the reference is of type B. Since B contains a method f(), the method call will be allowed at compile time. During execution it is determined that the object is of class C, and dynamic method lookup will cause the overridden method in C to be executed.

6.26 *(c)*

The program will print 1 when run. The f() methods in A and B are private and are not accessible by the subclasses. Because of this, the subclasses cannot overload or override these methods, but simply define new methods with the same signature. The object being called is of class C. The reference used to access the object is of type B. Since B contains a method g(), the method call will be allowed at compile time. During execution it is determined that the object is of class C, and dynamic method lookup will cause the overridden method g() in B to be called. This method calls a method named f(). It can be determined during compilation that this can only refer to the f() method in B, since the method is private and cannot be overridden. This method returns the value 1, which is printed.

6.27 *(c) and (d)*

The code as it stands will compile without error. The use of inheritance in this code is not justifiable since, conceptually, a planet *is-not-a* star. The code will fail if the name of the field starName is changed in the Star class since the subclass Planet tries to access it using the name starName. An instance of Planet is not an instance of HeavenlyBody. Neither Planet nor Star implements HeavenlyBody.

6.28 *(b)*

The code will compile without error. The use of aggregation in this code is justifiable. The code will not fail to compile if the name of the field starName is changed in the Star class, since the Planet class does not try to access the field by name, but instead uses the public method describe() in the Star class to do that. An instance of Planet is not an instance of HeavenlyBody since it neither implements HeavenlyBody nor extends a class that implements HeavenlyBody.

7 Nested Classes and Interfaces

7.1 *(e)*

The code will compile without error and will print 123 when run. An instance of the Outer outer will be created and the field secret will be initialized to 123. A call to the createInner() method will return a reference to a newly created Inner instance. This object is an instance of a non-static member class and is associated with the outer instance. This means that an object of a non-static member class has access to the members within the outer instance. Since the Inner class is nested in the class containing the field secret, this field is accessible to the Inner instance, even though the field secret is declared private.

7.2 *(b) and (e)*

A static member class is in many respects like a top-level class, and can contain non-static fields. Instances of non-static member classes are created in the context of an outer instance. The outer instance is inherently associated with the inner instance. Several inner class instances can be created and associated with the same outer instance. Static classes do not have any inherent outer instance. A static member interface, just like top-level interfaces, cannot contain non-static fields. Nested interfaces are always static.

7.3 *(e)*

The code will fail to compile, since the expression ((State) this).val in the method restore() of the class Memento is invalid. The correct way to access the field val in the class State, which is hidden by the field val in the class Memento, is to use the expression State.this.val. Other than that, there are no problems with the code.

7.4 *(d)*

The program will compile without error, and will print 1, 3, 4, in that order, when run. The expression B.this.val will access the value 1 stored in the field val of the (outer) B instance associated with the (inner) C object denoted by the reference obj. The expression C.this.val will access the value 3 stored in the field val of the C object denoted by the reference obj. The expression super.val will access the field val from A, the superclass of C.

7.5 *(c) and (d)*

The class Inner is a non-static member class of the Outer class, and its full name is Outer.Inner. The Inner class does not inherit from the Outer class. The method named doIt is, therefore, neither overridden nor overloaded. Within the scope of the Inner class, the doIt() method of the Outer class is hidden by the doIt() method of the Inner class.

7.6   *(e)*

Non-static member classes, unlike top-level classes, can have any accessibility modifier. Static member classes can only be declared in top-level or nested static member classes and interfaces. Only static member classes can be declared static. Declaring a class static only means that instances of the class are created without having an outer instance. This has no bearing on whether the members of the class can be static or not.

7.7   *(d) and (e)*

The methods labeled (1) and (3) will not compile, since the non-final parameter i is not accessible from within the inner class. The syntax of the anonymous class in the method labeled (2) is not correct, as the parameter list is missing.

7.8   *(a) and (d)*

No other static members, except final static fields, can be declared within a non-static member class. Members in outer instances are directly accessible using simple names (provided they are not hidden). Fields in nested static member classes need not be final. Anonymous classes cannot have constructors, since they have no names. Nested classes define distinct types from the enclosing class, and the instanceof operator does not take the type of the outer instance into consideration.

7.9   *(b)*

Classes can be declared as members of top-level classes. Such a class is a static member class if it is declared static, otherwise, it is a non-static member class. Top-level classes, local classes, and anonymous classes cannot be declared static.

8   Object Lifetime

8.1   *(e)*

An object is only eligible for garbage collection if all remaining references to the object are from other objects that are also eligible for garbage collection. Therefore, if an object obj2 is eligible for garbage collection and object obj1 contains a reference to it, then object obj1 must also be eligible for garbage collection. Java does not have a keyword delete. An object will not necessarily be garbage collected immediately after it becomes unreachable. However, the object will be eligible for garbage collection. Circular references do not prevent objects from being garbage collected, only reachable references do. An object is not eligible for garbage collection as long as the object can be accessed by any live thread. An object that has been eligible for garbage collection can be made non-eligible. This occurs if the finalize() method of the object creates a reachable reference to the object.

8.2　(b)

Before (1), the String object initially referenced by arg1 is denoted by both msg and arg1. After (1), the String object is only denoted by msg. At (2), reference msg is assigned a new reference value. This reference value denotes a new String object created by concatenating several other String objects. After (2), there are no references to the String object initially referenced by arg1. The String object is now eligible for garbage collection.

8.3　(b)

The Object class defines a protected finalize() method. All classes inherit from Object, thus, all objects have a finalize() method. Classes can override the finalize() method and, as with all overriding, the new method must not reduce the accessibility. The finalize() method of an eligible object is called by the garbage collector to allow the object to do any cleaning up, before the object is destroyed. When the garbage collector calls the finalize() method, it will ignore any exceptions thrown by the finalize() method. In all other cases, normal exception handling occurs when an exception is thrown during the execution of the finalize() method, that is, exceptions are not simply ignored. Calling the finalize() method does not in itself destroy the object. Chaining of the finalize() methods is not enforced by the compiler, and it is not mandatory to call the overridden finalize() method.

8.4　(d)

The finalize() method is like any other method, it can be called explicitly if it is accessible. However, the intended purpose of the method is to be called by the garbage collector in order to clean up before an object is destroyed. Overloading the finalize() method name is allowed, but only the method with the original signature will be called by the garbage collector. The finalize() method in Object is protected. This means that overriding methods must be declared either protected or public. The finalize() method in Object can throw any Throwable object. Overriding methods can limit the range of throwables to unchecked exceptions. Further overridden definitions of this method in subclasses will not be able to throw checked exceptions.

8.5　(b)

The finalize() method will never be called more than once on an object, even if the finalize() method resurrects the object. An object can be eligible for garbage collection even if there are references denoting the object, as long as the objects owning these references are also eligible for garbage collection. There is no guarantee that the garbage collector will destroy an eligible object before the program terminates. The order in which the objects are destroyed is not guaranteed. The finalize() method can make an object that has been eligible for garbage collection, accessible again by a live thread.

8.6   *(c), (e), and (f)*

Static initializer blocks (a) and (b) are not legal since the fields alive and STEP are non-static and final, respectively. (d) is syntactically not a legal static initializer block.

8.7   *(c)*

The program will compile without error and will print 50, 70, 0, 20, 0 when run. All fields are given default values unless they are explicitly initialized. Field i is assigned the value 50 in the static initializer block that is executed when the class is initialized. This assignment will override the explicit initialization of field i in its declaration statement. When the main() method is executed, the static field i is 50 and the static field l is 0. When an instance of the class is created using the new operator, the value of static field l (i.e., 0) is passed to the constructor. Before the body of the constructor is executed, the instance initializer block is executed, which assigns values 70 and 20 to fields j and l, respectively. When the body of the constructor is executed, the fields i, j, k, and l, and the parameter m, have the values 50, 70, 0, 20, and 0, respectively.

8.8   *(f)*

This class has a blank final boolean variable active. This variable must be initialized when an instance is constructed or else the code will not compile. The keyword static is used to signify that a block is a static initializer block. No keyword is used to signify that a block is an instance initializer block. (a) and (b) are not instance initializers blocks, and (c), (d), and (e) fail to initialize the blank final variable active.

8.9   *(c)*

The program will compile without error and will print 2, 3, and 1 when run. When the object is created and initialized, the instance initializer block is executed first, printing 2. Then the instance initializer expression is executed, printing 3. Finally, the constructor body is executed, printing 1. The forward reference in the instance initializer block is legal, as the use of the field m is on the left-hand side of the assignment.

8.10   *(e)*

The program will compile without error and will print 1, 3, and 2 when run. First, the static initializers are executed when the class is initialized, printing 1 and 3. When the object is created and initialized, the instance initializer block is executed, printing 2.

8.11   *(c) and (e)*

Line A will cause illegal redefinition of the field width. Line B uses an illegal forward reference to the fields width and height. The assignment in line C is legal. Line D is not a legal initializer since it is neither a declaration nor a block. Line E declares a local variable inside an initializer block.

9 Threads

9.1   *(c)*

Create a new Thread object and call the method start(). The call to the start() method will return immediately, and the thread will start executing the run() method asynchronously.

9.2   *(c)*

When extending the Thread class, the run() method should be overridden to provide the code executed by the thread. This is analogous to implementing the run() method of the Runnable interface.

9.3   *(b) and (e)*

The Thread class implements the Runnable interface and is not abstract. A program terminates when the last non-daemon thread ends. The Runnable interface has a method named run, but the interface does not dictate that implementations must define a method named start. Calling the run() method on a Runnable object does not necessarily create a new thread. Method run() is the method executed by a thread. Instances of the Thread class must be created to spawn new threads.

9.4   *(e)*

The program will compile without errors, and will simply terminate without any output when run. Two thread objects will be created, but they will never be started. The start() method must be called on the thread objects to make the threads execute the run() method asynchronously.

9.5   *(a) and (e)*

Because the exact behavior of the scheduler is undefined, the text A, B, and End can be printed in any order. The thread printing B is a daemon thread, which means that the program may terminate before the thread manages to print the letter.

9.6   *(a)*

No two threads can concurrently execute synchronized methods on the same object. This does not prevent one thread from executing a non-synchronized method while another thread executes a synchronized method on the same object. The synchronization mechanism in Java acts like recursive semaphores, which means that during the time a thread owns the lock, it may enter and re-enter any region of code associated with the lock.

9.7   *(b)*

One cannot be certain whether any of the letters i, j, and k will be printed during execution. For each invocation of the doit() method, each variable pair is incremented and their values are always equal when the method returns. The only way a letter could be printed would be if the method check() was executed between the time the first and the second variable were incremented. Since the check() method does not depend on owning any lock, it can be executed at any time, and the method doit() cannot protect the atomic nature of its operations by acquiring locks.

9.8 *(d)*

A thread dies when the execution of the run() method ends. The call to the start() method is asynchronous, that is, it returns immediately, and it enables the thread for running. Calling the sleep() or wait() methods will only block the thread temporarily.

9.9 *(b) and (d)*

The inner createThread() call is evaluated first, and will print 23 as the first number. The last number the main thread prints is 14. After the main thread ends, the thread created by the inner createdThread() completes its join() call and prints 22. After this thread ends, the thread created by the outer createThread() call completes its join() call and prints the number 12 before the program terminates.

9.10 *(e)*

The exact behavior of the scheduler is not defined. There is no guarantee that a call to the yield() method will grant other threads use of the CPU.

9.11 *(b)*

The notify() method is defined in the Object class.

9.12 *(a)*

The priority of a thread is set by calling the setPriority() method in the Thread class. No Thread constructor accepts a priority level as an argument.

9.13 *(a) and (c)*

A thread can hold multiple locks; for example, by nesting synchronized blocks. Invoking the wait() method on an object whose lock is held by the current thread will relinquish the lock for the duration of the call. The notify() method does not relinquish any locks.

9.14 *(c)*

An IllegalMonitorStateException will be thrown if the wait() method is called when the current thread does not hold the lock of the object.

9.15 *(a), (c), (d), and (e)*

The thread terminates once the run() method completes execution.

10 Fundamental Classes

10.1 *(b)*

The method hashCode() in the Object class returns a hash code value of type int.

10.2 *(e)*

All arrays are genuine objects and inherit all the methods defined in the Object class, including the clone() method. Neither the hashCode() method nor the equals() method is declared final in the Object() class, and it cannot be guaranteed that implementations of these methods will differentiate between all objects.

10.3 *(a)*

The clone() method of the Object class will throw a CloneNotSupportedException if the class of the object does not implement the Cloneable interface.

10.4 *(a), (c), and (d)*

The class java.lang.Void is considered a wrapper class, although it does not wrap any value. There is no class named java.lang.Int, but there is a wrapper class named java.lang.Integer. A class named java.lang.String also exists, but it is not a wrapper class since all strings in Java are objects.

10.5 *(c) and (d)*

The classes Character and Boolean are non-numeric wrapper classes and they do not extend the Number class. The classes Byte, Short, Integer, Long, Float, and Double are numeric wrapper classes that extend the Number class.

10.6 *(a), (b), and (d)*

All instances of wrapper classes are immutable.

10.7 *(b) and (c)*

All instances of wrapper classes except Void and Character have a constructor that accepts a string parameter. The class Object has only a default constructor.

10.8 *(e)*

While all numeric wrapper classes have the methods byteValue(), doubleValue(), floatValue(), intValue(), longValue(), and shortValue(), only the Boolean class has the booleanValue() method. Likewise, only the Character class has the charValue() method.

10.9 *(b) and (d)*

String is not a wrapper class. All wrapper classes except Boolean and Void have a compareTo() method. Only the numeric wrapper classes have an intValue() method. The Byte class, like all other numeric wrapper classes, extends the Number class.

10.10   *(b) and (d)*

The lines labeled (2) and (4) will print 11 exactly, since their expressions will return the int value 11. The expression `Math.ceil(v)` will return the double value 11.0, which will be printed as 11.0. The expression `Math.floor(v)` will return 10.0d.

10.11   *(a)*

The `Math` class does not have a method named tan2. However, it does have a method named atan2, which converts rectangular coordinates to polar coordinates.

10.12   *(a)*

The method `round(float)` will return a value of type int. A `round(double)` method also exists, which returns a value of type long.

10.13   *(c)*

The rounding function `ceil()` will return a value of type double. This is in contrast to the `round()` methods that will return values of integer types.

10.14   *(b)*

The value -0.5 is rounded up to 0 and the value 0.5 is rounded up to 1.

10.15   *(b), (c), and (d)*

The expression will evaluate to one of the numbers 0, 1, 2, or 3. Each number has an equal probability of being returned by the expression.

10.16   *(b) and (e)*

The operators - and & cannot be used in conjunction with a `String` object. The operators + and += perform concatenation on strings, and the dot operator accesses members of the `String` object.

10.17   *(d)*

The expression `str.substring(2, 5)` will extract the substring "kap". The method extracts the characters from index 2 to index 4, inclusive.

10.18   *(d)*

The program will print str3str1 when run. The `concat()` method will create and return a new `String` object, which is the concatenation of the current `String` object and the `String` object given as an argument. The expression statement `str1.concat(str2)` creates a new `String` object, but its reference value is not stored.

10.19   *(c)*

The `trim()` method of the `String` class returns a string where both the leading and the trailing white space of the original string have been removed.

10.20   *(a) and (c)*

The String class and all wrapper classes are declared final and, therefore, cannot be extended. The clone() method is declared protected in the Object class. String objects are immutable and, therefore, cannot be modified. The classes String and StringBuffer are unrelated.

10.21   *(a), (b), (c), and (e)*

The expressions ('c' + 'o' + 'o' + 'l') and ('o' + 'l') are of type int due to numeric promotion. Expression (d) is illegal since the String class has no constructor taking a single int parameter. Expression (a) is legal since string literals denote String objects and can be used just like any other object.

10.22   *(d)*

The constant expressions "ab" + "12" and "ab" + 12 will, at compile time, be evalutated to the string-valued constant "ab12". Both variables s and t are assigned a reference to the same interned String object containing "ab12". The variable u is assigned a new String object, created using the new operator.

10.23   *(a), (c), and (d)*

The String class does not have a constructor that takes a single int as a parameter.

10.24   *(e)*

The String class has no reverse() method.

10.25   *(d)*

The expression "abcdef".charAt(3) evaluates to the character 'd'. The charAt() method takes an int value as an argument and returns a char value. The expression ("abcdef").charAt(3) is legal. It also evaluates to the character 'd'. The index of the first character in a string is 0.

10.26   *(e)*

The expression "Hello there".toLowerCase().equals("hello there") will evaluate to true. The equals() method in the String class will only return true if the two strings have the same sequence of characters.

10.27   *(c)*

The variable middle is assigned the value 6. The variable nt is assigned the string "nt". The substring "nt" occurs three times in the string "Contentment!", starting at indexes 2, 5, and 9. The call s.lastIndexOf(nt, middle) returns the start index of the last occurrence of "nt", searching backwards from position 6.

10.28   *(b)*

The code will fail to compile since the expression (s == sb) is illegal. It compares references of two classes that are not related.

10.29   *(e)*

The program will compile without errors and will print have a when run. The contents of the string buffer are truncated down to 6 characters.

10.30   *(a), (b), and (d)*

The StringBuffer class does not have a constructor that takes an array of char as a parameter.

10.31   *(a)*

The StringBuffer class does not define a trim() method.

10.32   *(d)*

The program will construct an immutable String object containing "eenny" and a StringBuffer object containing " miny". The concat() method returns a reference value to a new immutable String object containing "eenny meeny", but the reference value is not stored. The append() method appends the string " mo" to the string buffer.

11 Collections and Maps

11.1   *(a), (d), and (e)*

Set, Collection and Map are core interfaces in the collections framework. LinkedList is a class that implements the List interface. There is no class or interface named Bag.

11.2   *(b) and (e)*

The java.util package provides map implementations named HashMap and TreeMap. It does not provide any implementations named HashList, ArraySet, and ArrayMap.

11.3   *(d)*

The List interface is implemented by collections that maintain sequences of possibly non-unique elements. Elements retain their ordering in the sequence. Collection classes implementing SortedSet only allow unique elements that are maintained in a sorted order.

11.4   *(a) and (c)*

Some operations on a collection may throw an UnsupportedOperationException. This exception type is unchecked, and the code is not required to explicitly handle unchecked exceptions. A List allows duplicate elements. An ArrayList implements a resizable array. The capacity of the array will be expanded automatically when needed. The List interface defines a get() method, but there is no method by that name in the Collection interface.

11.5   (d)

The program will compile without error, and will print all primes below 25 when run. All the collection implementations used in the program implement the Collection interface. The implementation instances are interchangeable when denoted by Collection references. None of the operations performed on the implementations will throw an UnsupportedOperationException. The program finds the primes below 25 by removing all values divisible by 2, 3, and 5 from the set of values from 2 through 25.

11.6   (a), (b), and (d)

The methods add(), retainAll(), and iterator() are defined in the Collection interface. The get() and indexOf() methods are defined in the List interface.

11.7   (b)

The remove() method removes the last element returned by either next() or previous(). The four next() calls return A, B, C, and D. D is subsequently removed. The two previous() calls return C and B. B is subsequently removed.

11.8   (b) and (d)

The methods add() and retainAll(), return the value true if the collection was modified during the operation. The contains() and containsAll() methods return a boolean value, but these membership operations never modify the current collection, and the return value indicates the result of the membership test. The clear() method does not have a return value.

11.9   (c) and (d)

The Map interface defines the methods remove() and values(). It does not define methods contains(), addAll(), and toArray(). Methods with these names are defined in the Collection interface, but Map does not inherit from Collection.

11.10   (b) and (d)

Although all the keys in a map must be unique, multiple identical values may exist. Since values are not unique, the values() method returns a Collection instance and not a Set instance. The collection objects returned by the keySet(), entrySet(), and values() methods are backed by the original Map object. This means that changes made in one are reflected in the other. Although implementations of SortedMap keep the entries sorted on the keys, this is not a requirement for classes that implement Map. For instance, the entries in a HashMap are not sorted.

11.11   (a)

[1, 3, 2] is printed. First, "1" and "2" are appended to an empty list. Next, "3" is inserted between "1" and "2", and then the list is duplicated. The original list is concatenated with the copy. The sequence of elements in the list is now "1", "3", "2", "1", "3", "2". Then a sublist view allowing access to elements from index 2 to index 5 (exclusive) is created (i.e., the subsequence "2", "1", "3"). The sublist is cleared, thus removing the elements. This is reflected in the original list and the sequence of elements is now "1", "3", "2".

11.12   (c) and (e)

The classes TreeSet and TreeMap implement the comparator() method. The comparator() method is defined in the SortedSet and SortedMap interfaces, and the TreeSet and TreeMap classes implement these interfaces.

11.13   (a) and (d)

The key of a Map.Entry cannot be changed since the key is used for locating the entry within the list. Although iterators obtained for the entry set of a map have a remove() method, the entries themselves do not. Map.Entry has a method named setValue, but its return type is Object.

11.14   (a) and (c)

(b) is eliminated since the hashCode() method cannot claim inequality if the equals() method claims equality. (d) and (e) are eliminated since the equal() method must be reflexive, and the hashCode() method must consistently return the same hash value during the execution.

11.15   (b), (d), and (e)

(a) and (c) fail to satisfy the properties of an equivalence relation. (a) is not transitive and (c) is not symmetric.

11.16   (c)

Of all the collection classes in the java.util package, only Vector and HashTable are thread-safe. The Collections class contains a static synchronized*CollectionType*() method that creates thread-safe instances based on collections, which are not.

11.17   (a) and (e)

(b) is not correct since it will throw an ArithmeticException when called on a newly created Measurement object. (c) and (d) are not correct since they may return unequal hash values for two objects that are equal according to the equals() method.

Solutions to Programming Exercises

•••

1 Basics of Java Programming

No programming exercises.

2 Language Fundamentals

2.1   The following program will compile and run without errors:

```java
package com.acme; // Correct ordering of package and import statements.

import java.util.*;

public class Exercise1 {
    int counter; // This is rather useless

    public static void main(String[] args) { // Correct main signature
        Exercise1 instance = new Exercise1();
        instance.go();
    }

    public void go() {
        int sum = 0;
        // We could just as well have written sum = 100
        // here and removed the if statement below.
        int i = 0;
        while (i<100) {
            if (i == 0) sum = 100;
            sum = sum + i;
            i++;
        }
        System.out.println(sum);
    }
}
```

2.2 The following program will compile and run without errors:

```java
// Filename: Temperature.java
/* Identifiers and keywords in Java are case-sensitive. Therefore, the
   case of the file name must match the class name, the keywords must
   all be written in lowercase. The name of the String class has a
   capital S. The main method must be static and take an array of
   String objects as an argument. */
public class Temperature {
    public static void main(String[] args) {  // Correct method signature
        double fahrenheit = 62.5;
        // /* identifies the start of a "starred" comment.
        // */ identifies the end.
        /* Convert */
        double celsius = f2c(fahrenheit);
        // '' delimits character literals, "" delimits string literals
        System.out.println(fahrenheit + "F = " + celsius + "C");
    }

    static double f2c(double fahr) {           // Note parameter type
        return (fahr - 32) * 5 / 9;
    }
}
```

3 Operators and Assignments

3.1 The following program will compile and run without errors:

```java
// Filename: Sunlight.java
public class Sunlight {
    public static void main(String[] args) {
        // Distance from sun (150 million kilometers)
        /* The max value for int is 2147483647, so using int here will
           work. */
        int kmFromSun = 150000000;

        // Again, using int for this value is OK.
        int lightSpeed = 299792458; // Meters per second

        // Convert distance to meters.
        /* The result of this equation will not fit in an int. Let's
           use a long instead. We need to ensure that the values that
           are multiplied really are multiplied using long
           data types, not multiplied as int data types and later
           converted to long. The L suffix on the 1000L integer
           literal ensures this. The value of kmFromSun will
           implicitly be converted from int to long to match the
           data type of the other factor. The conversion can be done
           implicitly by the compiler since the conversion represents
           a widening of the data type. */
        long mFromSun = kmFromSun * 1000L;
```

```
                    /* We know that the result value will fit in an int, but the
                       compiler does not. We use an explicit cast to convince the
                       compiler. The conversion must be specified explicitly, since
                       the conversion represents a narrowing of the data type. */
                    int seconds = (int) (mFromSun / lightSpeed);

                    System.out.print("Light will use ");
                    printTime(seconds);
                    System.out.println(" to travel from the sun to the earth.");
                }

                /* We leave this method alone. */
                public static void printTime(int sec) {
                    int min = sec / 60;
                    sec = sec - (min*60);
                    System.out.print(min + " minute(s) and " + sec + " second(s)");
                }
            }
```

3.2
```
        public class Binary {
            public static void main(String[] args) {
                System.out.println(makeBinaryString(42));
            }

            public static String makeBinaryString(int i) {
                /* This section could have been optimized using
                   StringBuffer, but is presented in this way for the
                   sake of simplicity. */
                String binary = "";
                do {
                    int lowBit = (i&1);
                    String newDigit = ((lowBit == 0) ? "0" : "1");
                    binary = newDigit + binary;
                    i >>>= 1;
                } while (i != 0);
                return binary;
            }
        }
```

3.3   The following program will operate as specified in the exercise. When given no
      arguments, the program will not print anything.

```
        public class ArgumentSkipper {
            public static void main(String[] args) {
                int count = args.length;

                // Iterate over the arguments skipping two places
                // forward between each step.
                for (int i=0; i < count; i+= 2) {
                    System.out.println(args[i]);
                }
            }
        }
```

4 Declarations and Access Control

4.1
```java
public class EditContext {

    private Object selected;

    public void setSelected(Object newSelected) {
        selected = newSelected;
    }

    public Object getSelected() {
        return selected;
    }
}
```

4.2
```java
public interface Tool {
    public void setContext(EditContext newContext);
    public boolean isActive();
}
```

4.3
```java
// Filename: Database.java

// Specify package
package com.megabankcorp.system;

// Allow usage of Account class simply by referring to the name Account.
import com.megabankcorp.records.Account;

// Class must be abstract since it has abstract methods.
public abstract class Database {
    // Abstract and available from anywhere.
    public abstract void deposit(Account acc, long amount);

    // Abstract and available from anywhere.
    public abstract void withdraw(Account acc, long amount);

    // Abstract and only available from package and subclasses.
    protected abstract long amount(Account acc);

    // Unmodifiable and only available from package.
    final void transfer(Account from, Account to, long amount) {
        withdraw(from, amount);
        deposit(to, amount);
    }
}
```

5 Control Flow, Exception Handling, and Assertions

5.1 Finding primes using for-loops.

```java
// Filename: ForPrimes.java
public class ForPrimes {
    final static int MAX = 100;
```

```java
    public static void main(String[] args) {
        numbers:
        for (int num = 1; num < MAX; num++) {
            int divLim = (int) Math.sqrt(num);

            for (int div = 2; div <= divLim; div++)
                if ((num % div) == 0) continue numbers;
            System.out.println(num);
        }
    }
}
```

Finding primes using while-loops.

```java
// Filename: WhilePrimes.java
public class WhilePrimes {
    final static int MAX = 100;

    public static void main(String[] args) {
        int num = 1;

        numbers:
        while (num < MAX) {
            int number = num++;

            int divLim = (int) Math.sqrt(number);
            int div = 2;
            while (div <= divLim)
                if ((number % div++) == 0) continue numbers;
            System.out.println(number);
        }
    }
}
```

5.2
```java
/** A PowerPlant with a reactor core. */
public class PowerPlant {
    /** Each power plant has a reactor core. This has package
        accessibility so that the Control class which is defined in
        the same package can access it. */
    Reactor core;

    /** Create and initialize the PowerPlant with a reactor core.  */
    PowerPlant() {
        core = new Reactor();
    }

    /** Sound the alarm to evacuate the power plant.  */
    public void soundEvacuateAlarm() {
        // ... implementation unspecified ...
    }

    /** Get the level of reactor output that is most desirable at
        this time. (Units are unspecified.)  */
    public int getOptimalThroughput() {
```

```
            // ... implementation unspecified ...
            return 0;
        }

        /** The main entry point of the program. Will set up a PowerPlant
            object and a Control object and let the Control object run the
            PowerPlant. */
        public static void main(String[] args) {
            PowerPlant plant = new PowerPlant();
            Control ctrl = new Control(plant);
            ctrl.runSystem();
        }
}

/** A reactor core that has a throughput that can be either decreased or
    increased. */
class Reactor {
    /** Get the current throughput of the reactor. (Units are
        unspecified.) */
    public int getThroughput() {
        // ... implementation unspecified ...
        return 0;
    }

    /** @returns true if the reactor status is critical, false otherwise. */
    public boolean isCritical() {
        // ... implementation unspecified ...
        return false;
    }

    /** Ask the reactor to increase throughput. */
    void increaseThroughput() throws ReactorCritical {
        // ... implementation unspecified ...
    }

    /** Ask the reactor to decrease throughput. */
    void decreaseThroughput() {
        // ... implementation unspecified ...
    }
}

/** This exception class should be used to report that the reactor is
    critical. */
class ReactorCritical extends Exception {}

/** A controller that will manage the power plant to make sure that the
    reactor runs with optimal throughput. */
class Control {
    PowerPlant thePlant;

    public Control(PowerPlant p) {
        thePlant = p;
    }

    /** Run the power plant by continuously monitoring the
        optimalThroughput and the actual throughput of the reactor. If
        the throughputs differ by more than 10 units, adjust reactor
        throughput. If the reactor goes critical, the evacuate alarm is
        sounded and the reactor is shut down.
```

```
    <p>The runSystem() method does handle the reactor core directly
    but calls methods needAdjustment(), adjustThroughput(), and shutdown
    instead.  */
public void runSystem() {
    try {
        while (true) { // infinite loop
            if (needAdjustment())
                adjustThroughput(thePlant.getOptimalThroughput());
        }
    } catch (ReactorCritical rc) {
        thePlant.soundEvacuateAlarm();
    } finally {
        shutdown();
    }
}

/** Reports whether the throughput of the reactor needs
    adjusting. This method should also monitor and report if the
    reactor goes critical.

    @returns true if the optimal and actual throughput values
    differ by more than 10 units.  */
public boolean needAdjustment() throws ReactorCritical {
/* We added the throws clause to the method declaration so that
   the method can throw a ReactorCritical exception if the reactor
   goes critical.  */
    if (thePlant.core.isCritical())
        throw new ReactorCritical();
    return (Math.abs(thePlant.getOptimalThroughput() -
                    thePlant.core.getThroughput())) > 10;
}

/** Adjust the throughput of the reactor by calling increaseThroughput()
    and decreaseThroughput() until the actual throughput is within 10
    units of the target throughput.  */
public void adjustThroughput(int target) throws ReactorCritical {
/* We added the throws clause to the method declaration so that
   the method can pass on ReactorCritical exceptions thrown by
   increaseThroughput(). We do this because the adjustThroughput
   does not want to handle the exception.  */
    while (needAdjustment()) {
        if (thePlant.getOptimalThroughput() >
                thePlant.core.getThroughput())
            thePlant.core.increaseThroughput();
        else
            thePlant.core.decreaseThroughput();
    }
}

/** Shut down the reactor by lowering the throughput to 0. */
public void shutdown() {
    while (thePlant.core.getThroughput() !=,0) {
        thePlant.core.decreaseThroughput();
    }
}
}
```

6   Object-oriented Programming

6.1
```java
// Filename: Exercise1.java
interface Function {
    public int evaluate(int arg);
}

class Half implements Function {
    public int evaluate(int arg) {
        return arg/2;
    }
}

public class Exercise1 {
    public static int[] applyFunctionToArray(int[] arrIn) {
        int length = arrIn.length;
        int[] arrOut = new int[length];

        Function func = new Half();

        for (int i=0; i< length; i++)
            arrOut[i] = func.evaluate(arrIn[i]);

        return arrOut;
    }
}
```

6.2
```java
// Filename: Exercise2.java
interface Function {
    public int evaluate(int arg);
}

class Half implements Function {
    public int evaluate(int arg) {
        return arg/2;
    }
}

class Print implements Function {
    public int evaluate(int arg) {
        System.out.println(arg);
        return arg;
    }
}

public class Exercise2 {
    public static void main(String[] args) {
        // Create array with values 1 .. 10
        int[] myArr = new int[10];
        for (int i=0; i<10;) myArr[i] = ++i;

        // Create a print function
        Function print = new Print();

        // Print array
        applyFunctionToArray(myArr, print);
```

```
                    // Half values
                    myArr = applyFunctionToArray(myArr, new Half());

                    // Print array again
                    applyFunctionToArray(myArr, print);
            }

            public static int[] applyFunctionToArray(int[] arrIn, Function func) {
                    int length = arrIn.length;
                    int[] arrOut = new int[length];

                    for (int i=0; i< length; i++)
                        arrOut[i] = func.evaluate(arrIn[i]);

                    return arrOut;
            }
    }
```

Output from the program:

```
    1
    2
    3
    4
    5
    6
    7
    8
    9
    10
    0
    1
    1
    2
    2
    3
    3
    4
    4
    5
```

7 Nested Classes and Interfaces

7.1
```
    // Filename: Exercise3.java
    interface Function {
        public int evaluate(int arg);
    }

    class Half implements Function {
        public int evaluate(int arg) {
            return arg/2;
        }
    }
```

```
class Print implements Function {
    public int evaluate(int arg) {
        System.out.println(arg);
        return arg;
    }
}

public class Exercise3 {
    /* Inner class that applies the function, prints the value, and
       returns the result. */
    static class PrintFunc extends Print {
        PrintFunc(Function f) {
            func = f:
        }

        Function func;

        public int evaluate(int arg) {
            return super.evaluate(func.evaluate(arg));
        }
    }

    // Inner class that just returns the argument unchanged.
    /* Use this when you want a PrintFunc object to print
       the argument as-is. */
    static class NoOpFunc implements Function {
        public int evaluate(int arg) {
            return arg;
        }
    }

    public static void main(String[] args) {
        // Create array with values 1 .. 10
        int[] myArr = new int[10];
        for (int i=0; i<10;) myArr[i] = ++i;

        // Print array without modification
        applyFunctionToArray(myArr, new PrintFunc(new NoOpFunc()));

        // Print halved values
        applyFunctionToArray(myArr, new PrintFunc(new Half()));
    }

    public static int[] applyFunctionToArray(int[] arrIn, Function func) {
        int length = arrIn.length;
        int[] arrOut = new int[length];

        for (int i=0; i< length; i++)
            arrOut[i] = func.evaluate(arrIn[i]);

        return arrOut;
    }
}
```

The output when run is the same as in Exercise 6.2.

8 Object Lifetime

No programming exercises.

9 Threads

9.1
```java
// Filename: Counter.java
/*
    Notice that the result of running this program
    may not be what you expect. Since both threads are
    working on full throttle it is possible that only one
    of the threads is granted CPU time.
*/
public class Counter implements Runnable {
    public static void main(String[] args) {
        Storage store = new Storage();
        new Counter(store);
        new Printer(store);
    }

    Storage storage;
    Counter(Storage target) {
        storage = target;
        new Thread(this).start();
    }

    public void run() {
        int i=0;
        while (true) {
            storage.setValue(i);
            i++;
        }
    }
}

class Printer implements Runnable {
    Storage storage;
    Printer(Storage source) {
        storage = source;
        new Thread(this).start();
    }

    public void run() {
        while (true) {
            System.out.println(storage.getValue());
        }
    }
}

class Storage {
    int value;
    void setValue(int i) { value = i; }
    int getValue() { return value; }
}
```

9.2

```
// Filename: Counter.java
/* Only the Storage class has been altered. */

/* No changes to this class */
public class Counter implements Runnable {
    public static void main(String[] args) {
        Storage store = new Storage();
        new Counter(store);
        new Printer(store);
    }

    Storage storage;
    Counter(Storage s) {
        storage = s;
        new Thread(this).start();
    }

    public void run() {
        int i=0;
        while (true) {
            storage.setValue(i);
            i++;
        }
    }
}

/* No changes to this class. */
class Printer implements Runnable {
    Storage storage;
    Printer(Storage s) {
        storage = s;
        new Thread(this).start();
    }

    public void run() {
        while (true) {
            System.out.println(storage.getValue());
        }
    }
}

/* This class now ensures that getting and setting are done
   in an alternating fashion.
 */
class Storage {
    int value;
    boolean isUnread = false;

    synchronized void setValue(int i) {
        ensureUnread(false);
        value = i;
        setUnread(true);
    }

    synchronized int getValue() {
        ensureUnread(true);
        setUnread(false);
        return value;
    }
```

```
                private void ensureUnread(boolean shouldHaveUnread) {
                    while (shouldHaveUnread != isUnread)
                        try { wait(); }
                        catch (InterruptedException ie) {}
                }

                private void setUnread(boolean b) {
                    isUnread = b;
                    notify();
                }
            }
```

10 Fundamental Classes

10.1
```
        /**
         * Aggregate pairs of arbitrary objects.
         */
        public final class Pair {
            private Object first, second;

            /** Construct a Pair object. */
            public Pair(Object one, Object two) {
                first = one;
                second = two;
            }

            /** Provides access to the first aggregated object. */
            public Object getFirst() { return first; }

            /** Provides access to the second aggregated object. */
            public Object getSecond() { return second; }

            /** @return true if the pair of objects are identical. */
            public boolean equals(Object other) {
                if (! (other instanceof Pair)) return false;
                Pair otherPair = (Pair) other;
                return first.equals(otherPair.getFirst()) &&
                        second.equals(otherPair.getSecond());
            }

            /** @return a hash code for the aggregate pair. */
            public int hashCode() {
                // XORing the hash codes to create a hash code for the pair.
                return first.hashCode() ^ second.hashCode();
            }

            /** @return the textual representation of aggregated objects. */
            public String toString() {
                return "[" + first + "," + second + "]";
            }
        }
```

```
10.2      public class Palindrome {
              public static void main(String[] args) {
                  if (args.length != 1) {
                      System.out.println("Usage: java Palindrome <word>");
                      return;
                  }
                  String word = args[0];
                  StringBuffer reverseWord = new StringBuffer(word);
                  reverseWord.reverse();
                  boolean isPalindrome = word.equals(reverseWord.toString());

                  System.out.println("The word " + word + " is " +
                                      (isPalindrome ? "" : "not ") +
                                      "a palindrome");
              }
          }
```

11 Collections and Maps

```
11.1      import java.util.*;

          public class UniqueCharacterCounter {

              /**
               * A cache, mapping strings to count results. The count values are
               * stored as Integer objects within the map.
               */
              static Map globalCache = new HashMap();

              public static int countUniqueCharacters(String aString) {
                  Object cachedResult = globalCache.get(aString);
                  if (cachedResult != null)
                      return ((Integer) cachedResult).intValue();

                  // Result was not in the cache, calculate it.
                  int length = aString.length();
                  Set occurred = new TreeSet();
                  Set duplicates = new TreeSet();

                  // Identify occurrences and duplicates for each character in string:
                  for (int i=0; i<length;i++) {
                      Character character = new Character(aString.charAt(i));
                      if (duplicates.contains(character)) continue;
                      boolean newOccurrence = occurred.add(character);
                      if (!newOccurrence) duplicates.add(character);
                  }

                  // Remove duplicates from occurrence count to obtain result:
                  occurred.removeAll(duplicates);
                  int result = occurred.size();

                  // Put result in cache before returning:
                  globalCache.put(aString, new Integer(result));
                  return result;
              }
```

```java
        /**
         * A simple main method for the purpose of demonstrating the
         * effect of the <code>countUniqueCharacters()</code>
         * method. Prints the result of applying the operation on each
         * command line argument.
         */
        public static void main(String[] args) {
            int nArgs = args.length;
            for (int i=0; i<nArgs; i++) {
                String argument = args[i];
                int result = countUniqueCharacters(argument);
                System.out.println(argument + ": " + result);
            }
        }
    }
```

11.2
```java
        import java.util.*;

        public class Concordance {

            /** Map for the concordance. */
            public Map index = new HashMap();

            /** Add each character and its index to the concordance */
            public Concordance(String input) {
                for (int i=0; i<input.length(); ++i) {
                    addEntry(input.charAt(i), i);
                }
            }

            /** Update the list of indices for a given character */
            void addEntry(char c, int pos) {
                Character key = new Character(c);
                List hits = (List) index.get(key);
                if (hits == null) {
                    hits = new ArrayList();
                    index.put(key, hits);
                }
                hits.add(new Integer(pos));
            }

            public static void main(String[] args) {
                StringBuffer input = new StringBuffer();
                for (int i=0; i<args.length; ++i)
                    input.append(args[i]);
                Concordance conc = new Concordance(input.toString());
                System.out.println(conc.index);
            }
        };
```

Mock Exam

• •

This is a mock exam for the Sun Certified Programmer for the Java 2 Platform (SCPJ2 1.4). It comprises brand new questions, which are similar to the questions that can be expected on the real exam. Working through this exam will give the reader a good indication of how well she is prepared for the real exam, and whether any topics need further study.

Q1   Given the following class, which statements can be inserted at position 1 without causing a compilation error?

```
public class Q6db8 {
    int a;
    int b = 0;
    static int c;

    public void m() {
        int d;
        int e = 0;

        // Position 1
    }
}
```

Select the four correct answers.

(a) a++;
(b) b++;
(c) c++;
(d) d++;
(e) e++;

- -

Q2   Which statements are true about the effect of the >> and >>> operators?

Select the three correct answers.

(a) For non-negative values of the left operand, the >> and >>> operators will have the same effect.
(b) The result of (-1 >> 1) is 0.

(c) The result of (-1 >>> 1) is -1.

(d) The value returned by >>> will never be negative if the left operand is non-negative.

(e) When using the >> operator, the left-most bit of the resulting value will always have the same bit value as the left-most bit of the left operand.

Q3 What is wrong with the following code?

```
class MyException extends Exception {}

public class Qb4ab {
    public void foo() {
        try {
            bar();
        } finally {
            baz();
        } catch (MyException e) {}
    }

    public void bar() throws MyException {
        throw new MyException();
    }

    public void baz() throws RuntimeException {
        throw new RuntimeException();
    }
}
```

Select the one correct answer.

(a) Since the method foo() does not catch the exception generated by the method baz(), it must declare the RuntimeException in a throws clause.

(b) A try block cannot be followed by both a catch and a finally block.

(c) An empty catch block is not allowed.

(d) A catch block cannot follow a finally block.

(e) A finally block must always follow one or more catch blocks.

Q4 What will be written to the standard output when the following program is run?

```
public class Qd803 {
    public static void main(String[] args) {
        String word = "restructure";
        System.out.println(word.substring(2, 3));
    }
}
```

Select the one correct answer.

(a) est

(b) es

(c) str

(d) st

(e) s

Q5 Given that a static method doIt() in the class Work represents work to be done, which block of code will succeed in starting a new thread that will do the work?

Select the one correct answer.

(a)
```
Runnable r = new Runnable() {
    public void run() {
        Work.doIt();
    }
};
Thread t = new Thread(r);
t.start();
```
(b)
```
Thread t = new Thread() {
    public void start() {
        Work.doIt();
    }
};
t.start();
```
(c)
```
Runnable r = new Runnable() {
    public void run() {
        Work.doIt();
    }
};
r.start();
```
(d)
```
Thread t = new Thread(new Work());
t.start();
```
(e)
```
Runnable t = new Runnable() {
    public void run() {
        Work.doIt();
    }
};
t.run();
```

Q6 What will be printed when the following program is run?

```
public class Q8929 {
    public static void main(String[] args) {
        for (int i=12; i>0; i-=3)
            System.out.print(i);
        System.out.println("");
    }
}
```

Select the one correct answer.

(a) 12
(b) 129630
(c) 12963
(d) 36912
(e) None of the above.

Q7   What will be the result of attempting to compile and run the following code?

```
public class Q275d {
    static int a;
    int b;

    public Q275d() {
        int c;
        c = a;
        a++;
        b += c;
    }

    public static void main(String[] args) {
        new Q275d();
    }
}
```

Select the one correct answer.

(a) The code will fail to compile since the constructor is trying to access static members.

(b) The code will fail to compile since the constructor is trying to use static field a before it has been initialized.

(c) The code will fail to compile since the constructor is trying to use field b before it has been initialized.

(d) The code will fail to compile since the constructor is trying to use local variable c before it has been initialized.

(e) The code will compile and run without any problems.

Q8   What will be written to the standard output when the following program is run?

```
public class Q63e3 {
    public static void main(String[] args) {
        System.out.println(9 ^ 2);
    }
}
```

Select the one correct answer.

(a) 81

(b) 7

(c) 11

(d) 0

(e) false

Q9   Which statements is true about the compilation and execution of the following program with assertions enabled?

```
public class Qf1e3 {
    String s1;
    String s2 = "hello";
    String s3;
```

```
Qf1e3() {
    s1 = "hello";
}

public static void main(String[] args) {
    (new Qf1e3()).f();
}

{
    s3 = "hello";
}

void f() {
    String s4 = "hello";
    String s5 = new String("hello");
    assert(s1.equals(s2)); // (1)
    assert(s2.equals(s3)); // (2)
    assert(s3 == s4);      // (3)
    assert(s4 == s5);      // (4)
}
}
```

Select the one correct answer.

(a) The compilation will fail.
(b) The assertion on the line marked (1) will fail.
(c) The assertion on the line marked (2) will fail.
(d) The assertion on the line marked (3) will fail.
(e) The assertion on the line marked (4) will fail.
(f) The program will run without any errors.

Q10 Which declarations of the main() method are valid in order to start the execution of an application?

Select the two correct answers.

(a) `public void main(String args[])`
(b) `public void static main(String args[])`
(c) `public static main(String[] argv)`
(d) `final public static void main(String [] array)`
(e) `public static void main(String args[])`

Q11 Under which circumstance will a thread stop?

Select the one correct answer.

(a) The run() method that the thread is executing ends.
(b) The call to the start() method of the Thread object returns.
(c) The suspend() method is called on the Thread object.
(d) The wait() method is called on the Thread object.

Q12 When creating a class that associates a set of keys with a set of values, which of these interfaces is most applicable?

Select the one correct answer.

(a) Collection
(b) Set
(c) SortedSet
(d) Map

Q13 What is the result of running the following code with assertions enabled?

```
public class Q1eec {
    static void test(int i) {
        int j = i/2;
        int k = i >>> 1;
        assert j == k : i;
    }

    public static void main(String[] args) {
        test(0);
        test(2);
        test(-2);
        test(1001);
        test(-1001);
    }
}
```

Select the one correct answer.

(a) The program executes normally and produces no output.
(b) An AssertionError with 0 as message is thrown.
(c) An AssertionError with 2 as message is thrown.
(d) An AssertionError with -2 as message is thrown.
(e) An AssertionError with 1001 as message is thrown.
(f) An AssertionError with -1001 as message is thrown.

Q14 What will be written to the standard output when the following program is run?

```
class Base {
    int i;
    Base() { add(1); }
    void add(int v) { i += v; }
    void print() { System.out.println(i); }
}

class Extension extends Base {
    Extension() { add(2); }
    void add(int v) { i += v*2; }
}

public class Qd073 {
    public static void main(String[] args) {
        bogo(new Extension());
    }
```

```
        static void bogo(Base b) {
            b.add(8);
            b.print();
        }
    }
```

Select the one correct answer.

(a) 9
(b) 18
(c) 20
(d) 21
(e) 22

- -

Q15 Which declarations of a native method are valid in the declaration of the following class?

```
    public class Qf575 {
        // Insert declaration of a native method here
    }
```

Select the two correct answers.

(a) native public void setTemperature(int kelvin);
(b) private native void setTemperature(int kelvin);
(c) protected int native getTemperature();
(d) public abstract native void setTemperature(int kelvin);
(e) native int setTemperature(int kelvin) {}

- -

Q16 Which collection implementation is suitable for maintaining an ordered sequence of objects, when objects are frequently inserted and removed from the middle of the sequence?

Select the one correct answer.

(a) TreeMap
(b) HashSet
(c) Vector
(d) LinkedList
(e) ArrayList

- -

Q17 Which statements can be inserted at the indicated position in the following code to make the program print 1 on the standard output when executed?

```
    public class Q4a39 {
        int a = 1;
        int b = 1;
        int c = 1;
```

```
class Inner {
    int a = 2;

    int get() {
        int c = 3;
        // Insert statement here.
        return c;
    }
}

Q4a39() {
    Inner i = new Inner();
    System.out.println(i.get());
}

public static void main(String[] args) {
    new Q4a39();
}
```

Select the two correct answers.

(a) c = b; ·
(b) c = this.a;
(c) c = this.b;
(d) c = Q4a39.this.a;
(e) c = c;

Q18   Which is the earliest line in the following code after which the object created in the
       line marked (0) will be a candidate for garbage collection, assuming no compiler
       optimizations are done?

```
public class Q76a9 {
    static String f() {
        String a = "hello";
        String b = "bye";          // (0)
        String c = b + "!";        // (1)
        String d = b;              // (2)

        b = a;                     // (3)
        d = a;                     // (4)
        return c;                  // (5)
    }

    public static void main(String[] args) {
        String msg = f();
        System.out.println(msg);   // (6)
    }
}
```

Select the one correct answer.

(a) The line marked (1).
(b) The line marked (2).
(c) The line marked (3).
(d) The line marked (4).

(e) The line marked (5).
(f) The line marked (6).

Q19 Which method from the String and StringBuffer classes modifies the object on
which it is invoked?

Select the one correct answer.

(a) The charAt() method of the String class.
(b) The toUpperCase() method of the String class.
(c) The replace() method of the String class.
(d) The reverse() method of the StringBuffer class.
(e) The length() method of the StringBuffer class.

Q20 Which statement, when inserted at the indicated position in the following code,
will cause a runtime exception?

```
class A {}

class B extends A {}

class C extends A {}

public class Q3ae4 {
    public static void main(String[] args) {
        A x = new A();
        B y = new B();
        C z = new C();

        // Insert statement here

    }
}
```

Select the one correct answer.

(a) x = y;
(b) z = x;
(c) y = (B) x;
(d) z = (C) y;
(e) y = (A) y;

Q21 Which of these are keywords in Java?

Select three correct answers.

(a) default
(b) NULL
(c) String
(d) throws
(e) long

Q22 A method within a class is only accessible by classes that are defined within the same package as the class of the method. How can such a restriction be enforced?

Select the one correct answer.

(a) Declare the method with the keyword public.
(b) Declare the method with the keyword protected.
(c) Declare the method with the keyword private.
(d) Declare the method with the keyword package.
(e) Do not declare the method with any accessibility modifiers.

Q23 Which code initializes the two-dimensional array tab so that tab[3][2] is a valid element?

Select the two correct answers.

(a)
```
int[][] tab = {
    { 0, 0, 0 },
    { 0, 0, 0 }
};
```
(b)
```
int tab[][] = new int[4][];
for (int i=0; i<tab.length; i++) tab[i] = new int[3];
```
(c)
```
int tab[][] = {
    0, 0, 0, 0,
    0, 0, 0, 0,
    0, 0, 0, 0,
    0, 0, 0, 0
};
```
(d) `int tab[3][2];`
(e) `int[] tab[] = { {0, 0, 0}, {0, 0, 0}, {0, 0, 0}, {0, 0, 0} };`

Q24 What will be the result of attempting to run the following program?

```
public class Qaa75 {
    public static void main(String[] args) {
        String[][][] arr = {
            { {}, null },
            { { "1", "2" }, { "1", null, "3" } },
            {},
            { { "1", null } }
        };

        System.out.println(arr.length + arr[1][2].length);
    }
}
```

Select the one correct answer.

(a) The program will terminate with an ArrayIndexOutOfBoundsException.
(b) The program will terminate with a NullPointerException.
(c) 4 will be written to standard output.

(d) 6 will be written to standard output.

(e) 7 will be written to standard output.

- -

Q25 Which expressions will evaluate to true if preceded by the following code?

```
String a = "hello";
String b = new String(a);
String c = a;
char[] d = { 'h', 'e', 'l', 'l', 'o' };
```

Select the two correct answers.

(a) (a == "Hello")

(b) (a == b)

(c) (a == c)

(d) a.equals(b)

(e) a.equals(d)

- -

Q26 Which statements are true about the following code?

```
class A {
    public A() {}

    public A(int i) { this(); }
}

class B extends A {
    public boolean B(String msg) { return false; }
}

class C extends B {
    private C() { super(); }

    public C(String msg) { this(); }

    public C(int i) {}
}
```

Select the two correct answers.

(a) The code will fail to compile.

(b) The constructor in A that takes an int as an argument will never be called as a result of constructing an object of class B or C.

(c) Class C defines three constructors.

(d) Objects of class B cannot be constructed.

(e) At most one of the constructors of each class is called as a result of constructing an object of class C.

- -

Q27 Given two collection objects referenced by coll and col2, which statements are true?

Select the two correct answers.

(a) The operation coll.retainAll(col2) will not modify the coll object.
(b) The operation coll.removeAll(col2) will not modify the col2 object.
(c) The operation coll.addAll(col2) will return a new collection object, containing elements from both coll and col2.
(d) The operation coll.containsAll(Col2) will not modify the coll object.

Q28 Which statements are true about the relationships between the following classes?

```
class Foo {
    int num;
    Baz comp = new Baz();
}

class Bar {
    boolean flag;
}

class Baz extends Foo {
    Bar thing = new Bar();
    double limit;
}
```

Select the three correct answers.

(a) A Bar is a Baz.
(b) A Foo has a Bar.
(c) A Baz is a Foo.
(d) A Foo is a Baz.
(e) A Baz has a Bar.

Q29 Which statements are true about the value of a field, when no explicit assignments have been made?

Select the three correct answers.

(a) The value of a field of type int is undetermined.
(b) The value of a field of any numeric type is zero.
(c) The compiler may issue an error if the field is used in a method before it is initialized.
(d) A field of type String will denote the empty string ("").
(e) The value of all fields which are references is null.

Q30 Which statements describe guaranteed behavior of the garbage collection and finalization mechanisms?

Select the two correct answers.

(a) An object is deleted as soon as there are no more references that denote the object.
(b) The finalize() method will eventually be called on every object.
(c) The finalize() method will never be called more than once on an object.
(d) An object will not be garbage collected as long as it is possible for a live thread to access it through a reference.
(e) The garbage collector will use a mark and sweep algorithm.

Q31 Which main() method will succeed in printing the last program argument to the standard output, and exit gracefully with no output if no program arguments are specified?

Select the one correct answer.

```
(a) public static void main(String[] args) {
        if (args.length != 0)
            System.out.println(args[args.length-1]);
    }
(b) public static void main(String[] args) {
        try { System.out.println(args[args.length]); }
        catch (ArrayIndexOutOfBoundsException e) {}
    }
(c) public static void main(String[] args) {
        int ix = args.length;
        String last = args[ix];
        if (ix != 0) System.out.println(last);
    }
(d) public static void main(String[] args) {
        int ix = args.length-1;
        if (ix > 0) System.out.println(args[ix]);
    }
(e) public static void main(String[] args) {
        try { System.out.println(args[args.length-1]); }
        catch (NullPointerException e) {}
    }
```

Q32 Which statements are true about the collection interfaces?

Select the three correct answers.

(a) `Set` extends `Collection`.
(b) All methods defined in `Set` are also defined in `Collection`.
(c) `List` extends `Collection`.
(d) All methods defined in `List` are also defined in `Collection`.
(e) `Map` extends `Collection`.

Q33 Which is the legal range of values for a short?

Select the one correct answer.

(a) -2^7 to 2^7-1
(b) -2^8 to 2^8
(c) -2^{15} to $2^{15}-1$
(d) -2^{16} to $2^{16}-1$
(e) 0 to $2^{16}-1$

Q34 What is the name of the method that threads can use to pause their execution until signalled to continue by another thread?

Fill in the name of the method (do not include a parameter list).

Q35 Given the following class definitions, which expression identifies whether the object referred to by obj was created by instantiating class B rather than classes A, C, and D?

```
class A {}
class B extends A {}
class C extends B {}
class D extends A {}
```

Select the one correct answer.

(a) `obj instanceof B`
(b) `obj instanceof A && !(obj instanceof C)`
(c) `obj instanceof B && !(obj instanceof C)`
(d) `!(obj instanceof C || obj instanceof D)`
(e) `!(obj instanceof A) && !(obj instanceof C) && !(obj instanceof D)`

Q36 What will be written to the standard output when the following program is executed?

```
public class Q8499 {
    public static void main(String[] args) {
        double d = -2.9;
        int i = (int) d;
```

```
                    i *= (int) Math.ceil(d);
                    i *= (int) Math.abs(d);
                    System.out.println(i);
                }
            }
```

Select the one correct answer.

(a) -12
(b) 18
(c) 8
(d) 12
(e) 27

. . . .

Q37   What will be written to the standard output when the following program is
executed?

```java
public class Qcb90 {
    int a;
    int b;
    public void f() {
        a = 0;
        b = 0;
        int[] c = { 0 };
        g(b, c);
        System.out.println(a + " " + b + " " + c[0] + " ");
    }

    public void g(int b, int[] c) {
        a = 1;
        b = 1;
        c[0] = 1;
    }

    public static void main(String[] args) {
        Qcb90 obj = new Qcb90();

        obj.f();
    }
}
```

Select the one correct answer.

(a) 0 0 0
(b) 0 0 1
(c) 0 1 0
(d) 1 0 0
(e) 1 0 1

. . . .

Q38 Given the following class, which are correct implementations of the hashCode() method? .

```java
class ValuePair {
    public int a, b;
    public boolean equals(Object other) {
        try {
            ValuePair o = (ValuePair) other;
            return (a == o.a && b == o.b)
                || (a == o.b && b == o.a);
        } catch (ClassCastException cce) {
            return false;
        }
    }
    public int hashCode() {
        // Provide implementation here.
    }
}
```

Select the three correct answers.

(a) return 0;
(b) return a;
(c) return a + b;
(d) return a - b;
(e) return a ^ b;
(f) return (a << 16) | b;

Q39 Which statements are true regarding the execution of the following code?

```java
public class Q3a0a {
    public static void main(String[] args) {
        int j = 5;

        for (int i = 0; i<j; i++) {
            assert i < j-- : i > 0;
            System.out.println(i*j);
        }
    }
}
```

Select the two correct answers.

(a) An AssertionError will be thrown if assertions are enabled at runtime.
(b) The last number printed is 4 if assertions are disabled at runtime.
(c) The last number printed is 20 if assertions are disabled at runtime.
(d) The last number printed is 4 if assertions are enabled at runtime.
(e) The last number printed is 20 if assertions are enabled at runtime.

Q40 Which of the following method names are overloaded?

Select the three correct answers.

(a) The method name yield in java.lang.Thread
(b) The method name sleep in java.lang.Thread
(c) The method name wait in java.lang.Object
(d) The method name notify in java.lang.Object

Q41 Which are valid identifiers?

Select the three correct answers.

(a) _class
(b) $value$
(c) zer@
(d) ångström
(e) 2much

Q42 What will be the result of attempting to compile and run the following program?

```
public class Q28fd {
    public static void main(String[] args) {
        int counter = 0;
        l1:
        for (int i=0; i<10; i++) {
            l2:
            int j = 0;
            while (j++ < 10) {
                if (j > i) break l2;
                if (j == i) {
                    counter++;
                    continue l1;
                }
            }
        }
        System.out.println(counter);
    }
}
```

Select the one correct answer.

(a) The program will fail to compile.
(b) The program will not terminate normally.
(c) The program will write 10 to the standard output.
(d) The program will write 0 to the standard output.
(e) The program will write 9 to the standard output.

Q43   Given the following interface definition, which definition is valid?

```
interface I {
    void setValue(int val);
    int getValue();
}
```

Select the one correct answer.

(a) ```
class A extends I {
    int value;
    void setValue(int val) { value = val; }
    int getValue() { return value; }
}
```

(b) ```
interface B extends I {
    void increment();
}
```

(c) ```
abstract class C implements I {
    int getValue() { return 0; }
    abstract void increment();
}
```

(d) ```
interface D implements I {
    void increment();
}
```

(e) ```
class E implements I {
    int value;
    public void setValue(int val) { value = val; }
}
```

Q44   Which statements are true about the methods notify() and notifyAll()?

Select the two correct answers.

(a) An instance of the class Thread has a method named notify that can be invoked.
(b) A call to the method notify() will wake the thread that currently owns the lock of the object.
(c) The method notify() is synchronized.
(d) The method notifyAll() is defined in class Thread.
(e) When there is more than one thread waiting to obtain the lock of an object, there is no way to be sure which thread will be notified by the notify() method.
```

Q45 Which statements are true about the correlation between the inner and outer
     instances of member classes?

     Select the two correct answers.

     (a) Fields of the outer instance are always accessible to inner instances, regardless
         of their accessibility modifiers.
     (b) Fields of the outer instance can never be accessed using only the variable
         name within the inner instance.
     (c) More than one inner instance can be associated with the same outer instance.
     (d) All variables from the outer instance that should be accessible in the inner
         instance must be declared final.
     (e) A class that is declared final cannot have any member classes.

Q46 What will be the result of attempting to compile and run the following code?

```
public class Q6b0c {
    public static void main(String[] args) {
        int i = 4;
        float f = 4.3;
        double d = 1.8;
        int c = 0;
        if (i == f) c++;
        if (((int) (f + d)) == ((int) f + (int) d)) c += 2;
        System.out.println(c);
    }
}
```

     Select the one correct answer.

     (a) The code will fail to compile.
     (b) The value 0 will be written to the standard output.
     (c) The value 1 will be written to the standard output.
     (d) The value 2 will be written to the standard output.
     (e) The value 3 will be written to the standard output.

Q47 Which operators will always evaluate all the operands?

     Select the two correct answers.
     (a) ||
     (b) +
     (c) &&
     (d) ? :
     (e) %

Q48   Which statement concerning the switch construct is true?

Select the one correct answer.

(a) All switch statements must have a default label.
(b) There must be exactly one label for each code segment in a switch statement.
(c) The keyword continue can never occur within the body of a switch statement.
(d) No case label may follow a default label within a single switch statement.
(e) A character literal can be used as a value for a case label.

Q49   Which modifiers and return types would be valid in the declaration of a main()
method that starts the execution of a Java standalone application?

Select the two correct answers.

(a) private
(b) final
(c) static
(d) int
(e) abstract
(f) String

Q50   Which of the following expressions are valid?

Select the three correct answers.

(a) System.out.hashCode()
(b) "".hashCode()
(c) 42.hashCode()
(d) ("4"+2).equals(42)
(e) (new java.util.Vector()).hashCode()

Q51   Which statement regarding the following method definition is true?

```
boolean e() {
    try {
        assert false;
    } catch (AssertionError ae) {
        return true;
    }
    return false;          // (1)
}
```

Select the one correct answer.

(a) The code will fail to compile since catching an AssertionError is illegal.
(b) The code will fail to compile since the return statement at (1) is unreachable.
(c) The method will return true under all circumstances.
(d) The method will return false under all circumstances.
(e) The method will return true if and only if assertions are enabled at runtime.

Q52   If str denotes a String object with the string "73", which of these expressions will convert the string to the int value 73?

Select the two correct answers.

(a) Integer.intValue(str)
(b) ((int) str)
(c) (new Integer(str)).intValue()
(d) Integer.parseInt(str)
(e) Integer.getInt(str)

- -

Q53   Insert a line of code at the indicated location that will call the print() method in the Base class.

```java
class Base {
    public void print() {
        System.out.println("base");
    }
}

class Extension extends Base {
    public void print() {
        System.out.println("extension");

        // Insert a line of code here.
    }
}

public class Q294d {
    public static void main(String[] args) {
        Extension ext = new Extension();
        ext.print();
    }
}
```

Fill in a single line of code.

- -

Q54   Given the following code, which statements are true?

```java
public class Vertical {
    private int alt;
    public synchronized void up() {
        ++alt;
    }
    public void down() {
        --alt;
    }
    public synchronized void jump() {
        int a = alt;
        up();
        down();
        assert(a == alt);
    }
}
```

Select the two correct answers.

(a) The code will fail to compile.
(b) Separate threads can execute the up() method concurrently.
(c) Separate threads can execute the down() method concurrently.
(d) Separate threads can execute both the up() and down() method concurrently.
(e) The assertion in the jump() method will not fail under any circumstances.

Q55 What will be written to the standard output when the following program is run?

```
public class Q03e4 {
    public static void main(String[] args) {
        String space = " ";

        String composite = space + "hello" + space + space;
        composite.concat("world");

        String trimmed = composite.trim();

        System.out.println(trimmed.length());
    }
}
```

Select the one correct answer.

(a) 5
(b) 6
(c) 7
(d) 12
(e) 13

Q56 Given the following code, which statements are true about the objects referenced through the fields i, j, and k, given that any thread may call the methods a(), b(), and c() at any time?

```
class Counter {
    int v = 0;
    synchronized void inc() { v++; }
    synchronized void dec() { v--; }
}

public class Q7ed5 {
    Counter i;
    Counter j;
    Counter k;
    public synchronized void a() {
        i.inc();
        System.out.println("a");
        i.dec();
    }
```

```
        public synchronized void b() {
            i.inc(); j.inc(); k.inc();
            System.out.println("b");
            i.dec(); j.dec(); k.dec();
        }

        public void c() {
            k.inc();
            System.out.println("c");
            k.dec();
        }
    }
```

Select the two correct answers.

(a) i.v is guaranteed always to be 0 or 1.
(b) j.v is guaranteed always to be 0 or 1.
(c) k.v is guaranteed always to be 0 or 1
(d) j.v will always be greater than or equal to k.v at any give time.
(e) k.v will always be greater than or equal to j.v at any give time.

Q57 Which statements are true about casting and conversion?

Select the three correct answers.

(a) Conversion from int to long does not need a cast.
(b) Conversion from byte to short does not need a cast.
(c) Conversion from float to long does not need a cast.
(d) Conversion from short to char does not need a cast.
(e) Conversion from boolean to int using a cast is not possible.

Q58 Which method declarations, when inserted at the indicated position, will not cause the program to fail during compilation?

```
    public class Qdd1f {
        public long sum(long a, long b) { return a + b; }

        // Insert new method declarations here.

    }
```

Select the two correct answers.

(a) public int sum(int a, int b) { return a + b; }
(b) public int sum(long a, long b) { return 0; }
(c) abstract int sum();
(d) private long sum(long a, long b) { return a + b; }
(e) public long sum(long a, int b) { return a + b; }

Q59 The 8859-1 character code for the uppercase letter A is the decimal value 65. Which code fragments declare and initialize a variable of type char with this value?

Select the two correct answers.

(a) char ch = 65;
(b) char ch = '\65';
(c) char ch = '\0041';
(d) char ch = 'A';
(e) char ch = "A";

Q60 What will be the result of executing the following program code with assertions enabled?

```java
import java.util.*;

public class Q4d3f {
    public static void main(String[] args) {
        LinkedList lla = new LinkedList();
        LinkedList llb = new LinkedList();
        assert lla.size() == llb.size() : "empty";

        lla.add("Hello");
        assert lla.size() == 1 : "size";

        llb.add("Hello");
        assert llb.contains("Hello") : "contains";
        assert lla.get(0).equals(llb.get(0)) : "element";
        assert lla.equals(llb) : "collection";
    }
}
```

Select the one correct answer.

(a) Execution proceeds normally and produces no output.
(b) An AssertionError with the message "size" is thrown.
(c) An AssertionError with the message "empty" is thrown.
(d) An AssertionError with the message "element" is thrown
(e) An IndexOutOfBoundsException is thrown.
(f) An AssertionError with the message "container" is thrown.

Q61 Which of these are keywords in Java?

Select the two correct answers.
(a) Double
(b) native
(c) main
(d) unsafe
(e) default

Answers to Questions

Q1 *(a), (b), (c), and (e)*

Only local variables need to be explicitly initialized before use. Fields are assigned a default value if not explicitly initialized.

Q2 *(a), (d), and (e)*

When the >> operator shifts bits to the right, it fills the new bits on the left with the bit value of the left-most bit of the original bit pattern. When the >>> operator shifts bits to the right, it always fills the new bits on the left with a bit value of 0. Thus, the >> and the >>> operators perform the same operation when the left-most bit of the original bit pattern has a bit value of 0. This occurs whenever the original value is non-negative.

The result of (-1 >> 1) is –1. A bit pattern consisting of all 1s (i.e., integer -1) will not change after being shifted by the >> operator.

The result of (-1 >>> 1) is 2147483647 which is $2^{31} - 1$. Shifting a bit pattern of all 1s one bit to the right using the >>> operator will yield a bit pattern of all 1s, except for the left-most bit which will be 0. This gives the non-negative value 2147483647, which is the maximum value of type int.

The >>> operator will shift 0s into the bit pattern from the left, thus giving the left-most bit a value of 0. Since a value of 0 in the left-most bit signifies a non-negative value, the >>> operator is guaranteed to return a non-negative number if a shift has actually occurred.

Q3 *(d)*

A try block must be followed by at least one catch or finally block. No catch blocks can follow a finally block. Methods need not declare that they can throw Runtime Exceptions, as these are unchecked exceptions.

Q4 *(e)*

Giving parameters (2, 3) to the method substring() constructs a string consisting of the characters between positions 2 and 3 of the original string. The positions are indexed in the following manner: position 0 is immediately before the first character of the string, position 1 is between the first and the second character, position 2 is between the second and the third character, and so on.

Q5 *(a)*

A Thread object executes the run() method of a Runnable object on a separate thread when started. A Runnable object can be given when constructing a Thread object. If no Runnable object is supplied, the Thread object (which implements the Runnable interface) will execute its own run() method. A thread is initiated using the start() method of the Thread object.

Q6 *(c)*

The loop prints out the values 12, 9, 6, and 3 before terminating.

Q7 *(e)*

The fact that a field is static does not mean that it is not accessible from non-static methods and constructors. All fields are assigned a default value if no initializer is supplied. Local variables must be explicitly initialized before use.

Q8 *(c)*

The ∧ operator will perform an XOR operation on the bit patterns 1001 and 0010, resulting in the bit pattern 1011, which will be written out in decimal form as 11.

Q9 *(e)*

All the "hello" literals denote the same String object. Any String object created using the new operator will be a distinct new object.

Q10 *(d) and (e)*

The main() method must be public and static, and take an array of String objects as parameter. It does not return a value and, therefore, should be declared void. The public and static modifiers must precede the keyword void. The (b) and (c) declarations will fail to compile due to error in the syntax of the method declaration.

Declaration (a) will compile, but it does not meet the criteria of a main() method to start the execution of an application. Declaration (d) meets the criteria although the method is declared final, which is redundant since the method is static. It also uses a different parameter name, but it is none the less also a valid main() method. Declaration (e) is the canonical form of the main() method.

Q11 *(a)*

Calls to methods suspend(), sleep(), and wait() do not stop a thread. They only cause a thread to move out of its running state. A thread will terminate when the execution of the run() method has completed.

Q12 *(d)*

The Map interface provides operations that map keys to values.

Q13 *(d)*

The >>> operator clears the sign bit, so for negative values i >>> 1 is not equivalent to i/2.

Q14 *(e)*

An object of the class Extension is created. The first thing the constructor of Extension does is invoke the constructor of Base, using an implicit super() call. All calls to the method void add(int) are dynamically bound to the add() method in the Extension class, since the actual object is of type Extension. Therefore, this method is called by the constructor of Base, the constructor of Extension and the bogo() method with the parameters 1, 2, and 8, respectively. The instance field i changes value accordingly: 2, 6, and 22. The final value of 22 is printed.

Q15 *(a) and (b)*

The native modifier can be specified in the same position as accessibility modifiers in method declarations. Thus, the order of tokens in (a) and (b) is correct. The (c) declaration is rejected since the native modifier is not allowed after the declaration of the return type. Declaration (d) is rejected since it tries to declare an abstract method within a non-abstract class. The (e) declaration is rejected because native method declarations, just like abstract method declarations, cannot have an implementation since this is defined elsewhere.

Q16   (d)

TreeMap and HashSet do not maintain an ordered sequence of objects. Vector and ArrayList require shifting of objects on insertion and deletion, while LinkedList does not. When objects are frequently inserted and deleted from the middle of the sequence, LinkedList gives the best performance.

Q17   (a) and (d)

Field b of the outer class is not shadowed by any local or inner class variables, therefore, (a) will work. Using this.a will access the field a in the inner class. Using this.b will result in a compilation error since there is no field b in the inner class. Using Q4a39.this.a will successfully access the field of the outer class. The statement c = c will only reassign the current value of the local variable c to itself.

Q18   (d)

At (1), a new String object is constructed by concatenating the string "bye" in the String object denoted by b and the string "!". After line (2), d and b are aliases. After line (3), b and a are aliases, but d still denotes the String object with "bye" from line (0). After line (4), d and a are aliases. Reference d no longer denotes the String object created in line (0). This String object has no references to it and is, therefore, a candidate for garbage collection.

Q19   (d)

String objects are immutable. None of the methods of the String class modify a String object. Methods toUpperCase() and replace() in the String class will return a new String object that contains the modified string. However, StringBuffer objects are mutable.

Q20   (c)

Statement (a) will work just fine, and (b), (d), and (e) will cause compilation errors. Statements (b) and (e) will cause compilation errors since they attempt to assign an incompatible type to the reference. Statement (d) will cause compilation errors since a cast from B to C is invalid. Being an instance of B excludes the possibility of being an instance of C. Statement (c) will compile, but will throw a runtime exception since the object that is cast to B is not an instance of B.

Q21   (a), (d), and (e)

String is a name of a class in the java.lang package, not a keyword. Java has a keyword null, but not NULL.

Q22   (e)

The desired accessibility is package accessibility, which is the default accessibility for members that have no accessibility modifier. The keyword package is not an accessibility modifier and cannot be used in this context.

Q23 *(b) and (e)*

For the expression tab[3][2] to access a valid element of a two-dimensional array, the array must have at least four rows and the fourth row must have at least three elements. Fragment (a) produces a 2×3 array. Fragment (c) tries to initialize a two-dimensional array as an one-dimensional array. Fragment (d) tries to specify array dimensions in the type of the array reference declaration.

Q24 *(a)*

The expression arr.length will evaluate to 4. The expression arr[1] will access the element { { "1", "2" }, { "1", null, "3" } }, and arr[1][2] will try to access the third sub-element of this element. This produces an ArrayIndexOutOfBoundsException, since the element has only two sub-elements.

Q25 *(c) and (d)*

String objects can have identical sequences of characters. The == operator, when used on String object references, will just compare the references and will only return true when both references denote the same object (i.e., are aliases). The equals() method will return true whenever the contents of the String objects are identical. An array of char and a String are two totally different types and cannot be compared using the equals() method of the String class.

Q26 *(b) and (c)*

Statement (d) is false since an object of B can be created using the implicit default constructor of the class. B has an implicit default constructor since no constructor has explicitly been defined. Statement (e) is false since the second constructor of C will call the first constructor of C.

Q27 *(b) and (d)*

The retainAll(), removeAll(), and addAll() methods do not return a new collection object, but instead modify the collection object they were called upon. The collection object given as an argument is not affected. The containsAll() does not modify either of the collection objects.

Q28 *(b), (c), and (e)*

An instance of the class Baz is also an instance of the class Foo since the class Baz extends the class Foo. A Baz has a Bar since instances of the class Baz contain an instance of the class Bar by reference. A Foo has a Baz since instances of the class Foo contain an instance of the class Baz by reference. Since a Foo has a Baz which has a Bar, a Foo has a Bar.

Q29 *(b) and (e)*

Unlike local variables, all fields are initialized with default initial values. All numeric fields are initialized to zero, boolean fields to false, char fields to '\u0000', and *all* reference fields to null.

Q30 *(c) and (d)*

Very little is guaranteed about the behavior of the garbage collection and finalization mechanisms. The (c) and (d) statements are two of the things that are guaranteed.

Q31   *(a)*

The `main()` method in (b) will always generate and catch an `ArrayIndexOutOfBounds-Exception`, since `args.length` is an illegal index in the args array. The `main()` method in (c) will always throw an `ArrayIndexOutOfBoundsException` since it is also uses `args.length` as an index, but this exception is never caught. The `main()` method in (d) will fail to print the argument if only one program argument is supplied. The `main()` method in (e) will generate an uncaught `ArrayIndexOutOfBoundsException` if no program arguments are specified.

Q32   *(a), (b), and (c)*

`Set` and `List` both extend `Collection`. A map is *not* a collection and `Map` does not extend `Collection`. `Set` does not have any new methods other than those defined in `Collection`. `List` defines additional methods to the ones in `Collection`.

Q33   *(c)*
The type short defines 16-bit signed values in the range from -2^{15} to $2^{15}-1$, inclusive.

Q34   *Filled in:*
     `wait`

Q35   *(c)*
The important thing to remember is that if an object is an instance of a class, then it is also an instance of all the superclasses of this class.

Q36   *(c)*
The expression `(int) d` evaluates to –2. The expression `Math.ceil(d)` evaluates to –2.0, giving the value –2 when converted to int. The expression `Math.abs(d)` evaluates to 2.9, giving the value 2 when converted to int.

Q37   *(e)*
Method `g()` modifies the field a. Method `g()` modifies the parameter b, not the field b, since the parameter declaration shadows the field. Variables are passed by value, so the change of value in parameter b is confined to the method `g()`. Method `g()` modifies the array whose reference value is passed as a parameter. Change to the first element is visible after return from the method `g()`.

Q38   *(a), (c), and (e)*

The `equals()` method ignores the ordering of a and b when determining if two objects are equivalent. The `hashCode()` implementation must, therefore, also ignore the ordering of a and b when calculating the hash value, that is, the implementation must return the same value even after the values of a and b are swapped.

Q39   *(c) and (d)*

The variable j is only decremented if assertions are enabled. The assertion never fails, since the loop condition ensures that the loop body is only executed as long as i<j is true. With assertions enabled, each iteration decrements j by 1. The last number printed is 20 if assertions are disabled at runtime, and the last number printed is 4 if assertions are enabled at runtime.

Q40   *(b) and (c)*

These names have overloaded methods that allow optional timeout values as parameters.

Q41   *(a), (b), and (d)*

Both $ and _ are allowed as characters in identifiers. Character @ is not allowed in identifiers. All characters considered letters in the Unicode character set are allowed. The first character of an identifier cannot be a digit.

Q42   *(a)*

The program will fail to compile since the label 12 cannot precede the declaration int j = 0. For a label to be associated with a loop, it must immediately precede the loop construct.

Q43   *(b)*

Classes cannot extend interfaces, they must implement them. Interfaces can extend other interfaces, but cannot implement them. A class must be declared abstract if it does not provide an implementation for one of its methods. Methods declared in interfaces are implicitly public and abstract. Classes that implement these methods must explicitly declare their implementations public.

Q44   *(a) and (e)*

The notify() and notifyAll() methods are declared in the class Object. Since all other classes extend Object, these methods are also available in instances of all other classes, including Thread. The method notify() is not synchronized, but will throw an IllegalMonitorStateException if the current thread is not the owner of the object lock.

Q45   *(a) and (c)*

Accessing fields of the outer instance using only the variable name works within the inner instance as long as the variable is not shadowed. Fields need not be declared final in order to be accessible within the inner instance.

Q46   *(a)*

The code will fail to compile because the literal 4.3 has the type double. Assignment of a double value to a float variable without an explicit cast is not allowed. The code would compile and write 0 to standard output when run, if the literal 4.3 was replaced with 4.3F.

Q47   *(b) and (e)*

The && and || operators exhibit short-circuit behavior. The first operand of the ternary operator (? :) is always evaluated. Based on the result of this evaluation, either the second or the third operand is evaluated.

Q48   *(e)*

No labels are mandatory (including the default label) and can be placed in any order within the switch body. The keyword continue may occur within the body of a switch statement as long as it pertains to a loop. Any constant non-long integral value can be used for case labels as long as the type is compatible with the expression in the switch expression.

Q49   *(b) and (c)*

The main() method must be declared static. It does not return a value and is, therefore, declared as void. It's accessibility modifier must be public. It has an array of String as parameter. Additionally it can be declared final, but that is not part of the requirement.

Q50   *(a), (b), and (e)*

Expressions (a), (b), and (e) all call the method hashCode() on valid objects. (c) is an illegal expression, as methods cannot be called on primitive values. The call in (d) to the equals() method requires an object as argument.

Q51   *(e)*

The method returns true if and only if assertions are enabled at runtime. It will only return false if assertions are disabled.

Q52   *(c) and (d)*

(d) shows how the static method parseInt() of the wrapper class java.lang.Integer can be used to parse an integer from its string representation. It is also possible to first construct an Integer object based on the string representation and then extract the int value, using the intValue() method, as shown in (c).

Q53   *Filled in:*

        super.print();

Overridden method implementations are accessed using the super keyword. Statements like print(), Base.print(), and Base.this.print() will not work.

Q54   *(c) and (d)*

Executing synchronized code does not guard against executing non-synchronized code concurrently.

Q55   *(a)*

Strings are immutable, therefore, the concat() method has no effect on the original String object. The string on which the trim() method is called consists of 8 characters, where the first and the two last characters are spaces (" hello "). The trim() method returns a new String object where the white space characters at each end have been removed. This leaves the 5 characters of the word "hello".

Q56   *(a) and (b)*

If a thread is executing method b() on an object, then it is guaranteed that no other thread executes methods a() and b() concurrently. Therefore, the invocation counters i and j will never show more than one concurrent invocation. Two threads can concurrently be executing methods b() and c(). Therefore, the invocation counter k can easily show more than one concurrent invocation.

Q57   *(a), (b), and (e)*

Widening conversion allows conversions (a) and (b) to be done without a cast. Conversion from a floating point value to an integer value needs a cast. So does conversion from short values (which are signed) to char values (which are unsigned). Conversion from a boolean value to any other primitive type is not possible.

Q58   (a) and (e)
       Declaration (b) fails since the method signature only differs in the return type. Declaration (c) fails since it tries to declare an abstract method in a non-abstract class. Declaration (d) fails since its signature is identical to the existing method.

Q59   (a) and (d)
       The literal 65 is parsed as a value of type int. The value is within the range of the char type. A char literal can be specified by enclosing the character in single quotes ('A'), as a Unicode value in hexadecimal notation ('\u0041'), or as an octal value ('\101'). The octal value cannot exceed '\377'. A char variable cannot be assigned a string, even if the string only contains one character.

Q60   (a)
       Execution proceeds normally and produces no output. All assertions are true.

Q61   (b) and (e)
       Note that keywords are case sensitive.

Number Systems and Number Representation

•••

G.1 Number Systems

Binary, Octal, and Hexadecimal Number System

Table G.1 lists the integers from 0 to 16, showing their equivalents in the binary (*base* 2), octal (*base* 8), and hexadecimal (*base* 16) number systems. The shaded cells in each column show the digits in each number system.

Table G.1 *Number Systems*

Decimal (base 10)	Binary (base 2)	Octal (base 8)	Hexadecimal (base 16)
0	0	0	0
1	1	1	1
2	10	2	2
3	11	3	3
4	100	4	4
5	101	5	5
6	110	6	6
7	111	7	7
8	1000	10	8
9	1001	11	9
10	1010	12	a

Continues

Table G.1   *Number Systems (Continued)*

Decimal (base 10)	Binary (base 2)	Octal (base 8)	Hexadecimal (base 16)
11	1011	13	b
12	1100	14	c
13	1101	15	d
14	1110	16	e
15	1111	17	f
16	10000	20	10

In addition to the decimal literals, Java also allows integer literals to be specified in octal and hexadecimal number systems, but not in the binary number system. Octal and hexadecimal numbers are specified with 0 and 0x prefix, respectively. The prefix 0X can also be used for hexadecimal numbers. Note that the leading 0 (zero) digit is not the uppercase letter 0. The hexadecimal digits from a to f can also be specified with the corresponding uppercase forms (A to F). Negative integers (e.g., -90) can be specified by prefixing the minus sign (-) to the magnitude, regardless of number system (e.g., -0132 or -0X5A). The actual memory representation of the integer values is discussed in Section on page 598.

Converting Binary Numbers to Decimals

A binary number can be converted to its equivalent decimal value by computing the *positional values* of its digits. Each digit in the binary number contributes to the final decimal value by virtue of its position, starting with position 0 (units) for the right-most digit in the number. The positional value of each digit is given by

$$digit \times base^{\,position}$$

The number 101001_2 corresponds to 41_{10} in the decimal number system:

$$101001_2 = 1 \times 2^5 + 0 \times 2^4 + 1 \times 2^3 + 0 \times 2^2 + 0 \times 2^1 + 1 \times 2^0$$
$$= 32 + 0 + 8 + 0 + 0 + 1$$
$$= 41_{10}$$

Converting Octal and Hexadecimal Numbers to Decimals

Similarly, octal (base 8) and hexadecimal (base 16) numbers can be converted to their decimal equivalents:

$$0132 = 132_8 = 1{\times}8^2 + 3{\times}8^1 + 2{\times}8^0 = 64 + 24 + 2 = 90_{10} \qquad \text{Octal} \rightarrow \text{Decimal}$$

$$0x5a = 5a_{16} = 5{\times}16^2 + a{\times}16^0 \quad = 80 + 10 \quad = 90_{10} \qquad \text{Hex} \rightarrow \text{Decimal}$$

The same technique can be used to convert a number from any base to its equivalent representation in the decimal number system.

G.2 Relationship between Binary, Octal, and Hexadecimal Numbers

From Table G.1 we see that 3 bits are needed to represent any octal digit, and 4 bits to are needed to represent any hexadecimal digit. We can use this fact to convert between binary, octal, and hexadecimal systems, as shown in Figure G.1.

The procedure for converting an octal to a binary is shown by the arrow marked (a). We can prove that replacing each octal digit by its 3-bit equivalent binary value gives the right result:

$$
\begin{aligned}
173_8 &= 1{\times}8^2 & &+ 7{\times}8^1 & &+ 3{\times}8^0 \\
&= 1{\times}(2^3)^2 & &+ 7{\times}(2^3)^1 & &+ 3{\times}(2^3)^0 \\
&= 1{\times}2^6 & &+ 7{\times}2^3 & &+ 3 \\
&= (001_2){\times}2^6 & &+ (111_2){\times}2^3 & &+ (011_2) \\
&= (0{\times}2^2+0{\times}2^1+1{\times}2^0){\times}2^6 & &+ (1{\times}2^2+1{\times}2^1+1{\times}2^0){\times}2^3 & &+ (0{\times}2^2+1{\times}2^1+1{\times}2^0) \\
&= 1{\times}2^6 & &+ 1{\times}2^5+1{\times}2^4+1{\times}2^3 & &+ 0{\times}2^2+1{\times}2^1+1{\times}2^0 \\
&= 1{\times}2^6 + 1{\times}2^5 + 1{\times}2^4 + 1{\times}2^3 + 0{\times}2^2 + 1{\times}2^1 + 1{\times}2^0 \\
&= 1111011_2
\end{aligned}
$$

Analogously, we can convert a hexadecimal number to its equivalent binary number by replacing each digit in the hexadecimal number by its 4-bit equivalent binary value, as shown by the arrow marked (b).

Figure G.1   *Converting between Binary, Octal, and Hexadecimal*

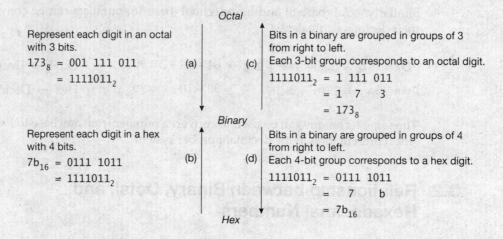

To convert a binary to it octal equivalent, we reverse the procedure outlined earlier (see arrow marked (c) in Figure G.1). The bits in the binary number are grouped into 3-bit groups from right to left. Each such group is replaced by its equivalent octal digit. This corresponds to reversing the computation shown above. Analogously, we can convert a binary to a hexadecimal number by replacing each 4-bit group by its equivalent hex digit (see arrow marked (d) in Figure G.1).

G.3   Converting Decimals

Converting Decimals to Binary Numbers

In order to convert decimals to binaries, we reverse the process outlined in Section G.1 for converting a binary to a decimal.

$41_{10} = 20 \times 2 + 1$ Dividing 41 by 2, gives the quotient 20 and remainder 1.

$20_{10} = 10 \times 2 + 0$ We again divide the current quotient 20 by 2.

$10_{10} = 5 \times 2 + 0$

$5_{10} = 2 \times 2 + 1$ We repeat this procedure until ...

$2_{10} = 1 \times 2 + 0$

$1_{10} = 0 \times 2 + 1$ ... the quotient is 0.

$41_{10} = 101001_2$

The divisor used in the steps above is the base of the target number system (binary, base 2). The binary value, 101001_2, is represented by the remainders, with the last remainder as the left-most bit. Back substitution of the quotient gives the same result:

$$41_{10} = (((((0 \times 2 + 1) \times 2 + 0) \times 2 + 1) \times 2 + 0) \times 2 + 0) \times 2 + 1$$
$$= 1 \times 2^5 + 0 \times 2^4 + 1 \times 2^3 + 0 \times 2^2 + 0 \times 2^1 + 1 \times 2^0$$
$$= 101001_2$$

Converting Decimals to Octal and Hexadecimal Numbers

Analogously, we can apply the above procedure for converting an octal to a binary. The conversion for the decimal number 90 can be done as follows:

$$90_{10} = 11 \times 8 + 2$$
$$11_{10} = 1 \times 8 + 3$$
$$1_{10} = 0 \times 8 + 1$$
$$90_{10} = 132_8 = 0132$$

The remainder values represent the digits in the equivalent octal number: 132_8. This can be verified by back substitution, which gives the following result:

$$90_{10} = ((0 \times 8 + 1) \times 8 + 3) \times 8 + 2$$
$$= 1 \times 8^2 + 3 \times 8^1 + 2 \times 8^0$$
$$= 132_8 = 0132$$

Conversion to hexadecimal is analogous:

$$90_{10} = 5 \times 16 + 10$$
$$5_{10} = 0 \times 16 + 5$$
$$90_{10} = 5a_{16} = 0x5a$$

The remainders represent the digits of the number in the hexadecimal system: 5a. Back substitution gives the same result:

$$90_{10} = (0 \times 16 + 5) \times 16 + 10$$
$$= 5 \times 16^1 + a \times 16^0$$
$$= 5a_{16} = 0x5a$$

G.4 Representing Integers

Integer data types in Java represent *signed* integer values, that is, both positive and negative integer values. The values of char type can effectively be regarded as *unsigned* 16-bit integers.

Values of type byte are represented as shown in Table G.2. A value of type byte requires 8 bits. With 8 bits, we can represent 2^8 or 256 values. Java uses 2's complement (explained later) to store signed values of integer data types. For the byte data type, this means values are in the range −128 (-2^7) to +127 (2^7-1), inclusive.

Bits in an integral value are usually numbered from right to left, starting with the least significant bit 0 (also called the *right-most bit*). When applying bitwise operators, the number of the most significant bit (also called the *left-most bit*) is dependent on the integral type; bit 31 for byte, short, char, and int, and bit 63 for long. The representation of the signed types sets the most significant bit to 1, indicating negative values. Adding 1 to the maximum int value 2147483647 results in the minimum value -2147483648, that is, the values wrap around for integers and no overflow or underflow is indicated.

Table G.2 *Representing Signed* byte *Values Using 2's Complement*

Decimal Value	Binary Representation (8 bit)	Octal Value with Prefix 0	Hexadecimal Value with Prefix 0x
127	01111111	0177	0x7f
126	01111110	0176	0x7e
...	...	...	...
41	00101001	0123	0x29
...	...	...	...
2	00000010	02	0x02
1	00000001	01	0x01
0	00000000	00	0x0
-1	11111111	0377	0xff
-2	11111110	0376	0xfe
...	...	...	...
-41	11010111	0327	0xd7
...	...	...	...
−127	10000001	0201	0x81
−128	10000000	0200	0x80

Calculating 2's Complement

Before we look at 2's complement, we need to understand 1's complement. 1 s complement of a binary integer is computed by inverting the bits in the number. Thus, 1's complement of the binary number 00101001 is 11010110. 1's complement of a binary number N_2 is denoted as $\sim N_2$. The following relations hold between a binary integer N_2, its 1's complement $\sim N_2$, and its 2's complement $-N_2$:

$-N_2 = \sim N_2 + 1$

$0 = -N_2 + N_2$

If N_2 is a positive binary integer, then $-N_2$ denotes its negative binary value, and vice versa. The second relation states that adding a binary integer N_2 to its 2's complement $-N_2$ equals 0.

Given a positive byte value, say 41, the binary representation of -41 can be found as follows:

	Binary Representation	Decimal Value
Given a value, N_2:	00101001	41
Form 1's complement, $\sim N_2$:	11010110	
Add 1:	00000001	
Result is 2's complement, $-N_2$:	11010111	−41

Similarly, given a negative number, say -41, we can find the binary representation of 41:

	Binary Representation	Decimal Value
Given a value, N_2:	11010111	−41
Form 1's complement, $\sim N_2$:	00101000	
Add 1:	00000001	
Result is 2's complement, $-N_2$:	00101001	41

Adding a number N_2 to its 2's complement $-N_2$ gives 0, and the carry bit from the addition of the most significant bits (after any necessary extension of the operands) is ignored:

	Binary representation	Decimal value
Given a value, N_2:	00101001	41
Add 2's complement, $\sim N_2$:	11010111	−41
Sum:	00000000	0

Subtraction between two integers is also computed as addition with 2's complement:

$$N_2 - M_2 = N_2 + (-M_2)$$

For example, calculating $41_{10} - 3_{10}$ (with the correct result 38_{10}) is computed as follows:

	Binary Representation	Decimal Value
Given a value, N_2:	00101001	41
Add $-M_2$ (i.e., subtract M_2):	11111101	−3
Result:	00100110	38

The previous discussion on byte values applies equally to values of other integer types: short, int, and long. These types have their values represented by 2's complement in 16, 32, and 64 bits, respectively.

About the CD

••

The CD accompanying the book contains resources that are meant to assist in the preparation for the Sun Certified Programmer for the Java 2 Platform 1.4 (SCPJ2 1.4, code CX-310-035).

The contents of the CD are divided into two parts. The first part contains the exam simulators developed by Whizlabs Software (http://www.whizlabs.com) for the SCPJ2 1.4 and the SCPJ2 Upgrade exams. The second part contains miscellaneous items from the book. Whizlabs products refer to the programmer exam by its more common name: SCJP (Sun Certified Java Programmer) exam.

H.1 Whizlabs Exam Simulators

The CD contains limited versions of the Whizlabs SCJP 1.4 and SCJP Upgrade exam simulators. Details concerning system requirements, installation, how to activate the software, and its usage, are all to be found on the CD.

Whizlabs SCJP 1.4 Exam Simulator

- Two complete SCJP 1.4 Mock Exams
- The PGJC2E Mock Exam, developed specifically from the Mock Exam in the book.
- Quick Revision Notes (abridged version)
- Interactive Quiz (20 questions)
- Tips and Tricks (abridged version), giving practical advice on taking the exam

Whizlabs SCJP Upgrade Exam Simulator

- One complete Upgrade Mock Exam
- The PGJC2E Upgrade Mock Exam, developed specifically from the Mock Exam in the book.
- Quick Revision Notes (abridged version)
- Interactive Quiz (20 questions)
- Tips and Tricks (abridged version)

Web-based Versions of the Exam Simulators

Web-based versions of the Whizlabs SCJP 1.4 and SCJP Upgrade exam simulators can be accessed at http://www.whizlabs.com/partners/awl.html.

Full Versions of the Exam Simulators

The full versions of the exam simulators have the following features:

- The complete Mock Exam Portfolio, which includes 12 practice exams, the PGJC2E exams, customizable mock exams, a diagnostic exam, a final exam, and also a special exam to enforce the new objectives included in the SCPJ 1.4 exam.
- Interactive Quiz (unabridged version)
- Quick Revision Notes (unabridged version)
- Tips and Tricks (unabridged version)
- Miscellaneous Reports (Mock Exam Score with various statistics, Objective-wise Score, Performance History)

Whizlabs is offering an exclusive 10% discount on full versions of its SCJP 1.4 and SCJP Upgrade exam simulators. Details about this special offer can be obtained by sending an e-mail to whizlabs_pgjc2e@whizlabs.com with the license numbers found in the documentation on the CD, or by visiting the Web site at http://www.whizlabs.com/partners/awl.html.

H.2 Items from the Book

The CD also contains the following items:

- Source code of all the examples
- Solutions to the programming exercises
- The PGJC2E mock exam engine, based on the Mock Exam in the book and developed by the authors.

Details of how to access and use these items are available on the CD.

Index

CD-ROM Warranty

Addison-Wesley warrants the enclosed disc to be free of defects in materials and faulty workmanship under normal use for a period of ninety days after purchase. If a defect is discovered in the disc during this warranty period, a replacement disc can be obtained at no charge by sending the defective disc, postage prepaid, with proof of purchase to:

Editorial Department
Addison-Wesley Professional
Pearson Technology Group
75 Arlington Street, Suite 300
Boston, MA 02116
Email: AWPro@awl.com

Addison-Wesley makes no warranty or representation, either expressed or implied, with respect to this software, its quality, performance, merchantability, or fitness for a particular purpose. In no event will Addison-Wesley, its distributors, or dealers be liable for direct, indirect, special, incidental, or consequential damages arising out of the use or inability to use the software. The exclusion of implied warranties is not permitted in some states. Therefore, the above exclusion may not apply to you. This warranty provides you with specific legal rights. There may be other rights that you may have that vary from state to state. The contents of this CD-ROM are intended for personal use only.

More information and updates are available at:
http://www.awprofessional.com/

Single-User License Agreement

••

Whizlabs Software Product License is a legal agreement between you (an individual) and Whizlabs Software Private Limited granting you a non-exclusive and non-transferable right for the software product it accompanies. By this agreement **only you (and no one else) are entitled to install, use, or copy** the software product, updates (if any), and the accompanying documentation (collectively known as the "Software"). Whizlabs retains exclusive rights to continue owning the software product that is protected by copyright and other international intellectual property laws. Unauthorized copying of the software product or failure to comply with this Agreement will result in automatic termination of this license and entitle Whizlabs to pursue suitable legal action.

Important Terms of Agreement

Under these terms **you may:**

a. Install and use the Software Product on only one computer or workstation.

b. Have only one user license per computer or workstation.

c. Make one (1) copy of the Software Product for backup purpose only.

Under these terms **you may not:**

a. Use the Software Product on more than one computer or workstation

b. Modify, translate, reverse engineer, decompile, decode, decrypt, disassemble, adapt, create a derivative work of, or copy the Software Product in any way (except one backup).

c. Sell, rent, lease, sublicense, or otherwise transfer or distribute the Software to any other person or entity without the prior written consent of Whizlabs.

d. Allow any other person or entity to use the Software or install the Software on a network of any sort (these will require a separate license from Whizlabs)

e. Remove or cover any proprietary notices, labels, or marks on the Software.

Tenure of the License Agreement

The term of the license shall commence upon your downloading, installing, copying, or using the Software Product. This license will expire on the completion of **six (6) months** after commencement or your discontinuation in using the Software, whichever occurs first.

Limited Warranty Under the License

Whizlabs warrants the media on which the Software Product is recorded for a period of thirty (30) days from the date of your receiving the software product. If the material of media is found defective or the workmanship is faulty, the media will be replaced free of cost within the warranty period.

Remedies Provided Under the License

The sole remedy under this agreement will be the replacement of defective media as set forth above. However Whizlabs makes no further warranties regarding the software, either express or implied including the merchantability, or fitness for a particular purpose. The software is licensed to you on an "as-is" basis.

Liabilities Under the License

Whizlabs exclusive and maximum liability for any claim by you or anyone claiming through or on behalf of you arising out of your order, use, or installation of the software shall not under any circumstance exceed the actual amount paid by you to Whizlabs for the software. In no event shall Whizlabs be liable to you or any person or entity claiming through you for any indirect, incidental, collateral, exemplary, consequential, or special damages or losses arising out of your order, use, or installation of the software or media delivered to you or out of the warranty, including without limitation, loss of use, profits, goodwill, or savings, or loss of data, files, or programs stored by the user. Some states do not allow the exclusion or limitation of incidental or consequential damages, so the above limitations may not apply to you.

Other Limitations Under the License

PLEASE READ CAREFULLY. THE FOLLOWING LIMITS SOME OF YOUR RIGHTS, INCLUDING THE RIGHT TO BRING A LAWSUIT IN COURT.

By accepting this Agreement, you and Whizlabs agree that all claims or disputes will be submitted to binding arbitration if demanded by either party. The arbitration will be handled by the courts of Delhi, INDIA and governed by its rules. This Agreement requiring arbitration (if demanded) is still fully binding even if a class action is filed in which you would be a class representative or member. You and

Whizlabs agree that the arbitration of any dispute or claim between us will be conducted apart from all other claims or disputes of other parties and that there will be no class or consolidated arbitration of any claims or disputes covered by this Agreement. You and Whizlabs also agree that this Agreement does not affect the applicability of any statute of limitations.

General Note

Indian Laws shall govern this agreement, including the limited warranty, the limited liability and the disclaimer of liability contained therein. All disputes are subject to exclusive jurisdiction of Courts in Delhi, India. You are responsible for installation, management and operation of the product.

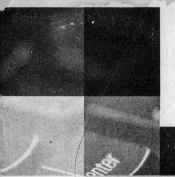